POPULAR FEATURES OF THE THIRTEENTH EDITION!

Education in the News

Highlights a recent news report about current topics in education.

PROFESSIONAL DILEMMA

Provides opportunities to analyze real-life problems that teachers encounter in their classrooms.

DEBATE

Two educators present opposing sides of an issue related to the chapter topic, and readers have an opportunity to register their opinions on each issue at the Companion Website.

RELEVANT RESEARCH

Showcases published research studies about education.

GLOBAL PERSPECTIVES

Provides preservice teachers with a better understanding of international educational practices and how they compare to practices in the United States.

INTRODUCTION TO THE FOUNDATIONS OF AMERICAN EDUCATION

13
EDITION

INTRODUCTION TO THE FOUNDATIONS OF AMERICAN EDUCATION

James A. Johnson
Northern Illinois University

Diann Musial
Northern Illinois University

Gene E. Hall
University of Nevada, Las Vegas

Donna M. Gollnick
National Council for the Accreditation of Teacher Education

Victor L. Dupuis
Pennsylvania State University

PEARSON

Boston • New York • San Francisco
Mexico City • Montreal • Toronto • London • Madrid • Munich • Paris
Hong Kong • Singapore • Tokyo • Cape Town • Sydney

Executive Editor and Publisher: Stephen D. Dragin
Senior Editorial Assistant: Barbara Strickland
Development Editor: Sonny Regelman
Marketing Manager: Tara Whorf
Associate Editor: Tom Jefferies
Production Editor: Michelle Limoges
Editorial-Production Service: Omegatype Typography, Inc.
Compositor: Omegatype Typography, Inc.
Composition and Prepress Buyer: Linda Cox
Manufacturing Buyer: Andrew Turso
Interior Design: Roy Neuhaus
Photo Research: PoYee Oster
Art Design: Maria Sas, NuGraphic Design
Cover Design: Linda Knowles

For related titles and support materials, visit our online catalog at www.ablongman.com.

Library of Congress Cataloging-in-Publication Data
Introduction to the foundations of American education / James A. Johnson . . . [et al.]—
    13th ed.
        p. cm.
    Includes bibliographical references and index.
    ISBN 0-205-39578-3
        1. Education—Study and teaching—United States. 2. Education—United States. 3.
Educational sociology—United States. 4. Teaching—Vocational guidance—United States. I.
Johnson, James Allen
LB17.I59 2005
370'.973—dc22

                                                                          2003070184

Printed in the United States of America

10 9 8 7 6 5 4 3 2 1 VHP 08 07 06 05 04

Contents

PART **I**

The Education Profession   1

1

A Teaching Career   2

PART II

Sociological Foundations of Education   40

2

Diversity in Society   42

3

Social Challenges in Schools   76

4

Education That Is Multicultural   110

PART III

Governance and Support of American Education   138

5   Organizing and Paying for American Education   140

PART IV

Historical Foundations of Education 232

7

The Evolution of American Education 234

PART V

Philosophical Foundations of Education   302

9

Philosophy: The Passion to Understand   304

Education in the News: High-Tech Cheating Hits Schools   305

Learning Outcomes   306

10

Educational Theory in American Schools: Philosophy in Action   334

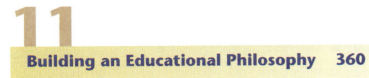

Building an Educational Philosophy   360

VI
PART

Curricular Foundations of Education   384

12

Standards-Based Education and Assessment   386

13

Designing Programs for Learners: Curriculum, Instruction, and Technology   420

14

Education in the Twenty-First Century 464

List of Features

RELEVANT RESEARCH

GLOBAL PERSPECTIVES

Preface

The thirteenth edition of *Introduction to the Foundations of American Education* is the product of the collaborative effort of five professional educators, each bringing her or his particular and general knowledge, both practical and scholarly, to the field of education and teaching. This team approach enriches the text by enlisting each author's valuable perspectives on a variety of educational topics. Like the twelfth edition, this edition uses the metaphor of a lens to give students a helpful way to study and interpret educational issues pertinent to schools, students, and the teaching profession.

As you know, a camera's zoom lens enables the photographer to view the world from different perspectives. Some lenses use tinted filters to clarify a scene or to enhance a particular view. Also, you can adjust the view through a camera lens to bring certain things into sharper focus. In this book, we use the wide-angle foundations of education lens to view education as a community of teachers and learners immersed in a complex system of institutions, norms, beliefs, social mores, laws, and instructional and assessment practices. The wide-angle lens helps us see underlying causes, examine issues of justice and equality, view education through big ideas, ask basic questions, clarify assumptions, and assess structures. This perspective is the basis of the six parts that comprise the overall structure of the book. The wide-angle view places the six parts in perspective, while the zoom ability focuses in on particular big ideas and questions in each chapter.

In addition to the lens perspective, each of the parts provides a unique filter or emphasis based on different disciplines of study. For example, the historical filter uses insights and concepts drawn from historical research, whereas the philosophical filter emphasizes philosophical ideas to enlighten an issue. Thus, students can examine each of the foundational areas in depth as the different filters bring education into sharper focus. We believe that students' understanding of education will be deepened by the six different parts with the particular lens perspective that we offer.

NEW TO THIS EDITION

- **Correlations to INTASC Standards!** The Learning Outcomes feature in each chapter opener includes **INTASC correlations** that indicate how the chapter content reflects the INTASC standards.
- **Classroom Application!** The new **School-Based Observations** feature at the beginning of each chapter suggests activities students can do during field practice.
- **Current Issues!** Back by popular demand, the chapter-opening **Education in the News** features are all new for this edition!

- **Updated Emphasis!** In response to readers' feedback, the organization of this edition focuses more on technology and the future of the teaching profession and education in the United States.
- **Teacher Certification!** The new **Preparing for Certification** feature at the end of each chapter provides activities to apply the chapter contents to Praxis and other state teacher certification tests.
- **Content Cross-References!** A new margin annotation feature called **Cross-Reference** indicates where topics are discussed elsewhere in the book and helps build a complete understanding of the information presented in the chapters.
- **Annotated References!** The new **Further Reading** feature and the **Websites** list at the end of each chapter are annotated to act as useful supplements to the information in the chapter.
- **Media Resources!** Chapter-ending correlations to Allyn & Bacon's **Themes of the Times!** newspaper archives provide media resources to expand student understanding.

FEATURES OF THE THIRTEENTH EDITION

- **Part openers** emphasize the lens metaphor, connecting the specific chapter topics to the broader foundations of education—professional, sociological, organizational and financial, historical, philosophical, and curricular. It also provides **Focus Questions** to preview the key concepts of the upcoming chapters.

- **Chapter openers** provide several features. **Education in the News** highlights a news report about current topics in education; **Learning Outcomes,** which are correlated to the INTASC Standards, identify the big ideas of the chapter; and **School-Based Observations** suggest chapter-appropriate activities that can be done during field practice.

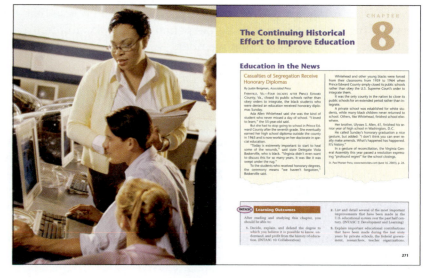

- **Professional Dilemma** features in each chapter provide opportunities to analyze real-life problems that teachers encounter in their classrooms. These features conclude with questions, which readers can answer on the Companion Website and e-mail to their professors.

- Each chapter contains a **Debate** feature, in which two educators present opposing sides of an issue related to the chapter topic. Readers also have an opportunity to register their own opinions on each issue at the Companion Website.

- **Relevant Research** features in each chapter showcase published research studies about education.

- **Global Perspectives** sections in every chapter provide preservice teachers with a better understanding of international educational practices and how they compare to practices in the United States.

- The margins of the thirteenth edition feature three types of resources. **Definitions of key terms** correspond to terms that appear in bold on the page; **quotations** provide thought-provoking comments about education; and **Cross-References** indicate where chapter topics are discussed elsewhere in the text.

- **Chapter-closing** material contains numerous resources as study aids, applications, and expansions of the chapter contents. **Summary** provides a brief chapter recap; **Discussion Questions** are thought-provoking suggestions for classroom discussion; **Journal Entries** are topics for personal reflection; **Portfolio Development** suggests artifacts for portfolios based on chapter information; **Preparing for Certification** provides sample questions for state teacher certification exams such as *Praxis*; **Websites** and **Further Reading** provide annotated bibliographies for additional information; **Themes of the Times!** correlations relate chapter contents to additional Allyn & Bacon media resources.

- Five **Appendixes** provide up-to-date resources for preservice teachers, including state certification websites, the NEA Code of Ethics, websites that list teaching positions, an educational history timeline, and professional organization websites.

A COMPREHENSIVE TEACHING AND LEARNING PACKAGE

Allyn & Bacon is committed to preparing the best supplements for its textbooks, and the supplements for the thirteenth edition of *Foundations of American Education* reflect this commitment. The following supplements provide an outstanding array of resources that facilitate learning about the foundations of education. For more information about the instructor and student supplements that accompany and support the text, ask your local Allyn & Bacon representative, or contact the Allyn & Bacon Sales Support Department (1-800-852-8024).

OUTSTANDING MEDIA RESOURCES

MyLabSchool Discover where the classroom comes to life! From video clips of teachers and students interacting to sample lessons, portfolio templates, and standards integration, Allyn & Bacon brings your students the tools they'll need to succeed in the classroom—with content easily integrated into your existing course.

Delivered within Course Compass, Allyn & Bacon's course management system, this program gives your students powerful insights into how real classrooms work and a rich array of tools that will support them on their journey from their first class to their first classroom.

VideoWorkshop for Foundations of Education CD-ROM Available free when packaged with the textbook, the CD-ROM contains eight modules of three- to five-minute digitized video clips featuring snapshots of teachers and students in real classroom settings. The VideoWorkshop CD comes with a Student Study Guide, containing all the materials needed to help students get the most out of this exciting media product. With questions for reflection before, during, and after viewing, this guide extends classroom discussion and allows for more in-class time spent on analysis of material. An Instructor's Teaching Guide is also available to provide ideas and exercises to assist faculty in incorporating this convenient supplement into course assignments and assessments. Visit www.ablongman.com/videoworkshop for more details.

Research Navigator™ (with ContentSelect Research Database) (Access Code Required) Research Navigator™ (www.researchnavigator.com) is the easiest way for students to start a research assignment or research paper. Complete with extensive help on the research process and three exclusive online databases of credible and reliable source material including EBSCO's ContentSelect™ Academic Journal Database, New York Times Search by Subject Archive, and "Best of the Web" Link Library, Research Navigator™ helps students quickly and efficiently make the most of their research time. Research Navigator™ is free when packaged with the textbook and requires an Access Code.

■ INSTRUCTOR SUPPLEMENTS: A COMPLETE INSTRUCTIONAL PACKAGE

A variety of teaching tools are available to assist instructors in organizing lectures, planning evaluations, and ensuring student comprehension.

- **Instructor's Resource Manual** Prepared by Francine Madrey, at Winston-Salem State University, the Instructor's Resource Manual includes a wealth of interesting ideas and activities designed to help instructors teach the course. Each chapter of the Manual includes at-a-glance grids, introducing the chapter, chapter overview and analysis, class activities, assignments, professional dilemma, diversity notes, journal reflection masters, and media resources.
- **Test Bank** The Test Bank has been thoroughly revised to include more challenging multiple choice, true/false, short answer, essay, case study, and alternative assessment questions. Page number references, suggested answers, and skill level have been added to each question to better help instructors create and evaluate student tests.
- **Computerized Test Bank** The printed Test Bank is also available electronically through our computerized testing system: TestGen EQ. Instructors can use TestGen EQ to create exams in just minutes by selecting from the existing database of questions, editing questions, or writing original questions.
- **Digital Media Archive for Education** This CD-ROM contains a variety of media elements that instructors can use to create electronic presentations in the classroom. It includes hundreds of original images, as well as selected art from Allyn & Bacon education texts, providing instructors with a broad selection of graphs, charts, and tables. For classrooms with full multimedia capability, it also contains video segments and Web links.
- **PowerPoint™ Presentation** Ideal for lecture presentations or student handouts, the PowerPoint™ presentation created for this text provides dozens of ready-to-use graphic and text images including illustrations from the text (available for download from Supplement Central at www.suppscentral.ablongman.com).
- **Allyn & Bacon Transparencies for Foundations of Education 2005** This revised package includes 100 acetates, most in full color.
- **Allyn & Bacon Interactive Video: Issues in Education** This video features news reports from around the country on topics covered in the text. The VHS video contains ten modules of up-to-date news clips exploring current issues and debates in education. Topics include teacher shortages, alternative schools, community–school partnerships, standardized testing, and bilingual classrooms. An accompanying instructor's guide outlines teaching strategies and discussion questions to use with the clips.
- **Online Course Management Systems** Powered by Blackboard and hosted nationally, Allyn & Bacon's own course management system, **CourseCompass,**

helps you manage all aspects of teaching your course. For colleges and universities with **WebCT**™ and **Blackboard**™ licenses, special course management packages are available in these formats as well. New for 2005, Allyn & Bacon is proud to offer premium content for Foundations of Education courses, ready to be uploaded to your online course (your sales rep can give you additional information).

STUDENTS SUPPLEMENTS: AN INTEGRATED LEARNING SYSTEM

Building on the study aids found in the text, Allyn & Bacon offers a number of supplements for students.

- **Companion Website (www.ablongman.com/johnson13e)** Prepared by [to come]. Students who visit the Companion Website that accompanies the text will find many features and activities to help them in their studies: web links, learning activities, practice tests, video and audio clips, and vocabulary flash cards. The website also features an interactive Foundations of American Education Timeline that highlights the people and events that have shaped education through history.
- **ResearchNavigator**™ **Guide for Education** This free reference guide includes tips, resources, activities, and URLs to help students use the Internet for their research projects. The first part introduces students to the resources on Research Navigator™. Part two includes information on how to correctly conduct online research. Part three includes many Internet activities that tie into the content of the text. Part four lists hundreds of special education Internet resources. It also includes Access Code for Research Navigator™.

ABOUT THE AUTHORS

James A. Johnson, professor of education emeritus at Northern Illinois University, has been an educator for more than thirty-five years, serving as a public school teacher, teacher educator, and university administrator. He has been coauthor of thirteen editions of *Introduction to the Foundations of American Education,* as well as author or coauthor of a dozen other college textbooks.

Diann Musial, professor of foundations of education and Northern Illinois University Distinguished Teaching Professor, has taught middle school science and mathematics in Chicago, served as principal of an Individually Guided Education elementary school, and worked in industry as director of training. She has directed more than twenty state and federally funded staff development grants, developed countless performance assessments and test item banks, and coauthored *Classroom 2061: Activity Assessments in Science Integrated with Mathematics and Language Arts* (Skylight Professional Development, 1995).

Gene E. Hall, dean of the College of Education at the University of Nevada at Las Vegas (UNLV), has served for more than thirty years as a teacher educator, researcher, and university administrator. He is active in assisting teacher education institutions in their efforts to become nationally accredited. He is also internationally known for his research on the change process in schools and other types of organizations. He is the lead architect of the widely used Concerns-Based Adoption Model (CBAM), which organizational leaders and staff developers employ in studying and facilitating the change process. In addition to coauthoring the last four editions of this text, he is coauthor of *Implementing Change: Patterns, Principles and Potholes* (Allyn & Bacon, 2001).

Donna M. Gollnick is senior vice president of the National Council for the Accreditation of Teacher Education (NCATE), where she oversees all accreditation activities. She is also past president of the National Association for Multicultural Education (NAME) and is a recognized authority in multicultural education. In addition to her work in teacher accreditation, she has taught in secondary schools and coauthored the last three editions of this text. She is also coauthor, with Philip C. Chinn, of *Multicultural Education in a Pluralistic Society,* Sixth Edition (Merrill, 2002).

Victor L. Dupuis, professor emeritus of curriculum and instruction and Waterbury Professor of Secondary Education at Pennsylvania State University, continues a professional career that began forty-five years ago. Currently, he serves as a private consultant in areas of staff development, Native American education, and curriculum development and evaluation with Dupuis Associates. He has also taught social studies and English and served as a school district curriculum director and teacher educator. In addition to coauthoring all twelve previous editions of this text, he has published widely in the areas of curriculum and instruction and Native American literatures.

ACKNOWLEDGMENTS

We are sincerely grateful to the many colleagues, reviewers, and editors who have helped us over the years to make this text the most popular and widely used book in the field. We thank our publisher, Allyn & Bacon, for its continued support over the years, and for enabling us to deliver the message that we, as professional educators, deem crucial for the preparation of teachers. In particular, we especially thank Sonny Regelman for her outstanding work as our developmental editor, as well as Steve Dragin, our series editor and longtime good friend, for his support and assistance. We also thank our colleagues and other members of the academic community for their assistance: Dr. Leslie Sassone for her advice on the philosophy section; Michele Clarke for research assistance; and Mary Ducharme for contributing the Preparing for Praxis features.

We also sincerely thank the following reviewers:

Barbara Burkhouse, *Marywood University*

G. Kathleen Chamberlain, *Lycoming College*

James L. Dawson, *Rochester College*

Rebecca L. Dye, *Culver-Stockton College*

Susan M. Ferguson, *University of Dayton*

Franklin B. Jones, *Tennessee State University*

Darrin Martin, *Concord College*

Thomas R. Oswald, *North Iowa Area Community College*

Mark Ryan, *National University*

Susan C. Scott, *University of Central Oklahoma*

Dale N. Titus, *Kutztown University of Pennsylvania*

INTRODUCTION TO THE FOUNDATIONS OF AMERICAN EDUCATION

 Chapter 1   A Teaching Career

The Education Profession

Viewing Education through Professional Lenses

 A lens metaphor is particularly useful in thinking about teaching, teachers, and the teaching profession. A lens can help us see things more clearly. A lens can be used to focus on certain spots, and the light that passes through a lens can contain a broad spectrum of colors. Both of these characteristics of lenses—focal point and broad spectrum—are easily applied to examining essential aspects of teaching as a profession. First of all, consider the question "What do we focus on?" Chapter 1 begins with a close-up view of teachers, society's concerns about the quality of teachers, and the teacher's working conditions.

Although this book attempts to help you personally, it also deals with what teachers should know and be able to do. This chapter also will help you focus on eventually finding a position as an educator and on the salary and fringe benefits that you may eventually receive.

As you read this book, whether the focus is personal or professional, you will find that it is focused on learning. As an aspiring teacher, you are now focusing on learning what the job of teaching entails and what you need to do to become an excellent and successful teacher. Answers to these and related important questions about the profession of teaching are the topics of Chapter 1.

Focus Questions

The following questions will help you focus your learning as you read Part I:

1. How do teachers and community members feel about the teacher's role in helping students learn at high levels?
2. What are key characteristics of the working conditions for teachers?
3. What are typical salaries and benefits for teachers?
4. In what content areas are there most likely to be position openings for new teachers?
5. What are some ways for outstanding teachers to receive extra recognition and reward?
6. If you were asked to prepare a portfolio about your potential to be an outstanding teacher, how would you go about it and what would you include?

A Teaching Career

Education in the News

The Average Teacher

Education Week, November 2002

ANYONE WHO WATCHES *BOSTON PUBLIC* EACH WEEK AND ISN'T an education professional would assume the following: Most U.S. teachers are hip, young things who work in schools of weapon-wielding, oversexed teens; and they spend much of their time obsessing about kids' personal problems rather than writing lesson plans. For a more accurate profile of teachers today, we turned to the U.S. Current Population Survey and the recently released Schools and Staffing Survey, which asked more than 42,000 public school teachers scores of questions about their work lives.[1] . . .

While those in the business know that there's nothing at all "average" about teachers, we've put together a picture of what she . . . and some of her colleagues look like. Not surprisingly, most spend abundant hours preparing for class, untangling red tape, and working to expand their knowledge and professionalism. And many, perhaps surprisingly, would return to the classroom if they had it all to do again. See if you recognize a little of yourself in this portrait of the "average" teacher.

Age: 42 years old

Gender: Female: 75%; Male: 25%

Race: White: 84.4%; Black: 7.6%; Hispanic origin: 5.6%; Asian: 1.6%; Other: 0.8%

Years of teaching experience: 15

Annual salary: $39,346

Degrees: Bachelor's: 99.3%; Master's: 46.3%; Doctorate: 0.7%

Hours worked before and after school and on weekends each week: 12

Class size: Self-contained: 21 students; Specialized subjects: 24 students

Minority student population at school: 34%

Threatened by a student in the past year: 10%

Work in a school where all kids pass through a metal detector daily: 2%

Students use computers in class: 69%

Have complete control over various areas of planning and teaching: 32%

Union member: Yes: 79.4%; No: 20.6%

Teach at least one student with an individualized education plan: 82%

Believe that lack of parental involvement is a serious problem: 24%

Strongly agree that routine duties and paperwork interfere with job: 29%

Married: 72%

Born outside the United States: 5%

Own a home: 82%

Plan to stay in teaching until retirement or as long as possible: 74%

Certainly would become a teacher again if had the chance to do it over: 40%

Reprinted with permission from *Education Week,* November 2002.

[1] *Sources:* Marital status, country of origin, and homeownership data compiled by Martye Scobee, a programmer at the Kentucky State Data Center, from the March 2000 *Annual Demographic Survey of the Current Population Survey,* conducted by the Bureau of the Census and the Bureau of Labor Statistics. All other data from the *1999–2000 Schools and Staffing Survey,* published by the National Center for Education Statistics of the U.S. Department of Education. SASS figures prepared by Jennifer Park, Editorial Projects in Education researcher. Most entries have been rounded to the nearest whole number.

Learning Outcomes

After reading and studying this chapter, you should be able to:

1. Identify the characteristics of professions and develop arguments for or against declaring teaching a profession.

2. Articulate the role demographics play in determining teacher supply and demand and identify areas in which teachers will be in high demand over the next decade.

3. Identify sources of evidence to show that you are developing the knowledge, skills, and dispositions outlined in the INTASC standards. (INTASC 1–10)

4. Outline the professional responsibilities of a teacher as viewed by the public, parents, and professional colleagues. (INTASC 1: Subject Matter)

5. Identify some of the challenges that affect teachers and not other professionals and clearly articulate why you plan to pursue a teaching career.

6. Identify the basic requirements for the initial teaching license in the state in which you plan to teach, including the type of tests and other assessments that will be required.

School-Based Observations

You may see these learning outcomes in action during your visits to schools:

1. Begin a list of the teaching challenges that you observe in schools. Discuss the challenges that you had not expected when you initially thought about teaching as a career and how those challenges may influence your decision to become a teacher. How much have the teaching challenges you have observed met your initial expectations?

2. Ask several teachers you are observing what they see as the major problems they face and about their greatest satisfactions as educators. Analyze their answers and think about the major challenges and satisfactions you may experience as an educator.

T eaching is a profession that is critical to the well-being of society. Many students indicate that they have chosen teaching as a career because they care about children and youth. Although teaching requires caring, it also requires competence in the subject being taught and in the teaching of that subject. Teachers' knowledge and skills should lead to the ultimate goal of successful teaching: student learning.

Educators must undergo stringent assessments and meet high standards to ensure high quality in the teaching profession. The teaching profession includes at least three stages of quality assurance, beginning with college-level teacher preparation programs, including the one in which you are now enrolled. Next, state teacher licensing systems give the public assurance that teachers are qualified and competent to do their work as educators.

The third stage of continuing professional development is tied to retaining the state license and seeking national certification. Each of these stages is accompanied by assessments of performance to determine whether individuals are qualified for the important job of teaching.

Reflection is one of the important characteristics of successful teachers. Professionals who reflect on and analyze their own teaching are involved in a process that is critical to improving as an educator. Individuals who are making either a lifelong or short-term commitment to teaching should consider the responsibilities and expectations of a teaching career. In this chapter, you will begin exploring the realities of what it means to be a teacher.

In addition to these concepts, Chapter 1 presents a number of big ideas about teaching. These include the fact that education is extremely important in our society, that educators are members of an established profession, that educators are generally well respected and valued by the public, and that the future job market for educators is complex but promising.

Teaching is a challenging, complex, and demanding profession that draws from the many diverse groups in the United States.

TODAY'S TEACHERS

More than three million teachers provide the instructional leadership for public and private schools in the United States. Most of today's new teachers must meet rigorous national and state standards for entering the profession that did not exist a decade ago. Requirements for entering teacher education programs in colleges and universities are now more stringent than admission requirements for most other professions. Grade point averages of 3.0 and higher are becoming more common requirements for admission; tests and other assessments must be passed before admission, at the completion of a program, and for state licensure. Clearly, not everyone can teach. The teaching profession is becoming one that attracts the best and brightest college students into its ranks.

Teacher candidates in colleges and universities today are diverse in age and work experience. Some of you are eighteen to twenty-two years old, the traditional age of college students, but still more of you are nontraditional students who are older and have worked for a number of years in other jobs or professions. Some of your classmates may have worked as teachers' aides in classrooms for years. Others may be switching careers from the armed forces, engineering, retail management, or public relations. Welcome to a profession in which new teachers represent such wonderfully diverse work experiences, as well as varying educational, cultural, and economic backgrounds.

If America's education goals are to be realized, our schools will need to recruit, hire, and develop the largest, best-prepared, and most diverse generation of teachers this nation has ever known.

Recruiting New Teachers

■ THE IMPORTANCE OF TEACHERS TO SOCIETY

Society has great expectations for its teachers. "Nine out of ten Americans believe the best way to lift student achievement is to ensure a qualified teacher in every classroom," according to a national survey.[1] In addition to guiding students' academic achievement, teachers have some responsibility for students' social and physical development. They are expected to prepare an educated citizenry that is informed about the many issues that are critical to maintaining a democracy. They help students learn to work together and try to instill the values that are critical to a just and caring society. Teachers are also asked to prepare children and youth with the knowledge and skills necessary to work in an **information age.**

Given these challenging responsibilities, teaching is one of the most important careers in a democratic society. Although critics of our education system sometimes give the impression that there is a lack of public support for schools and teachers, the public now ranks teaching as the profession that provides the most important benefit to society. Public perceptions of the importance of teaching have improved over the past years.[2] In fact, respondents to a survey ranked teachers first by more than a three-to-one margin over physicians,

information age

A period in which society must deal with vast amounts of rapidly changing information.

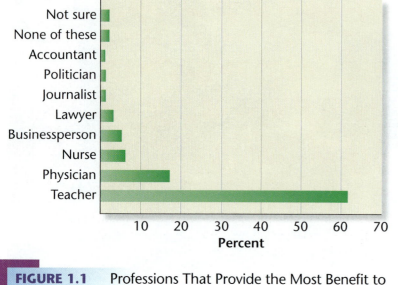

FIGURE 1.1 Professions That Provide the Most Benefit to Society According to Survey Respondents

Source: Based on data from Recruiting New Teachers, Inc., *The Essential Profession: A National Survey of Public Attitudes toward Teaching, Educational Opportunity and School Reform.* Belmont, MA: Author, 1998.

nurses, businesspeople, lawyers, journalists, politicians, and accountants, as shown in Figure 1.1.

Teachers were also given a vote of confidence in a recent Gallup Poll, which asked people to indicate the most trusted group of people in the country. The results, as shown in Figure 1.2, indicate that teachers were at the top of the most trusted groups in the country. This public trust should be both encouraging and perhaps a bit frightening to you as a future educator—encouraging because you will be entering a highly regarded and trusted professional group, and frightening because you will be responsible for helping to uphold this public trust.

THE PUBLIC VIEW OF TEACHERS AND SCHOOLS

Nine of ten Americans believe that the best way to improve student achievement is to have qualified teachers.[3] Teachers and the public agree that the quality of the teaching

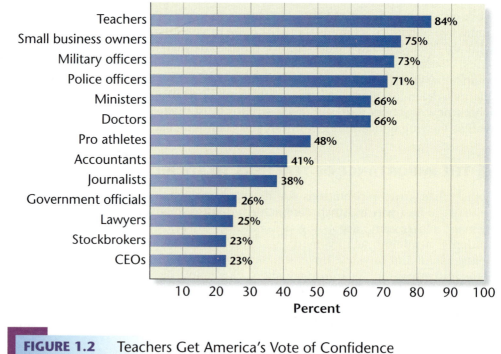

FIGURE 1.2 Teachers Get America's Vote of Confidence

You may not make as much as a CEO or a pro baseball player, but your stock has a lot more currency than theirs in the eyes of the American public.

In a recent Gallup Poll, Americans ranked teachers as the most trusted group of people in the country.

Source: Gallup Poll, July 2002, as reported in *NEA Today,* October 2002, p. 9.

staff is of primary importance in selecting a school.[4] Parents and students know who the effective teachers are in a school. Some parents do everything possible to ensure that their children are in those teachers' classes. At the same time, they know the teachers who are not as effective, and they steer their children into other classes if possible. They know the value of an effective teacher to the potential academic success of their children.

The annual Phi Delta Kappa/Gallup Poll survey on the public's attitudes toward public schools asks respondents to grade schools in both their local area and the nation as a whole. Figure 1.3 shows the results of this recent survey, which indicates that parents generally give relatively high grades to schools, especially so for their local schools.

This same annual PDK/Gallup Poll asks citizens to indicate the most serious problems facing our schools. The results of the 2002 survey are shown in Figure 1.4. Parents

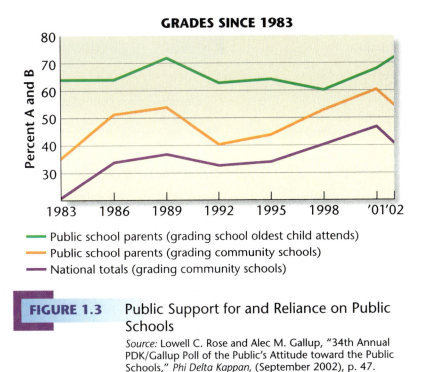

GRADES SINCE 1983

— Public school parents (grading school oldest child attends)
— Public school parents (grading community schools)
— National totals (grading community schools)

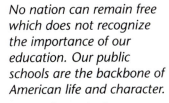

FIGURE 1.3 Public Support for and Reliance on Public Schools

Source: Lowell C. Rose and Alec M. Gallup, "34th Annual PDK/Gallup Poll of the Public's Attitude toward the Public Schools," *Phi Delta Kappan,* (September 2002), p. 47.

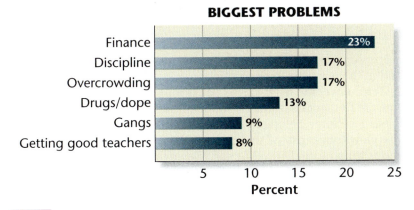

SERIOUSNESS OF PROBLEMS

Problem	Percent
Discipline	76%
Getting good teachers	73%
Overcrowding	71%
Gangs	63%

BIGGEST PROBLEMS

Problem	Percent
Finance	23%
Discipline	17%
Overcrowding	17%
Drugs/dope	13%
Gangs	9%
Getting good teachers	8%

No nation can remain free which does not recognize the importance of our education. Our public schools are the backbone of American life and character.

Samuel M. Lindsay

FIGURE 1.4 Problems Facing Community Schools

Source: Lowell C. Rose and Alec M. Gallup, "34th Annual PDK/Gallup Poll of the Public's Attitude toward the Public Schools," *Phi Delta Kappan* (September 2002), p. 49.

TABLE 1.1 What Would You Change to Improve the Public Schools in Your Community?

	Public (percent)	Teachers (percent)
Discipline/more control/stricter rules	12	6
More teachers/smaller class size	10	12
Funding	5	8
Better/more qualified teachers	7	*
Higher pay for teachers	3	5
More parent involvement	3	18
Prayer/God back in schools	4	*
Security	4	*
Academic standards/better education	3	2
Dress code/uniforms	3	*
More/updated equipment/books/computers	2	3
Curriculum/more offered	2	*

* = Less than 1 percent.

Source: Adapted from Carol A. Langdon and Nick Vesper, "The Sixth Phi Delta Kappa Poll of Teachers' Attitudes toward the Public Schools," *Phi Delta Kappan, 81*(8) (April 2000), pp. 607–611.

view discipline, getting good teachers, and overcrowding as major school problems, in their combined opinions.

Curiously, the public and teachers do not agree on all of the changes necessary to improve schools, as shown in Table 1.1. Teachers would like to see more parent involvement, whereas the public sees discipline and stricter rules as most important. Both groups agree on the importance of having more teachers and/or reducing class size. Over half of the respondents in another survey were concerned about student drug use, school violence, student drinking, lack of parental involvement, teenage pregnancy, and students' lack of basic skills. They were less concerned about large classes and poor-quality teachers. Latino and African American respondents were more likely than others to find the lack of teacher quality a serious and widespread problem. Respondents also affirmed the desire to "keep the guarantee of a free public education for every child."[5]

◼ WHO TEACHES?

Teachers should represent the diversity of the nation. However, white females are overrepresented in the teaching force, particularly in early childhood and elementary schools. Teachers come from varied backgrounds and hold a wide variety of views. Some are Democrats, some Republicans, and some members of the Reform and other parties. Some belong to unions, but others don't. They hold a variety of religious views. Because of these many differences, it is difficult to generalize about educators in the United States. However, some of the similarities and differences among teachers may help you to understand the current teaching profession.

PROFILE OF U.S. TEACHERS

Although demographic data are elusive and constantly changing, the following snapshot of educators in the United States should help you get an idea of the profile of U.S. teachers. The United States has about 2.7 million public school teachers, about 400,000 private school teachers, and about 932,000 college and

Instead of asking why women lag behind men in mathematics, we might ask the following: Why do men lag behind women in elementary school teaching, early childhood education, nursing, full-time parenting, and like activities? Is there something wrong with men or with schools that this state of affairs persists?

Nel Noddings

university faculty members. Over 60 percent of the teachers work at the elementary school level. In addition to teachers, our schools have about 411,000 administrative and education professionals, and about 1.25 million teachers' aides, clerks and secretaries, and service workers staff the nation's public schools. Another roughly million education-related jobs include education specialists in industry, instructional technologists in the military, museum educators, and training consultants in the business world. Altogether, there are approximately five million educators in the United States, making education one of the largest professions in the country.

In addition to being passionate about helping learners, teachers are good managers and take time to collaborate with their colleagues.

Nearly 75 percent of the nation's public school teachers are women. The percentage of male teachers is higher in grades 9–12, where about 46 percent of the teachers are men. Men are even better represented in vocational schools, making up about 63 percent of the teachers.

The percentage of white teachers is about 86.5, having increased by 2.4 percent during the past thirty years, whereas the number of white students in schools today is 62.7 percent. Only 7 percent of the teachers are African American; 6 percent are Latino, Asian American, or Native American. To further exacerbate the differences between the racial composition of students and that of the teaching force, projections show the teaching force becoming more white and the student body less white over the next decade.

The median age of teachers is between forty-five and fifty, higher than it has been for the past forty years. This graying of the teaching force will lead to large numbers of retirements over the next ten years, resulting in the need to replace about two million teachers. This means that there are, and will be, plenty of openings. Three-fourths of the teachers are married; about 12 percent are single; and another 12 percent are widowed, divorced, or separated.

More than half of the nation's teachers have a master's degree or higher; 2 percent have doctorates. Given the just-described demographics of age and formal education, at this time, in general, very experienced teachers are staffing our classrooms. Sixty-five percent of the teachers have been full-time teachers for more than ten years; 30 percent have over twenty years of full-time teaching experience. Public school teachers are older and more likely to have advanced degrees than are private school teachers.

ACADEMIC QUALITY OF TEACHERS AND OTHER PROFESSIONALS

Academically able teachers know the subjects they teach at a depth that allows them to draw on their **knowledge base** for examples and presentations to their students. They are excited about the subjects they teach, continue to study the subjects throughout their careers, and instill excitement about the subjects in their students.

However, a number of critics do not believe that most teachers are academically competent enough. Reports released during the past twenty years on the quality of education have often criticized teachers, reporting that they are the least academically able of college graduates. The facts challenge these unfounded perceptions of the nation's teachers.

knowledge base

Information that is supported by empirical research, disciplined inquiry, informed theory, and the wisdom of practice.

Most teachers enter and remain in their profession because of a desire to work with young people.

Researchers at the Educational Testing Service and American College Testing, Inc. examined the SAT and ACT scores of teacher candidates who had taken teacher licensure tests before admission to teacher education programs or before being licensed by a state. They found that candidates pursuing a license to teach a subject at the secondary and/or middle school level generally have college admissions test scores similar to those of all college students majoring in that academic area. Teacher candidates in mathematics and science have substantially higher SAT scores than all other college graduates. At the same time, teacher candidates in physical education, special education, and elementary education continue to have slightly lower SAT and ACT scores than other college graduates.[6]

Studies of academic prowess show that teachers perform at about the same level as other professionals. Teachers scored relatively high on measures of prose, document, and quantitative literacy tasks in a comparison with lawyers, electrical engineers, accountants, auditors, computer systems analysts, marketing professionals, financial managers, physicians, personnel and training professionals, social workers, and education administrators and counselors.[7] No significant differences were found between female and male teachers or between elementary and secondary teachers. In conclusion, research has shown that teachers are as academically able as members of other professions that are often perceived as more prestigious.

More than two hundred thousand new teachers graduate from colleges each year. Of them, about one-third never teach, about one-third teach for only a few years, and only the remaining one-third make teaching a career.

RETENTION IN THE PROFESSION

A relatively high percentage of teachers who begin working in a classroom decide that teaching is not the profession they wish to pursue. It is estimated that approximately 20 percent of the new teachers hired in a year are not teaching three years later. Teachers leave the classroom for a number of reasons. Some decide to return to school full time for an advanced degree. Others decide to pursue another career that might be more satisfying for them or pays a higher salary. Other factors for leaving teaching are related to poor working conditions in schools, including a lack of administrative support, perceived student problems, and little chance for upward mobility.

Like all other professionals, teachers become accomplished through experience. Most states do not grant a professional license to teachers until they have worked for at least three years. Teachers cannot seek national certification from the National Board for Professional Teaching Standards (NBPTS) until they have taught for three years. When teachers leave the profession in their first few years of practice, schools are losing an important developing resource. Induction and mentoring programs for new teachers increase the numbers of teachers who remain in the classroom. Good professional development programs for teachers such as **induction** programs also help to retain new teachers. When you search for your first teaching job, find out whether the school district provides induction, mentors, and professional development, especially for beginning teachers. These are services that help teachers improve their skills as well as the chances of being successful teachers and of remaining teachers over a longer period of time.

Many schools now have a system that provides **mentoring** among teachers. This peer mentoring system is designed to facilitate teachers helping one another. As part of a new teacher induction program, many of these schools assign an experienced master teacher to serve as a mentor to beginning teachers.

TEACHERS NEEDED

Many factors influence the number of teachers that a school district needs each year. The number of students in schools, the ratio of teachers to students in classrooms, immigration patterns, and migration from one school district to another influence the demand for teachers. The supply of teachers depends on the numbers of new teachers licensed, teachers who retired the previous year, and teachers returning to the workforce.

Sometimes the supply is greater than the demand, but various estimates for the next decade indicate a demand for new teachers beyond the number being prepared in colleges and universities. Overall, the United States does not have a teacher shortage. The problem is the distribution of teachers. School districts with good teaching conditions and high salaries do not face teacher shortages. However, inner cities and rural areas too often do not have adequate numbers of qualified and licensed teachers. There also are greater shortages of teachers in parts of the country with increasing populations, such as states in the Southwest.

TEACHER SUPPLY

The supply of new teachers in a given year consists primarily of two groups: new teacher graduates and former teacher graduates who were not employed as teachers in the previous year. Not all college graduates who prepared to teach actually teach. Generally, only about half of the college graduates who have completed teacher education programs actually take teaching positions in the first few years after graduation.

It is estimated that nearly half of the teachers hired by the typical school district are first-time teachers. One-third are experienced teachers who have moved from other school districts or from other jobs within the district. Experienced

The common teacher is not common at all. He (or she) is bulging with talent, with energy, and with understanding. What we human teachers have to give, ultimately, is ourselves—our own love for life, and for our subject, and our ability to respond to the personal concerns of our students.

Terry Borton, Reach, Touch, Teach

induction
The first one to three years of full-time teaching.

mentoring
One experienced professional helping a less experienced colleague.

teachers reentering the field make up the remainder of the new hires. Unfortunately, not all teachers who are hired have been even minimally prepared to teach before they take charge of a classroom. Over one-fourth of newly hired teachers are not qualified for the beginning license to teach. Some new hires do not have a license; others have a temporary, provisional, or emergency license.

NEW TEACHERS   A growing number of new teachers are not recent college graduates. They are applicants who are changing careers, such as retirees from the military or business. These older new teachers with years of work experience often have completed alternative pathways into teaching through school-based graduate programs that build on their prior experiences.

Still other new teachers have no preparation to teach; some do not even have a college degree. More often they have a degree in an academic area such as chemistry or history but have not studied teaching and learning or participated in clinical practices in schools. A number of states and school districts allow these individuals to teach with only a few weeks of training in the summer. Participants in these programs are more likely to be dissatisfied with their preparation than are teachers who have completed either regular or nontraditional programs for teacher preparation. They often have difficulty planning the curriculum, managing the classroom, and diagnosing students' learning needs, especially in their first years of teaching. Individuals who enter the profession through this path leave teaching at a higher rate than other teachers.

RETURNING TEACHERS   A number of licensed teachers drop out of the profession for a time but return later in life. These teachers constitute about 20 percent of the new hires each year. About 30 percent of the returning teachers were substitute teachers in the previous year; 15 percent were working in education but not in teaching roles. Others were working outside of education, attending college, or engaged in homemaking or child-rearing. Therefore, when you finish your teacher education program, you will be competing for teaching positions not only with other new graduates but also with experienced teachers who are returning to the classroom or moving from one school district to another.

TEACHER DEMAND

The demand for teachers in the United States varies considerably from time to time, from place to place, from subject to subject, and from grade level to grade level. One of the major factors related to the demand for teachers is the number of school-age children, which can be projected into the future on the basis of birthrates.

The number of school-age children in the United States is expected to increase to 54.2 million by 2009.

The projected demand for K–12 teachers through 2009 is shown in Figure 1.5. Many teachers will be retiring over the next decade, raising even further the number of new and reentering teachers needed to staff the nation's schools. As you plan your teaching career, you will want to consider a number of factors such as salary, fringe benefits, cost of living, workload, and so forth, that influence the demand for teachers. They may influence decisions you make about the subjects you will teach and the area of the country in which you will teach.

STUDENT-TO-TEACHER RATIOS Obviously, one measure of a teacher's workload is class size. The number of students taught by a teacher varies considerably from school to school and from state to state. Elementary teachers generally have more students in a class than secondary teachers, but secondary teachers have five to seven classes each day. Figure 1.6 shows average student-to-teacher ratios in public and private schools in the United States.

The demand for teachers has increased, in part, because some states and school districts are limiting the student-to-teacher ratio, especially in the primary grades. In large school districts, lowering the student-to-teacher ratio by even one student creates a demand for many more teachers. State initiatives to reduce the ratio have an even greater impact on the number of teachers needed.

LOCATION OF THE SCHOOL DISTRICT Even within a given metropolitan area, population shifts may be causing one school district to grow rapidly, build new schools, and hire new teachers because of new housing developments, while a neighboring school district is closing schools and reducing its number of teachers. Nevertheless, the greatest shortages are usually in urban schools with large proportions of low-income and culturally and linguistically diverse populations. Some teachers do not want to teach in large urban school districts because of poor working conditions in many schools and relatively low salaries as compared to schools in the wealthier suburbs. Many other teachers believe that teaching in a large city is challenging and fulfilling, with many advantages.

Urban schools are more likely than others to be staffed by unprepared teachers who have not met the qualifications for a state license. New, inexperienced teachers are disproportionately represented in the schools that need the best teachers. Attrition rates for new teachers in these districts are high in the first five years of teaching, leading to the constant need for replacements. To address this problem, some states have scholarships and loan-forgiveness programs to encourage teacher candidates to work in these high-demand areas.

Student enrollment also varies depending on the part of the country. By 2009, increases of more than 15 percent are expected in Arizona, Idaho, Nevada, and New Mexico; decreases are expected in most midwestern and northeastern states. Student enrollment in the District of Columbia, Maine, North Dakota, and West Virginia is projected to decrease by 7 to 12 percent.[8]

Almost all teachers can find a teaching position if they are willing to move to a place where jobs are available. One of the

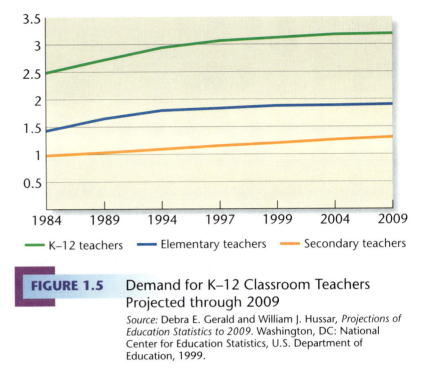

FIGURE 1.5 Demand for K–12 Classroom Teachers Projected through 2009

Source: Debra E. Gerald and William J. Hussar, *Projections of Education Statistics to 2009*. Washington, DC: National Center for Education Statistics, U.S. Department of Education, 1999.

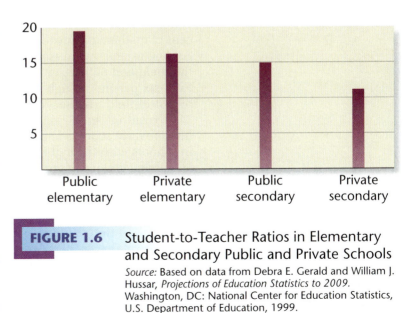

FIGURE 1.6 Student-to-Teacher Ratios in Elementary and Secondary Public and Private Schools

Source: Based on data from Debra E. Gerald and William J. Hussar, *Projections of Education Statistics to 2009*. Washington, DC: National Center for Education Statistics, U.S. Department of Education, 1999.

Bilingual teachers are in short supply throughout the United States— especially in southern and western states. What employment opportunities does this need present?

problems is that new teachers often want to remain close to home, which is more likely to be in small towns and suburban areas. To attract teachers to areas with teaching shortages, some school districts are offering signing bonuses and paying moving expenses. Others are exploring strategies to offer teachers housing and favorable mortgages.

TEACHING FIELD SHORTAGES Teacher shortages are more severe in some fields than others. For instance, the number of students diagnosed with various disabilities has increased considerably over the last decade and now totals more than five million throughout the country. As a percentage of the total public school enrollment, the number of students requiring special education has risen considerably in recent years. Consequently, most school districts report the need for more special education teachers.

There is also a critical shortage of bilingual teachers. The need for bilingual teachers is no longer limited to large urban areas and the southwestern states. Immigrant families with children have now settled in cities and rural areas across the Midwest and Southeast. The projected demographics for the country indicate a growing number of students with limited-English skills, requiring more bilingual and English as a second language (ESL) teachers than are available today.

Licensed mathematics and science teachers are prime candidates for job openings in many school districts. One of the problems in secondary schools especially is that teachers may have a state license but too often not in the academic area they are assigned to teach. The National Commission on Teaching and America's Future reported that:

- Nearly one-fourth (23 percent) of all secondary teachers do not have even a college minor in their main teaching field. This is true for more than 30 percent of mathematics teachers.
- Among teachers who teach a second subject, 36 percent are unlicensed in that field and 50 percent lack a minor.
- Fifty-six percent of high school students taking physical science are taught by out-of-field teachers, as are 27 percent of those taking mathematics and 21 percent of those taking English. The proportions are much higher in high-poverty schools and in lower-track classes.
- In schools with the highest minority enrollments, students have less than a 50 percent chance of getting a science or mathematics teacher who holds a license and a degree in the field he or she teaches.[9]

Teachers receive these out-of-field assignments when teachers with the appropriate academic credentials are not available. Sometimes the assignments are made to retain teachers whose jobs have been eliminated as enrollments shift and schools are closed. The tragedy is that students suffer as a result. It is difficult to teach what you do not know. The new federal legislation commonly referred to as the No Child Left Behind Act is designed to significantly reduce this out-of-field teacher assignment problem in the near future.

CROSS-REFERENCE
Much more detail regarding multicultural education is presented in Chapters 2 and 3.

CROSS-REFERENCE
This important federal legislation (No Child Left Behind) is discussed throughout the remaining chapters of this book.

TEACHERS FROM DIVERSE BACKGROUNDS   Although the student population is becoming more racially, ethnically, and linguistically diverse, the teaching pool is becoming less so. The number of Latino students is rapidly increasing, pulling almost even with the number of African American students in the 2000 census. The racial and panethnic composition of the student population and teaching force is shown in Figure 1.7.

Having teachers from different ethnic and cultural backgrounds is extremely important to the majority of people in the United States.[10] Most school districts are seeking culturally diverse faculties, and districts with large culturally diverse populations are aggressively recruiting teachers from diverse backgrounds. The federal government and some states provide incentives to colleges and universities to support the recruitment of a more diverse teaching force. Another implication of the demographics of increasing student diversity is that all teachers need to become skilled at teaching in diverse schools and classrooms.

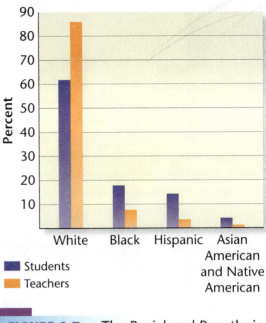

FIGURE 1.7   The Racial and Panethnic Composition of the Student Population and Teaching Force in Public Schools

Sources: Based on data from (1) National Center for Education Statistics, U.S. Department of Education, *The Condition of Education 2000.* Washington, DC: Author, 2000. (2) National Center for Education Statistics, U.S. Department of Education, *Digest of Education Statistics, 1999.* Washington, DC: Author, 1999.

TEACHING AS A PROFESSION

Historically, fields such as law, medicine, architecture, and accountancy have been considered professions, but teaching and nursing have sometimes been classified as semi-professions. This distinction is based in part on the prestige of the different jobs as reflected in the remuneration received by members of the profession. Although teaching salaries remain lower than those of other professionals in most parts of the country, most educators probably consider themselves professionals. The good news is that over the past decade the prestige of teaching has risen. Most teachers have master's degrees and continue to participate in professional development activities throughout their careers. For the most part, they manage their professional work, designing and delivering a curriculum during a school year. They develop their own unique teaching styles and methods for helping students learn. In this section, we will explore the factors that determine a profession and a professional and demonstrate that teaching itself is a full-fledged profession.

Teaching is a profession laden with risk and responsibility that requires a great deal from those who enter it.

John I. Goodlad

CHARACTERISTICS OF A PROFESSION

Professionals provide services to their clients, and their work is based on unique knowledge and skills grounded in research and practice in the field. Professions require their members to have completed higher education, usually at the advanced level. The competence of most professionals is determined in training by **authentic assessments** in real settings. Traditionally, they have had control of their work with little direct supervision.

PROFESSIONAL KNOWLEDGE

One of the characteristics of a profession is that its members have some generally agreed-upon knowledge bases for their work. This professional knowledge has evolved from research and practice in the field. Teachers who have prepared to

authentic assessment

An assessment procedure that uses real-world situations to assess students' ability to encounter those situations successfully, using journals, drawings, artifacts, interviews, and so on.

Each teaching discipline has unique requirements and knowledge bases needed for certification.

teach are more successful in classrooms than those who only have a degree in an academic discipline. These competent and qualified teachers are key to student learning. They also remain in the classroom for longer periods.

First and foremost, teachers must know the subjects they will be teaching. Secondary teachers often major in an academic area that they later will teach so that they learn the structure, skills, core concepts, ideas, values, facts, and methods of inquiry that undergird the discipline. They must understand the discipline well enough to help young people learn it and apply it to the world in which they live. If students are not learning a concept or skill, teachers must be able to relate the content to the experiences of students in order to provide meaning and purpose.

Elementary and middle school teachers usually teach more than one subject. A growing number of states and some colleges are requiring these teacher candidates to major in an academic area or have a concentration in one or more academic areas. Middle school teachers may teach one or two subjects; sometimes they team teach with others whose academic preparation is in other subjects. Elementary teachers, by contrast, often teach reading, English language arts, social studies, mathematics, and science in a self-contained classroom with few or no outside professional resources to assist them. In many schools, they are also expected to help students develop healthy lifestyles and an appreciation for music and art. To begin to have the academic knowledge to teach requires more than four years of college for many teacher candidates.

One of the primary cornerstones of the field of teaching is knowledge about teaching and learning and the development of skills and **dispositions** to help students learn. Therefore, teacher candidates study theories and research on how students learn at different ages. They must understand the influence of culture, language, and socioeconomic conditions on learning. In addition, they have to know how to manage classrooms, motivate students, work with parents and other colleagues, assess learning, and develop lesson plans built on the prior experiences of fifteen to thirty or more students in the classroom. Teaching is a complex field. There are seldom right answers that fit every situation. Teachers must make multiple decisions throughout a day, responding to individual student needs and events in the school and community. They must do so keeping in mind the professional ethics required by the education profession.

Qualified teachers have also had the opportunity to develop their knowledge, skills, and dispositions with students in schools. These field experiences and clinical practice such as student teaching and internships should be accompanied by feedback and mentoring from experienced teachers who know the subject they teach and how to help students learn. Work in schools is becoming more extensive in many teacher education programs. Some teacher candidates participate in yearlong internships in schools, ending in a master's degree. Others work in professional development schools in which higher education faculty, teachers, and teacher candidates collaborate in teaching and inquiry. In both of these cases, most, if not all, of the program is offered in the school setting.

The knowledge about teaching and learning, translated into student learning in the classroom, makes up the professional knowledge for teaching. People who begin to teach without this professional knowledge and the accompanying experiences for honing their skills in classrooms have difficulty in managing classrooms and teaching effectively.

dispositions

The values, commitments, and professional ethics that influence beliefs, attitudes, and behaviors.

STANDARDS

Standards are an important part of professions. They define, in part, what professionals should know and be able to do. They indicate the core values of the profession and the essential, agreed-upon knowledge and skills that professionals should have. Members of the profession develop standards to guide training, entry into the profession, and continuing practice in the profession. States also develop standards that define the minimal expectations to practice the profession in a particular state.

Standards and standards-based education are prevalent at all levels of education today. To finish your teacher education program, you will have to meet professional, state, and institutional standards that outline what you should know and be able to do as a novice teacher. When you begin teaching, you will be expected to prepare students to meet state or district standards. Assessments are designed to determine whether students meet the preschool–grade 12 standards at the levels expected. Most states require teacher candidates to pass standardized tests at a predetermined level before granting the first license to teach. Some states require beginning teachers to pass **performance assessments** based on standards in the first three years of practice in order to receive a professional license.

Standards developed by the profession can be levers for raising the quality of practice. When used appropriately, they can protect the least advantaged

CROSS-REFERENCE
Standards and assessment are discussed further in Chapter 12.

performance assessment
A comprehensive assessment system through which candidates demonstrate their proficiencies in the area being measured.

PROFESSIONAL DILEMMA
Who Is Cheating Now?

Testing is pervasive in our educational system today. Many school districts and states require students to pass tests to move from one grade to another grade. They must pass tests to graduate from high school and to enter most colleges and universities. Teacher candidates must pass numerous standardized tests to be licensed.

Not only are students and teacher candidates tested regularly and often, but also their schools and universities are held accountable for their performance on these tests. The aggregated results are published in newspapers and on websites. Schools and colleges are ranked within a state. Some are classified as low performing and lose part of their public funding. In some schools, teachers' and principals' jobs depend on how well their students perform on these standardized tests.

The standardized tests that are being used in elementary and secondary education are supposed to test for evidence that students are meeting state standards. For the most part, they are paper-and-pencil tests of knowledge in a subject area. Although the state standards are advertised as being developed by teachers and experts, many educators argue that many of the standards expect knowledge and skills that are developmentally inappropriate at some grade levels. In areas such as social studies, recall of specific facts that cover spans of hundreds of years is not an uncommon requirement.

It probably comes as no surprise that some teachers are teaching to the test, taking weeks out of the curriculum to coach students for the test. Too often, teachers and administrators are taking inappropriate steps to ensure higher scores. Test questions have been shared with students before the test. Students have been given additional time to complete a test. Low-performing students have been asked to stay at home on test days; high-performing students who are sick on test day are begged to come in anyway. As a result, teachers and principals are losing their jobs in cheating scandals across the country.

- What ethical issues are involved when educators interfere with the testing process?

- What are the limitations of standardized testing for high-stakes decisions about grade promotion, graduation, and teacher licensure?

- Why are standardized tests so pervasive in today's society?

- How would you respond if you knew that a teacher in your school was cheating in the way that he or she is preparing students for upcoming tests?

To answer these questions on-line and e-mail your answers to your professor, go to Chapter 1 of the companion website (**www.ablongman.com/johnson13e**) and click on Professional Dilemma.

The major goal of the No Child Left Behind legislation is to improve learning for all children.

students from incompetent practice.[11] Some educators view standards as a threat, especially when a government agency or other group holds individuals or schools to the standards, making summative judgments about licensure or approval. Others see standards as powerful tools for positive change in a profession or in school practices.

NO CHILD LEFT BEHIND

A new, sweeping piece of federal legislation, with the determined and optimistic title "No Child Left Behind," was signed into law by President George W. Bush on January 8, 2002. This act, which is actually a reauthorized version of the earlier Elementary and Secondary Education Act (ESEA), is built around four national education reform goals: stronger accountability for student learning results, increased educational flexibility and local control, expanded educational options for parents, and an emphasis on using teaching methods that have been proved to work. The act received overwhelming support by the U.S. Congress and the administration and is likely to guide much of our public education for at least the next decade. This far-reaching law will require the tracking of all students' progress from grades 3 to 8 and will also require every student to pass the state proficiency test(s) by the end of the 2013–14 school year.

Most important to you as a future teacher, this new legislation requires that every classroom have a highly qualified, competent teacher who is fully certified and licensed in the areas being taught in every classroom. Like all sweeping pieces of legislation, the No Child Left Behind Act is controversial and has many critics. Because it will have a considerable impact on your future as an educator and citizen, we highly recommend that you review it more closely (see www.nochildleftbehind.gov).

■ QUALITY ASSURANCE

One of the roles of professions and their standards is to provide quality control over who enters and remains in the profession. Most other professions, such as law, medicine, and dentistry, require candidates to graduate from an accredited professional school before they are even eligible to take a licensing examination to test the knowledge and skills necessary to practice responsibly. Some professions also offer examinations for certification of advanced skills, such as the CPA exam for public accountants, or for practice in specialized fields such as pediatrics, obstetrics, or surgery. The same quality assurance continuum now exists for teaching. Figure 1.8 depicts a comprehensive quality assurance system for teaching that includes complementary sets of standards and assessments for initial teacher preparation, state licensure, National Board certification, and continuing professional development.

ACCREDITATION

Both public schools and teacher education programs are subject to accreditation programs, some of which are mandated and some of which are voluntary.

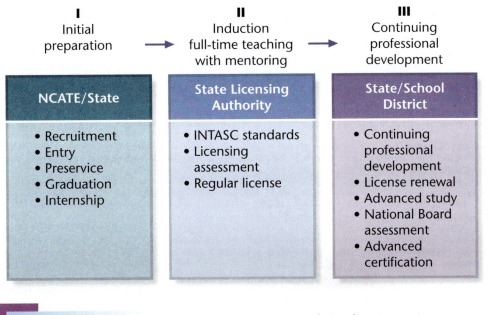

I Initial preparation	II Induction full-time teaching with mentoring	III Continuing professional development
NCATE/State	**State Licensing Authority**	**State/School District**
• Recruitment • Entry • Preservice • Graduation • Internship	• INTASC standards • Licensing assessment • Regular license	• Continuing professional development • License renewal • Advanced study • National Board assessment • Advanced certification

FIGURE 1.8   The Professional Continuum and Quality Assurance in Teaching

REGIONAL ACCREDITATION   The general concept of accreditation is related to an internal attempt on the part of a profession to examine and improve the quality of the profession that it serves. This is the case for the six regional accreditation bodies that offer accreditation to all K–12 schools and to colleges and universities. One of these six agencies, all of which are named by the general region in which they function, is functioning in your state right now. For instance, the North Central Association of Schools and Colleges (NCA) covers a large number of states in the upper central part of the nation. You might want to inquire whether your own institution is accredited by one of these six regional accrediting agencies. There is a good chance that the schools in which you will eventually teach will also be involved in some type of regional accreditation.

NCATE   Do you know whether the teacher education program you are in is part of an accredited institution? Your college or university is probably accredited by one of six regional accrediting bodies that apply standards to the university as a whole by reviewing its financial status, student services, and the general studies curriculum. However, professional accreditation in teacher education is granted to the school, college, or department of education that is responsible for preparing teachers and other educators. Fewer than half of the roughly 1,300 institutions that prepare teachers in the United States are accredited by the profession's accrediting agency, the National Council for Accreditation of Teacher Education (NCATE). In contrast, professional accrediting bodies accredit nearly all of the institutions that prepare physicians, architects, veterinarians, dentists, and lawyers. In most states, these professionals must have graduated from accredited schools to sit for state licensing tests. However, fewer than five states require all of their teacher education programs to be nationally accredited. To check on the accreditation status of your institution, visit NCATE's website at www.ncate.org.

Accreditation also can be the momentum for improvement in the profession, often provoking real change in the preparation of professionals. NCATE's standards, for example, hold schools of education responsible for the quality of the educators who complete programs. They expect the faculty to prepare candidates to meet professional and state standards as shown through successful practice in schools. Field experiences and clinical practice in schools must be designed for teacher candidates to help them develop the knowledge, skills, and dispositions necessary to be effective educators.

Accreditation also provides assurance to the public that graduates of programs are qualified and competent to practice. The proportion of accredited schools, colleges, and departments of education in a state has been found to be the best predictor of the proportion of well-qualified teachers in a state.[12] Because well-qualified teachers are the strongest predictor of student achievement on national achievement tests, accreditation is an important first step of a quality assurance system in the education field.

LICENSURE

When you graduate, you will be required to obtain a teaching license for the state in which you wish to teach. The requirements for your license are determined by the state in which you teach.

STATE TEACHER CERTIFICATION State licensure is a major component of a quality assurance system for professionals. To practice as a physician, nurse, lawyer, architect, or teacher, you must be granted a license from a state agency. A license to teach usually requires completion of a state-approved teacher education program and passing a standardized test of knowledge. A growing number of states require teacher candidates to major in an academic area rather than in education. In addition, student teaching or an internship must be completed successfully. Requirements for licensure differ from state to state. For this reason, if you plan to teach in a state different from the one in which you are going to school, you may want to contact that state directly for licensure information. Information on licensure requirements is available on the websites of state licensing agencies; for a list of agencies and contact information, see Appendix A at the end of this book. The certification officer at your institution should be able to provide you with licensure information and details about seeking a license in another state.

The initial license allows a new teacher to practice for a specified period, usually three to five years, or the induction period. On completion of successful teaching during that period and sometimes a master's degree, a professional license can be granted. Most states require continuing professional development throughout the teacher's career and periodical renewal of the license, typically every five years.

States traditionally required candidates to take specific college courses, complete student teaching, and successfully pass a licensure examination for a license. Most states are now in the process of developing **performance-based licensing** systems. These will not specify courses to be completed; instead, they will indicate the knowledge, skills, and sometimes dispositions that candidates should possess. Future decisions about granting a license will depend on the results of state assessments based primarily on licensure test scores.

INTASC Concerned about the limitations of standardized tests and their predictability of successful classroom practice, more than thirty states are participating in a consortium to develop performance-based licensure standards and assessments. The ten principles of the Interstate New Teacher Assessment and Support Consortium (INTASC) have been adopted or adapted for licensure by many states. Figure 1.9 shows these ten principles, which describe what teachers should know and be able to do in their first few years of practice. You should be developing this knowledge and skills in the college program in which you are currently enrolled. Before granting the professional license, some states are requiring teachers to submit **portfolios,** which are scored by experienced teachers, as evidence of teaching effectiveness. The portfolios that you begin to com-

---

performance-based licensing

A system of licensing professionals based on the use of multiple assessments that measure the candidate's knowledge, skills, and dispositions to determine whether he or she can perform effectively in the profession.

portfolio

A compilation of works, records, and accomplishments that teacher candidates prepare for a specific purpose to demonstrate their learnings, performances, and contributions.

1. The teacher understands the central concepts, tools of inquiry, and structures of the discipline(s) he or she teaches and can create learning experiences that make these aspects of subject matter meaningful for students.
2. The teacher understands how children learn and develop, and can provide learning opportunities that support their intellectual, social, and personal development.
3. The teacher understands how students differ in their approaches to learning and creates instructional opportunities that are adapted to diverse learners.
4. The teacher understands and uses a variety of instructional strategies to encourage students' development of critical thinking, problem solving, and performance skills.
5. The teacher uses an understanding of individual and group motivation and behavior to create a learning environment that encourages positive social interaction, active engagement in learning, and self-motivation.
6. The teacher uses knowledge of effective verbal, nonverbal, and media communication techniques to foster active inquiry, collaboration, and supportive interaction in the classroom.
7. The teacher plans instruction based on knowledge of subject matter, students, the community, and curriculum goals.
8. The teacher understands and uses formal and informal assessment strategies to evaluate and ensure the continuous intellectual, social, and physical development of the learner.
9. The teacher is a reflective practitioner who continually evaluates the effects of his/her choices and actions on others (students, parents, and other professionals in the learning community) and who actively seeks out opportunities to grow professionally.
10. The teacher fosters relationships with school colleagues, parents, and agencies in the larger community to support students' learning and well-being.

Each of these ten principles is accompanied in the full INTASC document with knowledge, dispositions, and performance expectations for candidates. INTASC content standards also have been developed for teachers of the arts, English language arts, mathematics, science, social studies, elementary education, and special education. INTASC standards can be accessed from the web at www.ccsso.org.

FIGURE 1.9   INTASC Principles: What Teachers Should Know and Be Able to Do

pile during your teacher education program could evolve into the documentation you will later need to submit for your first professional license.

PRAXIS   The Educational Testing Service (ETS) has developed a series of three examinations, commonly called the *Praxis Series*, that are designed to assess the knowledge and skills required to be an effective educator at various stages of a beginning teacher's career. Praxis I assesses academic skills, Praxis III assesses the subjects to be taught, and Praxis III assesses classroom performance. Some teacher education programs and most states make use of these tests as part of their admission, retention, graduation, and certification requirements. Perhaps you are familiar with these Praxis tests; you may even have taken some of them. You should become familiar with them, including Praxis II, which illustrates the subject matter that you should know in your particular teaching field. You can learn more about the *Praxis Series* by visiting its website at www.ets.org/praxis.

ADVANCED CERTIFICATION

Advanced certification has long been an option in many professions but is relatively new for teaching. Like all issues related to education, requiring advanced certification is a concept not supported by everyone.

STATE ADVANCED CERTIFICATION PROGRAMS   Many states now have an advanced certification option for educators. Some states actually require teachers to progress through a series of certification levels, whereas other states have either optional levels of certification that are made available to teachers or only one certification level. You should inquire about the certification levels required or available in your state. You obviously should also eventually clearly understand the certification requirements and options in any school district in which you might consider working.

NBPTS   The National Board for Professional Teaching Standards (NBPTS) was established in 1987 to develop a system for certifying accomplished teachers. The first teachers were certified in 1995; by 2000, over 4,800 experienced teachers had been board certified. The number of teachers seeking national certification continues to increase. Nearly 10,000 teachers were preparing documentation for certification in 2000.

The National Board standards outline what teachers should know and be able to do as accomplished teachers. These standards state that nationally certified teachers:

1. Are committed to students and their learning.
2. Know the subjects they teach and how to teach those subjects to students.
3. Are responsible for managing and monitoring student learning.
4. Think systematically about their practice and learn from experience.
5. Are members of learning communities.

Why then do teachers seek national certification? For one thing, recognition of accomplishment by one's peers is fulfilling. Nationally certified teachers are also aggressively being recruited by some school districts. Some school districts and half of the states pay an extra salary stipend that can be several thousand dollars annually to nationally certified teachers. Your current teacher education program should be providing the basic foundation for future national certification.

Teachers must have taught for at least three years before they are eligible for national certification. The process for becoming nationally certified is time-consuming and requires at least a year. You can learn the details about this opportunity by visiting the National Board website at www.nbpts.org.

The certification process requires the submission of portfolios with samples of student work and videotapes of the applicant teaching. In addition, the teachers must complete a number of activities at an assessment center. Experienced teachers score the various assessment activities. Many teachers do not meet the national requirements on the first try but report that the process is the best professional development activity in which they have participated. Overwhelmingly, teachers report that they have become better teachers as a result. More and more parents in the future will likely request a nationally certified teacher in the classrooms of their children.

■ PROFESSIONAL RESPONSIBILITIES

Being a professional carries many responsibilities. Professionals in most fields regulate licensure and practice through a professional standards board controlled by members of the profession rather than the government. Professional standards boards for teaching currently exist in about one-fourth of the states;

other agencies have this responsibility in the remaining states. These boards have a variety of titles and typically include many practicing educators. Not only do these boards set standards for licensure, but they also have standards and processes for monitoring the practice of teachers. They usually have the authority to remove a teacher's license.

DEVELOPING PROFESSIONAL COMMITMENTS AND DISPOSITIONS

Successful teachers exhibit dispositions that facilitate their work with students and parents. Teachers' values, commitments, and professional ethics influence interactions with students, families, colleagues, and communities. They affect student learning, motivation, and development. They influence a teacher's own professional growth as well. Dispositions held by teachers who are able to help all students learn include:

1. Enthusiasm for the discipline(s) she or he teaches and the ability to see connections to everyday life.
2. A commitment to continuous learning and engagement in professional discourse about subject matter knowledge and children's learning of the disciplines.
3. The belief that all children can learn at high levels.
4. Valuing the many ways in which people seek to communicate and encouraging many modes of communication in the classroom.
5. Development of respectful and productive relationships with parents and guardians from diverse home and community situations, seeking to develop cooperative partnerships in support of student learning and well-being.

EDUCATOR CODE OF ETHICS

One of the characteristics of a profession is the acceptance of a statement of ethics that professionals are expected to uphold. A number of professional associations have codes of ethics for individuals in a particular role, such as the special education teacher. Professional standards boards apply a code of ethics as they investigate complaints against teachers and other educators, sometimes removing an individual's license because of infractions. The code of ethics adopted by the largest organization of teachers, the National Education Association (NEA), outlines the critical values and behaviors expected of practicing teachers. This code of ethics can be found in Appendix B at the end of this book.

You are likely to have made some of these professional commitments when you decided to become a teacher. Your teacher education program should help you to further develop these dispositions and commitments and learn new ones. They are usually assessed as you work in classrooms with students and families.

▮ REFLECTING ON ONE'S PRACTICE

It is interesting, and perhaps useful to educators, to note that physicians proudly claim to "practice" medicine throughout their careers. Many people have suggested that teachers should borrow this concept and also proudly undertake to "practice" teaching throughout their careers. This interpretation of the word *practice* implies that teachers, like physicians, should constantly strive to improve their performance—something that all good teachers do. This section provides you with a few practical suggestions as you prepare to "practice" your profession as a teacher.

Given the trend to include students with disabilities in general education classrooms, it is likely that some of your students will have special needs, no matter what grade or subject you teach.

SYSTEMATIC OBSERVATION AND JOURNALING

As you proceed through your teacher education program, you should seize every opportunity to observe a wide variety of activities related to the world of education. For instance, in addition to the observation and participation assignments you will have as part of the formal teacher education program, you should seek out opportunities to visit and observe a wide variety of classrooms. You should also attempt to find summer employment that allows you to work with young people.

INFORMAL NOTE-TAKING   One of the most common ways to collect information is by writing down your observations. This type of note-taking can be done in a variety of ways. For instance, when you go into a classroom you could start by writing a brief description of the setting, such as the physical appearance of the room, the number of students, the teaching devices available, and so on. You can then systematically describe each of the things you observe. The more detail you can record, the more you will learn from your observations. Create a list of questions before you begin any given observation. If you are interested in how a teacher motivates students during a particular lesson, write down the question "What techniques does the teacher use to help motivate students?" Then record your observations under that question. The School-Based Observations feature, located at the beginning of each chapter of this book, will help you get an idea of the types of observations you can make.

STRUCTURED OBSERVATIONS   Observations that are conducted according to a predetermined plan are often referred to as **structured observations.** As your college or university sends you out into schools for various laboratory experiences, you should decide in advance what things you would like to observe. In fact, some colleges have developed structured observation forms that will guide you when participating in clinical experiences. We also recommend that you create your own structured observation forms around the questions that particularly intrigue you. In other words, if you are especially interested in classroom diversity, devise your own structured observation form to remind you to look for details concerning that particular topic the next time you are in a classroom. In fact, it might be fun to create some structured observation forms that you can use with the professors in your college classes. The more aware you are of what you are looking for as you observe a classroom, the more you are likely to learn about that particular topic.

OBSERVATION INSTRUMENTS   You might find it difficult to believe, but literally hundreds of structured observation instruments have been devised to help educators collect more valid data about classrooms. These observation instruments range from quite simple devices to extremely complex systems that require computers for analysis. Generally, however, they fall into two basic categories: structured interviews and **classroom analysis systems.**

STRUCTURED INTERVIEWS   Structured interviews consist of a series of specific questions that are asked of a respondent, as well as some provision for recording the respondent's answer. You could prepare a series of important questions that you would like to ask a principal, teacher, student, parent, or anyone else connected with the educational enterprise. Make sure that these questions are clear and that the respondent will understand what you are asking. You can then seek out a number of respondents and interview them with the same structured interview technique. Obviously, the more people you survey through such a technique, the more representative your data will be for the population in general. If you ask only one teacher the question "What is the single best dis-

structured observations
Observations that are conducted according to a predetermined plan.

classroom analysis systems
Clearly defined sets of procedures and written materials that educators can use to analyze the interaction between teachers and students.

cipline technique you use in your classroom?" you will glean only one idea; if you ask 100 teachers the same question, you will obtain much more representative data about effective discipline techniques.

ANALYSIS OF PRACTICE AND REFLECTION

Once you have collected observations of teaching, children, classrooms, and schools, take time to think about what you have seen. Several techniques exist for systematically analyzing your observations, but equally important is taking time to reflect on these analyses. In our rush to get everything done, we frequently fail to take time to examine our experiences and impressions. However, being serious about finding time for thoughtful reflection is an important part of becoming an excellent teacher, and some of the following processes can be helpful.

REFLECTIVE JOURNALING   Educators at all levels have come to realize that learners profit greatly from thinking reflectively about, and then writing down, what they learn in school. This process is called *reflective journaling.* If you are not now required to keep a journal in your teacher education program, we strongly recommend that you start doing so. If you are required to keep a journal, we urge you to take this assignment seriously because you will learn much in the process.

You can go about keeping a journal in many ways. All you need is something to write on and the will to write. A spiral notebook, a three-ring binder, or a computer works fine. Preferably at the end of each day (and at the very least once each week), briefly summarize your thoughts about and reactions to the major things you have experienced and learned. Spend more time thinking and reflecting, and write down only a brief summary. We believe that your journal should be brief, reflective, candid, personal, and preferably private, something like a personal diary. Try to be perfectly honest in your journal and not worry about someone evaluating your opinions.

When you start to work in schools, you will discover (if you have not already done so) that teachers in elementary and secondary schools are using journaling more and more with their students. Something about thinking and then writing down our thoughts about what we have learned helps us internalize, better understand, and remember what we have learned.

At the end of each chapter in this book, we offer several suggestions for entries in your journal. We sincerely hope that you will do reflective journaling throughout your teacher education program.

SUMMARIZING EDUCATIONAL INFORMATION   Regardless of the technique you use to record your educational observations, you should take the time to study them. The best way to do this is to reread your recorded data many times. Once you have become thoroughly familiar with the content of your recorded data, you are ready to begin summarizing your findings. This requires an open mind. You should strive to disregard any previous prejudices you may have had on the topic. Remember that your goal is to understand objectively the data from your observations. It is sometimes helpful to talk with fellow students about your findings. This type of peer brainstorming frequently will allow you to see data from a slightly different and perhaps more objective viewpoint. In fact, you might want to team up with classmates who are making the same observations using the same data collection technique so that you all have the same frame of reference. Your goal in summarizing your information is to draw accurate conclusions from the data you have collected.

FORMING HYPOTHESES   Once you have condensed and summarized your data, you are ready to draw conclusions and form hypotheses, or tentative interpretations, based on your observations. For example, if one of your original questions was "What techniques do teachers use to motivate their students?," obviously you will develop hypotheses to answer that particular question. The hypotheses you form at this stage in your development as an educator make worthwhile all the effort you make to verify for yourself some of what you have read and heard in your college classes. In addition, your hypotheses are the foundation on which you will eventually build your own teaching style.

TESTING YOUR CONCLUSIONS   Every belief, conclusion, or hypothesis that you develop as an educator should be considered tentative. In other words, it is important to formulate such beliefs at this point in your career, but you need to keep an open mind about them and continually revalidate them. The teacher who is constantly attempting to improve is also constantly forming new or modified beliefs, hypotheses, and conclusions about teaching. That is why it is critically important for you and all educators to observe and analyze classroom activity continually in an ongoing effort to understand more fully this complex field.

FOLIO/PORTFOLIO DEVELOPMENT

As you move through your teacher education program and into your career as a teacher, you will find that you have been collecting stacks, boxes, and files of information and "stuff" related to you, your teaching, and the accomplishments of the students you have taught. If you are like most teachers, you will not know for sure what to do with all of it, yet you will be reluctant to throw any of it away. Be very careful about discarding material until you have organized a folio and anticipated the needs of various portfolios that you might have to prepare. A *folio* is an organized compilation of all the products, records, accomplishments, and testimonies of a teacher and his or her students. Imagine the folio as a large file drawer with different compartments and file folders. Some of the material included is related directly to you and your background. Other items or artifacts are things that others have said about you. And some are examples of projects that your students have completed.

A *portfolio* is a special compilation assembled from the folio for a specific occasion or purpose, such as a job interview or an application for an outstanding teacher award. The portfolio might also be used by you and your professors throughout your teacher education program to document your performance in meeting state, professional, and institutional standards. Portfolios are required in some states as evidence that you should be granted a professional teaching license after the first few years of actual work in classrooms. Portfolios will also be required for National Board certification later in your career. The folio can be organized in any way you think will be most useful.

Many pieces of factual information about you belong in your folio. Demographic information, where you attended school, the states in which you are licensed to teach, and the record of your work experience are examples of these factual items. When organizing your folio, you should identify areas in which you should aim to add information. Now is the time to anticipate some of the material you might need in preparing a particular portfolio in the future. For example, when you apply for most teaching positions, a prospective employer will want to know the kinds of experiences you have had in schools and classrooms with diverse students. If you do not currently have any examples in your folio, plan to add some related experiences as your teacher education program unfolds. Your professors may expect to see evidence that you are meeting standards such as INTASC or those of a specialty professional association.

The occasions on which other people recognize your contributions and achievements are called *attestations*. Awards, letters of commendation, newspaper articles, elected positions, and committee memberships are examples of attestation items to keep in your folio.

Making Meaning of Educational Portfolios

STUDY PURPOSE/QUESTION: Can portfolios be used to help students make meaning of their experiences and provide an opportunity for an assessment of their work?

STUDY DESIGN: The research focused on the use of portfolios in two different projects. A kindergarten teacher studied the process she used throughout a school year in which her class developed portfolios of their "best" work and interacted with adults about the portfolios at the end of the year. In the second project, teacher candidates prepared portfolios that included entries that they believed represented themselves as teachers.

STUDY FINDINGS: The kindergarten teacher was surprised at the items that the children in her class selected as their best work; the students' selections were different from those the teacher would have selected as their best. "In the children's minds, 'best work' meant work that represented the people, objects, and events that were of most interest and importance to them" (p. 592). The teacher, by contrast, was looking for examples that showed learning and growth. For the students the portfolio activity was a "powerful learning tool"; it served as an authentic assessment for the teacher.

The portfolios presented by the teacher candidates varied greatly in their presentation and contents. The candidates found the preparation of portfolios to be a potent learning experience because the open-ended for-mat allowed them to discover the meaning of their experiences. A content analysis of the portfolios and candidate questionnaires indicated that candidates learned what was expected, though at different levels. The project also helped them to synthesize and reflect on their learning to develop a cohesive teaching philosophy.

IMPLICATIONS: Educational portfolios are "those that merge assessment with learning—the kind of learning that involves deep understanding, reflectivity, and multiple dimensions, including the moral and ethical." The researcher identified four essential elements of these portfolios. First, they allow for individuals to make their own meaning of their experiences. The contents to be included are clear but not prescriptive. The second essential element is that the contents and their meaning can be shared and discussed with others who matter. The portfolios have much more meaning when they are used for learning purposes, not assessments. Third, the process of preparing a portfolio occurs over a period of time. Finally, the portfolios are developed and presented in a context that is supportive of reflection and moral deliberation. Faculty and teachers who are designing portfolio activities should be clear about the purposes. Portfolios that are used for summative assessments are not always those that promote learning.

Source: Vicki Kubler LaBoskey, "Portfolios Here, Portfolios There . . . Searching for the Essence of 'Educational Portfolios,' " *Phi Delta Kappan, 81*(8) (April 2000), pp. 590–595.

Through your efforts as a teacher candidate and teacher, students complete assignments, assemble projects, achieve on examinations, and receive awards. In this part of the folio, compile the works and successes of the people you have worked with, along with photographs and video records of your classroom and student projects. You may want to include videotapes of your teaching with a description of your classroom context and analysis of your teaching. Also include copies of your best lesson plans, committee reports, grant proposals, and other products that have resulted from your leading the efforts of others.

PREPARING A PORTFOLIO   When the need arises to prepare a portfolio, such as for use in documenting that you meet standards or in your interview for a teaching position, you will be delighted that you did the advance work with your folio. Time always seems too short when a special portfolio needs to be developed. But when you do the folio work along the way, you will find it relatively easy to pull specific examples and documents to fit a particular job interview or to make final application for a teaching award. Also, when you

8. Continuing Professional Development
- Professional memberships
- Presentations
- Publications
- Conferences attended

10. Letters of Recommendation
- Letters from faculty members, advisor, employers

7. Letters of Appreciation/Commendation from Parents and Students

9. Community Service
- Volunteer service involving children or teaching
- Advisory boards
- Other community service

6. Student Teaching/Internship Evaluations/Recommendations

5. Samples of Student Work
- Completed tests, worksheets, projects*

*Be cautious about issues of confidentiality when using photos or documents containing students' or parents' names.

4. Teaching
- Sample unit plan
- Sample lesson plan
- Samples of homework, assessments, worksheets
- Photos of projects, manipulatives, bulletin boards

3. Philosophies
- Philosophy of education
- Discipline plan
- Classroom management plan

2. Awards/Honors
- Certificates/Letters (e.g., Dean's List)
- Awards (e.g., Outstanding Elementary Education Senior)
- Scholarship awards

1. Credentials
- Résumé
- Transcripts
- Child abuse clearance
- Criminal background clearance
- Teaching certificate

FIGURE 1.10   Sample Portfolio Contents

Source: Claude Netterville, "Sample Portfolio Contents," *2002 AAEE Job Search Handbook,* American Association for Employment in Education, Inc., Columbus, OH, p. 23. *Special thanks to Claude Netterville, University of Arizona, for suggesting the graphic presentation of portfolio contents.*

develop the folio with the broader array of items suggested in Figure 1.10, you will be able to prepare a higher-quality presentation of your accomplishments.

PORTFOLIO DEVELOPMENT TASKS   To help you start your folio, we have included at the end of each chapter several suggestions under the Portfolio Development section. These suggestions anticipate some of the items you may need to include in future portfolio presentations; we have selected topics and tasks that are important to you at this early point in your teacher education program.

CHALLENGES AFFECTING TEACHERS

The working conditions for teachers have improved measurably in recent years, and the following sections will show some of the ways in which these improvements are implemented. This information represents more good news for those who are preparing for careers in the education field.

■ SALARIES

Salaries vary considerably from state to state and from school district to school district. Table 1.2 shows average and beginning teacher salaries in each state. As

TABLE 1.2 Average and Beginning Teacher Salary in 2001–02 Ranked by Average Salary within Region

State	Average Salary	Beginning Salary	State	Average Salary	Beginning Salary
New England			**Southeast**		
Connecticut	$52,376	$34,551	Georgia	$43,933	$32,283
Rhode Island	51,619	30,272	North Carolina	42,118	29,359
Massachusetts	48,732	32,746	Virginia	41,752	31,238
New Hampshire	39,915	25,611	South Carolina	39,923	27,268
Vermont	39,771	25,229	Florida	39,275	30,096
Maine	37,300	24,054	Tennessee	38,515	28,857
			Kentucky	37,951	26,813
Mideast			Alabama	37,206	29,938
New York	$51,020	$34,577	West Virginia	36,775	25,633
District of Columbia	51,000	31,982	Louisiana	36,328	28,229
Pennsylvania	50,599	31,866	Arkansas	36,026	27,565
New Jersey	50,115	35,311	Mississippi	33,295	24,567
Delaware	49,011	32,868			
Maryland	48,251	31,828	**Rocky Mountains**		
			Colorado	$40,659	$28,001
Great Lakes			Idaho	39,194	25,316
Michigan	$52,497	$32,649	Utah	38,153	26,806
Illinois	49,679	31,761	Wyoming	37,853	26,773
Indiana	44,609	28,440	Montana	34,379	22,344
Ohio	44,266	29,953			
Minnesota	42,175	29,998	**Far West**		
Wisconsin	41,056	27,397	California	$54,348	$34,180
			Alaska	49,028	36,035
Plains			Oregon	46,033	31,026
Iowa	$38,230	$27,553	Nevada	44,621	28,734
Kansas	37,059	26,596	Hawaii	44,306	31,340
Nebraska	36,236	26,010	Washington	43,470	28,348
Missouri	36,053	27,554			
North Dakota	32,468	20,988	**Outlying Areas**		
South Dakota	31,383	23,938	Guam	$35,038	$28,054
			Virgin Islands	34,764*	22,751*
Southwest			Puerto Rico	22,164	18,000
Texas	$39,230	$30,938			
Arizona	38,510	27,648	**U.S. Average**	**$44,367**	**$30,719**
New Mexico	36,716	27,579			
Oklahoma	32,870	27,547			

*2000-01 salaries.

Source: American Federation of Teachers, AFL-CIO, Survey and Analysis of Teacher Salary Trends, 2002. Reprinted with permission.

you can see, salaries in most northeastern states are higher than those in other parts of the country. One reason for the higher salaries is a difference in the cost of living from one area to another. It is more expensive to live in a number of the northeastern states, Alaska, Hawaii, and large urban areas. However, cost of living alone does not explain the differences. Connecticut and school districts such as Rochester, New York, view teachers as professionals, have high expectations for them, support them through mentoring and professional development, use multiple assessments to determine teacher effectiveness, and pay salaries commensurate with those of other professionals.

SALARY DIFFERENCES

Each board of education is an agent of the state and is therefore empowered to set salary levels for employees of the school district it governs. Each school system typically has a **salary schedule** that outlines the minimum and maximum salary for several levels of study beyond the bachelor's degree and for each year of teaching experience. For example, a beginning teacher with a bachelor's degree might be paid $28,000, and one with a master's degree might be paid $35,000. Teachers with twenty years of experience might be paid $50,000 to $76,000, depending on the school district in which they are employees. Table 1.2 shows that, at the time it was composed, beginning teacher salaries ranged from $36,293 in Alaska to $20,675 in North Dakota and $18,700 in Puerto Rico.

Some people might argue that teachers are paid less because they do not work year-round. However, they earn less than most other professionals even when the number of weeks worked during a year is taken into account. Teachers between twenty-two and twenty-eight years of age earned an average $7,894 less in 1998 than other college-educated adults of the same age. By age forty-four to fifty, they earned $23,655 less than their counterparts in other occupations.[13] The difference is even greater between teachers with master's degrees and others with master's degrees; these teachers earned $43,313, compared to $75,824 earned by nonteachers.

GLOBAL PERSPECTIVES
Global Secondary Teacher Salaries

Salaries for teachers in the United States often lag behind those in other countries even though the workloads of U.S. teachers are usually heavier. What variables can help explain these differences from country to country? See Figure 1.11.

The somewhat lower salaries of teachers can become a deterrent for those who would like to teach. Some people argue that raising teachers' salaries will make no difference in the quality of the teaching force. Experiences in states such as Connecticut are contradicting those arguments. Higher salaries are attracting teachers to the state even though candidates must meet performance assessments required for licenses at high levels. As a result, students in the state's classrooms are also performing at higher levels.

The organization Recruiting New Teachers found that more than 75 percent of the public supported raising teachers' salaries. Over half of the respondents in this survey indicated that they would choose teaching as a career if they were guaranteed an annual income of $60,000. Further, they would recommend teaching as a career for members of their family if the salary was at this level.[14] These findings suggest that the pool of available teachers would be much larger if teachers' salaries were higher. With the pending shortage of teachers over the next few years, higher salaries will probably be needed to attract and retain the professionals we would like to have teaching the nation's children.

salary schedule

A printed and negotiated schedule that lists salary levels based on years of experience and education.

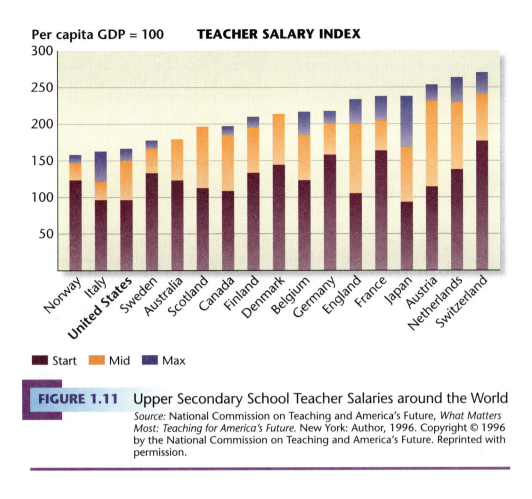

Per capita GDP = 100   **TEACHER SALARY INDEX**

Legend: ■ Start   ■ Mid   ■ Max

FIGURE 1.11   Upper Secondary School Teacher Salaries around the World

Source: National Commission on Teaching and America's Future, *What Matters Most: Teaching for America's Future.* New York: Author, 1996. Copyright © 1996 by the National Commission on Teaching and America's Future. Reprinted with permission.

SALARIES AND INFLATION

Although the average teacher's salary may sound good to a beginning teacher, experienced educators believe that their purchasing power has increased only slightly over the years. The average teacher salary has increased from around $10,000 in the mid-1970s to nearly $40,000 today, but inflation has caused the constant-dollar average teacher salary to increase only around $1,000. Of course, teacher salaries vary greatly from place to place; in some school districts, salaries have risen considerably since the 1970s, even when corrected for inflation.

FRINGE BENEFITS

Almost all full-time teachers receive fringe benefits that, when added to their basic salary, constitute their total compensation package. When you pursue your first teaching position, you will want to inquire about these benefits as well as the salary. Although the salary is usually of first concern to a teacher, the fringe benefits are equally important over the long term. Fringe benefits vary from school to school but frequently include some type of insurance benefits—hospitalization insurance, medical/surgical coverage, and major medical insurance. Somewhat less frequently, a teacher's medical insurance also includes dental care and prescription drugs; it may include coverage of eyeglasses and other types of less common medical services. Benefits often include a group life insurance policy as well.

Many school districts also provide some type of professional liability insurance for their teachers. In fact, some states require by law that school districts do so. The liability insurance covers teachers and other educators who may be sued for not providing appropriate services or other abuse of professional responsibilities.

Full-time public school teachers are usually eligible for retirement benefits as part of their total compensation package. These benefits vary from state to state. In some states, teachers receive a combination of state teacher retirement and social security retirement. In other states, a teacher's retirement may depend totally on a state program and be divorced entirely from the federal social security retirement system. It is sometimes possible for teachers who move from state to state to transfer their retirement benefits to the state in which they ultimately retire. A teacher's retirement package is an extremely important part of the total compensation package and needs to be well understood by everyone entering the profession.

School districts also usually provide special leave provisions for teachers. Leave policies should clearly indicate the number of days available with pay for personal illnesses, emergencies, and deaths. Some school systems allow a day or so of personal leave for special situations. Professional development leave may be available in some school districts to support the continuing education of teachers, but the availability of such leave varies greatly from district to district. Unfortunately, due to the lack of money and time, it is not easy for teachers in some school districts to participate in professional organizations and state and national activities.

RECRUITMENT INCENTIVES

The increasing shortage of teachers is leading to a number of innovative strategies for recruiting teachers. Job fairs are held in areas where there is an apparent surplus of teachers so that school districts from areas of shortage can interview prospective applicants. Technology is being used in innovative ways too. For example, the Clark County School District in Las Vegas, Nevada, will ship overnight a video telephone to an applicant so that he or she can be interviewed without having to travel to Las Vegas. In March 2000, the federal government began offering teachers 50 percent discounts on vacant homes in economically distressed neighborhoods. This program, which has also been offered to police officers, gives teachers an economic incentive to live and teach in low- and middle-income school districts. At the time, Federal Housing Administration chief Andrew Cuomo stated, "A good teacher can make a great neighbor as a mentor, an inspiring role model, and as a living link between the classroom and the community."[15]

WORKING CONDITIONS

Almost everyone feels better about his or her work when the environment is supportive and conducive to high-quality output. The same is true for teachers and students. Like other factors in education, working conditions differ greatly from school to school. Within a single school district, the conditions can change dramatically across neighborhoods. Some schools are beautiful sprawling campuses with the latest technology. In others, toilets are backed up, paint is peeling off the walls, classes are held in storage rooms, or administrators are repressive. Most teachers who begin their careers in the second type of setting either aggressively seek assignments in other schools as soon as possible or leave the profession.

Teachers do work under very different conditions from those of most other professionals. Secondary and middle school teachers usually work with students in forty-five- to fifty-five-minute time periods with brief breaks between classes. Elementary and early childhood teachers are usually in self-contained classrooms in which they have few breaks, and they even have to supervise students during recesses and lunch periods. They have little time during the school day to work with colleagues or to plan for the next lesson or the next day. In many schools, teachers have limited access to telephones or computers for support in their work.

One of the causes of these problems is aging school facilities that desperately need to be replaced. Recent federal legislation is providing some support for replacement and renewal of schools. With the student population growing dramatically over the next decade, additional resources will be required to provide working conditions that facilitate the work of educators. Public support will be needed to use taxes for these purposes.

BEGINNING AND CONTINUING A TEACHING CAREER

It is never too early to begin thinking about becoming licensed and finding a job. You can start by taking the appropriate courses and participating in activities that provide experiences for becoming licensed and being successful in your early years of teaching. One of the steps will be to collect and organize the materials that may be required for performance assessments throughout your teacher education program, job applications, and future renewal of your license.

■ BECOMING LICENSED

Teachers must obtain a license before they can legally teach in public schools. Each state determines its own licensure requirements. Although requirements may be similar from state to state, unique requirements exist in many states. You will need to check the requirements for the state in which you plan to work to ensure that you have completed an appropriate program and to determine the assessments that will have to be completed. Appendix A, located at the end of this book, lists these state certification websites.

LICENSURE TESTS

Most states require teacher candidates to pass one or more standardized tests at a specified level to be eligible for their first license to teach. Written assessments are required in many states, and many states require basic skills tests; in fact, many institutions require candidates to pass these tests before they are admitted into teacher education programs. Over half of the states require candidates to pass tests in both professional pedagogical and content or subject-area knowledge. The cutoff scores that determine passing are set by states and vary greatly. Teacher candidates who do not pass the test in one state may be able to pass in another state that has a lower cutoff score.

An increasing number of states are requiring future teachers to major in an academic area rather than in "education." Students complete courses in education, field experiences, and student teaching or an internship along with courses in the academic major to become eligible for a license when the program is completed. You should clearly understand the requirements for a license in the state in which you are attending school and in any states in which you may wish to teach.

ALTERNATIVE LICENSURE

As mentioned earlier in this chapter, some states have developed alternative licensure opportunities for people who wish to become teachers. In some states, due to severe teacher shortages, anyone with a bachelor's degree in just about any major can begin teaching with some type of provisional certificate. These teachers might be introduced to teaching and learning in intensive programs of a few weeks before they are responsible for a classroom. Some school districts do assign mentors to these teachers during their first year of practice, and the teachers are usually required to take education courses to retain their licenses over time. These alternative routes to licensure have come under considerable criticism from teachers and the teacher education establishment because they do not recognize the importance of learning about teaching and learning and practicing under the supervision of an experienced teacher before beginning to teach.

Should Districts Offer Signing Bonuses to Attract New Teachers?

Difficulty recruiting a sufficient number of teachers has led some school districts to offer contract signing bonuses to new teachers. Needless to say, this is a controversial practice that is opposed by some experienced teachers.

YES

Virginia Hoover is a school social worker with 11 years in the Guilford, North Carolina, schools. She was the state's School Social Worker of the Year in 1997–98 and the Student Services Support of the Year in 1999.

NO

Bob Kaplan teaches eighth-grade social studies at Jane Addams Junior High in Schaumburg, Illinois. He has taught for 23 years and served four times on bargaining teams, once as chairman, and most recently last spring.

Yes, I believe school systems should offer a sign-on bonus to staff. A bonus would definitely be an added attraction to new employees, whether they are graduating from college or just trying to get into education.

For new graduates, a bonus would help offset the expense of preparing their first classroom. Buying the materials and supplies needed to make classrooms inviting and exciting places for students can take a lot of money.

If a new teacher has to relocate to take the job, that's another expense. A bonus could relieve the stress of moving and help make the transition a more pleasant experience.

For the more seasoned staff person, a sign-on bonus would be a great help in meeting the expenses that come with taking a new job.

Many times, when a staff person accepts a new position in another system, the person ends up missing time from work. That time lost means less income. A bonus could help save a staff person from having to go deeper into debt after a job change.

What a relief it could be to have this extra money. I have a friend who recently accepted a position in another state. She and I discussed the burden that would have been lifted if the system had offered her a sign-on bonus. Moving expenses can be very taxing, especially if you're not in a superintendent's position.

Signing bonuses. What a great idea! What's next, no-cut contracts? Free agency? The traditional teacher pay scale may not be ideal, but it's fairer than having a rookie make more than a three-year veteran because the rookie teaches bilingual classes and the other teaches a multi-age elementary class.

If we were to have signing bonuses, who's going to determine what's more important for a bonus? Who's going to figure out how much of a bonus is deserved? Whatever happened to collective bargaining?

I can easily see a personnel director paying the extra dollars to fill a position. I can also foresee the same personnel director using these extra dollars as a backdoor to merit pay.

Our Association needs to represent all members. These first-year teachers aren't even members yet. How, as a labor organization, can we explain to our members in their second or third year, "Gee, sorry you were too late for a bonus, but remember to keep paying your dues dollars!"

Instead of offering signing bonuses, let's try to solve the underlying problem. If there are positions that are tough to fill, let's build the supply. How? Through academic advising in colleges and government financial support for students going into high-demand fields.

(continued)

Alternative routes are often designed to facilitate midcareer changes from other professions, such as business or the military, into the teaching profession. Candidates in these programs often participate in yearlong internships in which they are mentored by experienced teachers and work collaboratively with both higher education and school faculty in taking courses and working with students. These alternative route programs are available at many colleges and universities.

YES

The gesture of offering a bonus would also benefit the school system that makes the offer. It's a win–win situation. A bonus, once accepted by the new staff person, serves as a commitment to work for the school system—and helps prevent a staff person from going out the backdoor to accept a position with another system.

With a bonus in the balance, a school system wouldn't have to worry about whether a newly hired staff person is going to show.

On the other side, a staff person is going to think long and hard about leaving a school system that helped when help was most needed. Bonuses would help retain good and experienced staff.

A sign-on bonus would keep school systems from having to scramble in August to fill vacant positions. Scrambling school systems often just accept whoever is available at the last minute. With the sign-on bonus as an attraction, a system could have the best upon finding the best.

Staff, meanwhile, are seeking systems that are willing to offer something extra. A sign-on bonus would be an added recruiting incentive.

We need that incentive. With so much competition for graduating college students, districts need some added attraction to help fill the positions being vacated by our retiring educators.

As for me personally, I have no problem with systems offering such a sign-on bonus perk to attract capable people to education. I'm concerned about who will fill my role as social worker when I retire.

I won't be offended if my system begins offering a sign-on bonus to new staff. Those of us who are working hard pulling the load until vacant positions are filled would welcome the sight of quality applicants swarming to get those vacant jobs.

Source: "Should Districts Offer Signing Bonuses to Attract New Teachers?" *NEA Today* (April 2000), p.11.

NO

These steps, along with increased teacher pay throughout the salary schedule, would help increase the supply of new teachers. If more money will get better *new* teachers, then more money throughout the scale will serve as a motivator for *all* teachers.

Collective bargaining has brought us dramatically increased salaries, and we should stand by it. Any measure that would give special treatment to any segment of our members ought to be analyzed very closely.

I realize signing bonuses have been around for a long time in business and sports. But products in these fields are more measurable. I'm a much better teacher now than I was 23 years ago. Why don't we give me a bonus for that?

New teachers who have yet to step into the classroom are a risky investment. What is their average length of employment? What if these new teachers have difficulty and are released?

I guess we shouldn't worry. We'll just sign up some other untested new teacher with a signing bonus.

One final point: We already have huge salary discrepancies between school districts. Signing bonuses would increase those discrepancies. Wealthy districts would have much more money to dole out for bonuses than less affluent districts.

If signing bonuses become the rule, the rich will get richer, the poor will be stuck with vacancies. This isn't what public education should be all about.

Signing bonuses, on the surface, sound good. Administrators would love to fill tough positions by throwing money to a few.

But before we should even consider signing bonuses, we need standards and an effort to increase the supply for hard-to-fill positions. Let's use all this bonus money to reward teachers who have made and will continue to make a positive difference.

WHAT DO YOU THINK?
Should districts offer signing bonuses to attract new teachers?

To give your opinion, go to Chapter 1 of the companion website
(**www.ablongman.com/johnson13e**) and click on Debate.

SEARCHING FOR A TEACHING POSITION

Teacher education candidates should begin thinking about employment early in their college careers. A helpful resource is the *Job Search Handbook for Educators* from the American Association for Employment in Education (www.aaee.org); it may be available in your college's job placement office. This handbook contains suggestions for preparing your résumé, cover letters, and letters of inquiry; it also provides excellent practical suggestions for improving your interviewing techniques. Information on teacher supply and demand in different fields is included in the handbook as well. Appendix C found at the end of this book lists many teaching job websites that should be helpful to you.

School districts would like applicants to present evidence that responds to the following questions. Portfolios containing illustrations of performance are very helpful in this process.

1. Can the candidate do the job? Does the candidate have the necessary academic background? Can the candidate provide evidence that his or her students learned something? Does he or she know how to assess learning? Is he or she sensitive to the needs of diverse children? Can the candidate respond well to individual differences? How strong is he or she in regard to community activities?

2. Will the candidate do the job? What interview evidence does the candidate provide that communicates a professional commitment to getting the job done?

3. Will the candidate fit in? Is this candidate a good match for the needs of the district and the student needs as identified? How will the candidate work with other teachers and staff?

4. Will the candidate express well what he or she wants in a professional assignment? Does the candidate have personal and professional standards of his or her own?

5. Does the district's vision match the candidate's vision? Understanding the expectations of both the district and the candidate is critical if the candidate is to be successful.

Many state agencies that are responsible for teacher licensing and school districts have job openings listed on their websites. If you have a specific state and school district in mind, these job listings should be helpful in determining the possibilities and narrowing your search.

■ REMAINING A TEACHER

You are free to rise as far as your dreams will take you. Your task is to build the future of this country and of our world. You are our new global citizens.

Geraldine A. Ferraro

Teaching improves dramatically during the first five years of practice. Often teachers hone their skills alone as they practice in their own classrooms and take advantage of available professional development activities. A more promising practice is the assignment of mentors to new teachers to assist them in developing their skills during the early years of practice. Teachers who do not participate in an induction program (such as mentoring), who are dissatisfied with student discipline, or who are unhappy with the school environment are much more likely to leave teaching than are their peers.[16]

Continuing professional development is one of the ongoing activities of career teachers. Often teachers return to college for a master's degree that may help to increase their knowledge and skills related to teaching and learning and the subjects they teach. They learn new skills such as the use of the Internet to help students learn. They learn more about the subjects they teach through formal courses, reading on their own, exploring the Internet, working in related businesses in the summers, or traveling. They ask colleagues to observe their teaching and provide feedback for improving their work. They seek advice from other teachers and professionals with whom they work.

Experienced teachers see teaching as a public endeavor. They welcome parents and others to the classroom. As cooperating teachers and mentors, they become actively engaged with higher education faculty in preparing new teachers. They become researchers as they critically examine their own practice, testing various strategies to help students learn and sharing their findings with colleagues in faculty and professional meetings.

RENEWAL OF LICENSES

Most states require teaching licenses to be renewed periodically. A professional license is usually not granted until after several years of successful practice. Some states require a master's degree; a few require the successful completion of a portfolio with videotapes of teaching that are judged by experienced teachers. To retain a license throughout one's career, continuing professional development activities may be required.

SUMMARY

This chapter views the work of teachers through a professional lens. Total school enrollment is projected to increase throughout the next decade, resulting in a teacher shortage unless many more teachers are produced and the large numbers of teachers who have been certified but are not teaching return to the classroom. Although teachers do not yet earn salaries comparable to those of other professionals, teaching is evolving into a full profession that sets its own standards and monitors the practice of its members.

Successful teachers are reflective about their work, as shown in their ability to gather, analyze, and use data to improve their teaching. These teachers have a natural curiosity about their work and are continually searching for better answers to the challenges they face. Beginning in their teacher education programs, teachers write in reflective journals, collect and organize information and data, and compile information from these folios into portfolios for specific purposes such as performance assessments and job applications.

This chapter focuses on a variety of topics related to the professional aspects of the education profession. Several big ideas about the teaching profession grow out of this chapter, including the fact that education is extremely important to the development of our society and that teachers play the key role in this important profession.

DISCUSSION QUESTIONS

1. What are the characteristics of a profession? What are your arguments for or against recognizing teaching as a profession?

2. Why do shortages of teachers exist in some subjects and not in others?

3. What should national accreditation tell you about your teacher education program?

4. What is National Board certification and why is it important in a teacher's career?

5. Of what value are journals, folios, and portfolios in preparing to teach?

6. What support should school districts provide to teachers in the induction years to encourage retention in the profession beyond three years?

JOURNAL ENTRIES

1. Record your thoughts at this stage of your professional development about the teaching profession—its strengths and weaknesses, your interest in teaching as a career, and your excitement and doubts about working in the profession.

2. Think about teaching as compared to other well-established professions such as law, medicine, and ar-chitecture. Record your thoughts and arguments about teaching being a profession.

3. Record in your journal information about, and your reaction to, each of your visits to the classrooms you observe.

PORTFOLIO DEVELOPMENT

1. Your first folio development task is to find and organize the many materials, artifacts, and records that you currently have. If you are like most of us, the bits and pieces are stored in several different locations. Examples of term papers, transcripts, awards, letters of recognition, and journals of trips are scattered. Take some time now to find and begin organizing these materials. Organize them by categories that you think are

logical. Keep in mind the ultimate purpose of developing this folio. At various points in the future, you will be drawing items out of the folio to develop a portfolio for completion of student teaching or to apply for a teaching position or national certification.

2. The U.S. Department of Education now publishes each year a national teacher education report card, which includes information about all teacher education institutions in your state. Review the performance of candidates on state licensure tests in your field at your institution and other institutions in your state. Reflect on why there are differences in performance across institutions and whether state licensure tests are an appropriate measure of teaching competence.

PREPARING FOR CERTIFICATION

■ THE PRAXIS SERIES™

1. As mentioned in this chapter, many states require that prospective teachers take one or more standardized tests as part of certification. Some states, such as California, Massachusetts, and Texas, require their own tests; many other states require one or more tests in *The Praxis Series™*, published by the Educational Testing Service (ETS). Learn more about certification requirements, including testing requirements, in the state in which you plan to teach by visiting that state's website (see Appendix A).

2. The best way to prepare for Praxis or any other standardized test for certification is to understand the concepts covered in the test and how they relate to the content in each of your courses and field experiences. ETS provides a wealth of information about the Praxis assessments on their website. Learn more about the Praxis II assessments, including the test format and topics covered, by visiting their website (www.ets.org/praxis).

3. As you read further in this book, note how issues covered in the chapters relate to the topics covered in the Praxis II tests, particularly those on Principles of Teaching and Learning. Even if your state does not use Praxis, you will find the information useful; the topics covered on the test are important for Praxis-related documentation in your portfolio.

WEBSITES

Companion Website

www.ablongman.com/johnson13e The companion website for this textbook contains a wealth of enrichment material to help you learn more about the foundations of education.

www.rnt.org The website of Recruiting New Teachers, Inc. includes information about becoming a new teacher and offers a number of handbooks for people who are considering teaching as a career, including *Take This Job and Love It! Making the Mid-Career Move to Teaching.*

www.ncate.org A list of institutions with teacher education programs accredited by NCATE and information about becoming a teacher are available on this website. It also includes links to state agencies and their licensure requirements.

www.nbpts.org The website for the National Board for Professional Teaching Standards includes information on the process for seeking National Board certification as well as the board's standards, assessments, and publications.

www.nasdtec.org Information on licensure requirements and state agencies that are responsible for teacher licensing are available on this website of the National Association of State Directors of Teacher Education and Certification.

FURTHER READING

American Association for Employment in Education. *The Job Search Handbook for Educators.* Evanston, IL: Author, published annually. An excellent source of practical information for anyone searching for a teaching position.

Langdon, Carol A., and Vesper, Nick. (April 2000). "The Sixth Phi Delta Kappa Poll of Teachers' Attitudes toward the Public Schools." *Phi Delta Kappan, 81*(8), pp. 607–611. Interesting information on what teachers think about major educational issues. This survey is repeated and published in *Phi Delta Kappan* periodically.

National Board for Professional Teaching Standards. (1998). *What Teachers Should Know and Be Able to Do.* Detroit, MI: Author. The best source of definitive and most recent information on the NBPTS.

Rose, Lowell C., and Gallup, Alec M. (September 2002). "The 34th Annual Phi Delta Kappa/Gallup Poll of the Public's Attitude toward the Public Schools." *Phi Delta Kappan,* pp. 541–546. A wonderful annual source of information on the public's opinion on a wide variety of educational issues.

NOTES

1. Recruiting New Teachers, Inc., *The Essential Profession: A National Survey of Public Attitudes toward Teaching, Educational Opportunity and School Reform.* Belmont, MA: Author, 1998.
2. Ibid.
3. Ibid.
4. Carol A. Langdon and Nick Vesper, "The Sixth Phi Delta Kappa Poll of Teachers' Attitudes toward the Public Schools," *Phi Delta Kappan, 81*(8) (April 2000), pp. 607–611.
5. Recruiting New Teachers, Inc., ibid.
6. Drew H. Gitomer, Andrew S. Latham, and Robert Ziomek, *The Academic Quality of Prospective Teachers: The Impact of Admissions and Licensure Testing.* Princeton, NJ: Educational Testing Service, 1999.
7. Barbara A. Bruschi and Richard J. Coley, *How Teachers Compare: The Prose, Document, and Quantitative Skills of America's Teachers.* Princeton, NJ: Educational Testing Service, 1999.
8. Debra E. Gerald and William J. Hussar, *Projections of Education Statistics to 2009.* Washington, DC: National Center for Education Statistics, U.S. Department of Education, 1999.
9. National Commission on Teaching and America's Future, *What Matters Most: Teaching for America's Future.* New York: Author, 1996.
10. Recruiting New Teachers, Inc., ibid.
11. Linda Darling-Hammond, "Teaching for America's Future: National Commissions and Vested Interests in an Almost Profession," *Educational Policy, 14*(1) (January/March 2000), pp. 162–183.
12. National Commission on Teaching and America's Future, ibid.
13. "Who Should Teach? The States Decide," *Education Week, XIX*(18) (January 13, 2000), pp. 8–9.
14. Ibid.
15. Richard Wolf, quoted in Paul Leavitt, "Capitol Roundup," *USA Today* (March 13, 2000).
16. "Who Should Teach? The States Decide," ibid.

Sociological Foundations of Education

Viewing Education through Sociological Lenses

 The lens of sociology provides a way to examine and interpret human social behavior. Sociology investigates our origins and the ways we interact with one another. It describes how society has been organized to meet its needs and analyzes the components that are effective and those that are not in serving the needs of the population. Sociological thinking helps policymakers and professional educators make sense of practices that contribute to or make it difficult for us to meet the goals of society.

The sociological lens depends on the analysis of data about the population; groups in society; and institutions such as the government, businesses, and schools to help us understand who we are. It allows us to ask questions about critical issues that affect our lives and the lives of others. In this chapter, we explore the impact of sociology on education by examining issues that affect schools, families, and students. The filters through which we will examine sociology in education in this section include diversity, culture, family structures, challenges of youth, purposes of schools, democracy, equality, and social justice.

Focus Questions

The following questions will help you focus your learning as you read Part II:

1. Why is culture important in knowing yourself, your students, their families, and the community served by schools?
2. How do race, ethnicity, gender, and socioeconomic status interact to result in discrimination and inequity in society and schools?
3. What impact do society and culture have on the education process?
4. Why do some students not receive the same benefits from education as others?
5. Whose values are taught in schools?
6. What roles do diversity, equality, and social justice play in the delivery of education that is multicultural?
7. What is culturally relevant teaching and why is it important in a diverse society?
8. How do schools interact with the culture of students and communities to promote or limit student learning?
9. What is the digital divide and why do educators worry about it?

Diversity in Society

Education in the News

Culture Clash

By Mary Ann Zehr, *Education Week,* February 5, 2003

HARRISONBURG, VA.—LEONARD YAVNY BELIEVES DARWIN'S theory of evolution contradicts biblical truths. He also thinks youths shouldn't be taught about sex; if they learn about it, they might try it, he reasons. He requires his own children to be chaperoned on dates until they are married. And he doesn't want his children to be exposed to Halloween, which he believes is a holiday originating from the devil. Yavny, the 42-year-old father of five children between the ages of 10 and 19, finds that these particular beliefs conflict with those of many of the teachers or students at the public schools his children attend here. But he has never complained to school personnel.

Instead, he counteracts what his children face at school by pointing out to them what he believes to be false teaching, holding them to specific expectations, and occasionally pulling them out of school activities.

Last Halloween, for example, he and his wife, Galina, kept their children home from school.

Yavny is a conservative Christian and an immigrant from Ukraine who shares with many immigrants a critical view of the prevailing attitudes and beliefs that his children encounter in school.

Having received the largest number of immigrants ever in a single decade during the 1990s, the United States has become home to an increasing number of parents such as Yavny whose traditional values don't mesh well with the more liberal values that tend to permeate public schools.

Harrisonburg, a city of 42,000 set in a farming region of Virginia, has received an immigrant wave of its own as jobs in the poultry industry have drawn newcomers here. In five years, the population of language-minority children in the Harrisonburg schools has swelled from about 400 students, most of whom spoke Spanish, to 1,180 students who speak 39 different languages.

And so, it's not hard to find immigrant parents here who share Yavny's perspective. They resist assimilation and expect their children to follow their lead. "We are raising our kids in the United States," says Benita Castro, a native of Mexico who along with her husband recently threw an elaborate church ceremony and reception, or *quinceañera,* to celebrate her daughter Nancy's 15th birthday, "but we'll stick to our morals."

Aisha Rostem, a Kurdish Muslim who sends her two teenage daughters to schools here, says through an interpreter, "I'm praying that they will be safe—that they don't fight, that they don't get involved in bad things."

How these parents help their children make sense of the two worlds they live in—the world of school and the more traditional world of home and community—can have a huge effect on their children's academic success and school life. So also can schools' handling of this cultural clash make a difference in immigrant children's lives.

Reprinted with permission from *Education Week,* February 5, 2003.

Learning Outcomes

After reading and studying this chapter, you should be able to:

1. Describe culture and some of its characteristics. (INTASC 3: Diversity)

2. Identify the dominant culture in the United States and describe how it is influenced by and affects other cultures of groups in the United States.

3. Understand three theories and ideologies that describe ways in which schools respond to students who are not members of the dominant culture.

4. Identify microcultural groups to which students and teachers belong and explain why some are more important to their cultural identity than others.

5. Understand that student learning is influenced by language, culture, and family and community values. (INTASC 3: Diversity)

School-Based Observations

You may see these learning outcomes in action during your visits to schools:

1. Identify the microcultural memberships (e.g., race, ethnicity, language, gender, socioeconomic class, religion, physical and academic ability, and geographic background) of the students in a class that you are observing at the K–12 level. What are the differences within the ethnic groups represented in the class?

2. Examine the curriculum, textbooks, bulletin boards, and other materials used in the classroom to determine which microcultural groups are included and which never appear.

3. In a school with English language learners, interview two or more teachers about the strategies they use to ensure that students do not fall behind academically because their native language is not English.

More than a million new immigrants annually introduce different religions, languages, and ways of thinking and acting into schools and communities, including areas of the United States that previously lacked the rich diversity of urban areas. The **diversity** to which educators are exposed daily is much broader than the new immigrants themselves. It includes socioeconomic status, ethnicity, race, religion, language, gender, sexual orientation, academic and physical ability, age, and geography. Educators need to learn to incorporate the history, experiences, and perspectives of diverse groups into their teaching and to draw on students' diversity to help them learn. The big ideas that will help you understand diversity include culture, microcultural membership, and cultural identity. These concepts are covered in this chapter.

Children learn how to think, feel, speak, and behave through the **culture** in which they are raised. Their parents, teachers, and other adults in the neighborhood and in religious institutions they attend teach the culture and model the cultural norms. Furthermore, when schools use a different language or linguistic pattern from those used in the home, dissonance between schools and the home can occur. When students never see themselves in textbooks or stories, the culture of their families and communities is denigrated. As a result, students too often learn that their own culture is inferior to the official culture of the school or mainstream culture.

Each of us belongs to a number of different groups within our culture. We have not only an ethnic identity such as African American, Navajo, German American, or Korean American, but we also identify ourselves as male or female, heterosexual or homosexual, Christian, Muslim, atheist, or member of another religious group. Who we are is influenced by our place on a continuum from poor to wealthy and young to elderly, as well as by the geographic location in which we grew up and are living. Our behaviors in these groups are influenced by the culture in which we are raised and later live, and they may differ from one

diversity

The wide range of differences among people, families, and communities based on their cultural and ethnic backgrounds as well as their physical and academic abilities.

culture

Socially transmitted ways of thinking, believing, feeling, and acting within a group of people that are passed from one generation to the next.

culture to another. For example, expectations for men and women are influenced by ethnicity, religion, and socioeconomic status. Membership in these **microcultural groups,** the interaction across groups, and society's view of the group are critical factors in determining one's cultural identity. When we meet new people, we usually identify them immediately by their gender and race and maybe their ethnicity. We will not know their religion and its importance to them unless they are wearing something identified with a specific religion. We don't know the importance of their ethnicity, language, or socioeconomic status to their identity. Therefore, educators need to be very careful about stereotyping students and their families solely on the basis of factors that can be easily identified. Culture is far more complex, not allowing us to make assumptions based only on an individual's appearance.

microcultural groups

Distinct groups to which everyone belongs that are influenced by society and their own cultures.

enculturation

The process of learning the characteristics and behaviors of the culture of the group to which one belongs.

CULTURE AND SOCIETY

Society is composed of individuals and groups that share a common history, traditions, and experiences. Culture provides the blueprint for how people think, feel, and behave in society. A culture imposes rules and order on its members by providing patterns that help them know the meaning of their behavior. Members of the same cultural group understand the subtleties of their shared language, nonverbal communications, and ways of thinking and knowing. But they often misread the cultural cues of other groups, a problem that can lead to miscommunications and misunderstandings in society and the classroom.

All people around the world have the same biological and psychological needs, but the ways in which they meet these needs are culturally determined. For example, the location of the group, available resources, and traditions have a great influence on the foods eaten, grooming and clothing patterns, teaching and learning styles, and interactions of men and women and parents and children. The meaning and celebration of birth, marriage, old age, and death also depend on one's culture. In other words, culture affects all aspects of people's lives, from the simplest patterns of eating and bathing to the more complex patterns of teaching and learning.

■ CHARACTERISTICS OF CULTURE

Culture is learned, shared, adapted, and dynamic. People learn their culture through **enculturation.** Parents and other caretakers teach children the culture and the acceptable norms of behavior within it. Individuals internalize cultural patterns so well and so early in life that they have difficulty accepting different, but just as appropriate, ways of behaving and thinking. But when people live and actively participate in a second culture, they begin to see more clearly their own unique cultural patterns. Understanding cultural differences and learning to recognize when students do not share your own cultural patterns are critical steps in the provision of an equitable learning environment. Therefore, it is important to learn about your own culture as well as others.

An important aspect of culture is that it is dynamic and continually adapts to serve the

Parents are primary transmitters of their culture, as they interact with their children on a daily basis.

needs of the group. Individuals and families adapt their culture as they move from one section of the country to another or around the globe. The conditions of a geographic region may require adjustments to the culture. Technological changes in the world and society can also lead to changes in cultural patterns.

DOMINANT OR MAINSTREAM CULTURE

The dominant or mainstream culture in the United States is that of white, middle-class Protestants whose ancestors immigrated from Western Europe. Today, the dominant culture is primarily reflected in the lives of business managers or owners and professionals who are college educated and represent a number of ethnic and religious groups. The dominant culture is the one most financially successful families have grown up in or adopted.

The legal system, democratic elections, and middle-class values have their underpinnings in institutions and traditions of Western Europe. Historically, the male members of the group have dominated the political system and related government positions of authority. Policies and practices have been established both to maintain the advantages of the dominant culture and to limit the influence of other cultural groups.

What are some of the characteristics of the dominant culture today? Universal education and literacy for all citizens are valued. Mass communication, which has been enhanced by technology and electronic networks, influences people's view of themselves and the world. A job or career must be pursued for a person to be recognized as successful. Fun is usually sought as a relief from work. Achievement and success are highly valued and are demonstrated by the accumulation of material goods such as a house, car, boat, clothes, and vacations.

Individualism and freedom are core values that undergird the dominant culture in the United States. Members believe that individuals should be in charge of their own destiny and success. Freedom is defined as having control of one's own life with little or no interference by others, especially by government. Members of the dominant group rely on associations of common interest rather than strong kinship ties. Many people believe in absolute values of right and wrong rather than in degrees of rightness and wrongness.

Members of this group identify themselves as American. They do not see themselves as primarily white, Christian, English-speaking, middle class, male, or heterosexual. Many middle-class Catholics, Jews, and members of other faiths share values and behaviors similar to those of the dominant group, as do a number of middle-class African Americans, Latinos, Native Americans, and Asian Americans. Many low-income families also hold the same values but do not have the income to support a similar lifestyle. The mass media and international communications systems are contributing to the development of a universal culture that mirrors the dominant U.S. culture. Some people worry that the positive aspects of other cultures are losing ground as television and movies teach a common culture.

MICROCULTURAL GROUPS

Cultural identity is not determined by ethnicity and race alone. As shown in Figure 2.1, individuals are members of multiple microcultural groups. They are female or male and members of specific socioeconomic, religious, language, geographic, and age groups. In addition, mental and physical abilities help define who we are. Membership in these microcultural groups determines our cultural identity.

Students in U.S. schools are among the most diverse in the world. At the beginning of this century, one-third of the students in the nation's schools were young people of color. They will make up 40 percent of the school population by 2020 and half of the population by 2050. They are already the majority in schools in California, Texas, and the nation's largest cities. In many schools, the native languages of students are other than English. Some school districts can identify more than 100 languages used in the homes of their students. Religious diversity is no longer limited to the traditional Judeo-Christian roots as immigrants from Asia, Africa, and the Middle East bring their religious traditions to the mix. In addition, a growing number of students with disabilities are active participants in schools and society.

The relationship of individuals' group memberships to the dominant culture may have a great influence on how individuals perceive themselves and are viewed by others. Because of the importance of power relationships between groups in discussions of diversity and equality, educators should understand how they themselves are positioned in this dialogue. Educators need to know which groups they belong to and what influence those memberships have on their own identity. A critical self-examination is helpful in the identification of otherness and difference that pervade a culturally diverse society. Later in this chapter, we will look in some detail at several microcultural dimensions and their significance in U.S. education.

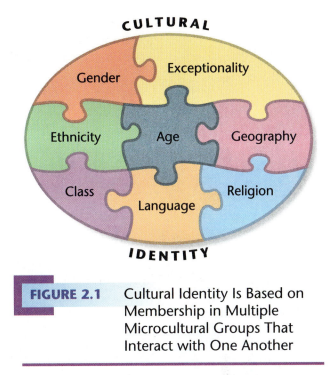

FIGURE 2.1 Cultural Identity Is Based on Membership in Multiple Microcultural Groups That Interact with One Another

DIVERSITY AND EDUCATION

Many people in this country celebrate the differences among groups and the contributions they have made to society. Others worry that these differences are leading to a divided society. The differences sometimes lead to misunderstandings, stereotypes, and even conflicts. At the same time, diverse groups share many characteristics, can learn what they have in common, develop common interests, and appreciate and value their differences.

Representatives of diverse groups have challenged the monocultural, universalist view of the world and society that has guided the country's laws and practices. They question the curriculum taught in schools, colleges, and universities. They ask why so many Latinos drop out of school, why students in poverty attend dilapidated and filthy schools with few licensed teachers who have majored in the subjects they are teaching, why so many young African American men are in jail, why single mothers do not earn enough to stay out of poverty, and why so few students with disabilities are in general education courses.

Diversity raises concerns about equality and inequality in society and schools. Concerned educators are exploring the intersections of race, ethnicity, gender, and class as they relate to individual and group identity. They work to overcome the stratification based on race, able-bodiedness, language, gender, and **socioeconomic status** that often tracks students into special education, gifted programs, advanced placement courses, low-level courses, and uninteresting, academically unchallenging courses. Educators who believe that all students can learn understand that the cultural backgrounds and experiences of their students must be respected and reflected in all aspects of the education process.

As an educator, you will encounter students from diverse ethnic, racial, language, religious, and economic groups and with different physical and mental abilities. The translation of this reality into educational practice leads to different strategies and outcomes. Ethnographic studies provide valuable information about how teachers and schools interact with students in the learning process. Researchers have discovered that schools often use teaching strategies that differ

socioeconomic status

The economic condition of individuals based on their (or their parents') income, occupation, and educational attainment.

Today's classroom reflects the diversity in U.S. society. Students may look similar but come from different cultural backgrounds and life experiences.

from those that are effective at home, particularly as they relate to language and learning styles.

Over time the relationship of groups to society has been described differently by sociologists, politicians, philosophers, and educators. These differing descriptions have led to the development of policies and practices that range along a continuum from promotion to condemnation of group differences. Assimilation, pluralism, and cultural choice are three prevalent theories and ideologies.

◼ ASSIMILATION

Assimilation is a process by which an immigrant group or culturally distinct group is incorporated into the mainstream culture. The group either adopts the culture of the dominant group as its own or interacts with it in a way that forges a new or different culture that is shared by both groups. Members of a group experience a number of stages in this process.

The first step involves learning the cultural patterns of the dominant group. The speed at which group members become assimilated is usually enhanced by interactions in settings such as work, school, and worship. In many cases, previous cultural patterns are shed—either enthusiastically or grudgingly—as those of the dominant group are adopted. Native languages and traditions can be lost within a few generations. Society usually requires an individual to take these steps in order to attain some modicum of financial success or achievement of the "good life" in the United States.

The final stage of assimilation is structural assimilation.[1] At this stage, members of the immigrant or culturally distinct group interact with the mainstream group at all levels, including marriage. They no longer encounter prejudice or **discrimination** and share equally in the benefits of society.

At the beginning of the twentieth century, the melting pot theory emerged as a description of how immigrants contributed to the evolution of a new American culture. This theory described the egalitarian state that is one of the core values of a democracy. Many immigrants believed that the prejudices and inequities they had experienced in their native countries would not exist in the United States and that they would become valued members of society. Although many European immigrants did merge into the mainstream, people of color were prevented by the prevailing racist ideology from "melting" or becoming structurally assimilated. Racism has prevented Native, African, Latino, and Asian Americans from becoming structurally assimilated for generations.

Assimilation remains the guiding principle in most schools. **Acculturation,** or learning of the dominant culture through immersion, is the prevailing strategy. School success usually depends on how well students are able to adjust to the dominant culture that permeates the curriculum and school activities. Their own unique cultural experiences and patterns are often not officially recognized, valued, or used in the teaching and learning process.

The poor academic performance of many students of color and students from low-income families is sometimes explained by a cultural deficit theory, in which students and their families are blamed for their failures. A problem, this theory suggests, is that these students have not been socialized to think and act like children of the dominant culture. Proponents of this theory blame the ed-

assimilation

A process by which an immigrant or culturally distinct group is incorporated into the dominant culture.

discrimination

Individual or institutional practices that exclude members of a group from certain rights, opportunities, or benefits.

acculturation

The process of learning the cultural patterns of the dominant culture.

ucational deficiencies of the home environment and such factors as single parents, teenage mothers, and inadequate child-rearing practices. The provision of equal educational opportunity is a policy response to this theory. Compensatory programs are offered to help students overcome both their educational and cultural deficiencies by making them more like students from the dominant culture. The perception exists that these families do not value education, as manifested by the lack of books in their homes or lack of parental participation in schools. However, education is valued in most communities. The problem is more likely the lack of financial resources and inability to take off work to meet with school officials. Some teachers and school leaders have become creative in overcoming these problems.

PLURALISM

Pluralism exists in societies in which the maintenance of distinct cultural patterns, including languages, is valued and promoted. Groups may be segregated, but they participate somewhat equally in politics, economics, and education. In some cases, groups have been able to establish and maintain their own political, economic, and educational systems.

Pluralism in its ideal form does not exist in the United States at this time. Although diversity does exist, parity and equality between groups do not. For example, some Native American nations do have their own political and educational systems, but they do not share power and resources equally with the dominant group. Some groups choose to maintain their native culture, religion, and language. This goal is more likely to be attained if families live in communities where there is a fairly large concentration of others from a similar cultural background; Little Italy, Chinatown, Harlem, East Los Angeles, and Amish and Hutterite communities provide these settings. Sometimes culturally distinct groups have been forced into segregated communities because of discriminatory housing patterns.

The implementation of pluralism in schools requires the recognition of the multiple cultures that make up society. Rather than the dominant culture being centered in the classroom and school, the cultures of the particular group or groups served by the school are the predominant focus of the curriculum. Examples include the Afrocentric and Native-centric programs that exist today in some urban areas and tribal-controlled schools. Also, some ethnic and religious groups have maintained their culture and history in private schools. The Amish and Hutterites, for example, operate their own schools to prevent the destruction of their cultures by the dominant group. Jewish and Islamic private schools promote religious study and practices; the rules of the religion guide student and teacher behavior.

Public schools generally teach only the dominant culture. The faculty might not represent the diversity of the students in the school and might have little, if any, knowledge about the cultures represented or personal experiences with them. Students who are from low-income

Ethnic and religious communities exist in many areas of the country. Group members in these neighborhoods are more likely to maintain the group's cultural traditions, language, and practices than members of the group who have moved into integrated communities.

families or from ethnic, racial, religious, or language groups other than the dominant culture too often do not achieve well academically in these schools.

A cultural difference theory helps explain the differential achievement of students of diverse backgrounds. Disjunctures in cultural patterns between the home and school may prevent academic success. Schools that focus only on the dominant culture expect all participants to operate as if they are members of that culture. This practice gives an advantage to students from the dominant group because the language and expected behaviors are the same as, or very similar to, those in their homes and communities. Students from other ethnic, racial, language, socioeconomic, and religious groups must reject their own cultural patterns or become bicultural to be successful at school. Some parents and communities have responded by establishing private or charter schools that reflect their own culture.

Schools in a pluralistic society are staffed by a diverse teaching force that at a minimum represents the cultures of students. Teachers who share the cultural backgrounds of students understand the students' language patterns. Teachers from different cultural backgrounds are expected to know multiple cultural patterns of communication and learning and be able to use them to help students learn.

■ CULTURAL CHOICE

Cultural choice is the freedom to choose and adapt the characteristics that determine one's cultural identity. Early in the twenty-first century, diversity in the United States is increasing. Some immigrants plan to assimilate into the dominant culture as soon as possible. They choose to adopt the new culture and shed the old. Others do not want to shed their unique cultural identity and patterns in order to be successful members of society. Many learn to be bicultural and bilingual, bridging two cultures and learning when it is appropriate to use the patterns of each. Others do not have a choice. Ideally, we could choose to assimilate, maintain our native culture, or become bicultural or multicultural and function effectively in more than one culture. Under cultural choice, society supports these choices and does not value one choice more than another or discriminate on the basis of group membership.

Unfortunately, this description does not match reality for large segments of the population. Many people of color are acculturated, but discrimination prevents them from being structurally assimilated even if they choose that route. Strong identity and affiliation with their cultural group has been necessary as a source of solidarity in the effort to combat inequities and obtain adequate housing and education. Although members of some cultural groups may be able to live almost solely within their distinct cultural milieu, most are forced to work within the dominant culture. Those who choose to assimilate might not be accepted by the dominant group and might also be rejected by the group into which they were born.

Equality across groups does not yet exist, but it continues to be a value espoused by society. Discrimination against groups prevents their members from having cultural choices. As the barriers to equality are reduced, there is likely to be greater individual choice and mobility across groups. We will move toward an open society in which cultural background determines who we are but is not the basis for discrimination. Cultural differences will be respected and encouraged to flourish.

Schools that value cultural choice consciously avoid promoting the dominance of a single culture. Such schools integrate the contributions and histories of diverse groups—particularly those represented in the school, but not limited to them—throughout the curriculum. Bilingualism and the use of dialects prevail in classrooms as well as school hallways. Students are the center of instruction, and teachers use students' cultural patterns to promote learning.

cultural choice

The freedom to choose and adapt the characteristics from one's own and other cultures in developing one's own cultural identity.

Students learn to operate comfortably in both their own and other cultures, including the dominant culture. Equality is manifested in the equal participation of all groups in courses and extracurricular activities, as well as in comparable achievement on academic assessments.

SOCIOECONOMIC STATUS

Most people want the "good life," which in the United States includes a decent job, affordable housing, good health, a good education for their family members, and periodic vacations. One way to estimate the good life is socioeconomic status, which is the primary determinant of the standard of living families are able to maintain. It also has a great impact on one's chances of attending college and attaining a job that ensures material comfort throughout life.

Socioeconomic status (SES) serves as a criterion to measure the economic condition of individuals. It is determined by one's occupation, income, and educational attainment. Wealth and power are other important factors that affect the way one is able to live, but these data are difficult to measure. We often can guess a family's socioeconomic status if we know such things as where they live, their jobs, the type of car they drive, the schools attended by their children, and the types of vacations they take.

SOCIAL STRATIFICATION

Most societies are characterized by **social stratification,** in which individuals occupy different levels of the social structure. Wealth, income, occupation, and education help define these social positions. However, high or low rankings are not based only on SES criteria. Race, age, gender, religion, and disability can contribute to lower rankings as well. Although members of most **ethnic groups** can be found at all levels of the socioeconomic status scale in the United States, those from western European backgrounds have a disproportionately high representation at the highest levels.

Social mobility remains one of the core values of the dominant culture. We are told that hard work will lead to better jobs, higher income, and a better chance to participate in the good life. We read the Horatio Alger stories of individuals who were born in poverty but through hard work became wealthy as a corporate president, prestigious publisher, successful writer, athlete, or entertainer. Although dramatic upward mobility continues to occur, the chances of moving from poverty to riches, no matter how hard one works, are low. Individuals who are born into wealthy families are likely to attend good schools, finish college, and find high-paying administrative jobs. They are raised with high expectations, have the economic resources to assist them in meeting these expectations, and usually end up meeting them.

CLASS STRUCTURE

The population can be divided into distinct classes in order for researchers to study inequities in society and the characteristics of individuals and families at these different levels. One of the early categorization systems identified the population as lower, middle, and upper class, with finer distinctions in each of the three groups. The "underclass" is the label sometimes given to the portion of the population that lacks a stable income and is persistently in poverty.

Individuals who do manual work for a living are sometimes described as the "working class." When farm laborers and service workers are included in the working class, this group represents 40 percent of the employed population. Most members of this class have little control over their work. Some of the jobs are

social stratification
Levels of social class ranking based on income, education, occupation, wealth, and power in society.

ethnic groups
Groups based on the national origin (that is, a country or area of the world) of one's family or ancestors in which members share a culture and sense of common destiny.

The combined wealth of the world's 225 richest people is the same as the annual income of the poorer half of the world population.
The State of the World Atlas, 1999

routine, mechanical, and not challenging. Work sometimes is sporadic and affected by an economy in which employees face layoffs, replacement by computerized equipment and other advances in technology, part-time work, and unemployment as jobs move to locations with cheaper labor. Fringe benefits such as vacation time and health plans are often limited. The education required for working-class jobs is usually less than that for many middle-class positions, except for skilled and crafts workers who have had specialized training and may have served apprenticeships. Even some of these skilled workers, however, work as long and hard as others, often working overtime and holding two jobs to make ends meet.

The middle class is large. Most people who don't perceive themselves as poor or rich define themselves as middle class. Annual middle-class incomes range from $30,000 to $80,000, encompassing 38 percent of the population.[2] It includes both blue-collar and professional or managerial workers. For most of the middle class, $80,000 would be the top of their earning potential, and this is often possible only because both spouses work. Families in this class have very different lifestyles at the opposite ends of the income continuum. Clerical workers, technicians, and salespeople in the group have less control over their jobs than the professionals, managers, and administrators who often supervise them. These workers tend to have somewhat better fringe benefits than do members of the working class. The professionals in this group expect to move beyond $80,000 in their careers with the goal of becoming one of the 17 percent of U.S. families earning $100,000 or more annually.

Many professionals, managers, and administrators receive incomes that are above $75,000, placing them in the upper middle class. They have become the affluent middle class, but they often believe that their condition is universal rather than unique. Many think that most of the U.S. population shares the same affluence, advantages, and comforts. A $75,000 salary in a neighborhood where most families earn over $200,000 seems low; in another neighborhood, a family making $75,000 would be considered well off. The professionals are men and women who have usually obtained professional or advanced degrees. They include teachers, lawyers, physicians, college professors, scientists, and psychologists. Excluding teachers, most of these families earn far above the median income of $50,890. Successful executives and businesspeople are the managers and administrators in this group. These workers usually have more autonomy over their jobs and working conditions than working- and lower-middle-class workers.

The upper class consists of wealthy and socially prominent families. The income and wealth of members of this class are far higher than those of the other classes, and the gap is growing. For example, in 1980 corporate chief executive officers earned 42 times as much as their manufacturing employees; by 1990 they earned 85 times as much; and by 1998 the multiple had grown to 419.[3] These great differences contribute to limited interactions with members of other classes. Children in this class rarely attend public schools, isolating them from peers of other social classes. Probably the greatest assimilation of lifestyles and values occurs among members of ethnically and culturally diverse groups who attain an upper-class status.

■ POVERTY

The U.S. government has established a poverty index that sets a conservative ceiling on poverty. Using this threshold, which is an annual income of $18,104 for a family of four, 31.1 million persons are in poverty—11 percent of the population. There are many myths about people who are poor. One is that they do not work. In reality, many work in full-time jobs that pay such low wages that they cannot pull their families out of poverty.

Children, the elderly, and persons of color suffer disproportionately from poverty, as shown in Figure 2.2. Sixteen percent of U.S. children live in poverty, which is more than double that of most other major industrialized nations, even

Just because a child's parents are poor or uneducated is no reason to deprive the child of basic human rights to health care, education, proper nutrition.

Marian Wright Edelman

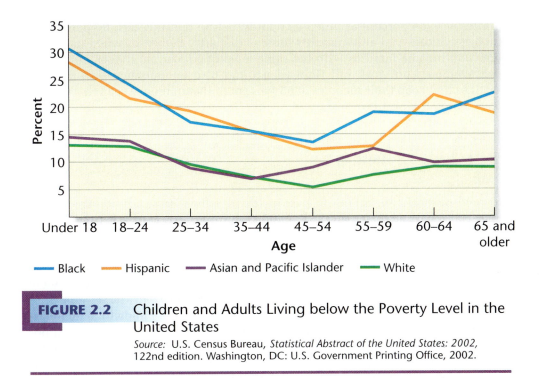

FIGURE 2.2 Children and Adults Living below the Poverty Level in the United States

Source: U.S. Census Bureau, *Statistical Abstract of the United States: 2002,* 122nd edition. Washington, DC: U.S. Government Printing Office, 2002.

though the United States has the highest gross domestic product per capita. Many industrialized nations have reduced child poverty levels to below 5 percent.[4]

Although 68 percent of the population living below the poverty level is white, only nine percent of all whites in the country are living in poverty. The percentage of other racial and ethnic groups in poverty is higher, as shown in Figure 2.3. The median income of Asian and Pacific Islanders was $61,511 in 2000 as compared to whites' median income of $53,256. African American

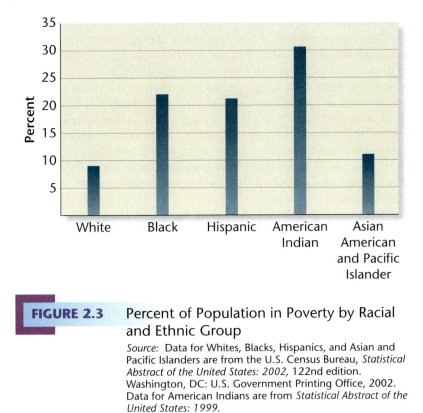

FIGURE 2.3 Percent of Population in Poverty by Racial and Ethnic Group

Source: Data for Whites, Blacks, Hispanics, and Asian and Pacific Islanders are from the U.S. Census Bureau, *Statistical Abstract of the United States: 2002,* 122nd edition. Washington, DC: U.S. Government Printing Office, 2002. Data for American Indians are from *Statistical Abstract of the United States: 1999.*

families earn 64 percent as much as whites; Latino families earn 66 percent as much as whites. And although this income disparity decreases when one compares two-income families with the same level of education, it does not disappear. Women who work full time year-round also encounter discriminatory practices that keep their incomes at 65 percent of that of men—a gap that has increased over the past few years.

RACE AND ETHNICITY

National origin is an important part of identity for many individuals. Native American tribes are the only indigenous ethnic groups in the United States; therefore, more than 99 percent of the U.S. population, or their ancestors, came from somewhere else at some time during the past 500 years. Many people can identify a country of origin, although the geographical boundaries may have changed since their ancestors immigrated. A growing number of people have mixed heritage, with ancestors from different parts of the world.

Although many people now identify themselves by their **panethnic membership** (for example, as African American or Asian American), race remains a political reality in U.S. society. It has become integrally interwoven into the nation's policies, practices, and institutions, including the educational, economic, and judicial systems. As a result, whites have advantages that are reflected in higher achievement on tests and higher incomes as adults. The issue of race encompasses personal and national discussions of affirmative action, immigration, desegregation, and a color-blind society. Race and ethnicity may be linked, but they are not the same. Both influence one's cultural identity and status in society.

RACE

Race and gender are among the first physical characteristics we notice when we meet another person. Although race is no longer accepted as a scientific concept for classifying people, it has become a social construction for identifying differences. We are asked to indicate our race or our panethnic identity on forms that we complete. Race is used inappropriately by many people to explain differences in behavior, language, socioeconomic standing, and academic achievement. Ideas about race are created from experiences in our own racial group and with other groups. They are informed by reflections of racial differences in the media. Ideas about race are politicized and institutionalized in the policies and actions of judges, teachers, legislators, police, employers, and others who are in charge of institutions that affect people's lives. Stereotyped views of race usually bestow positive attributes and high status on one's own race and negative attributes and low status on others.

Skin color is a signifier of race but does not capture the meaning of race. Many people have mixed racial backgrounds that place them along a continuum of skin color; they might not be obviously white, black, brown, or otherwise easily identifiable as one race or another. Historically, state laws declared a person's official race as nonwhite if a small percentage of his or her racial heritage was other than white. The official message was, and continues to be, that white is the ideal and that anything else, including small percentages of other races, is less than ideal. This example is one of many ways in which race affects our everyday lives and becomes an integral part of our identity, whether we like it or not. Race continues to be used to sort people in society.

People of color usually identify themselves by their race or ethnic group and are usually identified as such by others. They are confronted with their race almost daily in encounters with employers, salespeople, and colleagues or as they watch the evening news. Whites, on the other hand, are seldom confronted with their race; in fact, many see themselves as raceless. White has become the norm against which persons of color are classified as *other*. As a result, many whites are unable to see that they have been privileged in society. Their silence contributes to the maintenance of a racist society.

ETHNICITY

National origin is the primary determinant of one's ethnicity. Ethnic group members share a common history, language, traditions, and experiences in the United States. Identification with an ethnic group helps sustain and enhance the culture of the group. Ethnicity is strongest when members have a high degree of interpersonal associations with other members and share common residential areas.

Ethnic cohesiveness and solidarity are strengthened as members organize to support and advance the group, fight discrimination, and influence political and economic decisions that affect the group as a whole. In the 1960s, these struggles with the dominant culture led to calls for changes in schools, colleges, government programs, and employment to support equality across ethnic groups. During this period, African, Latino, Asian, and Native Americans called for recognition of their ethnic roots in the school curriculum. By the 1970s, European ethnic groups, especially those of southern and eastern European origins, had also joined this movement. Ethnic studies programs were established in colleges and universities and some high schools to study the history, contributions, and experiences of U.S. ethnic groups that had traditionally been excluded.

ETHNIC DIVERSITY

The U.S. Census Bureau reports population data on the five racial and ethnic groups shown in Figure 2.4. These broad classifications do not accurately describe the ethnic diversity of the United States. For example, there are more than 500 Native American tribes. Each of these panethnic classifications includes numerous ethnic groups with identities and loyalties linked to specific countries. Fifty-eight percent of the population identifies with a single ancestry, 22 percent with multiple ancestries, and 20 percent do not identify an ancestry.[5] Asian Americans include recent immigrants and people whose ancestors emigrated from countries as diverse as India, Korea, Japan, and the Philippines. Latinos include people from Mexico, Central American countries, Puerto Rico, Cuba, Spain, and South American countries. Although Africans continue to emigrate to the United States, most African Americans have long historical roots in this country; many have ancestors not only from Africa but also from Europe and Native American tribes. European Americans range from western Europeans who may have lived in the United States for several hundred years, to those from eastern Europe who immigrated in large numbers at the beginning of the twentieth century, to recent immigrants from Russia and other former Soviet countries.

In describing the United States, many people proudly refer to it as a land of immigrants who left their original homelands because of economic hardship or political repression. However, this picture is only partially true. The groups that are most oppressed in this country are those who are indigenous or whose ancestors entered the country involuntarily. Native Americans were here long before Europeans and others appeared. They suffered greatly as the foreign intruders took over the land, almost annihilating the indigenous population. Not

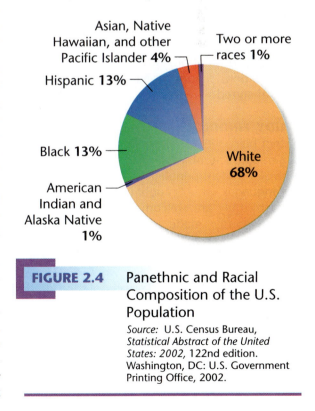

FIGURE 2.4 Panethnic and Racial Composition of the U.S. Population

Source: U.S. Census Bureau, *Statistical Abstract of the United States: 2002*, 122nd edition. Washington, DC: U.S. Government Printing Office, 2002.

until the year 2000 did the U.S. government admit to the near genocide of native peoples, when the head of the Bureau of Indian Affairs apologized for "the agency's legacy of racism and inhumanity that included massacres, forced relocations of tribes and attempts to wipe out Indian languages and cultures."[6]

Additionally, the ancestors of most African Americans were brought by slave traders as a commodity to be sold. They were not treated as full humans until well into the nineteenth century. Not until late in the twentieth century did Africans begin to voluntarily immigrate to the United States in any significant numbers. Similarly, Mexican Americans in the Southwest were inhabitants of lands that were annexed as part of the spoils for winning the Spanish-American War; they did not immigrate. Today, many Mexicans would like to immigrate to this country but, prevented by immigration laws, cross the border illegally to obtain jobs and have a better chance for economic stability. However, illegal immigrants constantly face possible deportation, loss of everything they have gained in this country, and separation from their families.

RELEVANT RESEARCH
Welcoming–Unwelcoming of Immigrant Students

STUDY PURPOSE/QUESTIONS: The focus of this study was to examine how students from Mexico, Bosnia, Sudan, and other countries fared in a middle school they attended for its English as a second language (ESL) program.

STUDY DESIGN: The researchers conducted a qualitative study that included observing and interviewing ESL teachers, the ESL program director, an administrator, and white students. Members of the local community and ESL students were also interviewed. The researchers attended ESL parent meetings, faculty meetings that focused on ESL issues, and school assemblies. In addition, documents on extracurricular participation, school discipline, and busing policies were analyzed.

STUDY FINDINGS: In the early 1980s, the school district placed its ESL program for immigrant students in a middle school, which had a predominantly white, high SES student population. The students, who spoke 12 languages, were "caught in a contradictory process whereby they are welcomed at the school and yet, simultaneously, made to feel unwelcome in many respects."

Community members spoke about the value of diversity in the school, but also worried about the students being a disruption. The school sponsored several welcoming events such as cultural fairs to help White students understand the countries from which the ESL students had come, but the events stereotyped groups and did not provide in-depth understanding of differences.

ESL classes lacked curricular materials, and class size was high (30 students) for providing the individualized attention needed in ESL. Most of the non-ESL teachers resisted having ESL students in their classrooms.

A pattern of segregation was found in school assemblies, the lunchroom, and classes. For example, during assemblies they were assigned to a secondary choir that sang a few songs, but not one of the ESL students participated in the main choir. None of the songs represented cultures other than the dominant U.S. culture.

ESL students traveled to the school from communities in other parts of the city. The fact that the buses arrived just before classes started and left immediately after classes made it difficult for the ESL students to participate in extracurricular activities. Suspension rates for immigrant students were more than four times as great as for white students. Students from Mexico and Africa were most likely to be disciplined.

IMPLICATIONS: Schools need to do more than offer ESL programs for immigrant students. They need to examine their policies and practices to ensure that these students are not excluded from the benefits available to students from the dominant group. In addition, teachers and administrators often need professional development to assist them in working effectively with ESL students.

Source: Andrew Gitlin, Edward Buendia, Kristin Crosland, Fode Doumbia, "The Production of Margin and Center: Welcoming–Unwelcoming of Immigrant Students." *American Educational Research Journal, 40*(1) (Spring 2003), pp. 91–122.

Who can immigrate or be admitted as a refugee is determined by Congress. Immigration policies have prevented or severely limited the immigration of some groups while favoring others. For example, people with either Chinese or Japanese heritage have been excluded at different times. Individuals fleeing Communist regimes have often been granted refugee status, but others have found it difficult to obtain such status when fleeing regimes supportive of the United States, even though those regimes may be dictatorships with numerous human rights violations. Immigration quotas historically were heavily weighted toward western Europeans; beginning in 1965, however, immigration became more open to people from other countries. As a result, the numbers of Latinos and Asians coming to the United States have grown dramatically.

Schools are early recipients of a growing number of new immigrants. Immigrants today are settling beyond the urban areas of California, Florida, Illinois, New Jersey, New York, and Texas. States that have had limited ethnic diversity in the past—among them Arkansas, Iowa, Montana, and Nebraska—are becoming home to students from other countries as immigrant families are sponsored by persons in these communities or settle in rural areas and small to medium-sized towns because of jobs. Many immigrants also believe that these communities have values more similar to their own.

LANGUAGE

Language interacts with our ethnic and socioeconomic background to socialize us into linguistic and cultural communities. Children learn their native language by imitating adults and their peers. By age five, they have learned the syntax of language and know the meaning of thousands of words. When cultural similarities exist between speaker and listener, spoken messages are decoded accurately. But when the speaker and listener differ in ethnicity or class, miscommunication can occur. Even within English, a word, phrase, or nonverbal gesture takes on different meanings in different cultural groups and settings. Educators need to recognize that miscommunications between themselves and students may be due to inaccurate decoding rather than lack of linguistic ability.

Who does not know another language, does not know his own.

Goethe

LANGUAGE DIVERSITY

English is not the native language for nearly 47 million residents of the United States. Spanish, Italian, and sign language are the most common languages other than English. A number of new immigrant students enter U.S. schools with no or very limited school experiences in their home countries.

The length of time required to learn English varies. Most students become conversationally fluent within two or three years.[7] However, young people may require five to seven years to reach the proficiency necessary for success in academic subjects such as social studies and English. Students who are conversationally fluent may be immersed in English-only classrooms without

Bilingual education uses both the native languages of students and English in classrooms to ensure that students learn the academic concepts being taught.

Should All Students Be Bilingual?

Many immigrant students enter school using a language other than English. The role of schools in teaching them English and encouraging the maintenance of their own native language has long been debated. Another side of the coin is the importance of native English speakers learning a second language so that they are fluent in at least two languages. This debate illustrates two teachers' perspectives on these issues.

YES

Douglas Ward is a bilingual learning disabilities resource teacher at William Nashold Elementary school in Rockford, Illinois. He is in his third year of teaching and is certified in bilingual special education and several other fields.

NO

Suzanne Emery retired last year after 35 years of teaching English and journalism, the last 25 at San Diego's Mira Mesa High School. She reviews questions for California's high school exit exam and edits the San Diego Education Association newsletter.

Yes, all students should be bilingual. Unfortunately, in the United States very few students become truly proficient in a foreign language. That is one reason for the shortage of foreign language and bilingual teachers.

Before the world wars, many immigrants in the United States used their native languages daily while they learned English. But the world wars and isolationist policies created a climate in which it was unpopular to speak anything but English. In some cities, fines were imposed on anyone caught speaking a foreign language in public business.

Many descendants of immigrants never learned their parents' or grandparents' native languages—in my case, Polish and German—because of these attitudes. My grandparents and parents, pressured by society, did not understand the importance of passing on their languages to me.

Learning a foreign language involves more than learning how to read, write, and speak. More important, it teaches students about a culture. Lack of understanding of cultural differences causes intolerance and war.

American education cannot be all things for all people.

We've agreed generally on the need to improve achievement in the basic curriculum. Bilingualism should not be added to the mix. Nor should it join all the other mandates that politically correct states and school districts impose: cultural holidays, parenting classes, good health activities, well-rounded social growth, adequate physical activities, proper nutrition, and suicide prevention.

A second language is always a luxury. It is needed only for the college bound and then only in certain majors.

We're told that European countries require two languages. But many European countries are very small, so bilingualism is a survival skill. And few other countries try to educate 100 percent of their children, as we do. In Europe, education is at the top of parents' priorities. Need we talk about the distractions here?

And what is the second language of bilingual children around the world? It is English. We need to edu-

(continued)

appropriate support to ensure that they can function effectively in academic work. The result is that these students may fall further behind their classmates in conceptual understanding of the subjects being taught.

As immigrants assimilate into the dominant culture of the United States, their native language is often replaced by English within a few generations. The native language is more likely to be retained when schools and the community value bilingualism. As commerce and trade have become more global, professionals and administrators have realized the advantages of knowing a competitor's culture and language. They are encouraging their children to learn a second language at the same time that many of our educational policies are discouraging native speakers from maintaining their native language while learning English. The movement in some states for English-only usage in schools, in

YES

The people of the United States and the world need to be, not just tolerant, but accepting of other cultures. We need to embrace and celebrate our many cultures. Studying a foreign language and becoming bilingual opens one's mind to new thinking and creates new opportunities to communicate with other people.

Language can be the key to a lasting peace between enemies. Learning another language is the best way to make friends.

Students in many other countries learn at least one foreign language in their public schools. In the United States, few schools even offer a foreign language in elementary school.

As global businesses and trade expand, the need to know a second language is growing tremendously. Many businesses in other countries want to do business with us. Their salespeople speak English and know our customs. We need people who know other languages and cultures so that our exports will increase and our economy will become stronger.

Learning another language may also spill over into other areas. Research shows that bilingualism leads to cognitive advantages that may raise scores on some intelligence tests.

Studies also show a correlation between knowing two languages and linguistic abilities that may facilitate early reading acquisition. That, in turn, could boost academic achievement.

Source: "Should All Students Be Bilingual?" *NEA Today* (May 2002), p. 11.

NO

cate our own kids for success in that universal language. Our schools can barely gather materials and teachers for the standard curriculum, let alone for another language.

If schools required a second language, what would it be? Spanish, Japanese, or French? How should we decide? What about all our students who speak Hmong, Farsi, or Tagalog? Would we mandate a third language for them?

Comfort in two languages is valuable in many venues and often desired for reasons of tradition. But families that want another language can do what they've always done: Saturday school, magnet schools, and temple classes.

If a district is so insular that it lacks the diverse quilt of contemporary America, its sterility and guilt should not be visited on the rest of the country.

So many American schools are like mine in San Diego where students regularly exchange videos with relatives in Vietnam, make the annual family pilgrimage to Mexico, edit the Islamic Center's youth newsletter, and produce pamphlets in graphic arts class for the Buddhist temple.

Here in California, with the nation's largest enrollment of newcomers, the challenge is to prepare all students for world-class competition, culminating with a high school exit exam in English, because English communication is key to success in academics and in adult life. That also applies to the rest of the country.

We cannot afford another diversion added to the overflowing plate of public education.

WHAT DO YOU THINK?
Should all students be bilingual?

To give your opinion, go to Chapter 2 of the companion website (**www.ablongman.com/johnson13e**) and click on Debate.

daily commerce, on street signs, and on official government documents highlights the dominance of English desired by some citizens.

American Sign Language (ASL) is officially recognized as a language with a complex grammar and well-regulated syntax. It is the natural language that has been developed and used for communication among individuals with hearing disabilities. As with oral languages, children learn ASL very early by imitating others who use the language. To communicate with people without hearing disabilities, many individuals with hearing disabilities also use signed English, in which the oral or written word is translated into a sign. ASL is a critical element in the identity of people with hearing disabilities. The language can be more important to their cultural identity than their membership in a particular ethnic, socioeconomic, or religious group.

DIALECTAL DIVERSITY

Standard English is the dialect used by the majority of dominant group members for official and formal communications. However, numerous regional, local, ethnic, and class (or socioeconomic status—SES) dialects are identifiable across this country. Each has its own set of grammatical rules that are known to its users. Although each dialect serves its users well, standard English is usually viewed as more credible in schools and the work world. For example, most individuals involved in the media use standard English. Although teachers may be bidialectal, they are expected to use standard English as the example that should be emulated by students.

Many Americans are bidialectal or multidialectal in that they speak standard English at work but speak their native or local dialect at home or when they are socializing with friends. Social factors have an influence on which dialect is appropriate in a specific situation. At one time, students were not allowed to use a dialect other than standard English in the classroom. Some schools have proposed using the dialect of the community as a teaching tool, but the proposal usually leads to a public outcry against it, as happened in Oakland, California, when administrators suggested using **Ebonics** in classrooms. Today, students are usually allowed to speak their dialects but are encouraged to learn standard English to provide them with an advantage when they seek employment in the dominant culture.

GENDER

Males and females are culturally different even when they are members of the same socioeconomic, ethnic, and religious group. For example, the two groups are often segregated at social gatherings, employed in different types of jobs, and expected to behave differently. The ways they think and act are defined in part by their gender identity.

DIFFERENCES BETWEEN FEMALES AND MALES

Because of our social circumstances, male and female are really two cultures and their life experiences are utterly different.

Kate Millett

Learning the gender of a baby is one of the important rites of parenthood. However, the major difference between boys and girls is the way adults respond to them. There are few actual physical differences, particularly before puberty. Primarily, the socialization process in child-rearing and schools determines gender identity and the related distinctive behaviors.

Some researchers attribute differences in mathematical, verbal, and spatial skills to different hormones that affect specific hemispheres of the brain. However, recent studies show that females and males are performing more alike, suggesting that the previously observed gender differences are not biologically determined. For example, no differences exist in quantitative abilities until the age of ten and then only slight differences that sometimes favor girls and sometimes favor boys in the middle school years. Males do perform better in high school, but the differences are declining as female students become more interested in mathematics. Gender differences in spatial abilities are also declining, and abilities in this area can be improved with training. There no longer appear to be gender differences in verbal abilities.[8]

By age two, children realize that they are a girl or a boy; by five or six, they have learned their gender and stereotypical behavior. In most cultures, boys are generally socialized toward achievement and self-reliance, girls toward nurturance and responsibility. In the United States, differences in the expectations and behaviors of the two genders may be rooted in different groups' ethnicity, religion, and socioeconomic status.

Ebonics

Also known as Black English, the dialect spoken by many African Americans.

A major difference between males and females is how they are treated in society. Society generally places men in positions of superiority, as evidenced by their disproportionate holding of the highest status and highest-paying jobs. Many times this relationship extends into the home, where the father and husband may both protect the family and rule over it. Sometimes this relationship leads to physical and mental abuse of women and children.

Although 90 percent of all women in the United States will work outside the home at some time, society's view of them as inferior to men has contributed to the current patterns of discrimination that keep many women in low-prestige and low-paying jobs. The jobs in which many women are concentrated are those that naturally extend their role as nurturers and helpers: nursing, teaching, and secretarial work. Job and wage discrimination is a critical issue for women, especially today when a large number of families are headed by women without the advantage of a second income. Women earn less than men throughout their life span, as shown in Figure 2.5. Families headed by single women are more likely to be in poverty than any other group; more than 27 percent of the persons in these families fall below the official poverty level. As barriers to professional education and employment are broken, the number of women in traditionally male occupations has increased. For example, the number of female physicians increased from 6.5 percent in 1950 to 29 percent in 2001; female attorneys and judges increased from 4 to 29 percent; and female principals in public schools increased from 20 percent in 1982 to 50 percent in 1998.

Schools often reinforce behavior that is stereotypically gender specific. Girls are expected to be quiet, follow the rules, and help the teacher. Boys and young men are expected to be rowdier and less attentive. Many working-class males develop patterns of resistance to school and its authority figures because schooling is perceived as feminine and as emphasizing mental rather than manual work.

Many males are also not well served by the current socialization patterns; some do not fit neatly in the dominant culture's stereotypical vision of maleness. For instance, some men would feel more comfortable working as preschool teachers, nurses, or librarians—traditionally female careers—but may have learned that those jobs are inappropriate for "real men."

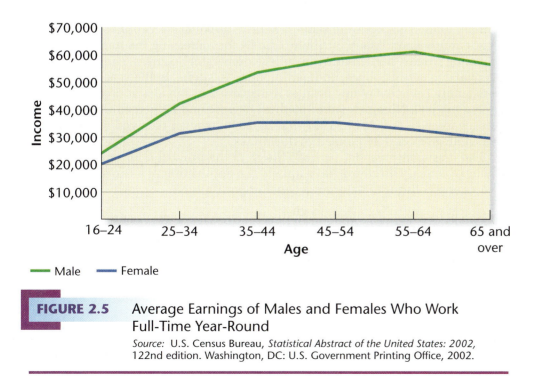

— Male — Female

FIGURE 2.5 Average Earnings of Males and Females Who Work Full-Time Year-Round

Source: U.S. Census Bureau, *Statistical Abstract of the United States: 2002,* 122nd edition. Washington, DC: U.S. Government Printing Office, 2002.

GLOBAL PERSPECTIVES
Women's Political Participation

Beginning in 1990, the global community agreed that gender equity was important in the development of a country. At the United Nation's World Education Forum in Dakar in 2002, gender equality became one of eight goals to eliminating poverty and hunger. The consensus among the world's leaders was that "no country's development can be judged satisfactory if women do not fully participate in community life, in society and in work."[9] Participants expect member countries to show women's progress in education, literacy, nonagricultural wage employment, and parliamentary representation.

A 2002 progress report by the United Nations Development Fund for Women (UNIFEM) shows limited progress in education, literacy, and employment. However, women's involvement in parliamentary bodies has made gains in a number of countries. Although women remain absent from these bodies in many countries, eleven have already reached the goal of 30 percent. They include Argentina, Costa Rica, Denmark, Finland, Germany, Iceland, Mozambique, the Netherlands, Norway, South Africa, and Sweden. The countries that met the benchmark did so by using quotas. The study also found that political participation is the only indicator in the gender equity goals that is not linked to poverty, which means that differences between wealthy and developing countries do not exist. For example, women's participation in legislative bodies in the United States, France, and Japan are 12 percent or less, which is behind thirteen of the countries in sub-Saharan Africa—countries suffering from great poverty.[10]

■ TITLE IX

Title IX of the 1972 Education Amendments is the major legislation that addresses the civil rights of girls and women in the education system. It requires federally funded colleges and schools to provide equal educational opportunity to girls and women. Many attribute Title IX for increasing the number of girls and young women participating in college preparatory courses, completing professional degrees in college, and participating in sports. In the year that Title IX passed, only 7 percent of law degrees were earned by females as compared to 46 percent in 2000. Nine percent of medical degrees and 25 percent of doctorates were awarded to females in 1977, but by 2000, women received 43 percent of medical degrees and 44 percent of doctorates.

The most controversial part of Title IX is the provision for equal opportunity in athletics. The courts have upheld the application of a three-part test by schools and colleges to determine equal opportunity:

1. The percentage of male and female athletes is substantially proportionate to the percentage of females and males in the student population.
2. The school has a history of expanding opportunities for underrepresented females to participate in sports.
3. Even if a school is not meeting the proportionate expectation in #1, the school is fully and effectively meeting the interest and abilities of female students.[11]

The number of girls and women participating in sports has increased dramatically since 1972. When Title IX was passed, 294,000 young women participated in high school sports. That number has increased by 847 percent, with nearly 2.8 million females now participating in high school sports.[12] The number of women in intercollegiate athletics has increased from 32,000 to 163,000, and the number of scholarships for female athletes jumped from a few to 10,000.[13] At the same time, some groups have argued that Title IX has led to the elimination of some men's sports as women's sports are expanded.

SEXUAL ORIENTATION

Sexual orientation is established early in life. It is not learned in adolescence or young adulthood, nor is it forced on others by immoral adults. The majority of gay adults report feeling different from other children before they entered kindergarten.[14] It has been estimated that 5 to 10 percent of the population is lesbian, gay, bisexual, or transgender (LGBT). However, many cultural groups place high value on heterosexuality and denigrate or outlaw homosexuality as part of their religious doctrine or community mores.

Title IX prevents discrimination in education programs based on sex. Schools must make provisions for girls and young women to participate in intramural, club, and interscholastic sports.

Gays and lesbians often face discrimination in housing, employment, and many social institutions, as evidenced when schools and universities prohibit the establishment of gay student clubs. Some states still have laws that make it illegal to engage in homosexual relations. Homophobia, as expressed in harassment and violence against gays and lesbians, is tolerated in many areas of the country. Society's prejudices and discriminatory practices result in many gays and lesbians hiding their homosexuality and establishing their own social clubs, networks, and communication systems to support one another.

Isolation and loneliness are the experiences of many gay and lesbian youth. If gays and lesbians openly acknowledge their sexual orientation or appear to be LGBT, they are likely to be harassed and face reprisals from peers and school officials. A 2001 study by the Gay, Lesbian and Straight Education Network (GLSEN) found that verbal, sexual, and physical harassment are common experiences for LGBT students in our schools. Eighty-three percent of LGBT students reported being verbally harassed (name calling, threats), 65 percent sexually harassed (sexual comments, inappropriate touching), 42 percent physically harassed, and 21 percent physically assaulted. Females and youth of color report even higher incidences of abuse when homophobia interacts with racism and sexism.[15]

Structures within the schools do not provide the same kind of support to LGBT students that is available to others. Nearly 70 percent of LGBT students fear for their safety in schools. However, students feel more comfortable and safer in schools when faculty and staff are supportive, LGBT people are portrayed in the curriculum, and gay–straight alliance or similar clubs exist.[16] Educators often know little about this group and have had few or no contacts with LGBT people who are out, or open about their sexual orientation. They may not have taught students whose parents are gay or lesbian. Without a better understanding of homosexuality, teachers may find it difficult to work effectively with LGBT students or the children of gay and lesbian parents.

EXCEPTIONALITIES

It doesn't matter who you are, there are some things you can do and some things you can't. It's about ability, not disability.

Christopher Reeve

More than 49 million people, or 19 percent of the population over five years old, have a **disability.** About one-fourth of the persons with a disability indicate that their disability existed at birth or developed before they were age twenty. The percent of the population increases with age, as shown in Figure 2.6. Individuals with a disability are often labeled by society by the classifications listed in Figure 2.7. Those with physical disabilities can be readily recognized by their use of supports such as a cane, braces, wheelchair, or sign language. Some individuals are labeled very early in their school careers as *mentally retarded* or *emotionally disturbed* and are placed in special programs that may prepare them for self-sufficiency but sometimes limit their potential. Critics of labeling declare this system to be demeaning and stigmatizing.

Some school systems require a determination as to whether a child with special needs is diploma-bound by the end of kindergarten. This early determination can lead to low academic expectations for students who can perform at high levels with appropriate accommodations for their disability. Seventy-two percent of persons with disabilities hold a high school diploma and 11 percent have college degrees.[17] Dropout rates for this population are relatively high. Persons with disabilities are disproportionately underrepresented in the labor force, sometimes because they are unable to go to work, but more often because the workplace has not made the accommodations that would make it possible for them to work productively.

Persons without a disability often react with disdain toward individuals with disabilities and view them as inferior. But like all other individuals, people with disabilities want to be recognized as persons in their own right. They have the same needs for love and the same desire to be successful as persons without disabilities. Instead, society has historically not accepted them as equals. Some individuals with severe disabilities are placed in institutions out of the sight of the public. Others are segregated in separate schools or classes. Too often they are rejected and made to feel inept and limited in their abilities.

Schools, which should be part of the solution, have often contributed to the problems of students with disabilities. Most classrooms are not physically designed to accommodate the special needs of all students. Chalkboards are too high for students in wheelchairs. Desks do not usually accommodate wheelchairs, and special ramps and elevators are often nonexistent. However, special equipment such as computers and amplification devices can make participation in learning possible for many students who were not provided that opportunity in the past.

disability

A long-standing physical, mental, or emotional condition that can make it difficult for a person to perform activities such as walking, climbing stairs, dressing, bathing, learning, or remembering.

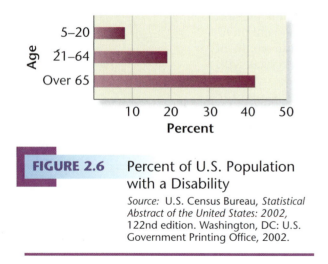

FIGURE 2.6   Percent of U.S. Population with a Disability

Source: U.S. Census Bureau, *Statistical Abstract of the United States: 2002,* 122nd edition. Washington, DC: U.S. Government Printing Office, 2002.

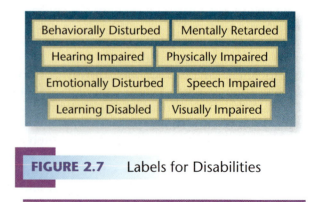

FIGURE 2.7   Labels for Disabilities

CULTURAL DIFFERENCES

Individuals with similar disabilities often find comfort and security with one another, forming their own culture. Those with hearing impairments share a language that is used by few people without hearing impairments; the language provides them with a strong sense of community. In some cities, many individuals with visual impairments live in the community near a school for the blind, where they can be close to potential work settings and provide mutual support. Individuals with mental retardation sometimes share group homes in which they can support one another and develop a degree of self-reliance. In these settings, they establish patterns of communication and behavior that are natural to them but may seem odd to nonmembers. Persons with disabilities have many publications, websites (for example, www.nod.org of the National Organization on Disability), and support systems developed by them, their families, and friends. Some activists participate in advocacy groups to promote their interests and issues and to ensure they are granted the civil rights that others expect.

INCLUSION

Inclusion is the practice of fully integrating all students into the educational process, regardless of their race, ethnicity, gender, class, religion, physical or mental ability, or language. Students see themselves represented in the curriculum as well as in classes for the gifted. Historically, inclusion referred primarily to the integration of students with disabilities in general education classrooms and schools. Inclusion of all students requires collaboration among the adults, including parents, who work with students with disabilities. Teachers should not be expected to serve as both the teacher and specialist. Ideally, teachers of general education collaborate with a special educator, often accompanied by a teacher's aide and appropriate specialists such as a speech/language pathologist, occupational therapist, physical therapist, vision specialist, adaptive physical education teacher, school psychologist, or school nurse. The team individualizes instruction for each student in an individualized educational plan (IEP). At times, students with disabilities may be pulled out of the classroom for special services, but these special sessions should be limited and should be used only to meet complex individual needs.

CROSS-REFERENCE

Legal requirements for education of students with disabilities are discussed in Chapter 6.

One of the goals of inclusion is to provide students with disabilities the same opportunities for learning academic content to which others are exposed. Most students with disabilities can achieve at the same levels as their peers without disabilities, but they require accommodations that allow them to access the content, the instruction, and the tools for learning. These accommodations may require physical changes in the classroom, such as increasing the height of a desk so that students in wheelchairs have a work space. It may require the provision of computers for students who cannot hold or control a pencil. It may require books in Braille, the use of sign language, and taped books.

Just because students with learning disabilities have difficulty reading

Many students with disabilities are included in classrooms and other school activities alongside students who do not have disabilities. All students benefit from this arrangement, with improved outcomes for students with disabilities and an enhanced appreciation for diversity among all students.

does not mean they can't learn. Educators must assist them in accessing mathematics, science, social studies, and other curricula through methods other than reading. Taped books, computer programs that assist students in reading, and the use of computers for writing are appropriate accommodations to assist students with learning disabilities in understanding academic content. Some students with disabilities have been assigned full-time aides to assist them. Successful

Over time, classroom teachers have been given increased responsibility for making sure the needs of a child with an IEP are met in their classroom. Although a child may enter the classroom with an IEP requiring support from special educators, ultimately and legally it is the teacher's responsibility to make sure the IEP is implemented in the classroom. It is also the teacher's responsibility to handle any behavior or social difficulties that may occur in the classroom. Furthermore, the teacher must work with the special educators to adapt lessons and assignments to the ability level of all of the students. Teachers must promote success for all learners rather than expecting failure.

Picture yourself as a teacher in an inner-city second-grade classroom. You have twenty-five students from low-income homes and several children for whom English is their second language. Among these students are three children with IEPs and four learners who are making limited academic progress but do not qualify for special education services.

The three children with IEPs have varied needs. One child is a girl in a wheelchair with physical needs requiring a nurse to accompany her in the classroom. Another child is an eight-year-old boy who was born with Down syndrome. He too has multiple needs, including speech/language therapy, occupational therapy to work on his fine-motor skills, and a behavior plan monitored by the school psychologist. The third child has attention deficit hyperactivity disorder (ADHD). His academic skills lag behind by a full year below grade level, and his attention span is minimal during periods of instruction.

In addition to these three children with IEPs, four children are reading at first-grade level. Although these children are obviously having difficulties with reading, writing, and spelling, they do not currently qualify for special education services as their performance level is

not two standard deviations below their intelligence quotient–derived ability level.

Unfortunately, there is no reading specialist in your school to help teach the learners performing below grade level. Furthermore, the special education teacher is only required to provide direct services to the students with IEPs for two hours a week. There is a special education assistant assigned to assist with the children with IEPs in your classroom, but her time is split between all twelve first- and second-grade classes, so you are lucky to have her assistance on a daily basis. If the special educator or assistant is out for any reason, a substitute is rarely provided.

- What would you do to include the student in the wheelchair in as many classroom activities as possible and to encourage social interactions with her peers?

- What would you do to make sure the child with Down syndrome is accepted and included by his peers?

- Where would you designate that the child with ADHD take his breaks in the classroom, and what would you provide to make him feel as though he were having a break?

- What would you do to differentiate instruction to meet the needs of the children who aren't reading on grade level but do not receive special education services?

- How will you meet the needs of all the students in your classroom and teach them at each of their ability levels?

Source: This Professional Dilemma was contributed by preschool special education teacher Michele Clarke.

To answer these questions on-line and e-mail your answers to your professor, go to Chapter 2 of the companion website **(www.ablongman.com/johnson13e)** and click on Professional Dilemma.

aides are those who encourage students to work independently so that they become self-sufficient in the process.

Researchers are finding improved student outcomes for students with disabilities who are in inclusive classrooms. Students without disabilities also receive positive benefits. Inclusion helps them become more tolerant of others, appreciate diversity, and be more responsive to the needs of others.[18]

■ DISPROPORTIONATE PLACEMENTS

Twelve percent of all students are provided with special education services. However, students in special education classes are likely to be students of color, English language learners, or whites from low-income families. Five percent of Asian American students are in special education, as compared to 14 percent of African American students. Students labeled *mentally retarded* or *emotionally disabled* disproportionately are from low-income families. Low-income children are also overrepresented in classes for seriously emotionally disturbed students. Middle-class students are more likely to be classified as *learning disabled*. This pattern is also found in the placement of males and students of color in special education and gifted classes. African American and Native American students are overrepresented in disability categories of learning disability, mental retardation, and emotionally disturbed, as are males in general. On the other hand, Latino, African American, and Native American students are underrepresented in gifted and talented programs. Educators need to monitor the reasons for their referrals of students to be tested for placement in these classes and provide equity in the delivery of education services.

Disproportionate placements of students in special education and gifted education programs may be due to a number of factors. Tests used for placement are often biased against low-income students, English language learners, and students who have not assimilated into the dominant culture. Some educators who recommend students for special programs are intolerant of cultural differences and do not want students in their classes who they believe will disrupt the classroom. Schools should monitor recommendations and placements to find out if students from some groups are being disproportionately placed in these programs and to take corrective action if needed.

RELIGION

Religion can have a great influence on the values and lifestyles of families and can play an important role in the socialization of children and young people. Religious doctrines and practices often guide beliefs about the roles of males and females. They also provide guidance regarding birthrates, birth control, child-rearing, friendships, and political attitudes.

By age five, children are able to generally identify their family's religious affiliation. Although 88 percent of the population regard their religious beliefs as very or fairly important, less than half attend a religious service on a weekly basis.[19] However, strong religious perspectives are reflected in the daily lives of many families.

■ RELIGIOUS PLURALISM

Religious pluralism flourishes in this country. Members of religions other than those with Judeo-Christian roots are increasing as more immigrants arrive from Asia and the Middle East. Other families declare themselves atheists or simply do not participate in an organized religion. Some individuals and families live in religious cults that are established to promote and maintain a religious calling.

Some religious groups believe that their religion is the only correct and legitimate view of the world. Other groups recognize that religious diversity has grown out of different historical experiences and accept the validity of diverse groups. At the same time, every major religion endorses justice, love, and compassion as virtues that most individuals and nations say they are trying to achieve.[20]

Although they are not as dominant as earlier in U.S. history, Protestants are still in the majority with 56 percent of the population. Two percent of the population are Jewish, and 27 percent are Catholic. Eight percent do not indicate a preference. Within each of the major religious groups, there are distinct denominations and sects that have the same general history but may differ greatly in their beliefs and perspectives on the correct way to live. Most Western religions are compatible with the values of the dominant culture; they usually promote patriotism and emphasize individual control of life.

With the influx of immigrants from Asia, Africa, and the Middle East over the past few decades, religious diversity among the population has increased further with the introduction of non-Western religions such as Islam, Hinduism, and Buddhism. The interaction of these faiths with Western religions and their impact on mainstream society have yet to be determined. In the meantime, students from diverse religious backgrounds appear in classrooms. Teachers need to respect these differences if they are going to serve the students and community well.

For many people, religion is an essential element, determining their cultural identity. For example, some religious groups, such as the Amish and Hutterites, establish their own communities and schools to maintain the religion, foster mutual support, and develop group cohesiveness. Members of groups such as the Mormons promote primary relationships and interactions with other members of the same faith. Most social activities are linked to religion, and institutions have been developed to reflect and support the religious beliefs. In many rural areas, the church is the center of social and community activities. Many religions expect their members to spend much of their nonworking hours in church and charity activities.

CROSS-REFERENCE

Issues and court cases related to religion in schools are presented in Chapter 6.

Public schools cannot advance a religion, but neither can religion be ignored in the curriculum. Diverse religious beliefs should be acknowledged and respected in classrooms and schools.

■ RELIGION IN SCHOOLS

The First Amendment of the U.S. Constitution, which requires the separation of church and state, is a cornerstone of American democracy. When it comes to schools, however, there is disagreement about the meaning of the amendment. Public schools cannot advance a religion, but they also cannot inhibit religion. Although schools must be neutral to religion, their policies and practices must protect the religious liberty of students. Religion cannot be ignored in the curriculum, but it should be acknowledged and taught about when appropriate.

Families appear satisfied with schools when the schools reflect the values that are important in their religion. But they may attack schools when the curriculum, assigned readings, holidays, school convocations, and graduation exercises are perceived to be in conflict with their religious values. Many court cases over the past century have helped to sort out these issues.

GEOGRAPHY

Communities and their schools differ from one region of the United States to another. Children and families may suffer culture shock in moving from one region to another and from urban to suburban to rural areas. People in different parts of the country sometimes behave differently, dress differently, and like different things even if they are from the same religious and ethnic backgrounds.

Over the past thirty years, many individuals and families have migrated from the Northeast and Midwest to states in the South and West. By 2010, 60 percent of the U.S. population will live in the South and West, compared to 48 percent in 1970. One-fourth of the population will live in California, Florida, and Texas alone. The population in rural areas of the upper Midwest is currently older than in other parts of the country, but by 2010, one-fifth of Florida's population will be over sixty-five years old, and 15 percent of the population in Arizona, Arkansas, Pennsylvania, and West Virginia will be retired.[21]

An examination of differences among rural, suburban, and urban communities captures some of the geographic variation. However, differences among communities are also found between the Northwest, Southwest, Midwest, South, and Northeast. Within these regions, states have their own cultural uniqueness. The geography of a state such as Colorado, for example, promotes the development of different cultural patterns among populations in the flat farmlands, urban centers, and mountains.

RURAL COMMUNITIES

Rural schools are often the center of rural life. Values tend to be conservative, and the immediate family is a cohesive unit. Children may travel long distances to school. By urban and suburban standards, rural families live long distances from one another. To the rural family, however, the distances are not great, and a feeling of neighborliness exists. The social structure is less stratified than in more populous geographical areas, and everyone may appear to know everyone else.

Workers in rural areas generally are poorly paid for their work, earning about three-fourths of the wages paid in urban areas. Although housing costs may be lower, other expenses are not much different. As a result, 17 percent of the rural population live in poverty,[22] although they are invisible to most people. Poverty is disproportionately high on Native American reservations but also exists on the midwestern plains, western ranches, and farms across the country.

Employment in manufacturing is limited in rural areas. However, increasing numbers of urban and suburban dwellers are choosing to live in the country and commute to their employment in the more populous metropolitan areas. These transplants are generally young and well educated. They are fleeing the complexities of city life to acquire self-reliance and self-confidence, to return to a

Children in farming communities experience aspects of life that are foreign to most city and suburban students.

physically healthier environment, or simply to be able to own an affordable home. In some instances, this exodus to the country has caused problems for rural schools because the newcomers' values have clashed with those of the rural community. Family living habits and expectations for school programs differ, and some newcomers demand increased social services. In many rural communities, it takes a considerable length of time for newcomers to be accepted into the social structure.

Despite the pivotal role of schools in rural life, these schools face real difficulties. Too often there are teacher shortages that result in the staffing of schools by teachers without a license or with limited academic background in the subject being taught. Teachers in rural areas sometimes feel isolated, especially if they are not from the area. As ethnic diversity increases in these areas, teachers will be confronted with cultures and languages to which they may have had little or no exposure.

SUBURBAN COMMUNITIES

Nearly half of the U.S. population now lives in the suburbs. The suburban population has become more diverse as middle-class families of color have moved from cities. It is becoming even more ethnically and linguistically diverse as new immigrants settle in the suburbs. The most dramatic change in the suburbs, however, is that poverty now exists there as well as in cities and rural areas. The National Center for Children in Poverty reports that 20 percent of suburban children under six years old live in families with incomes below the poverty level.

Suburbs are characterized by single-family homes, shopping centers, and space for parks and recreation activities. Funding for schools has traditionally been better in the suburbs than in other areas. As a result, most suburban schools are in good condition; some boast sprawling, beautiful, and technologically advanced campuses. Most teachers are licensed and generally teach the subjects they are qualified to teach. Students outperform their rural and urban counterparts on achievement tests, and more suburban students than students from other areas attend college. Safety is usually not a concern for students, parents, or teachers. With changing demographics in the suburbs, however, these conditions are beginning to change—particularly in suburban areas close to major cities. Suburban taxpayers sometimes are unwilling to pay adequately for the education of children in poverty. Retirees sometimes fight school bond issues that are needed to support public education. Already, a growing number of middle- and upper-middle-class parents in the suburbs are choosing private schools.[23]

URBAN COMMUNITIES

Urban areas are usually rich in educational and entertainment resources such as libraries, museums, theaters, professional sports, colleges, and universities. The urban population is ethnically and racially diverse, but many residential areas remain segregated. In many cities, people of color constitute the majority of the urban population. The majority of the foreign-born population live in cities. For example, foreign-born persons make up 41 percent of the population in Los Angeles, 37 percent in both San Francisco and San Jose, 36 percent in New York City, and 26 percent in Houston. Twenty percent of elementary and high school students have at least one foreign-born parent.

Class differences are evident across urban neighborhoods. Low-income families and families in poverty are often isolated in neighborhoods with few resources, inadequate police protection, and poorly maintained parks, schools, and public areas. Children who live in an underserved section of a city are often restricted by it, having few contacts outside the area. Their opportunities to participate in the educational and entertainment resources of the city are limited.

Although there are many single-family homes in a city, many children live in multifamily condominiums, apartments, and projects. Some city residents live comfortably by U.S. standards, but a disproportionate number of urban residents are economically oppressed. One of the reasons for high poverty rates among most groups in cities is the lack of academic credentials that qualify workers for better-paying jobs. Jobs that teenagers hold in other communities are filled in urban areas by adults for whom no other options are available. The result is high unemployment among youth from oppressed groups. Crime rates in many low-income neighborhoods exceed the national average. There are higher infant mortality rates, lower access to adequate health care, and a greater number of AIDS cases[24]—all factors that are common when people have inadequate incomes to support themselves and their families.

Public funding for city schools may be similar to that in other areas, but families in many urban neighborhoods are unable to contribute to schools at the same level as many suburban parents. Parents have less time to volunteer for school and community involvement or fund-raising projects. They often have more than one job. In some cases, they are caught in their own addictions and maladies exacerbated by the stress of poverty, violence, and lack of community support.

Many urban middle-class and upper-middle-class families opt for private schools over public schools. Children and youth in central cities of metropolitan areas are in poverty at higher rates than children in rural and suburban areas. African Americans make up 33 percent of central city school populations, and Latino students constitute 22 percent. A disproportionately high percentage of students are foreign-born or first-generation immigrants with limited English proficiency. Bilingual education and federally funded programs such as Title I for students from low-income families help to meet the needs of urban schools. Low-income students in urban areas are less likely to complete high school on time, although they complete postsecondary degrees at the same rates as their suburban and rural counterparts.[25]

Severe teacher shortages exist in urban schools. As a result, many teachers have not completed a teacher education program and are working on emergency licenses. A large percentage of teachers in city schools have had little or no preparation in the subjects they are assigned to teach; this problem is particularly severe for mathematics and science. Perhaps this is a major reason why urban students perform less well on national achievement tests.

SUMMARY

Culture determines the way individuals behave and think. Although characteristics and contributions of diverse cultural groups are reflected in U.S. society, white, Protestant, heterosexual, middle-class European Americans have had the greatest impact on societal values and behavioral expectations. Three ideologies describe the nature of diversity in the United States: assimilation, pluralism, and cultural choice.

The way students and their families live is greatly affected by their socioeconomic status, which is determined by income, wealth, occupation, and educational attainment. The population is socially stratified, providing some groups more advantage and prestige in society than others.

As a result of immigration from Asia, Mexico, Central America, and the Middle East, the United States is becoming more ethnically diverse. A growing number of English language learners are found in schools across the country. In addition, a number of students use a dialect that is not standard English in their home environments.

Although few biological differences exist between females and males, differences in economic status, jobs, and educational attainment continue to exist. Many educators are not knowledgeable about homosexuality and how to support LGBT students. Today's teachers are also likely to have students with disabilities in their classrooms. Like members of other underserved groups in society, students with disabilities are often labeled and stereotyped in ways not conducive to learning.

Religious diversity in the United States is expanding to include religions other than Christianity and Judaism. Families from other religious backgrounds seldom see their traditions and values reflected in the public schools and often feel discriminated against because of their religion. As the population shifts and ages, families are forced to move to a different part of the country. Because cultural traditions and values differ from one region of the country to another, teachers should be aware of these differences.

DISCUSSION QUESTIONS

1. Students and families bring their cultures into the classroom. To what degree do you think you should incorporate culture into the curriculum? How will you prevent your own cultural background from becoming the norm that dominates in the classroom?

2. Research shows that some students perform better academically and socially when they are segregated in single-sex classrooms. In what cases do you think such segregation is appropriate?

3. Which of the three ideologies related to the management of diversity in our society do you hope pervades the schools in which you will work in the future? Why?

4. How do you plan to manage your classroom to positively build on the racial, ethnic, gender, socioeconomic, and ability differences of students? What pedagogical strategies (e.g., cooperative learning) will you use? Why?

5. Most classrooms today include one or more students with disabilities. Where will you turn for assistance in providing the necessary accommodations to help those students learn at the levels they are capable of learning?

JOURNAL ENTRIES

1. Reflect on how your membership in the microcultural groups described in this chapter has contributed to your own cultural identity. Consider why membership in one or more groups is especially important in the identification of who you are.

2. Record an experience that you have had with members of another culture that has influenced how you think about that cultural group. Write your reflections on how your impressions have changed over time as you have had experiences with other members of that group.

PORTFOLIO DEVELOPMENT

1. Identify one microcultural group with which you have no or limited experience and write a paper on the group's historical and current experience in the United States. What other information will be helpful to you if students from this group are in your classroom when you begin teaching? How will you work effectively with the families from this group?

2. Contrast educational practices that have evolved to support different theories related to diversity and develop an argument for incorporating one or more of these practices into your own teaching.

PREPARING FOR CERTIFICATION

THE PRAXIS PLT TEST AND DIVERSITY

1. The Praxis II Principles of Teaching and Learning (PLT) test, which assesses a prospective teacher's knowledge about a variety of teaching-related skills, is required by many states. The test covers four broad categories: organizing content knowledge for student learning, creating an environment for student learning, teaching for student learning, and teacher professionalism. Learn more about the PLT test by reviewing the ETS *Test at a Glance* materials at www.ets.org/praxis/taags/prx0522.html.

2. Answer the following multiple-choice question, which is similar to items in Praxis and other state certification tests. If you are unsure of the answer, reread the Diversity and Education section in this chapter.

> Seven of Ms. Bishop's third-grade students are recent immigrants, all from different countries and all speaking little English. Ms. Bishop says her goal is for all seven students to learn English and American customs as quickly as possible so they can rapidly become part of U.S. society. Which ideology about diversity most closely corresponds to Ms. Bishop's beliefs?
>
> (A) cultural pluralism
> (B) assimilation
> (C) social stratification
> (D) cultural choice

3. Answer the following short-answer question, which is similar to items in Praxis and other state certification tests. After you've completed your written response, use the scoring guide in the *Test at a Glance* materials to assess your response. Can you revise your response to improve your score?

> Reread the chapter-opening Education in the News feature. The immigrant students mentioned who attend the Harrisonburg schools are members of several microcultural groups. Identify at least three microcultural groups for the Yavny and Castro families. How might membership in these groups affect the students' school experiences?

WEBSITES

www.adl.org The Anti-Defamation League fights anti-Semitism, bigotry, and extremism. Its website includes information on religious freedom, civil rights, and the Holocaust as well as resources for teachers on fighting hate.

www.cec.sped.org The Council for Exceptional Children is dedicated to improving educational outcomes for individuals with exceptionalities, students with disabilities, and/or the gifted. The website identifies resources for educators.

www.edc.org/womensequity The website of the Women's Educational Equity Association provides information about Title IX and women's equity issues, including links to additional resources.

www.glsen.org The website of the Gay, Lesbian and Straight Education Network provides resources and updates for ending bias against LGBT persons in schools and society.

www.lulac.org The League of United Latin American Citizens advances the economic condition, educational attainment, political influence, health, and civil rights of the Hispanic population of the United States. The website provides information on current issues.

www.ncai.org The National Congress of American Indians works to inform the public and Congress on the governmental rights of Native Americans and Alaska Natives. The website includes a directory of tribes in the United States.

FURTHER READING

Beykont, Zeynep F. (Ed.). (2000). *Lifting Every Voice: Pedagogy and Politics of Bilingualism.* Cambridge, MA: Harvard Education Publishing Group. An exploration of theories on bilingualism and pedagogical strategies for serving bilingual students by diverse and passionate voices from a variety of languages.

Gollnick, Donna M., and Chinn, Philip C. (2001). *Multicultural Education in a Pluralistic Society* (6th ed.). Columbus, OH: Merrill. A fundamental text with expanded descriptions and information about the seven microcultural groups outlined in this chapter. This book also discusses the pedagogical implications and applications for each group.

Hehir, Thomas. (Spring 2002). "Eliminating Ableism in Education." *Harvard Educational Review, 72*(1), pp. 1–32. An excellent discussion of ableism in schools that prevents students with disabilities from fully participating in the education system, having access to high levels of academic contact, and fully participating in society. Instead of accepting different ways of seeing, moving, and thinking, schools are guilty of ableism, which results in disvaluing persons with disabilities and treating them as inferior to others.

Ladson-Billings, Gloria. (1994). *The Dreamkeepers: Successful Teachers of African American Children.* San Francisco: Jossey-Bass. Descriptions and analysis of the culturally relevant strategies used by eight African

American and white teachers who have successfully taught African American children.

Orfield, Gary, and Lebowitz, Holly J. (Eds.). (1999). *Religion, Race and Justice in a Changing America.* New York: Century Foundation. A focus on the role of diverse religions and faiths in the civil rights movements of the past and today and a call for religious groups to inject their values of love, justice, and compassion in the fight against bigotry, discrimination, and racism in today's society.

NOTES

Unless otherwise indicated, the data reported in this chapter are from the U.S. Census Bureau, *Statistical Abstract of the United States: 2002,* 122nd edition. Washington, DC: U.S. Government Printing Office, 2002.

1. Milton M. Gordon, *Assimilation in American Life: The Role of Race, Religion, and National Origins.* New York: Oxford University Press, 1964.
2. Stephen J. Rose, *Social Stratification in the United States: The New American Profile Poster.* New York: New Press, 2000.
3. Sarah Anderson, John Cavanagh, Chuck Collins, Chris Hartman, and Felice Yeskel, *Executive Excess 2000: Seventh Annual CEO Compensation Survey.* Washington, DC: Institute for Policy Studies and United for a Fair Economy, August 2000.
4. " 'Children' Progress Elsewhere," *U.S. News & World Report* (August 28, 1995), p. 24.
5. U.S. Bureau of the Census, *Ancestry: 2000.* Census 2000 Summary File 3 (SF3)—Sample Data. Washington, DC: Author, 2000.
6. M. Kelley, Indian affairs head makes apology (September 8, 2000). The Free Press.
7. W. P. Thomas and Virginia P. Collier, *School Effectiveness for Language Minority Students.* Washington, DC: National Clearinghouse for Bilingual Education, 1997.
8. Myra Sadker, David Sadker, and Susan Klein, "The Issue of Gender in Elementary and Secondary Education," in Gerald Grant, ed., *Review of Research in Education,* vol. 17. Washington, DC: American Educational Research Association, 1991.
9. United Nations Educational, Scientific and Cultural Organization, *Education for All: Is the World on Track?* Paris, France: Author, 2002, p. 68.
10. United Nations Development Fund for Women, *Progress of the World's Women 2002: Volume 2: Gender Equality and the Millennium Development Goals.* New York: Author, 2002.
11. American Association of University Women, "Title IX" (www.aauw.org/takeaction/policyissues/titleix.cfm). Washington, DC: Author.
12. U.S. General Accounting Office, No. 01-297, *Intercollegiate Athletics: Four-Year Colleges' Experiences Adding and Discontinuing Teams.* Washington, DC: Author, March 2001, p. 7.
13. National Federation of State High School Associations, *2002 High School Athletics Participation Survey.* Indianapolis, IN: Author, 2002.
14. Francis Mark Mondimore, *A Natural History of Homosexuality.* Baltimore: Johns Hopkins University Press, 1996.
15. Gay, Lesbian and Straight Education Network, "The 2001 National School Climate Survey: Lesbian, Gay, Bisexual and Transgender Students and their Experiences in Schools." New York: Author, 2001.
16. Ibid.
17. U.S. Census Bureau, "Facts & Features: 12th Anniversary of Americans with Disabilities Act (July 26)," Press Release. Washington, DC: Author, July 12, 2002.
18. Dorothy Kerzner Lipsky and Alan Gartner, "Inclusion, School Restructuring, and the Remaking of American Society," *Harvard Educational Review* 66(4) (Winter 1996), pp. 762–796.

19. Gallup Organization, "Gallup Poll: How Important Would You Say Religion Is in Your Own Life?" Princeton, NJ: Author, August 2000.

20. Gary Orfield and Holly J. Lebowitz, eds., *Religion, Race and Justice in a Changing America*. New York: Century Foundation, 1999.

21. Joint Center for Housing Studies at Harvard University, *The State of the Nation's Housing: 1996*. Cambridge, MA: Author, 1996.

22. Sue Books, "The Other Poor: Rural Poverty and Education," *Educational Foundations 11*(1) (Winter 1997), pp. 73–85.

23. Jonathan Kaufman, "Suburban Parents Shun Many Public Schools, Even the Good Ones," *Wall Street Journal* (March 1, 1996).

24. The Urban Institute, *Improving Student Performance in the Inner City* (Policy and Research Report). Washington, DC: Author, 1996.

25. U.S. Department of Education, National Center for Education Statistics, *Urban Schools*. Washington, DC: U.S. Government Printing Office, 1996.

Social Challenges in Schools

Education in the News

Bye-Bye "Birdie": School Plays Get Serious

By Kimberly Edds, *The Washington Post,* May 12, 2003

CHULA VISTA, CALIF.—IT'S THE NIGHT OF THE SCHOOL SHOW, and 16-year-old Joshua Fountaine has his first starring role. There are the usual butterflies in the students' stomachs as they battle stage fright and get ready for the house lights to go down. Coincidentally, Fountaine is playing a high school student named Josh.

Not long after the curtain opens, Josh—the character is supposed to be an average but troubled teenager—pulls out a rifle and guns down four classmates. The student-actors slump to the floor. "More fun than droppin' dudes in a video game," Josh declares.

Parents sit silently in the audience, numb at the staged violence. A younger sibling of one of the student-actors sobs, believing his brother has been hurt. Then, slowly, the proud but slightly bewildered parents begin to applaud.

The show, *Bang Bang You're Dead,* has been staged in schools more than 15,000 times since it was written four years ago in response to a series of school shootings across the nation. Another play, *The Laramie Project,* has been performed by dozens of high schools this season. That one is based on interviews with residents of Laramie, Wyo., after the 1998 murder of Matthew Shepard, who was tied to a fence, pistol-whipped and left to die because he was gay.

The shows represent a new trend in high school drama. More and more schools are turning away from the innocence of *Bye Bye Birdie* or the antics of *The Music Man* for socially relevant—and frequently controversial—plays about school violence, homosexuality and racism.

From Anacortes, Wash., to Friendswood, Tex., from Lexington, Ky., to Salisbury, Md., high schools and some middle schools are producing the shows and following up with discussion groups for students and parents.

"This is *Our Town* for our time," Barbara Williams, a drama teacher at Newark Memorial High School, just south of San Francisco, said of *The Laramie Project.* High school directors have discovered the play is a way of combating intolerance in their schools.

"They're definitely not *Bye Bye Birdie* or *The Music Man,*" said Jeffrey Leptak-Moreau of the Ohio-based Educational Theatre Association. "It's not just frivolous fun. It's something with a message."

A Midsummer Night's Dream and *You Can't Take It with You* topped the theater association's list of the most-produced high school plays in 2001, but works like *Bang Bang You're Dead* and *The Laramie Project* are quickly gaining ground.

Students at Sheldon High School in Sacramento performed *God's Country,* which follows the rise and fall of the Order, a white supremacist group whose members assassinated Jewish radio host Alan Berg in 1984. The play calls for actors, some with freshly shaved heads and others in Ku Klux Klan and Nazi regalia, to let racial slurs roll easily off their tongues.

Since releasing *Bang Bang You're Dead* in 1999, playwright William Mastrosimone has received thousands of e-mails from kids. Many of the messages are disturbing, with a few of the young people saying they plan to kill themselves or others and have no one to talk to.

"I think kids need this [play] because they suffer and they need relief," said Mastrosimone, who won the New York Outer Critics Circle Award for his play *Extremities.* "Theater is a really good way to do it."

School-Based Observations

After reading and studying this chapter, you should be able to:

1. Understand that most white students and adults have advantages and benefits in society and schools because they are members of the dominant group.

2. Respect the differing family backgrounds from which students come and understand the importance of not stereotyping student behavior or academic potential on the basis of their family structure. (INTASC 3: Diversity)

3. Understand that young people need caring adults to help them maneuver through the tribulations and challenges of childhood and the teenage years. (INTASC 5: Motivation & Management)

4. Describe the role that schools play in the socialization of today's children and youth.

5. Understand that educational equality requires that all students learn and are represented proportionately in advanced placement and special education classes. (INTASC 10: Collaboration)

You may see these learning outcomes in action during your visits to schools:

1. In one of your next observations of a class in a school, identify and record the written and unwritten rules that guide the interactions of students with one another and with the teacher. What values do they reinforce? Who has the power in these interactions?

2. In your visits to a school, determine the types of programs available to students to assist them in handling issues of sexuality, drugs, or violence in their own lives. What approach is the school using to address these issues? What is the parental involvement in the development of these programs?

3. During one of your visits to a school, observe how students interact with other students and teachers from cultural backgrounds different from their own. Extend your observations beyond the classroom to the halls, the principal's office, and extracurricular activities. What is the nature of the interactions across ethnic, racial, gender, and socioeconomic groups? How does the school encourage positive, productive interactions? Students, teachers, and parents could be helpful informants in your data gathering; ask them for their perceptions.

A democratic society struggles with how to support individuality and yet develop a consciousness of shared concerns and actions that promote equality. This challenge is paramount in a society such as that of the United States, which includes many groups that affect and are affected by political, social, and economic systems. The big ideas that help us understand the challenges of education for a society include democracy, power, the changing nature of families, youth culture, and the roles of schools in educating young people.

In a democracy, citizens are called on to promote a common good. To ensure the participation of all citizens, power must be shared somewhat equally across groups in society. Although the United States describes itself as the premier model of a democratic society, it is governed primarily by members of the dominant culture. Most citizens are not privy to the same or similar benefits that allow others to meet basic needs, let alone get involved in governing their communities. In many instances, they have given up on equal participation in society, not even voting in elections. Nevertheless, most citizens continue to espouse the nation as a democracy with the goal of equality and prosperity for all, expecting schools to prepare students to engage in and promote the ideals of a democracy.

Power provides economic, educational, and political advantages for individuals and groups. Membership in some groups provides access to college, good jobs, and higher standards of living. Society raises barriers against members of other groups, making it difficult for them to finish high school and find a job that will adequately support a family. For example, children in low-income families suffer disproportionately from limited access to the best teachers, the best instruction in schools, good nutrition, safe environments, and community support and caring for their well-being.

Families and their children face many challenges in today's society. Many children live in single-parent households with limited income. Children are sometimes left on their own, especially in the period after school. Teenagers struggle with figuring out who they are. They are usually assisted in this process by parents and other responsible and caring adults, but a number of them learn about sexuality, drugs, and violence from the media and their peers. Teachers and other educators play an important role in helping children and youth maneuver through these challenges toward the goal of becoming responsible adults.

POWER IN SOCIETY

A democratic society is built on the principles of social equality and respect for individuals within society. However, many persons of color, limited English speakers, women, persons with disabilities, gays and lesbians, people with low incomes, and people affiliated with religions other than Protestantism do not experience the equality to which most members of the dominant group appear to be entitled. Why has the United States not yet been able to achieve the egalitarian ideal that should characterize democracy? A primary factor is the inequitable power relationships across groups.

Schools provide an example of institutions in which power relationships have been developed and maintained. Students' work and class rules are determined by teachers. Teachers are evaluated, and disciplined when necessary, by principals who report to a superintendent of schools. The rules and procedures for managing schools traditionally have been established by authorities who are not directly involved with the school and who may not even live in the community served by the school. Parents, especially in economically disadvantaged areas, often feel powerless in the education of their children.

Many people with power in U.S. society believe that they have achieved their status because of their individual abilities and accomplishments. They usually give no credit to their membership in the dominant group. Most whites do not think they have an advantage over members of other racial and ethnic groups. On the other hand, many people of color perceive whites as having excessive influence. There appears to be a large gap in the perceptions of power between the different groups in society.

Power not only allows domination over the powerless, but it also allows access to societal benefits such as good housing, tax deductions, the best schools, and social services. The powerful are not willing to give up this asset or readily share it with those whom they see as less deserving. A more equitable sharing of resources for schools

Teacher–student relationships, as with many others in U.S. society, are defined by one person or group having power over others.

would guarantee that all students, regardless of family income or ethnic background, would have qualified teachers, sufficient books and other instructional resources, well-maintained buildings and playgrounds, and access to high-level academic knowledge. Such equality does not exist across schools that students attend today. The great disparities between schools for advantaged and underserved students have been described graphically in Jonathan Kozol's book *Savage Inequalities: Children in America's Schools:*

> New Trier's physical setting might well make the students of Du Sable High School envious. *The Washington Post* describes a neighborhood of "circular driveways, chirping birds and white-columned homes." It is, says a student, "a maple land of beauty and civility." While Du Sable is sited on one crowded city block, New Trier students have the use of 27 acres. While Du Sable's science students have to settle for makeshift equipment, New Trier's students have superior labs and up-to-date technology. One wing of the school, a physical education center that includes three separate gyms, also contains a fencing room, a wrestling room and studios for dance instruction. In all, the school has seven gyms as well as an Olympic pool.
>
> The youngsters, according to a profile of the school in *Town and Country* magazine, "make good use of the huge, well-equipped building, which is immaculately maintained by a custodial staff of 48."
>
> It is impossible to read this without thinking of a school like Goudy, where there are no science labs, no music or art classes and no playground—and where the two bathrooms, lacking toilet paper, fill the building with their stench.[1]

■ ETHNOCENTRISM

Most of the time, we are not aware of the power or lack of power as a result of our cultural upbringing. This phenomenon often leads to **ethnocentrism,** in which members of a group view their culture as superior to all others—and perceive persons from other cultural groups as strange and unusual. Ethnocentrism is sometimes promoted in emotional calls for patriotism, especially at times when a country is involved in a political conflict with another country. The other country is often denigrated through name-calling based on negative stereotypes of its citizens.

Ethnocentrism is not limited to relations with other nations; it occurs often between groups within the United States. For example, homosexuals are victims of abuse by some radio talk show hosts and some religious groups. Members of some religious groups believe that their cultural values and lifestyles are the only correct ones; they do not tolerate alternative beliefs. Many members of the dominant culture believe that their culture is superior to those with non-European roots.

One of the manifestations of ethnocentrism is the inability to accept differences among groups as natural and appropriate. The values and behaviors of the dominant group become the norm against which others are measured. The dominant group often treats the differences as deficits that must be overcome through education and special programs.

For teachers to help all students learn, they must confront their own ethnocentrism. Many teachers do not recognize that they subtly, and sometimes overtly, transmit feelings of superiority over students and their cultural groups—through both curriculum content and classroom interactions. To be effective, teachers need to include in the curriculum the cultures and experiences of the community.

■ PREJUDICE AND DISCRIMINATION

Power relationships between groups influence young people's perceptions of themselves and the members of other groups. One of the struggles of youth is the construction of self, including identification and affiliation with one's gender and a racial or ethnic group. This process appears to be integrally tied to identifying "otherness," which involves assigning characteristics and behavior

ethnocentrism

The belief that members of one's own group are superior to the members of other groups.

to members of other groups to distinguish them from oneself. The construction of "others" places them either in a dominating or submissive role relative to the individual. This construction is often dependent on stereotypes that are promoted among peers and reinforced by society.

Our perceptions of others not only affect how we see ourselves in relationship to them but also have an influence on how society treats members of many groups. **Prejudice** is a preconceived negative attitude toward members of an ethnic, racial, religious, or socioeconomic group that is different from one's own. This prejudice sometimes extends to people with disabilities or of a different sexual orientation. Such negative attitudes are based on numerous factors, including information about members of a specific group that is stereotypical and many times not true. The prejudiced individual often has had little or no direct social contact with members of the other group.

An individual's prejudice may have a limited negative impact on members of the other group. However, these attitudes are passed on to children through the **socialization** process. Also, prejudiced attitudes can be transformed into discriminatory behavior that prevents members of a group from being interviewed for a job, joining a social club, or being treated like other professionals. Prejudices are often reinforced by schools in which a disproportionate number of students in low-achieving tracks are from low-income families and in which students in special education are disproportionately males, English language learners, and students of color. Because of this situation, some students form stereotypes of their low-income and foreign-born peers as academically inferior. Through this process, too, many students from low-income families and ethnic minority groups are prevented from gaining the skills and knowledge necessary to enter college or an apprentice trade.

Members of groups other than the dominant culture often have experienced discrimination through practices that exclude them from equal access to housing, jobs, and educational opportunities and through unfair treatment by store clerks or police officers. Having experienced discrimination, members of excluded groups can describe differential power relations among groups. Members of groups who do not experience discrimination have a more difficult time acknowledging the existence of the differences in power and advantage. As a result, rights based on group membership versus those of individuals are debated on college campuses, in board meetings of corporations, by politicians, and in many formal and informal neighborhood meetings. These discussions focus on programs that are perceived to favor one group over another, such as affirmative action, bilingual education, or equal funding for male and female athletes. An honest examination of power relationships and experiences with differences should highlight the struggles inherent in a democratic society.

INSTITUTIONAL DISCRIMINATION

In addition to supporting individual prejudice and discrimination, society has historically discriminated against members of powerless groups. Laws and systems that promote and support the dominant culture have been designed to help maintain its superiority and the power of its members. "English only" laws that prevent official documents and communications from being printed or spoken in any language other than English represent but one example of these efforts. Such practices have often become institutionalized in state and federal laws, the judicial system, schools, and other societal institutions. They have become so ingrained in the system that it is difficult to recognize them unless one is directly affected by the discriminatory policies.

RACISM

An assumption of superiority is at the center of **racism.** It is not a topic easily discussed in most classrooms. It is intertwined with the lived experiences of many people and evokes emotions of anger, guilt, shame, and despair. Most

Every American ought to have the right to be treated as he would wish to be treated, as one would wish his children to be treated.
John F. Kennedy

prejudice
Preconceived negative attitude toward the members of a group.

socialization
The process of learning the social norms of one's culture.

racism
The conscious or unconscious belief that racial differences make one group superior to others.

Racism is so universal in this country, so widespread and deep-seated, that it is invisible because it is so normal.

Shirley Chisolm

sexism

The conscious or unconscious belief that men are superior to women and subsequent behavior and action that maintain the superior, powerful position of males.

people have learned that the United States is a just and democratic society. Therefore, it is difficult to confront the societal contradictions that support racism. Educators must acknowledge the advantages, as well as the damage, caused by racism in order to overcome its negative impact on society.

Students and adults go through stages of racial identity as they address issues of discrimination and their own racial identification. Teachers should recognize that students will be moving back and forth across the stages outlined in Table 3.1 in their struggle to know themselves. One of the first steps in this process is to begin to confront one's own racial identity. How close is one to an internalization or autonomy stage? If educators have not struggled with issues of racism, how it affects their lives, and how they may contribute to its perpetuation, it will be impossible for them to develop antiracist classrooms.

SEXISM AND OTHER ISMS

Women of all racial and ethnic groups, people with disabilities, gays, lesbians, persons with low incomes, the elderly, and the young also suffer from discrimination and their lack of power in society. Many individuals are members of more than one of these powerless groups. For example, a low-income Latina may be triply harmed as a result of racism, classism, and **sexism**—the cultural

TABLE 3.1   Development of Racial Identity

Black Racial Identity	White Racial Identity
Preencounter: African American individuals have assimilated into the mainstream culture, accepting many of the beliefs and values of the dominant society, including negative stereotypes about blacks.	*Contact:* White individuals are not aware of themselves as racial beings and are oblivious to acts of individual racism. They have a color-blind view of race and racism.
Encounter: African Americans usually enter this stage when they are confronted directly by a racist act such as rejection by white peers or racial slurs or attacks. They are then forced to confront their own racial identity.	*Disintegration:* Whites usually enter this stage as a result of some experiences with race that lead to the recognition that race does matter, that racism exists, and that they are white. They may show empathy when blacks experience racial discrimination but often fail to understand their anger.
Immersion–Emersion: One's identification as an African American becomes paramount. At first this identification is manifested in anger against whites, but it evolves into a growing knowledge base about African American history and culture. The result of this exploration is an emerging security in a newly defined and affirmed sense of self.	*Reintegration:* Individuals believe consciously or unconsciously that whites are superior to people of color.
	Pseudoindependence: One begins the intellectual process of learning about and fighting against racism. One begins to understand that whites have responsibility for maintaining or eliminating racism.
Internalization: Individuals begin to build coalitions with members of other nonwhite or nondominant groups and to develop relationships with whites who respect and acknowledge them.	*Immersion–Emersion:* Individuals begin to grasp the need to challenge racism. They often experience feelings of guilt and shame for the racist ideas that they believed in the past.
Internalization–Commitment: Individuals are able both to maintain and to move beyond their personal racial identity—to be concerned with African Americans as a group.	*Autonomy:* White individuals have abandoned cultural, institutional, and personal racism. They have a more flexible view of the world, their own whiteness, and other racial groups. They value and seek out cross-racial/cultural experiences.

Sources: "Black Racial Identity" column is based on the five stages of black racial identity developed by W. E. Cross Jr. and described in Beverly Daniel Tatum, "Talking about Race, Learning about Racism: The Application of Racial Identity Development Theory in the Classroom," *Harvard Educational Review,* 62(1) (1992), pp. 1–24. "White Racial Identity" column is based on the six stages of white racial identity developed by J. F. Helms and described in Robert T. Carter, "Is White a Race? Expressions of White Racial Identity," in Michelle Fine, Lois Weis, Linda C. Powell, and L. Mun Wong, eds., *Off White: Readings on Race, Power, and Society.* New York: Routledge, 1997.

Race in a White School

STUDY PURPOSE/QUESTIONS: This study explored the role of race in a suburban school in which the student population was almost all white.

STUDY DESIGN: The researcher collected ethnographic data through observations in a fourth- and fifth-grade classroom during one academic year. Students, teachers, parents, administrators, and school staff were interviewed. The researcher also attended multiple staff meetings, Parent-Teacher Association (PTA) meetings, and other school events.

STUDY FINDINGS: Members of the school community saw themselves as color blind. They indicated that race did not matter in their community, primarily because little diversity existed there. At the same time, parents had selected this community because it was safe (as compared to the nearby city). Although they indicated that all people were the same, they talked about people of color as different than they in undesirable ways.

Teachers said that race was not a factor in the way they treated students; they treated all students the same. Teachers saw themselves as raceless and did not think that race had had any impact on their lives.

Although at least one of the teachers tried to address some multicultural issues in the curriculum, most saw no need to do so because the school population included so few students of color. The school did observe Black History Month by asking students to be involved in related projects, but attention to African Americans and other groups of color did not extend beyond that month.

The few students of color in the school did complain about name-calling by other students. Teachers did reprimand the name-callers, telling them that it was inappropriate to use such derogatory language. These incidents did not suggest to the involved educators that racism may have been the cause. In one case when a biracial student complained about her treatment in class, she was accused by the teacher and principal of playing the race card, and the incident did not lead to any interrogation by the educators of their own practices.

IMPLICATIONS: Just because a school has few or no students of color does not mean that a multicultural curriculum is not necessary. Students and teachers in settings with little racial diversity need to learn about the multicultural nation and world in which they live. They should learn to confront their stereotypical views and the racial realities that exist in society.

Source: Amanda E. Lewis, "There Is No 'Race' in the Schoolyard: Color-Blind Ideology in an (Almost) All-White School," *American Educational Research Journal, 38*(4) (2001), pp. 781–811.

---

attitudes and practices that devalue women. This woman's chances of reaching a comfortable standard of living may be severely limited by her circumstances and group membership.

Some persons with disabilities and their advocates argue that **ableism** greatly disadvantages them and their ability to live a full and productive life. Ableism not only leads to viewing persons with disabilities as inferior to others but also results in treatments and accommodations designed to help them become more like persons without disabilities. These efforts are not necessarily in the best interests of individuals with disabilities. For example, activists who are hearing disabled reject the view that they should become hearing through surgery and other aids if at all possible. Being deaf is their normality, even though it does not seem normal to those who hear. In other instances, teachers and aides without disabilities sometimes provide assistance or do things for persons with disabilities rather than encouraging them to do things for themselves. For educators, the strategy of overhelpfulness may be easier and less time-consuming; allowing individuals with disabilities to make the effort themselves may require a great deal of patience, but the long-term payoff for the student could be self-sufficiency.

ableism

The conscious or unconscious belief that persons with disabilities are inferior to persons without disabilities.

Families in the United States have changed dramatically in recent decades. In the 1950s, the norm was a working father and a mother at home with two or more school-aged children. Today only 68 percent of children aged eighteen or younger live in families with both biological parents. Families today include mothers working while fathers stay at home with the children, single-parent families, families with two working parents, remarried parents, childless marriages, families with adopted children, gay and lesbian parents, extended families, grandparents raising grandchildren, and unmarried couples with children.

The average age of parents is older than in the past; couples now marry later on average than they did in the 1950s. More than 80 percent of today's young people age eighteen to twenty-four years old have never been married. Most men and women have worked for a number of years before marrying; less than 5 percent never marry. Over one-third of first-time married couples have separated or divorced after ten years. Over half of divorced women remarry within five years and 75 percent of them by ten years.[2] Families are small with an average size of 3.17 members. Families of color have higher birthrates than white families. The average age of people of color is younger than that of whites; thus, a larger percentage of women of color are of childbearing age.

Most children live with two parents, even though one of them may be a stepmother or stepfather. Almost one-fourth of the children in the United States live with a single mother, a single father, grandparents, or another guardian. Ideally, it would be an advantage for children to have two caring and loving parents, but it is not essential. After reviewing research on the diversity of families, Frank Furstenberg concluded:

Family structure explains a relatively small amount of the variation in key outcomes of success such as educational attainment, mental health, or problem behavior, especially when single-parenthood does not expose children to poverty, conflict, and instability. Yet, we cannot gainsay the fact that in American society, where economic and social support for families of all types is meager, children are more likely to be disadvantaged when they grow up in a single-parent household. The reverse is just as true: children are more likely to grow up in a single-parent household when they are disadvantaged. Mounting evidence suggests that disadvantage breeds family instability by undermining confidence in marriage, necessitating improvised and impermanent arrangements, and restricting access to good neighborhoods, schools, and social services.[3]

Educators should avoid labeling a child as dysfunctional because he or she does not live with both parents. Too often, teachers develop a self-fulfilling prophecy about students in nontraditional families rather than maintaining—and demonstrating—high expectations for their success in school.

PARENTING

With the growing female influence in the family, the typical family structure is no longer as patriarchal as it once was. Many families are less autocratically controlled by adults and have become more egalitarian in the way they operate. In the past, nurturing children

Thirty percent of children under eighteen years of age live in nontraditional families who provide the love and support necessary to raise children.

was the primary responsibility of mothers. Today more fathers are actively involved in parenting as well.

Most parents want what's best for their children, but there is no simple guidebook for steering children through the complex terrain they will have to navigate to grow up. Often parents draw from their own experiences as children and adults, but they did not encounter the same pressures from peers and the mass culture faced by today's students. To increase students' chances of making it safely through childhood and adolescence, teachers and parents need to work together, setting high standards and helping young people meet them.

■ LATCHKEY KIDS

Most single parents work outside the home; and in many two-parent families, both parents work. Unless working parents have been lucky enough to arrange a flexible schedule that allows them to be home when their children are not in school, they are not available to care for their children during the period immediately after school. The result is children of all ages being left to care for themselves after school. Young children in these families have been referred to as latchkey kids because they carry their own house key.

Older students are more likely to care for themselves after school, as shown in Figure 3.1. Parents provide supervision after school for over half of the students in grades K–5. Other children stay with adults other than their parents,

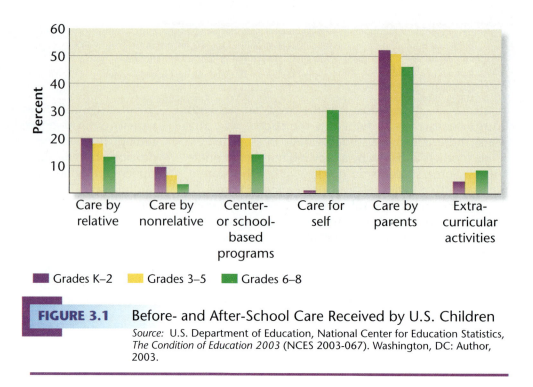

FIGURE 3.1   Before- and After-School Care Received by U.S. Children

Source: U.S. Department of Education, National Center for Education Statistics, *The Condition of Education 2003* (NCES 2003-067). Washington, DC: Author, 2003.

attend center-based programs, or participate in extracurricular activities such as sports, arts, or clubs. Children in poverty are slightly more likely to stay with relatives than other children; they are also less likely to care for themselves after school than children in families with higher incomes.

One-fifth of the children in kindergarten through fifth grade attend afterschool programs in centers or schools[4] with adult supervision and guidance on first aid, nutrition, health, homework, and being on their own at home. These programs are sometimes available at the child's school, or they may be organized by local houses of worship in cooperation with community groups. Young children may learn how to get home from school safely, how to use the telephone and be familiar with emergency telephone numbers, what to do in case of fire, how to deal with strangers, and how to use their time wisely. Often parents must pay a fee for their children to participate in these programs. Unfortunately, some families cannot afford the cost of such care.

Educators should be sensitive to the realities faced by children left alone after school. Children sometimes are frightened to be at home alone, especially when they have no siblings. The process of traveling from school to home can be dangerous and scary in neighborhoods where drugs are being sold and peers are tempting one another to misbehave. Adolescents may be tempted to experiment with drugs and sex while adults are not around. Television often becomes the babysitter, providing children with the opportunity to learn from educational programs—or from inappropriate programs. In most cases, children are thankful for caring adults who can provide supervision and assistance.

■ HOMELESSNESS

The National Law Center on Homelessness and Poverty estimates that up to three million people in the United States are without shelter at some point during a year. The homeless include men and women, families, children, and persons with disabilities, as shown in Figure 3.2. Parents who live in shelters are typically single mothers with one or two children under the age of six.[5] Like the

Increasing numbers of Americans are an illness, an accident, a natural disaster, or a paycheck away from becoming homeless.

Anonymous

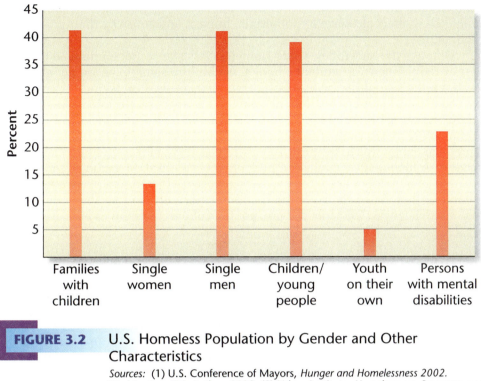

FIGURE 3.2   U.S. Homeless Population by Gender and Other Characteristics

Sources: (1) U.S. Conference of Mayors, *Hunger and Homelessness 2002*. Washington, DC: Author, 2002; (2) Urban Institute, *Homelessness: Programs and the People They Serve* (Summary Report of the Findings of the National Survey of Homeless Assistance Providers and Clients). Washington, DC: Author, 1999.

adult homeless, homeless young people live in shelters, in abandoned buildings, and on the street. Homelessness for most people is temporary, not a permanent condition.

One of the reasons for an increase in homelessness since the late 1970s is a shortage of affordable rental housing. Another is the large number of persons and families in poverty, which is further exacerbated by the reduction of governmental support for welfare over the past thirty years. One in five homeless persons are working, but employment is part time or sporadic or they are earning wages too low to afford necessary food, clothing, and housing. A full-time minimum wage job often does not provide enough income for a family to rent a one-bedroom unit at fair market prices in many areas.

Homelessness is devastating to families. Only 28 percent of the minor children of homeless parents live with the homeless parent;[6] these children may be placed in foster care or left with relatives or friends. Children who live in shelters and on the streets often suffer from inadequate health care. They may be surrounded by diseases such as whooping cough and tuberculosis. They are not always inoculated against common childhood diseases, making them more susceptible to illness than most other children. They suffer

Poverty and the lack of affordable housing are the major reasons for the growing number of homeless adults, children, and families in both rural and urban areas.

from asthma and ear infections at disproportionately high rates. Children in homeless shelters also face hypothermia, hunger, and abuse by their parents or other adults.

Although the McKinney-Vento Homeless Assistance Act eliminated the residency requirement for students, homeless children sometimes are not allowed to attend the school that would best serve their needs. Provision of transportation back to the student's school of origin is not always determined feasible by school systems. Homeless students are sometimes forced to wait to enroll in a school while personal records are collected. However, access to schools is less of a problem than it was in the past. Today's advocates focus on students' classroom success. A high-quality education offers homeless children a chance for academic and economic success. To ignore them because they do not have a home or are not well-groomed deprives them of the opportunity to rise above their current circumstances. They need more, not less, of our attention as educators.

■ ABUSE

The test of the morality of a society is what it does for its children.

Dietrich Bonhoeffer, German Protestant theologian

Domestic violence is often hidden or ignored by society. Just under one-third of the females murdered in this country are killed by a spouse, ex-spouse, or boyfriend, as contrasted to less than 6 percent of male murder victims being killed by someone they know intimately. This number has dropped by 68 percent since 1976, although the number of murdered women has remained about the same.[7] Physical violence against women and girls is near epidemic level in some countries. A report on domestic violence by UNICEF indicates that up to half of the females in some countries have been abused by a family member or boyfriend. Over 60 million females in these countries have been killed by their own families either deliberately or through neglect.[8] Domestic violence has become the primary cause of homelessness for women with children. More than one in five homeless families in the United States are fleeing domestic violence.[9]

Most children have probably been faced with angry parents who raise their voices or even spank them. But every year one of every hundred of the nation's children is the victim of serious abuse or neglect by parents, caretakers, or relatives. Nearly three million children were the subject of an investigation for abuse in 2000. Parents or caretakers are the murderers of over half of the children under age five who are killed every year.[10] Neglect is the cause of 60 percent of the reported abuse cases, one in five is the result of physical abuse, and sexual abuse is reported in 10 percent of the cases. Males are more likely to be the perpetrators of physical and sexual abuse. Sexual abuse is an especially insidious form of child abuse. Thirteen percent of girls and 3 percent of boys are sexually abused before they are eighteen years old. The sensational news stories report sexual abuse of children by strangers, but these represent less than one-fourth of the cases. Most often the abuser is a parent or friend.[11]

Children and youths who are abused or neglected may arrive at school hungry, bruised, and depressed. They may arrive early at school and seem to have little desire to leave the safety of the school. These children, like all others, need teachers who are caring, retain high expectations for them, and can provide hope for the future. School and other social service professionals may be the only adults available to support abused youngsters.

When old enough, many abused youths run away from home, choosing to confront possible abuse on the streets rather than the known abuse at home. Abused children also make up a large proportion of the adults seeking psychological and mental health treatment. For many of these children, the negative experiences and conditions of their childhood become the foundation for mental health problems and delinquent behaviors. These young people have learned abuse from the adults who were closest to them.

TODAY'S YOUTH

Young people face numerous challenges as they mature to adulthood. Changing family structures, alteration of what was once a societal set of expected values, and increased pressures to grow up quickly all have contributed to the difficulty of this period. Many students are able to draw on the support of friends, family, religion, and inner strength to resist being drawn into negative responses. Others find their own ways of countering circumstances over which they appear to have no control.

The love and care of adults help children and young people make a safe passage through childhood and adolescence. Teenagers are trying to figure out who they are and how they fit into the family, neighborhood, school, and larger world. They are searching for answers but in their own ways. One of the challenges for parents, caretakers, educators, and youth workers is to encourage young people to make sound choices among the unlimited possibilities while avoiding excessive interference.

WHO IS THIS GENERATION?

The great majority of U.S. teenagers are not the dangerous, drug-using, sexually promiscuous, nonproductive adolescents of the common stereotypes. Young people might not always agree with the adults with whom they interact, and sometimes they even break the rules, but they finish high school and attend college at higher rates than ever. And in many other respects, today's teens are more like their counterparts of past generations than different from them.

Many teens, especially inner-city youths, report that the messages they receive about themselves in the media and in schools are usually negative ones such as "You aren't worth anything."[12] They feel that adults and communities no longer care about them. This feeling is validated by cuts in funding of schools, parks, and community centers needed to assist youths in many communities.

Respect from adults is critical in helping youths to develop self-esteem. Teenagers don't always have appropriate adult support at home; their parents may be too tired or too busy or have too many problems themselves to care adequately for their children. For many teens, schools and neighborhood organizations are their primary sources of adult supervision and guidance. Teens need a "caring adult who recognizes a young person as an individual and who serves as a mentor, coach, gentle but firm critic, and advocate."[13] Yet many inner-city youths see school "as a place that has rejected and labeled them by what they are not [for example, not college-bound] rather than by what they are."[14]

Teenagers have complex identities that are influenced by their peers, family, neighborhoods, teachers, and other adults. Their identity is also influenced by their ethnic membership and the interaction of that membership with the dominant society. Out-of-school experiences are at least as important in these youngsters' development as school experiences. It is within these multiple contexts that young people define themselves as, for example, Latino, older sister, daughter, Catholic, smart, and athlete.

ECONOMIC REALITIES

Young people may be worried and somewhat pessimistic about their future economic conditions. However, they continue to seek out postsecondary education to improve their job and career opportunities. Sixty-three percent of high school graduates entered college immediately after graduation in 2000 as compared to 49 percent of the graduates in 1972.

Many young people begin to work while they are in high school. Forty-four percent of fifteen-year-olds work during the school year; by the time they are seventeen, 78 percent of them are working. Males are only slightly more likely to work

The number one thing young people in America—indeed young people around the world—have going for them is their sense of honesty, morality, and ethics. Young people refuse to accept the lies and rationalizations of the established order.

Dick Gregory

Many high school students work after school and in the summer.

than females, and white students are more likely to work than students from other racial or ethnic groups. There is evidence of a strong positive link between working in high school and obtaining a job after graduation. After-school jobs are particularly beneficial to students from low-income families who do not have family or school connections to help them find employment. Eight to ten years after high school, people who worked as teenagers earn more than their counterparts who did not.[15] Unfortunately, many students who could derive long-term benefits from working while in high school—those in inner-city areas—have limited access to jobs. The lack of employment opportunities contributes to low self-esteem and to pessimism about the future and the value of school. In addition, in communities in which there is high unemployment, many young people do not have opportunities to learn how to work either through their own experiences or through the modeling of working adults.

RESILIENCY

Many young people have the **resiliency** to overcome disastrous childhood and adolescent experiences and go on to become successful workers, professionals, and community leaders. These individuals' personal attributes give them strength and fortitude and help them confront overwhelming obstacles that seem designed to prevent them from reaching their potential. Resilient students are usually social, optimistic, energetic, cooperative, inquisitive, attentive, helpful, punctual, and on task.

■ CHALLENGES OF YOUTH CULTURE

Adults usually regard teenagers as too young to have the benefits of adulthood. They expect teenagers to enjoy youth, begin dating, develop friendships, plan for their future, and learn how to behave like responsible adults. Other adults see adolescents as teenage mothers, gang members, drug abusers, and troublemakers. Young people are bombarded by messages about themselves in music, movies, books, and television. Other potent influences are the circumstances in which teenagers live, which may include drugs, violence, and the lack of adult support. Young people must sort through all these influences as well as the messages given by significant peers and adults in their lives. This section explores some of the challenges with which most teens struggle and about which they make decisions, whether alone or with help from others.

SEXUALITY

The defining of one's sexuality—one's nature as a sexual being—begins in the early teens and continues throughout life. Coming to terms with one's sexuality often involves some turmoil both within oneself and with parents and caretakers during the teen years. Many young women will also be confronted with the danger of sexual assault. Even while trying to develop intimate relations with young men, young women may fear them. The development of a healthy sexual self is a complicated process.

resiliency

The ability to overcome overwhelming obstacles to achieve and be successful in school and life.

Many teenagers associate sex with the freedom and sophistication of adulthood. The decision to have sex is one that causes much consternation among youths. Their uncertainty is fueled by the mixed messages they receive from parents, teenage friends, religious doctrines, the media, and older adult friends. At the same time that one medium glamorizes sex, other voices tell teenagers that sex is sinful and that abstinence before marriage is the only moral option.

Girls and women often connect sex with being accepted, being attractive, and being loved. Many boys and men, by contrast, link sex with status, power, domination, and violence—a far cry from the loving relationship that many females have envisioned. Thus, ideal sexuality for men and for women may differ.

Teenage sex is not, however, as rampant as many believe. The sexual activity of both teenage females and teenage males decreased during the 1990s. In 1991 over half of our high school students had had sexual intercourse at least once; by 2001 the percentage had dropped to 43 percent for high school females and 49 percent for high school males. One of three high schoolers was sexually active (that is, had had sex in the past three months). Those teens who are sexually active are becoming more responsible about sex and using contraceptives more often.[16]

Concurrently, the number of teenage pregnancies and births is declining. Ninety-eight percent of junior high girls reach the age of fifteen without becoming pregnant; about 8 in 1,000 of ten- to fourteen-year olds do give birth. A recent study of younger teens found that 18 to 19 percent had sexual intercourse at least once before they were fifteen. Those who are more likely to become pregnant are young women who are sexually active and participate in other risk-taking behaviors such as smoking, drinking, and using drugs.[17] The data on all female teenagers show that 1 of 25 becomes pregnant, but of those nearly twice as many are older teens (eighteen to nineteen years old). Only 1 of 50 female teenagers actually becomes a parent.[18] The fathers of the majority of these babies are not teenage males. Instead, 62 percent of the men who father the children of teen's babies are in their twenties.[19]

Poverty appears to be the most important factor in determining teenage mothers. Of pregnant teenage girls, 83 percent are in poverty. Most unmarried teenage mothers continue to live with their parents, but their families are disproportionately low income. To reduce teenage pregnancy, family poverty may need to be reduced. Certainly, pregnancy has much less to do with age and ethnicity than with poverty.

Many teenage parents, especially mothers, are forced to take on adult responsibilities much earlier than society expects of its youth. Teenage mothers are sometimes forced to fend for themselves under poverty conditions. Their own parents can provide little or no support, and the fathers of their children are often absent and either not contributing or unable to contribute financially. Nevertheless, over 60 percent of these mothers are enrolled in school, have graduated, or have obtained a GED.[20] Staying involved in school is important. Otherwise, statistics show, "eight to 12 years after birth, a child born to an unmarried, teenage, high school dropout is 10 times as likely to be living in poverty as a child born to a mother with none of these three characteristics."[21]

Overall, teenagers are becoming more responsible about their sexual activity and are learning to use contraception to reduce the risk of pregnancy and the transmission of AIDS and other sexually transmitted diseases. School programs such as sex education

Motivated by the AIDS epidemic, many schools now offer programs that promote awareness of sexually transmitted diseases.

and health clinics are helpful, but they are not always supported by families and communities. Educators should be aware that the teen years are traumatic for many young people as they struggle with the development of their sexuality. Teenagers' apprehensions and activities related to sex may affect their school behavior and their ability to perform satisfactorily in school.

DROPPING OUT

Students drop out of high school and college for different reasons, but dropping out at either level is harmful to young people in the long term. The dropout rate has gradually decreased over the past three decades. In 2001, 89 percent of all eighteen- to twenty-four-year-olds had completed high school or GEDs. About 5 percent of students in the tenth to twelfth grades drop out each year—a figure that has fluctuated only slightly for nearly twenty years. However, the dropout rate in the United States varies across ethnic and racial groups, as shown in Figure 3.3.

Hispanic students continue to have a fairly high dropout rate. In 2001, 27 percent of Hispanic teenagers had dropped out of high school in the previous year. Hispanic students who speak English well are more likely to complete high school than are students whose English proficiency is limited. The largest proportion of Hispanic dropouts are immigrants who never attend U.S. schools; many have not completed more than elementary school in their countries of birth. Although first- and later-generation Hispanics graduate at higher rates than immigrants, they are still two to three times more likely to drop out of school than peers from other ethnic groups. Mexican American students drop out of high school at rates higher than other Hispanics.[22]

Students from low-income families drop out of high school at a rate seven times greater than that of students from middle- and high-income families. Students whose parents did not finish high school are three times as likely not to complete high school as those whose parents did graduate. More females finish high school than males, and a greater percentage of students without disabilities complete high school than students with disabilities. Students who complete high school are more likely than dropouts to be employed. Eighty-two percent of high school graduates are in the labor force as compared to 73 percent of the dropouts.

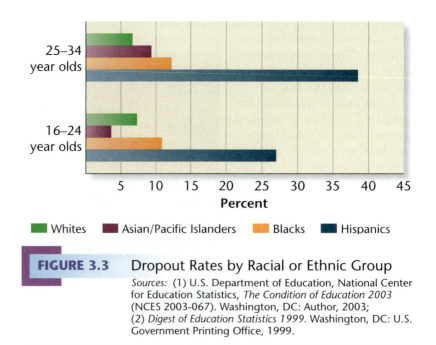

FIGURE 3.3 Dropout Rates by Racial or Ethnic Group

Sources: (1) U.S. Department of Education, National Center for Education Statistics, *The Condition of Education 2003* (NCES 2003-067). Washington, DC: Author, 2003; (2) *Digest of Education Statistics 1999.* Washington, DC: U.S. Government Printing Office, 1999.

Talented high school graduates who do not seek postsecondary training represent another type of dropout. The underdeveloped talent of students who don't seek postsecondary education or don't complete their programs represents a substantial loss to society.

DRUG USE

One of the questions with which many teenagers struggle is whether to experiment with cigarettes, alcohol, or drugs. Although not as glamorized in films and advertisements as in the past, drinking and smoking are still associated with independence and adult behavior. Teens use drugs for different reasons. Sometimes biological predispositions or psychological problems trigger drug use. In other cases, social pressures, family problems, or self-hate lead young people to drugs.

The public worries about drug use. In the 2003 Phi Delta Kappa/Gallup Poll of the Public's Attitudes Toward Public Schools, respondents ranked the use of drugs as the fourth greatest problem that public schools face. Drug use fell behind the lack of financial support for schools, lack of discipline, and overcrowding.[23] Parents worry particularly about drug usage that may lead to chemical dependency in the future. **Chemical dependency,** such as addiction to drugs, alcohol, or tobacco, is one of the causes of social and academic problems among youths. People are judged to be dependent when they find that their need for the chemical substance is constant and they can no longer control their use. Dependency can be difficult to overcome and often requires professional treatment.

A large percentage of teenagers do try one or more drugs, but alcohol is the favorite, being used more than twice as often as other drugs. Figure 3.4 shows the percentages of high school seniors who have used alcohol, marijuana, and other illicit drugs over the past twenty-five years. Fifty-three percent of twelfth graders have used an illicit drug at some time, but only one in four has used one or more drugs in the past month. Younger students also use drugs. Twenty-five percent of eighth graders have tried drugs, with 10 percent of them using in the

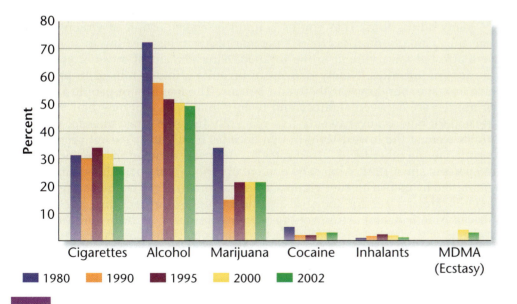

FIGURE 3.4 U.S. High School Seniors Reporting Use of Selected Substances in the Past Month

Sources: (1) National Center for Health Statistics, *Health, United States, 2002 with Chartbook on Trends in the Health of Americans* (DHHS #1232). Hyattsville, MD: Author, 2002; (2) L. D. Johnston, P. M. O'Malley, and J. G. Bachman, *Monitoring the Future National Results on Adolescent Drug Use: Overview of Key Findings, 2002.* Bethesda, MD: National Institute on Drug Abuse, 2002.

chemical dependency

The habitual use, for either psychological or physical needs, of a substance such as drugs, alcohol, or tobacco.

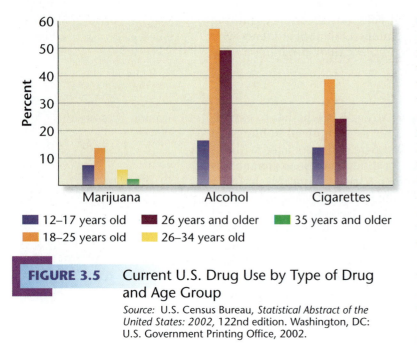

FIGURE 3.5 Current U.S. Drug Use by Type of Drug and Age Group

Source: U.S. Census Bureau, *Statistical Abstract of the United States: 2002,* 122nd edition. Washington, DC: U.S. Government Printing Office, 2002.

Chart legend: 12–17 years old, 18–25 years old, 26 years and older, 26–34 years old, 35 years and older. Categories: Marijuana, Alcohol, Cigarettes.

past month. Eleven percent of eighth graders also report using cigarettes in the past month. Although the rate of usage is higher than the public may find acceptable, current usage by all teenagers is down from what it was in the mid-1970s and throughout the rest of the twentieth century. Students who plan to attend college are less likely to use drugs. Male teenagers are more likely than females to use drugs other than cigarettes.[24] However, teens under age eighteen use illegal drugs other than marijuana less than adults in the U.S. population (see Figure 3.5). Drug use is much more prevalent among adults than teens.

Many state and national programs provide educators and students with information about drugs and the dangers of drug abuse. Generally, the most successful drug education programs are those that are adequately funded, involve parents and students, are taught by well-prepared teachers, and avoid preaching and moralizing. Some people suggest that programs should help students understand and control normal experimentation, in which the majority of teenagers participate, as well as emphasize the perils of self-destructive addiction.

VIOLENCE

Television news reports, newspapers, and politicians all proclaim that the nation is becoming more violent, presenting numerous examples to make the point. In fact, the United States is the most violent industrialized nation in the world. Children under age fifteen are twelve times more likely to be killed by firearms then children in twenty-five other industrialized countries.[25]

Many adults think that youths commit a larger portion of violent crime than they actually do. Less than 1 percent of juveniles ages ten to seventeen were arrested for a violent crime in 2000. Nine percent of those arrested for murder are juveniles. Ninety percent of juvenile crime is related to property such as arson, burglary, car theft, and larceny. The majority of people arrested for murder are between eighteen and twenty-four years old; over half of those arrested for rape are over twenty-five years old. Juvenile arrest rates for violent crimes were at the lowest level in two decades for all areas except aggravated assault. On the other hand, arrest rates for drug abuse violations has increased 145 percent since 1991. Almost 80 percent of serious and nonserious crimes are committed by males; murder victims are also more likely to be males. However, juvenile arrest rates for females are increasing while declining for males. African American and Latino youth are overrepresented in the juvenile system. Students with disabilities such as mental disorders, attention deficit hyperactivity disorder (ADHD), and learning disabilities are also overrepresented.[26]

Another myth is that most youths who are murdered are killed by their peers in gang shootings and other conflicts. In fact, automobile accidents account for at least three times as many teen deaths as homicides.[27] Furthermore, two-thirds of slain youths in the United States are victims of adult-perpetrated crime. Youths are the predominant perpetrators of street violence, but adults are the aggressors in home violence. Young people (twelve to nineteen years old) are over three times as likely to be victims as those over thirty-five.

Crime is related more directly to poverty than to the age of the criminal. At all age levels, persons with low incomes are more likely than persons with higher incomes to commit crimes. They are also more likely to be the victims of violent crimes. One reason for the higher crime rate for burglary and auto theft among teens is that a larger proportion of teens than adults live in poverty. Low-income teenagers commit crimes at about the same rate as adults who live in poverty. At the same time, most people in poverty do not commit crimes.

Gangs involve more students than ever. A 2000 survey of law enforcement agencies found a total of 24,500 gangs and nearly 750,000 gang members in the United States.[28] Gangs are found in all states and in most large cities; a growing number of smaller cities and rural areas are also becoming home to gangs. There are some female gangs, but most gangs comprise young men. For youths of both sexes, gangs can provide a sense of place and a feeling of importance as well as a strong identity structure. Gangs often provide a discipline that has been missing from the experience of many young people. Most gangs are not violent, but those that are violent are territorial.

Many schools are combating youth violence through conflict resolution and other programs that help students learn to respect others, stop harassment, and effectively handle interpersonal problems.

Suicide is another form of violence that affects the student population. However, the suicide rate for teenagers is lower than that for people over twenty-four years old. Nineteen percent of high schoolers report seriously considering suicide in 2001, but just over 6 percent actually attempted it. Latino and white teenagers are more likely to commit suicide than members of other groups. Female teens take their own lives nearly twice as often as their male peers.[29] Suicide attempts are often calls for help. Teachers should be alert for signs that may suggest the need for a referral to other professionals.

HARASSMENT AND BULLYING

Harassment by peers and teachers in schools is reported by students with disabilities and students who are male and LGBT, overweight, or different in ways that seem important to teenagers. Harassment is not rare in schools; it is a common occurrence for many students. Eighty percent of the students in a national survey indicated that they have been sexually harassed at school, with one in three experiencing it often. Sixteen percent of the students in this survey "said they avoided school or cut classes; 20 percent found it hard to pay attention; and 24 percent of students reported that they talked less in class."[30] The harassment of girls and young women in the hallways, classrooms, and cafeterias of schools ranges from name-calling to touching and, in some cases, rape. LGBT students report verbal, sexual, and physical harassment that sometimes ends in physical assault.

The most common harassment is in the form of verbal abuse. Almost all LGBT students report hearing homophobic remarks such as "that's so gay," "faggot," or "dyke" from other students. Nearly 25 percent of these students indicated that faculty or school staff also sometimes make homophobic remarks. In many schools, these homophobic remarks are applied to both LGBT and non-LGBT students as derogatory terms meant to call into question a student's masculinity or femininity. Students most often make these remarks when faculty and staff are not around. However, faculty do not always intervene when they hear students making homophobic remarks; students intervene even less often.[31]

Another form of aggression in schools is bullying by bigger and stronger students to establish dominance over their victims. For younger students, the bully may be the student who pushes them out of the cafeteria line so they can be at the front. The bully may be the student who forces others to turn over their money or do his or her homework. Such behavior cannot be excused as just "boys being boys." Bullying takes the form of belittling weaker students, calling them names, and harassing or threatening them. Sometimes the outcome of bullying is assault or murder. Bullies are 3.2 times more likely to carry weapons to schools and be involved in fights in and out of school. In a survey of over 15,000 sixth to tenth graders, nearly a third of the males and 6 percent of the females reported that they had been bullies, victims, or both in the previous thirty days. The small group of children who begin bullying classmates early in elementary school are rated by their teachers as more aggressive than their peers as they progress through school.[32] Psychologists report that victims of bullies experience anxiety, stress, and depression. Some wonder whether the males responsible for multiple shootings in schools are reacting violently to the students who bullied them. Other studies have found a link between bullying and violence later in life.[33] Educators cannot afford to ignore the bullying that occurs in schools.

School should be a safe haven for children and youth. For many students, however, schools are not safe, and sometimes they are dangerous. Educators can assist in the elimination of harassment, bullying, and other youth violence. Among the strategies recommended by the Sexual Harassment Task Force of the American Association of University Women (AAUW) Foundation are the following:

- Borrow or create your own sexual harassment curriculum. Integrate it into a civil rights, diversity, tolerance, or other unit, providing opportunities for students to discuss their ideas and feelings.
- Show a video addressing sexual harassment (such as *Flirting or Hurting*), following up with a classroom discussion.
- Compile a list of resources for students who may be experiencing harassment. Include articles, websites, and hotlines. Make the list and resources accessible in your classroom and office.
- Encourage students to form or join school leadership groups that work to educate others about and prevent sexual harassment.
- Support and validate students' feelings about their sexuality. Make yourself approachable or, if you are not comfortable doing so, refer students to someone who is. Educate yourself on sexuality and homophobia by reading or talking to peers who understand these issues and can communicate with young people about them.
- Model appropriate behavior with your students by avoiding sexual references, innuendos, and jokes.
- Report any harassment that you witness directly or indirectly to the appropriate complaint manager. Do not allow yourself to be a passive bystander.[34]

DEMOCRACY AND EDUCATION

Children learn to function in society through the process called *socialization.* Parents and families are usually the primary socialization agents, especially in the early years of a child's life. Children also learn culturally appropriate behaviors through religious training, the community, and even television. On the child's entrance in school, whether as an infant or at age six, teachers and other school personnel take on socializing roles during a large portion of the student's waking hours. At this point, the family shares the teaching function with professionals in schools.

Schooling and educators in a liberal democratic society face numerous tensions, in part because there is no one agreed-upon way to educate students. There is a strain between the public rights mandated by democratic principles and the private rights demanded by capitalist markets. Democracy calls for equality, whereas capitalism adapts to inequality. A liberal education for all is the goal of democracy; preparation for work is the goal of capitalism. Public schools tend to heed both sides and simultaneously promote some of both. Teachers confront these tensions in their schools and in the communities that have an influence on their work. Some of these issues are elaborated in this section.

ROLES OF SCHOOLS

Schools play many roles in society. They not only prepare students to be contributors to society, but they also reflect society's high ideals (universal education) and bad practices (differential opportunity based on race and income). One's philosophical and political perspectives determine how one views the roles of schools. The following questions identify different perspectives on the goals of schools:

1. Should schools present themselves as a model of our best hopes for society and as a mechanism for remaking that society in the image of those hopes?
2. Should schools focus on adapting students to the needs of society as currently constructed?
3. Should schools focus primarily on serving the individual hopes and ambitions of their students?[35]

In other words, should schools be supportive primarily of democratic equality, social efficiency, or social mobility? Advocates of democratic equality view education as a public good through which all students should be exposed to a liberal arts education and should learn to be productive citizens in a democracy. Proponents of social efficiency believe that schools should serve the private sector by preparing students for future jobs; this goal has probably been the most dominant in the past. However, many people now see promoting social mobility as a more important role of schools. People with this perspective view education as an asset that can be accumulated and used for social competition. Credentials become more important than what is learned; the purpose is to gain a competitive advantage over others to secure a desirable position in society.

REPRODUCTION

Traditionally, schools are expected to reproduce the cultural, political, social, and economic order of society. However, theorists differ in their views of how schools actually perform this reproduction role. Functionalism, conflict theory, and resistance theory provide contradictory descriptions of how schools carry out their reproductive role for society.

Functionalists view schools as important in supporting technological development, material well-being, and democracy. Since the release of the federal report *A Nation at Risk* in 1983, most reports calling for the reform of schools have referred to the need for an educated workforce. A less explicit message of those reports is that schools should socialize students for their roles as workers. Schools should also provide equal educational opportunity for all students and be a primary step in improving their social and economic status.

Conflict theorists also view schools as reproductive of society, but in ways less noble than those described by functionalists. The conflict theorists conclude that schools have been structured to maintain the power and dominance of the individuals and groups that benefit most from the current system. Rather than being benevolent institutions that provide all students an equal chance to succeed, schools legitimize existing inequities. Advantages depend greatly on ascribed characteristics. Students whose parents graduated from college are much more likely to graduate from college; students whose parents never finished high school are themselves more likely not to finish high school. The academic tracking systems in many schools reinforce this unequal distribution. The number of middle-class students in college preparatory and advanced placement courses is disproportionately high relative to the total school population. The number of males and students of color in special education classes is disproportionately high; students of color and those from low-income families are underrepresented in gifted and talented programs. It appears to conflict theorists that one group is being groomed for management positions in the labor market while the second group is being prepared to labor under the direction of the first. Thus, schools provide neither equal educational opportunity nor a chance to improve one's status to any appreciable degree except in rare individual cases.

Over the past decade, researchers working on resistance theory have investigated the interactions of students and teachers as schools carry out their reproduction function. These researchers have found that reproduction is not an automatic process that is implemented with systematic precision. Students sometimes resist domination by school authorities, not readily accepting their inferiority status. For example, they may resist following the rules and participating in some classes and activities.

Resistance theory suggests much more interaction between students and teachers in the reproduction process than has been explained by the previous two theories. It also allows for the possibility that people can change the system of reproduction by encouraging the development of schools that are not based on domination and submission and that actually model democracy. Through the process of resistance, students can become active participants who help define and redefine schools.

RECONSTRUCTIONISM

CROSS-REFERENCE

Reconstructionism is also discussed in Chapter 10.

Some educators believe that schools are able to do more than just reproduce society. They believe that schools need not merely reflect the inequities that prevail in the broader society; rather, schools can reconstruct or transform society. Reconstructionist educators believe that all students can learn at a high level regardless of their race, ethnicity, gender, or socioeconomic status. They also argue that education can make more of a difference in the lives of students than it currently does.

To implement a reconstructionist approach, classrooms and schools become democratic settings in which both students and teachers are active learners and participants. Students study problems confronting society and learn how to confront practices that are inequitable to some students. Teachers and other school personnel actively work with the community to overcome inequities and injustices to students and their families. Social justice, human rights, human dignity, and equity are critical values that guide the work of reconstructionism. In the reconstructionist process, the school itself becomes a model of democracy that leads, rather than follows, societal practices.

■ PURPOSES OF SCHOOLS

One's perceptions of shortcomings in the current education system are related to one's perception of the purposes of schooling. Depending on the speaker and the times, the reasons for schools' problems differ. Sometimes people point to the poor quality of the curriculum, the teachers, or the preparation of teachers. At other times, too much bureaucracy in the school system is the culprit. Some observers blame school problems on poverty, discrimination, and privilege in society. Some identify economic conditions, changing family values, or the gap between schools and families as the root cause of the lack of learning. To others, the fundamental problem is a lack of agreement about the desired outcomes of schools.

School boards, educators, parents, and communities have their own beliefs about the basic purposes of schools and the reasons for current problems in schools. These beliefs often draw on national reports calling for the reform of education. Through such reports and through discussions and debates among individuals and groups, U.S. society continually refines and redefines ideas about the purposes of schools. The five purposes described in the following sections are only a sampling of those most often mentioned by educators and the public. Most schools address each of these purposes, but in any given school, one purpose may receive more prominence than others at a given time.

CITIZENSHIP

Educators, parents, and policymakers agree that schools should help students become good citizens. There is less agreement about how schools should do this. In some schools, especially elementary schools, students receive a grade or rating on their citizenship within the classroom. Historically, students have taken a civics or government course or have studied citizenship issues in other social studies courses. The National Council for Social Studies includes a standard on civic ideals and practices. The focus in citizenship education or in civics and government courses is usually on the structure of the U.S. political system and on treasured documents such as the Constitution and Bill of Rights. Patriotism and loyalty to the United States are implicit values that often undergird both these courses and the school's **hidden curriculum.** A limitation of this patriotic approach is that students might not have the opportunity to grapple with the problems and issues that are inherent in democratic society. Students might learn the civic values but never be encouraged to discuss why inequities remain in society.

Preparation for citizenship cannot be taught in a single course. Schools should work to develop democratic citizens who respect others, believe in human dignity, are concerned about and care for others, and fight for justice, fairness, and tolerance. Students will learn through practice how to be active, involved citizens. What better place to model democratic practice and equitable participation than in our schools?

WORKFORCE READINESS

A number of national reports on education over the past two decades have expressed concern about the quality of the workforce. Although critics blamed schools for a lackluster economy in the 1980s, they did not credit schools for the booming economy of the 1990s. Some employers report that schools do not provide students with the basic skills and behaviors necessary to participate in today's economy. They report that many young people do not read, write, or compute at the level needed for the jobs available. In response, some employers have established their own programs to teach basic literacy.

A lack of agreement exists about the nature of these necessary skills, especially in an economy in which the greatest growth in jobs will be in the service sector, where people of color and women have disproportionately

hidden curriculum
The norms and values that define expectations for student behavior and attitudes and that undergird the curriculum and operations of schools.

Citizenship education in public schools implicitly values patriotism and loyalty to one's country.

Many students begin preparing for a day job by taking vocational courses in high school or at postsecondary vocational schools.

high representation. Most high schools prepare students either to attend college or to get a job soon after graduation. Many areas of the country have vocational high schools to teach occupational skills. Many school districts also have established magnet schools with single purposes, including career preparation in the arts, health fields, computing, and service areas such as foods, hotels, and tourism. A serious dilemma is the overrepresentation of low-income students, students of color, and females in nonacademic tracks.

Educators, policymakers, and the business community debate the "real" purpose of schools. Is it to help students learn a trade, learn how to learn, or learn how to take orders and follow the rules? This question is particularly important when conditions change as rapidly as they do in today's society. The vocation for which one is prepared initially may become obsolete within a few years. Perhaps students should be prepared to think, adjust to change, and be active participants in their life's work. They need to be able to handle change and adapt to new occupations and situations.

ACADEMIC ACHIEVEMENT

Media reports of student scores on achievement tests often highlight a schools' ability to offer students a strong academic background. Some school districts base their reputations on how well their students perform and how many are admitted to colleges. In some communities, parents camp out overnight to be first in line to enroll their children in a preschool that will provide the jump-start needed for success on future tests to ensure later admission to prestigious colleges and universities.

Countries and their education systems are compared through student scores on international tests. When the scores of U.S. students fall below those of students in other countries, parents and policymakers demand changes. Concern about performance in reading, writing, and mathematics periodically leads to a back-to-basics movement in which the traditional academic subjects are emphasized. "Frills" such as the development of self-esteem, leisure activities, and any other areas that take time away from academic study are condemned as a misuse of public funds. In response, states and school districts have increased the length of the school day to provide more time to learn academic subjects.

Attention to academic achievement in the 1990s focused on the development of national standards in academic areas, the arts, health, and physical education. As a result, many schools have revised their curricula to be standards-based. Test publishers have revised standardized tests used by states and school districts to reflect these standards. The emphasis in this decade is on testing of students annually to determine if they are at grade level. Low-income students, students of color, and females are expected to learn at the high levels historically expected of middle-class white males. School systems' reputations and their state funding are dependent on how well students perform on these tests. Educators and others struggle with the appropriateness of promoting students to the next grade when tests suggest they are not at the appropriate grade level.

SOCIAL DEVELOPMENT

Schooling provides opportunities for students to develop their social skills by interacting with other students. In this process, students should learn to respect others; they also learn a set of rules for working appropriately with peers and adults. Although schools usually do not provide a course that teaches skills in

CROSS-REFERENCE
For more information on standardized tests, see Chapter 12.

social development, appropriate behavior is constantly reinforced by teachers and other school personnel in the classroom and on the playground.

Teachers can give students opportunities to work with students from diverse cultural backgrounds and to learn about those differences in the process. Teachers can encourage interactions across groups through cooperative learning activities in which students from different groups are placed together. Other team projects allow students who might not seek one another out otherwise to work together. A part of teaching is helping students learn to work together positively.

Today's technology also opens many possibilities for interactions with students and adults in cultures beyond school boundaries. Internet and two-way video connections allow students in rural New Mexico to talk directly with students in inner-city Chicago or in Tokyo, Japan. Many teachers have developed these linkages themselves with the assistance of other knowledgeable teachers they have met in college classes and at professional meetings.

CULTURAL TRANSMISSION

Schools around the world are expected to transmit the culture of their nation to young people so that they can both maintain it and pass it on to the next generation. Schools have often approached this task by teaching history with an emphasis on important events and heroes. This emphasis helps children learn the importance of patriotism and loyalty. Formal and informal curricula reflect and reinforce the **values** of the national culture—the principles, standards, or qualities the culture endorses.

These national values and rules are so embedded in most aspects of schooling that most teachers and students do not realize they exist. The only exceptions may be students who do not belong to the dominant culture or whose families have recently immigrated. In these cases, students and families quickly learn that schools might not reflect or support aspects of their culture that differ from the culture of the dominant group. This dissonance between schools and families is most noticeable when students are from backgrounds other than western European ones. Students from religious backgrounds that have not evolved from Judeo-Christian roots are also likely to question the culture that is being transmitted at school. The challenge for educators is to transmit the national culture while including the richness and contributions of many who are not yet accepted as an integral part of that culture. In this way, schools begin to change and expand the national culture.

◼ WHOSE SCHOOLS?

Although schools are expected to transmit the culture of the United States to the younger generation, educators do not agree on *whose* culture. Is there really a national or common culture that diverse racial, ethnic, language, and religious groups in the country accept? Dialects, behaviors, and values vary within the same cultural group as well as across groups whose members live in different regions of the country. Cultural differences are even experienced by people who move from rural areas to the city or vice versa.

How can schools begin to accommodate all of these differences? Some conservative politicians and popular talk show hosts argue that schools should ignore diversity. These observers believe that all students should learn the common heritage and adopt the national culture as their own. In this approach, students who are not members of the dominant group are expected to assimilate.

Multicultural theorists and educators argue that the diversity of students enriches the school community. They believe that cultural differences should be valued and integrated throughout the curriculum and all activities of the school. In this approach, teachers draw on the cultural backgrounds and experiences of students to teach academic knowledge and skills.

Schools are microcosms of the societies that create them, and the dominant social values that prevail in a society will prevail in its schools.

Jing-Qui Liu

values

Principles, standards, or qualities that are considered worthwhile or desirable.

Can Retention Be Good for a Student?

Today's emphasis on academic achievement may lead to students who do not meet state standards as measured by standardized tests. What are the appropriate strategies for ensuring that students meet standards? These two educators debate the effectiveness of retention as an effective approach to help students learn at an acceptable level before being promoted to the next grade.

YES

Gwendolyn Malone, a fifth-grade teacher in rural Clarke County, Virginia, is president of the 133-member Clarke County Education Association. A teacher for five years when she wrote this piece, Malone works at Cooley Elementary. She can be reached at maloneg@clarke.k12.va.us.

NO

Philip Bowser, a past National Association of School Psychologists "school psychologist of the year," is an NEA activist in Roseburg, Oregon. Bowser can be reached at pbowser@orednet.org.

A child recently reached my fifth grade classroom without the ability to read even at a first grade level.

The child had been systematically promoted with his peers for years in the hopes that he would eventually pick up the necessary reading skills.

Every other student in the class knew the child couldn't read. The embarrassment was so painful the child cried every single time I called on him.

If this child had been retained at the primary grade level, he might have learned to read. He might have avoided years of humiliation. And he might have been more prepared for upper elementary skills, including risk-taking, guessing, context clueing, and the use of prior knowledge.

Social promotion set this child up for repeated failure, low self-esteem, and a high risk of becoming a drop-out statistic. Retention might have prepared this child for academic success.

For most struggling children, retention provides the opportunity to refresh, relearn, and acquire new skills that help them move to the next grade level.

Most important, if framed properly, retention gives students self-confidence and an "I can do this" attitude that's likely to boost their academic achievement for years to come.

But if grade retention is to be successful, educators must:

- Stop sitting back and hoping against all odds that children, if promoted, will eventually absorb the skills they need. It won't happen.
- Nip the problem in the bud by retaining students early in their school careers.

Imagine going to your physician with an illness. The doctor says, "There's an old treatment for your condition. At best, it helps only one in 10 who get it, but no one can predict which one.

"That one person will experience a little bit of relief for a short period of time," the doctor continues, "but then the problem will return. Everyone will have negative side effects, some of which can be severe, some lifelong."

The illness is underachievement. The treatment—if educators practice full disclosure—is grade retention.

It's easy to understand the appeal of holding back a student who fails to meet benchmarks. Retention can take a student from the bottom of a class to somewhere nearer the middle. That seems like progress, doesn't it?

The problem is that students are compared to the grade placement, not to their peers. The students have "caught up" to the wrong group!

Most likely, the learning problems that contributed to the original retention decision will persist, and the retained students, in a year or two, will be back at the bottom of the class.

As a districtwide school psychologist, I follow retained students for a few years. In my experience, grade retention is a dangerous gamble.

But you don't have to take my word for it. The research shows that:

- Retained students rarely make significant academic progress in the retained year.
- First or second graders who show improvement over nonretained, underachieving peers quickly

(continued)

YES

Kids get an essential educational foundation in kindergarten, first, and second grade. If they don't have a grasp of the basics at this age, they shouldn't be permitted to move on.

I'd like to call these three grades simply "primary grades," stop grading students in them, and instead provide a list of skills each child must master and knowledge they must acquire before advancing to third grade.

- Establish a way of transitioning students into the next higher grade when they're ready.

If children have mastered third grade skills or if retained children have "caught up," then they shouldn't have to remain in an unproductive or unchallenging setting. They should be moved within that academic year to an academically appropriate or age-appropriate level.

When kids see that there's a way out of a situation they don't like, they'll take it. Retained students will see the incentive to learn and be promoted with their peers.

Students who are retained early on with support and nurturing tend to feel better about themselves and enjoy school more than those who reach the later elementary levels not only unprepared but ashamed that other students are aware of their deficiencies.

Students who are promoted without the academic skills they need become embarrassed, hurt, angry, and defensive. That makes it even harder for them to catch up.

It would be easier, more academically sound, and even more economical to prevent dropouts by retaining these children in the primary grades.

Let's give these students what they need—a hand up, not a hand-out.

Source: "Can Retention Be Good for a Student?" *NEA Today* (March 1998), p. 43.

NO

lose that advantage. The two groups soon perform the same academically, but the retained group develops measurable mental health problems.

- A single retention increases a student's probability of dropping out by 21 to 27 percent.
- The stigma of retention damages self-concept and creates a negative attitude toward school to a much greater degree than most educators predict beforehand or recognize later.
- The most common retainee is a nonwhite male, small of stature, from a low-income family, with parents uninvolved in schooling.
- "Old for grade" adolescents are at increased risk for substance abuse, earlier sexual activity, behavioral problems, and emotional distress.

Those who frame the problem as a choice among grade retention, social promotion, or low academic standards don't see the variety of existing remedies with stronger therapeutic force and fewer side effects.

What if school districts took the cost of extending a student's career an extra year—on average, $5,000—and used the money for effective prevention and remediation programs?

What if teachers had decent class sizes and adequate time to reflect and plan individualized instruction?

What if schools involved parents earlier, gaining their support for additional tutoring, cross-grade groupings, and summer school?

Wouldn't these solutions be more effective than running kids through the same course of instruction that has already proven inadequate?

When parents and teachers decide to retain, they do so in the dark, in spite of ample evidence that they will be adding a significant risk factor to the life of a child. To me, that's not a chance worth taking.

WHAT DO YOU THINK?
Can retention be good for a student?

To give your opinion, go to Chapter 3 of the companion website (**www.ablongman.com/johnson13e**) and click on Debate.

WHOSE VALUES?

Parents' choices of private schools, home schooling, or segregated schools have been based in part on the values that parents believe schooling can impart. Although schools usually do not offer a course in which values are explicitly presented and discussed, values implicitly influence the formal and informal curriculum. Curricula usually support the current ideological, political, and economic order of U.S. society. For example, individualism is much more highly regarded than the rights of groups. The Protestant work ethic is evident in society's expectation of hard work and in the general belief that someone who works hard will be successful in life. Although these values may seem uncontroversial, they can be the cause of extensive debate and emotional pleas at meetings with groups of parents, school board meetings, and community forums.

CROSS-REFERENCE
See Chapter 6 for some of the court cases related to community values.

Some parents are concerned that the public school curriculum in the United States does not reflect their religious values; often, they think that their religion is purposefully denigrated in schools. These concerns are expressed most frequently by members of some fundamentalist Christian communities but also by Amish and Hutterite communities and by some Jewish, Muslim, and other non-Christian families and communities. On the other hand, atheists believe that religious values, especially Christian ones, pervade the school curriculum.

Additionally, the emphasis on individualism and competition that is prevalent in many schools is not compatible with the cooperative patterns practiced by Native American tribes and in many Latino and African American communities. These differences can lead to conflict between parents and schools and between groups within a community. Parents turn to the courts when they believe that schools have acted inappropriately. They may believe either that the schools do not have a democratic process in which they can be heard or that the majority of the community will not support their petitions. School prayer, creationism, the banning of books, sex education, and segregation are among the areas that have been tested in the courts.

Because parents and other groups in a community may vehemently disagree about the values to be reinforced in schools, teachers should be aware of their own values. Knowing their own values as well as those of the families represented in the school should help teachers prepare for potential conflicts. Expectations can vary greatly from one community or school to another.

GLOBAL PERSPECTIVES
Universal Values

One might wonder whether a diverse population can ever reach agreement on the values to be taught in schools. But one K–12 school in Lucknow, India, has been promoting diverse students' emotional and spiritual growth as well as academic excellence for nearly fifty years. The City Montessori School has 19,000 students in fifteen branches in a city with more than 1.5 million people and two very influential religious groups: Hindu and Muslim. Students learn and are expected to practice what the faculty and parents define as "universal values," which include "kindness, compassion, cooperation, responsibility, and other such values rooted in the world's religions."[36]

The school's approach integrates these universal values with excellence, global understanding, and service. In daily reflection times, students use texts and stories from many religions. They "visit India's holy places—Hindu, Sikh, Buddhist, Muslim, Christian, Jewish, Baha'i, and Jain—in order to learn tolerance for one another."[37] They also have exchange programs with schools in more than twenty countries. Students are expected to provide service to local communities and villages.

In developing this approach, those involved have drawn on effective practices from around the world. The school takes its teaching philosophy and its name from the Italian educator Maria Montessori. The mentoring aspect of teaching comes from Russia. The universal values are not those of one religious group but are basic to many religions. They also are the values of humanitarians around the globe, whether or not they are religious.

DEMOCRATIC SCHOOLS

Democratic schools are ones in which students practice democracy by being active participants in their education. These schools encourage the exchange and exploration of ideas from multiple perspectives. They develop the individual and collective capacity of students to develop the possibilities for resolving problems. Teachers in democratic classrooms teach students to analyze real-world ideas, problems, and policies. Students are involved in community issues, collecting and analyzing data, and often become involved in changes within the community. The goal is to understand that democracy is not so much an ideal to be pursued as an idealized set of values that we must live by and that must guide our life as a society.[38]

Democratic schools reflect democratic structures and processes and include a curriculum that provides students with democratic experiences. These schools require students, teachers, parents, and community members to be active participants in the educational process. Equity undergirds the structure of democratic schools. All students have access to all programs. Tracking, biased testing, and other practices that deny access to some students are eliminated. The emphasis on grades, status, test scores, and winning is replaced with an emphasis on cooperation and concern for the common good. Those involved in this democratic project also work toward the elimination of inequities in the broader community as well as in the school.

A democratic curriculum encourages multiple perspectives and voices in the materials used and the discussions that ensue. It respects differences in viewpoints. It does not limit information and study to the areas chosen by members of the dominant group. It includes discussions of inequities in society and challenges students and teachers to engage actively in eliminating them.

Establishing a democratic classroom or school is not an easy undertaking. Sometimes colleagues and parents resist it; some people believe that teachers should be all-knowing authorities so as to exert control over their students. Those who want schools to prepare students for social efficiency are supportive of stratified systems using grades and test scores to sort students into tracks that prepare them for future jobs. Supporters of schooling as a route to social mobility expect competition to determine which students deserve the greatest rewards, such as acceptance into the gifted program or admission to a prestigious college. Democratic schools, on the other hand, support equity, equal access, and equal opportunity for all students.

SUMMARY

Through historical and political developments, members of the dominant culture have benefited from the power that is possible through social and economic dominance. The results are prejudice and discrimination against members of the groups without power.

Students in schools today come from diverse family structures. Although a majority of children live with their mother and father, many live with single parents, grandparents, adoptive parents, foster parents, gay or lesbian parents, or relatives. Some have no home; others live in unsanitary, unsafe, and/or abusive conditions.

Teenagers are struggling with economic and social realities that can prove dangerous when they make inappropriate decisions. The poverty suffered by young people contributes to some of them engaging in violent acts and sometimes dropping out of school. At the same time, many young people exhibit amazing resiliency, allowing them to overcome economic and social hardships to finish school and become productive adults.

Theories of functionalism, conflict, and resistance provide different descriptions of the role of schools in reproducing culture and society. Reconstructionism suggests that schools can transform society by serving as model democratic and equitable institutions. Schools serve many purposes, including the development of citizenship, preparation for work, the development of academic and social competence, and the transmission of the culture to another generation.

Democratic schools and classrooms involve parents, students, teachers, administrators, and community members as partners in the design and delivery of education. The policies and practices of democratic schools promote equity for all students, abandoning practices that sort students and give privilege to those from advantaged backgrounds.

DISCUSSION QUESTIONS

1. How is power reflected in the schools with which you are most familiar? Who holds the power, how is it reinforced in school policies and practices, and which students are not well served as a result?

2. Families face a number of social and economic challenges that affect the well-being of children in this country. What are the factors that you think do the most damage to children? What should teachers and schools do to help students develop resiliency and be able to achieve academically under these adverse circumstances?

3. Teenagers need adult support as they cope with the challenges of adolescence. Who do you think should be providing this support? What should be the role of middle school and high school teachers in providing the support?

4. What are signs that teachers might see to make them wonder whether a child or adolescent is being abused? What steps should you take if you suspect abuse or other risk-taking behaviors?

5. You may be assigned to a school in which the community monitors the curriculum to ensure that their values are reflected. What curriculum content could spark debates in the community? How important will it be to keep parents and other community members informed?

JOURNAL ENTRIES

1. Describe the privileges or lack of privileges that you have had as a result of your membership in specific ethnic, racial, gender, economic, and religious groups. Why have these privileges been extended to or withheld from you?

2. Describe your perceptions of the students you would teach in an inner-city school in a large metropolitan area as compared to students in a wealthy suburban area. How do you think your perceptions might influence your academic expectations for the two groups of students?

3. Write a summary of what democracy means to you. How do common good and equality fit into your perception of democracy?

PORTFOLIO DEVELOPMENT

1. Write a paper that describes a classroom that operates on democratic principles; contrast it with traditional classrooms. The description should include the setup of the room, the interaction between the teacher and students, and the interactions of students, among other characteristics.

2. Select a school or community in which there has been debate regarding the values to be reflected in the curriculum. Analyze the fundamental differences between the groups in a paper, chart, or pictorial format. Identify strategies that could have prevented the conflict.

3. Based on your observations in a school, describe the purposes discussed in this chapter that are most valued within the school. What other purposes guide the school? What led you to these conclusions?

PREPARING FOR CERTIFICATION

■ STUDENT EXPERIENCES AND DEMOCRACY

1. One of the topics covered in the Praxis II Principles of Teaching and Learning (PLT) test is "becoming familiar with relevant aspects of students' background knowledge and experiences." Effective teachers identify methods and procedures for gathering background information about their students. What types of information will you want to have about your students and their backgrounds? What methods will you use to gather background information that will help you teach more effectively and also respect the privacy of students and their families?

2. Answer the following multiple-choice question, which is similar to items in Praxis and other state certification tests. If you are unsure of the answer, reread the Democracy and Education section of this chapter.

   James Bryant describes the focus of his U.S. history course: "I want students to know more than facts about history; I want them to understand the strengths and weaknesses of our country and be prepared to tackle social issues and challenge inequities in our society. I want students to become active citizens, committed to issues of social justice, human dignity, and human rights." Mr. Bryant's philosophy most closely resembles

   (A) reproduction theory
   (B) conflict theory
   (C) reconstructionism
   (D) functionalism

3. Answer the following short-answer question, which is similar to items in Praxis and other state certification tests. After you've completed your written response, use the scoring guide in the ETS *Test at a Glance* materials to assess your response. Can you revise your response to improve your score?

   What are two strategies that Mr. Bryant could use in his classroom that would promote his goal of students becoming active citizens? Explain the potential benefits of each of the two actions that you have identified.

WEBSITES

www.aauw.org   The website of the American Association of University Women (AAUW) addresses the education and lifelong learning of girls and women, including many suggestions and resources for fighting sexual harassment.

www.childrensdefense.org   The website of the Children's Defense Fund (CDF) includes data about the status of children in the United States. It also includes information on CDF's programs and activist work.

www.nationalhomeless.org   The website for the National Coalition for the Homeless has information bulletins on homelessness in the United States.

www.calib.com/nccanch/   The National Clearinghouse on Child Abuse and Neglect Information's website serves as a national resource for professionals seeking information on the prevention, identification, and treatment of child abuse and neglect.

www.cgcs.org   The Council of the Great City Schools is a coalition of the nation's largest urban public school systems. The website includes promising practices for serving students in urban schools.

www.nccj.org   The National Conference of Community and Justice is a human relations organization dedicated to fighting bias, bigotry, and racism in the United States. It promotes understanding and respect among all races, religions, and cultures through advocacy, conflict resolution, and education.

FURTHER READING

Children's Defense Fund. (2002). *The State of Children in America's Union: A 2002 Action Guide to Leave No Child Behind.* Washington, DC: Author. Information on the status of children today, including data on what happens to children daily in the United States. The report also includes a discussion of the No Child Left Behind Act and makes recommendations for families and others interested in the welfare of the nation's children.

Flores-Gonzalez, Nilda. (2002). *School Kids/Street Kids.* New York: Teachers College Press. Explores why Puerto Rican students in an urban high school stay, leave, and return to school. The implications of identification as a "school-kid" or "street-kid" are examined.

Kozol, Jonathan. (2000). *Ordinary Resurrections: Children in the Years of Hope.* New York: Crown. A description of living and being educated in the inner city through the experiences of inner-city children and the adults who try to assist them. The stories of individual children raise issues about recognizing the value and dignity of students as we teach.

Males, Mike A. (1999). *Framing Youth: 10 Myths about the Next Generation.* Monroe, ME: Common Courage Press. A debunking of myths about teenagers that have characterized them as the worst generation. Data about what teenagers are really like and what they need are a helpful resource for educators and parents.

Polakow, Valerie. (Ed.). (2000). *The Public Assault on America's Children: Poverty, Violence, and Juvenile Injustice.* New York: Teachers College Press. A fact-filled volume addressing the poverty, violence, and neglect that disproportionately attack our nation's children. It raises the question of how well our society cares for its children.

THEMES OF THE TIMES!

expect the world®

The New York Times

nytimes.com

Expand your knowledge of the concepts discussed in this chapter by reading current and historical articles from the *New York Times* by visiting the Themes of the Times! section of the companion website **(www.ablongman.com/johnson13e).**

NOTES

Unless otherwise indicated, the data reported in this chapter are from the U.S. Census Bureau, *Statistical Abstract of the United States: 2002,* 122nd edition. Washington, DC: U.S. Government Printing Office, 2002.

1. Jonathan Kozol, *Savage Inequalities: Children in America's Schools.* New York: Crown, 1991, p. 65.
2. M. D. Bramlett and W. D. Mosher, *Cohabitation, Marriage, Divorce, and Remarriage in the United States.* Washington, DC: National Center for Health Statistics, 2002.
3. Frank F. Furstenberg Jr., "Family Change and Family Diversity," in Neil J. Smelser and Jeffrey C. Alexander, eds., *Diversity and Its Discontents: Cultural Conflict and Common Ground in Contemporary American Society.* Princeton, NJ: Princeton University Press, 1999, pp. 147–165.
4. U.S. Department of Education, National Center for Education Statistics, *The Condition of Education 2003* (NCES 2003-067). Washington, DC: Author, 2003.
5. Homes for the Homeless. "Day to Day . . . Parent to Child: The Future of Violence among Homeless Children in America" (A Report of Homes for the Homeless). New York: Homes for the Homeless and the Institute for Children and Poverty, January 1998.
6. Urban Institute, *Homelessness: Programs and the People They Serve* (Summary Report of the Findings of the National Survey of Homeless Assistance Providers and Clients). Washington, DC: Author, 1999.
7. James Alan Fox and Marianne W. Zawitz, *Homicide Trends in the United States.* Washington, DC: U.S. Department of Justice, Bureau of Justice Statistics, 2002.
8. UNICEF, *Domestic Violence: An Epidemic.* New York: Author, 2000.
9. Homes for the Homeless, 1998.
10. Fox and Zawitz, 2002.
11. Office of Justice Programs, National Institute of Justice, *Youth Victimization: Prevalence and Implications.* Washington, DC: Author, 2003.
12. Shirley Brice Heath and Milbrey W. McLaughlin, *Identity and Inner-City Youth: Beyond Ethnicity and Gender.* New York: Teachers College Press, 1993.
13. Ibid, p. 61.
14. Ibid, p. 4.
15. Duncan Chaplin and Jane Hannaway, "High School Employment: Meaningful Connections for At-Risk Youth." Washington, DC: Urban Institute, 1996.
16. "Trends in Sexual Risk Behaviors among High School Students—United States, 1991–2001," *Morbidity and Mortality Weekly Report, 51*(38) (September 27, 2002), pp. 856–859.
17. Bill Albert, Sarah Brown, and Christine M. Glanigan, *14 and Younger: The Sexual Behavior of Young Adolescents.* Washington, DC: National Campaign to Prevent Teen Pregnancy, 2003.
18. "National and State-Specific Pregnancy Rates among Adolescents—United States, 1995–1997," *Morbidity and Mortality Weekly Report, 49*(27) (July 14, 2000), pp. 605–611.
19. Freya L. Sonenstein, ed., *Young Men's Sexual and Reproductive Health: Toward a National Strategy.* Washington, DC: Urban Institute, 2000.
20. Gregory Acs and Heather Koball, "TANF and the Status of Teen Mothers under Age 18," *New Federalism: Issues and Options for States,* Series A, No. A-62. Washington, DC: Urban Institute, 2003.
21. The Annie E. Casey Foundation, *Kids Count Data Book 2003.* Baltimore, MD: Author, 2003, p. 44.

22. National Center for Education Statistics, *Dropout Rates in the United States: 1995.* Washington, DC: U.S. Department of Education, 1997.

23. Lowell C. Rose and Alec M. Gallup, "The 35th Annual Phi Delta Kappa/Gallup Poll of the Public's Attitudes Toward the Public Schools," *Phi Delta Kappan, 85*(1) (September 2003), pp. 41–56.

24. National Center for Health Statistics, *Health, United States, 2002 with Chartbook on Trends in the Health of Americans.* Hyattsville, MD: Author, 2002, Table 65.

25. "Rates of Homicide, Suicide, and Firearm-Related Death among Children—26 Industrialized Countries," *Morbidity and Mortality Weekly, 46*(5) (February 7, 1997), pp. 101–106.

26. Laudan Y. Aron and Daniel P. Mears, "Addressing the Needs of Youth with Disabilities in the Juvenile System: The Current Status of Evidence-Based Research" (A Research Report). Washington, DC: National Council on Disability, 2003.

27. The Annie E. Casey Foundation, 2003.

28. Arlen Egley Jr., "National Youth Gang Survey Trends from 1996 to 2000" (OJJDP Fact Sheet). Washington, DC: Office of Juvenile Justice and Delinquency Prevention, U.S. Department of Justice, 2002.

29. National Center for Health Statistics, 2002.

30. "Harassment-Free Hallways: How to Stop Sexual Harassment in Schools: A Guide for Students, Parents, and Teachers, Section III for Schools." Washington, DC: American Association of University Women Educational Foundation, 2002, p. III-2.

31. Joseph G. Kosciw, *The 2001 National School Climate Survey: The School Related Experiences of Our Nations Lesbian, Gay, Bisexual and Transgender Youth.* New York: Gay, Lesbian and Straight Education Network, 2001.

32. Tonja R. Nansel, Mary D. Overpeck, Denise L. Haynie, June Ruan, and Peter C. Scheidt, "Relationships between Bullying and Violence among US Youth," *Archives of Pediatrics and Adolescent Medicine, 157*(4) (April 2003), pp. 348–357.

33. Ibid.

34. "Harassment-Free Hallways," p. III-9.

35. David F. Labaree, "Public Goods, Private Goods: The American Struggle over Educational Goals," *American Educational Research Journal, 34*(1) (Spring 1997), p. 81.

36. Carolyn Cottom, "A Bold Experiment in Teaching Values," *Educational Leadership, 53*(8) (May 1996), p. 54.

37. Ibid, p. 56.

38. James A. Beane and Michael W. Apple, "The Case for Democratic Schools," in Michael W. Apple and James A. Beane, eds., *Democratic Schools.* Alexandria, VA: Association for Supervision and Curriculum Development, 1995.

Education That Is Multicultural

Education in the News

Critics Are Too Hasty: All-Girls Schools May Help

USA Today, May 10, 2002

AS EARLY AS ELEMENTARY SCHOOL, THE DIFFERENT LEARNING styles of boys and girls are obvious. Most girls catch on to reading and writing skills faster than boys do. In fact, many boys never catch up in literacy skills.

Those differences are not a result of unfair educational opportunities. Gender-based learning differences are a fact of life. But they're overlooked by groups objecting to the Department of Education's decision this week to relax rules limiting same-sex education in public schools.

Many education experts believe that same-sex schools offer a promising alternative for boys who are easily distracted or intimidated by girls. If successful, they may offer a partial remedy to the sharp decline in the number of boys going to college.

Likewise, single-sex schools present a way for girls to develop self-confidence and leadership skills without being fearful of showing off their brains. Every educator knows girls who were brilliant in elementary school and then became cowed when competing with boys as a teen.

In many cities, however, expensive private schools are the only options for parents interested in single-sex education. The Bush administration wants to encourage more experimentation by removing the legal barriers that restrict all-boys and all-girls public schools. The Department of Education sees the move as a way to expand school choice.

But some civil-rights groups and women's organizations oppose the plans and argue that the changes are unnecessary and dangerous. The National Organization for Women, for example, maintains that separate schools will lead to unequal schools that discriminate by gender. Their worries have a legitimate historical basis, considering the nation's sordid history of providing inferior education to blacks while hiding behind the "separate but equal" mantle.

But the Education Department appears to be laying out tight rules to ensure that comparable courses would be offered for boys and girls. And same-sex schools must still comply with the equal-protection clause of the Constitution's 14th Amendment.

Done right, same-sex public schools could actually create opportunities and solve some problems in inner-city districts, where parents have the fewest school options.

Consider the success of the Young Women's Leadership School in New York's East Harlem, one of only 10 public same-sex schools in the country. The students at the all-girls school talk about the clean bathrooms and dearth of graffiti. Parents cite the safety. Everyone talks about the 100% passing rate on the challenging New York graduation tests and 100% college enrollment.

Critics say there's no reason those girls can't be just as successful in a well-run, mixed-sex school. Maybe not, but too often they're not. Critics also say those girls aren't learning the lessons they need to get along with men later in life. But they may be gaining valuable leadership opportunities and self-confidence that will prove even more valuable. At all-girls schools, the class leaders and yearbook editors are girls. Those same leadership advantages exist at all-boys schools. Plus, educators say boys in single-sex schools are more likely to try activities such as drama and choral singing.

Same-sex schools aren't right for all students. But for some students, the separation can lead to greater equality.

Learning Outcomes

After reading and studying this chapter, you should be able to:

1. Discuss the importance of diversity, equality, and social justice in delivering high-quality education for *all* students. (INTASC 3: Diversity)

2. Identify teaching practices that are culturally relevant. (INTASC 3: Diversity)

3. Understand the importance of bringing multiple perspectives to the curriculum. (INTASC 3: Diversity)

4. Describe and contrast approaches for teaching students who are learning English. (INTASC 3: Diversity)

5. Provide examples of teaching for social justice and discuss the role of social justice in schools and classrooms.

School-Based Observations

You may see these learning outcomes in action during your visits to schools:

1. Record the interactions between students from different ethnic backgrounds and the teacher. Describe the oral classroom participation patterns and the students' engagement with the subject matter.

2. Visit an inner-city school and a rural or suburban school and observe how student voices are incorporated in classes. Record the nature of the dialogue between students and teachers and among students; describe the degree of equality across the voices and whether any significant patterns of differences emerged.

3. Determine how multicultural education is being integrated in the classes you are observing. You can collect data from interviews with teachers and students in addition to reviewing the textbooks being used.

Diversity, equality, and social justice are the foundation for education that is multicultural. Provision of social justice and equality is a moral and ethical responsibility of educators; the goal is to help all students learn and reach their potential, regardless of their socioeconomic status, ethnicity, race, language, gender, religion, and ability. Teachers and administrators must view all aspects of education—including the hidden curriculum, staffing patterns, discipline, and extracurricular activities—through a multicultural lens to ensure that the needs of diverse students are an integral part of the education process.

Education that is multicultural provides equity in the curriculum, in relationships between teachers and students, in the school climate, in staffing patterns, and in relationships with parents and communities. In other words, it addresses all aspects of the school, including teaching students from diverse microcultural groups. *Multicultural education,* on the other hand, usually refers to the curriculum content, which should include human relations; the study of ethnic and other cultural groups; the development of critical thinking skills; and the examination of issues such as racism, power, and discrimination.

Curriculum and instructional practices in multicultural education value diversity, draw on the cultural experiences of students, include multiple ways of learning and viewing the world, and support democracy and **equity** in classrooms and schools. In culturally relevant teaching, teachers believe that all students can learn, and they place students at the center of teaching, drawing on their cultural backgrounds and experiences to develop meaningful learning experiences. Constant vigilance about the content and delivery of academic subjects is required. Many educators have mistakenly thought that **multicultural education** is only for students of color. Rather, it is for all students regardless of their microcultural memberships.

Many educators think they are "doing" multicultural education simply by including information about groups other than their own in a lesson. This additive approach is evident in black history and women's history months, or in

---

equity
The state of fairness and justice across individuals and groups; it does not mean the same educational strategies across groups but does expect equal results.

multicultural education
An educational strategy that incorporates the teaching of students from diverse backgrounds, human relations, and the study of ethnic and other cultural groups in a school environment that supports diversity and equity.

highlighted sections in textbooks that discuss, for example, Japanese Americans. In some schools, attention to multiculturalism begins and ends with tasting ethnic foods and participating in ethnic festivals. Although these activities can contribute to a superficial understanding of differences, they do not represent the integrated curriculum and school environment that is essential in multicultural education.

In education that is multicultural, all teaching is culturally relevant, and classrooms and schools are models of democracy and equity. This effort requires educators to:

1. Place the student at the center of the teaching and learning process;
2. Promote human rights and respect for cultural differences;
3. Believe that all students can learn;
4. Acknowledge and build on the life histories and experiences of students' microcultural memberships;
5. Critically analyze oppression and power relationships to help students understand racism; sexism; classism; and discrimination against persons with disabilities, gays, lesbians, the young, and the aged;
6. Critique society in the interest of social justice and equality; and
7. Participate in collective social action to ensure a democratic society.[1]

Although you should begin to struggle with these issues now, the process of learning about others and reflecting on one's attitudes and actions in these areas is a lifelong activity.

Many schools sponsor cultural events to show their commitment to diversity. However, these efforts are not multicultural education, which requires a deeper understanding of diversity and equality.

UNDERGIRDING TENETS

For centuries, women, people with low incomes, and members of oppressed ethnic and religious groups have fought for an education equal to that available to males of the dominant group. In the nineteenth century, courageous educators established schools to serve some of these students, often encountering opposition from the community at the time. Eighty years ago educators at the Intercultural Service Bureau in New York City were fighting for the incorporation of intercultural education into the curriculum to increase knowledge about new immigrants and to eliminate the prejudice against them. In 1954 the Supreme Court declared illegal separate-but-equal education for black and white students in the *Brown v. Board of Education* case. The civil rights struggles in the 1960s laid the groundwork for new curriculum content about African Americans, Latinos, Native Americans, and Asian Americans. Attention to equity for women, individuals with disabilities, and limited-English speakers soon followed.

These events became the foundation of multicultural education. Three core beliefs about schooling and society guide the development of education that supports democracy for all. One is the belief that cultural diversity is a national

Equality is the heart and essence of democracy, freedom, and justice.

A. Philip Randolph

strength that should be valued and promoted. Social justice and equality are other viable goals for society and should be modeled in classrooms and schools.

■ DIVERSITY

There has been much public and academic discussion of multiculturalism in recent years. Editorials, national news programs, radio talk shows, and debates among college students and faculty periodically focus on the importance of diversity in society and in the curriculum. Simply put, the argument on one side is that the recognition and promotion of cultural and ethnic diversity will strengthen the nation. The other side argues that the promotion of diversity will divide the nation and lead to even greater conflict among groups. This second group also argues that the Western tradition is denigrated as diversity is highlighted.

Campaigns for members of Congress, governors, and mayors include debates about immigration, provision of services to undocumented workers and their children, English-only policies, and gay rights. Multiculturalists argue that multicultural education will help unify a nation comprising many ethnic groups that has long discriminated against many. They believe that individuals should have the opportunity to learn more about one another and to interact on an equal basis in schools and society. They also believe that members of diverse groups can maintain their ethnic and cultural diversity while developing together a common civic culture. An outgrowth of these debates has been the establishment of general education requirements for ethnic, women's, and global studies in colleges and universities. Most states also expect teacher education candidates to study diversity and to be able to incorporate it into their teaching. Most of the developing state and national standards for preschool through college curricula include references to diversity.

What does the public think of incorporating diversity into the curriculum of our schools? A survey of the National Conference for Community and Justice found that whatever negative perceptions groups have about one another, many of the prerequisites of tolerance and intergroup cooperation are present in U.S. society. The majority of the population respects differences and is committed to increasing the understanding of those differences.[2]

The public believes not only that diversity should be incorporated in the curriculum but also that teachers in a school should represent different cultural groups.[3] A diverse student body and faculty make it possible for students not only to learn about others but also to interact in authentic settings with people from different backgrounds. The Internet has also created opportunities for students in schools with limited diversity to become acquainted with people from diverse backgrounds in other parts of the country and world.

■ SOCIAL JUSTICE

Justice can never be done in the midst of injustice.
Simone de Beauvoir

What is meant by *justice* in a society that places so much emphasis on individualism and the freedom to be left alone? Justice itself is related to fairness, moral rightness, and equity. Our judicial system is designed to guarantee legal justice for individuals and groups. Social justice, on the other hand, focuses on how we help others in the community who are less well off than we are. Most religions measure the quality of a society by the justice and care it gives to those in the greatest need—the homeless, the sick, the powerless, and the uneducated.

The ethic of social justice, especially as it relates to the teacher–student relationship, is essential in the profession of teaching, along with other moral commitments. Social justice in education requires schools to provide all students equal access to a high-quality education. Practices that perpetuate current inequities are confronted and strategies for eliminating them employed.

Schools reflect the inequities of the broader society. As you reflect on the inequitable conditions in schools, ask yourself the following questions:

- How fair is it for some students to attend school in dilapidated, foul-smelling, crowded buildings while others attend classes in beautiful buildings with future-oriented technology and well-groomed grounds?
- How fair is it for wealthier students to have the most experienced and best-qualified teachers, who also earn the highest of all teaching salaries?
- How fair is it that wealthier students are exposed to an intellectually challenging curriculum and experiences while many low-income students do not even have advanced placement classes offered in their school?
- How fair is it that students of color, especially males, and students with disabilities or limited English proficiency are pulled out of regular classes and isolated in segregated classes during much of the school day?
- How accurate are curricula and pedagogy that do not reflect the rich plurality of the people, histories, experiences, and perspectives of the groups that make up the United States and world?

Social justice calls for us to help those persons who have greater needs than we do.

These are among the numerous questions that educators ask themselves if they are serious about providing social justice in schools. A theory of social justice suggests that school systems give those students with the fewest advantages the most advantages in their education and schooling to begin to ensure an equal and fair playing field. The goal might be to use the best-funded and most successful schools as the norm for all schools, with the least advantaged receiving the greatest resources for their education.

EQUALITY

Although equality is an espoused goal of democracy, its meaning differs from one person to another. Many believe that each individual has an equal chance at success, which is often measured by the dominant group in terms of wealth and accumulated material goods. This system of **meritocracy** is built on the idea that with hard work, diligence, and persistence, an individual should be able to finish school, attend college, and obtain a well-paying job. Poverty and discrimination are obstacles that can be overcome.

A problem with the meritocratic approach is that not all individuals begin the game of life from the same starting line. Whites from the middle class and above start with advantages such as membership in the dominant culture, sufficient family income to support a college education, decent housing, adequate health care, and good schools with qualified teachers. The children of the wealthy have a much greater chance of being wealthy in their adulthood than do the children of low-income families.[4] The powerful are able to ensure that their children inherit their advantages. Therefore, equality of opportunity could begin to be realized only if the children from powerless groups are provided the same or similar advantages.

Critics of the public rhetoric on equality charge that U.S. institutions and political and economic systems are rigged to support the privileged few rather than the pluralistic majority. Both the shrinking middle class and the widening gap between wealth and poverty contribute to this problem. Nevertheless, some people still think that a more equitable society is not only desirable but also

meritocracy

A system based on the belief that individuals' achievements are based on their own personal merits and hard work and that the people who achieve at the highest levels deserve the greatest social and financial reward.

Is School the Best Place to Teach Tolerance?

Children learn about their own and other children's families before they enter school. Many families teach their children to respect and value others. Others teach hate and intolerance toward groups that they believe are inferior to them. The role of schools in teaching students to be tolerant is an issue still debated by some educators.

YES

Bettie Sing Luke, a multicultural trainer for the Eugene, Oregon, schools, works with teachers to help students develop tolerance and appreciation for each other's cultures. She has also worked in Seattle and, since 1973, has conducted diversity training in 30 states. E-mail: luke@4j.lane.edu.

NO

Barbara Joan Grubman is a speech specialist for the Los Angeles Unified School District at Grant High School in Van Nuys, California. She began teaching in New Jersey when Eisenhower was president and her salary was under $3,000. E-mail: bgrubman@lausd.k12.ca.us.

A resounding yes! on teaching tolerance in school! School is the only common institution, where *all* students can be touched and prepared to survive in our society's marvelous and sometimes maddeningly diverse mix.

We are less connected, as a society, than we were when travel and technology opportunities were more limited. Witness the recent instances of school violence, situations that cried out for tolerance.

Schools, I believe, can help redefine "family" and "belonging" and reinforce respect. They have to. It's unrealistic to depend on tolerance being taught at home.

Have you checked the percentages on single-parent and two-job families? Busy parents may have good ideals to pass on to their children, but we are no longer a society of "Dick and Jane" families sitting down for dinner and quality conversation each night.

Nor are all families models of tolerance. Some young people will reject the intolerant attitudes they might see at home, but what about children who are afraid to think beyond what they are told at home?

What if children never hear alternatives to intolerance at home—especially mainstream students, who can go through their entire lives and never be asked to reconsider their positions of privilege?

Religious or spiritual communities are a natural conduit for teaching tolerance, but in some localities there may be no religious leadership or opportunity to practice.

It is how your father treats the neighbors. It is how your mother welcomes the world into your childhood home. It is the words they use to talk about others— the words that help or heal, that allow you as a child to develop a sense of tolerance.

Long before a child's historic first day of school, the home provides a foundation of values. Those early years are made up of precious opportunities for teaching children acceptance of others.

I believe children cannot learn this lesson in school. They have to see tolerance modeled by those nearest and dearest to them. They have to hear the words and read the body language of those who care for them and nurture them from infancy.

Toddlers are sensitive to our every look. They know that "funny" glance, the hidden disdain, the lowered eyes of parents that say "this person is different." Spend a few minutes with a young child, and you'll know they don't miss much. Babies take in attitudes with mother's milk.

My maternal grandmother, Rose, was a frightened and prejudiced woman. I grew up as a lower-middle-class kid in the East Bronx, New York. My father's mother, a loving and tolerant woman, also lived nearby. But my mother's mother lived right across the street from us and it was there that I went home for lunch and after school.

(continued)

possible to achieve. Resources could begin to be more fairly distributed if all workers received a decent wage or even equal opportunities. In a study of literacy in the United States and other nations, researchers found that U.S. workers with the highest literacy skills were ten times more likely to receive training from their employers than those with the lowest skills. These researchers found that "our nation concentrates on producing and rewarding first-class skills and,

YES

Cultural beliefs about education can come into play as well.

In my culture, teachers have a highly elevated status. They are entrusted with children because their knowledge and wisdom are believed superior to those of parents.

Chinese heritage is imbued with the Confucian ethics of hierarchy. Parents do not sit and chitchat with their children—this just is not done in traditional families!

I observed, as a child, that my parents had to submit to bias and unfair treatment. If they didn't, they risked further harm to others who looked like us. Had I not had lessons from school, I might have acquiesced to the same fate.

Given these dynamics, schools are the prime choice for imparting tolerance. Dedicated teaching *can* overcome negative attitudes.

When I worked for the Seattle Public Schools, a rumble between Black and Asian students erupted in a middle school woodworking class. The conflict escalated and spilled out into the community.

I chose a Black male as an intervention partner and, together, we quelled the fears on both sides, letting the students know the school had adult advocates of their cultural group working on their behalf.

Young men of both groups were greeting each other in the halls within three weeks.

Schools can teach *all* children about tolerance and connectedness—through anti-bias programs and through *individual commitment* to tolerance, across the board, woven through all subjects.

Students, in turn, can then impact family and outside influences that may not be as tolerant.

Source: "Is School the Best Place to Teach Tolerance?" *NEA Today* (May 2000), p. 11.

NO

I can look back now with the perspective of time and see her fears, but then all I knew was that there were a lot of people out there she did not like, who did not "measure up" to what we were. From her, I learned that blacks were not to be trusted, German Jews were the chosen ones, and many people had what she termed "shifty eyes."

Even as I sat at her oil cloth-covered kitchen table, as she prepared dinner, I knew that those people could not all be bad. Hating the way she treated her foreign-born husband—my beloved grandfather—and hearing her unkind words directed toward my unconventional father, I silently vowed never to be like her. I felt as if I needed to protect them from her barbs. So, ironically, I learned from a very intolerant woman what it meant to be tolerant.

How do we teach our children that those who are different should not be feared—that the kid next to them holds the same fears, loves, emotions as they do?

You have to open your ears to the words of an Orthodox Jewish grandmother who you see has an open heart and a hand for all who come in her path. You have to start to discern from another grandmother that the way she looks at others is not the way you wish to, even when you are too young to put a name to it.

If we wait until we send our children off that first day of school, proud in their shiny new clothes, it is too late. The window of opportunity for teaching tolerance, while it may not be shut and locked, is already lowered.

Being exposed to the lesson of tolerance at school is better than not hearing it at all, but without the foundations laid by family, educators face an uphill battle.

A lesson at school can reinforce what a child already feels, but home is where the heart is.

WHAT DO YOU THINK?
Is school the best place to teach tolerance?

To give your opinion, go to Chapter 4 of the companion website **(www.ablongman.com/johnson13e)** and click on Debate.

as a result, is world class at the top; however, it spends a great deal to achieve this result. It accepts in fact, if not in rhetoric, a basic skills underclass. It spends meagerly to help adults with limited or restricted skills or on the next generation that will join their ranks."[5]

The application of civil rights laws and a drastic reduction in discriminatory practices would contribute greatly to the provision of fairness and justice

equal educational opportunity

Access to similar education for all students regardless of their cultural background or family circumstances.

in the distribution of societal benefits, including education. Schools should question whether their policies and practices are equitable. One step in this investigation might be an examination of how accessible gifted, talented, and honors programs are to students from diverse groups. A truly egalitarian society ensures not only that their schools are safe, adequately staffed, and support learning but also that the schools of other people's children have the same amenities. Such a society works toward the elimination of racism, sexism, and other forms of discrimination in education.

EQUAL EDUCATIONAL OPPORTUNITY

One way to address equality in the educational system is to offer **equal educational opportunity,** which should provide all students, regardless of their backgrounds, similar opportunities to learn and to benefit from schooling. The dilemma in this approach is the question of what constitutes equal educational opportunity. On the surface, it would seem that all students should have access to high-quality teaching, small classes, up-to-date technology, college preparatory courses, a building that supports learning, and a safe environment. In reality, most equal educational opportunity programs have struggled with overcoming educational deficiencies of underserved students by providing compensatory or remedial programs to reduce the educational gaps that have given advantaged students a head start. One of the foremost advocates for children, the Children's Defense Fund, reports that "equal educational opportunity is a myth in millennial America." This conclusion is based on the following key facts:

- The richest school districts spend 56 percent more per student than do the poorest.
- Thirty-eight percent of the nation's fourth graders do not read at basic level, according to National Assessment of Educational Progress (NAEP) studies.
- Seventy-seven percent of fourth graders, 73 percent of eighth graders, and 78 percent of twelfth graders scored below NAEP's writing proficiency level.
- While U.S. fourth graders score ahead of many other nations in both math and science, by the time they reach the twelfth grade, U.S. students are falling behind in both areas.[6]

Even when a school has the latest technology, is clean and well maintained, and is staffed by qualified professionals, equal opportunity is not automatically guaranteed. Many other factors need to be considered. What percentages of students in advanced mathematics and science classes are female and students of color? Who are the students who make up the college preparatory and advanced placement classes? Who is assigned to or chooses a general or vocational track? Who is referred to special education classes? Who has access to the best teachers? Who participates in which extracurricular activities? If the percentages of students from diverse groups in these various school settings are somewhat proportional to their representation in the school population as a whole, equal educational opportunity may be approaching the goal of its supporters.

OPPORTUNITY TO LEARN STANDARDS

CROSS-REFERENCE

National standards are discussed in greater detail in Chapter 12.

Schools today are expected to provide all students the opportunity to learn the skills outlined in national standards for mathematics, science, English, the arts, foreign languages, history, geography, civics, and economics. The expectation is that all students can learn. The provision of remediation for the underserved is no longer the focus. The general public also expects U.S. students to achieve better on international tests than students in any other part of the world. More optimistically, national standards could help prevent students from being tracked into courses and programs that limit their access to higher-level knowledge. They could encourage critical thinking and the ability to view the world and academic subjects from multiple perspectives.

EQUALITY OF RESULTS

Some theorists and educators argue that we must not stop at merely providing the opportunity to learn. Opportunity to learn places the burden on individuals, in that they choose whether to take advantage of the opportunity. But if the goal is to ensure equality of results, teachers would be expected to develop strategies for helping all students learn at a high level. They would start their careers with the disposition or belief that all children, regardless of their group memberships and environmental circumstances, are capable of learning. Students who were not performing well academically or otherwise would become the intellectual challenges for the teacher or a team of teachers and other support personnel. The goal would become developing strategies to ensure learning rather than simply moving students to a different class. This is the goal of the federal legislation in the No Child Left Behind Act, which requires schools to show evidence that all students are performing academically at grade level.

CROSS-REFERENCE
No Child Left Behind is discussed from different perspectives in Chapters 1, 6, 8, and 12.

CULTURE OF THE SCHOOL

The school itself is a cultural system that differs from the family and the broader community in which people participate. Despite individual differences in ability, rate of learning, and personal interest, most students are subjected to the same type of instruction. The school rules regulate classroom behavior as well as determine acceptable dress and speech. Although they differ across schools and communities, students and educators practice many common rituals in athletics, extracurricular clubs, graduation exercises, and school social events. The signs and emblems of the school culture are displayed in school songs, colors, and cheers.

TRADITIONS

Traditions in the school culture are associated with regional influences, the social structure of a community, and location in a rural, urban, or suburban area. Some schools are influenced greatly by the religion of the children's families, others by the presence of a large military base.

Regional interests may influence the sports activities that are fueled through school spirit. In the Midwest, for example, basketball is the favored sport. In other parts of the country, fierce athletic competition may be associated with football, swimming, wrestling, or gymnastics. Rural schools often emphasize Future Farmers of America clubs, agricultural programs, and 4-H clubs—activities usually not found in urban schools.

Schools with long histories have developed lasting traditions that are transferred from generation to generation. Extracurricular activities, clothing, proms, awards and graduation ceremonies, fund-raisers, school plays, bands, clubs, and school trips

Competition in regional athletics and other extracurricular activities often reflects the traditions of a school's culture.

take on different degrees of importance from one community to another and from one student to another. Some graduates retain lifelong feelings of pride about their schools. For others, the memories are of mediocrity and of never being challenged.

■ HIDDEN CURRICULUM

All schools offer a formal curriculum that includes coursework in numerous academic areas. In addition, there is a hidden curriculum that is seldom discussed. It includes the rules that guide the work of the school. This informal curriculum defines the behaviors and attitudes expected of both students and teachers. It is political in that it signifies which students are privileged by promoting their cultural values and patterns.

For most students from the dominant culture, the hidden curriculum reinforces behaviors expected by their families. These students fit fairly easily into the school culture. Students from different cultural backgrounds, however, may find school practices foreign and even contradictory to what they learn at home. The emphasis on competition between students is an example of one set of cultural assumptions being valued over another. Some students need to be taught the "rules" of competition to participate fully in the learning process because competition is not highly valued in the family's culture.

The informal curriculum could become more equitable and supportive of democratic principles if educators acknowledged that many school policies and practices are discriminatory in that they promote and reinforce only the dominant culture. Teachers who recognize their own prejudices and discriminatory practices in teaching and classroom management are able to develop strategies for eliminating them.

CULTURALLY RELEVANT TEACHING

All people have preferred learning and teaching styles that are embedded in their cultural background and experiences. Until teachers learn to recognize these differences and develop a repertoire of different strategies for teaching subject matter, some students will be deprived of appropriate assistance in the learning process. However, making generalizations about culturally diverse learners can be dangerous. Teachers need to be thoughtful about the role that culture—values, behaviors, and language—plays in learning; at the same time, teachers must avoid characterizing all students who appear to share the same ethnicity or class as being the same.

At first glance, it might seem that the guidelines for handling diversity in a classroom can be codified in a recipe book that clearly states what instruction is effective for students from a specific group. The problem with this approach is that not only are there differences across ethnic and cultural groups, but there are also many differences among members within the same group. The intragroup differences may be based on socioeconomic level, religion, language, and degree of assimilation. Therefore, descriptions of a group usually do not apply to all members of that group. The generalizations in the recipe book would lead to **stereotyping** and prejudging students. Knowledge about groups different from one's own can be greatly expanded by taking courses in ethnic or women's studies, reading books by female authors and authors of color, and participating in the institutions and activities of diverse communities.

Culturally relevant teaching is complex. A teacher cannot determine the learning styles, prior knowledge, or cultural experiences of students by simply knowing that they are from a specific ethnic group or socioeconomic level. The

stereotyping

The attribution of common traits, characteristics, and behavior to a group of people without acknowledgment of individual differences within the group.

teacher will need to observe and listen to students and their parents as well as assess student performance to develop the most effective teaching strategy. Culturally relevant teaching validates the cultures of students and communities. As a result, students begin to feel that teachers care about them, which is a first step in building a foundation for trust between teachers and students.

■ BUILDING ON CULTURAL CONTEXT

To demonstrate a respect for the students' backgrounds and experiences, teachers should be able to help students see the relationship between the subject matter and the world in which they live. Students should be able to see themselves in the representations (that is, books, examples, word problems, and films) used by teachers. Use of students' prior knowledge and experiences with the subject matter is also critical. Students make sense of information in different ways. Therefore, the teacher must be able to teach the same concept by explaining it in different ways, relating it to something meaningful in the student's life and demonstrating it with multiple representations. For most beginning teachers, these various explanations are rather limited; with experience, good teachers are able to draw on many different strategies to take advantage of each student's learning style and cultural patterns.

It is important to know what kind of knowledge, skills, and commitments are valued in the students' cultures. Some students rebel against academic study and school authority as a form of resistance against the values of dominant society and its institutions. For example, some white working-class families value common sense and working with one's hands. They place less value on academics than most middle-class families. Understanding these differences should help the teacher develop different strategies for presenting and discussing the subject matter.

Some of the conflict in student–teacher interactions results from lack of information and understanding about cultural differences in oral and nonverbal communications. People usually think that the way they communicate with members of their own culture is normal. They don't realize that there are many other ways to communicate. As long as people interact only with members of the same culture, they use the same cultural cues for, for example, whose turn it is to speak, the meaning of a raised eyebrow, or the seriousness of a statement.

Often teachers do not realize that they and their students are reading cultural cues differently. Students may even be punished for responding inappropriately when they may have read the teacher's intent differently based on their own cultural experiences. Recognizing that miscommunications may be based on cultural differences is a first step in improving cross-cultural communications. A next step is to be able to admit that you may be part of the problem. Next is the development of alternate means for communicating and understanding the messages from other cultures.

One approach is to systematically teach the communication patterns of the dominant culture to students who are not members of that culture. In this strategy, the students' communication patterns are still valued, but they learn when it is to their advantage to use

Teachers must be able to transcend their own cultural backgrounds to develop learning experiences that build on the cultural backgrounds of all their students.

the communication patterns of the dominant group. In other words, they become bicultural in that they are able to function in the different cultures of the school and their home. However, teachers who also learn to function effectively in more than one culture will gain respect from students and begin to genuinely model a multicultural pedagogy.

■ CENTERING THE CULTURES OF STUDENTS

A major dimension of multicultural education is the integration of principles of diversity and equality throughout the curriculum. The curriculum for all academic areas should reflect these principles. Adding a course on ethnic studies or women's studies to the curriculum is an easy way to introduce students to the culture, history, and experiences of others, but it is not enough. Many students will be more willing to learn if their cultures are integral to the curriculum. As they learn within their own cultural context, they see themselves and their cultures valued by the teacher and school authorities.

An inclusive curriculum begins to reflect the reality of our multicultural world rather than only the piece of it that belongs to the dominant group. For example, learning science and mathematics would be enhanced for Native American and other students if the knowledge and traditions of various Native American tribes and nations were incorporated into the curriculum. Researchers Sharon Nelson-Barber and Elise Estrin report that

> Many American Indian students have extensive knowledge of mathematics and science knowledge that is rooted in naturalist traditions common to Native communities and arrived at through observation and direct experience. Because many Indian communities follow traditional subsistence lifestyles, parents routinely expose their offspring to survival routines, often immersing the children in decision-making situations in which they must interpret new experiences in light of previous ones. Unfortunately, a majority of teachers recognize neither Indian students' knowledge nor their considerable learning strategies. Thus, not only is potentially important content knowledge ignored but well-developed ways of knowing, learning, and problem solving also go unrecognized.[7]

Some parents and communities have become so upset at schools' unwillingness to respect and validate their own cultures that they have established charter or private schools grounded in their own, rather than the dominant, culture. Afrocentric schools exist in a number of urban areas. Some Latino and Native American groups have set up schools in which their cultures are at the center of the curriculum. Jewish, Islamic, Black Muslim, Lutheran, Catholic, Amish, and other schools reinforce the values, beliefs, and behaviors of their religions in private schools across the country. Single-sex schools focus on developing the confidence, academic achievement, and leadership skills of young women or men by using the learning styles and cultural experiences central to their gender. Schools in some urban areas have been designed for African American young men to validate their culture and develop their self-esteem, academic achievement, and leadership capacities in order to confront the hostile environment they face in their interactions with the dominant society.

These schools are not multicultural in that they usually exclude some microcultural groups. But the centering of their culture in the curriculum does not necessarily mean that the curriculum is not multicultural. No matter how great or how limited the ethnic diversity is in a school or whose culture is centered in the curriculum, the curriculum should be multicultural. Rural white students should have the same opportunities to view the world and subject matter from multicultural and global perspectives as students in diverse urban settings. Because students in some schools do not have opportunities to interact directly with members of diverse groups, the curriculum often becomes their only source for the exploration of diversity, social justice, and related issues.

Pluralism in the curriculum is not a matter of trivial pursuit, nor is it primarily about self-esteem. It's about truth.

Asa Hilliard

■ VALIDATING STUDENT VOICES

In a democratic classroom, all participants have **voice.** Teachers do not dominate the dialogue. Students, especially low-income students and students of color, usually see teachers as representing the dominant cultural group and as not being open to hearing perspectives represented by the students' cultures.

Yet including student voices in the classroom dialogue is not always easy. Students usually have limited experience with active participation in their own learning. When the classroom climate begins to include student voices, students may express anger and be confrontative; they may even test the limits of the type of language that can be used and the subjects that can be broached. Allowing student voices to be an integral part of classroom discourse often tests the patience of teachers as they and their students figure out how to listen and contribute to the learning process. At the same time, tolerance, patience with one another, and the willingness to listen will develop as student voices contribute to the exploration of the subject matter.

Respect for differences is key in affirming student voices. For many educators, this affirmation requires relinquishing the power they have traditionally had as the voice of authority with the *right* answers. Class time can no longer be monopolized with teacher talk. The meaningful incorporation of student voices requires the development of listening skills and the validation of multiple perspectives, languages, and dialects. It should allow students to participate in the dialogue through speaking, writing, and artistic expression. It should allow them to use the modes of communicating with which they feel most comfortable while teaching them other modes as well.

The affirmation of student voices requires that educators listen to the voices of *all* students. It is particularly important to hear the voices of students of color, low-income students, girls and young women, English language learners (ELLs), and students with disabilities. The formal and hidden curricula have always validated the voices of the dominant groups. One of the goals of multicultural education is to validate the voices and stories of others too. Teachers

voice
The right and opportunity to speak and be heard as an equal.

The wise person can see a question from all sides without bias. The foolish person can see a question only from one side.
Confucius

Many educators must learn to relinquish their traditional role as the single voice of authority in order to allow student voices to be heard.

must ensure that these voices are not drowned out again in their classrooms. The stories or narratives of others will increase student knowledge and tolerance of differences. Many students will learn to value both their own culture and those of others. In the process, teachers and students will also learn that they have much in common.

CHALLENGES IN MULTICULTURAL CLASSROOMS

The challenges in delivering education that is multicultural are many. Because many teacher candidates have either no or limited experience with the ethnic and religious groups represented in their classrooms, they will face the unknown. The ideals of diversity, equality, and social justice will require that these teachers engage in continuous learning about and with these communities.

In some schools, of course, teachers still face fairly homogeneous student populations with little exposure to diversity and the multicultural nature of the country as a whole. But even with limited ethnic diversity, most schools will have males and females from different religious and economic backgrounds. The ethic of social justice is just as important in these settings as in those with great ethnic and language diversity. To provide a well-rounded and balanced curriculum for these students, teachers will need to work harder at bringing different perspectives to presentations and discussions. They will need to develop innovative strategies for providing direct exposure to diversity and issues of equality.

■ TECHNOLOGY AND EQUITY

Information technology is influencing the way many of us live and work today. We use the Internet to look and apply for jobs, shop, conduct research, make airline reservations, and explore areas of interest. We use e-mail and the Internet to communicate instantaneously with friends and business associates around the world. Computers are commonplace in many homes and the workplace. However, usage is not as widespread as we might expect. Members of oppressed groups are much less likely to have access to the knowledge, equipment, and skills necessary to compete successfully in an information society.

Although the number of Internet users is growing exponentially each year, most of the world's population does not have access to computers or the Internet. Only 6 percent of the population in developing countries are connected to telephones.[8] Although more than 94 percent of U.S. households have a telephone, only 56 percent have personal computers at home and 50 percent have Internet access. The lack of what most of us would consider a basic communications necessity—the telephone—does not occur only in developing nations. On some Native American reservations, only 60 percent of the residents have a telephone. The move to wireless connections may eliminate the need for telephone lines, but it does not remove the barrier of equipment costs.

Who has Internet access? The **digital divide** between the populations who have access to the Internet and information technology tools and those who don't is based on income, race, education, household type, and geographic location, but the gap between groups is narrowing. Eighty-five percent of households with an income over $75,000 have Internet access, compared with less than 20 percent of the households with incomes under $15,000. Over 80 percent of college graduates use the Internet as compared with 40 percent of high school completers and 13 percent of high school dropouts. Seventy-two percent of households with two parents have Internet access; 40 percent of female, single-parent households do. Differences are also found among households and families from different racial and ethnic groups. Fifty-five percent of white households, 31 percent of black households, 32 percent of Latino households, 68

information technology
Computer, software, telecommunications, and multimedia tools used to input, store, process, and communicate information.

digital divide
The difference in access to technology tools and the Internet between those with economic advantages and those without them.

percent of Asian or Pacific Islander households, and 39 percent of American Indian, Eskimo or Aleut households have access to the Internet. The number of Internet users who are children under nine years old and persons over fifty have more than tripled since 1997. Households in inner cities are less likely to have computers and Internet access than those in urban and rural areas, but the differences are no more than 6 percent.

Another problem that exacerbates these disparities is that African Americans, Latinos, and American Indians hold few of the jobs in information technology. Women hold about 20 percent of these jobs and are receiving fewer than 30 percent of the bachelor's degrees in computer and information science. The result is that women and members of the most oppressed ethnic groups are not eligible for the jobs with the highest salaries at graduation. Baccalaureate candidates with degrees in computer science are offered the highest salaries of all new college graduates.

Do similar disparities exist in schools? Ninety-eight percent of all schools in the country are wired with at least one Internet connection. The number of classrooms with Internet connections differs by the income level of students. Using the percentage of students who are eligible for free lunches at a school to determine income level, we see that schools with more affluent students have a higher percentage of wired classrooms than those with high concentrations of low-income students, as shown in Figure 4.1. Thus, the students who are most unlikely to have access at home also do not have access in their schools, increasing the divide between groups even further.

Access to computers and the Internet is important in reducing disparities between groups. It requires greater equity across diverse groups whose members develop knowledge and skills in computer and information technologies. The field today is overrepresented by white males. Schools will need to develop strategies for encouraging other students to participate in courses and experiences that help them develop the analytical, problem-solving, and creative skills necessary to use technology effectively. One of the problems may be that technology classes are not culturally relevant for many students. The American Association of University Women, for example, reports that girls are finding programming courses dull and uninviting and electronic games violent and unchallenging.[9] If the Internet is not being used in schools and communities to address the problems faced in those communities, it is not authentic or culturally relevant to students or their families.

Even more important, the Internet can open up access to knowledge beyond the official knowledge of dominant society. In a society that promotes equality, access should be available to all students, regardless of their family incomes; it also should be available to adults in libraries and community centers. The Children's Partnership, an advocacy group for children, has identified the following five key characteristics of a positive information society. It

1. is community driven and meets real community needs;
2. overcomes major content barriers facing the underserved;
3. provides people to help;
4. offers on-line content that is easy to use;
5. is sustainable.[10]

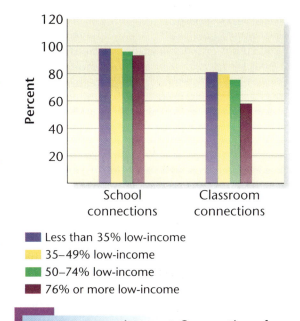

Legend	
■	Less than 35% low-income
■	35–49% low-income
■	50–74% low-income
■	76% or more low-income

FIGURE 4.1 Internet Connections for Students from Low-Income Families

Source: U.S. Census Bureau, *Statistical Abstract of the United States: 2002.* Washington, DC: U.S. Government Printing Office, 2002.

Most schools are now wired to the Internet, but a digital divide still exists among schools in low-income areas.

CROSS-REFERENCE
Technology in the curriculum is also discussed in Chapter 13.

If computers and the Internet are to be used to promote equality, they will have to become accessible to populations that cannot currently afford the equipment, which needs to be updated regularly. However, access alone is not enough. Students need to interact with the technology in authentic settings. As technology becomes a tool for learning in almost all courses, it will be seen as a means to an end rather than an end in itself. If it is used in culturally relevant ways, all students can benefit from its power.

GENDER-SENSITIVE EDUCATION

In the past, most girls and young women were prepared for the traditional female roles of wife and mother rather than for the male roles of wage earner and head of household. They were encouraged to choose the lower-paying "women's jobs" such as teacher, nurse, child care worker, librarian, or health care worker. When they had to become the primary wage earner because of the loss of a husband through divorce or death, women were at a significant disadvantage. They lacked the required skills or experiences necessary for jobs in which they could earn a wage high enough to maintain a comfortable living. However, over the past twenty-five years many women have broken those patterns.

Over 40 percent of the graduates from medical, dentistry, and law schools today are women. Men, on the other hand, are still not as likely as females to work in jobs that were traditionally women's. Society continues to need both males and females who are bright and committed in the education profession.

The rigid definitions of gender roles that remain in some jobs, schools, religions, and ethnic groups limit the options and potential of both males and females. Men and women do not prepare for all professions at the same rate. Only 29 percent of the graduates in theology are women. Fewer than 30 percent of the computer science degrees and 20 percent of the engineering degrees are earned by women. Even though more women are entering high-income professions that historically were dominated by men, women remain overrepresented at the other end of the income scale.

Schools have played an important role in helping more young women realize their potential during this period. Still, not all teachers and other school personnel are sensitive to gender differences that make a difference in learning. In some classrooms, students are separated and sorted by gender, reinforcing the stereotypical gender roles. Boys are expected to behave in one way, girls in another. Boys are expected to excel in sports competition, computer science, mathematics, and science. Girls are expected to perform better in English, reading, writing, and social studies.

If gender equity existed, females and males would be expected to participate at nearly the same rates in all courses, sports, and jobs. Let's look at some of today's realities:

- Girls and boys enroll in mathematics and science at about the same rate, but girls are more likely to stop with algebra II and less likely to take physics.
- Girls do not participate at the same rates as boys in computer courses; they are more likely to be in data entry and word-processing courses.
- Girls enroll in English at higher rates than boys; boys are more likely to be in remedial English courses.
- Both boys and girls from low-income families or ethnic backgrounds other than European are more likely to be in remedial classes than are affluent white students.
- Girls are more likely to be in gifted classes, but they drop out of them at higher rates than boys do.
- Boys and girls are involved in advanced placement and honors courses except for physics at about the same rate.
- Girls earn equal or higher grades in all subjects.
- Males score higher on SAT and ACT tests used for college admission.[11]

To promote gender equity, females should be encouraged to be involved in mathematics, science, and computer science. Males should be encouraged to participate in areas in which they are underrepresented: the fine arts, foreign languages, advanced English, and the humanities.

A gender-sensitive education provides equity to boys and girls, young women and young men. It does not mean that males and females are always treated the same. Different instructional strategies may be needed for the two groups to ensure participation and learning. Understanding cultural differences among females and males will be important in developing appropriate teaching strategies. Not all girls and young women respond to instruction in the same way. Their other microcultural groups intersect with their femaleness in determining their interaction with teachers and effective instructional strategies. Culturally relevant teaching will affirm students' gender and experiences in ways that promote learning for both males and females.

Teachers in gender-sensitive classrooms monitor interactions among girls and boys as well as their own interactions with the two genders. They intervene when necessary to equalize opportunities between them. If boys are not performing as well as girls in language arts or girls are not performing as well in mathematics, the challenge is to develop approaches that will improve their performance.

RELEVANT RESEARCH
Boys and Girls in Performance-Based Science Classrooms

STUDY PURPOSE/QUESTIONS: Do middle school girls and boys share equally in hands-on activities in science classes? Do performance behaviors account for changes in attitudes about science?

STUDY DESIGN: The researchers observed six middle school science classes in five schools twice a month, each month, for one academic year. Observers recorded students' behaviors as they worked with other students on hands-on activities. The number of male and female students was nearly equal and included European Americans, African Americans, Hispanic Americans, and Asian Americans.

STUDY FINDINGS: Both boys and girls exhibited leadership behaviors as shown in providing instructions to other members of the group or explaining a science concept. These leadership behaviors were predictors of positive science attitudes at the end of the year. Students who provided leadership had higher perceptions of their science abilities at the end of the year. Even with girls providing leadership at the same level as boys, girls' perceptions about their science abilities dropped over the school year. Boys' perceptions of their abilities did not change. These perceptual differences did not have any real effect on grades or abilities. The involvement of girls in the hands-on activities did differ from the boys' involvement. Boys tended to manipulate the equipment more than girls did, relegating the girls to following the boys' directions. Possibly because they were not actively engaged in the science activity, girls sometimes became bored with the activity, not fully participating. Thus, the performance-based science classes did not guarantee equal participation in the science activity.

IMPLICATIONS: Developing science activities that are hands-on and performance-based helps to develop positive attitudes about science for both boys and girls. However, teachers need to figure out how to help boys learn to share the science activity more equitably with girls rather than controlling the equipment, shutting girls out of direct involvement in the activity. Otherwise, girls become bored and may develop a perception that they are not as capable in science as the boys. Since boys seem to shut girls out of these activities, teachers might sometimes group girls together to conduct the performance-based activities so they have opportunities to manipulate the equipment themselves.

Source: Jasna Jovanovic and Sally Steinbach King, "Boys and Girls in the Performance-Based Science Classroom: Who's Doing the Performing?," *American Educational Research Journal,* 35(3) (1998), pp. 477–496.

bilingual education

An education strategy that uses English and the native language of students in classroom instruction.

Different educational strategies that draw on students' cultural strengths may be needed to equalize performance in knowledge and skill development for girls and boys. Although competitive strategies are effective for many white boys, most girls and boys from other racial groups are more successful in collaborative settings. Instruction should include hands-on laboratory experiences, collaborative learning, practical applications, group work, and authentic learning to build on the learning styles of different students. The goal is to help both females and males learn the subject matter. Teachers will need to draw on multiple teaching strategies to reach this goal.

EDUCATION FOR LANGUAGE DIVERSITY

A growing number of immigrant students are populating schools in large cities. Even small cities and rural areas are now home to immigrant families and their children. Eight percent of the U.S. population indicates they speak English less than "very well." The growing number of English language learners in U.S. schools calls for educators to understand language learning and how to help students learn English while they are learning math, science, and other subjects.

Differences between the languages used at home and at school can lead to dissonance between students, their families, and school officials. Many students who enter school with limited English skills are not only trying to learn a second language but also adjusting to a new culture. This is particularly true for recent immigrants. Figures 4.2 and 4.3 show the percentage of students who speak a language other than English at home and have difficulty with English in school.

The dropout rate for English language learners is two to two and a half times as great as for other students of the same age. Those who are most likely to drop out of school do not feel that they are part of the broader school culture. According to the National Association for the Education of Young Children (NAEYC), the problem for young children is the feeling of loneliness, fear, and abandonment that they may feel when they are thrust into settings that isolate them from their home community and language. The loss of children's home language may result in the disruption of family communication patterns, which may lead to the loss of intergenerational wisdom, damage to individual and community esteem, and children's potential nonmastery of their home language or English.[12]

NAEYC urges teachers to encourage "the development of children's home language while fostering the acquisition of English."[13] But not everyone agrees with NAEYC and other education associations that support **bilingual education.** Members of Congress, state legislators, and local school board members debate strategies for teaching English language learners.

The debate centers on whether to use students' native languages in instruction. Many school districts and some states require bilingual education if a specific number of students who speak the same native language are enrolled in a school. This approach requires teachers who are fluent in both English and the native language.

There are at least six different approaches to teaching academic content to English language learners.[14] Sheltered instruction, newcomer programs, and transitional bilingual education approaches are assimilationist in that they are designed to integrate students into the dominant or mainstream culture. Although the native language may be used for in-

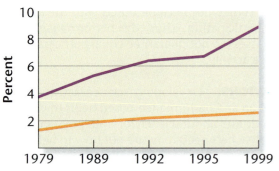

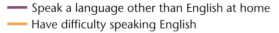

— Speak a language other than English at home
— Have difficulty speaking English

FIGURE 4.2 Students Who Speak a Language Other Than English at Home and Have Difficulty Speaking English

Source: U.S. Census Bureau, *Statistical Abstract of the United States: 2002.* Washington, DC: U.S. Government Printing Office, 2002, Table 217.

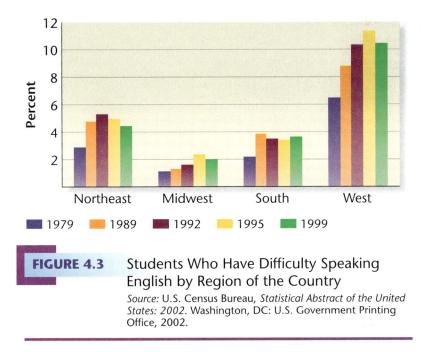

FIGURE 4.3 Students Who Have Difficulty Speaking English by Region of the Country

Source: U.S. Census Bureau, *Statistical Abstract of the United States: 2002.* Washington, DC: U.S. Government Printing Office, 2002.

struction early in the program, the goal is to move to English-only instruction as soon as possible, usually between one and four years. In sheltered instruction, teachers teach the academic subjects at the same time that they are teaching English to students. The newcomer programs are designed for new immigrants who have limited or no experience with English and often have limited literary skills in their native language. These programs are sometimes found within a school; some school districts have one or more schools specifically for new immigrants. The most successful programs are those in which students attend for as many as four years.[15] Teachers in these two approaches—sheltered and newcomer—should have knowledge and skills in **English as a second language (ESL).**

In transitional bilingual education, academic subjects are taught in the native language as students learn English. Gradually, more and more of the instruction is conducted in English. After a few years, students in transitional bilingual education move into classes with instruction in English only. Developmental bilingual education, by contrast, supports bilingualism and literacy in both English and the native language. Both English and the native language have equal status, and both are used for instructional purposes.

Two immersion language programs use a second language for instruction and help students understand and appreciate a second culture while maintaining their own native culture and language. Foreign/second language immersion is designed for English speakers who want to learn a second language in a classroom in which Spanish, French, Japanese, Farsi, or another language is used for instruction. Two-way immersion is used to develop bilingualism in all students as language training is integrated with academic instruction. Classes usually have an equal number of English speakers and speakers of another language.

As a school decides the appropriate approach for teaching English language learners, parents must be involved in the discussions and decisions. Together, educators and parents will have to decide whether they want to promote bilingualism among all students or only among the English language learners. Is the goal for English language learners to become competent in both English and

English as a second language (ESL)

An educational strategy for teaching English to speakers of other languages without the use of the native language for instruction.

Communicating with Parents of English Language Learners

At least 13 percent of all people over five years old in the United States use a language other than English at home. Many parents who do not speak English fluently are reluctant to visit schools because of their limited English skills. The reasons for not meeting with teachers are not that parents do not care about their children and their education. This dissonance between schools and parents is further exacerbated by the inability of most teachers to understand the language and culture of parents. Parents often are embarrassed and misunderstood by school officials. They sometimes cannot attend school events or conferences because they are working and employers will not give them the time off. Or they may have young children at home who cannot be left alone while the parent goes to school.

How then can teachers communicate with parents about their children and their social and academic development in school? Teachers might know only English and the parents only Spanish, Farsi, French, Japanese, Hmong, or Swahili. Even if the teacher visited the student's home, communications would be limited and possibly misinterpreted. Written notes or phone messages in English would have to be translated by parents, or for them by the child, placing the burden again on the family.

Some schools have hired bilingual teachers and aides who can help bridge the language differences.

When the number of bilingual education professionals is limited, schools may hire community liaisons who work with parents and teachers to bridge language and cultural differences. These community liaisons may accompany teachers on home visits and parents on school visits. These approaches may begin to affirm the diversity of a community and help it to move away from a cultural deficit approach in which students' cultures and languages are not valued and must be compensated. For example, some schools have begun to arrange transportation for parents to attend school events. Others are using ESL to teach English to parents before and after school. Students are the benefactors when families and educators work together to promote student learning and social development.

- How will you communicate with parents who speak a language different from your own?
- How will you learn about the resources available in your school district to assist you in working with families whose primary language is not English?
- How can you ensure that you don't misunderstand parents when their language and culture are different from your own?
- What responsibility do teachers have to understand and become comfortable in a culture other than their own?

Companion Website

To answer these questions on-line and e-mail your answers to your professor, go to Chapter 4 of the companion website (**www.ablongman.com/johnson13e**) and click on Professional Dilemma.

> Never doubt that a small group of thoughtful, committed citizens can change the world. Indeed it is the only thing that ever has.
>
> **Margaret Mead**

CROSS-REFERENCE
Teachers as change agents and leaders from a philosophical perspective are discussed in Chapter 11.

their native language or to move into English-only instruction as soon as possible? Each approach has learning implications for students and cost implications for school systems.

TEACHERS AS SOCIAL ACTIVISTS

Multicultural education requires educators to be active participants in the educational process. Social justice, democracy, power, and equity are more than concepts to be discussed in class; they are guides for action in the classroom, school, and community. Educators become advocates not only for their own empowerment but also for that of students and other powerless groups.

■ THINKING CRITICALLY

Educators who think critically ask questions about why inequities are occurring in their classrooms and schools. They wonder why girls are responding differently to the science lesson than boys. But they don't stop with wondering; they explore and try alternatives to engage the girls in the subject matter. They realize that teaching equitably does not mean teaching everyone the same way. (Nor, however, does it mean using thirty different lesson plans tailored to the individual learning style and cultural background of each student.) Teaching equitably may mean helping students function effectively in multiple cultural settings used by the students in the classroom. Teachers who think critically figure out ways to build on the diverse cultural backgrounds and experiences of the students, acknowledge the value of that diversity, and help them all learn.

Critical thinkers are able to challenge the philosophy and practices of the dominant society that are not supportive of equity, democracy, and social justice. They are open to alternative views; they are not limited by narrow parochialism that is based on absolutes and the notion of one right way. They question content for accuracy and biases, and they value multiple perspectives. They seek explanations for the educational meanings and consequences of race, class, and gender.

■ MODELING EQUITY IN THE CLASSROOM

Caring and fairness are two qualities that students praise when describing successful teachers. Students know whether teachers view them as special or as incompetent or worthless. Teacher perceptions may be based on a student's personal characteristics; sometimes they are based on group membership. A teacher may feel that homeless children who smell and arrive in dirty clothes have little chance of success. Teachers may pity children from one-parent homes and blame their lack of academic achievement on their not having two parents. Teachers may ignore English language learners until they learn English. Are these fair practices?

Teachers must model equity in the classroom if education that is multicultural is to become a reality.

A school that provides a multicultural education will not tolerate such unjust practices by teachers. Both the classroom and the school will be models of democracy in which all students are treated equitably and fairly. In such a school, teachers and instructional leaders confront their own biases and develop strategies for overcoming them in their own interactions with students and colleagues. They learn to depend on one another for assistance, both in developing a culturally relevant curriculum and in ensuring that students are not subject to discrimination. As a result, students learn to respect differences and to interact within and across ethnic and cultural groups as they struggle for social justice in the school and the community.

Teachers sometimes give more help to some students than to others. They might praise some students while correcting and disciplining others. Their expectations for academic success may differ depending on students' family income or ethnic group. However, most teachers do not deliberately set out to discriminate against certain students, especially in any harmful way. The problem is that everyone has been raised in a racist, sexist, and classist society in which biases are so embedded that it is difficult for people to recognize anything other than the very overt signs. Teachers often need others to point out their discriminatory practices.

CROSS-REFERENCE
Reflection is also addressed in Chapter 1.

A good pattern to begin to develop even now, early in your teacher education program, is to reflect on your practice and the practice of teachers you observe. Among the questions that you might ask are:

- Are students from different gender, economic, and ethnic groups treated differently? What are the differences?
- Are there fewer discipline and learning problems among the students who are from the same background as the teacher? What is contributing to the differences?
- Do the least advantaged students receive the most assistance from the teacher? What are the differences in the instruction given to various students?
- How well are male and female students from different ethnic and racial groups performing on the state standardized tests? How well are students with disabilities performing? How is the school making test-taking accommodations for English language learners and students with disabilities?

A key to ensuring that interactions with students are equitable is the ability to recognize one's own biases and make appropriate adjustments. Educators must be able to admit that they sometimes make mistakes. An ability to reflect on one's mistakes and why they occurred should lead to better teaching.

■ TEACHING FOR SOCIAL JUSTICE

Washing one's hands of the conflict between the powerful and the powerless means to side with the powerful, not to be neutral.

Paulo Freire

Culturally relevant teaching helps students struggle in class with social problems and issues that many students face daily in their lives both within and outside of school. Racism, sexism, classism, prejudice, and discrimination are felt differently by students of color than by members of the dominant group. Anger, denial, guilt, and affirmation of identity are critical elements of learning about and struggling with the pernicious practices that permeate most institutions. Although it is sometimes difficult to discuss these issues in classrooms, doing so means they are confronted in a system based on diversity and equality.

Most students of color, females, low-income students, students with disabilities, and gay students have probably already experienced discrimination in some aspect of their lives. They may have not acknowledged it, or they may be angry or frustrated by it. On the other hand, many students from the dominant group have never experienced discrimination and often do not believe that it exists. In most cases, they do not see themselves as advantaged; they do not think that they receive any more benefits from society than anyone else. These students will have a difficult time fighting social injustices if they have neither experienced them nor become aware of their existence. Are they receiving a good education if they are never exposed to the injustices that do exist or helped to confront their own biases?

In teaching for social justice, teachers help students understand the inequalities, oppression, and power struggles that are realities in society. But this kind of teaching does not stop there. It provides hope for a world that is more equitable and socially just. Students and teachers become engaged in confronting injustice and working to remove the obstacles that prevent equality as an academic subject is studied. Maxine Green writes:

Teaching for social justice helps students struggle through social problems and discrimination that many people face daily.

> To teach for social justice is to teach for enhanced perception and imaginative explorations, for the recognition of social wrongs, of sufferings, of pestilences wherever and whenever they arise. It is to find models in literature and in history of the indignant ones, the ones forever ill at ease, and the loving ones who have taken the side of the victims of pestilences, whatever their names or places of origin. It is to teach so that the young may be awakened to the joy of working for transformation in the smallest places, so that they may become healers and change their worlds.[16]

Students learn to apply the knowledge and skills they are learning to a local, regional, or global issue. The learning becomes authentic as it is related to the world that students care about. Students can take on community projects that examine pollution in their neighborhoods, political stances in their regional area, or the cost of food in their neighborhood versus another part of town. Students and teachers who tackle social justice as an integral part of their classroom work are providing multicultural education and reconstructionism. They are doing more than learning about the world; they are also working toward making it better for those who are least advantaged.

GLOBAL PERSPECTIVES

Social Justice in the Canadian Context

As early as 1971, Canada had adopted a national government policy that supported multicultural ideals in education. This action was followed by each province developing its own version of the policy in order to bring harmony across ethnic and racial groups. Currently, public debate is questioning the concept of multiculturalism as some citizens call for a return to assimilation, restriction of immigration, and upholding the traditional values of the dominant group. Amidst these attacks, researchers are arguing whether the traditional multicultural education should be replaced with antiracist education. Other scholars "have depicted social justice education as a highly divisive field of study, describing conflicts between MC [multicultural] and AR [antiracist] camps in dichotomous, oppositional terms."[17]

The supporters of antiracist education focus on the structure of the education system and on power relationships between the dominant European Canadian society and the powerless indigenous and immigrant groups. The traditional multicultural model in Canada has included short-term programs and supplemental curriculum materials to help students understand the cultures of different groups in the country. The antiracist camp accuses the multiculturalists of not critically addressing issues of oppression and racism in the country.

For the most part, social justice activists are aware of the academic debates and find them relevant to their work. However, while the academic debates flourish, most social justice activists are incorporating aspects of both antiracist and multicultural education into their work in schools.[18]

SUMMARY

Education that is multicultural is based on the principles of democracy, social justice, and equality. The goal is to ensure that all students participate equally in the education system. Educators value the diversity of students as they strive to provide educational equality in which all students are provided challenging and stimulating learning experiences.

The school itself is a cultural system with its own rules and traditions. Culturally relevant teaching occurs in schools that are multicultural as teachers incorporate the culture of students into the curriculum. Students' voices become an important part of classroom dialogue.

Bridging the digital divide between students who have access to computers and the Internet and those who do not is one of the challenges faced by educators in providing eq-

uity and social justice. A second challenge includes the delivery of gender-sensitive education that draws on different educational strategies to help male and female students perform at the highest possible levels. A third is the development of strategies for teaching English language learners that vary according to the goals of a school and community.

The time that teacher candidates spend in college to prepare to teach only begins to initiate them to working with students from diverse cultural backgrounds or delivering multicultural education. Beginning and experienced teachers will continue to learn about diversity, social justice, and equality and their implications for teaching and learning while they are in classrooms.

DISCUSSION QUESTIONS

1. Diversity, equality, and social justice are the major tenets of multicultural education. What conditions and practices in schools suggest that these tenets are not the principles that undergird the educational system as you know it? What are signs that these tenets are being addressed in schools?

2. Democratic schools validate the voices of students as they actively participate in their education. How do you think students voices can be effectively included in the classroom? What are the potential benefits and perceived dangers of allowing student voices to be an integral part of instruction?

3. Many people think multicultural education is primarily for students of color and English language learners. Which students do you think should be served through

multicultural education? Justify its importance to students who are members of the dominant group.

4. Reflect on your elementary and secondary education and identify ways in which your teachers delivered a culturally relevant curriculum. Would students from cultural backgrounds other than your own agree with your assessment? Why or why not?

5. Policymakers and politicians disagree on the importance of helping English language learners maintain their native languages. What is your position on this issue? What programs would schools provide to ELLs if your position became policy in a school district? What results would you expect if your position became a policy?

JOURNAL ENTRIES

1. Think about your high school and college experiences. How have they helped you clarify your thinking about racism, sexism, and classism in society and/or in schooling? Have they reinforced stereotypes? Or have they helped you understand how race, gender, and

class affect many policies and practices that affect one's life? Write your conclusions in your journal.

2. Discuss your perceptions of being a teacher who is a social activist. Why (or why not) is being a social activist an appropriate role for a teacher?

PORTFOLIO DEVELOPMENT

1. For the subject and level that you plan to teach, describe appropriate culturally relevant content that could be included in curriculum units.

2. Identify ways that social justice might be incorporated into your teaching. Explain the factors that might lead you to use or not use this approach in your own teaching.

3. Identify a list of five to ten criteria for determining whether educators in a school have seriously and successfully attended to diversity, equality, and social justice. Include a statement of the things you would observe to know that each criterion is being met.

PREPARING FOR CERTIFICATION

■ TEACHING FOR EQUALITY

1. One of the topics covered in the Praxis II Principles of Teaching and Learning (PLT) test is "structuring lessons based on the needs and characteristics of diverse populations." In this chapter, you were encouraged to develop culturally relevant teaching skills, including building on cultural context, centering on the cultures of students, and validating student voices. Think about the subject or grade level that you plan to teach. How might you incorporate these three principles into your future teaching?

2. Answer the following multiple-choice question, which is similar to items in Praxis and other state certification tests. If you are unsure of the answer, reread the Equality section of this chapter.

   Jim Blanchard is running for the local school board. In his campaign speech, he says, "I believe that everyone should be able to finish school, attend college, and get a well-paying job. All it takes is hard work, diligence, and persistence. It doesn't matter if you are rich or poor, black or white. In this country, everyone can succeed." Mr. Blanchard's perspective is most consistent with the concept of

   (A) equal educational opportunity
   (B) opportunity to learn standards
   (C) meritocracy
   (D) equality of results

3. Answer the following short-answer question, which is similar to items in Praxis and other state certification tests. After you've completed your written response, use the scoring guide in the ETS *Test at a Glance* materials to assess your response. Can you revise your response to improve your score?

   The hidden curriculum is the informal curriculum that defines the behaviors and attitudes of students and teachers. Give two examples of the hidden curriculum. Describe how each example might affect students from varied backgrounds or cultures differently.

WEBSITES

www.edchange.org/multicultural/index.html The Multicultural Pavilion links teachers with others who are dealing with issues related to multicultural education.

www.nabe.org The website of the National Association for Bilingual Education, which promotes educational excellence and equity through bilingual education, includes legislation, policies, and research related to language diversity.

www.naeyc.org The website of the National Association for the Education of Young Children provides a number of resources on teaching preschoolers and primary students from diverse racial and language groups as well as students with disabilities.

www.nameorg.org The website of the National Association for Multicultural Education includes definitions and policies for educators working in the field of multicultural education.

www.rethinkingschools.org The Rethinking Schools website was designed by a group of teachers who wanted to improve education in their own classrooms and schools as well as to help shape school reform that is humane, caring, multiracial, and democratic.

www.splcenter.org The Southern Poverty Law Center combats hate, intolerance, and discrimination through education and litigation against hate groups. It publishes *Teaching Tolerance,* which is available at no cost to teachers, and numerous other teaching resources.

FURTHER READING

Anti-Defamation League. (2000). *Hate Hurts: How Children Learn and Unlearn Prejudice.* New York: Author. A guide for parents and educators on understanding and respecting differences and fighting hate against others. The booklet includes stories about children who have experienced hate and provides guidelines for challenging biased materials.

Delpit, Lisa. (1995). *Other People's Children: Cultural Conflict in the Classroom.* New York: New Press. A helpful resource in understanding the culture and language patterns of students and their communities.

Grant, Carl A., and Sleeter, Christine E. (1999). *Turning on Learning: Five Approaches for Multicultural Teaching Plans for Race, Class, Gender, and Disability* (2nd ed.). Columbus, OH: Merrill. A companion to *Making Choices for Multicultural Education: Five Approaches to Race, Class, and Gender,* providing lesson plans and illustrations for incorporating multicultural education into the curriculum and classroom.

Multicultural Perspectives: The magazine of the National Association for Multicultural Education. A quarterly publication designed to advance the conversation about multicultural education. Each issue includes reviews of new resources for teachers.

Rethinking Schools. A news journal on teaching for equity and social justice published by Rethinking Schools. An activist publication written by teachers, parents, and students who care about equity and social justice in urban schools. Articles address current topics affecting students and schools and strategies for reforming classrooms and schools.

Teaching Tolerance: A Magazine for Teachers by the Southern Poverty Law Center. A publication for and by teachers for fighting hate and intolerance and fostering equity, respect, and understanding across diverse groups.

THEMES OF THE TIMES!

expect the world®
The New York Times
nytimes.com

Companion Website

Expand your knowledge of the concepts discussed in this chapter by reading current and historical articles from the *New York Times* by visiting the Themes of the Times! section of the companion website (**www.ablongman.com/johnson13e**).

NOTES

Unless otherwise indicated, the data reported in this chapter are from the U.S. Census Bureau, *Statistical Abstract of the United States: 2002.* Washington, DC: U.S. Government Printing Office, 2002.

1. Donna M. Gollnick and Philip C. Chinn, *Multicultural Education in a Pluralistic Society,* 5th ed. New York: Macmillan, 2001.
2. National Conference for Community and Justice, *Taking America's Pulse: A Summary Report of the National Conference Survey on Inter-Group Relations.* New York: Author, 1994.
3. Recruiting New Teachers, Inc., *The Essential Profession: A National Survey of Public Attitudes toward Teaching, Educational Opportunity and School Reform.* Belmont, MA: Author, 1998.
4. Stephen J. Rose, *Social Stratification in the United States: The New American Profile Poster.* New York: New Press, 2000.
5. Andrew Sum, Irwin Kirsch, and Robert Taggart, *The Twin Challenges of Mediocrity and Inequality: Literacy in the U.S. from an International Perspective.*

Princeton, NJ: Educational Testing Service, 2002, pp. 31–32.
6. Children's Defense Fund, "Key Facts about Education" Washington, DC: Author, June 12, 2003. Available at www.childrensdefense.org/keyfacts_education.htm.
7. Sharon Nelson-Barber and Elise Trumbull Estrin, "Bringing Native American Perspectives to Mathematics and Science Teaching," *Theory into Practice, 34*(3) (1995), pp. 174–185.
8. Worldwatch Institute, *State of the World 2000.* New York: W. W. Norton, 2000.
9. American Association of University Women (AAUW), *Tech-Savvy: Educating Girls in the New Computer Age.* Washington, DC: Author, 2000.
10. The Children's Partnership, *Online Content for Low-Income and Underserved Americans: The Digital Divide's New Frontier.* Santa Monica, CA: Author, 2000.
11. AAUW, 2000.
12. National Association for the Education of Young Children (NAEYC), *Responding to Linguistic and Cultural Diversity—Recommendations for Effective Early Childhood Education.* Washington, DC: Author, 1995.

13. Ibid, 1995.
14. Fred Genesee, ed., *Program Alternatives for Linguistically Diverse Students.* Washington, DC: Center for Research on Education, Diversity and Excellence, 1999.
15. Ibid.
16. Maxine Greene, "Introduction: Teaching for Social Justice," in William Ayers, Jean Ann Hunt, and Therese Quinn, eds., *Teaching for Social Justice.* New York: New Press, 1998, p. xlv.
17. Darren E. Lund, "Educating for Social Justice: Making Sense of Multicultural and Antiracist Theory and Practice with Canadian Teacher Activists," *Intercultural Education, 14*(1) (March 2003), pp. 3–16.
18. Ibid.

Governance and Support of American Education

Viewing Education through Organizational Lenses

 In Part III, you will view schools and the U.S. system of education through three different lenses. The first is structural, the focus being on how schools and school districts are organized. The second lens places the focus on the financing of education. Money has to be found to operate all the schools, which means taxation in a variety of forms. Through the third lens, we will view schools in terms of the laws of the United States. Schools are legally constituted entities. As professionals, teachers and administrators must know and understand how laws, policies, and court cases delimit what they can, should, and must do.

Focus Questions

The following questions will help you focus your learning as you read Part III:

1. What are the role and authority of the school principal? Who supervises the school principal?

2. Who is in charge of the school district: the superintendent or the school board?

3. Does a school district have to do what the state department of education says? Can the federal government tell schools what to do?

4. Property taxes have been the major source of revenue for schools. Is there something wrong with this?

5. Which three amendments to the U.S. Constitution provide the legal basis for public schools?

6. Can public funds be used to support students in parochial schools?

7. How is equal opportunity addressed in U.S. law?

8. Do school students in the United States have the same rights as adult citizens?

9. What protections, if any, do nontenured teachers have?

10. Is it legal for teachers to strike?

11. Do teachers and school administrators have to obtain a search warrant before they can search a student?

Organizing and Paying for American Education

Education in the News

Study Finds Skimpy Evidence on Vouchers

By Tamara Henry, *USA Today*, December 7, 2001

WASHINGTON—IN THE HEATED DEBATE OVER PRIVATE SCHOOL vouchers and charter schools, a new analysis by Rand researchers says both opponents and supporters lack evidence to back their claims.

Rand analysts Brian Gill, P. Michael Timpane and Dominic J. Brewer, in a 4-year study released Thursday, examined hundreds of reports and studies and concluded that "so many questions remain unanswered that neither the hopes of choice supporters nor the fears of its opponents can currently be confirmed." They add that "even the strongest evidence" is based on programs that have been operating only a short period, are too small or have uncertain results. Rand is a think tank. Its analysts focus on education.

Vouchers are financial grants given to students—mainly from low-income families—to attend public, private or parochial schools. Charter schools are semiautonomous public schools run by parents, teachers or others.

Proponents argue that the competition from school choice programs would force traditional public schools to improve. Opponents say vouchers and charter schools would skim off highly motivated students and their money.

The Rand study finds that a program's design can have a major impact and that funding correlates to the success. Rand researchers evaluated academic achievement, equitable access, integration and preparation for civic responsibilities to find:

- Charter school achievement results are mixed, but performance improves after the first year. Blacks benefit slightly, but all others do no better or worse on average. Researchers say long-term effects on academic skills in both voucher and charter programs are as yet unexamined.
- Parents are happy with the school choices.
- Students with disabilities are underrepresented.
- Virtually nothing is yet known about whether choice programs help students become responsible, democratically active citizens.

Reactions varied: "The study is more evidence that voucher schools are woefully unaccountable to the very people who are paying for these programs," says Marcus Egan of the National School Boards Association.

But Jeanne Allen of the Center for Education Reform notes that the Rand analysis shows parents are satisfied.

INTASC   Learning Outcomes

After reading and studying this chapter, you should be able to:

1. Describe the organizational structure of schools, school districts, and the authority relationships among schools, states, and the federal government. (INTASC 10: Collaboration)

2. Analyze pro and con arguments presented for increasing school choice. (INTASC 10: Collaboration)

3. Describe the relationship of teachers to their principal and how the responsibilities of the principal relate to those of the school district superintendent and the school board. (INTASC 10: Collaboration)

4. Summarize the key sources of funding for public schools and issues related to overreliance on any one of these sources. (INTASC 9: Reflection; INTASC 10: Collaboration)

5. Describe the underlying theme related to the large number of states that have court cases dealing with school finance. (INTASC 9: Reflection; INTASC 10: Collaboration)

6. Compare the spending for public schools in the United States with that of other developed countries. (INTASC 9: Reflection; INTASC 10: Collaboration)

School-Based Observations

You may see these learning outcomes in action during your visits to schools:

1. Find or develop an organization chart for the school. Place the names of people and their roles on the chart. For one or more people in each role group (e.g., teacher, library media specialist, resource teacher, secretary, cafeteria worker), find out who supervises and evaluates them. The purpose is to determine the line and staff relationships. Which people/roles have multiple organizational relationships?

2. Seek an opportunity to study a school budget. Determine the different sources of revenue (e.g., local, state, federal, grants, activity fees). What are the biggest line-item expenditures? Are some monies discretionary for teachers? Note that in most schools, especially high schools, there will be a surprising number of activities that generate cash. Inquire about the implications of having cash on hand, and ask how these amounts are secured and what policies guide their uses.

Several big ideas about education are developed in this chapter. The first addresses the American education system's structure. Although complex, school organization has an explainable pattern. On top of the local pattern is the organization of education within each state. The federal government also influences the way in which schools operate, and so a brief description of its involvement in and influence over schooling is presented. Another big idea developed in this chapter deals with the complexity of school finance. Key elements and critical issues in the financing of education make up the second topic. The funds to finance schooling come from several different sources. Each of these sources brings with it certain advantages and particular problems.

THE STRUCTURE OF THE AMERICAN EDUCATION SYSTEM

Descriptions of the U.S. education system generally start at the *top* of the organization chart, with the U.S. Department of Education; move *down* through the state structures; and ultimately arrive at the school district and school levels. This *top-down* approach reflects, in an organizational sense, the fact that it is easier to understand the pieces when you first have a view of the whole. Also, the top-down approach indicates that one has more authority and responsibility the further up one is in the structure. In many ways, this is true. However, in education, unlike many businesses, the "bottom" is composed of professionals (teachers and principals) who know as much or more about their business as those who are more removed from the day-to-day life in classrooms. Therefore, teachers and principals correctly argue, they should have a great deal of say in determining what happens

TABLE 5.1   The Policy-to-Practice Continuum in the U.S. Education System

Policy					Practice
Federal	State	Intermediate	District	School	Classroom
President	Governor	Director	Superintendent	Principal	Teacher
Congress	Legislature	Board	Board	Site council	Students
Secretary	Chief state school officer			Teachers	
U.S. Department of Education	State department of education		District office staff		

with their students on a day-to-day basis. Our decision to start this chapter with a description of schools, rather than at the federal level, is in some ways making a symbolic statement that teachers can be viewed as being at the top.

To avoid many of the problems implied in a vertical (top-down) picture of the education system, some theorists have advocated a horizontal perspective, as represented in Table 5.1. One important emphasis of this horizontal **policy-to-practice continuum** is that for education to improve, the agencies and people at each point along the continuum have to do their job well. A second critical feature is that all have to trust people and agencies at other points along the continuum. This means, for example, that teachers have to develop an understanding of the functions and purposes of other parts of the education system. Teachers cannot stay isolated in their classrooms, unaware of the issues and expectations of the school, the school district, the state, and increasingly the federal government. At the other end of the continuum, it is important that policymakers learn more about the work of teachers and what goes on in schools.

Another important organizational concept to keep in mind is the difference between line and staff relationships. In any organization, some people will have the job of being supervisors, bosses, managers, or directors. Other people will report to these persons. The supervisor typically has the authority, at least to some degree, to direct, monitor, and evaluate the work of the subordinate. When one person has this type of authority over another, there is a **line relationship.** But when there is no formal supervisory authority of one person over the other, they have a **staff relationship.** This distinction becomes important in education because in many instances it is not clear or absolute who has the authority or responsibility to direct the work of others. For example, teachers, as professionals, can legitimately claim more independence than can employees of other organizations. But teachers are not completely free to do whatever they want. If they were, the system of education would break down, at least as it is experienced by the students who must move through it.

◼ THE ORGANIZATION OF SCHOOLS

The basic building block of the U.S. education system is the school. To an amazing extent, schools are organized in the same way in each state. In fact, schools are organized pretty much the same in other countries too.

Each school consists of a set of classrooms, with corridors for the movement of students, and a central office. It has one or more large spaces for a cafeteria and gymnasium/auditorium. The school has outside spaces for a playground, staff parking, and a driveway for dropping off and picking up students. Wherever you go, you will find this basic architecture.

policy-to-practice continuum

The range of roles and responsibilities for education, from the development of national policy to teaching in classrooms.

line relationship

An organizational arrangement in which a subordinate is directly responsible to a supervisor.

staff relationship

An organizational arrangement in which one party is not under the direct control or authority of another.

This typical design of schools is frequently criticized for resembling an egg crate. If you viewed a school building with the roof off, you would see that it resembled an egg carton: a series of cells or pockets with routes running between them. Some educational critics see this architecture as interfering with the need to introduce new educational practices. For example, the walls restrict communication between teachers and channel the flow of student traffic.

Even when a school is built with modest attempts to change the interior space, teachers and students are able to preserve the egg-crate concept. For example, you may have visited an elementary school that had an open-space design. Instead of self-contained classrooms, there might be an open floor plan equivalent in size to three or four classrooms. However, if you observed the arrangement of furniture, bookshelves, and screens, you probably noted that teachers and students had constructed zones and areas that were equivalent to three or four self-contained classrooms.

This is not meant to criticize teachers for how they have adapted to new school architectures; rather, it is meant to point out how the organization of the space parallels the activities of the people who use it. There are many good reasons for organizing schools around self-contained classrooms. And in the case of the open-space concept, the noise from three or four teachers and 90 to 120 children can be so disruptive that little learning can occur. One key to the successful use of open-space plans, then, is to be sure the building is designed in ways that control and dampen noise.

The physical arrangement of a school into classrooms has organizational as well as instructional implications. For example, it is easy for teachers to be isolated in their classrooms. This geographic isolation contributes to their not knowing about or becoming engaged with issues that affect the whole school. Geographic isolation can affect the school as a whole too. The school staff might not be aware of community concerns or of what is going on in other schools across the district. Teachers and administrators must make deliberate efforts to learn about other parts of the education system.

> *A school can create a "coherent" environment, a climate, more potent than any single influence—teacher, class, family, neighborhood—so potent for at least six hours a day it can override almost everything else in the lives of children.*
>
> **Ron Edmonds**

THE ROLES AND RESPONSIBILITIES OF PRINCIPALS

The principal is in charge of the school. In law the principal is the final authority at the school. The principal is typically responsible for instructional leadership, community relationships, staff (including teachers, secretaries, and custodians), teacher selection and evaluation, pupil personnel, building and grounds, budgets, administration of personnel, provisions of contracts, administration of the attendance center office, and business management. The principal has a line relationship with the school district superintendent. In larger school districts, the principal may have an intermediate supervisor, such as an assistant superintendent or a director of elementary or secondary education.

Principals' tasks and responsibilities are expanding. For example, there has been a push to increase teacher and parent participation in making school decisions. This pressure has led to the creation of special committees of teachers and parents to work with the principal. This approach is called **site-based decision making (SBDM),** or school-based management (SBM). SBDM permits an individual school within a district to be more involved in decisions related to the educational operations of

The principal is responsible for the actions of all school personnel, as well as working with committees of parents and teachers.

that school—for example, budgeting, personnel selection, and curriculum design. This increase in decision-making authority may be granted by the school board or the state. An example of the latter is the Kentucky Education Reform Act, which includes a mandate for SBDM in all public schools in the state. Working with SBDM committees places new demands on the principal's time and generates new expectations for the types of leadership skills a principal needs to possess or develop.

site-based decision making (SBDM)

A school governance process that gives greater voice to teachers, parents, and community representatives in school policies.

ASSISTANT PRINCIPALS

Larger elementary schools and most junior high schools, middle schools, and high schools have one or more additional administrators. Normally, they are called assistant principals, although sometimes in high schools they are titled vice principals. Large high schools will have several assistant or vice principals and some other administrators that have "director" titles, such as director of athletics and director of counseling. These administrators share the tasks of the principal and provide additional avenues of communication between teachers, students, staff, parents, community, and the district office. In elementary schools, the job differentiation between the assistant principal and the principal is less clear, and both administrators will be a part of most operations. In the high school setting, specific roles and tasks will frequently be assigned to the different assistant principals. For example, one assistant principal might handle discipline or the evaluation of some teachers. In most districts, each teacher must be observed formally. This activity takes more time than the principal has available, so the assistant principal(s) observes some teachers. Usually, the principal concentrates on observing the new teachers because he or she makes the recommendation on rehiring beginning teachers.

DEPARTMENT HEADS AND TEAM LEADERS

Elementary schools normally have another, less formal level of leadership: grade-level or team leaders. These are full-time teachers who assume a communication and coordination role for their grade level(s) or team. Junior high schools and high schools have department chairs. Normally, departments are organized around the major subject areas (mathematics, science, English, and social studies) and the cocurricula (athletics and music). Teachers are members of one of the departments, and regular meetings are held to plan curriculum and to facilitate communication. In middle schools, the leaders of interdisciplinary teams likely serve in the same way. In each case, these department heads or team leaders meet with the principal from time to time and meet regularly with their teachers.

TEACHERS

The single largest group of adults in the school is the teachers. A typical elementary school has from 15 to 35 teachers, and a large high school has more than 100. Teachers are busy in their classrooms working with their students, and this is where the egg-crate architecture of schools can be a problem. Unless special mechanisms are used, such as team leaders or department chairs, individual teachers easily become isolated from the school as a whole. The self-contained classroom architecture and the work of attending to twenty to forty students in the classroom give each teacher little time or opportunity to communicate with other adults. As a consequence, the principal and all the teachers need to work hard with the other members of the school staff to facilitate communication. All must make an effort to work together to continually improve the school.

SCHOOL SUPPORT STAFF

A school has other personnel who support the administrators and teachers. One of the most important of these supporting roles is filled by the school secretary. Every teacher and principal will advise you to be sure to develop a good working relationship with the school secretary, who is at the nerve center of the running of the school. When a student has a problem, when a teacher needs some materials, when the principal wants a piece of information from the files, or when a student teacher wants to know about parking a car, the first person to contact is the school secretary. Another useful education professional in most schools is the library media specialist. This person is a good instructional resource for teachers and certainly is key to students being able to access information and become skilled in using technology. A third important resource is the custodians. The cleanliness of your classroom and school depend on the efforts of the custodians, and they also can be helpful to teachers in locating supplies and moving furniture. Keep in mind that they observe and talk with students. Frequently, custodians and other support staff will know about some-

RELEVANT RESEARCH
Does Class Size Make a Difference?

STUDY PURPOSE/QUESTION: Do students in the early grades who are assigned to smaller classes learn more each year and do better in their later years of schooling?

STUDY DESIGN: Beginning in the mid-1980s, the Tennessee legislature funded a multiyear study, which has become known as the Tennessee STAR (Student/ Teacher Achievement Ratio) Project. This long-term, statewide study included 79 schools, 328 classrooms, and about 6,300 students. Student achievement was compared in three types of classrooms: *standard classes* (a certificated teacher and more than 20 students); *supplemented classes* (one teacher and a full-time, noncertified teacher's aide); and *small classes* (one teacher and about 15 students). Since that time this study has continued to develop and is now seen as the "largest, best-designed field experiment that has ever appeared for education" (p. 6). Initially, student achievement was assessed in each of their first years in school. The students were then followed into the higher grades and their academic records were monitored.

STUDY FINDINGS: Results from *standard classes* and *supplemented classes* were quite similar. This means that there were few advantages in terms of student achievement from simply having untrained aides in classrooms. Results in the *small classes* were noteworthy. There were substantially higher levels of student achievement. The gains were also higher for those students who were in small classes for more years. In addition, the small class advantages were found for all types of students, and they were quite similar for boys and girls. Students from poverty, African American students, and inner-city students had even greater gains.

The findings from the follow-up studies as the small-class students moved into secondary schools are more significant. The small-class students earned better grades, fewer dropped out of school, fewer were retained, and once they were in high school, more took foreign languages and advanced-level courses, more were found to be in the top 25% of their classes, and more graduated from high school.

IMPLICATIONS: The findings from this large-scale, long-term study are clear: students who have small classes during their first four years of schooling achieve more in each of those years and do significantly better in the rest of their years in school. However, small classes means having approximately 15 students; simply reducing class size from the high 20s, or 30s, to the lower 20s does not fit the definition of small classes observed in this research. The skill of the teacher could be a factor as well. Still, with this level of support from research, one would think that states would expect all primary grade classes to be small. However, an analysis completed by Harris and Plank (2000) suggests that it would cost from $200 to $435 per student to universally reduce class size. This study looked only at the teacher salary costs. There are other major costs in adding small classes, including the cost of constructing additional classrooms. As often is the case, there are trade-offs. Research tends to support that students learn more in small classes, but it will cost significantly more to have more small classes.

Sources: (1) Bruce J. Biddle and David C. Berliner, "What Research Says about Small Classes & Their Effects," in *Policy Perspectives*. San Francisco: WestEd, 2002; (2) D. Harris and D. Plank, *Making Policy Choices: Is Class Size Reduction the Best Alternative?* East Lansing, MI: Education Policy Center, Michigan State University, 2000, available at www.epc.mus.edu.

thing that is going on before the teachers do. Cafeteria workers are another group of adult workers in the school who can make a positive difference in how the school feels and functions.

organization chart

A graphic representation of the line and staff relationships of personnel in a school, school district, or other type of organization.

THE SCHOOL ORGANIZATION CHART

All of the personnel described previously work in the school building. Their working relationships can be pictured in an **organization chart,** as shown in Figure 5.1. The principal is the single line authority for all of these adults *and* for all of the students! Most experts on organizations advocate that no more than five to seven people should be directly supervised by one administrator. Yet in nearly all schools, the principal is responsible for a minimum of 30 adults and several hundred students. In very large schools, the principal may have 200 to supervise. As you can see, the simple picture of top-down direction for education breaks apart when one considers the wide array of tasks and the sheer number of people at work in each school. A number of structures must exist for arranging the relationships among the varied role groups and facilitating coordination and communication.

WHEN TO TALK TO WHOM

When teachers have an idea about the school or want to try something different, it is important for them to talk with their principal. If department heads or team leaders are in place, then the first discussions should be with them. In any organization, including schools, it is normal protocol to talk first with the person at the next level above. When there is a concern or problem, teachers should use the official administrative system and contact the principal. If this method fails and a serious problem exists, then a teacher may continue up the line by contacting the principal's supervisor: the assistant superintendent or the superintendent. If a serious disagreement occurs, then a teacher may file a grievance through procedures outlined in the negotiated contract. In any instance, a beginning teacher, or one who is new to the system, is wise to seek advice from

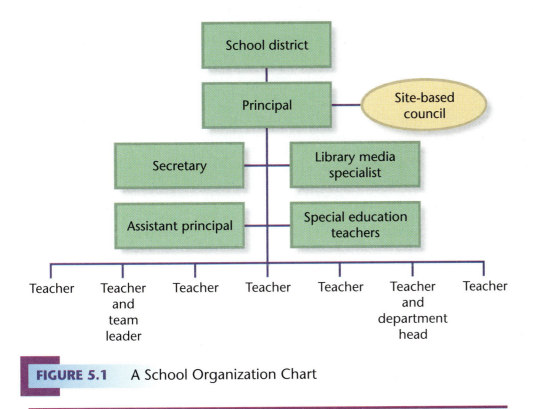

FIGURE 5.1 A School Organization Chart

experienced colleagues before taking action. In addition to knowing the system, one must know how the system works; colleagues and principals can be helpful in this regard.

ORGANIZATION OF THE SCHOOL DISTRICT

Public schools in the United States are organized into school districts, which have similar purposes but widely different characteristics. Some districts provide only elementary education; others provide only high school education; still others provide both elementary and secondary education. For the 2001–02 school year, 25 school districts enrolled 100,000 or more students, while 1,692 districts enrolled fewer than 150 students. Only 1.7 percent of the districts have an enrollment in excess of 25,000 students, yet these districts enroll about 33 percent of the total student population. Thousands of school districts have only one school campus; in comparison, a few urban districts have as many as 500 schools.

The school district is governed by a school board, and its day-to-day operations are led by a superintendent. Each district has its own district office that houses an array of administrative, instructional, financial, and clerical support staff. As the state and federal levels of government have become active in setting educational agendas, a concomitant response has occurred at the district level in the form of an ever-increasing list of tasks that must be accomplished. These additional tasks have brought more functions and personnel to the district office.

LOCAL BOARD OF EDUCATION

Legal authority for operating local school systems is given to local boards of education through state statutes. The statutes prescribe specifically how school board members are to be chosen and what duties and responsibilities they have in office. The statutes also specify the terms of board members, procedures for selecting officers of the board, duties of the officers, and procedures for filling any vacancies. Local citizens serving as school board members are official agents of the state.

About 92 percent of the school boards in the United States are elected by popular vote; most members are elected in special nonpartisan elections. About 7 percent are appointed. The percentage of appointed school boards is higher in school districts enrolling more than 25,000 pupils; yet even in three-fourths of these larger districts, the board members are elected.

Usually, teachers cannot be board members in the districts where they teach; however, they can be board members in districts where they live if they teach in different districts. The trend toward more teachers becoming board members most likely results from the goal of professional associations to secure seats on school boards.

POWERS AND DUTIES OF SCHOOL BOARDS

The powers and duties of school boards vary from state to state; the school codes of the respective states spell them out in detail. School boards' major function is the development of policy for the local school district—policy that must be in harmony with both federal and state law. Boards have only those powers granted or implied by statute that are necessary to carry out their responsibilities. These powers usually include the power to act as follows:

- Obtain revenue
- Maintain schools
- Purchase sites and build buildings
- Purchase materials and supplies
- Organize and provide programs of study

About 92 percent of the public school boards in the United States are elected by popular vote; about 7 percent are appointed.

- Employ necessary workers and regulate their services
- Admit and assign pupils to schools and control their conduct

Some duties of school boards are **mandatory,** whereas others are **discretionary.** Some duties cannot be delegated. If, for example, the state has given boards the power to employ teachers, they must do this; the power cannot be delegated— even to a school superintendent. Boards can delegate much of the hiring process to administrators, however, and then act officially on administrative recommendations for employment. An illustration of a discretionary power left to the local board is the decision whether to participate in a nonrequired school program—for example, a program of competitive athletics. Another illustration of discretionary power is the decision to employ only teachers who exceed minimum state certification standards.

Powers and duties granted to a board of education are granted to the board as a whole, not to individual members. An individual member of a board has no more authority in school matters than any other citizen of the community unless the school board legally delegates a task through official action to a specific member; in those instances, official board approval of final actions is necessary. A school board, as a corporate body, can act officially only in legally held and duly authorized board meetings, and these meetings usually must be open to the public. Executive or private sessions may be held, but ordinarily only for specified purposes such as evaluating staff members or selecting a school site. Usually, any action on matters discussed in private session must be taken officially in an open meeting.

SUPERINTENDENT OF SCHOOLS

One of the primary duties of the local board is to select its chief executive officer, the superintendent. There is one notable exception to the general practice of selection of the superintendent by school boards. In a few states, especially in the Southeast, school district superintendents are elected by the voters. In these situations, school superintendent selection is a political process just like that used for the election of mayors, county commissioners, some judges, and others. In either case, whether named by the board or elected by the people, the superintendent is responsible for the day-to-day operations of the school district, responding to school board members' interests, planning the district's budget, and defining the district's long-term aspirations. The superintendent is expected to be visible in the community and to provide overall leadership for the district.

THE CRITICAL IMPORTANCE OF LEADERSHIP

The importance of leadership by the superintendent and board members cannot be overemphasized. The quality of the educational program of a school district is influenced strongly by the leadership that the board of education and the superintendent provide. Without the communication and support of high expectations by boards and superintendents, high-quality education is not likely to be achieved. For example, offering curriculum programs over and above state-required minimums is discretionary. For a school district to excel, the local authorities, board members, and superintendent must convince their communities that specified school programs are needed and desirable.

CENTRAL OFFICE STAFF

The superintendent of schools works with a staff to carry out the program of education. Although the size of the staff varies with the school district, some kind of organization is necessary. Many school systems use a line and staff organization like that shown in Figure 5.2.

In this pattern, line officers hold the administrative power as it flows from the local board of education down to the pupils. Superintendents, assistant superintendents, and principals are line officers vested with authority over the

mandatory
Duties and responsibilities that must be accomplished.

discretionary
Duties and responsibilities that may be done by the designated body or may be delegated to another.

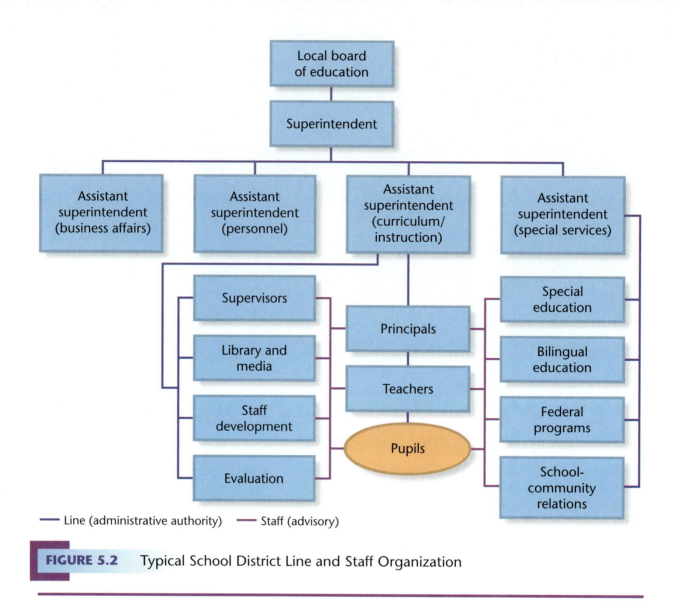

Line (administrative authority) — Staff (advisory)

FIGURE 5.2 Typical School District Line and Staff Organization

people below them on the chart. Each person is directly responsible to the official above and must work through that person in dealing with a higher official. This arrangement is frequently referred to as the *chain of command.*

Administrative staff positions are shown in Figure 5.2 as branching out from the direct flow of authority. Staff includes librarians, instructional supervisors, guidance officers, transportation officers, and others. They are responsible to their respective superiors but have no line authority over teachers. They assist and advise others from their special knowledge and abilities. Teachers are generally referred to as staff even though they are in the direct flow of authority. However, their authority in this arrangement prevails only over pupils.

ORGANIZATION OF EDUCATION AT THE STATE LEVEL

In certain countries, such as Taiwan, the national constitution specifies responsibility for education; but the U.S. Constitution does not specifically provide for public education. The Tenth Amendment has been interpreted as granting this power to the states. As a consequence, the states are the governmental units in the United States charged with the responsibility for education. Local school districts, then, receive through state law their empowerment to administer and operate the school system for their communities. State legislatures, within the limits expressed by the federal Constitution and by state constitutions, are the chief policymakers for education. State legislatures grant powers to state boards of education, state departments of education, chief state school officers, and local boards of education. These groups have only the powers granted to them by the legislature, implied powers from the specific grant of power, and the necessary powers to carry out the statutory purposes. The responsibilities and duties of intermediate units are also prescribed by the state legislatures. Figure 5.3 shows a typical state organization for education.

Stability, continuity, and leadership for education can come from the state board. However, as identified in Figure 5.3, many other individuals and groups are increasingly likely to engage in education issues. For example, many legislators have established records of heavy influence on the direction of education. Through their initiatives, new laws may affect any and all parts of the education system. There are "education governors" as well. Many state leaders have been very involved in supporting and attempting to shape education in their states. Suffice it to say, numerous participants and agencies and many kinds of influence have impacts on the shape and direction of the U.S. education system.

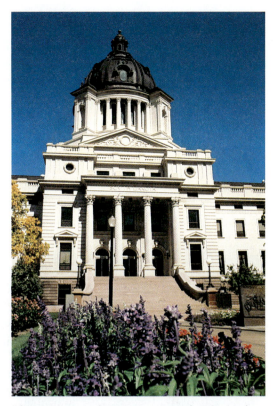

The states are the governmental units in the United States charged with the primary responsibility for education.

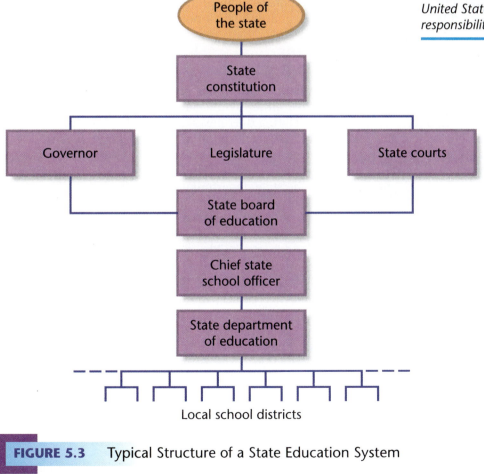

FIGURE 5.3 Typical Structure of a State Education System

■ STATE BOARDS OF EDUCATION

State boards of education are both **regulatory** and **advisory.** Regulatory functions include the establishment of standards for issuing and revoking teaching licenses, the establishment of standards for approving and accrediting schools, and the development and enforcement of a uniform system for gathering and reporting educational data. Advisory functions include considering the educational needs of the state, both long and short range, and recommending to the governor and the legislature ways of meeting these needs. State boards of education, in studying school problems and in suggesting and analyzing proposals, can be invaluable to the legislature, especially because the legislature is under pressure to decide so many issues. A state board can provide continuity for an educational program that ordinary legislative procedures don't accommodate. A state board can also coordinate, supplement, and even replace study commissions appointed by a legislature for advising on educational matters. These commissions frequently include groups studying textbooks, finance, licensure, student learning standards, school building standards, and teacher education.

STATE BOARD MEMBERSHIP

Members of state boards of education get their positions in various ways. Usually, they are appointed by the governor, with confirmation by the senate; or they may be elected by the people, the legislature, or the local school board members in a regional convention—also with confirmation by the senate. The terms of members of state boards of education are usually staggered to avoid a complete changeover at any one time. Board members usually serve without pay but are reimbursed for expenses. The policies of nonpayment and staggered terms are considered safeguards against political patronage.

CHIEF STATE SCHOOL OFFICERS

Every state has a chief state school officer, commissioner of education, or superintendent of public instruction. Some state superintendents are elected by the people, others are appointed either by the state board or by the governor.

Arguments advanced for electing the chief state school officer hold that, as an elected official, the person will be close to the people, responsible to them, and free from obligations to other state officials. An elected person will also be independent of the state board of education. Opponents of the election method argue that this method keeps the state department of education in partisan politics, that an elected official is obligated to other members of the same political party, and that many excellent candidates prefer not to engage in political contests. Those who advocate that the chief state school officer should be appointed by a state board of education claim that policymaking should be separated from policy execution, that educational leadership should not rest on the competence of one elected official, and that this method enhances the state's ability to recruit and retain qualified career workers in education.

Opponents of appointment by a state board of education claim mainly that an appointed chief school officer will not be responsible to the people. The principal objection to gubernatorial appointment is the inherent danger of the appointee's involvement in partisan politics. Another perspective on this issue is that an elected state school officer is legally an "official" of the state, whereas an officer appointed by a state board of education is generally an "employee," not a legal official.

STATE DEPARTMENTS OF EDUCATION

The state government carries on its activities in education through the state department of education, which is directed by the chief state school officer. These activities have been classified in five categories: operational, regulatory, service,

regulatory

Functions for which the state board has the authority to establish rules and regulations that limit and permit action.

advisory

Functions and areas in which the state board can only offer suggestions and indicate preference for action.

developmental, and public support and cooperation activities. Operational activities are those in which the state department directly administers schools and services, such as schools for the blind. Regulatory activities include making sure that teachers meet license standards, that school buses are safe, and that curricular requirements are fulfilled. Service activities include advising and consulting, disseminating research, and preparing materials (on state financial aid, for example). Developmental activities are directed to the improvement of the department itself and include planning, staffing, and research into better performance for the operational and regulatory as well as the service functions. Public support and cooperation activities involve public relations, political activities with the legislature and governor, and relations with various other governmental and nongovernmental agencies.

STATE LEGISLATURES

State legislatures are generally responsible for creating, operating, managing, and maintaining state school systems. The legislators are the state policymakers for education. State legislatures create state departments of education to serve as professional advisors and to execute state policy. State legislatures, though powerful, also operate under controls. The governors of many states can veto school legislation as they can other legislation, and the attorney general and the state judiciary system, when called on, will rule on the constitutionality of educational legislation.

State legislatures make decisions about how education is organized in the state; licensure standards and tenure rights of teachers; programs of study; standards of building construction for health and safety; financing of schools, including tax structure and distribution; and compulsory attendance laws.

State legislatures, in their legislative deliberations about the schools, are continually importuned by special-interest groups. These groups, realizing that the legislature is the focus of legal control of education, can exert considerable influence on individual legislators. Some of the representative influential groups are illustrated in Figure 5.4.

It is not uncommon for more than a thousand bills to be introduced each year in a state legislative session. Many of these bills originate with special-interest groups. In recent years, state legislatures have dealt with education bills on a wide range of topics, including accountability, finance, textbooks, adult basic education, length of the school year, legal holidays, lotteries, teacher and student testing, no-pass-no-play policies, and school standards of various sorts.

◼ THE FEDERAL GOVERNMENT'S ROLE IN EDUCATION

Under the Tenth Amendment to the U.S. Constitution, education is a function of the states. In effect, states have the primary responsibility for education, although the schools are operated by local governmental units commonly called school districts. Although the states have the primary responsibility for education and the schools are operated at the local level, the federal government has an ever-increasing involvement in education. In the 1960s and 1970s, the rationale for this interest and involvement was linked to national security and solving social problems. In the early 1990s, the rationale was based on economic competitiveness. In the late 1990s, the focus shifted to standards and testing, as well as concerns about funding of the crumbling infrastructure of schools. The result of this federal involvement has been the establishment of federal agencies, programs, and laws that address various aspects of the U.S. education system.

LEADERSHIP

The federal government has historically provided leadership in education in specific situations, usually in times of need or in crises that could not be fully addressed by the leadership in states or local school districts. In the

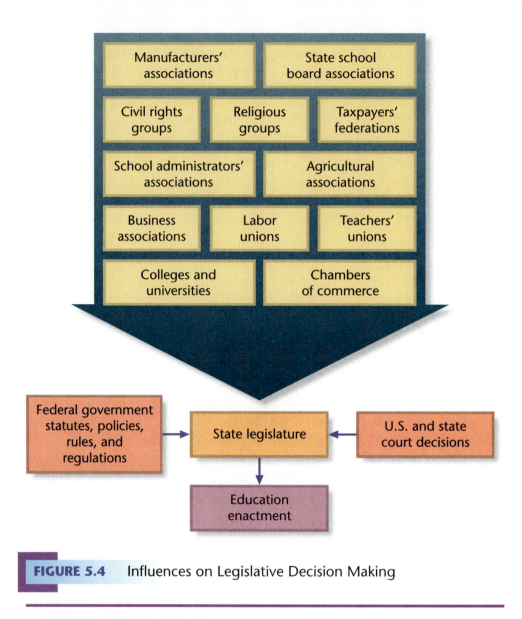

Manufacturers' associations	State school board associations
Civil rights groups	Religious groups	Taxpayers' federations
School administrators' associations	Agricultural associations
Business associations	Labor unions	Teachers' unions
Colleges and universities	Chambers of commerce

Federal government statutes, policies, rules, and regulations → State legislature ← U.S. and state court decisions

State legislature → Education enactment

FIGURE 5.4   Influences on Legislative Decision Making

In the past fifty years, the federal government has increased its activity in and leadership of education.

1980s, policymaker concerns over the quality of schools led to more active leadership on the part of the federal government, such as moves to establish national priorities in education and to raise major issues. *A Nation at Risk,* the report prepared by the National Commission on Excellence in Education, was published in 1983.

That report was not a mandate, nor was funding recommended; but it did sound an alarm, as well as providing recommendations to be considered by states and local school districts. Identifying national educational issues and encouraging forums on these issues at the state and local levels, along with soliciting responses, are appropriate federal activities. Other activities include research on significant national educational issues and dissemination of exemplary practices. Over the last fifty years, the federal government has insinuated itself more and more by tying school district access to federal funds to education mandates.

THE U.S. DEPARTMENT OF EDUCATION

The first-ever unit of education in the federal government, established in 1867 through the diligent efforts of Henry Barnard, was called the Department of Education. Later, it was called the Office of Education (1869); at another time, it was the Bureau of Education within the Department of the Interior. In 1939 the Office of Education became a part of the Federal Security Agency, which in 1953 became the Department of Health, Education, and Welfare, wherein the U.S. Office of Education was assigned. In October 1979, President Jimmy Carter signed legislation creating a cabinet-level federal agency, the Department of Education. The new Department of Education took on the functions of the U.S. Office of Education. The latest version of the Department of Education, in contrast with the first (1867), has the potential to become a powerful agency.

At this time, the U.S. Department of Education (ED) has 4,900 employees with about one-third of them stationed in ten regional offices. The organization of the department is presented in Figure 5.5. Information about grants, civil rights, education research, and education statistics is available through the various ED offices and programs.

There is no question that offering aid and awarding grants are effective ways to influence the goals of education nationally. However, there is continuing debate about whether the offices of the federal government should have a stronger or weaker influence on education. Some people maintain that the socioeconomic forces of society are not contained within local school districts or state boundaries and therefore that direct federal intervention is needed. Others advocate dissolution of the department, insisting that education is a state responsibility. As is easy to see with the No Child Left Behind legislation (NCLB), the clear trend in terms of acts of Congress and presidential leadership is toward a greater federal role in education.

EDUCATIONAL PROGRAMS OPERATED BY THE FEDERAL GOVERNMENT

The federal government directly operates some school programs. For example, the public school system of the District of Columbia depends on Congress for funds. The Department of the Interior has the educational responsibility for children of national park employees, for Samoa (classified as an outlying possession), and for the trust territories of the Pacific, such as the Caroline and Marshall Islands. Many of the schools on Native American reservations are financed and managed through the Bureau of Indian Affairs (BIA) of the Department of the Interior. Twenty-five of these schools have become what are called contract schools, in which the tribe determines the program and staff but the BIA supports the schools financially. The Department of Defense (DOD) is responsible for the Military Academy at West Point, the Naval Academy at Annapolis, the Coast Guard Academy at New London, and the Air Force Academy at Colorado Springs. The DOD also operates a school system (DOD Dependents Schools, or DoDDS) for the children of the military staff wherever members are stationed. The instruction supplied in the vocational and technical training programs of the military services has made a big contribution to the education of our nation as well.

The federal government also funds education research by individual university faculty and a set of ten Regional Education Laboratories, which provide curriculum development, technical assistance, and evaluation services to school districts and states. Another important resource for teachers has been the Education Resources Information Centers (ERIC). These centers are digital

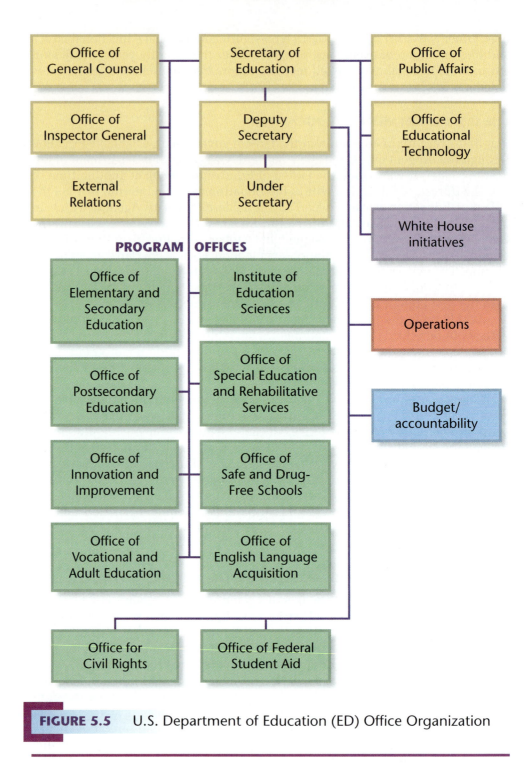

FIGURE 5.5 U.S. Department of Education (ED) Office Organization

archives of research reports and curriculum materials. Teachers can request specific information and literature searches from the ERIC databases.

NO CHILD LEFT BEHIND (NCLB)

The widest sweeping effort by the federal government to improve student learning and schools across the nation is the 2002 reauthorization of the Elementary and Secondary Education Act (ESEA). The first ESEA was passed by Congress in 1965 as one of President Lyndon Johnson's Great Society initiatives. Since then, the ESEA has been reauthorized every four or five years. Each time the scope of the bill has expanded. Unfortunately, although a major intent of the

ESEA was to increase the success of poor and minority students, the results over the last forty years have not been dramatic. With the leadership of President George W. Bush, the 2002 ESEA reauthorization represented a major rethinking based around the theme of No Child Left Behind (NCLB). Two major purposes of NCLB are to raise student achievement across the board and to eliminate the **achievement gap** between students from different backgrounds. The nearly 2,100 pages of this bill contain many directives and initiatives for states and school districts. Three of these are particularly important for future teachers to understand: HQT (highly qualified teachers), AYP (adequate yearly progress), and SINOI (school in need of improvement).

HIGHLY QUALIFIED TEACHERS (HQT)   The NCLB Act requires that school districts employ only teachers who are highly qualified. In its first year of implementation (2003), only schools with high proportions of poor students were required to be staffed with highly qualified teachers. However, by the end of the 2005–06 school year, states must ensure that all teachers of core academic subjects are highly qualified. The law specifies what "highly qualified" means:

- Public elementary and secondary teachers must be fully licensed or certified by the state and must not have any certification or licensure requirements waived on an emergency, temporary, or provisional basis.
- New public elementary school teachers must have at least a bachelor's degree and pass a rigorous state test demonstrating subject knowledge and teaching skills in reading, writing, mathematics, and other areas of any basic elementary school curriculum.
- New middle or secondary school teachers must have at least a bachelor's degree and demonstrate competency by passing a rigorous state test in each subject they will teach, or successfully complete a major, or graduate degree, or advanced certification in each subject they will teach.

ADEQUATE YEARLY PROGRESS (AYP)   This is the basis for determining whether schools, districts, and states are in compliance with the law. The primary criterion is student performance on standardized tests. A key difference from the past is that under NCLB all students must be making progress, and there must be improvement each year so that by the school year 2013–14, all students in all schools will be "proficient." Student test scores are to be **disaggregated** by the subgroups of:

- Economically disadvantaged students
- Major racial or ethnic groups
- Students with disabilities
- English language learners (ELL)

An additional step in the NCLB mandate is that student performance in the 2001–02 school year is to serve as the baseline. States then have twelve years to have all students meet the 2013–14 proficient level, which means that students within each subgroup who had test scores in 2001–02 below the proficient level need to, on average, improve by one-twelfth each year. This is where the AYP concept comes from; states have to report to the federal government each year that test scores for students in all subgroups are moving toward being at least proficient.

SCHOOLS IN NEED OF IMPROVEMENT (SINOI)   NCLB sets timelines and establishes consequences for states, school districts, and schools in which student performance on test scores does not meet the AYP targets. One unfortunate consequence is that these schools will be labeled as "low performing" or "failing" schools. Another consequence of the way AYP is defined is that sooner or later

achievement gap

The systematic difference in learning between majority and minority, or rich and poor, students.

disaggregated

The process of separating test scores based on student characteristics such as gender, ethnicity, and socioeconomic status.

Every time you stop a school, you will have to build a jail. What you gain at one end you lose at the other. It's like feeding a dog on his own tail. It won't fatten the dog.

Mark Twain

most schools are likely to be labeled as SINOI schools. Corrective actions for schools in need of improvement include:

1. Schools that fail to meet AYP for two consecutive years must be identified as "needing improvement."
2. Schools that fail to meet the state AYP standard for three consecutive years must offer pupils from low-income families the opportunity to receive instruction from a supplemental services provider of the parents' choice.
3. Schools that fail to meet AYP for four consecutive years must take one or more of the following corrective actions: replace school staff, implement a new curriculum, decrease management authority, appoint an outside expert to advise the school, extend the school day or year, or change the school's internal organizational structure.
4. Schools that fail to meet AYP standards for five consecutive years must be restructured, which includes reopening as a charter school, replacing all or most school staff, state takeover of school operations, or other "major restructuring" of school governance.

OTHER NCLB REQUIREMENTS　　Many more elements, mandates, and expectations are part of the 2002 version of the NCLB Act, such as annual testing of students in grades 3 through 8 in math and reading/language arts, as well as testing them three times in science by grade 12. Annual state report cards are required, and they must, among other things, name SINOI schools. Also, school districts must make available to parents, upon request, the following information about their child's classroom teacher:

- Whether the teacher has met state qualification and licensing criteria for the grade levels and subject areas taught
- Whether the teacher is teaching under emergency or other provisional status
- The baccalaureate degree of the teacher and any other graduate certification or degree held by the teacher, and the subject area of the certification or degree
- Whether the child is provided service by paraprofessionals and, if so, the paraprofessional's qualifications.

In summary, the No Child Left Behind Act is a far-reaching, long-lasting federal statute intended to improve schooling, as defined in terms of student performance on standardized state testing in all states, all school districts, all schools, and all classrooms.

■ OTHER TYPES OF EDUCATION AGENCIES

The organization of the U.S. education system described so far has been in a straight line from schools to the role of the federal government. Obviously, the whole system is not this simple. Many related agencies and organizations are important as well. Some that will play a more direct role in your work as a teacher are highlighted here.

INTERMEDIATE UNITS

The **intermediate unit** of school organization, which may consist of one or more counties, functions between the state department of education and the local school districts. These units have different names in different states. For example, in some states, such as New York and Colorado, they are called BOCES (Boards of Cooperative Educational Services); in Texas they are called Regional Service Centers; and in California, County Education Offices.

A fundamental purpose of the intermediate unit is to provide two or more local districts with educational services that they cannot efficiently or economically provide individually; cooperative provisions for special education and

intermediate unit

An education organization located between local districts and the state that delivers support services to one or more school districts.

vocational–technical education have been very successful. Other services that intermediate units can provide include audiovisual libraries, centralized purchasing, inservice training for teachers and principals as well as other school workers, health services, instructional materials, laboratories, legal services, and special consultant services. The inservice dimension of the intermediate units has escalated in some states in recent years, stimulated by educational reform.

FOUNDATIONS

The preceding educational agencies and organizations receive public funding (tax dollars). Private funds also support many activities in public schools, including an impressive array of foundations. Foundations are not as hamstrung by government regulations, so they are more able to support experimentation and novel educational activities. Some foundations are large and widely known, such as the Kellogg Foundation and, more recently, the Gates Foundation. Others are smaller or target their funding to particular states or topics. For example, the Hogg Foundation in Texas invests mainly in that state and primarily supports issues related to mental health. A very promising foundation in the Midwest is the Ewing Marion Kauffman Foundation and its Center for Entrepreneurial Leadership in Kansas City. One of its initiatives is to support the use of curriculum materials that introduce business and entrepreneurship concepts.

■ SCHOOL CHOICE: INCREASING OPTIONS ALONG WITH UNCERTAIN OUTCOMES

The newspaper article in the Education in the News feature at the beginning of this chapter foreshadows one of the hottest education topics across the United States: school choice. In the past, parents had no say in which public school their child would attend. Children were assigned to a school by the school district. Now increasing numbers and types of alternatives to the traditional neighborhood public school are becoming available. Nearly one in four students is exercising some form of choice within public or private schools. The problem for many parents now is not whether they have a choice but which one of the alternatives is best. Many of these options are being installed within public school districts, whereas other alternatives are found in private schools. Most of these options allow for increased parent and student involvement in school decision making. All represent, in some way, a break with the traditional public school and classroom structures. The creation of choices also causes competition between the alternatives, which some people believe will lead to more efficiency and effectiveness. However, the research to date, though limited, does not provide clear evidence of a trend toward higher student achievement. The findings do indicate that upper-income and more educated families are more likely to exercise choice.[1,2]

MAGNET SCHOOLS

Many school districts have been pressured by citizens and ordered by the courts to equalize the proportions of different racial groups in each school. One response, especially by large urban school districts such as those in Houston and Kansas City, has been to develop special academic programs and custom-designed facilities that will attract all students; hence the name *magnet* schools. Elementary, middle, and high school magnets exist. The program might emphasize the performing and visual arts, math and science, or the liberal arts. Whatever the theme, the faculty, curriculum, and all students

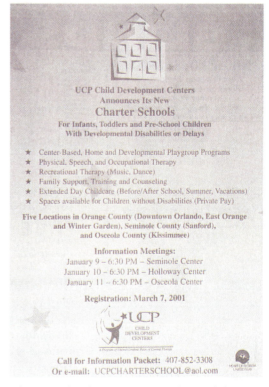

Charter schools are increasingly available as a competitive alternative to regular public schools.

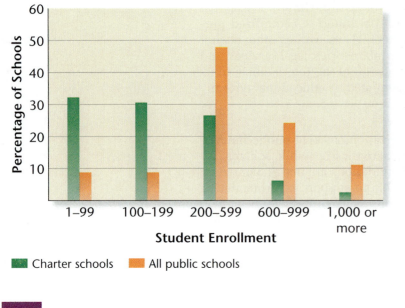

FIGURE 5.6 Estimated Distribution of School Size for Charter Schools and All Public Schools

Source: U.S. Department of Education, Office of Educational Research and Improvement, *The State of Charter Schools 2000.* Washington, DC: Author, 2000.

in the magnet school are there because of their interest in the school's theme.

CHARTER SCHOOLS

Charter schools are a relatively new approach to providing communities with alternative schools supported by public funds. These schools come into existence through a contract with either a state agency or a local school board. The school establishes a contract, or charter, that lays out how the school will operate in exchange for receiving public funding. Charter schools have greater autonomy than regular public schools and can be released from various district and state regulations. However, charter schools are still held accountable for student learning and, in most settings, having a diverse student body. Exponential growth in the number of charter schools has occurred since the first one was established in Minnesota in 1992. As of 1999, thirty-six states and the District of Columbia had passed legislation to permit the establishment of charter schools. For the 1998–99 school year, 250,000 students were enrolled, representing 0.8 percent of all public school students.[3] However, as shown in Figure 5.6, charter schools tend to have significantly smaller enrollments than public schools.

YEAR-ROUND SCHOOLS

The normal school year of nine to ten months with the full summer off is often criticized. One concern is that students will forget too much over the summer. Critics point out that the current school year was instituted back in the 1800s, when most people lived on farms and the children were counted on to perform summer chores. One interesting solution is the year-round school. This is not an extended school year in that students attend school for more days. Rather, year-round schools spread the time in school across twelve months. One way a school might do this is by having multiple "tracks" of six to eight weeks. During any one cycle, one-fourth to one-third of the students will be on vacation and the others will be attending classes. In this way, students have more frequent but shorter times away from school. An additional advantage is that the school site can handle more students on an annual basis. Curiously, much of the resistance to year-round schools comes from parents who are concerned about being able to schedule family vacations; however, once the schedule is implemented, they discover that being able to schedule vacations throughout the year has advantages.

VOUCHERS

Without a doubt, the most controversial choice alternative is school vouchers. At its simplest, a voucher program issues a check or a credit to parents that can be used to send their child to a private school. Most voucher programs are funded with state tax dollars. However, some voucher programs are funded by private foundations and occasionally individuals. For example, in the Edgewood Independent School District in San Antonio, Texas, a group of business executives offered $50 million over ten years for vouchers for low-income families to attend any private school or even public school in other school districts. The publicly financed programs have restrictions on who is eligible, as in Florida, where the state plan allowed vouchers to be used only after the state had designated the public school as a failing school. Typically, the amount of a voucher is equivalent to the amount the public school received for each student, in other words, $4,000 to $5,000. The debates about vouchers center on the use of public dollars to support private schools. The most serious point of contention is when the voucher funded with state education money is used to pay for a child to attend a religious school. This raises constitutional questions about the separation of church and state, which are discussed in detail in Chapter 6. The National Education Association has been active in opposition to voucher programs because it sees this choice as undermining public education. A useful summary of pros and cons about vouchers is presented in Table 5.2.

PRIVATE, PAROCHIAL, AND INDEPENDENT SCHOOLS

Alternative structures of schools exist outside the public school system too. These range from elite secondary schools (mainly in the Northeast), to dynamic alternative schools for high school dropouts, to church-supported schools, to schools that are operated for profit. As shown in Table 5.3, there has been a gradual increase in the number of private schools.

TABLE 5.2 Voucher Pros and Cons

Critics argue that:	Supporters argue that:
Only the most motivated students will use vouchers, increasing the segregation of students by race, economic status, and parents' educational background.	Low-income parents should be able to choose private schools over poorly performing public schools.
Vouchers weaken the public schools by diverting resources from them.	Increased competition from voucher schools will force public schools to improve, or risk closure.
Lack of accountability and quality control at voucher schools is a misuse of public money.	Private schools are unburdened by bureaucracy and regulations that hamstring the public school system.
Spending public money on religious education is unconstitutional.	Private schools provide more tailored services at a lower cost.
Transportation problems and difficulties in providing adequate information to all parents will make voucher systems inequitable.	Voucher systems allow parents more influence over their children's education.
Property taxes will rise as state aid to local districts is lost.	Voucher programs emphasize educational choices, not requirements dictated by the government.
Vouchers will increase overall costs. Private schools, like any other government contractor, will become even more dependent on and demanding of public funds, causing more spending.	Vouchers expand options for low-income parents, enhancing their feelings of empowerment and inclusion in society.
Vouchers do not really equalize the playing field, since no voucher program so far provides enough money for poor children to be able to attend the most expensive private schools.	

Source: *What We Know about Vouchers: The Facts behind the Rhetoric.* San Francisco: WestEd, 1999.

TABLE 5.3 The Increase in the Number of Public and Private Schools over Time

Elementary and Secondary Schools in the United States						
Characteristics	1980–81	1987–88	1990–91	1995–96	1997–98	1999–2000
All elementary and secondary schools	106,746	110,055	109,228	114,811	116,910	119,235
All public schools	85,982	83,248	84,538	87,125	89,508	92,012
All private schools	20,764	26,807	24,690	26,686	27,402	27,223

— = data not available.

Source: U.S. Department of Education, National Center for Education Statistics, *Digest of Education Statistics 1999, 2001.* Washington, DC: Author, Table 5, page 14.

INDEPENDENT SCHOOLS   Private education, which preceded public education in the United States, continues to be available as an alternative to the public schools. Private schools are increasingly being referred to as independent schools.[4] One source of information on these schools is the Council for American Private Education (CAPE), a coalition of fourteen private school organizations. Another is the National Association of Independent Schools (NAIS). The following description of independent schools is based on an NAIS publication.[5]

An **independent school** is a nonprofit institution governed by a board of trustees that depends almost entirely on private funds—tuition, gifts, grants—for its financial support. Most independent schools are accredited by their regional accrediting group and by state departments of education. All must meet state and local health and safety standards as well as the mandatory school attendance laws. Unlike public schools, independent schools are not involved in or part of large, formal systems. They do, however, share many informal contracts among themselves and with public schools. The vast majority offer programs that prepare students for college.

Independent schools vary greatly in purpose, organization, and size, and they serve students from all racial, religious, economic, and cultural backgrounds. Some are progressive and innovative; some are conservative and traditional. They are both large and small, day and boarding, single-sex and coeducational. Independent schools have been an integral part of our nation's educational resources since colonial times.

Because each independent school is free to determine and practice its own philosophy of education, spirit and environment vary from school to school, even though schools may display similar organizational structures and educational programs. This diversity among independent schools is one of their most distinctive characteristics.

GOVERNANCE OF INDEPENDENT SCHOOLS   Each independent school is incorporated as a nonprofit, tax-exempt corporation and governed by a board of trustees that selects its own members, determines the school's philosophy, selects the chief administrative officer, and bears ultimate responsibility for the school's resources and finances. The chief administrator responsible for the day-to-day operation of the school may be called the headmaster, headmistress, president, or principal. The head's duties are comparable to those of a public school superintendent.

HOME SCHOOLING

This rapidly growing form of schooling requires no public support; instead, children learn at home with one of their parents serving as the teacher. Home schooling is growing at the rate of 11 percent a year. In the most recent year studied, 1999, more than 850,000 students were being schooled at home. They represent 4 percent of the K–12 population, which may seem small, but represents the combined total number of children in Alaska, Delaware, Hawaii, Montana, New Hampshire, North Dakota, Rhode Island, South Dakota, Vermont, and Wyoming.[6] Teaching a home-schooled student requires relearning subjects, organizing each day's instruction, and then teaching it. One of the advantages, as well as potential weaknesses, is that in most states the subjects taught are self-determined. This can work in favor of students' interests but may also contribute to gaps in their education. Still, the evidence is clear that for many students home schooling is a success. For example, home-schooled fourth graders watch less television and in high school they score on average eighty points higher on the SAT.

POLITICS IN EDUCATION

So far this chapter has provided information about the formal structures of public education at the local, state, and federal levels. Although these organizational structures illustrate the line and staff relationships, another set of

independent school

A nonprofit, nonpublic school that is governed by a board of trustees.

relationships is important to consider and understand. Each of these levels is involved in politics—the politics of education. For example, local school districts are likely to be interested in federal educational programs and grants, so they will contact members of Congress to express their opinions. The purpose is to influence representatives' understanding of local needs and their actions on relevant legislation. The same activities take place at the state level. Local school districts and professional associations follow closely what is happening in their state legislature. These groups do not hesitate to let members in the legislature know their opinions or to urge action. It is not unusual for local school superintendents and board members to lobby their senators and representatives in person. These contacts with federal and state agencies are representative of political action. You also need to be aware of the many other types of education politics.

Special-interest groups organize to influence local school board elections by using fund-raising, mass communication, and grassroots campaigning.

THE INCREASING VOLATILITY OF ELECTION POLITICS

One common example of politics in education is found in school board elections. The individuals who serve on the school board can make a significant difference in what you can and cannot do as a teacher. Take, for example, the concerted efforts of the Religious Right to increase their voice in school matters by influencing school board elections. Religious Right groups are skilled at orchestrating campaigns to elect school board members who are favorably disposed to their agendas, which include demanding curriculum changes, challenging sex education programs, pushing for prayer in the classroom, and purging reading lists in libraries. These groups' political strategies are good examples of what politics are about. They are well organized and use state-of-the-art combinations of fund-raising, mass communication, and old-fashioned door-to-door campaigning. Because the general public tends not to be much interested in school board elections, a relatively small number of people (say, the membership of one or two churches) voting as a block can swing an election. The definition of what is fair in politics is not always clear. For example, the Religious Right has been criticized for running "stealth" candidates. In other words, the candidates do not say explicitly what they believe and what they plan to do if elected. Still, they are using the democratic process to influence policy and practice.

POLITICS AT THE SCHOOL DISTRICT LEVEL

The people who are likely to be involved in politics at the local level include school board members, superintendents, and community members. Politics begin for prospective board members when they decide to run for the school board. As President John F. Kennedy said, "the first thing you need to be is elected."

The motives expressed by those seeking board membership appear to be honorable. The encouragement to run for the school board by friends and neighbors, current school board members, and family members seems innocuous. In school district elections, however, depending on the circumstances and issues, bitterness and resentment can occur. The healing, when and if it happens, is likely to take place through the political process of talking about interests and needs. The same emphasis on talking and listening is important to becoming elected and facilitating development and implementation of good education policies.

SCHOOL BOARD POLITICS

Board members are expected to be accountable to their public constituency. However, some board members feel that they should be accountable to the entire community, whereas others feel they should be accountable only to a specific segment of the community. The two positions are not compatible and can create strife among board members and within the community. Political activity is the likely result.

Most school districts have at-large elections for board members. In at-large elections, every voter in a community casts a vote for each seat on the board. At-large elections allow the entire electorate to vote for each candidate or each board member who is running for election. A disadvantage of at-large elections is that there is less chance of a minority candidate winning a seat. When board members are elected as the representative of a particular region or district, there is likely to be greater diversity.

Often board members and the public have to deal with some political issues that are emotional and difficult. Among these are firing a superintendent, having a teacher strike, closing a school, opening a school-based clinic that provides sexual advice and contraceptives to teenagers, raising taxes, reducing staff and educational opportunities, busing students, admitting a child with AIDS, desegregating schools, and tolerating consistently losing athletic teams. Such issues are divisive and can result in political havoc until resolved. An additional area of political tension can develop between city government and the school district.[7]

THE SUPERINTENDENT'S POLITICS

The superintendent is the chief executive officer of the school district. The superintendent's formal power comes from the board of education, but he or she also gains power through access to various sources of information. In politics, one very important form of power is the control of information. For example, superintendents have access to expert information about curriculum and instruction. Generally, boards are considered to be policymakers, and superintendents implement the policies. Cooperative development of specific policies helps to establish the roles of both the board of education and the superintendent. However, specific educational (and other) issues can precipitate strenuous debate between the superintendent and the board and among board members. The superintendent with expert information may be able to help inform the debate and resolve related issues.

SCHOOL-BASED POLITICS

Politics always exist within the school site and between the school and the district office. For example, certain teachers will lobby the principal for a preferred schedule. Parents want certain teachers for their children. The principal would like to see a particular school reform model implemented. The SBDM council advocates for additional support for a marching band trip. The district office and the school board prefer one design for a necessary attendance boundary change, the school another. In each and every interaction there is an effort to influence and gain support. This is what politics are about.

POLITICS: NEITHER POSITIVE NOR NEGATIVE

Although many of the examples presented here might appear to be negative, keep in mind that politics are neither good nor bad. Instead, politics are the way that all organizations work. Areas of disagreement will always exist in educational organizations. People have varying interests that must be discussed. In many cases, there are basic differences in point of view, but a decision has to be made for the organization to move ahead. This is where political skill becomes a special strength for teachers and school administrators. Those who are skillful in talking with all parties and negotiating areas of agreement make significant

What Is the Appropriate Role for Teachers When the Politics Get Rough?

The education accountability movement of the last decade has demanded that teachers and school administrators make serious efforts to change the way schools operate and to implement new approaches to help students learn. Policymakers, business leaders, and citizens at large have demanded that schools "reform" and "restructure." As is discussed in Chapters 12 and 13, schools are now expected to implement curriculum standards and to administer newly created tests of student learning. Yet major changes in the structure and operation of schools are difficult to accomplish. It is hard for teachers to give up or change what they have been doing. It takes a great deal of time to work through the process that is necessary to develop a consensus among teachers, administrators, and parents about how a school should be restructured and what it should become. It also takes several years to work out the kinks when trying something new.

Suppose that after you had spent three years discussing and then two years implementing a major restructuring of your school and saw that it was working with students, a newly elected majority on the school board demanded that you return to the old way. As a teacher, what would you do?

This is not a hypothetical question. In one recent example, after more than three years of broad-based discussions involving teachers, administrators, students, parents, and community members, one school district's school board approved new performance-based graduation requirements for one of its high schools. The new requirements were based on student accomplishments rather than on seat-time. In fact, the high school had received national recognition for its efforts.

In November of the second year of implementation, three conservative members were elected to the five-member school board. A major theme in their election campaign was an attack on the new graduation requirements, which they promised to remove. In January the new majority on the school board proceeded to implement its campaign promise. Although students from the school, parents, and school staff members asked that the board not do this, or that the board at least allow the new graduation requirements to be optional, the board voted three to two to return to the traditional requirements. Remember that there were now students in their second year of high school who had been told that they were expected to meet the new graduation requirements.

The school board did not stop there. In the same month, January, the board terminated the superintendent, who was viewed as a very able educator by most and was well known and respected nationally. By the end of the school year, several school principals and teachers had taken positions elsewhere, and the district was running advertisements nationwide for principals and teachers who held "traditional" educational values. This might sound like an extreme case, but similar events have happened in other school districts, and similar cases will happen in one form or another during your years as an educator.

If you were a teacher in a school district where something like this occurred, what would you do? Your colleagues, the school, your students, and the innovative program have been challenged. It is clear that there is the potential for casualties, including your job. Of course, your actions will depend partly on which side of the issue you are on. Either way, what will you do?

- Will you speak out or wait for others to do so?
- What will you tell your students?
- Will you support your principal publicly or leave the principal on his or her own?
- How do you think you would feel the next time you were asked to invest four or five years in designing and implementing a major change in your school?

Companion Website

To answer these questions on-line and e-mail your answers to your professor, go to Chapter 5 of the companion website (**www.ablongman.com/johnson13e**) and click on Professional Dilemma.

---

contributions. Rather than judging "politics" as bad, successful teachers learn to understand how politics work and develop the skills to contribute to and influence the political process. Closing the classroom door guarantees that your positions and ideas will not be considered. Learn more about organizations and political processes and you will see politics as fascinating and, yes, fun.

■ ISSUES RELATED TO ORGANIZATION AND STRUCTURE

Pick up a newspaper or watch the television news, and you will quickly be confronted with one or more of the debates about what education *should* be doing or *should not* be doing. The following is a short list of hot topics and issues related to school organization.

ISSUE: LOCAL CONTROL

An important and unique feature of education in the United States is a belief in **local control:** the belief that educational decisions should be made at the local level rather than at the state or national level. The rationale is that people at the local level, including teachers and parents, know what is best for the students in that community. Those who advocate for more federal and state involvement argue that education is a responsibility of all of society. The mobility of the population and the interdependence of social elements have undermined the traditional concept that local people should have the sole voice in determining the directions of education. Some also argue that national survival requires centralized policies and programs laid down by states and the federal government.

The underlying questions have to do with power, authority, and what is best for students and society. The issue of local control has been more hotly debated in recent years as the states have assumed more control over curriculum, statewide testing, and school funding. Local control advocates are also concerned about the increasing involvement of the federal government in education. In the last fifty years, a consistent trend has grown toward increasing centralization of control over education at both the state and federal levels. The No Child Left Behind Act is the latest and heaviest centralization initiative by the federal government that includes many mandates to states and school districts.

Thoughtful critics and historians have offered some interesting comparisons between the original 1965 ESEA and the 2002 reauthorization. Some critics of the original ESEA say that it failed because it provided money without accountability, and the NCLB Act will succeed because it requires strict accountability. The ESEA of 1965 may have offered money without much educational accountability, but the NCLB Act demands heavy accountability without much greater federal financial and technical assistance—an approach no more likely to succeed.

In 1965, extensive federal requirements like those of NCLB would never have made it through Congress. At that time, the federal role in education was marginal, most state education agencies had limited authority and capabilities, and local people were extremely wary that more federal aid would bring federal control. Since then the federal and state roles in education have grown, and states and school districts recognize that accepting federal requirements goes along with receiving federal funding.

ISSUE: SCHOOL CHOICE IN PUBLIC SCHOOLS

In most school districts, parents have little or no choice about which public school their children attend. The school district makes the decision, usually based on where the children reside. Since the 1970s, however, there has been a movement toward parental choice. Some districts may include one or two alternative schools such as charter or magnet schools that parents can choose. In some districts, such as Cambridge, Massachusetts, all families list their top three schools; then the public authorities make assignments, balancing individual preferences against the state's interest in preventing overcrowding and in ensuring ethnic diversity within each school. Studies to date do not indicate that students show greater achievement when there is choice. However, parental satisfaction is higher. Choice is being pursued the most by parents who take an intense interest in their children's success at school. The issue, then, is one of equity and opportunity for children whose parents are not ac-

local control

Educational decision making by citizens at the local level rather than at the state or national level.

tively pursuing the available alternatives, because children who do not choose, and schools that are not chosen, could be left behind.[8] No Child Left Behind includes a number of choice initiatives, most of which are aimed at giving choice to parents who have children in consistently low-performing schools.

■ SUMMARY: ORGANIZATION OF SCHOOLS

So far in this chapter, the lens for describing the U.S. education system has used ideas and concepts related to organizational structure. Line and staff relationships, the role of school boards, the authority of state and federal governments, and the different positions and roles in schools and the district office have been described. We also introduced the theme that politics are a part of education, whether that means teachers talking in the staff lounge or the president and Congress writing new laws. You cannot escape politics whether at school, at home with your family, or at church. Rather than attempting to close the classroom door and ignoring school politics, effective teachers will learn how politics work and become skilled in participating and influencing.

FINANCING EDUCATION: SOURCES OF FUNDS AND THE MOVE FROM EQUITY TO ADEQUACY

When the financing of education is considered, the first question asked by many is "How much? How much do I have to pay, and how much do schools receive?" In the last decade, two other questions have sharpened the discussions about education finance: "Does each school have the same amount of funding?" This is the **equity** question. "Is there sufficient funding so that all students can achieve?" This is the **adequacy** question. The equity question was at the center of many school funding lawsuits in the 1980s and early 1990s. In 1989 a decision of the Kentucky Supreme Court brought the adequacy question to the front. That court decision held that every child in the state had the right to an "adequate" education. The direct consequence of that decision was the passing of the Kentucky Education Reform Act (KERA) by the state legislature. The significance of KERA is that it did not deal solely with equalizing spending by each school district— that is, equity. KERA went further by specifically connecting funding with implementation of school and curriculum reforms, specifying student outcomes and development of a statewide strategy for assessing academic achievement. Now questions related to the financing of education have to deal with all three questions: "How much?"; "Is there equity in the distribution?"; and "Are the resources adequate so that all students can achieve the identified outcomes?" We explore these finance questions in the remainder of this chapter.

The whole people must take upon themselves the education of the whole people and must be willing to bear the expense of it.

John Adams

■ A SYSTEM OF TAXATION AND SUPPORT FOR SCHOOLS

Money to support education comes from a variety of taxes paid to local, state, and federal governments. These governments in turn distribute tax money to local school districts to operate the schools. The three principal kinds of taxes that provide revenue for schools are property taxes, sales or use taxes, and income taxes. The property tax is generally a local tax, whereas the sales tax generally is a state and local mix, and the income tax is collected at the state and federal levels. More than $373 billion in revenues were raised by local, state, and federal governments to fund public education in the 1999–2000 school year.[9]

Each type of tax is a part of a system and has advantages and disadvantages, yet it is unlikely that any one of these taxes used by itself for education would be sufficient. In evaluating a system of taxes, one should consider the varying ability of citizens to pay, the economic effects of the taxes on the taxpayer, the

equity
Provision of the same amount of funding to all schools or students.

adequacy
Provision of sufficient funds so that all students can achieve.

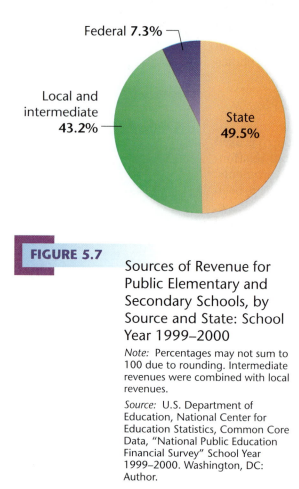

FIGURE 5.7

Sources of Revenue for Public Elementary and Secondary Schools, by Source and State: School Year 1999–2000

Note: Percentages may not sum to 100 due to rounding. Intermediate revenues were combined with local revenues.

Source: U.S. Department of Education, National Center for Education Statistics, Common Core Data, "National Public Education Financial Survey" School Year 1999–2000. Washington, DC: Author.

benefits that various taxpayers receive, the total yield of the tax, the economy of collection, the degree of acceptance, the convenience of paying, the problems of tax evasion, the stability of the tax, and the general adaptability of the system. Clearly, systems of taxation are complicated; each system is an intricately interdependent network.

Figure 5.7 diagrams the percentages of revenues that school systems nationwide receive from federal, state, and local sources. As you can see, public education is primarily funded by local and state sources of revenue.

PROPERTY TAXES AND LOCAL REVENUE

Until recently, the **property tax** has been the primary source of local revenue for schools. It is based on the value of property, both real estate and personal. Real estate includes land holdings and buildings such as homes, commercial buildings, and factories. Personal property consists of automobiles, machinery, furniture, livestock, and intangibles such as stocks and bonds. The property tax has both advantages and limitations.

PROPERTY TAXES: ADVANTAGES AND LIMITATIONS The main advantage of the property tax is its stability. Although the tax tends to lag behind changes in market values, it provides a steady, regular income for the taxing agency. Another advantage of taxing property is that it is fixed; it is not easily moved to escape taxation, as income might be. Also, because the owners of property pay the tax, it is easy to identify them.

The property tax has numerous limitations, however. It can have a negative impact on the value of housing: It tends to discourage rehabilitation and upkeep because both of these tend to raise the value of the property and therefore its taxes. The tax is often a deciding factor in locating a business or industry. And it is likely not to be applied equally on all properties.

DETERMINING THE VALUE OF PROPERTY One problem with the property tax lies in the potential unfairness of inconsistent property assessments. In some areas, assessors are local people, usually elected, with no special training in evaluating property. Their duty involves inspecting their neighbors' properties and placing values on them. In other areas, sophisticated techniques involving expertly trained personnel are used for property appraisal. In either circumstance, assessors are likely to be subject to political and informal pressures to keep values low in order to keep tax rates low.

The assessed value of property is usually only a percentage of its market value. This percentage varies from county to county and from state to state. Attempts are made within states to equalize assessments or to make certain that the same percentage of full cash value is used in assessing property throughout the state. In recent years, attempts have been made to institute full cash value for the assessed value. For the property tax to be a fair tax, equalized assessment is a necessity.

PROPERTY TAX: PROGRESSIVE OR REGRESSIVE Property tax is most generally thought of as a **progressive tax**—that is, one that taxes according to ability to pay; the more wealth one has in property, the more one pays. But because assessments can be unequal and because frequently the greatest wealth is no longer related to real estate, the property tax can be regressive. **Regressive taxes,** such as sales and use taxes, are those that affect low-income groups disproportionately. Some evidence supports the contention that people in the lowest in-

property tax

A tax based on the value of property, both real estate and personal.

progressive tax

A tax that is scaled to the ability of the taxpayer to pay.

regressive tax

A tax that affects low-income groups disproportionately.

come groups pay a much higher proportion of their income in property taxes than persons in the highest income groups.

INEQUITIES OF THE PROPERTY TAX   Significant support for schools across the nation has been provided by the property tax. However, as has been described, because of schools' heavy dependence on property taxes for financing, enormous discrepancies in resources and quality have built up between schools located in rich and in poor communities.

To illustrate the school finance consequences of differences in local wealth, look at a simple example. A school district having assessed property valuations totaling $30 million and a responsibility for educating 1,000 pupils would have $30,000 of assessed valuation per pupil. Property taxes are calculated on the basis of assessed valuations, so a district with a high assessed valuation per pupil is in a better position to provide quality education than is one with a low assessed valuation per pupil. If school district A has an assessed valuation of $90 million and 1,000 pupils, for example, and school district B has an assessed valuation of $30 million and 1,000 pupils, a tax rate of $2 per $100 of assessed valuation would produce $1.8 million for education in district A and only $600,000 in district B. School district A could therefore spend $1,800 per pupil, compared with $600 per pupil in school district B, with the same local tax effort.

THE PERSPECTIVE OF THE COURTS ON TAXATION AND EDUCATION   Can the property tax continue to be the primary base for financing schools? This question was asked of the U.S. Supreme Court in *San Antonio (Texas) Independent School District v. Rodriguez* (1979). Keep in mind that the U.S. Constitution does not mention education, so any litigation has to be based on indirect connections. In the *Rodriguez* case, the challenge was initiated under the Equal Protection Clause of the Fourteenth Amendment. This clause prohibits state action that would deny citizens equal protection. The U.S. Supreme Court, in a five-to-four decision, reversed the lower court decision in *Rodriguez* and thus reaffirmed the local property tax as a basis for school financing. Justice Potter Stewart, voting with the majority, admitted that "the method of financing public schools . . . can be fairly described as chaotic and unjust." He did not, though, find it unconstitutional. The majority opinion, written by Justice Lewis F. Powell Jr., stated, "We cannot say that such disparities are the product of a system that is so irrational as to be invidiously discriminatory." Justice Thurgood Marshall, in the dissenting opinion, charged that the ruling "is a retreat from our historic commitment to equality of education opportunity." Another part of the opinion in *Rodriguez* addressed the role of the states in supporting public education:

> The consideration and initiation of fundamental reforms with respect to state taxation and education are matters reserved for legislative processes of the various States, and we do no violence to the values of federalism and separation of powers by staying our hand. We hardly need add that this Court's action today is not to be viewed as placing its judicial imprimatur on the status quo. The need is apparent for reform in tax systems which may well have relied too long and too heavily on the local property tax. And certainly innovative thinking as to public education, its methods, and its funding is necessary to assure both a higher level of quality and greater uniformity of opportunity. These matters merit the continued attention of the scholars who already have contributed much by their challenges. But the ultimate solutions must come from the lawmakers and from the democratic pressures of those who elect them.

These comments in *Rodriguez* foreshadowed the continuing string of school finance suits that have been filed in most states.

STATE SOURCES OF REVENUE AND AID

On the average in the United States, the states provide about 49.5 percent of the fiscal resources for local schools. This money is referred to as **state aid,** and within most states all or a major portion of this money is used to help achieve equality of opportunity.

state aid

The money that states provide for the fiscal resources of local schools.

The main sources of tax revenue for states have been classified by the Department of Commerce in four groups: sales and gross receipt taxes, income taxes, licenses, and miscellaneous. Sales and gross receipt taxes include taxes on general sales, motor fuels, alcohol, insurance, and amusements; income taxes include both individual and corporate; licenses include those on motor vehicles, corporations, occupations, vehicle operators, hunting, and fishing. The miscellaneous classification includes property taxes, taxes on severance or extraction of minerals, and death and gift taxes. The two largest sources of state revenues are sales and income taxes.

SALES AND INCOME TAXES   Sales and income taxes are lucrative sources of state revenue, and it is relatively easy to administer both. The sales tax is collected bit by bit, in a relatively painless way, by the vendor, who is responsible for keeping records. The state income tax can be withheld from wages; hence, collection is eased. Income taxes are considered progressive taxes because they frequently are scaled to the ability of the taxpayer to pay. Sales taxes are regressive; they affect low-income groups disproportionately. All people pay the sales tax at the same rate, so people in low income groups pay as much tax as people in high income groups. Part of the advantage of sales taxes and income taxes is that they can be regulated by the legislature that must raise the money.

GAMBLING: AN INCREASING SOURCE OF REVENUE   In 1964, New Hampshire implemented a lottery. In 2003, thirty-nine states were operating lotteries. Legalized gambling in its many forms, from casinos and riverboats to horse racing, has become the newest source of state and local revenues. Gambling is an indirect source of revenue in the sense that it is not seen as a direct tax on citizens; instead, the revenues come through taxes on the games. Commercial casinos (not including Native American casinos), which operate in eleven states, paid $3.6 billion in taxes in 2001. Income for states from lotteries grew from $978 million in 1980 to $12.4 billion in 2001. In fifteen states, part or all of the net proceeds from the lottery are allocated to education. In some states, such as California, the original intent was for these funds to be used for educational enhancements. But within three years of the California lottery's implementation, in a tight budget year, the California legislature incorporated the lottery funds into the base education budget.

An early study of the Florida lottery found the same thing. In the 1989–90 school year, the level of state funding for education decreased, and approximately 56.8 percent of the lottery proceeds were used as a substitute for existing resources. The findings from the study also indicated that there was equity in the distribution of the funds. Clearly, lotteries and other games represent a potential new source of funds for education.[10] It also is clear that without careful wording in the original statutes and continuous monitoring, these funds may merely become another revenue stream to fund the general budget, rather than monies set aside for educational enhancements.

RECENT CHALLENGES TO SCHOOL FINANCE WITHIN THE STATES

The number of court cases related to school finance has increased in recent years. Some states have had new suits initiated, while others are continuing to struggle to respond to earlier court decisions and directives. In all, nearly forty states have experienced or are experiencing court cases that deal with school finance.

THE STATE PERSPECTIVE ON TAXATION AND EDUCATION   Equal protection challenges have been, or are currently being, made at the state level. In some states, the plaintiffs have emphasized a claim of equal protection; in others the focus has been on specific language in the state's constitution. In all cases, the issue is whether the state has fulfilled its constitutional obligation to provide for education. The answer by the state supreme courts in some states has been that education is not a fundamental right, and that as long as there is provision for a minimally adequate education, the equal protection clause is met. In *Serrano v. Priest* (1971), the California Supreme Court was called on to determine whether the California public school financing system, with its substantial dependence on local property taxes, violated the Fourteenth Amendment. In its six-to-one decision, the California court held that heavy reliance on unequal local property taxes "makes the quality of a child's education a function of the wealth of his parents and neighbors." Furthermore, the court declared, "Districts with small tax bases simply cannot levy taxes at a rate sufficient to produce the revenue that more affluent districts produce with a minimum effort." Officially, the California Supreme Court ruled that the system of school financing in California was unconstitutional but did not forbid the use of property taxes as long as the system of finance was neutral in the distribution of resources. Within a year of *Serrano v. Priest*, five other courts—in Minnesota, Texas, New Jersey, Wyoming, and Arizona—ruled similarly.

STATES' RESPONSIBILITY TO GUARANTEE EQUAL EDUCATIONAL OPPORTUNITY

In 1989 and 1990, several state supreme courts made significant decisions about school finance. In a number of states, the education finance systems were knocked down by the courts, and the state legislatures were directed to remedy the wrongs.

In Montana, in *Helena Elementary School District v. State* (1989), the Montana Supreme Court ruled that the state's school finance system violated the state constitution's guarantee of equal educational opportunity. The state's constitution article mandates that the state establish an educational system that will develop the full educational potential of each person. In 1990 the court delayed the effects of its decision to allow the legislature time to enact a new finance system.[11]

The Kentucky Supreme Court also ruled that the entire system of school governance and finance violated the state constitution's mandate for the provision of an efficient system of common schools throughout the state (*Rose v. The Council for Better Education Inc.*, 1989). The Kentucky Supreme Court's opinion stated that

> The system of common schools must be adequately funded to achieve its goals. The system of common schools must be substantially uniform throughout the state. Each child, *every child,* in this commonwealth must be provided with an equal opportunity to have an adequate education. Equality is the key word here. The children of the poor and the children of the rich, the children who live in poor districts and the children who live in the rich districts must be given the same opportunity and access to an adequate education. This obligation cannot be shifted to local counties and local school districts.

The court directed the state legislature to develop a new educational system, which was adopted as the Kentucky Education Reform Act (KERA) in 1990.

Throughout the 1990s, there continued to be suits, court actions, and legislative initiatives regarding how best to address funding inequities for public schools. Further, earlier court decisions have been revisited. For example, in a turnaround of earlier decisions, in 1994 the State Supreme Court of Arizona ruled that the state's property tax–based school financing system was unconstitutional because it created wide disparities between rich and poor school districts. As has been true in other states, the court left it up to the legislature to rectify the problem.

Undoubtedly, changes are occurring in the state provisions for financial support for education. Equal expenditures per pupil might not, because of other factors, ensure equal opportunity; but equal expenditures per pupil do in fact enhance the likelihood of equal opportunity.

A rapidly expanding source of financial support for schools is advertising, although accepting this type of funding is a topic of intense debate.

ENTREPRENEURIAL EFFORTS TO FUND EDUCATION

The combination of tight budgets, increasing enrollments, and demands for better educational services is pressuring schools, school districts, and state officials to search for new funding sources. Some sources that were highly controversial in the past, such as the lottery, have now become a regular part of the main revenue stream. Other potential new sources of funds are now being considered, debated, and utilized.

ADVERTISING: A NEW SOURCE OF REVENUE   School districts have found that they can raise money by selling space for advertising. In Colorado Springs, District 11, for example, soft drinks and fast foods are advertised on the sides of school buses. Other school districts are seeking corporate sponsorships to support music and sports programs. For example, the Denver public schools solicited $500,000 from four companies to sponsor education programs and ran the companies' ads on school buses and at the district's main football stadium. One school district near the Dallas–Fort Worth International Airport is even selling space for advertising on the rooftops of district buildings to catch the eye of travelers on incoming flights.

MORE STUDENT FEES   Expanded use of student fees, especially for noncore subjects and extracurricular activities, is prevalent. Fees for enrollment, gym clothes, yearbooks, and lab equipment have become standard. Fees for student parking are becoming routine as well. For parents with more than one child in a secondary school, these fees can total more than $500 a year. Through various fees, a large high school can increase its revenues by $50,000 to $250,000 annually, which can add up to $1 million in four years. Participation in an athletic program means yet more fees. For example, in the 1996–97 school year, each student athlete in the Eanes, Texas, school district paid a $100 fee.

MORE FUND-RAISING SCHEMES   The entrepreneurial spirit seems to have no bounds once school and school district administrators jump on the capitalist bandwagon. Bake sales and parent booster groups are routine compared to some of the more innovative approaches being tried around the United States. For example, several school districts in California sent students home with forms their parents could sign to switch their long-distance telephone carrier. The school's parent–teacher association would receive 10 percent of the long-distance payment from each family. If the students signed up friends, neighbors, and relatives, the school would gain more revenue. Projections were that through this mechanism a large school could gain as much as half a million dollars a year.

Several years ago, Del Oro High School in Loomis, California, tested a novel way of raising money to support its sports teams. At one fall football game, three cows were turned loose on the football field for "cow-chip bingo." The field was marked off in one-yard squares and chances were sold. The owners of squares where the cows made a "deposit" were the winners.

QUESTIONS ABOUT FUND-RAISING EFFORTS   Given the special place and role of schools in society, important questions are being raised about the appropriate-

Has Student Fund-Raising Gone Too Far?

As budgets have become tighter and tighter, schools have become increasingly entrepreneurial in their efforts to find extra dollars. Students, teachers, and parents are being pressed to sell cookies, candies, lottery chances, magazines, and tickets to special events. When does the effort to supplement or enhance school funding go too far?

YES

Mary Neff is an English teacher at Odessa High School in western Texas. A twenty-one-year teaching veteran and NEA activist, Neff coedits her local NEA newsletter in Ector County and has held local NEA office. Neff currently serves on her school district's policy and planning committee.

I know student fundraising is getting out of hand when:

- I cover a class for a fellow teacher, and, as her students enter my room, they immediately ask me if I sell anything to eat.
- Anxious teenagers plead with me to please buy a cookbook, candy bar, ham, fruit box, posters, even manure to fertilize my lawn.
- Students go beyond raising money for an academic competition across the state and, instead, raise funds to go to Disneyland.
- One of my seniors takes a school-sponsored cruise to the Bahamas. On the day they are to explore the islands, the student can't find his boarding pass and has to remain on the ship. For this, he misses three days of school.
- An 11-year-old New Jersey boy, last seen going door-to-door selling wrapping paper for a school fundraiser, is found murdered.

These events—and particularly this recent tragedy—should give us all pause. What are we really asking children to do when they're handed the "opportunity" to raise money for extras? What are we really selling?

Some say the real-world experience students gain from fundraising—and the travel it buys—builds character and broadens horizons.

But I often wonder if the students in Japan are out selling stationery and smoked sausage in the evenings. Are we, in America, so bereft of character-building opportunities that we must ask our children to go door-to-door?

My fantasy is a complete school year without fundraisers. Who would miss the bags of candy, brochures full of merchandise, lost or stolen collection envelopes, and teachers-turned-bill collectors?

NO

Clorinda Graziano teaches instrumental music at Frank Borman Middle School in Phoenix, Arizona. An NEA activist, she's served as chair of her local negotiations team for three years. Last year, Graziano helped her band students raise $160,000 so they could march in the New Year's Day Parade in London.

I have fond memories of selling Girl Scout cookies when I was in the third grade and going door-to-door with my mother raising money for various charities.

My biggest fundraising education came in high school, helping raise money for band and chorus annual trips. It's amazing to me, as I think back now, how much I learned from those experiences.

I learned about bookkeeping, banking, ordering, marketing, dealing with salespeople, budgeting, responsibility, working as a group, goal-setting, and achievement—all "real-life" skills.

If we didn't raise the money, we didn't go—that was the bottom line. That was a tremendous lesson to learn at a young age.

All the skills I learned as a student fundraiser have helped me immensely as a music instructor. Our schools always need money for something that's outside the spectrum of what the school district can provide.

Almost all of the handbell and handchime sets at individual schools are paid for through music student or PTA fundraisers. Students' summer music camp tuitions are routinely funded by candy sales.

By far the biggest fundraising project I've been involved in was our effort to send 104 junior high band students and chaperones to London to march in last year's New Year's Day Parade.

Each student and chaperone had to earn $1,525 to go. With more than 70 percent of our students on free or reduced-price lunch, there aren't a lot of families with extra money to shell out every time their children want something. We either help them earn their own way, or they can't go.

So we helped. We set up individual accounts for each student. What they raised was credited toward

(continued)

YES

I would welcome back the lost time and energy spent raising money. My time is better spent preparing for instruction. Students' time is better spent in the classroom and in after-school clubs that pursue interests, not dollars.

We should rely more on booster clubs made up of parents and patrons who raise money to supplement the activities that are important to them. And we should establish clearer priorities for our school systems and the communities that fund them.

Asking a community to finance any and all activities and materials that are not covered by the school budget is grossly unfair to everyone. We need to accept the simple fact that if it's not in the budget, perhaps we won't get it.

And perhaps we don't need it. Maybe we shouldn't raise money for unlimited student travel and laptops to keep athletic statistics, while at the same time issuing paperback books held together with rubber bands.

When we tell taxpayers they have to pay an additional $25 in property taxes, maybe we can understand why they rebel.

After all the fruit cakes, greeting cards, and bumper stickers they've already bought, why should they have a clear picture of what the public schools are trying to accomplish?

Let's face it: We are slowly bleeding money out of our communities to finance frills and dubious endeavors.

If you ask our school patrons what their goals for our schools are, I don't think a trip to Never-Never Land would be high on the list.

Source: "Has Student Fundraising Gone Too Far?" *NEA Today* (February 1998), p. 43.

NO

their own trip. Students sold candy, washed cars, held carnivals, sponsored volleyball tournaments, and more.

It paid off. Going to London was a great experience for all of us.

I know the students took the trip more seriously because they worked so hard to go, and because so many people had cared enough about them to send them on the trip of a lifetime.

I was amazed to hear so many parents tell me how much the fundraising had brought their families together. That unexpected benefit really boosted students' self-esteem.

Student fundraising does so much more than just raise money for school projects. It would be a shame if the appalling murder of a New Jersey boy while soliciting fundraising orders door-to-door forces an end to all student fundraising efforts.

It's not the school's fault that the child was alone, selling in a neighborhood to people he didn't know.

Schools have been trumpeting the message— "don't sell by yourself, don't sell to strangers, don't sell in strange neighborhoods"—for years. Plus, the child's parents should have known where he was on a Saturday afternoon and should have gone over the rules with him in advance.

A few unfortunate and preventable incidences shouldn't curtail the opportunities of all.

There are too many lifetime skills that can be learned and experiences gained to simply end student fundraising. What's at stake is much more than just a few dollars.

WHAT DO YOU THINK?
Has student fund-raising gone too far?

To give your opinion, go to Chapter 5 of the companion website
(**www.ablongman.com/johnson13e**) and click on Debate.

Companion Website

ness of many of these newer fund-raising efforts. Equity is one important issue. Schools in wealthy communities can raise more money than schools located in poor communities. If an important goal is to provide equal educational opportunity for all students, then the unequal distribution of funds and equipment is once again an issue. A second important question has to do with children being exposed to advertising in schools. A report by Consumers Union points out how the underfunding of schools has led to students being a captive audience for marketers.[12] Many educators are concerned that students are impressionable, unsophisticated consumers and are easily influenced. In the school context, many students will have difficulty distinguishing advertising from lesson messages. Because of budget pressures, however, schools and school districts will likely continue to develop their commercial bent.

EDUCATION SPENDING

Once funds for education are collected at the local, state, and federal levels, they are distributed to schools and school districts. Some of the funds are targeted by state and federal governments for specific activities and programs, but most decisions about allocations of funds are determined by each school district. In general, teachers and principals have little say in how monies will be spent.

The overall pattern of distribution of the public education dollar is shown in Figure 5.8. By far the largest proportion of the expenditures (61.7 percent) is directly related to instruction, teacher salaries being the major expense. One-third of the education dollar goes to support services, an amount that includes much of the expenses for operating the school district office.

Another frequently used statistic for examining and comparing school districts and states is per-pupil expenditure. For the 1999–2000 school year, the national average was $6,911 per pupil. However, as illustrated in Figure 5.9, per-pupil expenditures range from $4,378 in Utah to $10,337 in New Jersey.

STATE AID

State aid for education exists largely for three reasons: The state has the primary responsibility for educating its citizens; the financial ability of local school districts to support education varies widely; and personal wealth is now less related to real property than it once was. State aid can be classified as having general or categorical use. *General aid* can be used by the recipient school district as it desires; *categorical aid* is earmarked for specific purposes. Categorical aid may include, for example, money for transportation, vocational education, driver education, or programs for children with disabilities. Frequently, categorical aid is given to encourage specified education programs; in some states, these aid programs are referred to as *incentive programs.* Categorical aid funds may be granted

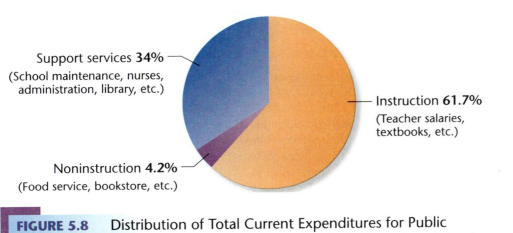

Support services **34%**
(School maintenance, nurses, administration, library, etc.)

Instruction **61.7%**
(Teacher salaries, textbooks, etc.)

Noninstruction **4.2%**
(Food service, bookstore, etc.)

FIGURE 5.8   Distribution of Total Current Expenditures for Public Elementary and Secondary Schools, by Function: School Year 1999–2000

Note: Percentages may not sum to 100 due to rounding. Other support included business office and research activities that did not appear in general administration. Percentage distribution of total current expenditures reported here may differ from a previously published report of such expenditures due to rounding.

Source: U.S. Department of Education, National Center for Education Statistics, Common Core Data, "National Public Education Financial Survey" School Year 1999–2000. Washington, DC: Author.

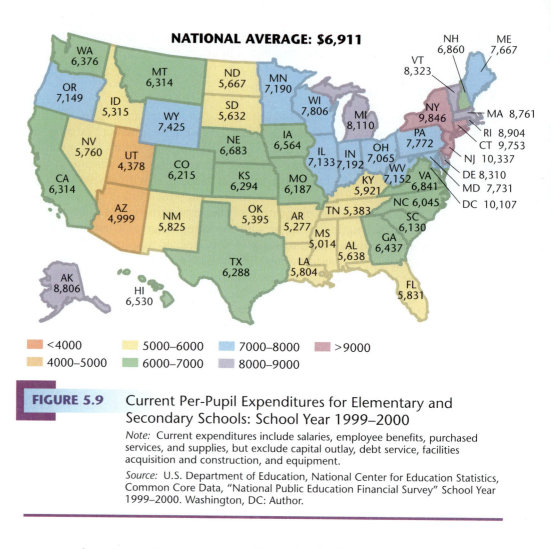

NATIONAL AVERAGE: $6,911

Color	Range
<4000	
4000–5000	
5000–6000	
6000–7000	
7000–8000	
8000–9000	
>9000	

FIGURE 5.9 Current Per-Pupil Expenditures for Elementary and Secondary Schools: School Year 1999–2000

Note: Current expenditures include salaries, employee benefits, purchased services, and supplies, but exclude capital outlay, debt service, facilities acquisition and construction, and equipment.

Source: U.S. Department of Education, National Center for Education Statistics, Common Core Data, "National Public Education Financial Survey" School Year 1999–2000. Washington, DC: Author.

on a matching basis; thus, for each dollar of local effort, the state contributes a specified amount. Categorical aid has undoubtedly encouraged development of needed educational programs.

GENERAL STATE AID: EQUALITY OF OPPORTUNITY

Historically, general aid was based on the idea that each child, regardless of place of residence or the wealth of the local district, is entitled to receive a basic education. General state aid was established on the principle of equality of opportunity and is usually administered through a foundation program. Creating a *foundation program* involves determining the dollar value of the basic education opportunities desired in a state, referred to as the foundation level, and determining a minimum standard of local effort, considering local wealth. The foundation concept implies equity for taxpayers as well as equality of opportunity for students.

HOW STATE FOUNDATION PROGRAMS WORK   Figure 5.10 shows how a foundation program operates. The total length of each bar represents the foundation level of education required per pupil, expressed in dollars. Each school district must put forth the same minimum local effort to finance its schools; this effort could be, for example, a qualifying tax rate that produces the local share of the foundation level. This tax rate will produce more revenue in a wealthy district than it will in a poor district; therefore, the poor district will receive more state aid than the wealthy district. Local school districts do not receive general state aid beyond that amount established as the foundation but are permitted in most instances to exceed foundation levels at their own expense.

STATE FOUNDATION PROGRAMS: LIMITED EFFECTIVENESS The effectiveness of using various state foundation programs to bring about fiscal equalization has been limited. A major limitation is that the foundation established is frequently far below the actual expenditure or far below the level needed to provide adequate educational opportunity. For example, if a state established a per-pupil foundation level of $1,500 and the average actual per-pupil expenditure was $3,000, equalization would not have occurred.

A second limitation is that most general state aid programs do not provide for different expenditure levels for different pupil needs. Special education and vocational education, for example, both require more money to operate than the usual per-pupil expenditure for the typical elementary or secondary school pupil.

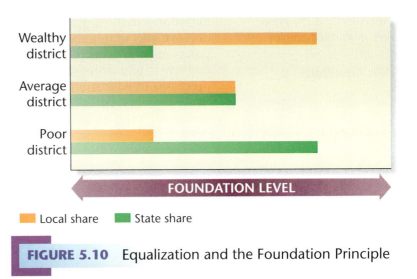

FOUNDATION LEVEL

■ Local share   ■ State share

FIGURE 5.10 Equalization and the Foundation Principle

FEDERAL AID

The United States has a history of federal aid to education, but it has been categorical and not general aid; it has been related to the needs of the nation at the time. Federal aid actually started before the U.S. Constitution was adopted, with the Northwest Ordinance of 1785, which provided land for public schools in "western territories." Such specialized federal aid has continued in a steady progression to the present. Almost 200 federal aid-to-education laws have been passed since the Northwest Ordinance.

■ ACCOUNTABILITY

With the arrival of the No Child Left Behind Act, states, school districts, and schools are being held accountable as never before. Although there are many

State aid for education is classified for general or categorical use, and general aid is often administered through a foundation program that will fund each school district up to a foundation level of education required per pupil.

definitions of the term **accountability,** in education it means that schools must devise a way of relating the vast expenditure made for education to the educational results, especially student performance on tests. For many years, the quality of education was measured by the number of dollars spent or the processes of education used. In other words, a school system that had a relatively high cost per pupil or used educational techniques judged to be effective was considered an excellent system. Seldom was the effectiveness of school systems judged by student outcomes—the educational achievements of students. Now those outcomes and their cost must be clearly accounted for.

ROOTS OF ACCOUNTABILITY

Accountability has its roots in two fundamental modern problems: the continuous escalation of educational costs and, closely related, the loss of faith in educational results. The failure of the U.S. educational system, particularly in the cities and in some remote rural areas, has been accurately documented. The expectations of citizens for their children have not been met. Although U.S. public schools historically have done the best job of any nation in the world in providing education for *all the children of all the people,* they still have failed for some of their constituents.

THE IMPORTANCE OF TEACHER ACCOUNTABILITY

Teachers play an important role in the quest for accountability. They are the primary contact with students, and they are directly responsible for instruction and student achievement. Therefore, they are expected to do their utmost to motivate students to learn and achieve. The assessment of accountability relies on data; therefore, teachers need to keep accurate records with respect to student achievement and be certain that instruction is well aligned with what is being tested.

REWARDS FOR BEING ACCOUNTABLE

The other side of the accountability coin is determining what will be the rewards for success and the sanctions for failure. In the 1980s, many reward programs consisted of bestowing special designations and plaques on schools. In the 1990s, there was a shift to the use of money as a reward or sanction. Under NCLB, few rewards exist. Instead, different forms of threats and sanctions hang over states, school districts, and schools that "need improvement."

REWARDING TEACHERS AND PRINCIPALS

Other accountability initiatives target teachers and principals directly through focused evaluation and training programs, as well as offering financial rewards. For example, the Texas Successful Schools program includes a Principals' Performance Incentive program that awards up to $5,000 to principals whose campuses meet performance gain criteria. Other states are considering similar programs.

SCHOOL AND SCHOOL DISTRICT REPORT CARDS

In the past, report cards were used only to evaluate students. A new element in the accountability movement is the use of new forms of report cards to "grade" schools, school districts, and states. Advocates of report cards argue that parents and voters need to know how well their school or school district is doing in comparison to others. They also point out that evaluating schools is complex; many factors need to be considered. A report card can incorporate many factors and present a clear picture. Opponents express concern that report cards still are overly simplistic representations. They argue that report cards increase competition, which is not supposed to be a part of public education. Proponents argue back that competition will make low-performing schools improve and/or inform parents so that they can make the choice of sending their children to another school.

accountability

A school's obligation to take responsibility for what students learn.

Clearly, an evaluation of schools needs to take into account a number of factors, some of which may be easy to score, whereas others require more subtlety. Class size, the amount of expenditures on technology, and test scores can be quantified. However, other factors, such as safety and the feel of the organizational culture, are not easily counted. This means that these report cards will likely become increasingly complex and less easy to understand. Still, teachers, parents, policymakers, and the public at large continue to need ways to evaluate how well schools are doing.

◼ PERENNIAL SCHOOL FINANCE ISSUES

The basic challenge in school financing is not likely to be different in the near future from what it has been in the past. That challenge is making an adequate public education system equally available to everyone, along with a system of taxation designed to be equitable—that is, a progressive tax plan, a system in which taxpayers are all called on to support education in proportion to their ability to pay. Both equal opportunity and equitable taxation are difficult to achieve, as illustrated earlier in this chapter.

Some issues from the 1990s have continued into the 2000s. These issues include increasing enrollments, taxpayer revolt, rewards for accountability, and the conditions of schools, all of which are likely to affect the adequacy of school funding and therefore further complicate the basic challenge in school finance—the challenge of providing an adequate education with equality of opportunity through an equitable system of taxation.

ISSUE: INCREASING ENROLLMENTS

Enrollment in elementary and secondary schools grew rapidly during the 1950s and 1960s and reached a peak in 1971. From 1971 to 1983, total enrollment decreased rapidly, reflecting the decline in the school-age population over that period. Enrollment reached a low of 44.9 million in 1984. Since then, enrollments have been increasing again. In 2000–01, enrollment in elementary and secondary education was 53.2 million and is projected to reach 53.7 million by 2011–12.[13]

Increased enrollments have effects on the amount of money needed to support education adequately. Although the new surge of students will be somewhat gradual, it will undoubtedly increase expenditures, and increased revenue is very likely to be needed to maintain the current level of expenditures per pupil. Furthermore, according to one educator, "the rising public school enrollments will include larger numbers and percentages of minority, limited-English-proficient, poor, and learning disabled students. All these special categories of students will require extra services to meet their needs."[14] Whether additional revenues will be available to provide educational services to the growing student population remains open to speculation.

ISSUE: TAXPAYER REVOLT

In the last thirty years, there have been a number of political initiatives by taxpayers to reduce their tax burden, especially the amount they pay in property taxes. This movement has been called the *taxpayer revolt*. A most dramatic instance of taxpayer revolt occurred in California in June 1978 with the passage of a citizens' ballot initiative called Proposition 13, which limited by constitutional amendment the property tax as a source of revenue. Subsequent and similar propositions have been added in other states. The trend is toward tax limitation, which reduces funds available for education. These efforts, along with a low success rate of local school bond referenda and the closing of school districts for periods of time because of insufficient operating funds, indicate problems ahead for the funding of public schools.

TABLE 5.4   Per-Pupil Spending on School Facilities by States

State	Per-Pupil Facilities Spending	State	Per-Pupil Facilities Spending
Alaska*	$2,254	New Mexico	93
Hawaii*	740	New Hampshire	84
Florida*	290	Wyoming	80
Connecticut	281	Mississippi	72
Delaware	275	New Jersey	61
Maine	203	North Dakota	48
North Carolina*	195	South Carolina	41
Massachusetts*	193	Ohio	38
New York	167	Idaho	30
Vermont	163	Utah	21
Indiana	155	Kansas	16
Minnesota*	153	Alabama	14
Washington	150	Michigan	13
Georgia*	123	Arkansas	11
Rhode Island	117	California	10[†]
Maryland*	113	Montana	6
Pennsylvania	105	West Virginia	0[‡]
Colorado	105	Tennessee	Not provided
Virginia	104	Arizona	Reported as unknown
Kentucky*	104	Wisconsin	Reported as unknown

Note: Illinois, Iowa, Louisiana, Missouri, Nebraska, Nevada, Oklahoma, Oregon, South Dakota, and Texas had no regular, ongoing program to assist districts with construction costs and are not included in the table.

*State has a comprehensive program, including facility-condition data, funding, and technical assistance and compliance review.

[†]California issues bonds every two years for school construction, but state officials report that sales scheduled in 1994 did not succeed; the amount shown represents the state's deferred-maintenance program, which does not depend on bond sales.

[‡]West Virginia provides state aid for school construction—$500 million since 1990—but provided none in 1994.

Source: U.S. General Accounting Office.

ISSUE: THE CONDITION OF SCHOOLS

For more than a decade, a frequent response to tight and reduced funding of schools has been to defer maintenance on buildings. A consequence of this tactic is that now thousands of school buildings across the nation need major repairs. Historically, states paid a large portion of the costs of school building construction; but with increased pressures from other sectors, such as criminal justice and welfare, state legislatures are backing away from supporting school construction and maintenance costs. One of the long-term effects on schools of the taxpayer revolt is now readily observed in states such as California, where 40 percent of the schools have roof and plumbing problems. Table 5.4 illustrates the dramatic differences among states' spending on school facilities.[15]

GLOBAL PERSPECTIVES

International Comparisons: Class Size as an Indicator

Debate continues about the amount of investment the United States makes in public education and how well this amount compares with what other countries invest. International comparisons are difficult to make, yet they need to be made. One clear indicator of investment is the number of students being taught by each teacher. How does the United States compare to other countries in terms of the number of students per teacher? This analysis for selected countries is presented in Figure 5.11. As with other international comparisons, there is a great deal of variation in class size, with the United States being neither at the top nor at the bottom. In the end, high levels of student performance are dependent on a number of indicators, including per-pupil expenditure, class size, and how schools and school districts are organized.

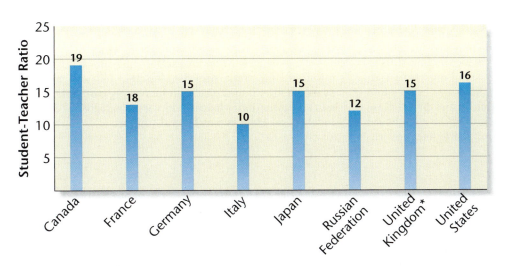

Ratio of full-time-equivalent students to full-time-equivalent teachers in public and private secondary schools, by country: 1999

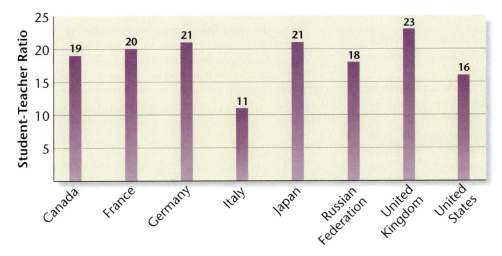

Ratio of full-time-equivalent students to full-time-equivalent teachers in public and private primary schools, by country: 1999

FIGURE 5.11 International Comparisons: Class Size

*Includes only general programs.

Note: The United Kingdom includes England, Northern Ireland, Scotland, and Wales.

Source: Organization for Economic Cooperation and Development. *Education at a Glance,* 2001, Table D 5.1.

SUMMARY

Two key ways to understand how the American education system works is to study its organization and financing. Teaching does not take place in a classroom that is an island, disconnected from the rest of the system. All parts are intertwined. What a teacher does in his or her classroom is affected by the rest of the school, the principal, the district, the state, and the federal government. Conversely, what you do in your classroom will affect the rest of the system.

Different levels of the organization of education exist in the United States. The organization of nearly all schools is by classrooms, with the principal being the line authority. At the school district level, each school reports to a superintendent, and school district policies are established by the school board. All schools, public and private, are under the authority of the state, including the state board of education and the state legislature. The federal government plays an ever-increasing role through its provision of funds for targeted educational needs and the establishment of laws such as NCLB. Teachers must understand the jobs and know the names of the key individuals in their school, district, and state. Teachers must maintain their line relationships by following through on tasks and assignments and being sure to communicate. A continuing issue of debate and concern is that of local control. As states and the federal government increase their involvement with and oversight of education, those at the local level have reduced opportunities to adjust to local needs.

The key issues of education finance are related to taxation, aid programs, and developing a fair and equitable system. Other issues deal with increasing certain taxes versus tax limitations, general aid versus categorical aid, and local versus state versus federal support.

DISCUSSION QUESTIONS

1. The No Child Left Behind Act is having a wide-ranging and continuing impact on schools, school districts, and states. What do you think about NCLB and its impacts? Do you think the federal government should be assuming such a strong role over states, school districts, and schools?

2. Have you had any firsthand experiences with site-based decision making? What do you see as the effects of this feature of school governance?

3. Is local control an issue in your state? What situations have you encountered that illustrate the tension between state and local education interests?

4. When is it appropriate for teachers to engage in politics? How can teachers influence what goes on in their schools? How can they influence decisions at the district and board levels?

5. What are the advantages of using sales and income taxes to fund elementary and secondary education instead of relying on the property tax?

6. Given the data that compare class size in different countries, how well do you think the United States is doing? Given the fact that reducing class size will require additional funds, where do you think policymakers should invest?

7. Explain why the federal government should or should not provide funds for the repair of school buildings.

JOURNAL ENTRIES

1. Develop an organizational chart for a school you are familiar with. Use solid lines to represent line relationships and dotted lines to signify staff relationships. Draw the arrangement of personnel in regard to each of the following decisions: (1) determining a child's grade on his or her report card, (2) expelling a student (hint—don't forget that the school is part of a school district), (3) deciding on the topic for a staff development day, and (4) determining whether a particular teaching activity will be used. After considering these different decisions, explain your thoughts and feelings about the authority and accountability of teachers within the school as an organization.

2. Develop a list of the concerns and issues that came to mind as you read the school finance sections of this chapter. What topics have implications for you as a teacher? What topics have implications for you as a taxpayer? Then write a journal entry examining your ideas about how schools should be funded.

PORTFOLIO DEVELOPMENT

1. One important component of the No Child Left Behind Act is the part mandating that each state set standards for highly qualified teachers (HQTs). Review the requirements for being an HQT in your state and then analyze your résumé. What will you need to accomplish to become an HQT?

2. School finance and spending will continue to be hot topics for school districts, state legislatures, and taxpayers. Start a file of articles from newspapers and newsmagazines and notes from television and radio news reports that deal with school finance and spending. Review the items in your file. Do certain topics and themes, such as school building construction, continue to be reported? When you are ready to apply for a position, having knowledge about finance and spending issues will make you better informed and prepared.

PREPARING FOR CERTIFICATION

■ SCHOOL ORGANIZATION AND CHOICE

1. The Praxis II Principles of Teaching and Learning (PLT) test includes cases and items that address "school-related issues (for example, school restructuring, school-based management plans, working in multidisciplinary teams, problems new teachers face, such as alienation and anxiety)." Reread this chapter's discussion of alternative school organizational structures. How might these alternative forms of school organization and management affect your role as a teacher? What skills will you need to function in such restructured schools?

2. Answer the following multiple-choice question, which is similar to items in Praxis and other state certification tests. If you are unsure of the answer, reread the School Choice: Increasing Options along with Uncertain Outcomes section of this chapter.

   Williams High School, located in a major U.S. city, has an academic curriculum that focuses on science and technology. The school has specialized science and computer laboratories, a carefully selected faculty, and an advanced curriculum. Students from across the district with interest and aptitude in science and technology can apply to attend. Williams High School is an example of a

   (A) charter school
   (B) independent school
   (C) pilot school
   (D) magnet school

3. Answer the following short-answer question, which is similar to items in Praxis and other state certification tests. After you've completed your written response, use the scoring guide in the ETS *Test at a Glance* materials to assess your response. Can you revise your response to improve your score?

   Some school reformers believe vouchers are an effective means of improving education. Describe the purpose of vouchers and how they work. List at least two arguments for and two arguments against the use of vouchers in public education.

WEBSITES

www.ed.gov/about/offices.jsp   The U.S. Department of Education is composed of a number of offices and institutes. Each of these offices can be located from this web page.

www.ed.gov/NCES/   The National Center for Education Statistics of the U.S. Department of Education provides on-line data and reports that describe many characteristics of schools, school finance, and international comparisons.

www.eric.uoregon.edu   The University of Oregon has an ERIC clearinghouse on educational management. It provides many reports and publications related to the organization of schools.

www.nasbe.org   The National Association of State Boards of Education is a good source for information about shared interests and topics of concern to state boards of education.

www.ecs.org   The Education Commission of the States is a policy study center for and association of the state governors. Many interesting and useful position papers and conference activities for state-level policymakers are sponsored by this commission.

www.edweek.org   *Education Week* is a newspaper that includes information about school finance and innovations in the organization of schools. Each week's issue contains several interesting articles dealing with these topics from local, state, and national perspectives.

www.ncsl.org/public/leglinks.cfm   The National Council of State Legislatures is an association that facilitates the interstate exchange of information about education policy. Use this website to find out about state legislatures and education-related policy initiatives.

FURTHER READING

Bolman, Lee G., and Deal, Terrence E. (2003). *Reframing Organizations: Artistry, Choice and Leadership.* San Francisco: Jossey-Bass. Many books about organization theory are complicated and provide few examples. This book is the exception. All of the theories and research about organizations and leadership are described in terms of four frames or perspectives. Each frame is described separately, along with plenty of interesting examples from all types of organizations, including schools. The focus throughout is the implications for teacher and administrator leadership.

Hanson, E. Mark. (2003). *Educational Administration and Organizational Behavior* (5th ed.). Boston: Allyn and Bacon. This text is written for educators who are interested in learning more about organization theory and research and its implications for schools and leaders. Each chapter is organized around a particular perspective, such as sociopolitical, professional–bureaucratic, and motivation and management.

Reeves, Douglas B. (2002). *The Daily Disciplines of Leadership: How to Improve Student Achievement, Staff Motivation, and Personal Organization.* San Francisco: Jossey-Bass. Leadership in schools is not solely the responsibility of the principal. Teachers have leadership responsibilities as well. Leadership as it unfolds daily is the theme for this book. The author describes four key leadership archetypes and offers a number of practical recommendations.

Wong, Kenneth K. (1999). *Funding Public Schools: Politics and Policies (Studies in Government and Public Policy).* Lawrence, KS: University Press. Instead of focusing on cost efficiency and the traditional topics of school finance, this book examines the politics of resource allocation at the federal, state, and local level. A set of "rules" is proposed that affects how funds are allocated. The role of politics, the dynamics of policy development, and implications for schools are described. Four models are described through which there could be an integration of political and educational accountability.

NOTES

1. B. Fuller, E. Burr, L. Huerta, S. Puryear, and E. Wexler, *School Choice: Abundant Hopes, Scarce Evidence on Results.* Berkeley, CA: Policy Analysis for California Education, 1999.

2. D. Goldhaber, "School Choice: An Examination of the Empirical Evidence on Achievement, Parental Decision Making, and Equity." *Educational Researcher* (December 1999), pp. 16–25.

3. B. Nelson, P. Berman, J. Ericson, N. Kamprath, R. Perry, D. Silverman, and D. Solomon, *The State of Charter Schools 2000.* Washington, DC: Office of Educational Research and Improvement, U.S. Department of Education, 2000.

4. *Private Independent Schools 2002, 55th Annual Edition.* Wallingford, CT: Bunting and Lyon, 2002.

5. Bobette Reed and William L. Dandridge, *Minority Leaders for Independent Schools.* Boston: National Association of Independent Schools.

6. John Cloud and Jodie Morse, "Home Sweet School," *Time, 158*(8) (2001), pp. 46–54.

7. Richard C. Hunter, "The Mayor versus the School Superintendent," *Education and Urban Society, 29*(2) (February 1997), pp. 217–232.

8. Jack Jennings, "Commentary," *From the Capital to the Classroom, State and Federal Efforts to Implement the No Child Left Behind Act.* Washington, DC: Center on Education Policy, 2003.

9. U.S. Department of Education, National Center for Education Statistics, *Revenues and Expenditures for Public Elementary and Secondary Education: School Year 1999–2000.* Washington, DC: Author, May 2002.

10. Steven Stark, Craig R. Wood, and David S. Honeyman, "The Florida Education Lottery: Its Use as a Substitute for Existing Funds and Its Effects on the Equity of School Funding." *Journal of Education Finance, 18* (Winter 1993), pp. 231–242.

11. *Helena Elementary School District v. State* (1989).
12. Consumers Union Education Services, *Captive Kids: Commercial Pressures on Kids at School.* Yonkers, NY: Consumers Union, 1996.
13. U.S. Department of Education, National Center for Education Statistics, *Projections of Education Statistics to 2012.* Washington, DC: U.S. Department of Education, October 2002.
14. Daniel U. Levine, "Educational Spending: International Comparisons," *Theory into Practice 33*(2) (Spring 1994), pp. 126–131.
15. *School Facilities: States' Financial and Technical Support Varies* (GAO/HEHS-96-27). Washington, DC: General Accounting Office, 1996.

Legal Foundations of Education

Education in the News

Copies of Student Newspaper Seized

The Associated Press, *Las Vegas Review Journal*, December 22, 2002

WOOSTER, OHIO—SCHOOL OFFICIALS IN A DISTRICT WHERE the policy is to allow students freedom of speech confiscated thousands of copies of the high school newspaper after learning it contained an article in which students talked about drinking alcohol at a party.

Student editors said the article quoted the daughter of a school board member saying she had consumed alcohol, and they believe that was the reason about 4,500 copies of the bi-weekly *Wooster Blade* were seized Thursday.

James Jackson, the principal at Wooster High School, confirmed Saturday that the papers were taken after a teacher told him about a possible confidentiality problem with the story.

Federal law forbids naming students who face disciplinary action without parents' permission, and at least one student claimed to have been misquoted, Jackson said. Violating privacy rights could leave the school vulnerable to lawsuits, he said.

The student journalists disagreed and called the Student Press Law Center. Mike Hiestand, an attorney for the Arlington, VA-based center, said he reviewed the reporting at the student editors' request and saw nothing in the *Blade* that violated libel laws.

"It's very good reporting," Heistand said. "It's just another one of those cases of school officials wanting nothing but happy news in the newspaper and abusing their authority."

According to a policy under "Student Publication Rights" on the Wooster City School District's Web site, an "unfettered student press" is essential and "student journalists shall be afforded protection against prior review and/or censorship."

It says that freedom does not extend to material that is obscene or defamatory, or would disrupt school activities. "I feel very privileged to have an open forum policy, but personally I am disappointed that it has been violated," said Darcy Draudt, 17, a senior and editor of the *Wooster Blade.*

Whether school administrators can insist on prior review of a students' publication has been a hot issue in high school journalism since 1988, when the U.S. Supreme Court ruled limits can be set on the free press rights of high school students.

(INTASC) **Learning Outcomes**

After reading and studying this chapter, you should be able to:

1. Explain the relationships between the U.S. Constitution and the role and responsibilities of the states in ensuring the availability of public schools for all children. (INTASC 7: Planning)

2. Describe critical issues about the role of public schools for which the courts are being used to resolve points of debate. (INTASC 9: Reflection)

3. Identify and describe court-established guidelines related to the use of public funds for private schools. (INTASC 9: Reflection)

4. Identify and describe court-established guidelines related to religious activities in public schools. (INTASC 7: Planning)

5. Outline the role of statutes and court decisions related to civil rights and affirmative action as they relate to schools. (INTASC 9: Reflection)

6. Summarize key components of the rights and responsibilities of teachers as determined by

key U.S. Supreme Court decisions. (INTASC 9: Reflection)

7. Be clear about a teacher's responsibilities and liabilities related to negligence. (INTASC 7: Planning)

8. Distinguish between students' rights and responsibilities as citizens and their rights and responsibilities as students. (INTASC 9: Reflection)

School-Based Observations

You may see these learning outcomes in action during your visits to schools:

1. Beginning teachers do not have the same rights as tenured teachers, but they do have rights. With a partner, compare and contrast the rights of beginning teachers in two school districts. Some of the items to check are length of the probationary period, the basis for tenure decision, how the tenure decision-making process works, and the rights of probationary teachers.

2. Interview an experienced teacher about students' rights. Ask him or her to provide examples of situations in which it was important for the teacher to be aware of student rights. What were the critical points to be considered? What were the related responsibilities of the teacher? What advice would this teacher have for today's beginning teachers?

Aspiring teachers typically do not consider the fact that there is a legal aspect to teaching. As citizens of the United States, teachers are, of course, subject to the laws of the land. However, in addition, teachers are employees and as such have specified protected rights and responsibilities. Also, teachers are responsible not only for children learning but also for their safety and protecting their rights. In each of these areas, elements of the legal system, its processes, and its rulings come into play. As illustrated in the Education in the News feature, schools and educators are frequently drawn into areas of debate that reflect society at large. All too frequently, it seems, the courts are turned to for resolution. Hot areas of debate include prayer in schools, racial equality, and teachers' and children's rights as citizens versus their rights in school.

The first big idea addressed in this chapter emphasizes that the legal foundations of education are the U.S. Constitution and the Bill of Rights. All else evolves from interpretations of the Constitution. Another big idea has to do with the rights and responsibilities of teachers as employees. For example, teachers are protected from termination without cause. A related important big idea is teacher responsibility, including providing safe and well-supervised educational activities for students. Teachers also need to understand that children retain their rights as citizens while having related rights and responsibilities as students. Another big idea is that policymakers such as Congress, state legislatures, and local school boards also establish laws in the forms of statutes, policies, rules, and procedures. Teachers must know about and understand how these affect classroom practice as well.

To illustrate each of these ideas, this chapter presents an important set of social, political, and educational issues that have been debated within and addressed by the legal system. It examines topics such as the appropriateness of using public funds to support private education, desegregation, teachers' rights, and students' rights. The chapter draws on excerpts from the Constitution, state statutes, and court decisions to point out some of the important issues that have been addressed through the legal system. Each of the topics presented in this chapter, as well as the legal processes behind it, applies directly to what you can do and should not do as a teacher and a school district employee. The chapter is organized into three major sections: the legal basis and framing of the public education system, the legal rights and responsibilities of teachers, and the rights and responsibilities of students.

LEGAL ASPECTS OF EDUCATION

The legal foundation of the United States is the U.S. Constitution, and a pivotal part of the Constitution is the Bill of Rights. Within the boundaries of U.S. law, each state is guided by its own constitution. Several additional sources of laws exist at the federal, state, and local levels, and there are a number of processes for addressing disputes. As illustrated in Figure 6.1, in many ways the teacher is the implementer at the intersection between those who enact laws and those who interpret them. Some, but not all, laws are developed out of the legislative process. These are referred to as **enabling laws**, or those that provide opportunity or make it possible for educators to do certain things. Also, laws can impose mandates or prohibitions. Once legislation is enacted into law, if a question of interpretation is raised, then the **judicial interpretive process** is engaged. If an administrative interpretation is not accepted, then the judicial process can come into play. The judicial process also is used when it appears that a law has been violated. The interpretations of the state and federal court systems form a body of case law. The sampling of legal topics presented in this chapter includes examples from constitutional law, state and federal statutes, and case law based on court interpretations. All apply directly to schools, teachers, and students.

■ LEGAL PROVISIONS FOR EDUCATION: THE U.S. CONSTITUTION

The educational systems of the United States, both public and nonpublic, are governed by law. The U.S. Constitution is the fundamental law for the nation, and a state legislature has no right to change the Constitution. When a state legislature makes laws that apply to education, these laws must be in accordance with both the U.S. Constitution and that state's constitution.

Three of the amendments to the U.S. Constitution are particularly significant to the governance of education, both public and private, in the United States. Interpretations of each of these amendments—the First, Tenth, and Fourteenth—by the courts have had profound impacts on the role and purpose of schools, the opportunities of all students to have access to an education, and the responsibilities and rights of teachers, students, and school administrators.

TENTH AMENDMENT

The U.S. Constitution does not specifically provide for public education; however, the Tenth Amendment has been interpreted as granting this power to the states. The amendment specifies that "The powers not delegated to the United States by the Constitution, nor prohibited by it to the States, are reserved to the States respectively, or to the people." Therefore, education is legally the responsibility and the function of each of the fifty states. Education in the United States is not nationalized as it is in many other nations of the world.

ENABLING AND LEGISLATIVE AGENTS

- People of the state and their rights under the U.S. Constitution
- Constitution of the state
- Statutes of the state legislature
- State school board policies
- Local school board policies

The Classroom Teacher

INTERPRETIVE AND ADMINISTRATIVE AGENTS

- Local administrative officers
- State superintendent of public instruction
- Opinions of the attorney general
- Decisions of the state court
- Decisions of the U.S. Supreme Court

FIGURE 6.1 Sources of Legal Control in U.S. Education as They Affect the Classroom Teacher

enabling laws
Laws that make it possible for educators to do certain things.

judicial interpretive process
The judicial process of drawing conclusions about the intent of the wording in the Constitution and statutes.

Each state, reflecting its responsibility for education in its state, has provided for education either in its constitution or in its basic statutory law. For example, Part 6, Section 2 of the Ohio Constitution reads:

> The General Assembly shall make such provisions, by taxation, or otherwise, as, with the income arising from the school trust fund, will secure a thorough and efficient system of common schools throughout the state; but no religious or other sect, or sects, shall ever have any exclusive right to, or control of, any part of the school funds of this state.

The Utah Constitution, Section 1, Article X reads:

> The Legislature shall provide for the establishment and maintenance of a uniform system of public schools, which shall be open to all children of the State, and be free from sectarian control.

Through such statements, the people of the various states commit themselves to a responsibility for education. The state legislatures are obliged to fulfill this commitment. While the interpretation of the Tenth Amendment places the responsibility for education on the states, the rights of citizens of the United States are protected by the Constitution and cannot be violated by any state.

FIRST AMENDMENT

The First Amendment ensures freedom of speech, of religion, and of the press, as well as the right to petition. It specifies:

> Congress shall make no law respecting an establishment of religion, or prohibiting the free exercise thereof; or abridging the freedom of speech, or of the press; or the right of the people peaceably to assemble, and to petition the Government for redress of grievances.

As illustrated in the cases presented later in this chapter, two important clauses in the First Amendment have been applied repeatedly to issues confronting public education: (1) the *establishment clause,* "Congress shall make no law respecting an establishment of religion," and (2) the *free speech clause,* which has direct implications for teacher and student rights.

FOURTEENTH AMENDMENT

The Fourteenth Amendment protects specified privileges of citizens. It reads in part:

> No state shall make or enforce any law which shall abridge the privileges or immunities of citizens of the United States; nor shall any State deprive any person of life, liberty, or property without due process of law; nor deny to any person within its jurisdiction the equal protection of the laws.

The application of the Fourteenth Amendment to public education as considered in this chapter deals primarily with the equal protection clause: "nor shall any State . . . deny to any person within its jurisdiction the equal protection of the laws." Equal educational opportunity is protected under the Fourteenth Amendment. In effect, the rights of citizens of the United States are ensured by the Constitution and cannot be violated by state laws or action.

■ CHURCH AND STATE

Our nation has a strong religious heritage. For example, in colonial times, education was primarily a religious matter; furthermore, much of this education was conducted in private religious schools. Many private schools

The U.S. Constitution laid the groundwork for the notion of equal access to education for all.

today are under religious sponsorship. But debate about the rightful role of religion in public education continues. Should public funds be used to support students in religious schools? Can there be prayer at high school commencement services or in classrooms? Does the teaching of creationism amount to public support for religion, or is it merely the presentation of an alternative scientific view? Agreements have not been reached through the debate process, so proponents of differing viewpoints have turned to the courts.

Court cases concerned with separation of church and state most frequently involve both the First and Fourteenth Amendments of the U.S. Constitution. The First Amendment is interpreted as being applicable to the states by the Fourteenth Amendment. For example, a state law requiring a daily prayer to be read in classrooms throughout the state could be interpreted as "depriving persons of liberty" (see the Fourteenth Amendment due process clause) and as the state establishing a religion, or at least "prohibiting the free exercise thereof" (see the First Amendment establishment clause). States are not permitted to make laws that abridge the privileges of citizens, and the right to the free practice of religion must be ensured.

Court cases related to the separation of church and state can be classified in three categories: (1) those dealing with the use of public funds to support religious education, (2) those dealing with the practice of religion in public schools, and (3) those dealing with the rights of parents to provide private education for their children. Key cases related to each of these categories are presented next.

PUBLIC FUNDS AND RELIGIOUS EDUCATION

The use of public funds to support religious schools has been questioned on many occasions. Typically, state constitutions deny public funds to sectarian institutions or schools. However, public funds have been used to provide transportation for students to church schools and to provide textbooks for students in parochial schools.

Approximately 85 percent of the students who attend nonpublic schools are attending church-related schools. Of this number, some 70 percent are enrolled in parochial (Catholic) schools. In states with relatively large enrollments in parochial schools, there have been continuing efforts to obtain public financial assistance of one form or another for nonpublic school students. These attempts have often been challenged in the courts. We will present a sampling of these cases and issues here to illustrate the reasoning and to assess trends in this difficult area. A summary of cases related to the use of public funds for private education is presented in Table 6.1.

TRANSPORTATION FOR STUDENTS OF CHURCH SCHOOLS

The landmark case on the use of public funds to provide transportation for students to church schools was *Everson v. Board of Education,* ruled on by the U.S. Supreme Court in 1947. The Court held that in using tax-raised funds to reimburse parents for bus fares expended to transport their children to church schools, a New Jersey school district did not violate the establishment clause of the First Amendment. The majority of the members of the Court viewed the New Jersey statute permitting free bus transportation to parochial school children as "public welfare legislation" to help get the children to and from school safely and expeditiously. Since the *Everson* decision, the highest courts in several states, under provisions in their own constitutions, have struck down enactments authorizing expenditures of public funds to bus children attending denominational schools; others have upheld such enactments.

THE *LEMON* TEST: EXCESSIVE ENTANGLEMENT

A useful rubric emerged from the U.S. Supreme Court decision in *Lemon v. Kurtzman* (1971). This case dealt with an attempt by the Rhode Island legislature to provide a 15 percent salary supplement to teachers who taught secular

Religion, morality, and knowledge being necessary to good government and happiness of mankind, schools and the means of education shall forever be encouraged.

Northwest Ordinance, 1787

TABLE 6.1 — Selected U.S. Supreme Court Cases Related to the Use of Public Funds for Private Education

Case	Issue	Decision
Everson v. Board of Education (1947)	Use of tax-raised funds to reimburse parents for transportation of students to church schools	Court ruled that reimbursement did not violate the First Amendment.
Lemon v. Kurtzman (1971)	Legislation to provide direct aid for secular services to nonpublic schools, including teacher salaries, textbooks, and instructional materials	Court ruled the legislation unconstitutional because of the excessive entanglement between government and religion.
Wolman v. Walter (1977)	Provision of books, standardized testing and scoring, diagnostic services, and therapeutic and remedial services to nonpublic school pupils	Court ruled that providing such materials and services to nonpublic school pupils was constitutional.
	Provision of instructional materials and field trips to nonpublic school pupils	Court ruled that providing such materials and services to nonpublic school pupils was unconstitutional.
Grand Rapids School District v. Ball (1985), and *Aguilar v. Felton* (1985)	Instruction of nonpublic school students in supplementary education by public school teachers	Court ruled that the action violated the establishment clause in that it promoted religion.
Zobrest v. Catalina Foothills School District (1993)	Provision of a school district interpreter for a deaf student attending a Catholic high school	Court ruled that government programs that neutrally provide benefits to a broad class of citizens without reference to religion are not readily subject to an establishment clause challenge.
Board of Education of Kiryas Joel Village School District v. Grumet (1994)	Creation and support of a public school district for Hasidic Jews by New York State	Court ruled that the district violated the establishment clause in that it was a form of "religious favoritism."
Agostini v. Felton (1997)	School districts' provision of Title I teachers to serve disadvantaged students in religious schools	Court overturned ban provided the district assigns teachers without regard to religious affiliation, all religious symbols are removed from classrooms, teachers have limited contact with religious personnel, and public school supervisors make monthly unannounced inspections.

subjects in nonpublic schools and a statute in Pennsylvania that provided reimbursement for the cost of teachers' salaries and instructional materials in relation to specified secular subjects in nonpublic schools. The Court concluded that the "cumulative impact of the entire relationship arising under the statutes in each state involves excessive entanglement between government and religion." The Court pointed out another defect of the Pennsylvania statute: It provided for the aid to be given directly to the school. In the *Everson* case, the aid was provided to the students' parents, not to the church-related school. The Court posed three questions that have since become known as the *Lemon* test: (1) Does the act have a secular purpose? (2) Does the primary effect of the act either advance or inhibit religion? (3) Does the act excessively entangle government and religion? Most subsequent cases dealing with the use of public funds in nonpublic school settings have referred to this test.

SPECIAL SITUATIONS   The U.S. Supreme Court seems to have wavered from a strict application of the *Lemon* test in two more recent cases: *Zobrest v. Catalina* and *Kiryas Joel v. Grumet.*

In a 1994 case, *Board of Education of Kiryas Joel Village School District v. Grumet,* the U.S. Supreme Court ruled that a New York State law that created a public school to serve children with disabilities in a village of Hasidic Jews was a form of "religious favoritism" that violated the First Amendment. Interestingly, in this case, as in some others recently, the justices ignored the *Lemon* test in making the decision. Instead, the focus was on the legislature's creation of a special school district; the justices noted the risk that "the next similarly situated group seeking a school district of its own will receive one." Another implication of this decision was the indication that the court would be willing to revisit *Aquilar v. Felton* (1985) and *Grand Rapids v. Ball* (1985), which invalidated sending public school teachers to private religious schools to provide supplemental instruction.

Whether a public school district could provide an interpreter for a student who was deaf attending a Catholic high school was the central question in *Zobrest v. Catalina Foothills School District* (1993). Under a federal statute, the Individuals with Disabilities Education Act (IDEA), students who are deaf are entitled to have a sign language interpreter in all regular classes. In *Zobrest v. Catalina,* the Court concluded that no establishment clause violation occurred because the provision of the interpreter was a "private decision of individual parents." In terms of the federal statute, the Court determined that this was a situation in which "government programs that neutrally provide benefits to a broad class of citizens defined without reference to religion are not readily subject to an establishment clause challenge just because sectarian institutions may also receive an attenuated benefit."

In Zobrest v. Catalina *the Supreme Court ruled that no establishment clause was violated in the case of providing an interpreter for a student who was deaf attending a Catholic school.*

CHILD BENEFIT THEORY   The use of public funds to provide secular services has led to a concept referred to as **child benefit theory.** Child benefit theory supports the provision of benefits to children in nonpublic schools with no benefits to the schools or to a religion. More recent decisions supporting the use of public funds for transportation and textbooks for students in private schools have generally been based on the child benefit theory; this theory emerged out of commentary about the *Everson v. Board of Education* case. The reasoning was that transportation and books provide benefits to the children and not to the school or to a religion. Those opposed to the child benefit theory argue that aid to children receiving sectarian education instruction is effectively aiding the institution providing instruction.

The child benefit theory, as supported by the U.S. Supreme Court, has penetrated federal legislation. For example, the Elementary and Secondary Education Act of 1965 (ESEA) and its subsequent amendments, including No Child Left Behind, provide assistance to both public and nonpublic school children. Title I of ESEA, which deals with assistance for the education of children from low-income families, states that children from families attending private schools must be provided services in proportion to their numbers. When a school is demonstrated to be failing, the school district is required to provide transportation and access to other schools.

TITLE I TEACHERS IN RELIGIOUS SCHOOLS   In one recent decision, *Agostini v. Felton* (1997), the U.S. Supreme Court seemed to be providing increased flexibility and easing the tensions created by *Aguilar v. Felton* (1985). In *Aguilar* the court struck down the use of Title I funds to pay public school teachers who taught in programs to help low-income students in parochial schools. But in *Agostini,* the court decided that under specific safeguards Title I teachers can be sent to serve disadvantaged students in religious schools; refer to Table 6.1.

child benefit theory

A criterion used by the U.S. Supreme Court to determine whether services provided to nonpublic school students benefit children and not a particular school or religion.

TABLE 6.2	Summary Statements on Church and State Related to Public Funds and Religious Education

- Laws and policies that have the effect of establishing religion in the schools will not be upheld by the courts.
- Public tax funds to pay for secular textbooks for loan to students and transportation of religious school children have been upheld by the courts.
- Public tax funds to pay for salaries of teachers in religious schools have not been upheld by the courts.
- Using public funds to pay tuition of religious school children has not been upheld; in Minnesota, a tax deduction has been upheld for parents of children in public *and* private schools.
- Special support services such as speech and hearing teachers may be provided to students in religious schools.
- Religious schools may be reimbursed for administrative costs of standardized tests, test scoring, and record keeping required by the state.
- Public tax funds may not be used in support of public school teachers offering remedial or enriched instruction in religious schools.

The issue of public aid to church-related schools is still in the process of being settled. Although it is clear that aid for certain secular services (such as transportation, textbooks, and—under prescribed circumstances—testing, diagnostic, therapeutic, and remedial services) can be provided, it is not yet absolutely clear what further aid will be approved. In fact, the whole body of law in this area continues to be somewhat confused and contradictory. Some state legislatures are continuing to try to find new ways to provide aid to religious schools without violating the First Amendment. See Table 6.2 for a summary of statements related to public funds and religious education.

RELIGIOUS ACTIVITIES IN PUBLIC SCHOOLS

The limits and boundaries of the First Amendment in relation to public schools have been and will continue to be tested in the courts, especially in relation to religion. Several cases have dealt with the teaching of creationism and evolution, the practice of religion, and the religious use of public facilities. Each case has contributed to a gradual process of clarification of what can and what should not be done to ensure the separation of church and state. Table 6.3 is a summary of U.S. Supreme Court judgments in some of these cases.

PRAYER IN SCHOOL A number of attempts have been and continue to be initiated by school districts to incorporate some form of prayer into public school classrooms and activities. One such case began when the school district for Santa Fe High School, in Texas, adopted a series of policies that permitted prayer initiated and led by a student at all home athletic games. In June 2000, the U.S. Supreme Court ruled in *Santa Fe In-*

A continuing topic of debate and judicial action is the place of prayer in public schools as determined by the First Amendment.

TABLE 6.3 Selected U.S. Supreme Court Cases Related to the Practice of Religion in Public Schools

Case	Issue	Decision
Creationism		
Edwards v. Aguillard (1987)	Balanced treatment of biblical and scientific explanations of the development of life	A state cannot require that schools teach the biblical version of creation.
Practice of Religion		
Wallace v. Jaffree (1985)	Legislation authorizing prayer in public schools, led by teachers, and a period of silence for meditation or voluntary prayer	Court held that state legislation authorizing a minute of silence for prayer led by teachers was unconstitutional.
Mozert v. Hawkins County Public Schools (1987)	Request that fundamentalist children not be exposed to basal reading series in the public schools of Tennessee	Rejected by the Court of Appeals for the Sixth Court, which reasoned that the readers did not burden the students' exercise of their religious beliefs.
Board of Education of the Westside Community Schools v. Mergens (1990)	The right of a student religious club to hold meetings at a public school	Court ruled that based on Equal Access Act (EAA) of 1984, if only one non-curriculum-related student group meets, then the school may not deny other clubs.
Lee v. Weisman (1992)	Inclusion of a religious exercise in a graduation ceremony where young graduates who object are induced to conform	Prayers as an official part of graduation exercises are unconstitutional.
Use of Facilities		
Police Department of the City of Chicago v. Mosley (1972)	Government's refusal of use of a public forum to people whose views it finds unacceptable	"There is an equality of status in the field of ideas," and "government must afford all points of view an equal opportunity to be heard."
Lamb's Chapel v. Center Moriches Union Free School District (1993)	A church's screening of a family-oriented movie on public school premises after school hours	The district property had been used by a wide variety of audiences, so there was no danger of the district's being perceived as endorsing any given religion.
Santa Fe Independent School District, Petitioner v. Jane Doe (2000)	School district policy supporting student-led prayer before football games	"The policy is invalid on its face because it establishes an improper majoritarian election on religion, and unquestionably has the purpose and creates the perception of encouraging the delivery of prayer at a series of important school events."

dependent School District, Petitioner v. Jane Doe that the clear intent of the district policies was in violation of the establishment clause. The six-to-three majority observed, "the District, nevertheless, asks us to pretend that we do not recognize what every Santa Fe High School student understands clearly—that this policy is about prayer." Later in the decision, the Court noted, "This policy likewise does not survive a facial challenge because it impermissibly imposes upon the student body a majoritarian election on the issue of prayer." In other words, the district would be imposing a particular religious activity of the majority on all, a clear violation of the establishment clause. "It further empowers the student body majority with the authority to subject students of minority views to constitutionally improper messages. The award of that power alone, regardless of the students' ultimate use of it, is not acceptable." In concluding, the Court stated, "the policy is invalid on its face because it establishes an improper

Our examination of those circumstances above leads to the conclusion that this policy does not provide the District with the constitutional safe harbor it sought.

Santa Fe Independent School District, Petitioner v. Jane Doe

TABLE 6.4 Guiding Principles for the Association of Prayer and Religion in Public Schools

- Students may pray when not engaged in school activities or instruction, subject to the same rules designed to prevent material disruption of the educational program that are applied to other privately initiated expressive activities.

- Students may organize prayer groups, religious clubs, and "see you at the pole" gatherings before school to the same extent that students are permitted to organize other noncurricular student activities groups.

- Such groups must be given the same access to school facilities for assembling as is given to other noncurricular groups, without discrmination because of the religious content of their expression.

- When acting in their official capacities as representatives of the state, teachers, school administrators, and other school employees are prohibited by the establishment clause from encouraging or discouraging prayer and from actively participating in such activity with students.

- If a school has a "minute of silence" or other quiet periods during the school day, students are free to pray silently, or not to pray, during these periods. Teachers and other school employees may neither encourage nor discourage students from praying during such times.

- Schools have the discretion to dismiss students to off-premises religious instruction, provided that schools do not encourage or discourage participation in such instruction or penalize students for attending or not attending.

- Students may express their beliefs about religion in homework, artwork, and other written and oral assignments free from discrimination based on the religious content of their submissions. Such home and classroom work should be judged by ordinary academic standards of substance and relevance and against other legitimate pedagogical concerns identified by the school.

- School officials may not mandate or organize prayer at graduation or select speakers for such events in a manner that favors religious speech such as prayer.

Source: U.S. Department of Education, *Guidance on Constitutionally Protected Prayer in Public Elementary and Secondary Schools.* Washington, DC: U.S. Education Department, 2003.

CROSS-REFERENCE
The philosophical and legal arguments about the place of religion in public schools are addressed in Chapter 11.

The Louisiana Creationism Act advances a religious doctrine by requiring either the banishment of the theory of evolution from public school classrooms or the presentation of a religious viewpoint that rejects evolution in its entirety. The Act violates the Establishment Clause of the First Amendment because it seeks to employ the symbolic and financial support of government to achieve a religious purpose.

Edwards v. Aguillard

majoritarian election on religion, and unquestionably has the purpose and creates the perception of encouraging the delivery of prayer at a series of important school events."

In an attempt to clarify what is and is not permissible in relation to prayer and other religious activities in public schools, the U.S. Department of Education has published a set of guidelines for religious expression. Points from these guidelines are summarized in Table 6.4.

CREATIONISM VERSUS EVOLUTION   One of the most famous trials involving religion and a teacher occurred in Tennessee in 1925, when a science teacher, John Scopes, was found guilty of teaching evolution. Although the decision was later reversed on a technicality, the Scopes "monkey trial" has been kept alive in the theater and through the more recent efforts of certain religious groups advocating that creation be taught in place of, or along with, the scientific construct of evolution. Creationists advance an interpretation of the origin of human life that is based on the Bible. In 1968 the Court ruled against states that had attempted to ban the teaching of evolution and then in 1987 ruled in *Edwards v. Aguillard* that the Arkansas legislature violated the Establishment Clause of the First Amendment when it required equal time for the teaching of creationism and evolution. Still, creationists have continued to push their agenda. For example, in 1999 the Kansas state board of education removed evolution from the science standards. This action then became a major election issue because in Kansas state board members are elected, and several conservative board members lost. As can readily be seen in Figure 6.2, a clear majority of the public supports the teaching of evolution. In fact, 83 percent of those surveyed believed that evolution should be taught in school, whereas fewer than 30 percent wanted creationism taught as science in public schools.

Regardless of past Supreme Court decisions, some topics, such as the posting of the Ten Commandments in classrooms and Bible reading in public schools, continue to be challenged by legislatures, individuals, and various groups. One of the outcomes of these ongoing challenges is an accumulating series of judicial interpretations that can serve as guidelines about what can and cannot be done. The summary statements presented in Table 6.5 outline the overall pattern of the many judicial decisions related to religion and the public schools.

SEGREGATION AND DESEGREGATION

A troublesome problem for U.S. society has been the history of legal and social separation of people based on their race; in other words, **segregation.** Up until the middle of the twentieth century, the public school systems in many states contributed to this problem through the operation of two separate sets of schools, one for whites and one for African Americans ("Negroes"). Segregated schools were supported by state laws and by the official actions of state and local government administrators. This kind of segregation, based in legal and official actions, is called **de jure segregation.**

Since 1954 the courts and communities have made intensive efforts to abolish the racial segregation of school students, a process that has been called **desegregation.** A major instrument the courts have used to accomplish this end has been **integration,** the busing of students to achieve a balanced number of students, in terms of race, in each school within a school district. A second instrument has been the use of magnet schools, which are schools that emphasize particular curriculum areas, disciplines, or themes. The hope is that these schools will attract a diverse set of students. These efforts to integrate the schools have had mixed success, and now there is increasing concern over the **resegregation** of schools based on where people live. Segregation—or resegregation—caused by housing patterns and other nonlegal factors is called **de facto segregation.**

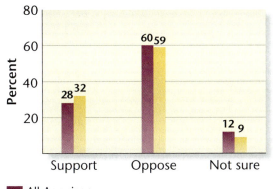

QUESTION: "The Kansas state board of education has recently voted to delete evolution from their new state science standards. Do you support or oppose the decision?"

■ All Americans
■ Parents with children in public schools

FIGURE 6.2 Public Support for the Teaching of Evolution
Source: People for the American Way Foundation.

segregation
Legal and/or social separation of people on the basis of their race.

de jure segregation
The segregation of students on the basis of law, school policy, or a practice designed to accomplish such separation.

desegregation
The process of correcting illegal segregation.

integration
The process of mixing students of different races in school.

resegregation
A situation in which formerly integrated schools become segregated again because of changes in neighborhood population patterns.

de facto segregation
The segregation of students resulting from circumstances such as housing patterns rather than law or school policy.

TABLE 6.5 Summary Statements on Church and State and the Practice of Religion in Public Schools

- To teach the Bible as a religion course in the public schools is illegal, but to teach about the Bible as part of the history of literature is legal.
- To dismiss children from public schools for one hour once a week for religious instruction at religious centers is legal.
- Reading of scripture and reciting prayers as religious exercises are in violation of the Establishment Clause.
- Public schools can teach the scientific theory of evolution as a theory; a state cannot require that the biblical version of evolution be taught.
- If school facilities are made available to one group, then they must be made available to all other groups of the same general type.

"SEPARATE BUT EQUAL": NO LONGER EQUAL

Before 1954 many states had laws either requiring or permitting racial segregation in public schools (de jure segregation). Until 1954 lower courts adhered to the doctrine of "separate but equal" as announced by the Supreme Court in *Plessy v. Ferguson* (1896). In *Plessy v. Ferguson,* the Court upheld a Louisiana law that required railway companies to provide separate but equal accommodations for the black and the white races. The Court's reasoning at that time was that the Fourteenth Amendment implied political, not social, equality.

THE FAILURE OF THE SEPARATE-BUT-EQUAL DOCTRINE This separate-but-equal doctrine appeared to be the rule until May 17, 1954, when the Supreme Court repudiated it in *Brown v. Board of Education of Topeka.* The Court said that in education the separate-but-equal doctrine has no place and that separate facilities are inherently unequal. In 1955 the Court rendered the second *Brown v. Board of Education of Topeka* decision, requiring that the principles of the first decision be carried out with all deliberate speed.

From 1954, the time of the *Brown* decision, to 1964, little progress was made in eliminating segregated schools. On May 25, 1964, referring to a situation in Prince Edward County, Virginia, the Supreme Court said, "There has been entirely too much deliberation and not enough speed in enforcing the constitutional rights which we held in *Brown v. Board of Education.*" The Civil Rights Act of 1964 added legislative power to the 1954 judicial pronouncement. The act not only authorized the federal government to initiate court suits against school districts that were laggard in desegregating schools but also denied federal funds for programs that discriminated by race, color, or national origin.

Subsequently, many efforts have been made to meet the expectations of the Court decisions and legislation. The objective of these initiatives has been to promote integration, that is, to achieve a representative mix of students of different races in schools. In the fifty years since *Brown,* there have been many efforts by school districts and communities, and many additional lawsuits. Table 6.6 summarizes some key Supreme Court decisions on school desegregation and integration.

One of the positive long-term effects of desegregation can be seen in today's highly diverse schools and classrooms.

TABLE 6.6 Selected U.S. Supreme Court Cases Related to School Desegregation and Integration

Case	Issue	Decision
Plessy v. Ferguson (1896)	Whether a railway company should be required to provide equal accommodations for African American and white races	The Court indicated in its decision that the Fourteenth Amendment implied political, not social, equality. Thus the doctrine of "separate but equal" was established.
Brown v. Board of Education of Topeka (1954)	Legality of separate school facilities	The separate-but-equal doctrine has no place in education, and dual school systems (de jure segregation) are inherently unequal.
Griffin v. County School Board of Prince Edward County (1964)	Whether a county may close its schools and provide assistance to private schools for whites only	The Court instructed the local district court to require the authorities to levy taxes to reopen and operate a nondiscriminatory public school system.
Board of Education of Oklahoma City Public Schools v. Dowell (1991)	The conditions under which a school district may be relieved of court supervision	Court supervision was to continue until segregation was removed from every facet of school operations.
Freeman v. Pitts (1992)	Whether court supervision may be withdrawn incrementally, and whether a school district is responsible for segregation based on demographic changes (de facto segregation)	A district court is permitted to withdraw supervision in discrete categories in which the district has achieved compliance; also "the school district is under no duty to remedy imbalance that is caused by demographic factors."

RELEASE FROM COURT ORDERS

After fifty-plus years of court actions related to desegregation and school district responses, questions were raised about the conditions that must be in place for a school district to be released from federal court supervision. Three cases in the 1990s offered instances of conditions under which the courts would back away. *Board of Education of Oklahoma City Public Schools v. Dowell* (1991) is important for at least three reasons: First, the U.S. Supreme Court made it clear that "federal supervision of local school systems was intended as a temporary measure to remedy past discrimination." Second, the Court stated that in relation to desegregation, "the District Court should look not only at student assignments, but to every facet of school operations—faculty, staff, transportation, extracurricular activities and facilities." And third, for the first time the Court defined what full compliance with a desegregation order would mean:

> In the present case, a finding by the District Court that the Oklahoma City School District was being operated in compliance with the commands of the equal protection clause of the Fourteenth Amendment, and that it was unlikely that the school board would return to its former ways, would be finding that the purposes of the desegregation litigation had been fully achieved.

Two other cases added additional clarity to what the Court expects in order to release a school district from supervision. In *Freeman v. Pitts* (1992), the U.S. Supreme Court ruled that districts do not have to remedy racial imbalances caused by demographic changes, but the districts still have the burden of proving that their actions do not contribute to the imbalances. The third case was a return to *Brown*. The Court had ordered the Court of Appeals for the Tenth Circuit to reexamine its 1989 finding that the Topeka district remained segregated. In 1992 the appellate court refused to declare Topeka successful. The court concluded that the district had done little to fulfill the duty to desegregate that was

Multiethnic education requires reform of the total school.

James A. Banks

first imposed on it in 1954. The judges wrote that to expect the vestiges of segregation to "magically dissolve" with so little effort "is to expect too much."

These three cases in combination made it clear that it is possible for school districts to be released from court order. The decisions also made it clear that school districts have to make concerted efforts across time to address any and all remnants of de jure segregation. Further, it now appears that school districts are not expected to resolve those aspects of de facto segregation that are clearly beyond their control.

INTEGRATION FIFTY-FIVE YEARS LATER

At present there are more than 500 formerly segregated school districts under some federal court jurisdiction. Table 6.7 presents a summary of the legal reasoning behind several key cases. Unfortunately, while de jure segregation has been removed, it has been replaced in many situations with a more virulent form of segregation. The demographics and economic conditions of the country have changed in ways that have not facilitated integration in local schools. Many strategies have been tested, and there are some indicators of success, but the goal is still a dream in many ways.

THE RISK OF RESEGREGATION   Currently, there is concern in several regions of the country about apparent trends toward resegregation, which occurs when a recently integrated school population returns to being almost totally a minority school population. The historic progress that has been made toward integration of African Americans appears to be slowly eroding because of a combination of demographic, economic, and social factors. In addition, more Hispanic students are attending schools with decreasing proportions of white students. Interpreting these trends is difficult. Still, there is reason to be concerned if this trend toward resegregation continues.

THE SUCCESSES OF THE DESEGREGATION AGENDA   Desegregation has had some measurable benefits. For example, African Americans who graduated from integrated schools have higher incomes than those who graduated from segregated schools. They are more likely to graduate from college and to hold good jobs. In addition, the number of middle-class black families is growing. Still,

---

TABLE 6.7   Summary Statements on Segregation and Desegregation

- The assignment of a child to a school on the basis of race is in violation of the equal protection clause of the Fourteenth Amendment.
- Where school boards have indirectly contributed to segregated communities, the school district can be required to desegregate.
- Desegregation plans that have the effect of delaying integration of the school have not been upheld by the courts.
- Busing may be required for the operation of a desegregated school system.
- Once a school district has been fully desegregated, the school board does not need to draw up a new plan if resegregation occurs because of demographic shifts.
- The merger of school districts may be required where the involved districts helped create the segregated school systems.
- The neighborhood school concept is not in conflict with the Equal Protection Clause.
- Once the district has achieved desegregation in all facets of school operations, it can be released from court supervision.

there is a long way to go before the dream of full socioeconomic equality is achieved. It seems certain that schools will continue to be a primary vehicle for advancing this dream from the points of view of the courts.

EQUAL OPPORTUNITY

The Equal Protection Clause of the Fourteenth Amendment has been instrumental in shaping many court cases and federal statutes that are directed toward preventing discrimination in schools. Table 6.8 is a summary of key events in the nation's efforts to eradicate discrimination. A judgment of **discrimination** can be defined as a determination that an individual or a group of individuals—for example, African Americans, women, or people with disabilities—has been denied constitutional rights. In common usage, the term applies to various minorities or to individual members of a minority who lack rights typically accorded the majority. The principle that discrimination violates the Equal Protection Clause was reinforced in Titles VI and VII of the Civil Rights Act of 1964 and in Title IX of the Education Amendments Act of 1972. Title VI of the Civil Rights Act states:

> No person in the United States shall, on the ground of race, color, or national origin, be excluded from participation in, be denied the benefits of, or be subjected to discrimination under any program or activity receiving federal financial assistance.

Title VII states:

> It shall be an unlawful employment practice for an employer (1) to fail or refuse to hire or to discharge any individual, or otherwise to discriminate against any individual with respect to his compensation, terms, conditions, or privileges of employment, because of such individual's race, color, religion, sex, or national origin; or (2) to limit, segregate, or classify his employees or applicants for employment in any way which would deprive or tend to deprive any individual of employment opportunities or otherwise adversely affect his status as an employee, because of such individual's race, color, religion, sex, or national origin.

All provisions of federal, state or local law requiring or permitting discrimination in public education must yield.

Earl Warren, Chief Justice, U.S. Supreme Court (1955)

CROSS-REFERENCE
Chapters 2, 3, and 4 describe the many ways in which our society is becoming diverse and the need for equal educational opportunity for all.

TABLE 6.8	Events in the History of Affirmative Action

1941: President Roosevelt issues an executive order prohibiting discrimination by government contractors.

1961: President Kennedy makes the first reference to affirmative action in an order mandating that federal contractors make employment practices free of racial bias.

1964: Congress passes the Civil Rights Act.

1965: President Johnson outlines specific steps federal contractors must take to ensure hiring equality.

1970: The Nixon administration orders federal contractors to set "goals and timetables" for hiring minorities.

1972: Congress passes Title IX of the Education Amendments Act that states that no person can be excluded from participation based on their sex.

1978: In *University of California v. Bakke,* the Supreme Court rules that colleges can consider race as one factor in admissions.

1995: The Supreme Court limits racial preferences in federal highway contracts.

2003: The Supreme Court rules that race can be considered by colleges in their efforts to have a diverse student body, but it cannot be done through a set formula or quota.

discrimination
Denial of constitutional rights to an individual or group.

Title IX of the Education Amendments Act of 1972 states:

> No person in the United States shall, on the basis of sex, be excluded from participation in, be denied the benefits of, or be subjected to discrimination under any education program or activity receiving federal financial assistance.

AFFIRMATIVE ACTION

In the years since the 1964 Civil Rights Act, numerous statutes and court cases have encouraged steps designed to ensure that underrepresented populations have equal opportunity. These **affirmative action** initiatives have included such actions as formalizing and publicizing nondiscriminatory hiring procedures and setting aside a certain number of slots in hiring or college admissions programs. Over time, concern has increased about the possibility of **reverse discrimination**—situations in which a majority or an individual member of a majority is not accorded equal rights because of different or preferential treatment provided to a minority or an individual member of a minority. This concern has resulted in a new set of court cases, such as *University of California v. Bakke* (1978), each of which is attempting to redress what is perceived as a new imbalance.

The legal basis for affirmative action is found in Titles VI and VII of the Civil Rights Act of 1964 and in Title IX of the Education Amendments Act of 1972. However, affirmative action procedures and methods continue to be clarified and, in some instances, questioned. For example, in 1996 the citizens of California passed Proposition 209, which bans the state and its local governments from using racial and gender preferences in hiring, contracting, and college admissions. Proposition 209 and other legal initiatives will be examined in the courts.

In 2003 the U.S. Supreme Court clarified further the extent to which race can be considered when it ruled that the University of Michigan could consider race in its admissions programs (*Grutter v. Bollinger; Gratz v. Bollinger*). However, this consideration must be done within the context of striving to achieve a racial mixture on campus and cannot be applied to all applications through a fixed point system or quota. Instead, each application must be considered individually and race must be just one of the factors considered.

OPPORTUNITIES FOR STUDENTS WITH DISABILITIES

The judicial basis for current approaches to the education of students with disabilities also is closely linked to the civil rights and equal opportunity initiatives. In addition, several specifically targeted statutes address the education of people with disabilities. Three particularly important statutes are Section 504 of the Rehabilitation Act; Public Law 94-142, the Education for All Handicapped Children Act (EAHCA); and the Individuals with Disabilities Education Act (IDEA).

SECTION 504 OF THE REHABILITATION ACT   Under this civil rights act established in 1973, recipients of federal funds are prohibited from discriminating against "otherwise qualified individuals." Note that Section 504 is a federal statute and regulations, not a court decision. Three important themes addressed in Section 504 are equal treatment, appropriate education, and handicapped persons. Equal treatment, as in other civil rights contexts, must be addressed. However, this does not necessarily mean the *same* treatment. For example, giving the same assessment procedure to students with disabilities and other students may not be equal treatment. Educational judgments in relation to students with disabilities require a "heightened standard." The measures must fit the students' circumstances, and procedural safeguards must be employed. Appropriate education means that the school system and related parties must address

affirmative action

Policies and procedures designed to compensate for past discrimination against women and members of minority groups; for example, assertive recruiting and admissions practices.

reverse discrimination

A situation in which a majority or an individual of a majority is denied certain rights because of preferential treatment provided to a minority or an individual of a minority.

individual needs of students with disabilities as adequately as do the education approaches for other students. In Section 504, a "handicapped person" is

> Any person who (i) has a physical or mental impairment which substantially limits one or more major life activities, (ii) has a record of such an impairment, or (iii) is regarded as having such an impairment. (34 CFR 104.3)

PUBLIC LAW 94-142 (EAHCA)   Passed by Congress in 1975, Public Law 94-142 has been amended several times since. This law assures "a free appropriate public education" to all children with disabilities between the ages of three and twenty-one. Children with exceptional needs cannot be excluded from education because of their needs. The law is very specific in describing the kind and quality of education and in stating that each child with a disability is to have an individually planned education. Details of this plan must be spelled out in a written Individualized Education Plan (IEP), formulated by general and special education teachers, and subject to the parents' approval. Originally, the law provided for substantial increases in funding; in subsequent years, however, the funding authorizations have been lower than the original commitment. Two priorities for funding were identified: (1) the child who currently receives no education and (2) the child who is not receiving all the services he or she needs to succeed. These priorities place the emphasis on need rather than on the specific disability.

THE INDIVIDUALS WITH DISABILITIES EDUCATION ACT (IDEA)   This act (1992) developed tighter specifications for the delivery of educational services to children with disabilities. At the time, more than half of children with disabilities were not receiving appropriate educational services. The purpose of IDEA is to make available to all children with disabilities a free appropriate public education. IDEA establishes at the federal level an Office of Special Education Programs headed by a deputy assistant secretary. Further, the act makes clear that states are not immune under the Eleventh Amendment of the Constitution from suit in federal court for a violation of the act. The act encourages the education of individuals with disabilities by making grants to states and local education agencies for children ages three to five, requires the federal government to be responsive to the increasing ethnic diversity of society and those with limited English proficiency, and funds programs to provide education to all children with disabilities.

AIDS AS A DISABILITY

The 1990 Americans with Disabilities Act expanded the definition of *disability* in such a way as to include people with AIDS. Also, under IDEA the courts have found that AIDS is a disabling condition. But AIDS is an issue charged with emotion, as was desegregation. People do not always approach these difficult situations with calmness or equanimity. The courts, as well as school administrators and teachers, are constantly struggling to determine what is appropriate education for students with AIDS and what are suitable educational environments for children with AIDS-related disabilities. Some exceptional and spiritually strong children, such as Ryan White, have challenged the educational system's capabilities. Ryan White was an Indiana adolescent with AIDS who, because of attitudes within his school, was forced to leave town to get an education. Because of Ryan's example, others with disabilities will have the courage to challenge the limits of school systems. In these situations, educators, the courts, and policymakers will be further tested—but at the same time will have the opportunity to move the educational system ahead by developing creative approaches and innovative practices. Calm heads will be needed, as will wisdom, from all the players for the education system to succeed for all its students. The Centers for Disease Control is a useful resource for information about AIDS (phone: 800-342-2437; website: www.cdc.gov/hiv/dhap.htm).

Should Teachers Have the Authority to Remove Disruptive Students from Their Classes Permanently?

From a legal perspective, all students have a right to an education. But what can a teacher do when a student is very disruptive? When should teachers be able to expel a student from class?

YES

Tracey Jones Saxon is in her fourth year teaching sixth grade at Walker Upper Elementary School in Charlottesville, Virginia. She is vice president of the Charlottesville Education Association.

I have always been amazed at how people—teachers, parents, and administrators alike—sometimes get tunnel vision when it comes to disruptive students. In our constant efforts to make sure that every child has the "right to learn," the rights of some children get trampled by disruptive children. Disruptive students steal time. They steal patience. They steal the fun a lot of the time.

I had a parent say to me, "Why did you send my child out of your class? Sitting in the hall won't teach him anything! He has the right to learn, and if you don't let him stay in your class, I'll go to Central Office."

What about the other 20 kids in the room who were interrupted as I gave him three warnings and moved his seat? They have rights, too.

That parent never asked what the student was doing that made me give him a new seat and three warnings. The child's disruption was not the issue to the parent, but it was the major issue to me and my other students. Every time I stopped to deal with this one student, 20 kids lost their train of thought. Some children in that class had to really struggle to focus on their work. They were trying to stay with me, trying to participate, but they lost time and focus.

As teachers, our job is to help prepare our students for the real world—you have to follow rules. If you disrupt

NO

Noel Richardson is the student services coordinator at Ilima Intermediate School in Ewa Beach, Hawaii, and a member of the NEA's IDEA cadre, which helps state and local associations. He has worked in special education for six years.

Our monumental task as educators goes beyond teaching reading, writing, and arithmetic. We need to instill in children the social skills that will enable them to be productive in society. This can be the most frustrating task for new and seasoned teachers alike. We have many disruptive students. But much as we may want to send them on their merry way to the office, that will not teach them the essential social skills.

Sometimes the consequences we impose only make things worse. If the child's goal is to get out of class, sending him or her to the office only reinforces the behaviors you don't want. The child has associated acting out with getting out.

You may feel you have tried everything, but have you really? Are you doing this by yourself or are you receiving help from other teachers? Disruptive behavior is the result of a need. Find out what it is and try to meet that need. Ask other teachers whether the student acts the same way in their classrooms. If not, find out what is different.

In one case, we found by observing the classroom that the teacher was yelling at the disruptive student. He did not realize this, and after some simple suggestions, the classroom was fine.

(continued)

due process

The legal procedures that must be followed to safeguard individuals from arbitrary, capricious, or unreasonable policies, practices, or actions.

TEACHERS' RIGHTS AND RESPONSIBILITIES

Teachers have the same rights as other citizens. The Fourteenth Amendment gives every citizen the right to **due process** of law: both *substantive due process* (protection against the deprivation of constitutional rights such as freedom of expression) and *procedural due process* (procedural protection against unjustified deprivation of substantive rights). Most court cases related to teachers

YES

a movie in a theater, they don't give you three warnings and ask you to move your seat—they throw you out! If you do it enough times, you can be banned from returning. Kids need to know that. We need to help them, but we must also let the other members of our class "enjoy the movie," so to speak. Classroom environments should have clear rules and expectations for everyone.

The decision to remove a child permanently should not rest on any one person. But the teacher should have the final say because he or she knows firsthand what the "disruptive child" can do to the learning of the other children.

Some disruptive students may have special problems, and they should receive special education services for those problems. But special education should not be a dumping ground for disruptive students!

I am talking about the child who refuses to stop talking, who bothers other kids, picks at things that don't belong to him or her, shows a general indifference to the educational process, and—this is the key—makes the choice not to follow classroom rules.

My father, a former teacher and administrator, gave me the best teaching advice: "Do what is best for your class. Always put the kids first."

I believe I am doing just that every time I make the decision to remove a disruptive child from my class.

A disruptive student's right to learn ends when it interferes with his classmates' right to learn.

Source: "Should Teachers Have the Authority to Remove Disruptive Students from their Classes Permanently?" NEA Today (January 2002), p. 11.

NO

It is not always so easy. By no means should you tackle the problem on your own.

Yes, if the behavior is totally out of control and the team has exhausted all possible interventions, then perhaps it's time to look at another less restrictive environment. But that should be a team decision. Usually, removing the child is not necessary.

In our school, three years ago, we started to use "student support teams" for all students with special needs, even those who have not been formally referred under IDEA. In the team, we talk about the reasons for the disruptive behavior. We bring in whatever help is needed.

Teachers come out of these sessions saying, "I learned an intervention that makes sense." They come back after trying the new approach saying, "This part is okay but I need more help in that area." And we work on it more.

We have cut the number of students referred under IDEA by three-quarters.

There was once a handsome little kindergarten student who gave his teacher a hard time. He would pester other students, disrupt the class, and basically frazzle the teacher to her wit's end. Then she found out the boy's mother had taught him all the skills he would need up to first grade. He was bored. So the teacher gave the student harder work. This simple modification kept him focused. He went on to fly helicopters in the U.S. Marines. Later, he became a teacher of special needs students. How do I know? The little boy was me!

Don't give up on disruptive kids. You never know which of them will go on to become teachers!

WHAT DO YOU THINK?
Should teachers have the authority to remove disruptive students from their classes permanently?

To give your opinion, go to Chapter 6 of the companion website (**www.ablongman.com/johnson13e**) and click on Debate.

evolve from either liberty or property interests. Liberty interests are created by the Constitution itself; property interests are found in forms of legal entitlement such as tenure or certification.

Teachers also have the same responsibilities as other citizens. They must abide by federal, state, and local laws and by the provisions of contracts. As professionals they must also assume the heavy responsibility for educating young people. We will discuss specific court cases briefly here to illustrate some of the issues and decisions related to aspects of teacher rights and responsibilities. Note that the cases selected do not necessarily constitute the last word regarding

TABLE 6.9 Selected U.S. Supreme Court Decisions Related to Teachers' Rights and Responsibilities

Case	Issue	Decision
Discrimination		
North Haven Board of Education v. Bell (1982)	Allegation by former women faculty members of sex discrimination in employment	Court ruled that school employees as well as students are protected under Title IX.
Cleveland Board of Education v. LeFleur (1974)	Rights of pregnant teachers	Court struck down the board policy forcing all pregnant teachers to take mandatory maternity leave.
Burkey v. Marshall County Board of Education (1981)	Paying female coaches half the salary of male coaches	Court ruled that the policy violated the Equal Pay Act, Title VII of the Civil Rights Act of 1964.
Contract Rights		
Board of Regents of State Colleges v. Roth (1972)	Rights of nontenured teachers	Teacher had been hired under a one-year contract. Court concluded that he did not have a property interest that would entitle him to procedural rights under the Fourteenth Amendment.
Perry v. Sindermann (1972)	Rights of nontenured teachers	Court ruled that a state employee may acquire the property interest if officially fostered customs, rules, understandings, and practices imply a contract promise to grant continuing contract status and thus establish a de facto tenure system.
Bargaining		
Hortonville Joint School District No. 1 v. Hortonville Education Association (1976)	Rights of boards of education to dismiss teachers who are striking illegally	Court said the law gave the board power to employ and dismiss teachers as a part of the municipal labor relations balance.
Academic Freedom		
Pickering v. Board of Education (1968)	Dismissal of an Illinois teacher for criticizing a school board and superintendent in a letter published by a local newspaper	Court upheld teacher's claim that his First and Fourteenth Amendment rights were denied.

teacher rights but rather provide an overview of some of the issues that have been decided in the courts. Table 6.9 summarizes the issues and decisions in selected cases involving teacher rights and responsibilities. This summary table is not intended to provide a complete understanding of the court decisions cited; please read the text for better comprehension. Note also that most of the court cases were decided in the 1970s and 1980s; more recently, new federal statutes have been the defining force.

◼ CONDITIONS OF EMPLOYMENT

Many conditions must be met for you to be hired as a teacher. These include your successful completion of a professional preparation program, being credentialed or licensed by the state, and receiving a contract from the hiring school district. In each of these instances, you have rights established in law and statute, as well as responsibilities.

TEACHER CERTIFICATION AND LICENSURE

teacher certification and licensure

The process whereby each state determines the requirements for certification and for obtaining a license to teach.

The primary purpose of **teacher certification and licensure** is to make sure there are qualified and competent teachers in the public schools. Certification laws usually require, in addition, that the candidate show evidence of citizenship, good moral character, and good physical health. A minimum age is frequently specified. All states have established requirements for teacher certification and licensure. Carrying out the policies of certification is usually a function of a state professional standards board. The board first has to make certain that applicants meet legal requirements; it then issues the appropriate license/certificates. Certifying agencies may not arbitrarily refuse to issue a certificate to a qualified candidate. The courts have ruled that local boards of education may prescribe additional or higher qualifications beyond the state requirements, provided that such requirements are not irrelevant, unreasonable, or arbitrary. A teaching certificate or license is a privilege that enables a person to practice a profession—it is not a right. But teacher certification is a property interest that cannot be revoked without constitutional due process.

A big moment: signing a contract to teach is a professional commitment by the teacher and a legal one for the school district.

TEACHER EMPLOYMENT CONTRACTS

Usually, boards of education have the statutory authority to employ teachers. This authority includes the power to enter into contracts and to fix terms of employment and compensation. In some states, only specific members of the school board can sign teacher contracts. When statutes confer the employing authority to boards of education, the authority cannot be delegated. It is usually the responsibility of the superintendent to screen and nominate candidates to the board. The board, meeting in official session, then acts officially as a group to enter into contractual agreement. Employment procedures vary from state to state, but the process is fundamentally prescribed by the legislature and must be strictly followed by local boards. A contract usually contains the following elements: the identification of the teacher and the board of education, a statement of the legal capacity of each party to enter into the contract, a definition of the assignment specified, a statement of the salary and how it is to be paid, and a provision for signature by the teacher and by the legally authorized agents of the board. In some states, contract forms are provided by state departments of education, and these forms must be used; in others, each district establishes its own.

Teachers are responsible for making certain that they are legally qualified to enter into contractual agreements. For example, a teacher may not enter into a legal contract without having a valid teaching certificate issued by the state. Furthermore, teachers are responsible for carrying out the terms of the contract and abiding by them. In turn, under the contract they can legally expect proper treatment from an employer.

CROSS-REFERENCE
See Chapter 1 for additional information about becoming a licensed teacher.

TEACHER TENURE

Teacher tenure legislation exists in most states. In many states, tenure or fair dismissal laws are mandatory and apply to all school districts without exception. In other states, they do not. The various laws differ not only in extent of coverage but also in provision for coverage.

Tenure laws are intended to provide security for teachers in their positions and to prevent removal of capable teachers by capricious action or political motive. Tenure statutes generally include detailed specifications necessary for granting tenure and for dismissing teachers who have tenure. These statutes have been upheld when attacked on constitutional grounds. The courts reason that because state legislatures create school districts, they have the right to limit their power.

BECOMING TENURED AND TENURE RIGHTS   A teacher becomes tenured by serving satisfactorily for a stated time. This period is referred to as the **probationary period** and typically is three years. The actual process of acquiring tenure after

tenure

A system of school employment in which educators retain their positions indefinitely unless they are dismissed for legally specified reasons through clearly established procedures.

probationary period

The required time, typically one to three years, during which a beginning teacher must demonstrate satisfactory performance as a basis for seeking tenure.

serving the probationary period depends on the applicable statute. In some states, the process is automatic at the satisfactory completion of the probationary period; in other states, official action by the school board is necessary. Teachers may be dismissed for any one of numerous reasons, including "nonperformance of duty, incompetency, insubordination, conviction of crimes involving moral turpitude, failure to comply with reasonable orders, violation of contract provisions or local rules or regulations, persistent failure or refusal to maintain orderly discipline of students, and revocation of the teaching certificate."[1]

A school board in Tennessee dismissed Jane Turk from her tenured teaching position after she was arrested for driving under the influence of alcohol (DUI).[2] Turk's appeal was upheld by the lower-court judge because there was no evidence of an adverse effect on her capacity and fitness as a teacher. The school board appealed to the Tennessee Supreme Court, which rejected the board's appeal, finding that the school board "acted in flagrant disregard of the statutory requirement and fundamental fairness in considering matters that should have been specifically charged in writing." Tennessee law requires that before a tenured teacher can be dismissed, "the charges shall be made in writing specifically stating the offenses which are charged." Nevertheless, teacher tenure may be affected by teacher conduct outside school as well as inside. This issue, in a sense, deals with the personal freedom of teachers: freedom to behave as other citizens do, freedom to engage in political activities, and academic freedom in the classroom.

Tenure laws are frequently attacked by those who claim that the laws protect incompetent teachers. There is undoubtedly some truth in the assertion, but it must be stated clearly and unequivocally that these laws also protect the competent and most able teachers. Teachers who accept the challenge of their profession and dare to use new methods, who inspire curiosity in their students, and who discuss controversial issues in their classrooms need protection from politically motivated or capricious dismissal. Incompetent teachers, whether tenured or not, can be dismissed under the law by capable administrators and careful school boards that allow due process while evaluating teacher performance.

RIGHTS OF NONTENURED TEACHERS   Although due process has been applicable for years to tenured teachers, nontenured teachers do not, for the most part, enjoy the same rights. As you can see in Table 6.10, there are significant differences from state to state. In general, tenured teachers enjoy two key rights: protection from dismissal except for cause as provided in state statutes, and the right to prescribed procedures. Nontenured teachers may also have due process rights if these are spelled out in state statutes; however, in states that do not provide for due process, nontenured teachers may be nonrenewed without any reasons being given. If a nontenured teacher is dismissed (as distinguished from nonrenewed) before the expiration of the contract, the teacher is entitled to due process. Twenty-two states afford nontenured teachers the right both to know the reasons for their nonrenewal and to meet with the school board or superintendent to argue to keep their jobs. Cases in Massachusetts[3] and Wisconsin[4] point to the necessity of following due process in dismissing nontenured teachers. In the Massachusetts case, the court said: "the particular circumstances of a dismissal of a public school teacher provide compelling reasons for application of a doctrine of procedural due process."[5] In the Wisconsin case, the court said:

> A teacher in a public elementary or secondary school is protected by the due process clause of the Fourteenth Amendment against a nonrenewal decision which is wholly without basis in fact and also against a decision which is wholly unreasoned, as well as a decision which is impermissibly based.

In 1972 the Supreme Court helped to clarify the difference between the rights of tenured and nontenured teachers. In one case (*Board of Regents v. Roth,* 1972), it held that nontenured teachers were assured of no rights that were

TABLE 6.10 Employment Rights of Nontenured Teachers, K–12

	Right to Know Reasons for Nonrenewal	Right to Meet with Administration	Mandatory Evaluation of Job Performance	Mandatory Plan of Improvement	Violation of Evaluation Procedure Results in Contract Renewal	Union Can Bargain Just Cause Protection
Y Alabama						
X Alaska	✔	✔	✔	✔		✔
Arizona	✔		✔			
X Arkansas	✔	✔	✔	✔	✔	✔
Y California						
Y Colorado	✔		✔	✔		
Connecticut	✔	✔	✔			
X Delaware	✔	✔	✔	✔	✔	✔
Y Fed. Ed. Assn.			✔			
Y Florida			✔	✔		
Z Georgia	✔		✔	✔		
X Hawaii	✔	✔	✔		unclear	✔
X Idaho	✔	✔	✔		✔	✔
Y Illinois	✔		✔			
X Indiana	✔	✔	✔		✔	✔
X Iowa	✔	✔	✔		unclear	✔
Kansas			✔			✔
X Kentucky	✔		✔	✔	✔	✔
Louisiana	✔		✔	✔	✔	
Y Maine			✔			
Y Maryland			✔			
Y Massachusetts			✔			unclear
X Michigan			✔	✔	✔	✔
Minnesota	✔		✔			✔
Z Mississippi	✔	✔				
Y Missouri	✔		✔			
Montana						✔
X Nebraska	✔	✔	✔	✔	✔	unclear
X Nevada	✔		✔	✔	unclear	✔
Y New Hampshire						unclear
X New Jersey	✔	✔	✔	✔		
Y New Mexico	✔		✔			
New York	✔				✔	

(continued)

TABLE 6.10 (continued)

	Right to Know Reasons for Nonrenewal	Right to Meet with Administration	Mandatory Evaluation of Job Performance	Mandatory Plan of Improvement	Violation of Evaluation Procedure Results in Contract Renewal	Union Can Bargain Just Cause Protection
Y North Carolina	✔		✔			
North Dakota	✔	✔	✔		unclear	✔
X Ohio	✔	✔	✔	✔	✔	✔
X Oklahoma	✔	✔	✔	✔	✔	
X Oregon	✔	✔	✔	✔		✔
X Pennsylvania	✔	✔	✔		✔	✔
Rhode Island	✔	✔				✔
South Carolina		✔	✔	✔		
Y South Dakota						unclear
Tennessee			✔	✔		unclear
Z Texas		✔	✔		✔	
Y Utah			✔	✔		
X Vermont	✔	✔				✔
Virginia	✔	✔	✔			
X Washington	✔	✔	✔	✔		unclear
X West Virginia	✔	✔	✔	✔	✔	
Wisconsin	✔	✔				✔
Y Wyoming	✔		✔			

Note:
X = States with substantial job protections for beginning teachers.
Y = States with few or no rights in connection with nonrenewal decisions.
Z = Three states have no state tenure laws, even for veteran teachers.

Source: "'Where Should I Teach?' How Each State Views New Teachers" (brochure). Washington, DC: National Education Association.

not specified in state statutes. In this instance, the only right that probationary teachers had was the one to be notified of nonrenewal by a specified date. In a second case (*Perry v. Sindermann,* 1972), the Court ruled that a nontenured teacher in the Texas system of community colleges was entitled to due process because the language of the institution's policy manual was such that an unofficial tenure system was in effect. Guidelines in the policy manual provided that a faculty member with seven years of employment in the system acquired tenure and could be dismissed only for cause.

Whether or not a teacher is tenured, that person cannot be dismissed for exercise of a right guaranteed by the U.S. Constitution. A school board cannot dismiss a teacher, for example, for engaging in civil rights activities outside school, speaking on matters of public concern, belonging to a given church, or running for public office. These rights are guaranteed to all citizens, including teachers. However, if a teacher's behavior is disruptive or dishonest, a school board can dismiss the person without violating the right to freedom of speech.

DISCRIMINATION

School districts are prohibited from using discriminatory practices in the hiring, dismissal, promotion, or demotion of school personnel. In addition to court decisions, federal statutes, such as the Civil Rights Acts of 1964 and 1991, have had a defining influence on the legal basis for judgments of discrimination. For example, the 1991 law expanded protection beyond race to include discrimination based on sex, disability, medical conditions, religion, and national origin. Further, employment decisions must be "job-related for the position in question." The 1991 law also places the burden on the defendant (schools) to show that a legitimate nondiscriminatory reason exists for any personnel decision that may be challenged.

CROSS-REFERENCE
See www.nasdtec.org and Chapter 1 for additional information about each state's certification and licensure requirements.

RIGHT TO BARGAIN COLLECTIVELY

The right of teachers to bargain collectively has been an active issue since the 1960s. In the past, teacher groups met informally with boards of education to discuss salaries and other teacher welfare provisions. Sometimes the superintendent was even the spokesperson for such teacher groups. In more recent years, however, formal collective procedures have evolved. These procedures have been labeled collective bargaining, professional negotiation, cooperative determination, and collective negotiation. Teachers' groups have defined collective bargaining as a way of winning improved goals and not the goal itself. The right of employees to bargain collectively and the obligation of the district to bargain are not constitutionally granted but are typically guaranteed by statute.

A contract arrived at by a teachers' union means that salaries, working conditions, and other matters within the scope of the collective bargaining agreement can no longer be decided unilaterally by the school administration and board of education. Instead, the contract outlines how the teachers' union and its members will participate in formulating the school policies and programs under which they work.

The first teachers' group to bargain collectively with its local board of education was the Maywood, Illinois, Proviso Council of West Suburban Teachers, Union Local 571, in 1938. In 1957 a second local, the East St. Louis, Illinois, Federation of Teachers was successful in negotiating a written contract. The breakthrough, however, came in December 1961, when the United Federation of Teachers, Local 2 of the American Federation of Teachers (AFT), won the right to bargain for New York City's teachers. Since then, collective bargaining agreements between boards of education and teacher groups have grown phenomenally. Both the AFT and the National Education Association (NEA) have been active in promoting collective bargaining. Today, approximately 75 percent of the nation's teachers are covered by collective bargaining agreements.

RIGHT TO STRIKE

Judges have generally held that public employees do not have the right to strike. For example, the Supreme Court of Connecticut[6] and the Supreme Court of New Hampshire[7] ruled that teachers may not strike. The court opinion in Connecticut stated:

> Under our system, the government is established by and run for all of the people, not for the benefit of any person or group. The profit motive, inherent in the principle of free

Although the number of collective bargaining agreements between boards of education and teacher groups has grown phenomenally, many states have statutes that prohibit teachers from striking.

enterprise, is absent. It should be the aim of every employee of the government to do his or her part to make it function as efficiently and economically as possible. The drastic remedy or the organized strike to enforce the demands of unions of government employees is in direct contravention of this principle.

A few states permit strikes in their collective bargaining statutes. At least twenty states have statutes that prohibit strikes, however. Whether or not there are specific statutes prohibiting strikes, boards of education threatened by strikes can usually get a court injunction forestalling them. Both the NEA and the AFT view the strike as a last-resort technique, although justifiable in some circumstances.

In 1976, by a six-to-three vote, the U.S. Supreme Court ruled that boards of education can discharge teachers who are striking illegally. Ramifications of this decision, which involved a Wisconsin public school, are potentially far-reaching. The Court viewed discharge as a policy question rather than an issue for adjudication: "What choice among the alternative responses to the teachers' strike will best serve the interests of the school system, the interests of the parents and children who depend on the system, and the interests of the citizens whose taxes support it?" The Court said that the state law in question gave the board the power to employ and dismiss teachers as a part of the balance it had struck in municipal labor relations (*Hortonville Joint School District No. 1 v. Hortonville Education Association*, 1976).

One can argue that strikes are unlawful when a statute is violated, that the courts in their decisions have questioned the right of public employees to strike, and that some teachers and teacher organizations consider strikes unprofessional. In any given case, the question before teachers seems to be whether the strike is a justifiable and responsible means—after all other ways have been exhausted—of declaring abominable educational and working conditions and trying to remedy them.

■ ACADEMIC FREEDOM

CROSS-REFERENCE
See Chapter 13 for information about how curriculum and instruction can be offered in ways that include teacher creativity.

A sensitive and vital concern to the educator is **academic freedom**—freedom to control what one will teach and to teach the truth as one discovers it without fear of penalty. Academic freedom is thus essentially a principle of pedagogical philosophy that has been applied to a variety of professional activities. A philosophical position, however, is *not necessarily* a legal right. Federal judges have generally recognized certain academic protections in the college classroom while exhibiting reluctance to recognize such rights for elementary and secondary school teachers. For example, the contract of a history teacher at the University of Arkansas–Little Rock was not renewed after he announced that he taught his classes from a Marxist point of view. The court ordered that the teacher be reinstated in light of the university's failure to advance convincing reasons related to the academic freedom issue to warrant his nonrenewal.[8] In another case, a university instructor claimed that he was denied tenure because he refused to change a student's grade. He argued that awarding a course grade was the instructor's right of academic freedom. Because the university had given several valid reasons for the nonrenewal of the instructor's contract, however, the court did not order a reinstatement.[9]

ACADEMIC FREEDOM FOR ELEMENTARY AND SECONDARY TEACHERS

academic freedom
The opportunity for a teacher to teach without coercion, censorship, or other restrictive interference.

Although federal courts generally have not recognized academic freedom for elementary and secondary school teachers, the most supportive ruling was made in 1980[10] in a case that involved a high school history teacher whose contract was not renewed after she used a simulation game to introduce her students to the characteristics of rural life during the post–Civil War Reconstruction era. Although the role playing evoked controversy in the school and the community, there was no evidence that the teacher's usefulness had been impaired. Therefore, the school erred in not renewing the teacher's contract, and she was ordered reinstated.

In *Pickering v. Board of Education* (1968), the U.S. Supreme Court dealt with academic freedom at the public school level. Marvin L. Pickering was a teacher in Illinois who, in a letter published by a local newspaper, criticized the school board and the superintendent for the way they had handled past proposals to raise and use new revenues for the schools. After a full hearing, the board of education terminated Pickering's employment, whereupon he brought suit under the First and Fourteenth Amendments. The Illinois courts rejected his claim. The U.S. Supreme Court, however, upheld Pickering's claim and, in its opinion, stated:

> To the extent that the Illinois Supreme Court's opinion may be read to suggest that teachers may constitutionally be compelled to relinquish the First Amendment rights they would otherwise enjoy as citizens to comment on matters of public interest in connection with the operation of the public schools in which they work, it proceeds on a premise that has been unequivocally rejected in numerous prior decisions of this Court.

It is difficult to define precisely the limits of academic freedom. In general, the courts strongly support it yet recognize that teachers must be professionally responsible when interacting with pupils. In most instances, teachers are not free to disregard a school board's decision about which textbook to use, but they are able to participate more when it comes to their choice of supplementary methods. Teachers have usually been supported in their rights to criticize the policies of their local school boards, wear symbols representing stated causes, participate in unpopular movements, and live unconventional lifestyles. But where the exercise of these rights can be shown to have a direct bearing on a teacher's effectiveness, respect, or discipline, these rights may have to be curtailed. For example, a teacher may have the right to wear a gothic costume to class, but if the wearing of the outfit leads to disruption and an inability to manage students, the teacher can be ordered to wear more conventional clothes.

In summary, academic freedom for teachers is more limited than it is for higher education faculty. First Amendment protection of free speech is increasingly limited to a teacher's actions outside of the classroom and school. Before arguing for academic freedom and free speech in the classroom, a teacher must show that she or he did not defy legitimate state and local curriculum directives, followed accepted professional norms, and acted in good faith when there was no precedent or policy.

BOOK BANNING AND CENSORSHIP

Ever since the United States has had public schools, some people have taken issue with what has been taught, how it has been taught, and the materials used. The number of people challenging these issues and the intensity of their feeling have escalated since the mid-1970s. Well-organized and well-financed pressure groups have opposed the teaching of numerous topics, including political, economic, scientific, and religious theories; the teaching of values grounded in religion, morality, or ethnicity; and the portrayal of stereotypes based on gender, race, or ethnicity. Some complaints have involved differences of opinion over the central role of the school—whether the school's job is to transmit traditional values, indoctrinate students, or teach students to do their own thinking.

Several court cases since the 1970s have involved the legality of removing books from the school curriculum and school libraries. The courts have given some guidance but have not fully resolved the issue. In 1972 a court of appeals held that a book does not acquire tenure, so a school board was upheld in its removal of *Down These Mean Streets.* The Court of Appeals for the Seventh Circuit in 1980 upheld the removal of the book *Values Clarification,* ruling that local

When standards are set in place, a successful school is one that provides both excellence and equity—a challenging education for every child. When a school adopts high standards for all, it is telling each of its students clearly, "We respect you and believe that you can learn."

Diane Ravitch

boards have considerable authority in selecting materials for schools. Removal of books on the basis of the vulgar language they contain has also been upheld.

The U.S. Supreme Court treated this issue in 1982.[11] The decision disappointed people who had hoped that the justices would issue a definitive ruling on the banning of books. Instead, Justice William Brennan ruled that students may sue school boards on the grounds of denial of their rights, including the right to receive information. The Court also indicated that removal of a book because one disagrees with its content cannot be upheld. The net effect of this decision was that the school board decided to return the questionable books to the library.

The latest censorhip battleground has to do with limiting access to the World Wide Web. Many school districts and schools are applying filters that restrict access to particular types of websites. New questions related to defining what is meant by "responsible use" and who decides—teachers, principals, or school districts—are now occupying school boards, legislative bodies, and the courts.

FAMILY RIGHTS AND PRIVACY ACT

In 1974, Congress passed the Family Educational Rights and Privacy Act (FERPA), which also is called the **Buckley Amendment.** This statute addresses the maintenance of confidentiality of student records. The statute makes it clear that schools and teachers may not release any information or records of students without written permission of the parents. The statute also mandates that parents have the right to inspect the official records, files, and data related directly to their children, including academic and psychological test scores, attendance records, and health data. Parents must be able to challenge the content of their child's school records to ensure that they are accurate and that they are not misleading or in violation of the privacy or other rights of students. This statute does not prohibit teachers, principals, and other education professionals from making student information available for educational purposes as long as they take steps to maintain privacy of the information.

SCHOOL RECORDS   Before November 19, 1974, the effective date of the Buckley Amendment, the law regarding the privacy of student records was extremely unclear. Even today many school administrators—and most parents—do not realize that parents now have the right to view their children's educational records. Many teachers, too, are not yet aware that their written comments, which they submit as part of a student's record, must be shown at a parent's request, or at a student's request if the student is eighteen or older.

The law (P.L. 93-380 as amended by P.L. 93-568) requires that schools receiving federal funds must comply with the privacy requirements or face loss of those funds. What must a school district do to comply? According to a 1976 clarification by HEW, the Buckley Amendment requires that the school district

- Allow all parents, even those not having custody of their children, access to each educational record that a school district keeps on their child.
- Establish a district policy on how parents can go about seeing specific records.
- Inform all parents of what rights they have under the amendment, how they can act on these rights according to school policy, and where they can see a copy of the policy.
- Seek parental permission in writing before disclosing any personally identifiable record on a child to individuals other than professional personnel employed in the district (and others who meet certain specific requirements).[12]

STUDENTS GRADING ONE ANOTHER'S PAPERS   A common instructional practice for teachers is to have students grade one another's work. As common as the practice is, it resulted in a suit that went all the way to the U.S. Supreme Court. In *Owasso Independent School District v. Falvo,* the plaintiff alleged violations of FERPA in regard to "peer review." The suit was funded by the Rutherford Institute, a national conservative organization. The Court of Appeals for the Tenth Circuit agreed with an Oklahoma parent that students should not grade other students' work. In 2002 the Supreme Court was unanimous in overturning the circuit court and said that the privacy law was directed at records "kept in a filing cabinet in a records room or on a permanent secure database," not the grades on a classroom paper. The Court observed:

> Correcting a classmate's work can be as much a part of the assignment as taking the test itself. It is a way to teach material again in a new context, and it helps show students how to assist and respect fellow pupils. By explaining the answers to the class as the students correct the papers, the teacher not only reinforces the lesson but also discovers whether the students have understood the material and are ready to move on. We do not think FERPA prohibits these educational techniques.

TEACHER RESPONSIBILITIES AND LIABILITIES

With about 47 million students enrolled in elementary and secondary schools, it is almost inevitable that some will be injured in educational activities. Each year, some injuries will occasion lawsuits in which plaintiffs seek damages. Such suits are often brought against both the school districts and their employees. Legal actions seeking monetary damages for injuries are referred to as *actions in tort*. Technically, a **tort** is a legal wrong—an act (or the omission of an act) that violates the private rights of an individual. Actions in tort are generally based on alleged negligence; the basis of tort liability or legal responsibility is negligence. Understanding the concept of negligence is essential to understanding liability.

Legally, *negligence* is a failure to exercise or practice due care. It includes a factor of foreseeability of harm. Court cases on record involving negligence are numerous and varied. The negligence of teacher supervision of pupils is an important topic that includes supervision of the regular classroom, departure of the teacher from the classroom, supervision of the playground, and supervision of extracurricular activities. **Liability** is the responsibility for negligence—responsibility for the failure to use reasonable care when such failure results in injury to another.

EDUCATIONAL MALPRACTICE

Culpable neglect by a teacher in the performance of his or her duties is called **educational malpractice.** The courts of California[13] and New York[14] dismissed suits by former students alleging injury caused by educational malpractice. The plaintiffs claimed that they did not achieve an adequate education and that this was the fault of the school district. In the California case, the student, after graduating from high school, could barely read or write. The judge in his opinion stated:

> The science of pedagogy itself is fraught with different and conflicting theories . . . and any layman might—and commonly does—have his own emphatic viewpoints on the subject. . . . The achievement of literacy in the schools, or its failure, is influenced by a host of factors from outside the formal teaching process, and beyond the course of its ministries.

In essence, the judge stated that there was no way to assess the school's negligence. In the New York case, the judge said, "The failure to learn does not bespeak a failure to teach." In the twenty-first century, with the continuing push for accountability, there are likely to be more tests of the educational malpractice question.

tort
An act (or the omission of an act) that violates the private rights of an individual.

liability
Responsibility for the failure to use reasonable care when such failure results in injury to another.

educational malpractice
Culpable neglect by a teacher in the performance of his or her duties.

Although negligence is a vague concept, courts have ruled that teachers were responsible in specific cases of injury to students on school field trips.

NEGLIGENT CHEMISTRY TEACHER

In a California high school chemistry class, pupils were injured while experimenting with the manufacture of gunpowder.[15] The teacher was in the room and had supplemented the laboratory manual instructions with his own directions. Nevertheless, an explosion occurred, allegedly caused by the failure of pupils to follow directions. A court held the teacher and the board of education liable. Negligence in this case meant the lack of supervision of laboratory work, a potentially dangerous activity requiring a high level of "due care."

FIELD TRIP NEGLIGENCE

In Oregon a child was injured while on a field trip.[16] Children were playing on a large log in a relatively dry area on a beach. A large wave surged up onto the beach, dislodging the log, which began to roll. One of the children fell seaward off the log, and the receding wave pulled the log over the child, injuring him. In the subsequent court action, the teacher was declared negligent for not having foreseen the possibility of such an occurrence. The court said:

> The first proposition asks this court to hold, as a matter of fact, that unusual wave action on the shore of the Pacific Ocean is a hazard so unforeseeable that there is no duty to guard against it. On the contrary, we agree with the trial judge, who observed that it is common knowledge that accidents substantially like the one that occurred in this case have occurred at beaches along the Oregon coast. Foreseeability of such harm is not so remote as to be ruled out as a matter of law.

Although liability for negligence is a vague concept involving due care and foreseeability, it is defined more specifically each time a court decides such a case.

GOVERNMENTAL IMMUNITY FROM LIABILITY

Historically, school districts have not been held liable for torts resulting from the negligence of their officers, agents, or employees while the school districts are acting in their governmental capacity. That immunity was based on the doctrine that the state is sovereign and cannot be sued without its consent. A school district, as an arm of state government, would therefore be immune from tort liability. Unlike school districts, however, employees of school districts have not been protected by immunity; teachers can be held liable for their actions. Teachers must act as reasonable and prudent people, foreseeing dangerous situations. The degree of care required increases with the immaturity of the pupil. Lack of supervision and foresight forms the basis of negligence charges.

Recent decades have seen a trend away from governmental immunity. As of 1986, more than half of the states had abrogated governmental immunity either judicially, statutorily, or through some form of legal modification. There has also been an increase in the number of lawsuits.

LIABILITY INSURANCE

Many states authorize school districts to purchase insurance to protect teachers, school districts, administrators, and school board members against suits. It is important that school districts and their employees and board members be thus protected, either through school district insurance or through their own per-

TABLE 6.11 Summary Statements on Teachers' Rights and Responsibilities

- Prospective teachers must fulfill the requirements of laws and policies regarding certification before being employed as teachers.

- Boards of education have the authority to employ teachers, including the authority to enter into contracts and to fix terms of employment and compensation.

- School districts are prohibited from use of discriminatory practices; discrimination in employment and salary of teachers on the basis of sex is in violation of Title IX of the Education Amendments Act.

- Most states have tenure laws that provide teachers with protection against arbitrary dismissal; rights of nontenured teachers are found in state laws.

- Teachers may speak out on matters of public concern, even in criticism of their school board, as long as their speech is not disruptive or a lie.

- Boards of education may remove books from library shelves under their authority to select materials for schools; however, the removal of a book merely because someone disagrees with its content was not upheld by the U.S. Supreme Court.

- Many states provide for school boards and teacher unions to bargain collectively on wages, hours, and terms and conditions of employment.

- Teacher strikes are unlawful when a statute is violated; in some states, it is legal for teachers to strike.

- Teachers are expected to exercise due care in foreseeing possible accidents and in working to prevent their occurrence; teachers may be sued for their negligence that led to pupil injury.

sonal policies. The costs of school district liability insurance have increased so dramatically in recent years that many school districts are contemplating the elimination of extracurricular activities. Consequently, state legislatures are being pressured to fix liability insurance rates for school districts; they are also being asked to pass laws to limit maximum liability amounts for school-related cases. For teachers, membership in the state affiliates of the NEA and membership in the AFT include the option of liability insurance programs sponsored by those organizations.

In summary of the discussion of this section, Table 6.11 lists brief statements related to the rights and responsibilities of teachers.

STUDENTS' RIGHTS AND RESPONSIBILITIES

The Professional Dilemma feature dealing with testing student athletes for drugs reflects how the rights of students have changed since the late 1960s. Before 1969, school authorities clearly had the final say as long as what they decided was seen as reasonable. A key U.S. Supreme Court decision in 1969 changed the balance by concluding that students do not "shed their constitutional rights to freedom of speech or expression at the schoolhouse gate." Going further on behalf of student rights, in 1975 the Court decided that the principle of due process applied to students. These decisions led to several successful student challenges of school policies and procedures. In the late 1980s, Court decisions moved back toward increasing the authority of public school officials. Along the way, student life has become more complex, not only because of such threats as the increased use of drugs and the presence of weapons and gangs, but also because a diverse multicultural and shifting political context has

Drug Testing of Student Athletes: Prevention or Problem?

States, school districts, and schools have clear policies and rules that address the problem of student uses of drugs. Even with strong laws and policies, many students use alcohol, so-called recreational drugs, and other illicit substances. Student athletes represent a special case in that they are more apt to use anabolic steroids and other substances that are percieved to enhance performance. One response by both policymakers and educators has been to advocate for drug testing programs.

Over the last twenty-five years, testing for drugs has become common in sports. For example, most professional sports test athletes for drugs, as does the U.S. Olympic Committee. But what about having required drug testing of student athletes? Is it legal? Is it an invasion of privacy? Should there be advance notice? Should the testing be random or applied to all students equally? And, most important, are such policies effective?

The answer to the legality of drug testing is "yes." The U.S. Supreme Court in *Vernonia School District 47 v. Acton* (1995) upheld drug testing of adolescents engaged in sports. As a result, schools and school districts are implementing a variety of approaches, especially random testing.

What do you think?

- As a teacher, do you think your students should be subject to random drug testing?

- Should the testing be done across all students?

- Researchers who study policy talk about two kinds of consequences: intended and unintended. For any policy such as random drug testing there will be both kinds of consequences. What would you predict to be some of the intended and unintended consequences of random drug testing?

Read the next paragraph *after* you have developed your thoughts about this professional dilemma.

Researchers have compared drug use and attitudes of athletes in schools with and without random drug testing. The findings are that illicit drug use for athletes in the testing school decreased across the school year (the intended consequence). At the same time, the tested athletes had a larger reduction in positive attitudes toward school and more preference for risky drug use behavior, and they saw authority figures as more tolerant of drug and alcohol use (unintended consequences). Also, the researchers found no differences in the uses of alcohol and tobacco.

Source: Linn Goldberg et al., Drug Testing Athletes to Prevent Substance Abuse: Background and Pilot Study Results of the SATURN (Student Athlete Testing Using Random Notification Study), *Journal of Adolescent Health, 32*(1) (2003), pp. 16–25.

To answer these questions on-line and e-mail your answers to your professor, go to Chapter 6 of the companion website **(www.ablongman.com/johnson13e)** and click on Professional Dilemma.

made it more difficult to determine what is and what is not appropriate to be able to do and say within a school environment.

To illustrate some of the issues and decisions related to student rights and responsibilities, we present specific court cases here. Note that the cases do not necessarily constitute the last word regarding student rights, but rather provide an overview of some of the issues that have been decided by the courts. Table 6.12 is a summary of key cases; however, it is not intended to provide a complete understanding of the court decisions. You should read the following subsections and pursue references provided in the notes and bibliography to learn more about these and other student rights issues.

STUDENTS' RIGHTS AS CITIZENS

Through a series of court decisions, all children in the United States have been granted the opportunity for a public school education. Further, although school officials have a great deal of authority, children as students maintain many of the constitutional rights that adult citizens enjoy all the time. As obvious as each of these points might seem, each has been the subject of debate and court decision.

**TABLE 6.12   Selected U.S. Supreme Court Decisions Related to Students'
Rights and Responsibilities**

Case	Issue	Decision
Plyler v. Doe (1982)	Rights to education of illegal aliens	Court struck down Texas law that denied a free public education to children of illegal aliens.
Goss v. Lopez (1975)	Suspension of high school students without a hearing	Court ruled that only in an emergency can a student be suspended without a hearing.
Wood v. Strickland (1975)	Question of whether school board members can be sued for depriving students of their constitutional rights (through suspension)	Students can seek damages from individual school board members but not from the school district.
Tinker v. Des Moines Independent Community School District (1969)	Free speech rights of students to wear black armbands to protest U.S. involvement in Vietnam	Court ruled against school district—recognized to an extent constitutional rights of pupils.
Board of Education, Island Trees Union Free District No. 26 v. Pico (1982)	School board's decision to remove books from the school library	Court issued decision that under certain circumstances, children may challenge board's decision to remove books.
Ingraham v. Wright (1977)	Power of states to authorize corporal punishment without consent of the student's parent	Court ruled that states may constitutionally authorize corporal punishment.
Bethel School District No. 403 v. Fraser (1986)	Power of school officials to restrain student speech	School officials may discipline a student for making lewd and indecent speech in a school assembly attended by other students.
Hazelwood School District v. Kuhlmeier (1988)	School district control of student expression in school newspapers, theatrical productions, and other forums	School administrators have broad authority to control student expression in the official student newspaper, which is not a public forum but is seen as part of the curriculum.
Honig v. Doe (1988)	Violation of the Education for All Handicapped Children Act (P.L. 94-142); school indefinitely suspended and attempted to expel two emotionally disturbed students	P.L. 94-142 authorizes officials to suspend dangerous children for a maximum of ten days. Justice Brennan said, "Congress very much meant to strip schools of unilateral authority to exclude disturbed students."
New Jersey v. T.L.O. (1985)	Search and seizure	School officials must have a reasonable cause when engaged in searches.

STUDENTS' RIGHT TO AN EDUCATION

American children have a right to an education; this right is ensured in many state constitutions. It has been further defined by court decisions and is now interpreted to mean that each child has an equal opportunity to pursue education.

The right to an education, however, is not without certain prerequisites. Citizenship alone does not guarantee a free education. Statutes that establish public school systems also generally establish how operating costs will be met. Real estate taxes are the usual source of funds, so proof of residence is necessary for school attendance without tuition. *Residence* does not mean that the student, parent, or guardian must pay real estate taxes; it means that the student must live in the school district in which he or she wants to attend school. Residence, then, is a prerequisite to the right of a free public education within a specific school district.

HOMELESS CHILDREN HAVE THE RIGHT TO GO TO SCHOOL   There are more than 500,000 homeless children in the United States. Because access to public school usually requires a residence address and a parent or guardian, as well as transportation, in the past homeless children were squeezed out of the system. Congress addressed this growing problem in 1987 with passage of the Stewart B.

in loco parentis

Meaning "in the place of a parent," this term describes the implied power and responsibilities of schools.

McKinney Homeless Assistance Act, which requires that "each State educational agency shall assure that each child of a homeless individual and each homeless youth have access to a free, appropriate public education." The law was amended in 1990 to require each school district to provide services to the homeless that are comparable to the services offered other students in the schools. These services include allowing homeless children to finish the school year in the school they were in before they lost their housing, providing transportation to school, tutoring to help catch students up, and giving homeless children the opportunity to take part in school programs offered to other children.

STUDENTS' RIGHT TO SUE

The U.S. Supreme Court has affirmed that students may sue school board members who are guilty of intentionally depriving students of their constitutional rights. In *Wood v. Strickland* (1975), the Supreme Court held that school officials who discipline students unfairly cannot defend themselves against civil rights suits by claiming ignorance of pupils' basic constitutional rights. As a result of this decision, Judge Paul Williams, a federal judge in Arkansas, ordered that certain students who had been suspended could seek damages from individual school board members—though not from the school district as a corporate body. The judge also ruled that the school records of these pupils must be cleared of the suspension incident. From these decisions, it is apparent that the U.S. Supreme Court is taking into account the rights of students.

STUDENTS' RIGHT TO DUE PROCESS

Much of the recent involvement of the courts with student rights has concerned due process of law for pupils. Due process is guaranteed by the Fourteenth Amendment. The protection clause states, "nor shall any state . . . deny to any person within its jurisdiction the equal protection of the laws." Due process of law means following those rules and principles that have been established for enforcing and protecting the rights of the accused. As explained earlier, due process falls under two headings—procedural and substantive. *Procedural* due process has to do with whether the procedures used in disciplinary cases are fair; *substantive* due process is concerned with whether the school authorities have deprived a student of basic substantive constitutional rights such as personal liberty, property, or privacy.[17]

The application of due process to issues in schools is a recent phenomenon. Historically, schools functioned under the doctrine of **in loco parentis** ("in the place of a parent"). This doctrine meant that schools could exercise almost complete control over students because they were acting as parent substitutes. Under the doctrine of in loco parentis, the courts have usually upheld the rules and regulations of local boards of education, particularly about pupil conduct. However, the courts have not supported rules that are unconstitutionally "vague" and/or "overboard." The following cases illustrate the difficult balance between protecting students' right to due process and giving schools sufficient authority to pursue their mission.

Students have procedural due process rights, including the opportunity for some kind of hearing.

PROCEDURAL DUE PROCESS IN CASES OF SUSPENSION AND EXPULSION   Zero tolerance policies, such as those described in the Relevant Research feature, have complicated the local schools' ability to balance students' right to due process and serving students' ed-

Zero Tolerance, Zero Sense

STUDY PURPOSE/QUESTIONS: Legal research begins with the analysis of incidents and cases related to a particular statute or interpretation of the U.S. Constitution, in this case zero tolerance. In response to the tragedy at Columbine High School, many state legislatures and school districts have mandated that there be no flexibility when it comes to students making threats or bringing weapons to schools, that is, **zero tolerance.** Most of the established policies mandate that the student be expelled.

STUDY DESIGN: Stories from many individual situations were summarized. For example, one six-year-old made national news when he was expelled for bringing a weapon to kindergarten. The "weapon" was a plastic knife in his lunch sack, which his grandmother had put there so that he could spread peanut butter. Then there was the high school potential valedictorian who was expelled for making a "terrorist threat" on a student government election campaign poster. In this study, state statutes and district policies were examined as well.

STUDY FINDINGS: "Kids whose misbehaviors in the past would have occasioned oral reprimands from a teacher or perhaps a trip to the principal's office are now being labeled a threat to school safety. And, those very same kids-will-be-kids incidents are now prompting punishments ranging from suspension to expulsion to referral to the juvenile court system for behaviors that even the schools agree do not actually compromise safety." Another finding is that parents think of zero tolerance as keeping guns and drugs out of schools. However, zero tolerance, in many settings, has become a catch phrase for schools that are unable or unwilling to prevent school violence. This approach is also making students less inclined to confide in teachers and administrators

IMPLICATIONS: As with many policies, there needs to be a commonsense approach to zero tolerance. Teachers and administrators, those closest to the action, need to have flexibility in judging the seriousness of perceived threats and in dispensing consequences. Texas has been innovative in its approach by identifying three levels of severity and three levels of response. At the most serious level, bringing a gun, knife, or drugs to school and aggravated assault result in expulsion. At the middle level, simple assault, use of alcohol, and a few other violations result in temporary removal from school. For the lowest-level offenses, school officials have discretion to determine the severity of the offense and the punishment. Zero tolerance has become a widespread policy approach. To what extent should school officials have flexibility in determining the severity of a threat? Or should there be a universal mandated response? Where should the line be drawn, if there is to be one?

Source: Margaret Graham Tebo, "Zero Tolerance, Zero Sense," *American Bar Association Journal* (April 2000), pp. 119–120.

---

ucational needs. Procedural due process is scrutinized especially in cases of suspension and expulsion. These cases most often result from disciplinary action taken by the school, which may or may not have violated a pupil's substantive constitutional rights. For example, in *Goss v. Lopez* (1975) the U.S. Supreme Court dealt with the suspension of high school students in Columbus, Ohio. In that case, the named plaintiffs claimed that they had been suspended from public high school for up to ten days without a hearing. The action alleged deprivation of constitutional rights. Two students who were suspended for a semester brought suit charging that their due process rights were denied—because they were not present at the board meeting when the suspensions were handed out.

In ruling that students cannot be suspended without some kind of hearing, the Court said:

> The prospect of imposing elaborate hearing requirements in every suspension case is viewed with great concern, and many school authorities may well prefer the untrammeled power to act unilaterally, unhampered by rules about notice and hearing. But it would be a strange disciplinary system in an educational institution if no communication was sought by the disciplinarian with the student in an effort to inform him of his defalcation and to let him tell his side of the story in order to make sure that an injustice is not done. Fairness can rarely be obtained by secret,

one-sided determination of the facts decisive of rights. . . . Secrecy is not congenial to truth-seeking and self-righteousness gives too slender an assurance of rightness. No better instrument has been devised for arriving at truth than to give a person in jeopardy of serious loss notice of the case against him and opportunity to meet it.

Procedural due process cases usually involve alleged violations of the Fourteenth Amendment, which provides for the protection of specified privileges of citizens, including notice to the student, impartiality of the hearing process, and the right of representation. These cases might also involve alleged violations of state constitutions or statutory law that call for specific procedures. For example, many states have procedures for expulsion or suspension. Expulsion usually involves notifying parents or guardians in a specific way, perhaps by registered mail, and giving students the opportunity for a hearing before the board of education or a designated hearing officer. Suspension procedures are usually detailed as well, designating who has the authority to suspend and the length of time for suspension. Teachers and administrators should know due process regulations, including the specific regulations of the state where they are employed.

SUBSTANTIVE DUE PROCESS AND STUDENTS' RIGHTS TO FREE SPEECH   Substantive due process frequently addresses questions of students' constitutional rights to free speech versus the schools' authority to maintain order in support of education. The *Tinker* case (*Tinker v. Des Moines Independent Community School District,* 1969) was significant. It involved a school board's attempt to keep students from wearing black armbands in a protest against U.S. military activities in Vietnam. In 1969 the U.S. Supreme Court ruled against the Des Moines school board. The majority opinion of the Court was that

> the wearing of armbands in the circumstances of this case was entirely divorced from actually or potentially disruptive conduct by those participating in it. It was closely akin to "pure speech" which, we have repeatedly held, is entitled to comprehensive protection, under the First Amendment. . . . First Amendment rights, applied in the light of the special characteristics of the school environment, are available to teachers and students. It can hardly be argued that either students or teachers shed their constitutional rights to freedom of speech or expression at the schoolhouse gate.

In the *Tinker* opinion, the Court clearly designated that the decision "does not concern aggressive, disruptive action or even group demonstrations." The decision did make it clear that whatever their age, students have constitutional rights; and the decision has had a widespread effect on the operation of schools in the United States. Schools have had to pay attention to U.S. law. Educators as well as lawyers have been guided by the principles set forth in the decision regarding the constitutional relationship between public school students and school officials.

A more recent U.S. Supreme Court decision appears to have at least narrowed the breadth of application of the *Tinker* ruling. The case involved Matthew Fraser, a high school senior in a school outside Tacoma, Washington. In the spring of 1983, Fraser was suspended from school for two days after he gave a short speech at a school assembly nominating a friend for a position in student government. School officials argued that Fraser's speech contained sexual innuendos that provoked other students to engage in disruptive behaviors unfavorable to the school setting. The U.S. District Court for the Western District of Washington held that Fraser's punishment violated his rights to free speech under the First Amendment and awarded him damages. The U.S. Court of Appeals for the Ninth Circuit affirmed the decision, holding that Fraser's speech was not disruptive under the standards of *Tinker*.[18] However, the Supreme Court reversed the decision. In the majority opinion in *Bethel School District No. 403 v. Fraser* (1986), Chief Justice Warren Burger wrote, "The determination of what manner of speech in the classroom or in school assembly is inappropriate properly rests with the school board."

STUDENTS' RIGHTS AND RESPONSIBILITIES IN SCHOOL

The right, or privilege, of children to attend school also depends on their compliance with the rules and regulations of the school. To ensure the day-to-day orderly operation of schools, boards of education have the right to establish reasonable rules and regulations controlling pupils and their conduct. Boards' actions have been challenged in numerous instances, however. Challenges have concerned questions such as corporal punishment, the rights of married students, dress codes, student publications' freedom of expression, and involvement with drugs.

DRESS CODES AND GROOMING

Lower-court cases dealing with grooming have been decided in some instances in favor of the board of education—in support of their rules and regulations—and in other instances in favor of the student. A general principle seems to be that if the dress and grooming do not incite or cause disruptive behavior or pose a health or safety problem, the court ruling is likely to support the student. Dress codes, once very much in vogue, are less evident today. Although the U.S. Supreme Court has yet to consider a so-called long-hair case, federal courts in every circuit have issued rulings in such cases; half of them found regulations on hair length unconstitutional, and half upheld them. In all, over a two-decade period, federal and state courts decided more than 300 cases on this subject. If there is a trend, it is that students have won most of the cases that dealt with hairstyle. The courts have usually refused to uphold dress and hair length regulations for athletic teams or extracurricular groups unless the school proves that the hair or dress interfered with a student's ability to play the sport or perform the extracurricular activity.[19]

In the late 1970s and continuing through the 1980s, courts entertained fewer challenges to grooming regulations. The later decisions, however, continued to be consistent with earlier court rulings. Courts have supported school officials who attempted to regulate student appearance if the regulation could be based on concerns about disruption, health, or safety. Presumably, controversy over the length of students' hair or grooming in general is no longer critical because officials and students have a more common ground of agreement about what is acceptable. However, as the new century begins, new questions could be raised in relation to school efforts to control the clothing and other grooming symbols of gangs.

CORPORAL PUNISHMENT

In 1977 the U.S. Supreme Court ruled on and finally resolved many of the issues related to corporal punishment (*Ingraham v. Wright,* 1977). The opinion established that states may *constitutionally* authorize corporal punishment without prior hearing or notice and without consent by the student's parents, and may as a matter of policy elect to prohibit or limit the use of corporal punishment. It also held that corporal punishment is not in violation of the Eighth Amendment (which prohibits "cruel and unusual punishments").

In response to the greater sensitivity to student rights, many school districts have

Court cases dealing with student grooming have found in favor of both school boards and students.

adopted administrative rules and regulations to restrict the occasions, nature, and manner of administering corporal punishment. Some school districts specify that corporal punishment can be administered only under the direction of the principal and in the presence of another adult.

SEX DISCRIMINATION

Until relatively recently, educational institutions could discriminate against females—whether they were students, staff, or faculty. In 1972 the Ninety-Second Congress enacted Title IX of the Education Amendments Act to remove sex discrimination against students and employees in federally assisted programs. The key provision in Title IX states, "No person in the United States shall, on the basis of sex, be excluded from participation in, be denied the benefits of, or be subjected to discrimination under any education program or activity receiving federal financial assistance." Title IX is enforced by the Department of Education's Office of Civil Rights. An individual or organization can allege that any policy or practice is discriminatory by writing a letter of complaint to the secretary of education. An administrative hearing is the next step in the process. Further steps include suing for monetary damages under Title IX, which the U.S. Supreme Court affirmed in *Franklin v. Guinneth County Schools* (1992).

MARRIAGE AND PREGNANCY

A recipient (e.g., a school district) shall not apply any rule concerning a student's actual or potential parental, family, or marital status which treats students differently on the basis of sex.

Title IX of the Education Amendments Act of 1972

In the past, it was not unusual for school officials to expel students who married. Some educators reasoned that marriage brought on additional responsibilities, such as the establishment of a household, and therefore that married students could not perform well in school. They also believed that exclusion would help deter other teenagers from marrying. Courts tended to uphold school officials in these positions. Both courts and school officials acted consistently in not rigidly enforcing compulsory attendance statutes for underage students who married.

School officials today cannot prohibit a student from attending school merely because he or she is married. This position is based on the above-mentioned Title IX and on the notion that every child has a right to attend school. Public policy today encourages students to acquire as much education as they can. Not only are married students encouraged to remain in school, but they are also entitled to the same rights and privileges as unmarried students. Thus, they have the right to take any course the school offers and to participate in extracurricular activities open to other students. That is, participation in extracurricular activities cannot be denied a student solely on the basis of married status. However, a student's attendance and participation rights can be removed if his or her behavior is deleterious to other students.

Today's schools also enroll more pregnant students than ever before. Title IX prohibits their exclusion from school or from participation in extracurricular activities. Many school systems have reorganized their school programs so that courses can be offered during after-school hours or in the evenings to accommodate married and pregnant students. This arrangement makes it easier for students to work during the day and complete their education at a time that is convenient for them. Such programs often include courses and topics aimed at the specific audience, as well as counseling programs to assist students with their adjustment to marriage and family life.

CHILD ABUSE AND NEGLECT

Government bodies in the United States have the right to exercise police power, which means that government is entrusted with the responsibility of looking after the health, safety, and welfare of all its citizens. In effect, each state acts as a guardian over all its people, exercising that role specifically over individuals not able to look after themselves. This guardianship extends to care for children who have been either abused or neglected by their parents. All fifty states have statutes dealing with this issue. These statutes generally protect children under the age of eighteen, but the scope of protection and definitions of abuse and neglect vary considerably among the states. In 1974, Congress passed the Child Abuse Prevention and Treatment Act, which provides financial assistance to states that have developed and implemented programs for identifying, preventing, and treating instances of child abuse and neglect.

The severity of this problem has been highlighted by the requirement of mandatory reporting of suspected abuse and neglect. Formerly, this reporting was limited mainly to physicians, but today educators are also required to report instances of suspected abuse and neglect. Some teachers are reluctant to do so because they fear a breakdown in student–teacher–parent relationships and the possibility of lawsuits alleging invasion of privacy, assault, or slander. Their fear should be diminished, however, by statutes that grant them immunity for acting in good faith.

STUDENT PUBLICATIONS

A significant decision relative to "underground" student newspapers was made in Illinois in 1970.[20] Students were expelled for distributing a newspaper named *Grass High,* which the students produced at home and which criticized school officials and used vulgar language. The students were expelled under an Illinois statute that empowered boards of education to expel pupils guilty of gross disobedience or misconduct. A federal court in Illinois supported the board of education, but on appeal the Court of Appeals for the Seventh Circuit reversed the decision. The school board was not able to validate student disruption and interference as required by *Tinker.* The expelled students were entitled to collect damages. An implication is that the rights of students regarding newspapers they print at home are stronger than their rights of free expression in official school publications.

Early in 1988, in a landmark decision (*Hazelwood School District v. Kuhlmeier*), the U.S. Supreme Court ruled that administrators have broad authority to control student expression in official school newspapers, theatrical productions, and other forums that are part of the curriculum. In reaching that decision, the Court determined that the *Spectrum,* the school newspaper of the Hazelwood District, was not a public forum. A school policy of the Hazelwood District required that the principal review each proposed issue of the *Spectrum.* The principal objected to two articles scheduled to appear in one issue. One of the articles was about girls at the school who had become pregnant; the other discussed the effects of divorce on students. Neither article used real names. The principal deleted two pages of the *Spectrum* rather than delete only the offending articles or require that they be modified. He stated that there was no time to make any changes in the articles and that the newspaper had to be printed immediately or not at all.

Three student journalists sued, contending that their freedom of speech had been violated. The Supreme Court upheld the principal's action. Justice Byron White decided that the *Spectrum* was not a public forum, but rather a supervised learning experience for journalism students. In effect, the censorship of a student press was upheld by the Supreme Court. In Justice White's words,

> schools must be able to set high standards for the student speech that is disseminated under [their] auspices—standards that may be higher than those demanded by some newspaper publishers and theatrical producers in the "real" world—and may refuse to disseminate student speech that does not meet those standards.
>
> Accordingly, we hold that the standard articulated in *Tinker* for determining when a school may punish student expression need not also be the standard for determining when a school may refuse to lend its name and resources to the dissemination of student expression.

The issue of institutional control over publications has not yet been fully resolved. In response to questions about student publications and their distribution, school boards have endeavored to write rules and regulations that will withstand judicial scrutiny. A prompt review and reasonably fast appeal procedures are vital. Students should also be advised of distribution rules and abide by them.

RIGHTS OF STUDENTS WITH DISABILITIES

Before the early 1970s, the access to education of students with disabilities was left to the discretion of different levels of government. In the early 1970s, court decisions established the position that students with disabilities were entitled to an "appropriate" education and to procedural protections against arbitrary treatment. Congress subsequently specified a broad set of substantive and procedural rights via Section 504 of the Rehabilitation Act and Public Law 94-142, the Education for All Handicapped Children Act (EAHCA). Since that time there has been a continuing series of legislative and legal refinements and extensions of the intents to see that students with special needs have appropriate educational opportunities. The problem has been to define what is meant by "appropriate." This examination and clarification process continues to unfold.

One recent case regarding student rights dealt with a violation of P.L. 94-142. That law requires public school officials to keep disruptive or violent students with disabilities in their current classrooms pending hearings on their behavior. In the decision made in *Honig v. Doe* (1988), the U.S. Supreme Court upheld lower-court rulings that San Francisco school district officials violated the act in 1980 when they indefinitely suspended and then attempted to expel two students who were emotionally disturbed and who the officials claimed were dangerous.

The act authorizes officials to suspend dangerous children with disabilities for a maximum of ten days. Longer suspensions or expulsions are permissible only if the child's parents consent to the action taken or if the officials can convince a federal district judge that the child poses a danger to himself or herself or to others. The rules under which school officials must operate also are more limiting if the misbehavior is a manifestation of the student's disability.

It is clear that Congress meant to restrain the authority that schools had traditionally used to exclude students with disabilities, particularly students who are emotionally disturbed, from school. But P.L. 94-142 did not leave school administrators powerless to deal with dangerous students.

STUDENT AND LOCKER SEARCHES

Most courts have refused to subject public school searches to strict Fourth Amendment standards. In general, the Fourth Amendment protects individuals from search without a warrant (court order). Many lower courts, however, have decided in favor of a more lenient interpretation of the Fourth Amendment in school searches. The rationale is that school authorities are obligated to maintain discipline and a sound educational environment and that that responsibility, along with their in loco parentis powers, gives them the right to conduct searches and seize contraband on reasonable suspicion without a warrant. First, however, school officials may only search for evidence that a student has violated a school rule or a law. Also, there must be a valid rule or law in place.

School authorities do not need a warrant to search a student's locker or a student vehicle on campus. For searches of a student's person, however, courts apply a higher standard. Where reasonable suspicion exists, a school official will likely be upheld. Reasonable suspicion exists when one has information that a student is in possession of something harmful or dangerous, or when there

Where reasonable suspicion exists, school authorities do not need a warrant to search a student's locker or a student's vehicle on campus.

is evidence of illegal activities such as drug dealing (money, a list of customers, or selling papers). The second consideration is the way in which the search of a student's person is conducted. School officials are advised to have students remove contents from their clothing rather than having a teacher or administrator do it. A further caution is not to force students to remove all their clothing or undress to their underwear. To date, courts have not upheld school officials in strip searches; these cases evoke the greatest judicial sympathy toward student claims for damages on grounds of illegal searches.[21]

PEER SEXUAL HARASSMENT

Title IX prohibits sex discrimination, and this includes students' harassing other students. Teasing, snapping bra straps, requesting sexual favors, making lewd comments about one's appearance or body parts, telling sexual jokes, engaging in physical abuse, and touching inappropriately are examples of peer sexual harassment. It is important for teachers to make it clear that sexual harassment will not be tolerated. School districts are supposed to have in place a grievance procedure for sex discrimination complaints. Students and/or their parents can file a complaint with the Office of Civil Rights also. All allegations must be investigated promptly, and schools must take immediate action in cases in which harassment behaviors have been confirmed. Keep in mind that sexual harassment is not limited to high school students; middle school and in some cases elementary school children are also sexually harassed. In summary of the topics covered in this section, Table 6.13 lists brief statements related to the rights and responsibilities of students.

TABLE 6.13   Summary Statements on Students' Rights and Responsibilities

- State constitutions provide that a child has the right to an education; to date, students have been unsuccessful in suing school board members on the ground that they have not learned anything.
- The due process clause provides that a child is entitled to notice of charges and the opportunity for a hearing prior to being suspended from school for misbehavior.
- Students enjoy freedom of speech at school unless that speech is indecent or leads to disruption; courts are in agreement that school officials can regulate the content of student newspapers. Underground newspapers are not subject to this oversight.
- Students may be awarded damages from school board members for a violation of their constitutional rights if they can establish that they were injured by the deprivation and that the school official deliberately violated those rights.
- The use of corporal punishment is not prohibited by the U.S. Constitution, but excessive punishment may be barred by the Fourteenth Amendment.
- Students may be restricted in their dress when there are problems of disruption, health, or safety.
- Assignments of students to activities or classes in general on the basis of sex is not consistent with Title IX. These assignments may be made in such areas as sex education classes or when sports are available for both sexes.
- Restricting a student's activities on the basis of marriage or pregnancy is inconsistent with the equal protection clause and Title IX.
- Teachers are required to report to proper authorities suspected instances of child abuse and neglect.
- Parents have the right to examine their children's educational records. Students age eighteen or older have the right to examine their records.
- School officials may search students, lockers, and student property without a search warrant, but they must have reasonable grounds for believing that a student is in possession of evidence of a violation of a law or school rule.

Legal Aspects of Education in Other Countries

The legal aspects of school systems in other countries offer some interesting differences in comparison to the U.S. system. For example, other democratic countries do not have the apparently never-ending debates about the separation of church and state. As nearby as provinces of Canada and as far away as Belgium and the Netherlands, public dollars fund nondenominational and church-based schools. In the Dutch system, there are three separate school systems: public, Catholic, and Protestant. Each is supported with public funds, yet each is governed independently.

Germany incorporates instruction in religion in all schools. In fact, often one teacher is hired specifically to teach religion in regularly scheduled classes. Students have to take instruction on religion and are given a choice of Protestant or Catholic classes. In the higher grades, this instruction shifts toward more emphasis on human values.

Also, in Germany there are no school boards, and there are no publicly elected state boards of education. The school system is run by government bureaucracies. The curriculum and exams are set by the state. However, parents are actively involved in the education of their children at the school site. For example, when there is a parent evening, *both* parents will attend. At these evenings, much of the talk between parents will be about the homework assignments their children have been doing. This level of involvement is possible because parents are expected to help their children with homework. In Germany children have three to four hours of homework assignments *every day*. The school day ends at 1:00 P.M. Children return home and work on their homework during the afternoon.

Germany takes a different approach to consideration of special-needs children. These children either have tutors or are assigned to different schools. If a child cannot keep up with the others at a school, he or she is told, "You do not belong here." The parents and the child will then either have to work harder at keeping up or move to a different school.

Another legal aspect of the education system in Germany is that teachers, as government employees, cannot be sued. One consequence is that teachers do not supervise children during nonteaching times. Also, as government employees teachers are not evaluated after their first year of teaching. As this description of schooling in Germany illustrates, the legal aspects of education and schools can be very different from country to country. Be careful not to assume that schools are the same everywhere.

SUMMARY

The legal foundation for education in the United States, including the rights and responsibilities of teachers and students, is the U.S. Constitution. Education is not mentioned directly in the U.S. Constitution, but the Tenth Amendment has been interpreted as assigning responsibility to each state for the education of its citizens. Following from the U.S. Constitution are the many other forms of law, including state constitutions, federal and state statutes, and the policies of school boards.

The legal rights and responsibilities of teachers are the same as those of other citizens. For example, the courts have said that a teaching certificate is a license to practice a profession that cannot be revoked without constitutional due process. At the same time, the courts have ruled that local boards of education may prescribe requirements beyond the state requirements for licensure.

All students, including students with disabilities, have the right to a public school education; but they must behave in ways that ensure an orderly and safe school environment. Students have the right to see their school records, to sue, and to receive procedural and substantive due process. Students must not dress in ways that are disruptive or present a risk to health or safety, harass other students, or violate school standards in school publications.

In summary, the legal lens offers an important view of education, schools, teaching, and learning. From the U.S. Constitution through state statues to school board policies, school administrators and teachers are surrounded with protected rights and identified responsibilities. Most of these rights and responsibilities apply to nontenured teachers and to teacher education students. However, it is of the utmost importance that you learn about and keep in mind the legal specifics of the school districts and school where you will be teaching. As in other parts of life, ignorance of the law is not an acceptable defense for teachers.

DISCUSSION QUESTIONS

1. Each year state legislators offer up many bills related to the operation of public schools. What are some current or recent examples in your state or another of proposed bills that the courts would probably find unconstitutional?

2. The appropriate place for prayer in public schools continues to be a source of contention. What will you say and do if a parent wants you to have a moment of prayer in your classroom?

3. How should you as a teacher accommodate the religious interest of children in your class who are of a religion other than Christianity, such as Judaism, Muslim, or Buddhism?

4. In *Ingraham v. Wright* (1977), the U.S. Supreme Court ruled that states may authorize the use of corporal punishment as school policy. The U.S. military has not allowed corporal punishment for 100 years; why should it be disallowed in the military but be permissible in schools? Is it ever appropriate in schools?

5. Each fall, teacher strikes somewhere in the country delay the opening of school. Have you ever been involved in a strike of any kind? What do you think are the most critical consequences of teacher strikes? If your association/union leaders called for a strike, would you join the picket line or teach your classes?

6. What are your thoughts about the balancing of student rights against school officials' need to maintain an environment conducive to learning? Should school officials have more authority? Should students have greater freedom?

7. AIDS is a legally recognized disability. If, as a teacher, you are to have an HIV-positive student in your classroom, what are that student's rights under the law? What are your responsibilities as a teacher?

JOURNAL ENTRIES

1. Prayer in public schools is the subject of seemingly endless debates. As a teacher, you will probably be asked to offer an opinion or be asked to include a moment of silence in your classroom. Now is the time for you to prepare your position. Certainly, you have a personal position as to whether prayer should be permitted/encouraged/required in public schools. On one page, list the key points in your personal position. Then review the position of the courts as outlined in this chapter. Is your personal position consistent with legal precedent? Annotate your list to indicate which points are supported or refuted by law.

2. Academic freedom is a complex idea with uncertain legal foundation, especially for schoolteachers; most court cases involving academic freedom have dealt only with college faculty. Issues related to academic freedom are more uncertain still for beginning teachers. For the first several years, you will be a probationary teacher—in other words, untenured. What are your thoughts about the amount of academic freedom you will have during those first years? Do you plan to select the topics you will teach? What about the lesson designs and specific activities you will use? What are the chances of your slipping into some area of controversy? How will you guard against this happening? Take fifteen minutes or so to prepare a journal entry on this topic.

PORTFOLIO DEVELOPMENT

1. Pick a school district where you think you would like to be employed as a teacher. Obtain a copy of the teacher employment contract from the district human resources/personnel office and study it. What does the contract say about your rights as a district employee and as a teacher? What does it say about your responsibilities? There may be references to other legal documents such as an employee handbook and board

policies; if so, become familiar with those documents too. Together, these documents set the parameters for what you can, should, and should not do as a teacher. Place these documents and your notes in a folio file folder and save them for later uses.

2. From time to time, newspapers and weekly news-magazines carry reports about disagreements between students and school officials. Collect these reports, paying special attention to the legal interpretations drawn by each side, and consider the implications for you. In all instances, keep in mind that both teachers and students have legal responsibilities as well as rights. These clippings and notes may be a useful resource for you someday, when as a teacher you are confronted with a question about student and teacher rights.

PREPARING FOR CERTIFICATION

TEACHERS' AND STUDENTS' RIGHTS

1. The Praxis II Principles of Teaching and Learning (PLT) test includes cases and items that address "teachers' and students' legal rights inside and outside the classroom." Review the tables in this chapter that present key legal decisions affecting teachers' and students' rights, then list the five law-related parameters that you think will influence you the most in the subject area or geographical location in which you plan to teach.

2. Answer the following multiple-choice question, which is similar to items in Praxis and other state certification tests. If you are unsure of the answer, reread the Teachers' Rights and Responsibilities section of this chapter.

    The Buckley Amendment

    (A) permits corporal punishment as long as district policies and procedures are in place.

    (B) allows all parents access to their children's academic records.
    (C) establishes that married or pregnant students have the same rights and privileges as other students.
    (D) states that all students with disabilities are entitled to an "appropriate" education.

3. Answer the following short-answer question, which is similar to items in Praxis and other state certification tests. After you've completed your written response, use the scoring guide in the ETS *Test at a Glance* materials to assess your response. Can you revise your response to improve your score?

    What are the arguments for and against tenure for teachers? What is your position, and why?

WEBSITES

catalog.loc.gov The Library of Congress Catalog provides a quick way to access the text of government bills, including those related to education.
janweb.icdi.wvu.edu and **www.schoolnet. ca/sne** There are many websites with information on special education topics. The ADA (Americans with Disabilities Act) Document Center and the Special Needs Education Network are two useful sites to check first.
www.abanet.org The American Bar Association's website provides access to its journal, analyses of court decisions, and a large database of court decisions.

www.lawschool.cornell.edu The Cornell Law School website is easy to use and provides access to court decisions, news related to court cases, directories, and current awareness items.
www.cnn.com/LAW CNN operates a number of useful websites including Law Center, which reports on state, national, and international court proceedings.
www.nea.org The National Education Association website offers legal information and a number of teaching supports for beginning teachers.

FURTHER READING

Essex, Nathan L. (2002). *School Law and the Public Schools: A Practical Guide for Educational Leaders* (2nd ed.). Boston: Allyn and Bacon. This book presents issues and topics briefly, and for each it provides a table called "Administrative Guide" that summarizes legal points and suggests appropriate steps to take.

Fraser, James W. (2000). *Between Church and State: Religion and Public Education in a Multicultural America.* New York: St. Martin's Press. An informative and useful analysis of the views and legal parameters related specifically to the place of religion in public schools.

LaMorte, Michael W. (2002). *School Law: Cases and Concepts* (7th ed.). Boston: Allyn and Bacon. Each chapter presents an in-depth analysis of cases and points of law related to public education, teacher rights, and student rights.

School Law Yearbook: Reference Guide to Education Law. (2000). Frederick, MD: Aspen Publishers. An easy-to-read reference to education law.

Yudof, Mark G., Kirp, David L., Levin, Betsy, and Moran, Rachel F. (2002). *Educational Policy and the Law* (4th ed.). Belmont, CA: Wadsworth Group, West Thomson Learning. A well-developed and thorough analysis of legal issues and relevant cases.

Zirkel, Perry A. "Courtside." *Phi Delta Kappan.* A regular column in the *Phi Delta Kappan* providing timely and pertinent information about legal issues.

THEMES OF THE TIMES!

expect the world®

The New York Times

nytimes.com

Expand your knowledge of the concepts discussed in this chapter by reading current and historical articles from the *New York Times* by visiting the Themes of the Times! section of the companion website **(www.ablongman.com/johnson13e).**

NOTES

1. Michael LaMorte, *School Law: Cases and Concepts,* 7th ed. Boston: Allyn and Bacon, 2000, p. 177.
2. *Turk v. Franklin Special School District* (1982).
3. *Lucia v. Duggan* (1969).
4. *Gouge v. Joint School District No. 1* (1970).
5. Haskell C. Freedman, "The Legal Rights of Untenured Teachers," *Nolpe School Law Journal, 1* (Fall 1970), p. 100.
6. *Norwalk Teachers Association v. Board of Education* (1951).
7. *City of Manchester v. Manchester Teachers' Guild* (1957).
8. *Cooper v. Ross* (1979).
9. *Hillis v. Stephen F. Austin University* (1982).
10. *Kingsville Independent School District v. Cooper* (1980).
11. *Board of Education, Island Trees Union Free District No. 26 v. Pico* (1982).
12. Lucy Knight, "Facts about Mr. Buckley's Amendment," *American Education, 13* (June 1977), p. 7.
13. *Peter W. v. San Francisco Unified School District* (1976).
14. *Donahue v. Copiague Union Free School District* (1978).
15. *Mastrangelo v. West Side Union High School District* (1935).
16. *Morris v. Douglas County School District* (1966).
17. Lee O. Garber and Reynolds C. Seitz, *The Yearbook of School Law, 1971.* Danville, IL: Interstate, 1971, p. 253.
18. Thomas J. Flygare, "De Jure," *Phi Delta Kappan, 68* (October 1986), pp. 165–166.
19. *Long v. Zopp* (1973).
20. *Scoville v. Board of Education* (1970).
21. William D. Valente, *Law in the Schools.* Columbus, OH: Merrill, 1980, p. 282.

Historical Foundations of Education

Viewing Education through Historical Lenses

 This part of the book briefly surveys the history of education. As you read these history chapters, remember that historians see past events through various lenses. And they interpret history, including the history of American education, according to the particular lens through which they view it.

Celebrationist historians, for instance, tend to see the brighter side of historical events and may tend, for example, to praise schools for past accomplishments. Some might suggest that celebrationist historians view history through "rose-colored" lenses. By contrast, *liberal* historians tend to study educational history through lenses that focus on conflict, stress, and inconsistencies. *Revisionist* historians use yet another lens, seeing celebrationist history as fundamentally flawed and concluding that we often learn more by studying what has been wrong with education than by rehearsing what has been right. *Postmodernist* historians believe that a person sees the history of education through the unique lenses of her or his social class, race, ethnicity, gender, age, and so on.

Some historians provocatively argue that it is really not possible to "know" history because it can only be viewed through somewhat clouded lenses; so we can only make assumptions about the past.

Although this part of the book presents many interesting and potentially useful details about the history of education, each of the following two chapters also proposes several big ideas about history that we hope will be particularly useful generalizations for you.

In addition, we challenge you to think critically as you read the next two chapters and to formulate your own opinions about the content, major ideas, and relevancy of this historical material, thereby eventually developing your own informed and unique lens through which to view educational history.

Focus Questions

The following questions will help you focus your learning as you read Part IV:

1. Who were some of the most important early educators in the world, and what lessons might we learn from them today?
2. What was life probably like for colonial American parents, students, and teachers? In what ways was it different and yet similar to today?
3. What role(s) have American governmental agencies played in education down through history?
4. What major changes have taken place in our educational systems during the past half century?
5. What are the really important big ideas in educational history?
6. How might an understanding of educational history be used to improve the work of educators today?

The Evolution of American Education

Education in the News

"Summer Fellows" Learn Lessons Teaching in City

By Ana Beatriz Cholo, *Chicago Tribune,* July 21, 2003.

HEATHER HARTZ IS A SUN-BRONZED 21-YEAR-OLD WHO LOVES hanging out at the beach with her friends. But this summer the Florida State University student is teaching in the Chicago public schools, working with some of the city's most academically challenged pupils.

"This is a great thing to put on my résumé," she said enthusiastically before her first day in the classroom. "It's only going to make me a better person."

Hartz and 146 other young adults are part of a six-week summer program, just out of its pilot phase, that is one of the Chicago Public Schools' efforts to lure quality teachers into the system.

All aspiring teachers, most of whom are still in college, these "summer fellows" seem to share Hartz's idea that, armed with knowledge and passion, they can change the world—student by student.

It isn't long before Hartz is standing before more than a dozen rambunctious kids who are at risk of being retained in 6th grade for another year.

Some are blatantly insolent and loud. They snicker behind the young woman's back and, de-spite warnings to throw out their gum, the chewing is incessant. Others just can't seem to stop giggling.

But no matter what they do, Hartz's steely resolve does not soften, and her smile always stays strong.

"These are my babies; these are my kids," she said, her eyes guarded against saying anything negative. "They all have bad days and good days, just like me. You just have to be sensitive to that."

The "summer fellows" represent schools as diverse as the University of Iowa, Chicago State University, the University of Tennessee and Harvard University. Most are female and white, although the recruiting effort visited historically black colleges.

The fellows are paid $12 an hour and are housed in university dorms. The program also involves professional development training, twice-weekly field trips to local museums, a weekly visit to a local neighborhood and an unlimited-use CTA fare card.

About 90 percent of the interns will receive job offers in August, officials said, with salaries that start at $34,538 for graduates with a bachelor's degree.

INTASC   **Learning Outcomes**

After reading and studying this chapter, you should be able to:

1. List some of the most important early educators in the world and explain their contributions to education. (INTASC 4: Teaching Methods)

2. Detail the major educational accomplishments of the early Eastern societies, the ancient Greeks, the ancient Romans, and the Europeans of the Middle Ages, Renaissance, Reformation, and Age of Reason. (INTASC 3: Diversity)

3. Analyze what life was like for the colonial schoolteacher, student, and parent.

4. Articulate the roles government (local, state, and national) played in colonial America soon after winning the War of Independence, in the 1800s, and in the early twentieth century.

5. Analyze how an understanding of early American educational history might be used to improve teaching today. (INTASC 9: Reflection)

School-Based Observations

You may see these learning outcomes in action during your visits to schools:

1. Over two hundred years ago, Jean-Jacques Rousseau advocated that children be taught with love, patience, understanding, and kindness. As you work in the school, experiment with this basic approach to see whether it is effective. You might also wish to observe experienced teachers: To what extent do they teach children with love, patience, understanding, and kindness? We suggest that you experiment with other constructive ideas in this chapter as you observe and participate in the classroom.

2. As you work in schools, observe how they have changed relative to schools of the past. How are schools today similar to those of the past? How much and in what ways are students today similar to their historical counterparts? In what ways are they probably different?

3. While you are in the schools, visit with experienced teachers and administrators to discuss the ways in which schools have changed over the years. Also ask how students, teaching methods, and parents have changed.

The first part of this chapter will briefly look at some of the antecedents of our current U.S. educational systems. There is much to be learned from past successes and failures in education. Remember that there are various methods of **historical interpretation,** various lenses through which to view the past, and that historians often disagree when attempting to understand history. History is not an exact science by any means; rather, it is open to different interpretations.

Although this chapter presents detailed information about the development of education in what is now the United States, it does so around a number of major historical ideas. The first idea is that since the beginning of time, adults have always informally educated their children in an attempt to prepare them for adult life. Another idea is that as people developed a written language, they created a need for schools as a means of teaching these writing skills and passing on knowledge to succeeding generations. A third major historical idea presented in this chapter relates to the fact that countless early societies throughout the world developed unique educational programs to serve their perceived needs. For instance, the early American colonists brought their educational ideas and practices with them from Europe. In other words, nearly all of the educational practices and educational materials were essentially the same as those found in Europe at that time. The religious motive was extremely strong in colonial America, and it permeated colonial education.

The last big idea presented in this chapter is that education has played a critical role in the historical development of the United States. The framers of our Constitution clearly recognized that our new democracy was dependent on an educated citizenry. Progress and advancement in every society has been and still is, in large part, dependent on education.

We challenge you to think creatively and critically about the history presented in this and the next chapter. Strive to learn the historical facts and then make your own historical interpretations.

historical interpretation
Different ways to study and understand history, such as celebrationist, liberal, revisionist, and postmodernist historians' approaches.

EDUCATION IN OTHER CULTURES

It is generally believed that human beings have been on earth for several million years. But not until about ten thousand years ago did people start to raise food, domesticate animals, build canoes, and live in some semblance of community life; and not until approximately six thousand years ago was written language developed.

THE BEGINNINGS OF EDUCATION (TO 476 CE)

It would be unfair, and simply not historically accurate, to overlook the informal education that has been provided for children down through the ages by aboriginal peoples throughout the world. All people, regardless of their time and place in history, have cared for their young and prepared them for life at that time. This was true even of the very earliest humans, who fed and protected their children and informally taught them—probably by example and admonition—the skills they needed to survive as adults. For in-

The aboriginal ancestors of today's Native Americans, like other aboriginal peoples, probably taught their children by admonition and example.

stance, Native Americans, who lived and flourished in North America for thousands of years before the first Europeans arrived and established formal schools, educated generations of their children. Many other early societies (in China, Africa, and South America, for example) also successfully provided the education that their children needed to help build their flourishing cultures. Unfortunately, records do not exist that would help us better understand these earliest informal educational systems. If such records did exist, we would probably be quite impressed with the educational efforts of our aboriginal ancestors.

Once there was written language, humans felt the need for a more formal education. As societies became more complex and the body of knowledge increased, people recognized a need for schools. What they had learned constituted the subject matter; the written language allowed them to record this knowledge and pass it from generation to generation.

GLOBAL PERSPECTIVES

Educational Ideas Borrowed from around the World

The educational ideas now implemented in the United States had their inception a long time ago. Our contemporary schools are a mixture of educational ideas, concepts, and practices borrowed from around the world. Much of whatever credit and accolades our current American educational system receives must be shared with those who long ago conceived of the idea of formal education and who then slowly developed and refined these educational concepts.

This chapter is devoted to a brief review of some of the early educational developments that occurred long before any formal education took place in the United States.

NON-WESTERN EDUCATION

It is impossible to determine the date that schools first came into existence. However, the discovery of cuneiform mathematics textbooks dated to 2000 BCE suggests that some form of school probably existed in Sumeria (now part of Iraq) at that time. There is also evidence to suggest that formal schools existed in China during the Hsia and Shang dynasties, perhaps as early as 2000 BCE. Let's briefly explore several examples of these early educational efforts.

HINDU EDUCATION   The ancient Hindu societies were deeply rooted in the caste system, in which family status determined a person's social and vocational position in life. The Hindu religion emphasized nonearthly values; this resulted in little interest in education for anyone but boys from the highest castes. Priests were in charge of what formal education existed. Clues from the writing of Buddha suggest that education involved a heavy emphasis on morals, writing with a stick in the sand, and frequent punishments with a rod. Further education was reserved for the priestly caste, which, over the ages, gradually cultivated such disciplines as logic, rhetoric, astronomy, and mathematics. Many of our contemporary educational values, including our European languages, are partially derived from those of the early Hindu societies.

HEBREW EDUCATION   Perhaps no culture has historically valued education more than the Hebrew societies. Hebrew education was derived from the Jewish Scriptures, which taught religious faithfulness and strict adherence to Old Testament laws. Discipline was harsh both at home and in school and was justified by many Bible verses such as the proverb "He that spareth his rod, hateth his son." Early Hebrew schools taught boys to read and write and girls to prepare food, spin, weave, sing, and dance. Teachers were greatly respected; the Talmud dictates, "If your teacher and your father have need of your assistance, help your teacher before helping your father, for the latter has given you only the life of this world, while the former has secured for you the life of the world to come." From Hebrew society we have inherited, at least in part, the value we place on education.

CHINESE EDUCATION   It has been said that China has been civilized longer than any other society in the world. The Chinese invented printing, gunpowder, and the mariner's compass, among other things. Chinese education has always been characterized by tradition, formality, and conformity—all designed to help students function in a regular, mechanical, and predictable routine.

In the sixth century BCE, two philosophers/reformers exerted enormous influence on Chinese thinking and education through their writings. One of these was Lao-tszu, who wrote,

> Certain bad rulers would have us believe that the heart and the spirit of man should be left empty, but that instead his stomach should be filled; that his bones should be strengthened rather than the power of his will; that we should always desire to have people remain in a state of ignorance, for then their demands would be few. It is difficult, they say, to govern a people that are too wise.
>
> These doctrines are directly opposed to what is due to humanity. Those in authority should come to the aid of the people by means of oral and written instruction; so far from oppressing them and treating them as slaves, they should do them good in every possible way.

Another Chinese reformer, K'ung-Fu-tzu (551–478 BCE), who later became known as Confucius, is perhaps the most famous Asian philosopher. Since his time, all Chinese students have been taught Confucius's five cardinal virtues (universal charity, impartial justice, conformity, rectitude of heart and mind, and pure sincerity) as well as many of his famous sayings, such as "There are three thousand crimes . . . of these no one is greater than disobedience to parents." Interestingly, early Chinese education did not include geography, history, science, language, or mathematics—all subjects that are highly valued by early Western societies. Also, unlike many of their Western counterparts, early Chinese educators placed little importance on the individual. From early Chinese educational traditions we have inherited our respect for others and for authority and patience, as well as advances in written language.

EGYPTIAN EDUCATION In Egypt, civilization and intellectual advancement occurred very early. There, as in most early societies, education was provided only for privileged males. The fact that the pyramids were built several thousand years before Christ attests to the skills of this ancient civilization. In addition, several notable Greek philosophers, including Pythagoras, Plato, Lycurgus, and Solon, completed their education in Egypt.

Egyptian society was divided into castes, with priests holding the highest position and receiving instruction in philosophy, astronomy, geometry, medicine, history, and law. The priests also provided education for others who were considered worthy of that privilege.

Most of the great early Eastern civilizations developed educational systems long before Western civilizations did. Eastern civilizations contributed substantially to the development of knowledge, education, and schools in the world.

WESTERN EDUCATION

It was not until about 500 BCE that a Western society advanced sufficiently to generate an organized concern for formal education. This happened in Greece during the **Age of Pericles,** 455–431 BCE. Greece consisted of many city-states, one of which was Sparta, a militaristic state whose educational system was geared to support military ambitions. Spartan infants were exposed to the elements for a stated period; if they survived the ordeal, they were judged sufficiently strong for soldiering if male or to bear healthy children if female. From the ages of eight to eighteen, boys were wards of the state. During this time, they lived in barracks and received physical and moral training. Between the ages of eighteen and twenty, boys underwent rigorous war training, after which they served in the army. All men were required to marry by the age of thirty so that they might raise healthy children to serve the state. The aims of Spartan education centered on developing such ideals as courage, patriotism, obedience, cunning, and physical strength. Plutarch (46–120 CE), a writer of later times, said that the education of the Spartans "was calculated to make them subject to command, to endure labor, to fight, and to conquer." There was very little intellectual content in Spartan education.

In sharp contrast to Sparta was Athens, another Greek city-state, which developed an educational program that heavily stressed intellectual and aesthetic objectives. Between the ages of eight and sixteen, some Athenian boys attended a series of public schools. These schools included a kind of grammar school, which taught reading, writing, and counting; a gymnastics school, which taught sports and games; and a music school, which taught history, drama, poetry, speaking, and science as well as music. Because all city-states had to defend themselves against aggressors, Athenian boys received citizenship and military training between the ages of sixteen and twenty. Athenian girls were educated in the home. Athenian education stressed individual development, aesthetics, and culture.

The Western world's first great philosophers came from Athens. Of the many philosophers that Greece produced, three stand out: Socrates (470–399 BCE), Plato (427–347 BCE), and Aristotle (384–322 BCE).

SOCRATES Socrates left no writings, but we know much about him from the writings of Xenophon and Plato. He is famous for creating the **Socratic method** of teaching, in which a teacher asks a series of questions that leads the student to a certain conclusion. This method is still commonly used by teachers today.

Socrates traveled around Athens teaching the students who gathered about him. He was dedicated to the search for truth and at times was very critical of the existing government. In fact, Socrates was eventually brought to trial for inciting the people against the government by his ceaseless questioning. He

The very spring and root of honesty and virtue lie in good education.
Plutarch

Age of Pericles

A period (455–431 BCE) of Greek history in which sufficiently great strides were made in human advancement to generate an organized concern for formal education.

Socratic method

A way of teaching that centers on the use of questions by the teacher to lead students to certain conclusions.

Of the many ancient Greek philosophers, Socrates stands out the most.

History illuminates reality, vitalizes memory, provides guidance in daily life. . . .

Marcus Cicero (first century BCE)

was found guilty and given a choice between ending his teaching or being put to death. Socrates chose death, thereby becoming a martyr for the cause of education. Socrates' fundamental principle, "Knowledge is virtue," has been adopted by countless educators and philosophers throughout the ages. Incidentally, some historians speculate that Socrates might not really have existed, but rather might have been a mythical character created by other writers, something that many writers did at that time, as evidenced by the rich Greek mythology we now treasure.

PLATO   Plato was a student and disciple of Socrates. In his *Republic,* Plato set forth his recommendations for the ideal society. He suggested that society should contain three classes of people: artisans, to do the manual work; soldiers, to defend the society; and philosophers, to advance knowledge and to rule the society. Plato's educational aim was to discover and develop each individual's abilities. He believed that each person's abilities should be used to serve society. Plato wrote, "I call education the virtue which is shown by children when the feelings of joy or of sorrow, of love or of hate, which arise in their souls, are made conformable to order." Concerning the goals of education, Plato wrote, "A good education is that which gives to the body and to the soul all the beauty and all the perfection of which they are capable."

ARISTOTLE   Like Plato, Aristotle believed that a person's most important purpose in life was to serve and improve humankind. Aristotle's educational method, however, was scientific, practical, and objective, in contrast to the philosophical methods of Socrates and Plato. Aristotle believed that the quality of a society was determined by the quality of education found in that society. His writings, which include *Lyceum, Organon, Politics, Ethics,* and *Metaphysics,* were destined to exert greater influence on humankind throughout the Middle Ages than the writings of any other person.

Insight into some of Aristotle's views concerning education can be obtained from the following passage from *Politics:*

> There can be no doubt that children should be taught those useful things which are really necessary, but not all things; for occupations are divided into liberal and illiberal; and to young children should be imparted only such kinds of knowledge as will be useful to them without vulgarizing them. And any occupation, art, or science, which makes the body or soul or mind of the freeman less fit for the practice or exercise of virtue, is vulgar; wherefore we call those arts vulgar which tend to deform the body, and likewise all paid employments, for they absorb and degrade the mind.[1]

The early Greek philosophers, including Plato and Aristotle, articulated the idea that females and slaves did not possess the intelligence to be leaders and therefore should not be educated. Unfortunately, our world's current struggle with racism and sexism, deeply rooted in Western civilization, is traceable to the ancient world.

WESTERN EDUCATION—THE ROMANS

In 146 BCE, the Romans conquered Greece, and Greek teachers and their educational system were quickly absorbed into the Roman Empire. Many of the educational and philosophical advances made by the Roman Empire after that time were actually inspired by enslaved Greeks.

ROMAN SCHOOLS   Before 146 BCE, Roman children were educated primarily in the home, though some children attended schools known as *ludi,* where the rudiments of reading and writing were taught. The Greek influence on Roman education became pronounced between 50 BCE and 200 CE, during which time an entire system of schools developed. Some children, after learning to read and write, attended a *grammaticus* school to study Latin, literature, history, mathematics, music, and dialectics. These **Latin grammar schools** were somewhat like twentieth-century secondary schools in function. Students who were preparing for a career of political service received their training in schools of rhetoric, which offered courses in grammar, rhetoric, dialectics, music, arithmetic, geometry, and astronomy.

The Roman Empire contained numerous institutions of higher learning that were continuations of former Greek institutions. A library founded by Vespasian about 70 CE later came to be known as the Athenaeum and eventually offered studies in law, medicine, architecture, mathematics, and mechanics. Even though the Romans developed a rather extensive system of schools, few Roman children profited from these institutions.

QUINTILIAN One of the most influential Roman educators was a man named Quintilian (35–95 CE). In a set of twelve books, *The Institutes of Oratory,* he described current educational practices, recommended the type of educational system needed in Rome, and listed the great books that were in existence at that time.

Quintilian had considerable insight into educational psychology; concerning the punishment of students, he wrote,

> I am by no means in favor of whipping boys, though I know it to be a general practice. In the first place, whipping is unseemly, and if you suppose the boys to be somewhat grown up, it is an affront to the highest degree. In the next place, if a boy's ability is so poor as to be proof against reproach he will, like a worthless slave, become insensible to blows. Lastly, if a teacher is assiduous and careful, there is no need to use force. I shall observe further that while a boy is under the rod he experiences pain and fear. The shame of this experience dejects and discourages many pupils, makes them shun being seen, and may even weary them of their lives.[2]

Regarding the motivation of students, Quintilian stated,

> Let study be made a child's diversion; let him be soothed and caressed into it, and let him sometimes test himself upon his proficiency. Sometimes enter a contest of wits with him, and let him imagine that he comes off the conqueror. Let him even be encouraged by giving him such rewards that are most appropriate to his age.[3]

These comments apply as well today as they did when Quintilian wrote them nearly 2,000 years ago. Quintilian's writings were rediscovered in the 1400s and became influential in the humanistic movement in education.

The Romans had a genius for organization and for getting the job done. They made lasting contributions to architecture, and many of their roads, aqueducts, and buildings remain today. This genius for organization enabled Rome to unite much of the ancient world with a common language, a religion, and a political bond—a condition that favored the spread of education and knowledge throughout the ancient world.

■ EDUCATION IN THE MIDDLE AGES (476–1300)

By 476 CE (the fall of the Roman Empire), the Roman Catholic Church was well on the way to becoming the greatest power in government and education in the Western world. In fact, the rise of the church to a very powerful position is often cited as a main cause of the Western world's plunge into the Dark Ages. As the church stressed the importance of gaining entrance to heaven, life on earth became less important. Many people viewed earthly life as nothing more than a way to a better life hereafter. You can see that a society in which this attitude prevailed would be unlikely to make intellectual advances, except perhaps in areas tangential to religion.

This section will briefly review the history of education in the Dark Ages and the revival of learning that eventually followed. We begin by sketching the

Latin grammar school

An early type of school that emphasized the study of Latin, literature, history, mathematics, music, and dialectics.

achievements of two educators who lived during the Dark Ages: Charlemagne and Alcuin.

THE DARK AGES (400–1000)

As the name implies, the Dark Ages was a period in the Western world when human learning and knowledge didn't just stand still but actually regressed. This regression was due to a variety of conditions, including political and religious oppression of the common people. However, there were some examples of human progress during this time. In fact, some historians believe this historical period was not "dark" at all but rather an era of considerable human progress—another example of the differing lenses through which various historians view the past.

CHARLEMAGNE   During the Dark Ages, one of the bright periods for education was the reign of Charlemagne (742–814). Charlemagne realized the value of education; and as ruler of a large part of Europe, he was in a position to establish schools and encourage scholarly activity. In 768, when Charlemagne came into power, educational activity was at an extremely low ebb. The church conducted the little educating that was carried on, mainly to induct people into the faith and to train religious leaders. The schools where this religious teaching took place included *catechumenal schools,* which taught church doctrine to new converts; *catechetical schools,* which at first taught the catechism but later became schools for training church leaders; and *cathedral* (or *monastic*) *schools,* which trained clergy.

ALCUIN   Charlemagne sought far and wide for a talented educator who could improve education in the kingdom, finally selecting Alcuin (735–804), who had been a teacher in England. While Alcuin served as Charlemagne's chief educational advisor, he became the most famous educator of his day. His main educational writings include *On Grammar, On Orthography, On Rhetoric,* and *On Dialectics.* In addition to trying to improve education generally in the kingdom, Alcuin headed Charlemagne's Palace School in Frankland. It is reported that Charlemagne himself often sat in the Palace School with the children, trying to further his own meager education.

Roughly during Alcuin's time, the phrase **seven liberal arts** came into common usage to describe the curriculum that was then taught in some schools. The seven liberal arts consisted of the *trivium* (grammar, rhetoric, and logic) and the *quadrivium* (arithmetic, geometry, music, and astronomy). Each of these seven subjects was defined broadly, so collectively they constituted a more comprehensive study than today's usage of the term suggests. The phrase *liberal arts* has survived time and is commonly used now as a reference to general education as opposed to vocational education.

THE REVIVAL OF LEARNING

Despite the efforts of men such as Charlemagne and Alcuin, little educational progress was made during the Dark Ages. However, between 1000 and 1300—a period frequently referred to as the "age of the revival of learning"—humankind slowly regained a thirst for education. Two events supported this revival of interest in learning: the rediscovery of the writings of some of the ancient philosophers (mainly Aristotle) and renewed interest in them and the reconciliation of religion and philosophy. Before this time, the church had denounced the study of philosophy as earthly and ungodly.

THOMAS AQUINAS   Thomas Aquinas (1225–1274), more than any other person, helped to change the church's views on learning. This change led to the creation of new learning institutions, among them the medieval universities.

seven liberal arts

A medieval curriculum that consisted of the trivium (grammar, rhetoric, logic) and the quadrivium (arithmetic, geometry, music, astronomy).

The harmonization of the doctrines of the church with the doctrines of philosophy and education was rooted in the ideas of Aristotle. Himself a theologian, Aquinas formalized **scholasticism,** the logical and philosophical study of the beliefs of the church. His most important writing was *Summa Theologica,* which became the doctrinal authority of the Roman Catholic Church. The educational and philosophical views of Thomas Aquinas were made formal in the philosophy Thomism—a philosophy that has remained important in Roman Catholic parochial education.

MEDIEVAL UNIVERSITIES The revival of learning brought about a general increase in educational activity and a growth of educational institutions, including the establishment of universities. These medieval universities, the true forerunners of our modern universities, included the University of Bologna (1158), which specialized in law; the University of Paris (1180), which specialized in theology; Oxford University (1214); and the University of Salerno (1224). By the time Columbus sailed to North America in 1492, approximately eighty universities already existed in Europe.

Although the Middle Ages produced a few educational advances in the Western world, we must remember that much of the Eastern world did not experience the Dark Ages. Mohammed (569–632) led a group of Arabs through northern Africa and into southern Spain. The Eastern learning that the Arabs brought to Spain spread slowly throughout Europe over the next few centuries through the writings of such scholars as Avicenna (980–1037) and Averroës (1126–1198). These Eastern contributions to Western knowledge included significant advances in science and mathematics, including the Arabic numbering system.

■ EDUCATION IN TRANSITION (1300–1700)

Two very important movements took place during the educational transition period of 1300–1700: the Renaissance and the Reformation. The Renaissance represented the protest of individuals against the dogmatic authority the church exerted over their social and intellectual life. The Renaissance started in Italy (around 1300) when humans reacquired the spirit of free inquiry that had prevailed in ancient Greece. The Renaissance slowly spread through Europe, resulting in a general revival of classical learning called *humanism.*

The second movement, the Reformation, represented a reaction against certain beliefs of the Roman Catholic Church, particularly those that discouraged learning and that, in consequence, kept lay people in ignorance.

THE RENAISSANCE

The common people were generally oppressed by wealthy landowners and royalty during the eleventh and twelfth centuries. In fact, the common people were thought to be unworthy of education and to exist primarily to serve landed gentry and royalty. The Renaissance represented a rebellion on the part of the common people against the suppression they experienced from both the church and the wealthy who controlled their lives.

VITTORINO DA FELTRE One important and influential educator from the Renaissance period was a man from the eastern Alps by the name of Vittorino da Feltre (c. 1378–1446).[4] Da Feltre studied at the University of Florence, where he developed an interest in teaching. He also developed a keen interest in classical literature and, along with other educators of that time, began to believe that people could be educated and also be Christians at the same time—a belief that the Roman Catholic Church generally did not share.

Da Feltre established several schools, taught in a variety of others, and generally helped to advance the development of education during his lifetime. He

scholasticism

The logical and philosophical study of the beliefs of the church.

Erasmus (1466–1536) was one of the most famous educators of the Renaissance.

believed that education was an important end in itself and thereby helped to rekindle an interest in the value of human knowledge during the Renaissance.

ERASMUS   One of the most famous humanist educators was Erasmus (1466–1536), and two of his books, *The Right Method of Instruction* and *The Liberal Education of Boys,* formed a humanistic theory of education. Erasmus had a good deal of educational insight. Concerning the aims of education, he wrote:

> The duty of instructing the young includes several elements, the first and also the chief of which is that the tender mind of the child should be instructed in piety; the second, that he love and learn the liberal arts; the third, that he be taught tact in the conduct of social life; and the fourth, that from his earliest age he accustom himself to good behavior, based on moral principles.[5]

THE REFORMATION

It is difficult for people today to imagine the extent to which the Roman Catholic Church dominated the lives of the common people through most of what we think of as Europe during the fifteenth and sixteenth centuries. The Roman Catholic Church and the pope had an enormous amount of influence over European royalty during this time. In fact, some historians suggest that the pope and other officials of the Roman Catholic Church were in some ways more powerful than many individual kings and queens. After all, the Roman Catholic Church could and frequently did claim that unless members of royalty abided by its rules, they were destined to spend eternity in hell—an extremely frightening prospect for any human being. Consequently, it is understandable that the church came to be a powerful influence throughout most of Europe.

What can only be taught by the rod and with blows will not lead to much good; they will not remain pious longer than the rod is behind them.

Martin Luther

Martin Luther (1483–1546) was an early supporter of state-sponsored, state-controlled education for all people.

LUTHER AND MELANCTHON   The Protestant Reformation had its formal beginning in 1517. In that year, Martin Luther (1483–1546) published his ninety-five theses, which stated his disagreements with the Roman Catholic Church. One of these disagreements held great implications for the importance of formal education. The church believed that it was not desirable for each person to read and interpret the Bible for himself or herself; rather, the church would pass on the "correct" interpretation to the laity. Luther felt not only that the church had itself misinterpreted the Bible, but also that people were intended to read and interpret the Bible for themselves. If one accepted the church's position on this matter, formal education remained relatively unimportant for the masses. If one accepted Luther's position, however, education became necessary for all people so that they might individually read and interpret the Bible for themselves. In a sense, education became important as a way of obtaining salvation.

It is understandable that Luther and his coworker in education, Philipp Melanchthon (1497–1560), soon came to stress universal elementary education. Melanchthon's most important educational writing was *Visitation Articles* (1528), in which he set forth his recommendations for schools. Luther and Melanchthon felt that education should be provided for all, regardless of class, and should be compulsory for both sexes. They also believed that it should be state controlled, state supported, and centered on classical languages, grammar, mathematics, science, history, music, and physical education. Luther's argument for increased governmental support for education has a familiar contemporary ring:

> Each city is subjected to great expense every year for the construction of roads, for fortifying its ramparts, and for buying arms and equipping soldiers. Why should it not spend an equal sum for the support of one or two schoolmasters? The prosperity of a city does not depend solely on its natural riches, on the solidity of its walls, on the elegance of its mansions, and on the abundance of arms in its arsenals; but the safety and strength of a city reside above all in a good education, which furnishes it with instructed, reasonable, honorable, and well-trained citizens.[6]

Is "Abstinence-Only" the Best Sex Education Policy for Schools to Implement?

Early school curricula were historically driven by a desire to help children read the Bible and develop strict moral standards. The debate about how to best help students develop socially acceptable sexual behavior carries on today, as shown in this debate.

YES

Elizabeth Bradley teaches math at Lewiston High School in Lewiston, Maine, and won a Presidential Award in 2000 for her work. She has taught for 15 years, interrupted by eight years as a business applications programmer.

NO

Eileen Toledo has taught English in middle shcools for 14 years, currently at the Pablo Avila Junior High School in Camuy, Puerto Rico. She runs the "Baby, Think It Over" program one period a week and wrote a master's thesis on it.

Consider this:

"Good morning, class. Today we're going to talk about how to drive a car safely, even if you've been drinking. Now, it's really better not to drink and drive, because you might end up dead, but there are some ways to do it so that you cut your risk of becoming injured or dying."

The fact is that the true message sent by adults, the media, and the schools is the exact opposite: "Don't drink and drive." And we don't offer training in how to do it safely.

Now, let's change the scene just a little.

"Good morning, class. Today we're going to learn how to have safe sex (now referred to as "safer sex" because safe sex doesn't really exist).

"We'll show you how to put a condom on a banana, and some other things you can do to minimize your risk of contracting an incurable disease, which may make you sterile (chlamydia), be a precursor to cervical cancer (HPV), or cause death (HIV).

"Oh, and you might end up pregnant. Then your choices are abortion ("one dead, one wounded," to quote a recent bumper sticker), adoption (a lifelong hole in your heart), or parenthood (a 24/7 commitment that will make school, college, work, independence, and emotional stability very difficult)."

Why can't we take the drinking and driving approach of "Just don't do it"? Statistics show that kids do care about what the adults in their lives have to say.

To me, teen promiscuity is in the same category as Russian roulette, and promoting safe sex is just handing them the gun.

If you knew that within the next 12 months your child would have a child, an incurable disease, or be HIV positive, how far would you be willing to go today to prevent that? We are talking about 4

The reality is that more students are becoming sexually active at earlier ages. As an educator, I had to get involved. I have been using "Baby, Think It Over" at my junior high school for five years. Pregnancy dropped from 15 the first year, to three last semester, and zero this year! This program has a "baby" simulator. Students, male and female, are given "baby" to take home for five days. They experience the endless cries, waking at night, feeding, changing diapers.

Meanwhile, at school, we talk about child abuse, how to place babies to sleep correctly, and more. Students budget the weekly costs of caring for a baby. They inquire about jobs available to them at their age (13–16). Students realize how hard raising a baby can be for them.

One girl who loved baby-sitting became so frustrated after two days that "baby" was thrown in a clothes hamper and covered to drown out the cries. Her parents explained the consequences had this been a real baby. The student learned that this is not the time for her to become a parent.

We also discuss STDs, and we talk about how making love is different from sex, which is what teens are having. Making love is a beautiful experience in a true relationship between adults ready and able to take on responsibilities, not teens who got pregnant by mistake. We do role-plays: You're with your boyfriend, lose control, go all the way and don't even think about birth control, and a while later the girl is pregnant and all dreams are now put on hold. Or, things get hot but you stop and say, "Wait a second, I'm not ready for this."

Yet I cannot be so naive as not to see that most teens become sexually active at an early age. So I must also talk about birth control. But schools that accept federal "abstinence-only" funds are not allowed to

(continued)

The textbooks written by Comenius (1592–1670) were among the first to contain illustrations.

My whole method aims at changing the school drudgery into play and enjoyment.

Comenius

IGNATIUS OF LOYOLA   To combat the Reformation movement, Ignatius of Loyola (1491–1556) organized the Society of Jesus (Jesuits) in 1540. The Jesuits worked to establish schools in which to further the cause of the Roman Catholic Church, and they tried to stem the flow of converts to the Reformation cause. Although the Jesuits' main interest was religious, they soon grew into a great teaching order and were very successful in training their own teachers. The rules by which the Jesuits conducted their schools were stated in the *Ratio Studiorum;* a revised edition still guides Jesuit schools today. The improvement of teacher training was one of the Jesuits' main contributions to education.

Another Catholic teaching order, the Brothers of the Christian Schools, was organized in 1684 by Jean Baptiste de la Salle (1651–1719). Unlike the Jesuits, who were primarily interested in secondary education, de la Salle and his order were interested in elementary schools and in preparing elementary school teachers. De la Salle was one of the first educators to include student teaching in the preparation of teachers.

COMENIUS   Among many other outstanding educators during the transition period was Johann Amos Comenius (1592–1670). Comenius is perhaps best remembered for his many textbooks, including *Orbis Pictus,* which were among the first to contain illustrations. The invention and improvement of printing during the 1400s made it possible to produce books, such as those of Comenius, more rapidly and economically, a development that was essential to the growth of education. Much of the writing of Comenius reflected the increasing interest that was then developing in science.

LOCKE   John Locke (1632–1704) was an influential English educator during the late seventeenth century. He wrote many important educational works, including *Some Thoughts on Education* and *Essay Concerning Human Understanding.* He viewed a young child's mind as a blank slate *(tabula rasa)* on which an education could be imprinted. He believed that teachers needed to create a nonthreatening learning environment—a revolutionary idea at that time.

■ MODERN PERIOD (1700–PRESENT)

As we have suggested, educational progress in the world was slow and developed in only a few places through the seventeenth century. This section will show why many of our current educational ideas can be traced to the early 1700s.

THE AGE OF REASON

The first movement of the early modern period that influenced education was a revolt of the intellectuals against the superstition and ignorance that dominated people's lives at the time. This movement became the keynote of the period known as the **Age of Reason**; and François-Marie Arouet (1694–1778), a Frenchman who wrote under the name Voltaire, was one of its leaders. Those who joined this movement became known as *rationalists* because of the faith they placed in human rational power. The implication for education in the rationalist movement is obvious: If one places greater emphasis on human ability to reason, then education takes on new importance as the way by which humans develop this power.

DESCARTES AND VOLTAIRE   The work of René Descartes (1596–1650) laid the foundations for rationalism. This philosophy evolved three axioms that gradually became well accepted by thinking people. These axioms were (1) that reason was supreme, (2) that the laws of nature were invariable, and (3) that truth could be verified empirically—verified by exact methods of testing. These ideas became the basis for disputing some of the traditional teaching of the church and for resisting the bonds that royalty had traditionally placed on the common people. These axioms also influenced the thinking of Voltaire. Voltaire was an articulate writer who was also brilliant, clever, witty, and vain—qualities that helped him become extremely influential. In fact, many authorities give him considerable credit for both the American and French Revolutions, which took place during his lifetime.

Although Voltaire was not technically an educator, his writings helped bring about a renewed interest in learning and a conviction that knowledge, and therefore education, was extremely powerful in shaping the lives of people. His views contributed to the development of educational philosophies such as rationalism and empiricism, which helped elevate the importance of education in the Western world.

FREDERICK THE GREAT   One of the influential leaders during the Age of Reason was Frederick the Great (1712–1786). Frederick was a friend of Voltaire and supported the notion that education was of value. He was a liberal thinker for his time and one of the few leaders who did not attempt to force the common people into a particular form of religion. Frederick also permitted an unusual amount of freedom of speech for his era and generally allowed the common people a degree of liberty that most rulers considered dangerous.

As a consequence, education had an opportunity to develop, if not flourish, during his reign, as leader of Prussia. During Frederick's reign, Prussia passed laws regarding education and required teachers to obtain special training as well as licenses to teach.

The progress of education during Frederick's reign was meager in comparison to what we know today; nevertheless, given his time, Frederick must be given considerable credit for contributing to the development of schools during the Age of Reason. Concerning education for all children, Frederick stated, "In the open country it is sufficient if they learn to read and write a little; if they know too much they will go to towns and become secretaries and such like." Though it is true that Frederick did not place much value on education for young children beyond learning to read and write, it is interesting to note that he was particularly interested in better training for teachers.

Age of Reason

The beginning of the modern period of educational thought: a period in which European thinkers emphasized the importance of reason. The writing of Voltaire strongly influenced the rationalist movement.

THE EMERGENCE OF COMMON MAN

The second pivotal trend of the early modern period that affected education was the influential concept sometimes called the **Emergence of Common Man.** Whereas the Age of Reason was sparked by a revolt of the learned for intellectual freedom, the thinkers who promoted the emergence of common man argued that common people deserved a better life—politically, economically, socially, and educationally.

Philosopher Jean-Jacques Rousseau (1712–1778) felt that education should seek to return humans to their natural state.

ROUSSEAU One of the leaders in this movement was Jean-Jacques Rousseau (1712–1778), whose *Social Contract* (1762) became an influential book in the French Revolution. Scholars have suggested that *Social Contract* was also the basal doctrine of the American Declaration of Independence.[7] Rousseau was a philosopher, not an educator, but he wrote a good deal on the subject of education. His most important educational work was *Émile* (1762), in which he states his views concerning the ideal education for youth. Rousseau felt that the aim of education should be to return human beings to their "natural state." His view on the subject is well summed up by the opening sentence of *Émile:* "Everything is good as it comes from the hand of the author of nature: but everything degenerates in the hands of man." Rousseau's educational views came to be known as *naturalism.* Concerning the best method of teaching, Rousseau wrote,

> Do not treat the child to discourses which he cannot understand. No descriptions, no eloquence, no figures of speech. Be content to present to him appropriate objects. Let us transform our sensations into ideas. But let us not jump at once from sensible objects to intellectual objects. Let us always proceed slowly from one sensible notion to another. In general, let us never substitute the sign for the thing, except when it is impossible for us to show the thing. . . . I have no love whatever for explanations and talk. Things! Things! I shall never tire of saying that we ascribe too much importance to words. With our babbling education we make only babblers.[8]

Rousseau's most important contributions to education were his belief that education must be a natural process, not an artificial one, and his compassionate, positive view of the child. Rousseau believed that children were inherently good—a belief in opposition to the prevailing religiously inspired belief that children were born full of sin. The contrasting implications for teaching methods suggested by these two views are self-evident, as is the educational desirability of Rousseau's view over that which prevailed at the time. Although Rousseau never taught a day of school in his life, he likely did more to improve education through his writing than any of his contemporaries.

Rousseau saw children through a different set of lenses than most educators of his day. As a result, his views of children were not quickly accepted. In fact, many of his counterparts belittled his notion that children were born good and became "degenerate" at the hands of society. Eventually, of course, nearly all educators came to believe that Rousseau's views of children were correct. This raises an interesting question for contemporary educators: To what degree should one stand by and defend one's educational convictions—even when others do not accept them?

PESTALOZZI Johann Heinrich Pestalozzi (1746–1827) was a Swiss educator who put Rousseau's theory into practice. Pestalozzi established two schools for boys, one at Burgdorf (1800–1804) and the other at Yverdun (1805–1825). Educators came from all over the world to view Pestalozzi's schools and to study his teaching methods. Pestalozzi enumerated his educational views in a book entitled *Leonard and Gertrude.* Unlike most educators of his time, Pestalozzi believed that a teacher should treat students with love and kindness:

> I was convinced that my heart would change the condition of my children just as promptly as the sun of spring would reanimate the earth benumbed by the win-

Emergence of Common Man

A period during which developed the idea that common people should receive at least a basic education as a means to a better life.

Herbartian teaching method

An organized teaching method based on the principles of Pestalozzi that stresses learning by association and consists of five steps: preparation, presentation, association, generalization, and application.

ter.... It was necessary that my children should observe, from dawn to evening, at every moment of the day, upon my brow and on my lips, that my affections were fixed on them, that their happiness was my happiness, and that their pleasures were my pleasures.... I was everything to my children. I was alone with them from morning till night.... Their hands were in my hands. Their eyes were fixed on my eyes.[9]

Key concepts in the Pestalozzian method included the expression of love, understanding, and patience for children; compassion for the poor; and the use of objects and sense perception as the basis for acquiring knowledge.

Swiss educator Johann Heinrich Pestalozzi (1746–1827) put Rousseau's theory into practice.

HERBART   One of the educators who studied under Pestalozzi and was influenced by him was Johann Friedrich Herbart (1776–1841). Whereas Pestalozzi had successfully put into practice and further developed Rousseau's educational ideas, it remained for Herbart to organize these educational views into a formal psychology of education. Herbart stressed apperception (learning by association). The **Herbartian teaching method** developed into five formal steps:

1. *Preparation:* Preparing the student to receive a new idea
2. *Presentation:* Presenting the student with the new idea
3. *Association:* Assimilating the new idea with the old ideas
4. *Generalization:* Generalizing the new idea derived from the combination of the old and new ideas
5. *Application:* Applying the new knowledge

Herbart's educational ideas are contained in his *Science of Education* (1806) and *Outlines of Educational Doctrine* (1835).

Johann Friedrich Herbart (1776–1814) was a German philosopher, educator, and author who expanded the work of Pestalozzi.

FROEBEL   Friedrich Froebel (1782–1852) was another European educator who was influenced by Rousseau and Pestalozzi and who made a significant contribution to education. Froebel's contributions included the establishment of the first kindergarten (or *Kleinkinderbeschaftigungsanstalt*), an emphasis on social development, a concern for the cultivation of creativity, and the concept of learning by doing. He originated the idea that women are best suited to teach young children. Froebel wrote his main educational book, *Education of Man,* in 1826.

Two other developments in the late 1800s were also important European antecedents of American education: the maturing of the scientific movement, hastened by the publication of Charles Darwin's *On the Origin of Species* (1859), and the formulation of educational psychology near the end of the century.

The student of educational history must realize that even though many educational advances had been made by 1900, the average European received a pathetically small amount of formal education, even at that late date. Historically, education had been available only to the few who were fortunate enough to be born into the leisure class; the masses of people in the working class had received little or no education up to that time. What little formal education the working person might have received was usually provided for religious purposes by the church.

Friedrich Froebel (1782–1852) was a German educator and author who founded the kindergarten.

THE IMPORTANT ROLE OF EDUCATION IN OUR DEVELOPING NATION

The earliest settlers to America from Europe brought with them a sincere interest in providing at least rudimentary education for their children. Naturally, they brought their European ideas about education with them and, soon after arrival, created educational programs throughout colonial America. This section will briefly examine these early colonial school programs.

■ COLONIAL EDUCATION

The early settlements on the East Coast were composed of groups of colonies: the Southern Colonies, centered in Virginia; the Middle Colonies, centered in New York; and the Northern Colonies, centered in New England. Each of these colonies evolved a somewhat unique educational system.

SOUTHERN COLONIES

The Southern Colonies soon came to be made up of large tobacco plantations. Because of the size of the plantations, people lived far apart, and few towns grew up until later in the colonial period. There was an immediate need for cheap labor to work on the plantations; and so in 1619, only twelve years after Jamestown was settled, the colony imported the first boatload of slaves from Africa. Other sources of cheap labor for the Southern Colonies included white Europeans from a variety of backgrounds, people who purchased passage to the New World by agreeing to serve a lengthy period of indentured servitude on arrival in the colonies. There soon came to be two very distinct classes of people in the South—a few wealthy landowners and a large mass of laborers, most of whom were slaves.

The educational provisions that evolved from this set of conditions were precisely what one would expect. No one was interested in providing education for the slaves, with the exception of a few missionary groups such as the English Society for the Propagation of the Gospel in Foreign Parts. Such missionary groups tried to provide some education for slaves, primarily so that they could read the Bible. The wealthy landowners usually hired tutors to teach their children at home. Distances between homes and slow transportation precluded the establishment of centralized schools. When the upper-class children grew old enough to attend college, they were usually sent to well-established universities in Europe.

MIDDLE COLONIES

The people who settled the Middle Colonies came from various national (Dutch, Swedish) and religious (Puritan, Mennonite, Catholic) backgrounds. This is why the Middle Colonies have often been called the melting pot of the nation. This diversity of backgrounds made it impossible for the inhabitants of the Middle Colonies to agree on a common public school system. Consequently, the respective groups established their own religious schools. Many children received their education through an apprenticeship while learning a trade from a master already in that line of work. Some people even learned the art of teaching school through apprenticeships with experienced teachers.

NORTHERN COLONIES

The Northern Colonies were settled mainly by the Puritans, a religious group from Europe. In 1630 approximately one thousand Puritans settled near Boston. Unlike people in the Southern Colonies, people in New England lived close to one another. Towns sprang up and soon became centers of political and social life. Shipping ports were established, and an industrial economy developed that demanded numerous skilled and semiskilled workers—a condition that eventually created a large middle class.

EARLY SCHOOL LAWS

These conditions of common religious views, town life, and a large middle class made it possible for the people to agree on common public schools and led to very early educational activity in the Northern Colonies. In 1642 the General Court of Massachusetts enacted a law that stated:

> This Co^t [Court], taking into consideration the great neglect of many parents & masters in training up their children in learning . . . do hereupon order and decree, that in every towne y chosen men . . . take account from time to time of all parents and masters, and of their children, concerning their . . . ability to read & understand the principles of religion & the capitall lawes of this country.

This law did nothing more than encourage citizens to look after the education of children. Five years later (1647), however, another law was enacted in Massachusetts that required towns to provide education for the youth. This law, which was often referred to as the **Old Deluder Satan Act** because of its religious motive, stated:

> It being one chiefe proiect of y ould deluder, Satan, to keepe men from the knowledge of y Scriptures. . . . It is therefore orded [ordered], ye evy [every] towneship in this jurisdiction, aft y Lord hath increased y number to 50 household, shall then forthw appoint one w [with] in their towne to teach all such children as shall resort to him to write & reade . . . & it is furth ordered y where any towne shall increase to y numb [number] of 100 families or houshould, they shall set up a grammar schoole, y m [aim] thereof being able to instruct youth so farr as they shall be fited for y university [Harvard].

These Massachusetts school laws of 1642 and 1647 served as models for similar laws that were soon created in other colonies.

TYPES OF COLONIAL SCHOOLS

Several different kinds of elementary schools sprang up in the colonies, such as the **dame school,** which was conducted by a housewife in her home; the writing school, which taught the child to write; a variety of church schools; and charity, or pauper, schools taught by missionary groups.

To go back a few years, in 1635 the Latin Grammar School was established in Boston—the first permanent school of this type in what is now the United States. This school was established when the people of Boston, which had been settled only five years before, voted "that our brother Philemon Pormont, shal be intreated to become scholemaster, for the teaching and nourtering of children with us." The grammar school was a secondary school, its function was college preparatory, and the idea spread quickly to other towns. Charlestown opened its first grammar school one year later, in 1636, by contracting William Witherell "to keep a school for a twelve month." Within sixteen years after the Massachusetts Bay Colony had been founded, seven or eight towns had Latin grammar schools in operation. Transplanted from Europe, where similar schools had existed for a long time, these schools were aimed at preparing boys for college and "for the service of God, in church and commonwealth."

HARVARD

Harvard, the first colonial college, was established in 1636 for preparing ministers. Other early American colleges included William and Mary (1693), Yale (1701), Princeton (1746), King's College (1754), College of Philadelphia (1755), Brown (1764), Dartmouth (1769), and Queen's College (1770). The curriculum in these early colleges was traditional, with heavy emphasis on theology and

Old Deluder Satan Act

An early colonial educational law (1647) that required colonial towns of at least fifty households to provide education for youth.

dame school

A low-level primary school in the colonial and other early periods, usually conducted by an untrained woman in her own home.

the classics. An example of the extent to which the religious motive dominated colonial colleges can be found in one of the 1642 rules governing Harvard College, which stated: "Let every Student be plainly instructed, and earnestly pressed to consider well, the maine end of his life and studies is, to know God and Jesus Christ."

■ THE STRUGGLE FOR UNIVERSAL ELEMENTARY EDUCATION

When the colonists arrived in this country, they simply established schools like those they had known in Europe. The objectives of colonial elementary schools were primarily religious. These early colonial schools were meager by today's standards, but nevertheless, they were important forerunners to our contemporary schools.

CHRISTOPHER DOCK

A good idea of what a colonial elementary school was like, and the extent to which religion dominated its curriculum, can be gleaned from the following account of a school conducted in 1750 by Christopher Dock, a Mennonite school teacher in Pennsylvania:

> The children arrive as they do because some have a great distance to school, others a short distance, so that the children cannot assemble as punctually as they can in a city. Therefore, when a few children are present, those who can read their Testament sit together on one bench; but the boys and girls occupy separate benches. They are given a chapter which they read at sight consecutively. Meanwhile I write copies for them. Those who have read their passage of Scripture without error take their places at the table and write. Those who fail have to sit at the end of the bench, and each new arrival the same; as each one is thus released in order he takes up his slate. This process continues until they have all assembled. The last one left on the bench is a "lazy pupil."
>
> When all are together, and examined, whether they are washed and combed, they sing a psalm or morning hymn, and I sing and pray with them. As much as they can understand of the Lord's Prayer and the Ten Commandments (according to the gift God has given them), I exhort and admonish them accordingly.[10]

MONITORIAL SCHOOLS

In 1805, New York City established the first *monitorial school* in the United States. The monitorial school, which originated in England, represented an attempt to provide economical mass elementary education for large numbers of children. Typically, the teacher would teach hundreds of pupils, using the better students as helpers. By 1840, however, nearly all monitorial schools had been closed; the children had not learned enough to justify continuance of this type of school.

HORACE MANN

Between 1820 and 1860, an educational awakening took place in the United States. This movement was strongly influenced by Horace Mann (1796–1859). As secretary of the state board of education, Mann helped to establish **common elementary schools** in Massachusetts. These common schools were designed to provide a basic elementary education for all children. Among Mann's many impressive educational achievements was the publication of one of the very early professional journals in this country, *The Common School Journal*. Through this journal, Mann kept educational issues before the public.

In 1852, Massachusetts passed a compulsory elementary school attendance law, the first of its kind in the country, requiring all children to attend school. By 1900, thirty-two other states had passed similar **compulsory education** laws.

Financing public education has always been a challenge in America. As early as 1795, Connecticut legislators decided to sell public land and create a

---

Beyond the power of diffusing old wealth, education has the prerogative of creating new. It is a thousand times more lucrative than fraud; and adds a thousand fold more to a nation's resources than the most successful conquest.

Horace Mann

common elementary school

Schools designed to provide a basic elementary education for all children, originated in the mid-nineteenth century.

compulsory education

School attendance that is required by law on the theory that it is to the benefit of the state or commonwealth to educate all the people.

permanent school fund to help finance public schools. As more and more children attended school, other states soon took action to establish school funding plans as well.

HENRY BARNARD

The first U.S. commissioner of education was a prominent educator named Henry Barnard (1811–1900). He was a longtime supporter of providing common elementary schools for all children and wrote enthusiastically about the value of education in the *Connecticut Common School Journal* and in the *American Journal of Education,* which he founded. He had also served as the Rhode Island commissioner of public schools and as the chancellor of the University of Wisconsin before holding the prestigious position of commissioner of education for the entire United States. Barnard also strongly supported kindergarten programs for very young children as well as high school programs for older students.

REFLECTION ON U.S. ELEMENTARY EDUCATION

If we look back at the historical development of U.S. elementary education, we can make the following generalizations:

1. Until the late 1800s, the motive, curriculum, and administration of elementary education were primarily religious. The point at which elementary education began to be more secular than religious was the point at which states began to pass compulsory school attendance laws.
2. Discipline was traditionally harsh in elementary schools. The classical picture of a colonial schoolmaster equipped with a frown, dunce cap, stick, whip, and a variety of abusive phrases is more accurate than one might expect. It is no wonder that children historically viewed school as an unpleasant place. Pestalozzi had much to do with bringing about a gradual change in discipline when he advocated that love, not severe punishment, should be used to motivate students.
3. Elementary education was traditionally formal and impersonal. The ideas of Rousseau, Pestalozzi, Herbart, and Froebel helped change this condition gradually and make elementary education more student centered; this was becoming apparent about 1900.
4. Elementary schools were traditionally taught by poorly prepared teachers.
5. Although the aims and methodology varied considerably from time to time, the basic content of elementary education was historically reading, writing, and arithmetic.

Horace Mann (1796–1859) helped to establish common schools designed to provide a basic elementary education for all children in Massachusetts.

The right beginning of this work of school improvement is in awakening, correcting, and elevating public sentiment in relation to it.

Henry Barnard

GLOBAL PERSPECTIVES

Educational Transplantation from Europe

The ideas of Pestalozzi and Herbart considerably affected elementary education when they were introduced into the United States in the late 1800s. Pestalozzianism emphasized teaching children with love, patience, and understanding. Furthermore, children should learn from objects and firsthand experiences, not from abstractions and words. Pestalozzian concepts soon spread throughout the country. Herbartianism was imported into the United States at the Bloomington Normal School in Illinois by students who had learned about the ideas of Herbart while studying in Germany. Herbartianism represented an attempt to make a science out of teaching. The more formal system that Herbartianism brought to the often disorganized elementary teacher was badly needed at the time. Unfortunately, Herbartianism eventually contributed to an extreme formalism and rigidity that characterized many U.S. elementary schools in the early 1900s. One school administrator of that time bragged that at a given moment in the school day he knew exactly what was going on in all the classrooms. One can infer from this boast that teachers and students often had a strict, rigid educational program imposed on them.

■ THE NEED FOR SECONDARY SCHOOLS

Contemporary U.S. high schools have a long and proud tradition. They have evolved from a series of earlier forms of secondary schools that were created to serve the needs of society at various points in the nation's history.

LATIN GRAMMAR SCHOOL

The first form of secondary school in the American colonies was the *Latin grammar school* mentioned previously, first established in Boston in 1635, only five years after colonists settled in the area. The Latin grammar school focused largely on teaching Latin and other classical subjects, such as Greek, and was strictly college preparatory.

Harvard was the only university in the colonies at that time. The entrance requirements to Harvard showed the emphasis placed on classical subjects:

> When any Scholar is able to understand Tully, or such like classicall Latine Author extempore, and make and speake true Latine in Verse and Prose, suo ut aiunt marte; and decline perfectly the Paradigms of Nounes and Verbes in the Greek tongue; let him then, and not before, be capable of admission into the college.

European colleges and later colonial colleges also demanded that students know Latin and Greek before they could be admitted. For instance, in the mid-eighteenth century the requirements for admission to Yale stated:

> None may expect to be admitted into this College unless upon Examination of the President and Tutors, they shall be found able Extempore to Read, Construe, and Parce Tully, Vergil and the Greek Testament; and to write true Latin in Prose and to understand the Rules of Prosodia, and Common Arithmetic, and Shal bring Sufficient Testimony of his Blameless and inoffensive Life.

Because Latin grammar schools were designed to prepare students for college, it is little wonder that the curriculum in these schools was so classical and traditional. Needless to say, a very small percentage of boys attended Latin grammar school because very few could hope to attend college. Girls did not attend because colleges at that time did not admit them. As late as 1785, there were only two Latin grammar schools in Boston, and the combined enrollment in these two schools was only sixty-four young men.

AMERICAN ACADEMY

By the middle of the eighteenth century, there was a need for more and better-trained skilled workers. Benjamin Franklin (1706–1790), recognizing this need, proposed a new kind of secondary school in Pennsylvania. This proposal brought about the establishment, in Philadelphia in 1751, of the first truly American educational institution: the *American Academy*. Franklin established this school because he thought the existing Latin grammar schools were not providing the practical secondary education that youth needed. The philosophy, curriculum, and methodology of Franklin's academy were all geared to prepare young people for employment. Eventually, similar academies were established throughout America, and these institutions eventually replaced the Latin grammar school as the predominant secondary education institution. They were usually private schools, and many of them admitted girls as well as boys. Later on, some academies even tried to train elementary school teachers.

The excellent become the permanent.

Jane Addams

HIGH SCHOOL

In 1821 an *English Classical School* (which three years later changed its name to *English High School*) opened in Boston, and another distinctively American educational institution was launched. This first high school, under the direction of George B. Emerson, consisted of a three-year course in English, mathematics, science, and history. The school later added to its curriculum the philosophy of history, chemistry, intellectual philosophy, linear drawing, logic, trigonometry, French, and the U.S. Constitution. The school enrolled about one hundred boys during its first year.

The high school was established because of a belief that the existing grammar schools were inadequate for the day and because most people could not afford to send their children to the private academies. The high school soon replaced both the Latin grammar school and the private academy, and it has been with us ever since.

JUNIOR HIGH/MIDDLE SCHOOL

About 1910 the first *junior high schools* were established in the United States. A survey in 1916 showed 54 junior high schools in thirty-six states. One year later a survey indicated that the number had increased to about 270. More recently, some school systems have abandoned the junior high school in favor of what is called the *middle school,* which usually consists of grades 6, 7, and 8.

◾ FEDERAL INVOLVEMENT IN EDUCATION

The federal government of the United States has had a long and extensive involvement in educational affairs. In fact, it has historically supported education at all levels in a variety of ways and continues to do so today. This section will look briefly at some of the early federal efforts to help provide education for U.S. citizens.

U.S. CONSTITUTION

The U.S. Constitution does not mention education. Therefore, by virtue of the Tenth Amendment—which states, "The powers not delegated to the United States by the Constitution, nor prohibited by it to the states, are reserved to the states respectively, or to the people"—education is a function of each state. There is some question whether the makers of the Constitution thoughtfully intended to leave education up to each state or whether they merely forgot to mention it. Some historians believe that the founders wisely realized that local control of education would build better schools and a better nation. Other historians believe that the framers of the Constitution were so preoccupied with what they believed were more important issues that they never thought to make national provision for education.

NORTHWEST ORDINANCE

Even though the Constitution does not refer to education, the federal government has been active in educational affairs from the very beginning. In 1785 and 1787, the Continental Congress passed the Northwest Ordinance Acts. These acts provided for disposing of the Northwest Territory and encouraged the establishment of schools in the territory by stating, "Religion, morality and knowledge being necessary to good government and the happiness of mankind, schools and the means of education shall forever be encouraged." As the various states formed in the Northwest Territory, they were required to set aside the sixteenth section of each township to be used for educational purposes.

MORRILL LAND GRANT

In 1862, when it became apparent that existing colleges were not providing the vocational education needed, the federal government passed the Morrill Land

Comprehensive high school gave millions a shot at careers.

Mortimer B. Zuckerman

CROSS-REFERENCE
Information about current school organization is presented in Chapter 5.

The Past is Prologue.

Engraved on the National Archives in Washington, D.C.

Grant Act to provide for schools that served this purpose. The Hatch Act of 1887 established agricultural experimental stations across the country, and the Smith-Lever Agricultural Extension Act of 1914 carried the services of land grant colleges to the people through extension services. These early federal acts did much to improve agriculture and industry at a time when the rapidly developing nation badly needed such improvement.

SMITH-HUGHES ACT

CROSS-REFERENCE
The more recent role of the federal government in educational affairs is discussed in Chapters 5 and 6.

In 1917 the federal government passed the first act providing financial aid to public schools below the college level, the Smith-Hughes Act. This act provided for high school vocational programs in agriculture, trades and industry, and homemaking. High schools were academically oriented then, and the Smith-Hughes Act stimulated the development of badly needed vocational programs.

The 1930s were Depression days, and the government was trying to solve national economic difficulties. Legislation was enacted during these years to encourage economic development, and this legislation indirectly provided financial aid to education. Five relief agencies related to education during this time included the Civilian Conservation Corps, National Youth Administration, Federal Emergency Relief Administration, Public Works Administration, and Federal Surplus Commodities Corporation.[11]

RELEVANT RESEARCH
Critiquing Historical Sources

STUDY PURPOSE/QUESTIONS: As you prepare for your teaching career, you should have an opportunity to read and think about original historical research sources. Such historical materials constitute the "relevant research" sources for those who strive to understand and learn from the past—something all educators should do.

STUDY DESIGN: The following letter, written in 1712 by Nathaniel Williams, briefly describes the curriculum of the first Latin grammar school established in the colonies—the Boston Latin Grammar School, which was created in 1635, soon after the first colonists settled in the area.

STUDY FINDINGS:

Curriculum of the Boston Latin Grammar School (1712)
The three first years are spent first in Learning by heart & then acc: to their capacities understanding the Accidence and Nomenclator, in construing & parsing acc: to the English rules of Syntax Sententiae Pueriles Cato & Cordcrius & Aesops Fables.

The fourth year, or sooner if their capacities allow it, they are entered upon Erasmus to which they are allou'd no English . . . & upon translating English into Latin out of m^r Garreston's Exercises.

The fifth year they are entred upon Tullies Epistles . . . the Elegancies of which are remarked and improv'd in the afternoon of the day they learn it, by translating an English which contains the phrase somthing altered, and besides recited by heart on the repetition day. . . .

The sixth year they are entred upon Tullies Offices & Luc: Flor: for the forenoon, continuing the use of Ovid's Metam: in the afternoon, & at the end of the Year they read Virgil. . . . Every week these make a Latin Epistle, the last quarter of the Year, when also they begin to learn Greek, & Rhetorick.

The seventh Year they read Tullie's Orations & Justin for the Latin & Greek Testam^t Isocrates Orat: Homer & Hesiod for the Greek in the forenoons & Virgil Horace Juvenal & Persius afternoons . . . Every fortnight they compose a theme. . . .

IMPLICATIONS: Each reader must deliberate and decide the implications of this small bit of original historical documentation of the Boston Latin Grammar School curriculum. What was the apparent function of the Boston Latin Grammar School? For whom was this curriculum apparently intended, and for what purpose? In what ways was this curriculum similar to that of secondary schools throughout the world today? In what ways was it different? What, if anything, can contemporary educators learn from the Boston Latin Grammar School?

Source: "Letter from Nathaniel Williams to Nehemia Hobart," in Robert F. Seybold, *The Public Schools of Colonial Boston.* Cambridge, MA: Harvard University Press, 1935, pp. 69–71.

■ THE EVOLUTION OF TEACHING MATERIALS

As we have said, the first schools in colonial America were poorly equipped. In fact, the first elementary schools were usually conducted by housewives right in their homes. The only teaching materials likely to be found then were a Bible and perhaps one or two other religious books, a small amount of scarce paper, a few quill pens, and perhaps hornbooks.

THE HORNBOOK

The **hornbook** was the most common teaching device in early colonial schools (see Figure 7.1). Hornbooks differed widely but typically consisted of a sheet of paper showing the alphabet, covered with a thin transparent sheet of cow's horn and tacked to a paddle-shaped piece of wood. A leather thong was often looped through a hole in the paddle so that students could hang the hornbooks around their necks. Hornbooks provided students with their first reading instructions. Records indicate that hornbooks were used in Europe in the Middle Ages and were common there until the mid-1700s.

As paper became more available, the hornbook evolved into a several-page "book" called a *battledore.* The battledore, printed on heavy paper, often resembled an envelope. Like the hornbook, it typically contained the alphabet and various religious prayers and/or admonitions.

THE NEW ENGLAND PRIMER

The first real textbook to be used in colonial elementary schools was the *New England Primer.* Records show that the first copies of this book were printed in England in the 1600s. Copies of the *New England Primer* were also printed as early as 1690 in the American colonies. An advertisement for the book appeared in the *News from the Stars Almanac,* published in 1690 in Boston (see Figure 7.2). The oldest extant copy of the *New England Primer* is a 1727 edition, now in the Lenox Collection of the New York Public Library.

The *New England Primer* was a small book, usually about 2 by 4 inches, with thin wooden covers covered by paper or leather. It contained fifty to one hundred pages, depending on how many extra sections were added to each edition. The first pages displayed

FIGURE 7.1 Hornbook

The hornbook was the most common teaching device in colonial American schools.

ADVERTISEMENT.
There is now in the Press, and will suddenly be extant, a Second Impression of *The New-Eng-land Primer enlarged,* to which is added, more *Directions for Spelling*: the *Prayer of* K. *Edward the* 6th. and *Verses* made by Mr. Rogers the Martyr, left as a Legacy to his Children.
Sold by *Benjamin Harris,* at the *London Coffee-House* in *Boston.*

FIGURE 7.2 1690 Advertisement

This 1690 advertisement promotes the *New England Primer,* the first true textbook to be used in colonial American elementary schools.

hornbook

A single written page containing the alphabet, syllables, a prayer, and other simple words, tacked to a wooden paddle and covered with a thin transparent layer of cow's horn; used in colonial times as a beginner's first book or preprimer.

FIGURE 7.3   Page from the *New England Primer*

How does this page from the *New England Primer* reveal the religious motive in colonial American education?

the alphabet, vowels, and capital letters. Next came lists of words arranged from two to six syllables, followed by verses and tiny wood-cut pictures for each letter in the alphabet. Figure 7.3 shows a sampling of these pictures and verses. The contents of the *New England Primer* reflect the heavily religious motive in colonial education.

BLUE-BACKED SPELLER

The primer was virtually the only reading book used in colonial schools until about 1800, when Noah Webster published *The American Spelling Book.* This book eventually became known as the *Blue-Backed Speller* because of its blue cover. It eventually replaced the *New England Primer* as the most common elementary textbook. In fact, Noah Webster's *American Spelling Book* is the third biggest selling book the world has ever known, having sold about 100 million copies, compared to *Quotations from the Works of Mao Tse-tung,* which has sold about 800 million copies, and the Bible, which has sold an estimated 2 billion copies. Figure 7.4 shows a page from a *Blue-Backed Speller* printed about 1800. A later series of school books, *The McGuffey Readers,* authored by William Holmes McGuffey, sold about 60 million copies. The speller was approximately 4 by 6 inches; its cover was made of thin sheets of wood covered with light blue paper. The first part of the book contained rules and instructions for using the book; next came the alphabet, syllables, and consonants. The bulk of the book was taken up with lists of words arranged according to syllables and sounds. It also contained rules for reading and speaking, moral advice, and stories of various sorts.

Very few textbooks were available for use in colonial Latin grammar schools, academies, and colleges, although various religious books, including the Bible, were often used. A few books dealing with history, geography, arithmetic, Latin, Greek, and certain classics were available for use in colonial secondary schools and colleges during the eighteenth century. Harvard College had a large library for its day because John Harvard, its benefactor, had bequeathed his entire collection of four hundred volumes to the school.

TEACHING MATERIALS IN AN EARLY SCHOOL

By 1800, nearly two hundred years after the colonies had been established, school buildings and teaching materials were still very crude and meager. You can understand something of the physical features and equipment of an 1810 New England school by reading the following description written by a teacher of that school:

> The size of the building was 22 × 20 feet. From the floor to the ceiling it was 7 feet. The chimney and entry took up about four feet at one end, leaving the schoolroom itself 18 × 20 feet. Around three sides of the room were connected desks, arranged so that when the pupils were sitting at them their faces were toward the instructor and their backs toward the wall. Attached to the sides of the desks nearest to the instructor were benches for small pupils. The instructor's desk and chair occupied the center. On this desk were stationed a rod, or ferule; sometimes both. These, with books, writings, inkstands, rules, and plummets, with a fire shovel, and a pair of tongs (often broken), were the principal furniture. . . .
>
> The room was warmed by a large and deep fireplace. So large was it, and so efficacious in warming the room otherwise, that I have seen about one-eighth of a cord of good wood burning in it at a time. In severe weather it was estimated that the amount usually consumed was not far from a cord a week. . . .
>
> The school was not infrequently broken up for a day or two for want of wood. The instructor or pupils were sometimes compelled to cut or saw it to prevent the closing of the school. The wood was left in the road near the house, so that it often

was buried in the snow, or wet with rain. At the best, it was usually burnt green. The fires were to be kindled about half an hour before the time of beginning the school. Often, the scholar, whose lot it was, neglected to build it. In consequence of this, the house was frequently cold and uncomfortable about half of the forenoon, when, the fire being very large, the excess of heat became equally distressing. Frequently, too, we were annoyed by smoke. The greatest amount of suffering, however, arose from excessive heat, particularly at the close of the day. The pupils being in a free perspiration when they left were very liable to take cold. . . .

Instructors have usually boarded in the families of the pupils. Their compensation has varied from seven to eleven dollars a month for males; and from sixty-two and a half cents to one dollar a week for females. Within the past ten years, however, the price of instruction has rarely been less than nine dollars in the former case, and seventy-five cents in the latter. In the few instances in which instructors have furnished their own board the compensation has been about the same, it being assumed that they could work at some employment of their own enough to pay their board, especially the females.[12]

SLATES

About 1820 a new instructional device was introduced in American schools: the slate. These school slates were thin, flat pieces of slate stone framed with wood. The pencils used were also made of slate and produced a light but legible line that was easily erased with a rag. The wooden frames of some of the slates were covered with cloth so that noise would be minimized as students placed the slates on the desk. There were even double slates made of two single slates hinged together with cord or leather. Students wrote their assignments on the slates, just as today's students write on tablet paper. Later on, large pieces of slate made up the blackboards that were added to classrooms.

By about 1900, pencils and paper had largely replaced the slate and slate pencil as the writing implements of students. The invention of relatively economical mass production of pencils in the late 1800s made them affordable for student use and thereby had a considerable impact on schools.

McGUFFEY'S *READER*

In the same way that Noah Webster's *Blue-Backed Speller* replaced the *New England Primer,* McGuffey's *Reader* eventually replaced the *Blue-Backed Speller.* These readers were carefully geared to each grade and were meant to instill in children a respect for hard work, thrift, self-help, and honesty. McGuffey's *Readers* dominated the elementary school book market until approximately 1900, when it was gradually replaced by various newer and improved readers written by David Tower, James Fassett, William Elson, and others.

During the twentieth century, teachers have gradually adopted a variety of tools to assist them in educating young people. This variety has come about partly through the influence of Pestalozzi, John Dewey, and others, who demonstrated that children learn best by firsthand experiences. Likewise, school buildings have become larger, more elaborate, and better designed to encourage

FABLE I. *Of the Boy that stole Apples.*

AN old Man found a rude Boy upon one of his trees stealing Apples, and desired him to come down; but the young Sauce-box told him plainly he wou'd not. Won't you? said the old Man, then I will fetch you down; so he pulled up some tufts of Grass, and threw at him; but this only made the Youngster laugh, to think the old Man should pretend to beat him out of the tree with grass only.

Well, well, said the old Man, if neither words nor grass, will do, I must try what virtue there is in Stones; so the old Man pelted him heartily with stones; which soon made the young Chap, hasten down from the tree and beg the old Man's pardon.

MORAL.

If good words and gentle means will not reclaim the wicked, they must be dealt with in a more severe manner.

FIGURE 7.4 Page from the *Blue-Backed Speller*

Noah Webster's *Blue-Backed Speller* came to replace primers around 1800. In addition to the alphabet, syllables, consonants, lists of words, and rules for reading and speaking, the *Speller* contained stories like the one shown here.

learning. Today, many schools are equipped with an impressive array of books, laboratory equipment, movie projectors, filmstrip projectors, tape recorders, television devices, single-concept films, teaching machines, computers, programmed materials, and learning devices of all kinds. Some modern school buildings are not only excellent from an educational standpoint, but magnificent pieces of architecture as well. One cannot help but be awed by the contrast between U.S. education today and its humble beginning centuries ago. One wonders what schools will be like in the distant future.

■ MEAGER EDUCATION FOR DIVERSE POPULATIONS

It is sad but true that students of color, girls, and students with disabilities have been historically badly underserved by our educational system, and typically not even allowed to attend school until relatively recently.

EDUCATION OF AFRICAN AMERICANS

Unfortunately, general efforts have been made only recently in this country to provide an education for African Americans. In the following section, we will briefly explore why this was the case and discuss some of the early African American educators who struggled to correct this injustice.[13]

SLAVERY In 1619, only a dozen years after Jamestown was established, the first boatload of enslaved people arrived in the colonies. In that year, John Rolfe wrote in his *Journal* that the captain of a Dutch ship "sold us twenty Negroes." These enslaved people were imported as a source of cheap labor for the new colonies.

Early efforts to provide formal education for African American children were few. The African American Children's School, shown here, was one example.

The number of imported slaves steadily increased; between 1700 and 1750, thousands of Africans were brought to the American colonies each year. By the Revolutionary War, there were approximately 700,000 enslaved Africans in the colonies; by 1860 there were about 4.5 million.

EARLY CHURCH EFFORTS TO EDUCATE AFRICAN AMERICANS   Probably the first organized attempts to educate the African Americans in colonial America were by French and Spanish missionaries. These early missionary efforts set an example that influenced the education of both African Americans and their children. Educating slaves posed an interesting moral problem for the church. The English colonists had to find a way to overcome the idea that converting enslaved people to Christianity might logically lead to their freedom. The problem they faced was how to eliminate an unwritten law that a Christian should not be a slave. The church's governing bodies and the bishop of London settled the matter by decreeing that conversion to Christianity did not lead to formal emancipation.

The organized church nevertheless provided the setting in which a few African Americans were allowed to develop skills in reading, leadership, and educating their brethren. Often African Americans and whites attended church together. Eventually, some preachers who were former slaves demonstrated exceptional skill in "spreading the gospel." The Baptists in particular, by encouraging a form of self-government, allowed African Americans to become active in the church. This move fostered the growth of African American congregations; thus, Baptist congregations gave enslaved as well as free African Americans an opportunity for education and development that was not provided by many other denominations.

The efforts of the English to educate enslaved people were carried out largely by the society for the Propagation of the Gospel in Foreign Parts. This society was created by the Church of England in 1701. In 1705 the Reverend Samuel Thomas of Goose Creek Parish in South Carolina established a school fostered by the society, enrolling sixty African American students. Nine years later the society opened a school in New York City where two hundred African American pupils were enrolled. Despite vigorous opposition from many whites, who believed that educating enslaved people was a "dangerous business," the society went on to establish other schools for African Americans. The degree of success of these early efforts varied greatly. Initially, many people were not generally opposed to educating African Americans; however, education seemed to make enslaved people aware of their plight. In the South, many people attributed the growing unrest concerning slavery to the education of enslaved people. Insurrections, uprisings, and threats to overseers, masters, and their families produced fear among the whites. Consequently, some states even passed legislation that forbade any form of education for enslaved people.

BENJAMIN BANNEKER   Benjamin Banneker (1731–1806), a distinguished African American, was born in Baltimore County, Maryland, in 1731. Baltimore maintained a liberal policy toward educating African Americans, and Banneker learned to read, write, and do arithmetic at a relatively early age; he eventually became very well educated. One of his accomplishments was to manufacture the first clock made in the United States, in 1770. He then turned his attention specifically to astronomy. With the help of books borrowed from a supportive white inventor, Banneker soon was able to calculate eclipses of the sun and moon. His accuracy far excelled that of any other American, and his astronomical calculations received much acclaim after they were published. George Washington appointed him to help survey what became Washington, D.C. The outstanding works of this inventor aroused the curiosity of Thomas Jefferson, who in 1803 invited Banneker to his home, Monticello. The acknowledgment of an African American's achievement by a noted U.S. leader was yet another small milestone in the education of African Americans.

Frederick Douglass (1817?–1895) was an influential antislavery lecturer, writer, and consultant to President Lincoln.

FREDERICK DOUGLASS   Born in slavery in Maryland in 1817, Frederick Douglass (1817–1895) ran away and began talking to abolitionist groups about his experiences in slavery. He attributed his fluent speech to listening to his master talk. Douglass firmly believed that if he devoted all his efforts to improving vocational education, he could greatly improve the African Americans' plight. He thought that previous attempts by educators to combine liberal and vocational education had failed, so he emphasized vocational education solely.

EARLY SCHOOLS FOR AFRICAN AMERICAN CHILDREN   One of the first northern schools established for African Americans appears to have been that of Elias Neau in New York City in 1704. Neau was an agent of the Society for the Propagation of the Gospel in Foreign Parts.

In 1807 several free African Americans, including George Bell, Nicholas Franklin, and Moses Liverpool, built the first schoolhouse for African Americans in the District of Columbia. Not until 1824, however, was there an African American teacher in that district—John Adams. In 1851, Washington citizens attempted to discourage Myrtilla Miner from establishing an academy for African American girls. However, after much turmoil and harassment, the white schoolmistress from New York did found her academy; it is still functioning today as the School of Education at the University of the District of Columbia.

Boston, the seat of northern liberalism, established a separate school for African American children in 1798. Elisha Sylvester, a white man, was in charge. The school was founded in the home of Primus Hall, a "Negro in good standing." Two years later, sixty-six free African Americans petitioned the school committee for a separate school and were refused. Undaunted, the patrons of Hall's house employed two instructors from Harvard; thirty-five years later, the school was allowed to move to a separate building. The city of Boston opened its first primary school for the education of African American children in 1820—one more small milestone in the history of African American education.

JOHN CHAVIS   African Americans' individual successes in acquiring education, as well as their group efforts to establish schools, were greatly enhanced by sympathetic and humanitarian white friends. One African American who was helped by whites was John Chavis (1763–1838), a free man born in Oxford, North Carolina. Chavis became a successful teacher of aristocratic whites, and his white neighbors sent him to Princeton "to see if a Negro would take a college education." His rapid advancement under Dr. Witherspoon soon indicated that the venture was a success. He returned to Virginia and later went to North Carolina, where he preached among his own people. The success of John Chavis, even under experimental conditions, represented another step forward in the education of African Americans.

PRUDENCE CRANDALL   A young Quaker, Prudence Crandall (1803–1890), established an early boarding school in Canterbury, Connecticut. The problems she ran into dramatize some of the northern animosity to educating African Americans. Trouble arose when Sarah Harris, a "colored girl," asked to be admitted to the institution. After much deliberation, Miss Crandall finally consented, but white parents objected to the African American girl's attending the school and withdrew their children. To keep the school open, Miss Crandall recruited African American children. The pupils were threatened with violence, local stores would not trade with her, and the school building was vandalized. The citizens of Canterbury petitioned the state legislature to enact a law that would make it illegal to educate African Americans from out of state. Miss Crandall was jailed and tried before the state supreme court in July 1834. The court never gave a final decision because defects were found in the information prepared by the attorney for the state; the indictment was eventually dropped. Miss Crandall continued to work for the abolition of slavery, for women's rights, and for African American education. Prudence Crandall became well known, and she deserves considerable credit for the advances made by minorities and women in the United States.

EARLY AFRICAN AMERICAN COLLEGES   Unfortunately, despite these efforts, African Americans received pathetically little formal education until the Emancipation Proclamation, issued by President Abraham Lincoln on January 1, 1863. At that time, the literacy rate among African Americans was estimated at 5 percent. Sunday school represented about the only opportunity most African Americans had to learn to read. In the late 1700s and early 1800s, some communities did set up separate schools for African Americans; however, only a very small percentage ever attended the schools. A few colleges such as Oberlin, Bowdoin, Franklin, Rutland, and Harvard admitted African American students; but, again, very few attended college then. There were even a few African American colleges such as Lincoln University in Pennsylvania (1854) and Wilberforce University in Ohio (1856); however, the efforts and opportunities for the education of African Americans were pathetically few relative to the size of the African American population.

BOOKER T. WASHINGTON   Booker T. Washington (1856–1915) was one of the early African American educators who contributed immensely to the development of education in the United States. He realized that African American children desperately needed an education to compete in society, and he founded Tuskegee Institute in 1880. This Alabama institution provided basic and industrial education in its early years and gradually expanded to provide a wider-ranging college curriculum. It stands today as a proud monument to Booker T. Washington's vision and determination concerning the education of African American youth.

Although there was no great rush to educate African Americans, the abolishment of slavery in 1865 signaled the beginning of a slow but steady effort to improve their education. By 1890, African American literacy had risen to 40 percent; by 1910 it was estimated that 70 percent of African Americans had learned to read and write. These statistics showing the rapid increase in African American literacy are impressive; however, they are compromised by a report of the U.S. commissioner of education showing that by 1900, fewer than 70 of every 1,000 public high schools in the South were provided for African Americans. Even worse, while educational opportunities for African Americans were meager, for other minority groups such as Native Americans and Hispanic Americans they were practically nonexistent.

■ PRIVATE EDUCATION IN AMERICA

Private education has been extremely important in the development of the United States. In fact, private schools carried on nearly all of the education in colonial times. The first colonial colleges such as Harvard, William and Mary, Yale, and Princeton were all private institutions. Many of the other early colonial schools, which can be thought of as **religion-affiliated schools,** were operated by churches, missionary societies, and private individuals.

THE RIGHT OF PRIVATE SCHOOLS TO EXIST

In 1816 the state of New Hampshire attempted to take over Dartmouth College, which was a private institution. A lawsuit growing out of this effort ultimately resulted in the U.S. Supreme Court's first decision involving the legal rights of

"Give me your tired, your poor, / Your huddled masses yearning to breathe free, / The wretched refuse of your teeming shore, / Send these, the homeless, tempest-tossed to me: / I lift my lamp beside the golden door."
Emma Lazarus

CROSS-REFERENCE
Multicultural education is presented in Chapters 2, 3, and 4.

Booker T. Washington (1856–1915), an early African American educator, founded the Tuskegee Institute in Alabama in 1880 to help African American children acquire the education they needed to compete in society.

religion-affiliated school

A private school over which, in most cases, a parent church group exercises some control or to which the church provides some subsidy.

PROFESSIONAL DILEMMA

How Can the Busy Teacher Keep Up with Historical and Contemporary Research?

Ask any teacher what her or his major problems are and "not having enough time" will likely be near the top of the list. So it is perhaps not surprising that many teachers find it difficult to keep up with current research that may help educators do a better job. And yet one of the important hallmarks of a professional is finding, evaluating, and implementing the results of valid and reliable research. For instance, when a person goes to a medical doctor, he or she expects that physician to be using knowledge based on the most recent medical research. By the same token, parents have a right to expect, when they send their children to school, that teachers will be using the most recent educational research in their educational practice. Thus, the professional dilemma is: How do busy teachers locate, read, evaluate, and implement the best research results into their teaching? This task is made even more difficult by the fact that although a great volume of education research is constantly being conducted, a fair amount of it is not necessarily valid or reliable.

Teachers who are determined to put good research results into practice must first be able to read, understand, and evaluate educational research. To learn how to do this, you will probably need to take some basic research courses at a nearby college or university. You will also need to read research reports found in a variety of professional journals in your specialty fields. This may mean subscribing to such journals or getting your school to make them available. Probably you will also wish to attend a variety of professional meetings where research is presented and discussed. And after you locate good research findings, you will need to do careful planning when you implement these research results in your classroom.

Unfortunately, there is no simple solution to this professional dilemma. We know that because we, too, struggle with this problem. However, we are convinced that the first step to solving this dilemma is becoming determined to offer your clients (your students and their parents) the very best education possible. We also are convinced that to do so requires a knowledge of the best and most recent educational research.

- What are your feelings about this professional dilemma at this point in your career development?

- What might you be able to do at this time to help you prepare to deal with this dilemma?

- To what degree do you feel your current teachers are keeping up with, and using, research in their teaching?

To answer these questions on-line and e-mail your answers to your professor, go to Chapter 7 of the companion website (**www.ablongman.com/johnson13e**) and click on Professional Dilemma.

---

a private school. The Supreme Court decided that a private school's charter must be viewed as a contract and cannot be broken arbitrarily by a state. In other words, the Court decided that a private school could not be forced against its will to become a public school.

Subsequent court decisions have reconfirmed the rights of private education in a variety of ways. Generally speaking, for instance, courts have reconfirmed that private schools have a right to exist and in some cases even to share public funds, as long as these funds are not used for religious purposes. Examples of such actions include the use of state funds to purchase secular textbooks and to provide transportation for students to and from private schools. Chapter 5 contains more information about the legal status of private schools.

Not until after the Revolution, when there was a strong sense of nationalism, did certain educators advocate a strong public school system for the new nation. However, such recommendations were not acted on for many years. In the meantime, some Protestant churches continued to expand their schools during the colonial period. For instance, the Congregational, Quaker, Episcopal, Baptist, Methodist, Presbyterian, and Reformed churches all, at various times and in varying degrees, established and operated schools for their youth. It was the Roman Catholics and Lutherans, however, who eventually developed elaborate **parochial school** systems, which were operated by their respective denominations.

parochial school
An educational institution operated and controlled by a religious denomination.

PAROCHIAL SCHOOLS

As early as 1820 there were 240 Lutheran parochial schools in Pennsylvania. Although the number of Lutheran schools in that particular state eventually dwindled, Henry Muhlenberg and other Lutheran leaders continued to establish parochial schools until the public school system became well established. The Missouri Synod Lutheran Church has continued to maintain a well-developed parochial school system. Currently, there are approximately 1,700 Lutheran elementary and secondary schools, which enroll about 200,000 pupils, in the United States, and most of these schools are operated by the Missouri Synod Lutheran Church.

The Roman Catholic parochial school system grew rapidly after its beginnings in the 1800s. Enrollment in Catholic schools mushroomed between 1900 and 1960 from about 855,000 to over five million students. The Roman Catholic parochial school system in the United States is now the largest private school system in the world.

A number of other religious groups have developed and operated their own parochial schools from time to time, some of which still do today. Examples of such religious groups include the Mormons, Mennonites, and Quakers.

THE IMPORTANCE OF PRIVATE EDUCATION IN AMERICA

The concept of public education—that is, education paid for by various governments (local, state, and federal)—is a relatively new idea in the history of U.S. education. For many years, if parents or religious groups wanted to provide education for their children, they had to do so with their own resources. In this part of the book, there have been many references to private schools and private education; at this juncture, we simply wish to reiterate the tremendous importance of private education. In fact, were it not for private education as the predecessor, it is difficult to imagine how we would have evolved a public education system. Private education still plays an enormously important role at all levels of education in the United States.

The major shift from private to public education occurred during the nineteenth century. For instance, in 1800 there was no such thing as a state system of public education anywhere in the United States—no public elementary schools, secondary schools, or state colleges or universities. In fact, until the nineteenth century, all forms of education were private in nature—from elementary school through graduate school. By the year 1900, however, nearly all states had developed a public system of education running from elementary school through graduate school.

Many historians suggest that the overriding motive for private education has always been religious in nature. Initially, parents wanted their children to learn to read so that they could study and understand the Bible and thus gain salvation. Even the earliest colleges were designed primarily to prepare ministers. Harvard College, for instance, was created in 1636 for the express purpose of training ministers.

Likewise, Benjamin Franklin created his unique academy as a private institution to provide technical training to young men because there was no public institution yet created to do so. It was not until 1874 that the Michigan State

Supreme Court established that it was legal for school districts to tax citizens for general support of public high schools. By that time, private schools had been providing secondary education for our nation's youth for two centuries.

■ LEARNING FROM HISTORY

As in all chapters in this book, you should ask how this chapter on historical antecedents of our educational system might be of practical use to you as a contemporary educator. In an attempt to help you begin searching for answers to this critical question, we offer the following for your consideration:

1. If it is true, as many people have suggested, that you cannot really understand something unless you understand its past, then historical information about the antecedents of our educational system should help you better understand today's schools and the education profession.
2. A common characteristic of our most successful educators is that they are proud of their profession; an understanding of the essential role and accomplishments of schools and teachers throughout history helps to build appreciation for, and genuine pride in, the teaching profession.

In what other ways, if any, do you think this chapter might be of use to you?

SUMMARY

Any study of the beginnings of formal education should start with recognition of the fact that parents have always attempted to provide, in one way or another, the informal education their children need to survive in their society. Formal schools very likely did not come into existence until four or five thousand years ago, as humans developed written languages.

Current evidence suggests that one of the first well-organized, educational systems was that evolved by the Greeks during what is commonly called the Age of Pericles today. Greek knowledge and schools eventually blended into Roman schools and libraries.

During the later part of the Middle Ages, there was a revived interest in learning. This period of educational history is commonly divided into two time periods: the Renaissance and the Reformation. The Renaissance represented a rebellion on the part of the common people against the economic, educational, and religious suppression under which the royalty and landed gentry made them live. These common people gradually demanded a better life and developed a spirit of inquiry, which created an interest in education and schooling.

The last three centuries have seen a sometimes erratic, but nevertheless fairly continuous, progression of educational development and advancement throughout the world. In the Western world, this period is often divided into the Age of Reason, which emphasized people's rational and scientific abilities, and the Emergence of Common Man, which sought to create a better education and life for all people.

Our earliest colonists brought their educational ideas and expectations with them from Europe and, soon after arriving in the New World, set about creating schools that fulfilled their needs. These efforts varied widely, from private tutorial education for plantation owners' children in the South, to religious schools in the Middle Colonies, to public schools in the North. Most education was driven by religious motives, and much of the formal education beyond that needed to read the Bible was provided only for boys from the more well-to-do families. Our federal government has played an increasing role in education over time, even though our U.S. Constitution does not mention education and therefore supposedly leaves education up to the states.

This chapter has suggested that history can be viewed through different lenses, each of which will likely produce slightly different views and opinions of historical events. We have also proposed a number of big historical ideas that grow out of the more detailed education history discussed in the chapter. These included the idea that adults in early societies provided the informal education that they felt necessary for children to succeed in their society; more formal schools likely came into existence only as people developed written languages; all societies around the world have developed their own forms of education, down through the ages, designed to fulfill their unique needs; and human progress has, in large part, depended on education.

DISCUSSION QUESTIONS

1. What were the major contributions of several ancient societies to the development of education?

2. What factors contributed to the decline of education during the Dark Ages?

3. What were the strengths and weaknesses of Jean-Jacques Rousseau's ideas about children and education?

4. Discuss the evolution of elementary schools.

5. What historical conditions led to that uniquely American institution, the comprehensive high school?

6. What are the highlights of the history of education of African Americans?

7. Discuss the roles that private schools have played in U.S. education.

JOURNAL ENTRIES

1. Select a person mentioned in this chapter (or another individual from the history of education who is of interest to you) and learn more about that person and her or his influence on today's schools. Make journal entry notes about what you learn.

2. Try to learn more about the historical development of education in the particular grade or subjects you are thinking of teaching. Record in your journal any especially pertinent things you learn.

3. List some of the most important things you learned from this chapter. Which, if any, of the items you listed will likely have practical value for you as a future educator? In what ways?

PORTFOLIO DEVELOPMENT

1. Make a list of historical educational ideas mentioned in this chapter that are still valid and useful for educators today.

2. Summarize the evolution of the goals of public schools in colonial America and the United States. Develop a chart that creatively portrays this evolution.

3. Write an essay on the importance of education in the historical development of the United States.

PREPARING FOR CERTIFICATION

▪ THE EVOLUTION OF U.S. SCHOOLS

1. One of the topics in the Praxis II Principles of Teaching and Learning (PLT) test is "structuring a climate for learning (for example, attention to interpersonal relations, motivational strategies, questioning techniques, classroom and school expectations, rules, routines, and procedures)." In this chapter, you learned about the evolution of schools in the United States from colonial times to the present. Compare the climate for learning in early American schools with schools of today. How are schools' climates similar and different?

2. Answer the following multiple-choice question, which is similar to items in Praxis and other state certification tests. If you are unsure of the answer, reread The Evolution of Teaching Materials section of this chapter.

   The McGuffey readers were commonly used in U.S. schools in the 1800s. What was their major characteristic that contributed to modern curriculum development?

   (A) The materials in each reader were sequenced by grade level and level of difficulty.
   (B) They were the first materials to focus on phonics.
   (C) They emphasized multicultural themes.
   (D) They emphasized the concepts of learning by firsthand experience.

3. Answer the following short-answer question, which is similar to items in Praxis and other state certification tests. After you've completed your written response, use the scoring guide in the ETS *Test at a Glance* materials to assess your response. Can you revise your response to improve your score?

Reread the Relevant Research feature of this chapter, which describes the curriculum of the Boston Latin Grammar School in 1712. List three ways in which the curriculum of the Boston Latin Grammar School is similar to that of U.S. secondary schools today and three ways in which it differs.

WEBSITES

www.cedu.niu.edu/blackwell The Blackwell History of Education Museum and Research Collection is one of the largest collections of its kind in the world. Much of the collection is listed on this website. The Blackwell Museum has developed a variety of instructional materials (also listed on its site) designed to help you learn more about the antecedents of American education.

www.historyofeducation.org.uk The *History of Education* journal of the History of Education Society, located in England. A useful general source of educational history.

www.cr.nps.gov/nr/twhp/wwwlps/lessons/58iron/58iron.htm A historical website about Iron Hill School, an African American one-room school in northern Delaware.

FURTHER READING

Bial, Raymond. (1999). *One-Room School.* Boston: Houghton Mifflin. An interesting book about the history of one-room schools.

Cremin, Lawrence. (1961). *The Transformation of the School: Progressivism in American Education, 1876–1957.* New York: Knopf. This and the next two entries are authored by one of the most respected educational historians of the twentieth century.

Cremin, Lawrence A. (1970). *American Education: The Colonial Experience, 1607–1783.* New York: Harper & Row.

Cremin, Lawrence. (1990). *American Education: The National Experience, 1793–1976.* New York: Harper & Row.

Holmes, Madelyn, and Weiss, Beverly J. (1995). *Lives of Women Public Schoolteachers: Scenes from American*

Educational History. New York: Garland. A well done book about the important role of women educators.

Morgan, Harry. (1995). *Historical Perspectives on the Education of Black Children.* Westport, CT: Praeger. A useful book containing a good deal of information about the history of African American children.

Szasz, Margaret Connell. (1988). *Indian Education in the American Colonies 1607–1783.* Albuquerque: University of New Mexico Press. An excellent source of information about the education of Native Americans during the colonial period.

THEMES OF THE TIMES!

expect the world®
The New York Times
nytimes.com

Expand your knowledge of the concepts discussed in this chapter by reading current and historical articles from the *New York Times* by visiting the Themes of the Times! section of the companion website **(www.ablongman.com/johnson13e).**

NOTES

1. Paul Monroe, *Source Book of the History of Education.* New York: Macmillian, 1901, p. 282.
2. Quintilian, *The Institutes of Oratory,* tran. W. Guthrie. London: Dewick and Clark, 1905, p. 27.
3. Ibid., p. 12.
4. Glenn Smith et al., *Lives in Education.* Ames, IA: Educational Studies Press, 1984, pp. 84–88.
5. Gabriel Compayre, *History of Pedagogy,* trans. W. H. Payne. Boston: Heath, 1888, pp. 12–13, 88–89.
6. Ibid., p. 115.

7. Paul Monroe, *History of Education.* New York: Macmillan, 1905, p. 283.
8. Compayre, *History of Pedagogy,* p. 299.
9. Compayre, *History of Pedagogy,* p. 425.
10. Monroe, *Source Book.*
11. Roe L. Johns and Edgar L. Morphet, *Financing the Public Schools.* Englewood Cliffs, NJ: Prentice-Hall, 1960.
12. Monroe, *Source Book,* p. 282.
13. Portions of the material dealing with the history of African Americans up to the signing of the Emancipation Proclamation (1863) was adapted from the doctoral dissertation of Samuel David, *Education, Law, and the Negro.* Urbana: University of Illinois, 1970.

The Continuing Historical Effort to Improve Education

Education in the News

Casualties of Segregation Receive Honorary Diplomas

By Justin Bergman, *Associated Press*

FARMVILLE, VA.—FOUR DECADES AFTER PRINCE EDWARD County, Va., closed its public schools rather than obey orders to integrate, the black students who were denied an education received honorary diplomas Sunday.

Ada Allen Whitehead said she was the kind of student who never missed a day of school. "I loved to learn," the 55-year-old said.

But she had to stop going to school in Prince Edward County after the seventh grade. She eventually earned her high school diploma outside the county in 1963 and is now working on her doctorate in special education.

"Today is extremely important to start to heal some of the wounds," said state Delegate Viola Baskerville, who is black. "Virginia didn't even want to discuss this for so many years. It was like it was swept under the rug."

To the students who received honorary degrees, the ceremony means "we haven't forgotten," Baskerville said.

Whitehead and other young blacks were forced from their classrooms from 1959 to 1964 when Prince Edward County simply closed its public schools rather than obey the U.S. Supreme Court's order to integrate them.

It was the only county in the nation to close its public schools for an extended period rather than integrate.

A private school was established for white students, while many black children never returned to school. Others, like Whitehead, finished school elsewhere.

Her brother, Ulysses S. Allen, 61, finished his senior year of high school in Washington, D.C.

He called Sunday's honorary graduation a nice gesture, but added: "I don't think you can ever really make amends. What's happened has happened. It's history."

In a gesture of reconciliation, the Virginia General Assembly this year passed a resolution expressing "profound regret" for the school closings.

St. Paul Pioneer Press, www.twincities.com (June 16, 2003), p. 2A.

INTASC | **Learning Outcomes**

After reading and studying this chapter, you should be able to:

1. Decide, explain, and defend the degree to which you believe it is possible to know, understand, and profit from the history of education. (INTASC 10: Collaboration)

2. List and detail several of the most important improvements that have been made in the U.S. educational system over the past half century. (INTASC 2: Development and Learning)

3. Explain important educational contributions that have been made during the last sixty years by private schools, the federal government, researchers, teacher organizations,

teacher educators, and other groups that have helped to improve U.S. schools.

4. List and explain several of the major ideas regarding the history of U.S. education.

5. Explain why knowledge of the history of education is important to educators and how it might be used to improve education today. (INTASC 7: Planning)

School-Based Observations

You may see these learning outcomes in action during your visits to schools:

1. Most of the developments discussed in this chapter are so recent that they continue to influence contemporary classrooms. As you work in the schools, look to see how the continuing struggle for equal educational opportunity is progressing. Also, analyze what you observe in order to determine the degree to which teaching has been professionalized—a movement that has gained impetus during the last sixty years. Finally, as you participate in classrooms, look for evidence that the work of educational pioneers discussed in this chapter (such as Bloom, Montessori, Skinner, and Piaget) has made an impact in U.S. classrooms.

2. Discuss with experienced educators the changes they have observed during their careers. Visit with veteran educational administrators to discuss changes they have seen in education over the years. Ask older people about their school experiences as students.

Many dramatic changes have occurred in education in the United States over the past sixty years. Examples of these rapid and often controversial changes will be briefly discussed in this chapter. However, the big historical ideas presented in this chapter focus on such facts as that (1) there has been phenomenal growth in both the size and complexity of U.S. educational establishments in the last sixty years; (2) the current information age has placed tremendous new demands and expectation on our schools and teachers; (3) providing excellent equal educational opportunities to all students continues to be a major, yet unrealized challenge to our society and to our schools; and, perhaps most important, (4) an understanding of the history of education is of very practical value in helping contemporary educators improve education.

MORE STUDENTS AND BIGGER SCHOOLS

Since World War II, U.S. education has been characterized by a great deal of growth and change: growth in terms of school enrollment, educational budgets, complexity, and federal influence; change in terms of court decisions, proliferation of school laws, confusion about goals, school financial difficulties, struggles for control, and diversification of curricula.

THE RAPID GROWTH OF THE EDUCATIONAL ENTERPRISE

Perhaps the single most dramatic change that has occurred in education over the past sixty years is the sheer expansion in size of the educational enterprise, which took place in many ways.

ENROLLMENT GROWTH

The total number of public school students in the United States has about doubled over the past sixty years. Although part of this rapid growth in school enrollment was attributable to overall population growth, a good part was due to the fact that greater percentages of people were going to school. Furthermore, people were staying in school much longer, as shown by the almost doubled enrollment in higher education.

NEED FOR MORE SCHOOLS

As school enrollment dramatically increased, the need for new classrooms and buildings to house these students also increased. This need for new schools was generally concentrated in cities and suburbs. In fact, because of increased busing, school district consolidation, and shifting population, some smaller rural schools were no longer needed, while more densely populated areas saw a drastic shortage of classrooms. Many schools had to resort to temporary mobile classrooms. Other strategies for coping with classroom shortages included larger classes, split scheduling that started some classes very early and others very late in the day, and classes held in a variety of makeshift areas such as gymnasiums, hallways, and storage closets. Many schools also rented additional space in nearby buildings. Fortunately, over time taxpayers were generally willing to approve the necessary bond referenda to provide the needed additional schools during this period of rapid growth in student enrollment.

NEED FOR MORE TEACHERS

Naturally, this surge in student enrollment required many additional teachers, and at times colleges simply could not produce enough. In this situation, states lowered teacher certification requirements, sometimes to the point at which no professional education training was required at all. Over time, however, the nation managed to meet the demand for more teachers.

As one would expect, the increased numbers of students and teachers cost a great deal more money. More buses had to be purchased, more books and other instructional materials had to be obtained, more school personnel had to be hired—more of everything required to provide education was needed.

■ SCHOOL DISTRICT CONSOLIDATION

The consolidation of school districts was one notable administrative trend over the past sixty years. The number of separate school districts was reduced from 117,000 in 1940 to about 14,000 today. There was a corresponding decline in the number of one-teacher schools over this same period.

ONE-ROOM SCHOOLS

For many years, the **one-room school,** a single classroom taught by one teacher and encompassing all grades, symbolized traditional education in the United States, especially from 1700 to 1900.

Dr. Mark DeWalt completed a study that yielded surprising results: The private one-room school made a modest comeback in the 1980s. This phenomenon is shown in Figure 8.1, which indicates that there was considerable growth in the number of private one-room schools between 1971 and 1987. DeWalt attributes this growth, at least in part, to the U.S. Supreme Court's decision in *Wisconsin v. Yoder* (1972), which upheld Amish parents' rights to educate their own children.

one-room school

A school in which all grade levels are taught by a single teacher in a single room.

A person who wants to learn will always find a teacher.

Persian proverb

This is one of thousands of one-room country schools established to educate rural children during the westward movement in America.

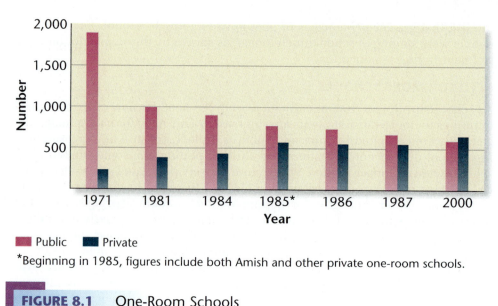

*Beginning in 1985, figures include both Amish and other private one-room schools.

FIGURE 8.1   One-Room Schools

Source: Education Week, February 1, 1989, p. 3.

This decision opened up the opportunity for Amish parents, as well as other parents with similar levels of commitment, to establish their own private elementary schools.

In terms of longer trends, of course, the overall number of one-room schools has diminished greatly. There were approximately 150,000 public one-room schools in 1930, compared to 423[1] today.

Although school consolidation undoubtedly had many educational advantages and saved school dollars in some ways, it did necessitate the busing of more students over greater distances.

GROWTH OF BUSING

Both the number and the percentage of students who were bused increased considerably over the past sixty years, as did the total cost and per-pupil cost of busing. In addition to the general busing of students necessitated by school district consolidation, integration efforts have often involved busing students out of their neighborhood schools.

Busing students to school is still a big operation for the U.S. educational enterprise. It is estimated that about 60 percent of all students are bused to school by about 450,000 school buses.

BIGGER SCHOOL BUDGETS

Educational growth has driven the nation's public education costs to record heights. This rapid increase is illustrated by the fact that the approximate cost of public education was $2 billion in 1940, $5 billion in 1950, $15 billion in 1960, $40 billion in 1970, $97 billion in 1980, and $208 billion in 1990. Even if the figures are corrected for inflation, public education has become considerably more expensive: The percentage of the gross domestic product spent on education rose from 3.5 percent in 1940 to 7 percent by 1980.[2]

■ GROWTH OF PROGRAMS

CROSS-REFERENCE
See Chapter 5 for more information about the current costs of education.

As enrollments increased and schools became larger, more diverse curricula and programs also developed in U.S. schools. This rapid growth of programs placed a great deal of work and pressure on teachers, school administrators, and school boards.

CURRICULAR GROWTH

Curricular growth, like most change, was the result of an accumulation of many smaller events. One such event was the publication in 1942 of the report of the Progressive Education Association's Eight-Year Study (1932–1940) of thirty high schools. The study showed that students attending "progressive" schools achieved as well as students at traditional schools. This report helped to create a climate that was more hospitable to experimentation with school curricula and teaching methodologies. The publication of a series of statements on the goals of U.S. education (the 1938 "Purposes of Education in American Democracy," the 1944 "Education for All American Youth," and the 1952 "Imperative Needs of Youth") helped broaden our schools' curricular offerings.

In 1958, shortly after the Soviet Union launched *Sputnik*, the world's first artificial satellite, Congress passed the National Defense Education Act (NDEA). This act provided a massive infusion of federal dollars to improve schools' science, mathematics, engineering, and foreign language programs. Eventually, innovative curricula such as SMSG mathematics, BSCS biology, and PSCS physics grew out of these programs. Other school programs, such as guidance, were later funded through the NDEA. Note that in the case of the NDEA the federal government called on the schools to help solve what was perceived to be a national defense problem. Regardless of the motive, the NDEA represented another milestone that contributed significantly to the growth of the U.S. educational enterprise.

If one were to compare today's school curriculum with that in any school sixty years ago, one would find impressive changes. The 1940 curriculum was narrow and designed primarily for college-bound students, whereas today's curriculum is broader and designed for students of all abilities. This growth in the school curriculum has come about through the dedicated work of many people and represents one of the truly significant accomplishments in education in the United States.

GROWTH OF SPECIAL EDUCATION PROGRAMS

Perhaps curriculum growth is best illustrated in the area of special education. Public schools historically did not provide special education programs for children with disabilities; rather, they simply accommodated such children as best they could, usually by placing them in regular classrooms. Teachers had little or no training to help them understand and assist the special child. In fact, relatively little was known about common disabilities.

Not until the federal government passed a series of laws during the later twentieth century—including Public Law 94-142, the Education for Handicapped Children Act—did schools begin to develop well-designed programs for students with disabilities. These new special education programs required teachers who had been trained to work with students with visual or hearing impairments, students with behavior disorders, and so forth. States and colleges then developed a wide variety of teacher-training programs for special educators. The percentage of public school students enrolled in various special education programs increased from 1.2 percent in 1940 to 11.4 percent in 1990. In actual numbers of students, this represented a total of about 310,000 special education students in 1940 compared to about 4,641,000 in 1990.

Special education has developed rapidly over a relatively short period in our recent history. It continues to evolve today and will likely do so in the future. And as you can imagine, those who believe we should continue to put a high priority on special education programs view these programs through lenses shaped by their own knowledge, experiences, and historical perspective.

ASIAN AMERICAN EDUCATION

The Second World War brought about what many consider to have been unwarranted discrimination against Japanese Americans when the U.S. government placed more than 100,000 Japanese American citizens in internment camps and

In the new brain-powered economy, education will be the world's largest, most important industry.
Morton Egol

CROSS-REFERENCE
See Chapter 2 for more information about education and exceptionalities.

The number of Asian students is increasing rapidly throughout the United States.

in some cases confiscated their property. Not until 1990 did the government officially apologize and pay restitution for having done so. In hindsight, many believe that this treatment of U.S. citizens of Japanese background constituted a form of discrimination.

In the decades following the Korean and Vietnam wars, the number of Asian immigrants to the United States has increased dramatically. Large numbers of Vietnamese, Cambodians, Laotians, and Thais have been included in this recent migration. Although many of these Asian immigrants have experienced considerable success, the majority have struggled to learn English, receive an education, and find suitable jobs. Many feel that they have been discriminated against and have not received equal educational and employment opportunities. Yet many of the highest-achieving high school students are Asian Americans, proof of the fact that their families typically place a high value on education.

Of course, the first Asian immigrants arrived in colonial America at a very early stage—especially Chinese immigrants. Asians came, like most immigrants from around the globe, seeking jobs and a better life. Also like most immigrants, the Asians arrived as poor and relatively uneducated people. Unfortunately, many of them were often discriminated against and were seldom offered equal educational opportunity. In 1882, in fact, the U.S. government passed the Chinese Exclusion Act in an attempt to limit the number of Chinese immigrants. Despite these many obstacles, like many other immigrant groups Asians typically found ways to earn a living and to educate their children; and through hard work many became very successful in a variety of vocations.

HISPANIC AMERICAN EDUCATION

The number of Hispanic American students in U.S. schools has increased dramatically over the past sixty years. But the historical background of this increase can actually be traced to the very first formal schools in North America. The earliest formal schools on this continent were started and conducted by Spanish missionaries in Mexico and the southwestern part of what is now the United States in the sixteenth century. Some historians even assert that the Spanish had established several "colleges" in North America before Harvard was founded in 1636. This assertion is probably true if one defines a mission school as a college, because some of them prepared boys for the ministry. As with the other early schools in the Americas, the missionaries established these early Spanish schools primarily for religious purposes: to help people read the Bible and thus gain salvation. Early mission schools in what is now Mexico and in Florida, Cuba, California, Arizona, New Mexico, and elsewhere were taught by the Catholic priests in the Spanish language. After the United States won its independence and grew to include what we now think of as the Southwest, these early Spanish schools gradually became part of the larger English-speaking U.S. school system.

Many important Hispanic Americans have made significant contributions to the development of education. For example, Rafael Cordero, a self-taught free black Hispanic, established an early (1810) school in San Germán, Puerto Rico. He realized that black and Hispanic children, who were denied a formal education because of their skin color, would profit greatly from schooling. Cordero's schools and his teaching methods eventually became so highly respected that they also attracted the children of the white upper class.

George Sanchez is another example of a Hispanic American educational pioneer. After graduation from the Albuquerque, New Mexico, high school in 1923, Sanchez began his teaching career at age sixteen. He taught in one-room schools to which he traveled on horseback, continuing to attend college whenever possible. Sanchez eventually obtained a master's degree and a doctorate, after which he held various professorships and government positions; he then became the minister of education in Venezuela. After returning to the United States, he worked in various capacities to advocate the improvement of education for Hispanic American children. Through the courts and through writing, speaking, and advising, Sanchez eventually was able to bring about significant improvements in Mexican American education.

Unfortunately, Hispanic American education did not develop as quickly or as well as it did for the majority population. This discrepancy was due at least in part to the fact that many Hispanic Americans were in the lower income brackets, immigrated to the United States without well-developed English language skills, and in many instances suffered discrimination. Like other minority groups in the United States, Hispanic Americans have not historically been afforded equal educational opportunities. Schools in the southern and southwestern parts

CROSS-REFERENCE
More information about multicultural education is found in Chapters 2 and 3.

of the United States now have huge numbers of Hispanic American students, and in many of these schools Hispanic American students are, or will become, the majority in the relatively near future.

The education of immigrants from all over the world remains an important challenge for our educational system today as it has throughout our history. For example, about eighteen million immigrants came to the United States in the three decades between 1890 and 1920, whereas about twelve million have come in the 1980s and 1990s.

THE DEVELOPMENT OF THE TEACHING PROFESSION

The field of education has taken giant strides toward becoming a profession since World War II. In the following pages, we will briefly explore the increasing complexities of educational systems in the United States and look at some of the recent developments that have contributed to the professionalization of the field of education.

THE INCREASING COMPLEXITY OF THE EDUCATIONAL ENTERPRISE

The current U.S. educational system is much more complex than school systems of the past, and this complexity is manifested in many different ways.

INCREASING FEDERAL INVOLVEMENT

As we noted earlier, the federal government has played important roles in the development of national educational programs. This federal involvement in education has gradually increased over the years, and it reached a peak during the past sixty years.

The 1940s saw the nation at war, which provided the impetus for the federal government to pass a number of laws that affected education. The Vocational Education for National Defense Act was a crash program to prepare workers needed in industry to produce goods for national defense. The program operated through state educational agencies and trained more than seven million workers. In 1941 the Lanham Act provided funds for building, maintaining, and operating community facilities in areas where local communities had unusual burdens because of defense and war initiatives.

GI BILL The GI Bill of 1944 provided for the education of veterans of World War II. Later, similar bills assisted veterans of the Korean conflict. The federal government recognized a need to help young people whose careers had been interrupted by military service. These federal acts afforded education to more than ten million veterans at a cost of almost $20 billion. Payments were made directly to veterans and to the colleges and schools the veterans attended. In 1966 an-

World War II veterans returned to college motivated by their war experiences and assisted by the federal GI Bill of Rights.

other GI Bill was passed for veterans of the war in Vietnam. The initial cost of these acts amounted to a wonderful national investment because the government was repaid many times over by the increased taxes eventually paid by the veterans who received this financial aid and later were employed.

NATIONAL SCIENCE FOUNDATION   The National Science Foundation, established in 1950, emphasized the need for continued support of basic scientific research. It was created to "promote the progress of science; to advance the national health, prosperity, and welfare; to secure the national defense; and for other purposes." The Cooperative Research Program of 1954 authorized the U.S. commissioner of education to enter into contracts with universities, colleges, and state education agencies to carry on educational research.

CATEGORICAL FEDERAL AID   Beginning in 1957, when the first Soviet space vehicle was launched, the federal government further increased its participation in education. The National Defense Education Act of 1958, the Vocational Education Act of 1963, the Manpower Development and Training Act of 1963, the Elementary and Secondary Education Act of 1965, and the International Education Act of 1966 are examples of increased federal participation in educational affairs. Federally supported educational programs such as Project Head Start, the National Teacher Corp, and Upward Bound are further indications of such participation.

All these acts and programs have involved categorical federal aid to education—that is, aid for specific uses. Some people believe that federal influence on education has recently been greater than either state or local influence. There can be no denying that through federal legislation, U.S. Supreme Court decisions, and federal administrative influence, the total federal effect on education is indeed great. Indications are that this effect will be even more pronounced in the future. It will remain for historians to determine whether this trend in U.S. education is a beneficial one.

CROSS-REFERENCE
Chapters 5 and 6 present more information on the administrative and financial aspects of federal involvement in education.

THE STRUGGLE FOR EQUAL EDUCATIONAL OPPORTUNITY   The past half century has also been characterized by an increasing struggle for **equal educational opportunity** for all children, regardless of race, creed, religion, or sex. This struggle was initiated by the African American activism movement, given additional momentum by the women's rights movement, and eventually joined by many other groups such as Hispanic Americans, Native Americans, and Asian Americans. Other chapters of this book discuss the details of this relatively recent quest for equal educational opportunity. We mention it briefly at this point simply to emphasize that the struggle for equal educational opportunity represents an important but underrecognized recent historical movement in education. Today, many observers are pointing out that with the accelerated growth of minority subcultures within this nation, our economic and political survival depends to a great degree on educational opportunities and achievements for all segments of U.S. society.

NO CHILD LEFT BEHIND   One of our federal government's recent major efforts to improve education and to help children learn, especially disadvantaged children, is the sweeping legislation commonly referred to as No Child Left Behind. This law is discussed in more detail throughout this book, but it is mentioned here as yet another example of increasing federal involvement in education.

THE PROFESSIONALIZATION OF TEACHING

Formal teacher training is a relatively recent phenomenon. Teacher-training programs were developed during the late nineteenth century and the first half of the twentieth century. By the midpoint of the century, each state had established teacher certification requirements. Since then, teacher training and certification

equal educational opportunity

Access to a similar education for all students, regardless of their cultural background or family circumstances.

What Have We Learned about Homework and Students with Disabilities?

INTRODUCTION: Throughout history, teachers have worked to provide the right type and amount of homework for each student; and they are still striving to do so.

STUDY PURPOSE/QUESTIONS: Today, partly as a result of educational reform, many students are receiving increased amounts of homework. For students with disabilities, homework may pose significant challenges. Some of these problems are related to a student's ability to maintain attention, sustain acceptable levels of motivation, demonstrate effective study skills, and manifest positive attitudes toward homework. Others are related to factors such as how homework is assigned and the quality of communication between home and school about homework.

· · ·

William Bursuck, researcher at Northern Illinois University, has been studying how practitioners and families can make homework a more successful experience for students with disabilities. One thing is clear—parent involvement is critical if homework is to be beneficial.

STUDY DESIGN: With his colleagues, Bursuck conducted a series of studies to identify problems parents and schools were experiencing in communicating about homework, as well as recommendations for ameliorating these problems.

STUDY FINDINGS: Teachers encountered the following problems:

- Insufficient time and opportunity to communicate.
- Too many students on a given teacher's caseload.
- Need for additional knowledge to facilitate communication (e.g., students' needs, whom to contact).
- Other factors that hindered communication, such as lack of phones in teachers' classrooms.

Recommendations for improvement grew out of the discussions.

· · ·

Teachers identified useful adaptations for students with disabilities. They also suggested strategies for ensuring that homework was clear and appropriate.

In addition, the surveys indicated that teachers preferred the following strategies to maintain effective communication:

- Use technology to aid communication (e.g., use answering machines or e-mail, and establish homework hotlines).
- Encourage students to keep assignment books.
- Provide a list of suggestions on how parents might assist with homework. For example, ask parents to check with their children about homework daily.

Preferred Homework Adaptations

- Provide additional one-on-one assistance to students.
- Monitor students' homework more closely.
- Allow alternative response formats (e.g., audiotaping rather than writing an assignment).
- Adjust the length of the assignment.
- Provide a peer tutor or assign the student to a study group.
- Provide learning tools (e.g., calculators).
- Adjust evaluation standards.
- Give fewer assignments.

Tips for Assigning Homework

- Make sure the students can complete the homework assignment.
- Write the assignment on the chalkboard.
- Explain the assignment clearly.
- Remind students of due dates periodically.
- Assign homework in small units.
- Coordinate with other teachers to prevent homework overload.
- Make sure students and parents have information regarding your policy on missed and late assignments, extra credit, and available adaptations. Establish a set routine at the beginning of the year.
- Provide parents with frequent communication about homework.
- Use written modes of communication (e.g., progress reports, notes, letters, forms).
- Encourage the school administration to provide incentives for teachers to participate in face-to-face meetings (e.g., release time, compensation).
- Suggest that the school district offer after-school and/or peer tutoring sessions to give students extra help with homework.
- Share information with other teachers regarding student strengths and needs and necessary accommodations.

IMPLICATIONS: If students, teachers, and parents do not find homework strategies palatable, they may not use them. "The ultimate impact of these homework practices on students may depend largely on how favorably teachers, parents, and the students themselves perceive them," Bursuck adds. "Our research underscores the need to check out practices with all stakeholders. Simply put, practices that are not acceptable will not be used."

Source: Research Connections: In Special Education, ERIC Clearinghouse on Disabilities and Gifted Education, U.S. Office of Education, No. 8 (Spring 2001), pp. 2–3.

have been characterized by a "refinement" or "professionalization" movement. Teacher salaries have also improved considerably over this period.

In addition to teacher education, this professionalization movement touched just about all facets of education: curriculum, teaching methodology, training of school service personnel (administrators, counselors, librarians, media and other specialists), inservice teacher training, teacher organizations, and even school building construction. To understand clearly this professionalization movement, one need only compare pictures of an old one-room country school with a modern school building, read both a 1940 and a 1998 publication of the AFT or NEA, contrast a mid-twentieth-century high school curriculum with one from today, or compile a list of the teaching materials found in a 1940 school and a similar list for a typical contemporary school.

home schooling
Teaching children at home rather than in formal schools.

CONTINUED IMPORTANCE OF PRIVATE SCHOOLS

As explained in Chapter 7, nearly all early schools were private and religion was the main purpose of education in colonial America. Children were taught to read primarily so that they could study the Bible, and most early colleges were private and established primarily to train ministers.

As the public school system developed, however, the religious nature of education gradually diminished to the point where relatively few American children attended religious schools. There have always been certain religious groups, however, that have struggled to create and maintain their own private schools so that religious instruction could permeate all areas of the curriculum. The most notable of these religious groups has long been the Roman Catholic Church. Over the past twenty-five years, though, enrollment in non-Catholic religious schools has grown dramatically while Catholic school enrollment has declined.

Despite this recent trend, some Roman Catholic dioceses operate extremely large school systems, sometimes larger than the public school system in the same geographical area. The Chicago Diocese operates the largest Roman Catholic school system, enrolling approximately 150,000 students.

With rare exceptions, private and parochial schools struggle to raise the funds they need to exist. They typically must charge a tuition fee, rely on private contributions, and conduct various fund-raising activities. In recent years, some school districts have made tuition vouchers available to parents who choose not to send their children to the public school.

We should begin improving our schools by appreciating how well they have, in most places and most times, done so far.

Gerald W. Bracey

CROSS-REFERENCE
The highly controversial subject of vouchers was presented in Chapter 5.

HOME SCHOOLING

Many years ago, about the only parents who taught their children at home were those who lived so far from a school that it was impossible for their children to attend. In the past several decades, however, a growing number of parents have been choosing to educate their children at home—at least through the elementary grades and sometimes even through high school. The motivation for **home schooling** varies, but often it stems from a concern that children in the public schools may be exposed to problems such as drugs, alcohol, smoking, or gangs. Other parents have religious motives, wanting their children to be taught in a particular religious context. Still other parents, who may have had bad experiences with public schools, simply feel they can provide a better education for their children at home. Recent laws

Home schooling is a rapidly growing phenomenon.

CROSS-REFERENCE

Chapter 5 provides more information on private schooling in the United States.

and court cases have generally upheld the right, within certain parameters, of parents to educate their children if they choose to do so. The number of parents providing home schooling has grown an estimated 15 percent each year in the last decade. The Home Legal Defense Association estimates that over 1.5 million children are now schooled at home. As one would expect, the value of home schooling is widely debated in our society.

CONTINUING/ADULT EDUCATION

Many forms of education for adults have existed for at least two centuries in this country. Shortly after the United States became a nation, a need to help new immigrants learn English caused schools, churches, and various groups to offer English language instruction; factories found a need to offer job and safety training; churches taught adult religious instruction; and so forth. The New York public schools, as well as many other large schools, developed large English language programs as well as adult vocational programs for the unemployed. Adult education took a great variety of forms and quickly grew into a vast network of programs dealing with nearly all aspects of life in the United States.

An example of a large early adult education development can be found in the Chautauqua movement at Lake Chautauqua, New York. Started in 1874 by the Methodist Sunday school, this adult education effort expanded to include correspondence courses, lecture classes, music education, and literary study on a wide variety of subjects throughout the eastern part of the nation.

Public schools increasingly offered adult education classes during the nineteenth century. Some of the larger public school systems, such as that in Gary, Indiana, developed adult educational programs with an emphasis on vocational and technical training. Gradually, nearly all schools serving rural areas developed adult agricultural programs to improve farming methods.

In 1964 the Economic Opportunity Act provided adult basic education funding to help adults learn to read and write. Since that time there has been a proliferation of continuing/adult education programs of all types throughout the United States. These programs serve an increasingly important purpose in our rapidly changing society. They help new immigrants learn the English language, provide job training for the unemployed, update job skills, teach parenting skills, enable people to move to higher-level employment, help people explore new hobbies, provide enrichment programs for retired folks, and generally make the world of education available to nearly all citizens regardless of age. The exploding popularity of the Elderhostel programs and other activities now offered for senior citizens and the crowded evening parking lots at high schools and colleges throughout the country attest to the popularity and success of continuing/adult education programs. In the future, as the world becomes increasingly complex and as more people remain active and healthy in old age, we predict that such adult/continuing education programs will continue to grow.

EVOLUTION OF EDUCATIONAL TESTING

Educators have undoubtedly attempted to measure and assess student learning from the very beginning

Adult education programs have been common in the United States since the seventeenth century, but they burgeoned during the late twentieth and early twenty-first centuries. Many such programs are offered through public schools.

of formal education. However, it is only in the last sixty years that educational assessment has taken on vastly more importance, to the point in contemporary education that many feel assessment has become the tail that wags the educational dog. Let's briefly review this recent evolution of educational assessment.

Many historians suggest that the increased attention given to educational testing in the past sixty years was sparked by James Conant, who had become president of Harvard University in 1933. Conant and his colleagues were influenced by the developments in mental testing done by Alfred Binet in France and by Lewis Terman in the United States, which were used extensively by the U.S. Army to test recruits.

Conant seized on a relatively new test called the Scholastic Aptitude Test (SAT), developed by Carl Bright at Princeton University, as a way to assess a student's potential for success at Harvard. He also helped to create a new organization, called the Educational Testing Service (ETS), which became—and remains—the major power in the educational assessment area. By the 1960s, over a million high school students were taking the SAT test, which most colleges used as one criterion for admission.

Many so-called standardized tests have been developed over the past sixty years in an attempt to measure different kinds of aptitude, learning, motivation, and virtually every aspect of education. These standardized tests have come under much criticism by many educators, parents, and others, who question their fairness and accuracy. Even so they continue to be heavily used today.

Educators have faced increasing pressure in recent years to develop improved ways to assess student learning. Much of this pressure has come from taxpayers, government, and the industrial world, often in a demand for greater accountability. Most states have implemented a required system of achievement testing. The results of these achievement tests are commonly used to evaluate and compare schools—a controversial and unfair practice, according to many educators.

In fact, while agreeing that accurate educational assessment is absolutely essential to the educational enterprise, a growing number of educators are questioning many aspects of the increasing emphasis on educational assessment. This important topic is discussed more in various places throughout the text. Suffice it to point out here that educational assessment has grown rapidly and taken on increasing importance, for better or worse, in the past sixty years.

Through public education we can in this century hope in no small measure to regain that great gift to each succeeding generation, opportunity, a gift that once was the promise of our frontier.

James Conant

CROSS-REFERENCE
See Chapter 12 for more information on educational assessment.

CHANGING AIMS OF EDUCATION

The aims of education in the United States have gradually changed over the years. During colonial times, the overriding aim of education at all levels was to enable students to read and understand the Bible, to gain salvation, and to spread the gospel.

After the colonies won independence from England, educational objectives—such as providing U.S. citizens with a common language, attempting to instill a sense of patriotism, developing a national feeling of unity and common purpose, and providing the technical and agricultural training the developing nation needed—became important tasks for the schools.

COMMITTEE OF TEN

In 1892 a committee was established by the National Education Association (NEA) to study the function of the U.S. high school. This committee, known as the **Committee of Ten,** made an effort to set down the purposes of the high school at that time and made the following recommendations: (1) High school should consist of grades 7 through 12; (2) courses should be arranged sequentially; (3) students should be given very few electives in high school; and (4) one unit, called a Carnegie unit, should be awarded for each separate course that a student takes each year, provided that the course meets four or five times each week all year long.

Each generation must define afresh the nature, direction, and aims of education to assure such freedom and rationality as can be attained for a future generation.

Jerome S. Bruner

Committee of Ten
A historic National Education Association (NEA) committee that studied secondary education in 1892.

The Committee of Ten also recommended trying to graduate high school students earlier to permit them to attend college sooner. At that time, the recommendation implied that high schools had a college preparatory function. These recommendations became powerful influences in the shaping of secondary education.

SEVEN CARDINAL PRINCIPLES

Before 1900, teachers had relatively little direction in their work because most educational goals were not precisely stated. This problem was partly overcome in 1918 when the Commission on Reorganization of Secondary Education published the report *Cardinal Principles of Secondary Education,* usually referred to as the Seven Cardinal Principles. In reality, the Seven Cardinal Principles constitute only one section of the basic principles discussed in the original text, but it is the part that has become famous. These principles stated that the student should receive an education in the following seven fields: health, command of fundamental processes, worthy home membership, vocation, civic education, worthy use of leisure, and ethical character.

THE EIGHT-YEAR STUDY

The following goals of education, or "needs of youth," were listed by the Progressive Education Association in 1938 and grew out of the Eight-Year Study of thirty high schools conducted by the association from 1932 to 1940:

Educational opportunity had become a measure of the aspirations and possibilities of American democracy.

Marvin Larerson

1. Physical and mental health
2. Self-assurance
3. Assurance of growth toward adult status
4. Philosophy of life
5. Wide range of personal interests
6. Esthetic appreciations
7. Intelligent self-direction
8. Progress toward maturity in social relations with age-mates and adults
9. Wise use of goods and services
10. Vocational orientation
11. Vocational competence

"PURPOSES OF EDUCATION IN AMERICAN DEMOCRACY"

Also in 1938, the Educational Policies Commission of the National Education Association set forth the "Purposes of Education in American Democracy." These objectives stated that students should receive an education in the four broad areas of self-realization, human relations, economic efficiency, and civic responsibility.

"EDUCATION FOR ALL AMERICAN YOUTH"

In 1944 this same commission of the NEA published another statement of educational objectives, entitled "Education for All American Youth":

Schools should be dedicated to the proposition that every youth in these United States—regardless of sex, economic status, geographic location, or race—should experience a broad and balanced education which will

1. equip him to enter an occupation suited to his abilities and offering reasonable opportunity for personal growth and social usefulness;
2. prepare him to assume full responsibilities of American citizenship;
3. give him a fair chance to exercise his right to the pursuit of happiness through the attainment and preservation of mental and physical health;
4. stimulate intellectual curiosity, engender satisfaction in intellectual achievement, and cultivate the ability to think rationally; and
5. help to develop an appreciation of the ethical values which should undergird all life in a democratic society.

"IMPERATIVE NEEDS OF YOUTH"

In 1952 the Educational Policies Commission made yet another statement of educational objectives, entitled "Imperative Needs of Youth":

1. All youth need to develop salable skills and those understandings and attitudes that make the worker an intelligent productive participant in economic life. To this end most youth need supervised work experience as well as education in the skills and knowledge of their occupations.
2. All youth need to develop and maintain good health and physical fitness.
3. All youth need to understand the rights and duties of the citizen of a democratic society, and to be diligent and competent in the performance of their obligations as members of the community and citizens of the state and nation.
4. All youth need to understand the significance of the family for the individual and society and the conditions conducive to successful family life.
5. All youth need to know how to purchase and use goods and services intelligently, understanding both the values received by the consumer and the economic consequences of their acts.
6. All youth need to understand the methods of science, the influence of science on human life, and the main scientific facts concerning the nature of the world and of man.
7. All youth need opportunities to develop their capacities to appreciate beauty in literature, art, music, and nature.
8. All youth need to be able to use their leisure time well and budget it wisely, balancing activities that yield satisfactions to the individual with those that are socially useful.
9. All youth need to develop respect for other persons, to grow in their insight into ethical values and principles, and to be able to live and work cooperatively with others.
10. All youth need to grow in their ability to think rationally, to express their thoughts clearly, and to read and listen with understanding.

These various statements concerning educational objectives, made over the last century, sum up fairly well the history of the aims of U.S. public education. These changing aims also show how perspectives on the purposes of education have evolved over time; this is yet another example of viewing education through different lenses.

■ PREPARATION OF TEACHERS

Because present-day teachers have at least four—and often five to eight—years of college education, it is difficult to believe that teachers have historically had little or no training. One of the first forms of teacher training grew out of the medieval guild system, in which a young man who wished to enter a certain field of work served a lengthy period of apprenticeship with a master in the field. Some young men became teachers by serving as apprentices to master teachers, sometimes for as long as seven years.

GLOBAL PERSPECTIVES
European Beginnings of Teacher Training

The first formal teacher-training school in the Western world of which we have any record was mentioned in a request to the king of England, written by William Byngham in 1438, requesting that "he may yeve withouten fyn or fee (the) mansion ycalled Goddeshous the which he hath made and edified in your towne of Cambridge for the free herbigage of poure scolers of Gramer."[3]

Byngham was granted his request and established Goddeshous College as a teacher-training institution on June 13, 1439. Students at this college gave demonstration lectures to fellow students to gain practice teaching. Classes were even conducted during vacations so that country schoolmasters could also attend. Byngham's college still exists today as Christ's College of Cambridge University. At that early date of 1439, Byngham made provision for two features that are still considered important in teacher education today: scheduling classes so that teachers in service can attend and providing some kind of student teaching experience. Many present-day educators would probably be surprised to learn that these ideas are nearly 600 years old.

COLONIAL TEACHERS

Elementary school teachers in colonial America were very poorly prepared; in fact, more often than not, they had received no special training at all. The single qualification of most of them was that they themselves had been students. Most colonial college teachers, private tutors, Latin grammar school teachers, and academy teachers had received some kind of college education, usually at one of the well-established colleges or universities in Europe. A few had received their education at an American colonial college.

Teachers in the various kinds of colonial elementary schools typically had only an elementary education themselves, but a few had attended a Latin grammar school or a private academy. It was commonly believed that to be a teacher required only that the instructor know something about the subject matter to be taught; therefore, no teacher, regardless of the level taught, received training in the methodology of teaching.

Teaching was not considered a prestigious occupation, and the pay was poor. Consequently, many schoolteachers viewed their jobs as only temporary. For young women who taught elementary school, the "something better" was usually marriage. Men frequently left teaching for careers in the ministry or business. Not uncommonly, career teachers in the colonies were undesirable people. Records show that many teachers lost their jobs because they paid more attention to the tavern than to the school or because of stealing, swearing, or conduct unbecoming to a person in such a position.

Because many colonial schools were conducted in connection with a church, the teacher was often considered an assistant to the minister. Besides teaching, other duties of some early colonial teachers were "to act as court messenger, to serve summonses, to conduct certain ceremonial services of the church, to lead the Sunday choir, to ring the bell for public worship, to dig the graves, and to perform other occasional duties."

TEACHERS AS INDENTURED SERVANTS

Sometimes the colonies used white indentured servants as teachers; many people who came to the United States bought passage by agreeing to work for some years as indentured servants. The ship's captain would then sell the indentured servant's services, more often than not by placing an ad in a newspaper. Such an ad, shown in Figure 8.2, appeared in a May 1786 edition of the *Maryland Gazette.*

Records reveal that there were many indentured servants and convicted felons among early immigrants who were advertised and sold as teachers. In fact, it has been estimated that at least one-half of all the teachers in colonial America may have come from these sources. This is not necessarily a derogatory description of these early teachers when we remember that many poor people bought their passage to the colonies by agreeing to serve as indentured servants for a period of years and that in England at that time, hungry and desperate people could be convicted as felons and deported for stealing a loaf of bread.

Men and Women Servants

JUST ARRIVED

In the ship *Paca,* Robert Caulfield, Master, in five Weeks from Belfast and Cork, a number of healthy Men and Women SERVANTS.

Among them are several valuable tradesman, viz.

Carpenters, Shoemakers, Coopers, Blacksmiths, Staymakers, Bookbinders, Clothiers, Diers, Butchers, Schoolmasters, Millrights, and Labourers.

Their indentures are to be disposed of by the Subscribers,

Brown, and Maris
William Wilson

FIGURE 8.2 1786 Advertisement for Indentured Servants

TEACHING APPRENTICESHIPS

Some colonial teachers learned their trade by serving as apprentices to schoolmasters. Court records reveal numerous such indentures of apprenticeship; the following was recorded in New York City in 1772:

> This Indenture witnesseth that John Campbel Son of Robert Campbel of the City of New York with the Consent of his father and mother hath put himself and by these presents doth Voluntarily put and bind himself Apprentice to George Brownell of the Same City Schoolmaster to learn the Art Trade or Mastery—for and during the term of ten years. . . . And the said George Brownell Doth hereby Covenant and Promise to teach and instruct or Cause the said Apprentice to be taught and instructed in the Art Trade or Calling of a Schoolmaster by the best way or means he or his wife may or can.

TEACHER TRAINING IN ACADEMIES

One of Benjamin Franklin's justifications for proposing an academy in Philadelphia was that some of the graduates would make good teachers. Speculating on the need for such graduates, Franklin wrote,

> A number of the poorer sort [of academy graduates] will be hereby qualified to act as Schoolmasters in the Country, to teach children Reading, Writing, Arithmetic, and the Grammar of their Mother Tongue, and being of good morals and known character, may be recommended from the Academy to Country Schools for that purpose; the Country suffering at present very much for want of good Schoolmasters, and obliged frequently to employ in their schools, vicious imported servants, or concealed Papists, who by their bad Examples and Instructions often deprave the Morals and corrupt the Principles of the children under their Care.

The fact that Franklin said some of the "poorer" graduates would make suitable teachers reflects the low regard for teachers typical of the time. The academy that Franklin proposed was established in 1751 in Philadelphia, and many graduates of academies after that time did indeed become teachers.

NORMAL SCHOOLS

Many early educators recognized this country's need for better-qualified teachers; however, it was not until 1823 that the first teacher-training institution was established in the United States. This private school, called a **normal school** after its European prototype, which had existed since the late seventeenth century, was established by the Reverend Mr. Samuel Hall in Concord, Vermont.

normal school
The first type of American institution devoted exclusively to teacher training.

First State Normal School was adapted from European teacher training schools and is still standing in Lexington, Massachusetts.

Hall's school did not produce many teachers, but it did signal the beginning of formal teacher training in the United States.

The early normal school program usually consisted of a two-year course. Students typically entered the normal school right after finishing elementary school; most normal schools did not require high school graduation for entrance until about 1900. The nineteenth-century curriculum was much like the curriculum of the high schools of that time. Students reviewed subjects studied in elementary school, studied high school subjects, had a course in teaching (or "pedagogy" as it was then called), and did some student teaching in a model school, usually operated in conjunction with the normal school. The subjects offered by a normal school in Albany, New York, in 1845 included English grammar, English composition, history, geography, reading, writing, orthography, arithmetic, algebra, geometry, trigonometry, human physiology, surveying, natural philosophy, chemistry, intellectual philosophy, moral philosophy, government, rhetoric, theory and practice of teaching, drawing, music, astronomy, and practice teaching.

Horace Mann was instrumental in establishing the first state-supported normal school, which opened in 1839 in Lexington, Massachusetts. Other public normal schools, established shortly afterward, typically offered a two-year teacher-training program. Some of the students came directly from elementary school; others had completed secondary school. Some states did not establish state-supported normal schools until the early 1900s.

STATE TEACHERS' COLLEGES

During the early part of the twentieth century, several factors caused a significant change in normal schools. For one thing, as the population of the United States increased, so did the enrollment in elementary schools, thereby creating an ever-increasing demand for elementary school teachers. Likewise, as more people attended high school, more high school teachers were needed. To meet this demand, normal schools eventually expanded their curriculum to include secondary teacher education. The growth of high schools also created a need for teachers who were highly specialized in particular academic subjects, so normal schools established subject matter departments and developed more diversified programs. The length of the teacher education program was expanded to two, three, and finally four years; this longer duration fostered development and diversification of the normal school curriculum. The demand for teachers increased from about 20,000 in 1900 to more than 200,000 in 1930.

The United States gradually advanced technologically to the point at which more college-educated citizens were needed. The normal schools assumed a responsibility to help meet this need by establishing many other academic programs in addition to teacher training. As normal schools extended their programs to four years and began granting baccalaureate degrees, they also began to call themselves *state teachers' colleges.* For most institutions, the change in name took place during the 1930s.

TEACHER EDUCATION IN THE MID-TWENTIETH CENTURY

Universities entered the teacher preparation business on a large scale around 1900. Before then, some graduates of universities had become high school teachers or college teachers; but not until about 1900 did universities begin to

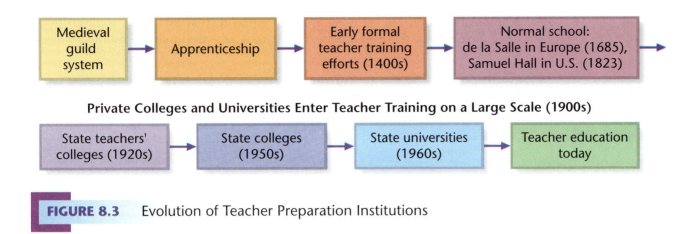

| Medieval guild system | → | Apprenticeship | → | Early formal teacher training efforts (1400s) | → | Normal school: de la Salle in Europe (1685), Samuel Hall in U.S. (1823) | → |

Private Colleges and Universities Enter Teacher Training on a Large Scale (1900s)

| State teachers' colleges (1920s) | → | State colleges (1950s) | → | State universities (1960s) | → | Teacher education today |

FIGURE 8.3 Evolution of Teacher Preparation Institutions

establish departments of education and add a full range of teacher education programs to the curriculum.

Just as the normal schools expanded in size, scope, and function until they became state teachers' colleges, so the state teachers' colleges expanded to become *state colleges.* This change in name and scope took place for most institutions around 1950. The elimination of the word *teacher* really explains the story behind this transition. The new state colleges gradually expanded their programs beyond teacher education and became multipurpose institutions. One of the main reasons for this transition was that a growing number of students coming to the colleges demanded a more varied education. The state teachers' colleges developed diversified programs to try to meet their demands.

Many of these state colleges later became state universities, offering doctoral degrees in a wide range of fields. Some of our largest and most highly regarded universities evolved from normal schools. Figure 8.3 diagrams the evolution of U.S. teacher preparation institutions.

Obviously, establishing the teaching profession has been a long and difficult task. Preparation of teachers has greatly improved over the years from colonial times—when anyone could be a teacher—to the present, when people such as you must meet rigorous requirements for permanent teacher certification.

■ EDUCATION OF WOMEN

Historically, women have not been afforded equal educational opportunities in the United States. Furthermore, many authorities claim that U.S. schools have traditionally been sexist institutions. Although there is much evidence to support both these assertions, it is also true that an impressive list of women have made significant contributions to educational progress.

Colonial schools did not provide education for girls in any significant way. In some instances girls were taught to read, but females could not attend Latin grammar schools, academies, or colleges. We will look briefly at a few of the many outstanding female educators who helped to develop our country's educational system, in spite of their own limited educational opportunity.

EMMA WILLARD

Whereas well-to-do parents hired private tutors or sent their daughters away to a girls' seminary, girls from poor families were taught only to read and write at home (provided someone in the family had these skills). Emma Willard (1787–1870) was a pioneer and champion of education for females during a time when there were relatively few educational opportunities for them. She opened one of the first female seminaries in 1821 in Troy, New York, and this

Emma Willard (1787–1870) was a pioneer in female higher education who established Middlebury Female Seminary, Waterford Female Academy, and Troy Female Seminary.

school offered an educational program equal to that of a boys' school. In a speech designed to raise funds for her school, she proposed the following benefits of seminaries for girls:

1. Females, by having their understandings cultivated, their reasoning power developed and strengthened, may be expected to act more from the dictates of reason and less from those of fashion and caprice.
2. With minds thus strengthened, they would be taught systems of morality, enforced by the sanctions of religion; and they might be expected to acquire juster and more enlarged views of their duty, and stronger and higher motives to its performance.
3. This plan of education offers all that can be done to preserve female youth from contempt of useful labor. The pupils would become accustomed to it, in conjunction with the high objects of literature and the elegant pursuits of the fine arts; and it is to be hoped that both from habit and association they might in future life regard it as respectable.
4. The pupils might be expected to acquire a taste for moral and intellectual pleasures which would buoy them above a passion for show and parade, and which would make them seek to gratify the natural love of superiority by endeavoring to excel others in intrinsic merit rather than in the extrinsic frivolities of dress, furniture, and equipage.
5. By being enlightened in moral philosophy, and in that which teaches the operations of the mind, females would be enabled to perceive the nature and extent of that influence which they possess over their children, and the obligation which this lays them under to watch the formation of their characters with unceasing vigilance, to become their instructors, to devise plans for their improvement, to weed out the vices of their minds, and to implant and foster the virtues. And surely there is that in the maternal bosom which, when its pleadings shall be aided by education, will overcome the seductions of wealth and fashion, and will lead the mother to seek her happiness in communing with her children, and promoting their welfare.[4]

Many other female institutions were established and became prominent during the mid- and late 1800s, including Mary Lyon's Mount Holyoke Female Seminary; Jane Ingersoll's seminary in Cortland, New York; and Julia and Elias Mark's Southern Carolina Collegiate Institute at Barhamville, to name just a few. Unfortunately, not until well into the twentieth century were women generally afforded access to higher education.

Even though women eventually could attend college, they were not given equal access to all fields of study. Considerable progress has been made in recent years, but remnants of this problem still exist today.

GLOBAL PERSPECTIVES
Maria Montessori

Maria Montessori (1870–1952), born in Italy, became first a successful physician and later a prominent educational philosopher. She developed her own theory and methods of educating young children. Her methods utilized child-size school furniture and specially designed learning materials. She emphasized independent work by children under the guidance of a trained directress. Private Montessori schools thrive in the United States today.

Maria Montessori (1870–1952) developed a theory and methods for educating young children that are still practiced in the United States.

ELLA FLAGG YOUNG

Yet another example of an outstanding early female educator is Ella Flagg Young (c. 1845–1918). Overcoming immense obstacles, she earned a doctorate at the age of fifty under John Dewey, was appointed head of the Cook County

Normal School in Illinois, and became superintendent of the gigantic Chicago public school system in 1909—all achievements that were unheard of for a female at that time. She was also elected the first female president of the male-dominated National Education Association.

MARY McLEOD BETHUNE

Mary McLeod Bethune (1875–1955) was one of seventeen children born to African American parents in Mayesville, South Carolina, the first family member not born in slavery. She received her first formal schooling at age nine in a free school for African American children. It is reported that she would come home from school and teach her brothers and sisters what she had learned each day. She came to believe that education was the key to helping African American children move into the mainstream of American life, and she devoted her life to improving educational opportunities for young African American women. She eventually started the Daytona Normal and Industrial School for Negro Young Women and later Bethune-Cookman College, for which she served as president until 1942. She also believed that education helps everyone to respect the dignity of all people, regardless of color or creed, and is needed equally by Caucasian Americans, African Americans, and all other Americans. Mary McLeod Bethune went on to serve as founder and head of the National Council of Negro Women, director of the Division of Negro Affairs of the National Youth Administration, President Franklin D. Roosevelt's special advisor on minority affairs, and special consultant for drafting the charter of the United Nations. Mary McLeod Bethune was an effective, energetic human rights activist throughout her life and also a dedicated and professional career educator.

The fact that women have made significant contributions to our educational progress through the years has been well documented. In addition to the examples just mentioned and those discussed elsewhere in this book, we can add the following: Catharine Beecher (who founded the Hartford Female Seminary), Jane Addams (who proposed an expanded school as part of her new liberal social philosophy), Susan Anthony (who was a teacher in her early professional life), and Margarethe Meyer Schurz (who founded the first kindergarten in this country).

THE NINETEENTH AMENDMENT

The first great interest, on the part of various groups, in advancing the cause of females came about in the mid-1800s in the United States. The women's rights convention held at that time passed twelve resolutions that attempted to spur interest in providing females more equal participation and rights in U.S. society. The Civil War also furthered interest in the rights of women throughout the country, very likely as a spin-off of the abolition of slavery. It is interesting to note that not all of the people in favor of doing away with slavery supported improved rights for women. For instance, not until 1920, when the Nineteenth Amendment passed, did women have the right to vote.

Unfortunately, the right to vote did not necessarily do much to improve the status of women; females continued to be denied equal educational and employment opportunities. The civil rights movement after World War II served as another impetus to the women's movement and gave rise to an additional round of improvements for females in U.S. society. Some authorities would trace the emergence of the current feminist movement to the 1960s, when a variety of activist groups coalesced to work against discrimination of all kinds in U.S. society. Some groups and individuals feel that adequate educational provisions and opportunities for females, minorities, and those with disabilities are still lacking in our school systems today at all levels. What do you think?

Mary McLeod Bethune (1875–1955) believed that education was the key to helping African American children move into the mainstream of American life.

The school is an institution in which female status would be nurtured and encouraged.

Catharine Beecher

RECENT TRENDS IN EDUCATION

Education experienced a major change following World War II when John Dewey, George Counts, William Bagley, W. W. Charters, Lewis Terman, and other intellectuals who had held sway during the first half of the twentieth century yielded to a somewhat less philosophically oriented breed of researchers represented by Abraham Maslow, Robert Havighurst, Benjamin Bloom, J. P. Guilford, Lee Cronbach, Jerome Bruner, Marshall McLuhan, Noam Chomsky, and Jean Piaget.[5] The Progressive Education Association closed its doors, and a series of White House conferences on children, youth, and education were inaugurated in an attempt to improve education.

No school system on earth has been scrutinized, analyzed, and dissected as profoundly and as mercilessly as that in the United States. From the late 1940s to the mid-1950s, educational institutions at all levels were not only flooded with unprecedented numbers of students but also censored and flailed unmercifully by self-ordained critics (Hyman Rickover, Arthur Bestor, and Rudolph Flesch). In retrospect this frantic rush to simultaneously patronize and criticize the institution seems a curious contradiction. The public schools were characterized as "godless, soft, undisciplined, uncultured, wasteful, and disorganized." Critics who remembered the high failure rates on tests given to World War II draftees were determined to raise the public's levels of physical fitness and literacy; others who detected a weakening of moral and spiritual values were eager to initiate citizenship and character education programs. The enrollments in nonpublic schools doubled, correspondence schools of all kinds sprang into existence, and the popular press carried articles and programs designed to help parents augment the basic skills taught within the school program. In 1955 there were an estimated 450 correspondence schools serving 700,000 students throughout the country.

NEW EMPHASES IN EDUCATION

Fortunately, although some people were highly critical of the schools, not everybody panicked. There were physical fitness programs, character education projects, a general tightening of educational standards, and much more. J. P. Guilford, E. Paul Torrence, Jacob Getzels, and others explored the boundaries of creativity; Alfred Barr and D. G. Ryans carried out exhaustive studies of teacher characteristics; and just about everybody experimented with new patterns of organization. There were primary block programs; inter-age groupings; plans devised by and named for George Stoddard and J. Lloyd Trump; core programs; and a host of other patterns or combinations of plans structured around subject areas, broad groupings of subjects, or pupil characteristics. There were programs for the gifted and the not-so-gifted, and there was a new concern for foreign language instruction as well as the functional use of English. There was also a limited resurgence of Montessori schools and several one-of-a-kind experimental schools such as Amidon and Summerhill. While all this was taking place within the schools, the school systems themselves were consolidating; by 1960 there were only about one-third as many school districts as had existed twenty years earlier.

Automation was highly regarded during the 1950s, but the tools that gave education its biggest boost were more diverse. Social psychologists provided more advanced sociometric tools, which offered new insights into the functioning of groups; reading specialists and psychologists developed highly refined diagnostic instruments for use in studying learning disabilities; and statisticians devised new formulas and designs for controlling and analyzing data with the help of modern computers. New research tools such as regression formulas and factoral analysis yielded data that had been unobtainable earlier. On a somewhat less sophisticated level, more interesting and more flexible teaching tools were developed—audiovisual devices, learning games, more beautifully illustrated books, instructional television, machines for programmed instruction, and computers. Additional personnel such as teacher aides, counselors, social workers, and school psychologists became part of the school scene as well.

ANALYSIS OF TEACHING

Another emphasis found expression in the **analysis of teaching.** For half a century, researchers had been attempting to identify the characteristics and teaching styles that were most closely associated with effective instruction. Hundreds of studies had been initiated, and correlations had been done among them. During the 1950s, the focus began changing from identification of what ought to occur in teaching to scrutiny of what actually does occur. Ned Flanders and other researchers developed observational scales for assessing verbal communications between and among teachers and students. The scales permitted observers to categorize and summarize specific actions on the part of teachers and students. These analyses were followed by studies of nonverbal classroom behaviors.

Another series of investigations involving the wider range of instructional protocols was patterned after the time-and-motion studies used earlier for industrial processes. Dwight Allen and several other educators attempted to analyze teacher behaviors, delineate the components of effective teaching, and introduce teacher candidates to the elements judged most important to good teaching. The change in focus from studies of teacher characteristics to analyses of what actually occurs in classrooms has offered educators highly fruitful insights into teaching and learning and has provided usable instruments for further investigations of classroom behavior. It is now possible to assess the logical, verbal, nonverbal, affective, and several attitudinal dimensions of instruction as well as the intricate aspects of cognition and concept development.

TEACHER EFFECTIVENESS

Research has focused even more closely on the instructional patterns of effective teachers. A review by Marjorie Powell and Joseph Beard, *Teacher Effectiveness: An Annotated Bibliography,* catalogs more than 3,000 investigations into instructional competencies. The **effective teaching** movement based on this research offers today's teachers important skills. In common with the schoolteachers of sixty years ago, today's teachers learn to be strong leaders who direct classroom activities, maximize the use of instructional time, and teach in a clear, businesslike manner.

Effective teachers now employ structured, carefully delineated lessons. They break larger topics into smaller, more easily grasped components, and they focus on one thought, point, or direction at a time. They check prerequisite skills before introducing new skills or concepts. They accompany step-by-step presentations with many probing questions. Teachers offer detailed explanations of difficult points and test students on one point before moving on to the next. They provide corrective feedback where needed and stay with the topic under study until students comprehend the major points or issues. Effective teachers use prompts and cues to assist students through the initial stages of acquisition.

This recent emphasis on demonstration, prompting, and practice is a far cry from the relatively unstructured classroom activities of the recent past. We now emphasize carefully created learning goals and lesson sequences. It will be interesting to see whether the educational pendulum swings back to a new focus on student concerns and initiatives at some time in the future.

analysis of teaching
Procedures used to enable teachers to critique their own performance in the classroom.

effective teaching
A movement to improve teaching performance based on the outcomes of educational research.

"Never Smile before Thanksgiving"— Is That a Good Policy?

Historically, schools have been places where discipline has been rather harsh. The Roman educator Quintilian (35–95 CE) showed he was an early critic of harsh disciplinary practices when he suggested that students should be treated with kindness and patience. Teachers today still must develop their own philosophy of discipline. This debate explores one approach.

YES

Pat Morse-McNeely retired two years ago after 24 years as a secondary social studies, language arts, and special education teacher and guidance counselor in San Antonio, Stockdale, and Dallas, Texas. She also writes poetry.

I warn new teachers, "Don't be 'nice.'"

That is, be aware that you are a target. When school begins, you are being checked out on all sides. If you are looking back at those "mean" teachers of your school days and thinking you aren't going to be like them, better forget it! Those kids will know all the spots to hit in your personality by the time you pass out the supply list! This is not a sales pitch for meanness—no, no. It is a warning that a teacher must be on guard.

Students love to scope out ways to set you off, addle you, divert you from your goals for learning. Given the opening (however tiny), they will work you like a violin! Of course, you want to smile! Go ahead—but put something of "you'll be sorry if . . ." behind that smile that conveys very definitely who calls the shots. Laugh

NO

Christine Gold teaches English at Freedom High School in Tampa, Florida. She has taught for 10 years and was her district's Teacher of the Year for 2001–2002. In 2001, she won a Dow Jones Newspaper Fund award as an outstanding student newspaper advisor.

Two of my three brothers were teachers briefly—very briefly. When I decided to become an English teacher, they thought I had lost my mind. One brother's sage advice: "When you get your first class, remember not to smile until Thanksgiving." His adage wasn't exactly original. It represents many teachers' philosophies. In fact, many of my own teachers seemed grim-mouthed throughout the first semester each year. But, I must say, those were not the teachers who influenced me the most.

Many teachers seem to believe that being warm and friendly and maintaining rigorous academic standards are mutually exclusive. They assume that the well-liked teacher is a pushover. The notion that stu-

(continued)

SOCIOLOGICAL STUDIES

A major breakthrough in education has resulted from a series of sociological studies relating to social class, social perceptions, and academic achievement. James Coleman was among the first to demonstrate that it is not teaching equipment as much as children's social relationships that make the difference. Students' parents and peer groups at home and at school mold their perceptions and regulate their performances. These findings and those of Alan Rosenthall and Christopher Jencks have given new direction to schools' efforts. Educators' concerns have changed, at least partially, from educational hardware to studies of pupil populations.

STUDY OF THE LEARNING PROCESS

Several leading educational researchers in the United States and Europe have sought to analyze and describe how children learn. All of these investigators have stressed the importance of successful early learning patterns and the problems associated with serious learning deficits. They also believe that important

YES

NO

if you want to—but watch out for the trap that may be hidden behind the effort to get you to laugh.

Don't smile until Thanksgiving, but through your sternness, get across to your students: "You are important, you are capable, I expect the best from you, and yes, I love you."

Better than a smiling, cajoling, candy-dispensing, reward-giving teacher is one who may talk like you'll be skinned alive if you twitch your nose, but whose actions show he or she is in charge, expects the best from students, and can also be trusted to see you through a tough time.

One day when I was dressing down my students for their behavior, one of them blurted out, "But you love us anyway, don't you, Mrs. McNeely?" Since he was one of the central targets, I asked him "Why would I love you? Look at you!" He laughed and responded "But you do, don't you?" I laughed, too, and said, "Yes, I do—but I'll kill you anyway if you don't behave." And I truly did love him and most of the others—and oh, I still miss them and wonder if they are okay.

Funny—those who were the most troublesome, the actors, always in the soup—were the ones who came calling years later and said, "I learned a lot from you."

Source: " 'Never Smile before Thanksgiving'—Is That a Good Policy?" *NEA Today* (September 2002), p. 30.

dents will eat you alive if you appear kind and nurturing fosters an us-versus-them mentality.

The first two ideas I relay to my students are that they are welcome members in a learning community and that my academic standards are lofty. The establishment of my classroom as an academic haven is essential to my pedagogy. In order for scholarly ideas to flow freely, students must understand that their ideas are encouraged and valid. If those ideas are met with a cheerless demeanor, the student may feel intimidated and lose intellectual confidence.

Today's teachers are no longer mere purveyors of information. In our classrooms, we must create an atmosphere where students thrive academically, emotionally, and socially, and maintain high standards despite budget cuts, high-stakes testing, overcrowded classrooms, and a lack of parent support.

For many of my students, the five hours I spend with them in the classroom each week is considerably more time than they spend with their parents. As the family unit has continued to disintegrate, teachers have become the constant adult figures in children's lives. Our role as nurturers is unquestionable; it is a responsibility we should accept with a smile from the time a student walks across the threshold of our classroom until the day he or she crosses the stage, diploma in hand.

WHAT DO YOU THINK?
"Never smile before Thanksgiving"—is that a good policy?

To give your opinion, go to Chapter 8 of the companion website (**www.ablongman.com/johnson13e**) and click on Debate.

elements within the environment may be changed or modified to promote learning.

Robert Havighurst, a University of Chicago professor, identified specific developmental tasks that he believes children must master if they are to develop normally. He even suggests there may be periods during which certain tasks must be mastered if they are to become an integral part of children's repertoire of responses. There may also be "teachable moments" (periods of peak efficiency for the acquisition of specific concepts/skills) during which receptivity is particularly high. Havighurst, like Piaget, has caused educators to look carefully at the motivations and needs of children.

A contemporary of Havighurst, Jerome Bruner of Harvard, has also postulated a series of developmental steps or stages that he believes children encounter as they mature. These involve action, imagery, and symbolism. Bruner's cognitive views have stressed student inquiry and the breaking down of larger tasks into components.

Benjamin Bloom, author of Bloom's Taxonomy of Educational Objectives and distinguished service professor at the University of Chicago, has attempted

cognitive development
A learner's acquisition of facts, concepts, and principles through mental activity.

behavioral theory
A theory that considers the outward behavior of students to be the main target for change.

to identify and weigh the factors that control learning. He believes that one can predict learning outcomes by assessing three factors: (1) the cognitive entry behaviors of a student (the extent to which the pupil has mastered prerequisite skills), (2) the affective entry characteristics (the student's interest in learning the material), and (3) the quality of instruction (the degree to which the instruction offered is appropriate for the learner). Bloom's research is reflected in models of direct instruction, particularly mastery learning, in which teachers carefully explain, illustrate, and demonstrate skills and provide practice, reinforcement, corrective feedback, and remediation.

GLOBAL PERSPECTIVES

Jean Piaget

Jean Piaget (1896–1980), a Swiss psychologist, was educated at the University of Paris. Through his work with Alfred Binet, who developed one of the first intelligence tests, Piaget became interested in how children learn. He spent long hours observing children of different ages and eventually created a theory of mental or **cognitive development.** Piaget believed that children learn facts, concepts, and principles in four major stages. Up until about age two, he suggested, a child is at the *sensorimotor stage* and learns mainly through the hands, mouth, and eyes. From about two to seven years of age, a child is at the *preoperational stage* and learns primarily through language and concepts. Between ages seven and eleven, a child's learning is characterized by *concrete operations,* which involve the use of more complex concepts such as numbers. The final learning stage identified by Piaget is called the *formal operations* phase. This stage typically begins between ages eleven and fifteen and continues throughout adulthood. During this final stage, the learner employs the most sophisticated and abstract learning processes. Although children do not all fit neatly into these categories, Piaget's work has contributed much to educators' understanding of the learning process and has helped teachers develop more appropriate teaching strategies for students at different developmental stages.

Jean Piaget (1896–1980) was a Swiss developmental psychologist who researched children's stages of learning.

B. F. SKINNER

Burrhus Frederic (B. F.) Skinner (1904–1990) became one of the foremost early educational psychologists in U.S. education. He developed a **behavioral theory,** which was a theory focusing on outward behavior that suggested students could be successfully trained and conditioned to learn just about anything a teacher desired. This required the teacher to break down the learning into small sequential steps. Skinner even experimented with teaching machines that presented the learner with small sequential bits of information—an idea that has been revived today in computer-assisted instruction. Skinner published many works including *The Technology of Teaching, Beyond Freedom and Dignity,* and *Walden Two.* He contributed much to present-day understanding of human learning and helped to advance the technology of teaching.

Psychologist B. F. Skinner (1904–1990) developed a behavioral theory that suggested students could be trained, or conditioned, to learn just about anything a teacher desired.

◼ EDUCATIONAL CRITICS

Another development in education was triggered by a phalanx of critics, including Edgar Friedenberg *(Coming of Age in America);* Charles Silberman *(Crisis in the Classroom);* Jonathan Kozol *(Death at an Early Age);* Ivan Illich *(Deschooling Society);* John Holt *(How Children Fail);* and a government report, *A Nation at Risk* (1983), which focused on low educational standards. Some critics, such as Silberman, urge schools to refurbish what they already have; others, including Illich, want to abandon the schools altogether. These critics have not gone unnoticed. Friedenberg's call for alternatives to traditional education, Silberman's endorsement of open education, and Kozol's plea for equal opportunity are all reflected to some degree in innovative programs from coast to coast.

SCHOOL REFORM

Schools have constantly evolved, changed, and been reformed down through the ages, usually slowly, but sometimes rather quickly. The last several decades have witnessed relatively rapid school changes and reform in the United States. Some advocates of school reform would probably claim that there has been more talk about school reform than action. There is certainly some truth in this assertion, in large part because of talk on the part of politicians at all levels of government. Unfortunately, these same politicians have not always been willing to provide sufficient funding to improve our schools. In fact, political talk about school reform is often motivated by a desire to cut taxes.

Nevertheless, countless efforts to reform U.S. education have gone forward over the past sixty years. These have included small local efforts, many statewide mandated efforts, and even many national efforts, usually advocated by the federal government and/or the courts. Many of these more recent reform efforts are reported throughout this book. The past sixty years may well eventually be called "the school reform era" by future educational historians.

SCHOOL PUBLIC OPINION OVER THE PAST SIXTY YEARS

A public opinion survey, first conducted in 1950 and repeated in 1999, revealed the following interesting shifts over this sixty-year span: In 1950, 24 percent of those surveyed thought that teachers should be asked their political beliefs, whereas in 1999 only 9 percent thought so; in 1950, 39 percent said that religion should be taught in the public schools, whereas in 1999 the number had increased to 50 percent; in 1950, 44 percent said that teachers were underpaid, whereas in 1999, 61 percent said so; and in 1950, 67 percent of those polled thought that students were being taught more worthwhile and useful things in school than were children twenty years before, but in 1999 only 26 percent thought so. These shifts in public opinion about public schools provide food for thought for contemporary educators.

MAJOR EDUCATIONAL EVENTS OF THE PAST CENTURY

As we moved into the twenty-first century, many people reflected on educational accomplishments in the United States over the past hundred years. As would be expected, opinions differ considerably on this subject. Ben Brodinsky, an education journalist, has suggested that the GI Bill of Rights should perhaps be thought of as the single most important educational event of the past century. He lists the desegregation of schools as the second most important and the federal Education for All Handicapped Children Act as the third most important educational event of the twentieth century.

Undoubtedly, many important educational events and accomplishments occurred during the twentieth century—the list could go on and on. One example of significant progress made by the U.S. educational system in the past sixty years is reflected in the increase in the percentage of students completing high school: from about 50 percent in 1940 to about 70 percent in 1990. What would you put on your list of the most important educational events and/or accomplishments of the last century?

It is difficult to draw meaningful inferences from recent events that have not yet stood the test of time. Implications of recent educational events will eventually be found in the answers to questions such as these: What should be the role of the federal government in education? How can equal educational opportunity be achieved in the United States? How professionalized should the school system be? To what degree should educational policy and practice be influenced by litigation? How will school reform movements change the practice of education? The answer to these questions, and other questions you may have in mind, will be colored by the lenses through which people view the world, children, and schools. We believe that viewing all educational questions through well-informed historical lenses yields more valid answers.

■ THE VALUE OF HISTORY

CROSS-REFERENCE
Appendix D at the back of this book presents a brief, selected chronology of the history of education.

One rather obvious way in which historical knowledge can be useful to an educator is to help her or him capitalize on historical educational successes and avoid past educational failures. If a school district is contemplating moving to a new student grouping system, for instance, teachers would greatly profit from knowing the experiences of other schools that have used those student grouping systems in the past.

Many people have attempted to point out how knowledge of history can have practical uses and might help improve student learning. Sam Wineburg claims that knowledge of history has the potential of helping to humanize people. Building on this idea, Carl Degler suggests that knowledge of history might help a person better understand what it means to be human. Paul Gagnon asserts that developing some understanding of history helps a person mature, helps to hearten a person, and helps to set people free. David McCullough suggests that history has the potential to enlarge and intensify life and reminds us that history is by far the greatest part of human experiences. William McNeill points out that history tells us who we are and how to behave and that knowledge of past successes and failures has the potential to help us make correct choices more easily.

We hope that these ideas about the value of historical knowledge will help convince you that all educators can profit from a better understanding of the history of education and that such knowledge can help you improve student learning.

SUMMARY

Over the past sixty years, the U.S. education system has experienced unprecedented growth in both size and complexity. The great increase in numbers of students over these years has created a challenging need for more school buildings and many more teachers. Population increases and shifts from rural settings to cities require bigger schools and large, elaborate school busing systems. There has also been an amazing expansion of educational curricula and program diversification for different types of students at all levels over the past sixty years. All of this growth in size and programs has resulted in a tremendous increase in school budgets.

Programs for students with special needs have increased tremendously in recent history. There has also been notable growth in other educational programs de-

signed to better serve the needs of the increasingly diverse student population now found in our schools.

Our U.S. educational systems have also grown in complexity over the last sixty years, especially in funding and control. Our federal government has increased its involvement in public education through legislation such as the GI Bill, the National Science Foundation, the National Defense Education Act, the Elementary and Secondary Education Act, Project Head Start, Upward Bound, and the National Teacher Corp, to name just a few. And each of these federal acts, while providing funds for specific school programs, has also placed new demands and regulations on our schools.

Our court systems at all levels have made countless rulings over the last sixty years that have greatly affected our school systems. Notable among these court decisions have been those dealing with school racial integration, equal educational opportunity, parents' and students' rights, teachers' rights, the legal rights of various special populations, and the constitutionality of some laws.

Many other recent trends in education were also discussed in this chapter. These included professional advancements such as analysis of the teaching act, teacher effectiveness research, sociological studies, the development of new learning theories, and other research efforts designed to help us better understand and improve student learning. There have been an increasing number of

widely read critics of our schools over the past sixty years; examples include Friedenberg, Silberman, Kozol, Illich, and Holt. Various governmental agencies at the state and national levels have also been critical of our schools in recent years, resulting in many reports and calls for school reforms.

And finally, we sincerely hope that the historical lenses through which we have viewed education in this chapter, and the big historical ideas we have shared with you, have been of interest and will be of value to you as you continue on your professional journey.

DISCUSSION QUESTIONS

1. Other than those mentioned in this chapter, what additional recent educational developments seem particularly important to you? Why are they important?

2. Has the increased federal involvement in education been good or bad for schools? How so?

3. In your opinion, how much progress has the United States really made in providing equal educational opportunity? Defend your answer.

4. In what respect, if any, has education become professionalized, in your opinion?

5. What is happening in education at this very moment that is likely to be written about in future history of education books?

JOURNAL ENTRIES

1. Interview a retired teacher about the educational changes she or he has observed over the past sixty years. Ask what advice this retired educator has for beginning teachers today, and record the answers.

2. Describe and evaluate a learning experience you remember from your own elementary school days. What made the experience memorable, and what role did the teacher play in the learning process?

PORTFOLIO DEVELOPMENT

1. Prepare a creative educational history project (using a poster, videotape, audio recording, slide presentation, or some other creative medium) dealing with a topic, person, or idea that is of interest to you. Design your project so that it can be used as part of your job placement credentials.

2. Create a list of the most useful outcomes of U.S. education over the past sixty years. What can you as a beginning teacher learn, if anything, from your list?

PREPARING FOR CERTIFICATION

RESEARCH AND THEORIES OF LEARNING

1. One of the topics in the Praxis II Principles of Teaching and Learning (PLT) test is "encouraging students to extend their thinking" through an understanding of "stages and patterns of cognitive and cultural devel-

opment." In this chapter, you learned about the several researchers who developed theories about child development and learning processes. Make a list of the theorists and write two or three sentences about how they contributed to our understanding about how students think and learn.

2. Answer the following multiple-choice question, which is similar to items in Praxis and other state certification tests. If you are unsure of the answer, reread the Teacher Effectiveness section of this chapter.

The effective teaching movement was based on research focusing on the instructional patterns of effective teachers. Which of the following instructional patterns was *not* emphasized in the effective teaching movement?

(A) Teachers emphasize demonstration, prompting, and practice in their teaching.

(B) Teachers focus on student concerns and initiatives when constructing the lessons.

(C) Teachers check prerequisite skills before introducing new skills or concepts.

(D) Teachers emphasize carefully created learning goals and lesson sequences.

3. Answer the following short-answer question, which is similar to items in Praxis and other state certification tests. After you've completed your written response, use the scoring guide in the ETS *Test at a Glance* materials to assess your response. Can you revise your response to improve your score?

Reread the 1952 list of "Imperative Needs of Youth." Think about the relevance of this list for students today. Select the two objectives that you believe are most important today and two of the objectives that you believe are least important today and explain your choices.

WEBSITES

www.scholastic.com/Instructor The Scholastic Instructor site contains a variety of educational materials such as articles, contests, free materials for teachers, and chats with other educators on any subject, including the history of education.

www.si.edu This site provides links to each museum of the Smithsonian Institution in Washington, D.C., and includes much historical information.

www.cdickens.com/articles/dickjane.htm Information about the Dick and Jane readers that were used in many schools.

FURTHER READING

Campbell, John Martin. (1996). *The Prairie Schoolhouse.* Albuquerque: University of New Mexico Press. Contains information about rural schoolhouses common during the westward expansion of the United States.

Capella, Gladys, Geismar, Kathryn, and Nicoleau, Guitele (Eds.). (1995). *Shifting Histories: Transforming Schools for Social Change.* Cambridge, MA: Harvard Educational Publishing Group. A more detailed treatment of the history of education as it relates to social change in the United States.

Ravitch, Diane. (1983). *The Troubled Crusade: American Education 1945–1980.* New York: Basic Books. An excellent account of the history of relatively recent (1945–1980) education in the United States, written by a well-respected educational historian.

Spring, Joel. (1994). *The American School 1642–1990.* White Plains, NY: Longman. A useful survey of the history of education in the United States.

"The Struggle for Integration." (1999, March 24). *Education Week,* Part 3 of an excellent yearlong series dealing with the history of education.

Youniss, James, and McLellan, Jeffery A. (1999, October). "Catholic Schools in Perspective." *Phi Delta Kappan,* 81, 105–113. An article dealing with the history of Roman Catholic parochial schools.

THEMES OF THE TIMES!

expect the world®

The New York Times
nytimes.com

Expand your knowledge of the concepts discussed in this chapter by reading current and historical articles from the *New York Times* by visiting the Themes of the Times! section of the companion website (**www.ablongman.com/johnson13e**).

NOTES

1. "Teaching No Longer a Solitary Job," *The Christian Science Monitor* (July 22, 2003), p. 12.
2. U.S. Dept. of Commerce, Bureau of the Census, *Digest of Education Statistics 1982*. Washington, DC: U.S. Government Printing Office, 1982, p. 23.
3. W. H. G. Armytage, "William Byngham: A Medieval Protagonist of the Training of Teachers," *History of Education Journal, 2* (Summer 1951), p. 108.
4. Emma Willard, "A Plan for Improving Female Education" in *Women and the Higher Education.* New York: Harper & Brothers, 1893, pp. 12–14.
5. We thank Dr. Donald Barnes for many of the ideas presented in this section.

PART V

Philosophical Foundations of Education

Viewing Education through Philosophical Lenses

 The lens of philosophy provides a way to examine and interpret the world—to ask basic questions about human nature, beauty, principles of right and wrong, and how knowledge and reality are defined. Philosophical thinking helps to uncover the essentials—the basic principles that undergird teaching and learning.

The philosophical lens is especially important because our personal philosophy of life is seldom explicit. Rather, philosophy lives in peoples' minds and hearts and is seldom expressed in words or specific ideas. Our personal philosophy becomes evident in the manner in which we respond to everyday problems and questions. For example, we all conform to authority at least sometimes; some of us resist authority and tradition, and a few of us even seek out challenges to innovate or to defend our social order. But rarely do we examine our lives to find out what kinds of answers are evidenced by our actions, our hesitations, and our indifferences. The lens of philosophy helps us to focus on the underlying issues and assumptions and beliefs that are not always evident to us in the hectic pace of contemporary life.

Because philosophy deals with underlying values and beliefs, it naturally pervades all aspects of education. The lens of philosophy presents opposing views about human nature, knowledge, and the world in which we live. By examining these different, often opposing views, you will be able to identify your own philosophical position and state it in clearer language and concepts.

Focus Questions

The following questions will help you focus your learning as you read Part V:

1. What is knowledge? Is it merely the mastery of facts or is it the ability to solve problems?
2. Is knowledge the understanding of big ideas or is it the mastery of large quantities of information?
3. What are the implications of different views of knowledge for the teaching methods and assessment procedures that you choose to use?
4. Are children innately good, needing only gentle encouragement and guidance, or are children self-centered individuals who need to be disciplined and socialized?
5. What knowledge, skills, and attitudes are of most worth and should be part of every school curriculum?
6. Do teachers have a responsibility to question societal values and actively bring about social change or should they represent and articulate the current views of society to their students?

Philosophy: The Passion to Understand

Education in the News

High-Tech Cheating Hits Schools

MSNBC, February 18, 1999

THERE HAS ALWAYS BEEN SOME CHEATING ON TESTS—CRIB notes, or copying off another paper—but it's gotten so sophisticated and so widespread that it's raising serious questions about the integrity of young people and their education.

Espionage on campus is turning Joe College into James Bond as students try literally to steal better grades. The cutting-edge tools at their disposal include tiny spy cameras, noticeable only on extremely close inspection, hidden in beepers, watches and baseball caps.

Florida private eye Gregg Colton has seen it all. He chases such cheats for a living, exposing cameras hidden in jackets, on ties and in purses.

"These cameras are easily worn by anyone wanting to walk into a room. And they are capable of either direct recording onto a VCR, or transmission outside of the building to a waiting car," says Colton.

He says the cord to such a camera, and the power source, can come out of the back of a tie and is usually worked down through a person's pants and into a pocket where the recorder, or a transmitter, and a power source are kept.

From his pocket, the test taker can then broadcast the test to people waiting outside, who then quickly compute the answers. That's where the pagers come in.

Pagers are put in a quiet reception mode and then carefully rigged to reveal a string of test answers, one answer at a time, in the order the test was given.

When they have the opportunity, Colton says, test takers will either go to the restroom and look at the answer string, or simply take the pager off their belt during the exam and look at the strings and copy them down.

"This is a pager worn by almost everybody today in the United States. Very common," says Colton.

Colton also talks of secret "cram schools," one in particular in California, which was caught engraving answer keys for cheaters on pencils they take into exams.

A Widespread Problem

The Center for Academic Integrity says 70 percent of American college students admit to cheating on tests.

"It's big money. You pay between $250 and $9,000 to $10,000 to get this advance look at the exam that you're going to take," says Colton.

Students say it's the pressure that entices many to cheat.

Not Just Tests

But it's not just tests that students cheat on. The same study says 84 percent of college students cheat on term papers as well.

"I had to write a paper on *Pride and Prejudice* for an English class that I was not interested in at all," says one young woman, a senior from a major midwestern university who refused to identify herself. "I really did not like the teacher so I was doing everything I could to avoid doing this paper. And I had heard stories about getting papers off the Internet, but I didn't know how. And I couldn't believe how easy it was. I literally went to Yahoo!, typed in 'term papers' and I got a site to do it from."

The woman says she got a B+ on the term paper—which she did not write.

"There are so many Web sites out there that any college kid with a credit card can buy any paper," says University of Iowa professor Tom Rocklin, who wrote an academic paper that he published on the Internet titled, "Downloadable Term Papers: What's a Professor to Do?"

Teachers say cheaters are only cheating themselves.

"They have taken a transactional approach to their education," Rocklin said. "I give you something; you give me something. That's not what it's about. Education is "we help you grow."

What's more, some American educators fear that students are learning only what it takes to pass the test—even if it means using the tools of a spy.

"We adults are establishing a climate in which we show through our behavior and through what we emphasize that the thing that matters most is me, myself, [is] getting ahead," says Steven Carter, a Yale University law professor and the author of a book on integrity.

"Our children watch how their parents behave and what they learn is that the key to being a successful adult is making sure that nothing like a mere law or moral principle gets in the way of getting what I want," says Carter.

INTASC Learning Outcomes

After reading and studying this chapter, you should be able to:

1. Define philosophy and describe methods of inquiry used by philosophers. (INTASC 1: Subject Matter)

2. List major philosophical questions associated with the three major branches of philosophy: metaphysics, epistemology, and axiology. (INTASC 1: Subject Matter)

3. Elaborate on the major tenets of idealism, realism, pragmatism, and existentialism. (INTASC 1: Subject Matter)

4. Relate philosophical concepts to teaching and learning. (INTASC 4: Teaching Methods; INTASC 5: Motivation & Management; INTASC 8: Assessment)

5. Compare writers from different schools of philosophy: Plato, Kant, Martin, Aristotle, Locke, Whitehead, Peirce, Dewey, Rorty, Sartre, Nietzsche, and Greene. (INTASC 1: Subject Matter)

6. Describe the characteristics of Eastern and Native North American ways of knowing. (INTASC 3: Diversity; INTASC 9: Reflection)

School-Based Observations

You may see these learning outcomes in action during your visits to schools:

1. Many schools have written statements describing their philosophy of education. Ask several schools to send you a copy of their philosophy of education. When you receive them, look for similarities and differences among the philosophical statements.

2. As you visit schools and classrooms, be alert for indications of philosophical concepts and different philosophical views. Examine the lesson plans that teachers have developed and consider whether their focus is on subject matter acquisition, the development of character, or the development of skills. These emphases can be a clue to the type of philosophy that teacher endorses. You might wish to talk with teachers about their educational ideas.

3. As you visit schools and classrooms, focus on the discipline approaches that teachers employ. What do these approaches imply about teachers' views of human nature?

Although there are many different ways of defining philosophy, it is best thought of as a passion to understand the underlying meaning of everything. Derived from the Greek *philos*, which means "love," and *sophos*, which means "wisdom," the word *philosophy* means "love of wisdom." Early philosophers were fond of pointing out that they did not claim to be wise—they were merely lovers of wisdom. To many philosophers, conveying information is not as important as helping others in their own search for wisdom.

Searching for wisdom is closely related to the essence of multiculturalism. Philosophy demands a habit of mind that is always searching to understand and incorporate different points of view, different voices. Philosophy compels us to consider the beauty and cohesion of seemingly diverse worlds of thought and existence.

In this chapter, you will explore different ways of looking at the world in which you live. Such big ideas as metaphysics, epistemology, axiology, schools of philosophy, human nature, ways of knowing, and analytic and prophetic thinking will offer very different perspectives about yourself and your place in the larger world. This chapter presents a unique way of thinking about societal issues and education. You will see how the art of asking larger questions about the nature of things can either clarify or challenge your personal beliefs about teaching and learning, about values and societal norms, about discipline and motivation.

STRUCTURE AND METHODOLOGY OF PHILOSOPHY

Education is inextricably intertwined with a passion to understand. Both philosophy and education are vitally concerned with a search for truth. By its very name, education calls teachers "to lead from ignorance." Philosophy compels teachers to lead students in a direction that is meaningful and of most worth. Philosophy reminds teachers to continue the search for truth and not be satisfied with pat answers, even answers that are provided by so-called experts. To a philosopher, an expert is not one who professes truth or beauty; an expert is one who searches and questions.

Education presupposes ideas about human nature, the nature of reality, and the nature of knowledge. These questions are ultimately of a philosophical character. Teachers must constantly confront the underlying assumptions that guide conduct, determine values, and influence the direction of all existence. Hence, the study of philosophy is at the heart of the study of education.

THE BRANCHES OF PHILOSOPHY

Philosophy is not a collection of sterile, objective facts. Rather, it is like an internal desire; it drives persons to search for better answers and better understandings. At its deepest level, philosophy consists of sets of profound and basic questions that remain constant because the basic dilemmas posed by these questions are yet to be answered adequately. At this basic level, philosophy does not provide answers; rather, it offers a range of possibilities or arguments that can be examined and used to guide decisions.

Because the questions of philosophy are so important, the study of philosophy is structured around them. Philosophy includes branches that investigate large and difficult questions—questions about reality or being, about knowledge, about goodness and beauty and living a good life. Throughout the centuries, entire branches of philosophy have evolved that specialize in and center on major questions. For example, questions about the nature of reality or existence are examined in metaphysics, questions about knowledge and truth are considered in epistemology, and questions about values and goodness are central to axiology.

METAPHYSICS

Metaphysics is a branch of philosophy that is concerned with questions about the nature of reality. Literally, *metaphysics* means "beyond the physical." It deals with such questions as "What is reality?"; "What is existence?"; "Is the

metaphysics

An area of philosophy that deals with questions about the nature of ultimate reality.

universe rationally designed or ultimately meaningless?" Metaphysics is a search for order and wholeness—a search applied not to particular items or experiences but to all reality and to all existence.

In brief, metaphysics is the attempt to find coherence in the whole realm of thought and experience. Concerning the world, metaphysics includes the question of what causes events in the universe to happen, including the theories of creation and evolution. Metaphysics also involves questions concerning the nature of humans. Is human nature physical or spiritual? What is the relationship between mind and body? Does a person make free choices, or do events and conditions force one into determined decisions?

The questions in metaphysics, especially those about humanity and the universe, are extremely relevant to teachers and students of education. Theories about how the universe came to be and about what causes events in the universe are crucial if scholars are to interpret the physical sciences properly. George F. Kneller writes about the power of metaphysics in generating questions that lack scientific answers.

> Teachers often say, "If Johnnie kept his mind on his work, he would have no trouble in school." But what does the teacher mean here by "mind"? Is the mind different from the body? How are the two related? Is the mind the actual source of thoughts? Perhaps what we call "mind" is not an entity at all. Physiological and psychological studies of the brain have given us factual information and cyberneticians have compared the mind (or brain) to a computer. But such comparisons are crude; they do not satisfy our concern about the ultimate nature of the mind. Here again, knowing metaphysics and being able to think metaphysically helps the teacher when considering questions of ultimate meaning.[1]

A teacher's classroom approach will be linked to the teacher's metaphysical beliefs. If, for example, the teacher believes that very specific basic knowledge is crucial to the child's intellectual development, it is likely that this teacher will focus on the subject matter. If, on the other hand, the teacher holds that the child is more important than any specific subject matter, it is likely that this teacher will focus on the child and allow the child to provide clues as to how he or she should be instructed.

EPISTEMOLOGY

Epistemology is a branch of philosophy that examines questions about how and what we know. What knowledge is true, and how does knowledge take place? The epistemologist attempts to discover what is involved in the process of knowing. Is knowing a special sort of mental act? Is there a difference between knowledge and belief? Can people know anything beyond the objects with which their senses acquaint them? Does knowing make any difference to the object that is known?

Because epistemological questions deal with the essence of knowledge, they are central to education. Teachers must be able to assess what is knowledge to determine whether a particular piece of information should be included in the curriculum. How people know is of paramount importance to teachers because their beliefs about learning influence their classroom methods. Should teachers train students in the scientific methods, deductive reasoning, or both? Should students study logic and fallacies or follow intuition? Teachers' knowledge of how students learn influences how they will teach.

AXIOLOGY

Axiology is a branch of philosophy that deals with the nature of values. It includes such questions as "What is good?" and "What is beautiful?" Questions about what should be or what values we hold are highlighted in axiology. This study of values is divided into ethics (moral values and conduct) and aesthet-

Many important decisions we make have ethical dimensions: What should we teach? How should we treat students, parents, teachers, and administrators? In order to address such matters, we must conceive of moral bases on which to make these decisions and try to forecast the potential ramifications of them for individuals and society.

Gail McCutcheon

epistemology

An area of philosophy that examines questions about how and what we know

axiology

An area of philosophy that deals with the nature of values. It includes questions such as "What is good?" and "What is value?"

ics (values in the realm of beauty and art). Ethics deals with such questions as "What is the good life?" and "How should we behave?" One major question to be examined is "When does the end justify any means of achieving?" Aesthetics deals with the theory of beauty and examines such questions as "Is art public and representative, or is it the product of private creative imagination?"[2] Good citizenship, honesty, and correct human relations are all learned in schools. Sometimes these concepts are taught explicitly; but often students learn ethics from *who* the teacher is as well as from *what* the teacher says.

Both ethics and aesthetics are important issues in education. Should a system of ethics be taught in the public school? If so, which system of ethics should be taught? Aesthetics questions in education involve deciding which artistic works should or should not be included in the curriculum and what kind of subject matter should be allowed or encouraged in a writing, drawing, or painting class. Should teachers compromise their own attitudes toward a piece of artwork if their opinion differs from that of a parent or a school board?

■ THINKING AS A PHILOSOPHER

Philosophy provides the tools people need to think clearly. As with any discipline, philosophy has a style of thinking as well as a set of terms and methodologies that distinguish it from other disciplines. Philosophers spend much of their energy developing symbols or terms that are both abstract (apply to many individual cases) and precise (distinguish clearly). Developing ideas that embrace more and more instances (abstraction) while at the same time maintaining a clear and accurate meaning (precision) is difficult, but this tension is at the heart of the philosopher's task. The entire process is what is meant by understanding: uncovering the underlying, the foundational, and the essential principles of reality.

In the physical sciences, experimenters try to do the same thing when they devise a theory. The major difference between the scientist who empirically examines the material world and the philosopher who examines all reality is that the physical scientist mainly targets particular events or things in the material world and then tries to explain these events by some theory. The philosopher, on the other hand, strives to clarify the underlying principles for all events, material or immaterial, that are logically related. Philosophers tend to search for concepts that are larger than what the physical scientist is researching, and they also examine not only what seems to be but what ought to be.

There is great variety in the ways philosophers think. Hence it is difficult to set forth a simple set of rules or thinking steps that can accurately be labeled philosophical thinking. To give you a sense of philosophical thinking, it is easier (and more accurate) to describe two different thinking styles that philosophers use interchangeably as they wrestle with large, unstructured questions. The first way of thinking can be labeled **analytic thinking.** Philosophers employ this style when they attempt to examine questions of the "what seems to be" type. A second philosophical style of thinking is called **prophetic thinking.** It focuses on questions of the "what ought to be" type.

ANALYTIC WAYS OF THINKING IN PHILOSOPHY

When philosophers encounter a contemporary problem, they often spend time analyzing it, attempting to clarify or find the "real" problem, not just the surface issues. To do so, philosophers use abstraction, imagination, generalization, and logic. These analytic thinking processes help focus the problem clearly and precisely.

ABSTRACTION   The notion of **abstraction** covers a multitude of meanings. The word *abstract* is derived from the Latin verb *abstrahere*, meaning to "draw

Being a philosopher, I have a problem for every solution.
Robert Zend

analytic thinking

A thinking strategy that focuses on questions of the "what seems to be" type; includes abstractions, imagination, generalization, and logic.

prophetic thinking

A thinking strategy that focuses on questions of the "what ought to be" type; includes discernment, connection, tracking hypocrisy, and hope.

abstraction

A thought process that involves drawing away from experiences to a conceptual plane.

away." Abstraction, then, involves drawing away from a concrete level of experience to a conceptual plane of principles or ideas. The process of abstraction can be thought of as a three-step process that moves thinking from singular concrete instances to more general, universal ideas. The three steps involve (1) focusing attention on some feature within one's experience, (2) examining the precise characteristics of the feature, and (3) remembering the feature and its characteristics later so as to apply them to other instances or combine them with other ideas.

In general, philosophers distinguish between two basic types of abstraction: (1) parts, or abstractions of characteristics that could also be physically removed (features such as tabletops, legs, drawers, and the like), and (2) attributes, or abstractions of characteristics that cannot be physically removed, such as shape, structure, or form. This second type of abstract thinking is the stuff of philosophers; they seek to understand the essential aspects of both material and immaterial things. These underlying, substantial aspects are sometimes referred to as qualities, relations, and functions.

When teachers are asked to examine a new textbook series, for example, they will often be presented with promotional material about the important subject matter and learning tools that the series contains. The process of abstraction helps teachers pull away from the "bells and whistles" or the concrete examples in the text. Abstraction enables teachers to consider the underlying themes that are implicit and that provide a cohesive structure to the entire text series. Abstraction helps teachers uncover hidden messages.

IMAGINATION AND GENERALIZATION   According to Herbert Alexander,[3] the second step of analytic thinking is the use of imagination. Imagination can be thought of as the altering of abstractions. In philosophy the use of imagination assists the process of abstraction by filling in the details of an idea, selecting details, and relating ideas to one another.

Imaginative explorations occur in many different ways. Usually, they occur when a person first focuses on some abstraction or idea. Ideas come when one makes observations, reflects about past experiences, reads, views a dramatic work or piece of art, or converses with others. Once ideas are selected, imaginative explorations can be made about them. Basic assumptions about things can be examined, arguments can be justified or clarified, and ideas can be distinguished from or related to other ideas. Experiential evidence, logical consistency, and a host of other criteria can be employed. The outcome of the whole imaginative process is the development of a system of ideas that has greater clarity and more interrelationships to other ideas or sets of propositions. This last step of the imaginative exploration process is sometimes referred to as *generalization,* because it ultimately results in the development of a comprehensive set of ideas.

Generalization sets ranges and limits to the abstractions that have been altered by imagination. As one's imagination relates more and more ideas to one another, the process of generalization determines which relationships should be emphasized or de-emphasized.

As an example of the analytical thinking process, consider a simple chair that is located in a kitchen. First, the philosopher would abstract from the chair some idea on which to focus; for instance, the idea of support. Support is an underlying substantial characteristic of all chairs. Second, the philosopher might imagine how many physical parts of a chair could be removed without loss of the chair's ability to provide support. Are four legs always necessary for support? What must be supported for an object to be a chair? As the philosopher ponders these questions (which are spurred by the imagination), precise generalizations can be made about basic aspects of the concept of support. New questions or hypotheses can be developed. For example, how does the support

Creativity consists largely of rearranging what we know in order to find out what we normally take for granted. Hence, to think creatively, we must be able to look afresh at what we normally take for granted.

George Kneller

provided by chairs relate to the support that a teacher should provide to students? What does teaching support really mean?

When teachers consider new ways to support student motivation, they can use the same analytic thinking processes. For example, teachers often imagine different types of mathematics contests or science Olympiads that might spur students' interests. As they imaginatively apply these contests to the classroom setting, teachers might abstract the competitiveness component as a necessary aspect of contests and Olympiads. Teachers might then wonder about the hidden messages of winning at the expense of others' losses. Teachers might generalize that the competitive approach could bring about knowledge wars; knowledge contests might make students less willing to share what they know with others. To complete this inquiry, teachers need to use logic.

LOGIC Philosophy deals with the nature of reasoning and has designated a set of principles called *logic.* Logic examines the principles that allow us to move from one argument to the next. There are many types of logic, but the two most commonly studied are deductive and inductive logic. Deduction is a type of reasoning that moves from a general statement to a specific conclusion. Induction is a type of reasoning that moves in the opposite direction, from the particular instance to a general conclusion.

Philosophy provides the tools people need in order to think clearly. It is important for educators to have a philosophy, both as a means of developing their ability to think clearly about what they do on a day-to-day basis and as a means of seeing how their workaday principles and values extend beyond the classroom to the whole of humanity and society. Figure 9.1 describes how analytic ways of thinking help teachers solve a classroom problem. Studying philosophy enables you to recognize the underlying assumptions and principles of things so you can determine what is significant.

PROPHETIC WAYS OF THINKING IN PHILOSOPHY

In contrast to the search for underlying universal principles that is the focus of an analytic way of thinking, *prophetic thinking* seeks to uncover multiple, even divergent realities or principles. Prophetic thinking has emerged as a counterpoint to the highly successful but rigid analytic thinking style. According to Cornel West, a prophetic thinker is one who goes beyond abstraction. A prophetic thinker lives in multiple realities, feeling and touching these realities to such a degree that understanding is ultimately achieved. And a prophetic thinker understands multiple realities so well that bridges can be built between and among the multiple worlds. In his book *Prophetic Thought in Postmodern Times,* West identifies four basic components of prophetic thinking: discernment, connection, tracking hypocrisy, and hope.[4]

DISCERNMENT Discernment is the capacity to develop a vision of what should be out of a sophisticated understanding of what has been and is. This

Specific Problem Confronts a Teacher
"Why do some students in my classroom fail to complete their homework?"

ABSTRACTION

Draw Away from the Specifics
- What motivates my students?
- What inhibits my students from completing any work at home?
- What motivates human beings?

IMAGINATION AND GENERALIZATION

Consider Possibilities
- People like freedom.
- People enjoy completing tasks that they do well.

LOGIC

Rationally Evaluate
- I need to allow more choices for students.
- I need to examine the home context of students who repeatedly fail to complete their homework.

FIGURE 9.1 Analytic Ways of Thinking: Focus and Solve Problems Clearly and Precisely

Teachers not only teach content but also find ways to help students seek connections to the world around them and apply ideas to their daily lives.

first component of prophetic thought is quite different from the abstract approach of the analytic thinker. The prophetic thinker is more concerned with the concrete, specific aspects of reality. To discern a situation is to take the entire situation into account to get beyond abstract principles. A discerning teacher is one who sees beyond mere test scores, beyond simple classroom rules. A discerning teacher examines the total content of a child's life and makes decisions based on this context. An outsider could criticize a discerning teacher for bending rules or being inconsistent. Yet a prophetic thinker would applaud the teacher for being wise. The prophetic thinker is a bit of a historian, building the future on the best of the past and present.

CONNECTION   A prophetic thinker must relate to or connect with others. Rather than considering humankind in the abstract, prophetic thinkers value and have empathy for other human beings. They show empathy, the capacity to get in contact with the anxieties and frustrations of others.

Many teachers really do care and work hard to help students. However, they are often unable to make the connection that would complete caring relations with their students. Teachers' willingness to empathize with students is often thwarted by society's desire to establish teaching on a firm scientific footing. But to students, the failure to connect means that teachers sometimes look as though they simply do not care. According to Nel Noddings,[5] both teachers and students have become victims in the search for the one best method of instruction.

Hypocrisy—Prejudice with a halo.

Ambrose Bierce

TRACKING HYPOCRISY   Although the relationship between empathy and teaching is important, it is equally important for the prophetic teacher to identify and make known "the gap between principles and practice, between promise and performance, between rhetoric and reality."[6] Tracking hypocrisy ought to be done in a self-critical rather than in a self-righteous manner. It takes boldness as well as courage to point out inconsistencies between school policies and practices, but when doing so a prophetic teacher remains open to others' points of

Should Morals and Values Be Taught in Public Schools?

Should a teacher instruct students about values and matters of right and wrong? You may feel that this question demands an obvious affirmative answer. A problem arises, however, when you are asked to clarify the specific values that should be taught. How do you, as a teacher in a multicultural school setting, determine what moral values should be the focus of instruction?

One school of thought, influenced largely by the work of Lawrence Kohlberg, endorses direct instruction in moral development. The educational theorists who endorse this position contend that there exists a body of morals that spans all cultures. This body of morals can be articulated at any point in time and should be taught directly to students in public schools. People—especially parents—may also feel that children are faced with an increasingly complex and dangerous society and cannot be expected simply to absorb the proper morals and values from the world around them. Because of this, the schools should step in.

In contrast to this point of view, those influenced by the educational theories proposed by Syd Simon in

his text *Values Clarification* reject the direct instruction of morals on the grounds that democracy demands that its citizens be free to clarify their own sets of values. This school of thought calls for public schools to refrain from the direct instruction of morals and asks teachers to help students define their own sets of individually selected values. The approach requires teachers to remain neutral in their presentations of opposing value systems. The teacher's role is simply to assist students in the clarification of the consequences of selecting any one set of morals or values.

This difficult problem of teaching morals and values is especially problematic for a democracy.

- Who shall select the set of values to be taught?
- If the majority is given this right, then what becomes of the individual rights of minorities?
- Yet is it possible to teach a value-free curriculum?
- Does the very act of instruction imply a certain value system expressed and upheld by the individual teacher?

To answer these questions on-line and e-mail your answers to your professor, go to Chapter 9 of the Companion Website (**www.ablongman.com/johnson13e**) and click on Professional Dilemma.

---

view. New evidence might reveal that one's position is no longer valid, or it might enhance one's original thinking. Figure 9.2 describes how prophetic ways of thinking help teachers solve a classroom problem.

The important aspect of tracking hypocrisy is not being right or wrong but helping others and oneself examine the relationship between what is said and what is practiced. Recently, for example, the hypocrisy of standardized norm-referenced testing has been tracked by many prophetic educators. Although to date no clear alternatives have been uncovered, there is increased interest in and experimentation with new forms of testing, thanks to the courage of critical educators.

HOPE   The fourth and perhaps most important component of prophetic thought is simply hope. West admits that given the numerous and horrific examples of people's inhumanity to one another, it is hard to take hope seriously. Still, without it, all thought is meaningless. West says:

> To talk about human hope is to engage in an audacious attempt to galvanize and energize, to inspire and to invigorate world-weary people. Because that is what we are. We are world-weary; we are tired. For some of us there are misanthropic skeletons hanging in our closet. And by misanthropic I mean the notion that we have given up on the capacity to do anything right; the capacity of human communities to solve any problem.[7]

Specific Problem Confronts a Teacher
"Why do some students in my classroom fail to complete their homework?"

DISCERNMENT

Develop a Vision of What Should Be

Children and adults should be free to develop in a variety of ways and according to individual needs.

CONNECTION

Relate and Show Empathy to Others

I have felt constrained by school assignments and rigid academic requirements.

TRACKING HYPOCRISY

What Is the Gap between Principles and Practice?

Why do I require homework? Do I allow for student choice?

HOPE

The World Can Change for the Better

I will examine our school's philosophy and mission and discuss the implications for our children with my fellow teachers.

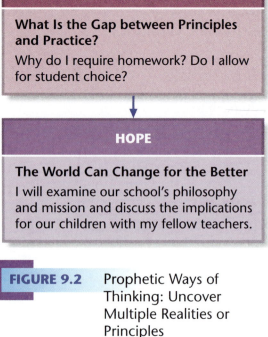

FIGURE 9.2 Prophetic Ways of Thinking: Uncover Multiple Realities or Principles

West challenges educators to see "skeletons" as challenges, not as conclusions. Even when confronted with educators' failures at creating a better community of scholars, the prophetic teacher must remember that the world is unfinished, that the future is open-ended, and that what teachers think and do can make a difference.

RELIGION AND PHILOSOPHY

The relationship between religion and philosophy is complex. One way to approach this relationship is to consider religious beliefs as a *filter* through which persons evaluate different philosophic ideas. Depending on one's faith, a person will tend to endorse certain points of view and philosophical arguments or reject certain points of view. In this approach, religious beliefs provide a framework or set of criteria against which to determine if a philosophic argument or idea is valid. This approach implies that religion is separate from philosophy but exerts an external force against which philosophic ideas are deemed acceptable or unacceptable.

Another way of thinking about the relationship between religion and philosophy is to use philosophy as a *means to support* one's religious beliefs. As in the filter view, religion remains a prior value and philosophy is subordinate. When philosophy is viewed as a means to support, it is an integral aspect of religion because through philosophic thinking, religious tenants are strengthened.

A third way of thinking about the relationship between philosophy and religion is to view the two as an *integrated* way of thinking about the nature of the world and our relationship to the world. In this integrated view, philosophy and religion work hand in hand. Neither beliefs nor philosophical principles have a prior place; both beliefs and principles contribute to an understanding about the nature of all reality. Religious beliefs change and philosophic principles are modified conjointly.

SCHOOLS OF PHILOSOPHY AND THEIR INFLUENCE ON EDUCATION

As philosophers attempt to answer questions, they develop answers that are clustered into different schools of thought. These schools of philosophical thought are somewhat contrived; they are merely labels developed by others who have attempted to show the similarities and differences among the many answers philosophers develop. Throughout the centuries, these schools of philosophic thought have been used as organizing frameworks for the diversity of responses from so many thinkers. As you examine the schools of thought described in this section, keep in mind that the philosophers who represent these schools are individual thinkers, like yourself, who do not limit their thinking to the characteristics of any one label or school of thought. Four well-known schools of thought are idealism, realism, pragmatism, and existentialism. In addition to these, we will touch on Eastern thought and Native North American thought. Technically, these two final clusters of thought are not termed *schools* because they encompass greater diversity and often extend beyond the limits of philosophy into beliefs, customs, and group values.

idealism

A school of philosophy that considers ideas to be the only true reality.

IDEALISM

The roots of idealism lie in the thinking of the Greek philosopher Plato. Generally, idealists believe that ideas are the only true reality. It is not that idealists reject the material world; rather, they hold that the material world is characterized by constant change and uncertainty, whereas ideas endure throughout time. Hence, **idealism** is a school of philosophy that holds that ideas or concepts are the essence of all that is worth knowing. The physical world we know through our senses is only a manifestation of the spiritual world (metaphysics). Idealists believe in the power of reasoning and de-emphasize the scientific method and sense perception, which they hold suspect (epistemology). They search for universal or absolute truths that will remain constant throughout the centuries (axiology).

EDUCATIONAL IMPLICATIONS OF IDEALISM

The educational philosophy of the idealist is idea-centered rather than subject-centered or child-centered because the ideal, or the idea, is the foundation of all things. Knowledge is directed toward self-consciousness and self-direction and is centered in the growth of rational processes about the big ideas. Some idealists note that the individual, who is created in God's image, has free will and that it is this free will that makes learning possible. The idealist believes that learning comes from within the individual rather than from without. Hence, real mental and spiritual growth do not occur until they are self-initiated.

Idealists' educational beliefs include an emphasis on the study of great leaders as examples for us to imitate. For idealists the teacher is the ideal model or example for the student. Teachers pass on the cultural heritage and the unchanging content of education, such as knowledge about great figures of the past, the humanities, and a rigorous curriculum. Idealists emphasize the methods of lecture, discussion, and imitation. Finally, they believe in the importance of the doctrine of ideas.

No one philosopher is an idealist. Rather, philosophers answer questions, and some of their answers are similar. These similarities are what make up the different schools of philosophy. To describe adequately any one school of philosophy, such as idealism, one needs to go beyond these general similarities to examine the subtle differences posed by individual thinkers. Plato and Socrates, Immanuel Kant, and Jane Roland Martin represent different aspects of the idealist tradition.

PLATO AND SOCRATES

According to Plato (c. 427–c. 347 BCE), truth is the central reality. Truth is perfect; it cannot, therefore, be found in the world of matter because the material world is both imperfect and constantly changing. Plato did not think that people create knowledge; rather, they discover it. In one of his dialogues, he conjectures that humanity once had true knowledge but lost it by being placed in a material body that distorts and corrupts that knowledge. Thus, humans have the arduous task of trying to remember what they once knew.

The modern world knows the philosophy of Socrates only through Plato, who wrote about him in a series of texts called "dialogues." Socrates (c. 470–399 BCE) spoke of himself as a midwife who found humans pregnant with knowledge, but knowledge that had not been born or realized. This Socratic "Doctrine of Reminiscence" speaks directly to the role of the educator.

Idealists—Foolish enough to throw caution to the winds . . . have advanced mankind and have enriched the world.
Emma Goldman

Ideals are like stars: you will not succeed in touching them with your hands, but like the seafaring man on the desert of waters, you choose them as your guides, and following them you reach your destiny.
Carl Schurz

RELEVANT RESEARCH
Using Socratic Dialogue to Enhance Reflective Learning

STUDY PURPOSE/QUESTIONS: The ancient philosophers Socrates and Plato believed that learning is best achieved through dialogue. Both philosophers contended that a teacher's main task is to ask good questions. By so doing the learner would reason to new knowledge. Socratic dialogue has been the topic of research studies in contemporary education and is now described as a dual-way communication between a teacher or tutor and a learner. The teacher does not teach a subject by direct exposition. Instead, learners' beliefs are challenged by the teacher through a series of questions that lead learners to reflect on their beliefs, induce general principles, and discover gaps and contradictions in their beliefs.

Using this type of questioning strategy is difficult when attempting to teach precise mathematical, scientific relationships. Researchers have proposed a Pictorial Socratic Dialogue coined to refer to a Socratic dialogue involving only graphics (e.g., drawings of objects or Cartesian graphs).

STUDY DESIGN: All student participants were asked to investigate a Spring Balance System on their own. The Spring Balance System models a set of experimental apparatus that is employed for the verification of Archimedes' Principle in a physics laboratory. Students were randomly assigned to three different learning conditions. Prior to beginning the experiment, all students were pretested on the mathematical and physics principles surrounding Archimedes' Principle. One group of students investigated the Spring Balance System with the help of a teacher who assumed the role of a Socratic tutor and who prescribed immediate and intelligent feedback based on the Socratic questioning method. A second group of students investigated the Spring Balance System with the help of a Socratic tutor as well as the assistance of an articulation tool. The articulation tool offers different problems that have similar solutions (DPSS) and similar problems with different solutions (SPDS). The Socratic tutor not only provided questions but also used the different DPSS and SPDS problems to guide the learning of the students.

STUDY FINDINGS: After both groups of students investigated the Spring Balance System, students were post-tested. Results showed that all students improved their understanding of Archimedes' Principle. However, students who only received the help of Socratic Dialogue improved their understanding on a surface level and did not achieve a more abstract understanding of critical attributes. Students who were assisted by both Socratic Dialogue and the DPSS and SPDS problems significantly improved both surface level and abstract understanding concerning Archimedes' Principle.

IMPLICATIONS: Socratic dialogue is an effective teaching tool. When teachers guide the development of students' understandings, learning occurs. However, when teachers wish to help students understand technical, abstract principles, Socratic dialogue needs to be enhanced by carefully structured, supporting problems that are designed to make explicit to the learner underlying critical entities that might be missed.

Source: Ah-Lian Kor, John Self, and Ken Tait, "Pictorial Socratic Dialogue and Conceptual Change," 2001 International Conference on Computers in Education, AACE-APC (Association for the Advancement of Computing in Education-Asia Pacific Chapter) Computer-Based Learning Unit, University of Leeds, Woodhouse Lane, Leeds LS29JT,UK., www.icce2001.org/cd/pdf/P02/UK002.pdf.

Teachers need to question students in such a way as to help them remember what they have forgotten. In the dialogue *Meno*, Plato describes Socrates' meeting a slave boy and through skillful questions leading the boy to realize that he knows the Pythagorean theorem, even though he does not know that he knows it. This emphasis on bringing forth knowledge from students through artful questioning is sometimes called the Socratic method.

Socrates' and Plato's ideas have stimulated a great deal of thinking about the meaning and purpose of humankind, society, and education. Their ideas have influenced almost all philosophers who came after them, whether others supported or rejected their basic ideas. Alfred North Whitehead even stated that modern philosophy is but a series of footnotes to Plato.

Writing in the *Republic,* Plato depicts his central ideas about knowledge in an allegory about human beings living in a cave:

> If I am right, certain professors of education must be wrong when they say that they can put knowledge into the soul which was not there before, like sight into a blind eye. . . . Whereas, our argument shows that the power and capacity of learning exists in the soul already; and that just as the eye was unable to turn from darkness to light without the whole body, so too the instrument of knowledge can only by the movement of the whole soul be turned from the world of becoming into that of being, and learn by degrees to endure the sight of being, and of the brightest and best of being, or in other words, of the good.[8]

IMMANUEL KANT

The German philosopher Immanuel Kant (1724–1804), in the *Metaphysics of Morals* and the *Critique of Practical Reason,* spelled out his idealistic philosophy. Kant believed in freedom, the immortality of the soul, and the existence of God. He wrote extensively on human reason and noted that the only way humankind can know things is through the process of reason. Hence, reality is not a thing unto itself but the interaction of reason and external sensations. Reason fits perceived objects into classes or categories according to similarities and differences. It is only through reason that we acquire knowledge of the world. Once again, it is the idea or the way that the mind works that precedes the understanding of reality.

In the *Critique of Pure Reason,* Kant clarifies the relationship between *a priori* and *a posteriori* knowledge:

> But, though all our knowledge begins with experience, it by no means follows that all arises out of experience. For, on the contrary, it is quite possible that our empirical knowledge is a compound of that which we receive through impressions, and that which the faculty of cognition supplies for itself (sensuous impressions given merely the *occasions*), an addition which we cannot distinguish from the original element given by sense, till long practice has made us attentive to, and skillful in separating it. It is, therefore, a question which requires close investigation, and is not to be answered at first sight—whether there exists a knowledge all together independent of experience, and even of all sensuous impressions? Knowledge of this kind is called *a priori,* in contradistinction to empirical knowledge, which has as its sources *a posteriori,* that is, in experience.[9]

JANE ROLAND MARTIN

Often labeled a feminist scholar, Jane Roland Martin (1929–) is a contemporary disciple of Plato's dialogues. In "Reclaiming a Conversation,"[10] Martin describes how women have historically been excluded from the "conversation" that constitutes Western educational thought. Martin advocates a return to Plato's approach. Dialogues such as the *Apology,* the *Crito,* and the *Phaedo* illustrate educated persons—well-meaning people of good faith, people who trust and like one another, people who might even be called friends—getting together and trying to talk ideas through to a reasonable conclusion. They engage in conversation, learning something from one another and from the conversation itself.

For Martin, to be educated is to engage in a conversation that stretches back in time. Education is not simply something that occurs in a specific building at

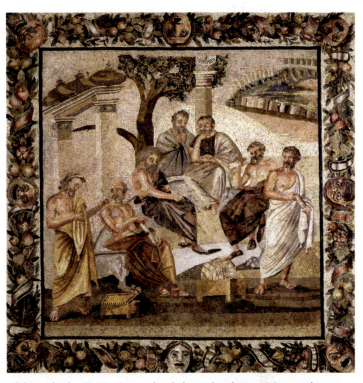

Although the Socratic method dates back to 400 BCE, the art of asking probing questions and using dialogue to enhance learning is still widely used today.

German philosopher Immanuel Kant (1724–1804) believed in freedom, the immortality of the soul, and the existence of God.

a specific time. Nor is it simply training or preparation for the next stage in life. Education is the development of the intellectual and moral habits, through the give-and-take of the conversation, that ultimately give "place and character to every human activity and utterance." Education—the conversation—is the place where one comes to learn what it is to be a person.

Cast in this light, Martin's charge about the historical exclusion of women from the conversation is serious. To exclude any group is to deny members of that group the right to become persons. In addition, the educational conversation requires a multiplicity of perspectives and a diversity of voices. Without such diversity, people will all look and sound and think alike, and eventually the conversation will wind down.

The following excerpt illustrates Jane Roland Martin's ideas about the predominance of a masculine voice in the world of education:

> Education is also gender-related. Our definition of the function of education makes it so. For if education is viewed as preparation for carrying on the processes historically associated with males, it will inculcate traits the culture considers masculine. If the concept of education is tied by definition to the productive process of society, our ideal of the educated person will coincide with the cultural stereotype of a male human being, and our definitions of excellence in education will embody "masculine" traits.[11]

■ REALISM

Realism's roots lie in the thinking of Aristotle. **Realism** is a school of philosophy that holds that reality, knowledge, and value exist independent of the human mind (metaphysics). In other words, realism rejects the idealist notion that ideas are the ultimate reality. Refer to Figure 9.3, which illustrates the dualistic position of idealism and realism.

EDUCATIONAL IMPLICATIONS OF REALISM

Realists place considerable importance on the role of the teacher in the educational process. The teacher should be a person who presents content in a systematic and organized way and should promote the idea that there are clearly defined criteria one can use in making judgments (axiology). Contemporary realists emphasize the importance of scientific research and development. Curriculum has reflected the impact of these realist thinkers through the appearance of standardized tests, serialized textbooks, and a specialized curriculum in which the disciplines are seen as separate areas of investigation.

Realists contend that the ultimate goal of education is advancement of human rationality. Schools can promote rationality by requiring students to study organized bodies of knowledge, by teaching methods of arriving at this knowledge, and by assisting students to reason critically through observation and experimentation (epistemology). Teachers must have specific knowledge about a subject so that they can order it in such a way as to teach it rationally. They must also have a broad background to show relationships that exist among all fields of knowledge.

Thus, the realist curriculum would be a subject-centered curriculum and would include natural science, social science, humanities, and instrumental subjects such as logic

---

The direction in which education starts a man will determine his future life.

Plato

realism

A school of philosophy that holds that reality, knowledge, and value exist independent of the human mind. In contrast to the idealist, the realist contends that physical entities exist in their own right.

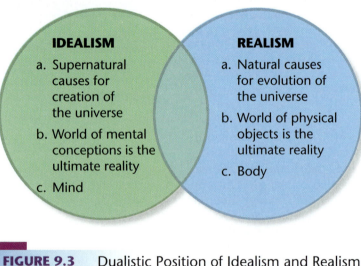

IDEALISM
a. Supernatural causes for creation of the universe
b. World of mental conceptions is the ultimate reality
c. Mind

REALISM
a. Natural causes for evolution of the universe
b. World of physical objects is the ultimate reality
c. Body

FIGURE 9.3 Dualistic Position of Idealism and Realism

and inductive reasoning. Realists employ experimental and observational techniques. In the school setting, they would promote testing and logical, clear content. To understand the complexity of the realist philosophy, we must once again turn to the ideas of individual thinkers: Aristotle, Locke, and Whitehead.

ARISTOTLE

Aristotle (384–322 BCE) thought that ideas (forms) are found through the study of the world of matter. He believed that one could acquire knowledge of ideas or forms by investigating matter. To understand an object, one must understand its absolute form, which is unchanging. To the realist, the trees of the forest exist whether or not there is a human mind to perceive them. This is an example of an independent reality. Although the ideas of a flower can exist without matter, matter cannot exist without form. Hence, each tulip shares universal properties with every other tulip and every other flower. However, the particular properties of a tulip differentiate it from all other flowers.

Aristotle's writings are known for their analytic approach. In contrast to Plato, whose writings are in the form of a conversation, Aristotle took great care to write with precision. In *Nicomachean Ethics,* Aristotle discusses the nature of moral responsibility:

> It is sometimes difficult to determine what ought to be chosen or endured in order to obtain or avoid a certain result. But it is still more difficult to abide by our decisions; for it generally happens that the consequences we expect are painful or the act we are forced to do is shameful; therefore we receive blame or praise according as we yield or do not yield to the constraint.
>
> What class of acts then may rightly be called compulsory? Acts may be called absolutely compulsory whenever the cause is external to the doer and he contributes nothing. But when an act, though involuntary in itself, is chosen at a particular time or for a particular end, and when its cause is in the doer himself, then, though the act is involuntary in itself, it is voluntary at that time and for that end.[12]

Ancient Greek philosopher Aristotle (384–322 BCE) believed that one could acquire knowledge of ideas or forms through an investigation of matter.

JOHN LOCKE

John Locke (1632–1704) believed in the tabula rasa (blank tablet) view of the mind. Locke stated that the mind of a person is blank at birth and that the person's sensory experiences make impressions on this blank tablet. Locke distinguished between sense data and the objects they represent. The objects, or things people know, are independent of the mind or the knower insofar as thought refers to them and not merely to sense data. Ideas (round, square, tall) represent objects. Locke claimed that primary qualities (such as shapes) represent the world, whereas secondary qualities (such as colors) have a basis in the world but do not represent it.

> The little or almost insensible impressions on our tender infancies have very important and lasting consequences: and there it is, as in the fountains of some rivers, where a gentle application of the hand turns the flexible waters into channels, that make them at first, in the source, they receive different tendencies, and arrive at last at very remote and distant places.
>
> I imagine the minds of children as easily turned, this or that way, as water itself; and though this be the principal part and our main care should be about the inside yet the clay cottage is not to be neglected. I shall therefore begin with the case and consider first the health of the body.[13]

John Locke (1632–1704) believed that a person's mind is like a blank tablet at birth and that a person's sensory experiences make impressions on this tablet.

ALFRED NORTH WHITEHEAD

Alfred North Whitehead (1861–1947), a philosopher and mathematician, attempted to reconcile some aspects of idealism and realism. He proposed "process" to be the central aspect of realism. Unlike Locke, Whitehead did not see objective reality and subjective mind as separate. He saw them as an organic

Philosopher and mathematician Alfred North Whitehead (1861–1947) attempted to reconcile idealism and realism.

unity that operates by its own principles. The universe is characterized by patterns, and these patterns can be verified and analyzed through mathematics.

Culture is activity of thought and receptiveness to beauty and humane feelings. Scraps of information have nothing to do with it. . . . In training a child to activity of thought, above all things we must beware of what I will call "inert ideas"—that is to say, ideas that are merely received into the mind without being used, or tested, or thrown into fresh combinations.

In the history of education, the most striking phenomenon is the schools of learning, which at one epoch are alive with a ferment of genius, in a succeeding generation exhibit merely pedantry and routine. The reason is that they are overladen with inert ideas. Education with inert ideas is not only useless: it is, above all things, harmful—*Corruptio optimi, pessima.* Except at rare intervals of intellectual ferment, education in the past has been radically infected with inert ideas. . . . Every intellectual revolution which has ever stirred humanity into greatness has been a passionate protest against inert ideas.[14]

◼ PRAGMATISM

Pragmatism is a late-nineteenth-century American philosophy that affected educational and social thought. It differs from most forms of idealism and realism by a belief in an open universe that is dynamic, evolving, and in a state of becoming (metaphysics). It is a process philosophy, which stresses becoming rather than being. Wedded as they are to change and adaptation, pragmatists do not believe in absolute and unchanging truth. For pragmatists, truth is what works. Truth is relative because what works for one person might not work for another, just as what works at one time or in one place or in one society might not work in another (axiology).

EDUCATIONAL IMPLICATIONS OF PRAGMATISM

Like the realist, the pragmatist believes that we learn best through experience; but pragmatists are more willing to put that belief into practice. Whereas realists are concerned with passing organized bodies of knowledge from one generation to the next, pragmatists stress applying knowledge—using ideas as instruments for problem solving (epistemology). Realists and idealists call for a curriculum centered on academic disciplines, but pragmatists prefer a curriculum that draws the disciplines together to solve problems—an interdisciplinary approach. Refer to Figure 9.4, which illustrates the relationships among realism, idealism, and pragmatism.

CHARLES SANDERS PEIRCE

Charles Sanders Peirce (1839–1914) is considered the founder of pragmatism. He introduced the principle that belief is a habit of action undertaken to overcome indecisiveness. He believed that the purpose of thought is to produce action and that the meaning of a thought is the collection of results of actions. For example, to say that steel is "hard" is to mean that when the operation of scratch testing is performed on steel, it will not be scratched by most substances. The aim of Peirce's pragmatic method is to supply a procedure for constructing and clarifying meanings and to facilitate communication.

Peirce wrote with great precision. He carefully crafted arguments in an effort to show that human thought and the external world

pragmatism

A late-nineteenth-century American school of philosophy that stresses becoming rather than being.

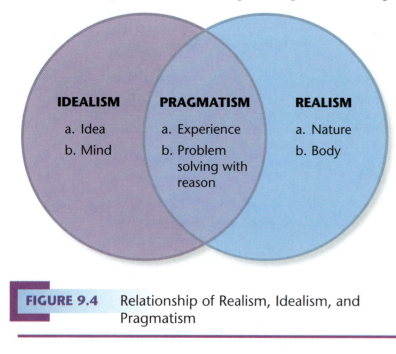

IDEALISM	PRAGMATISM	REALISM
a. Idea	a. Experience	a. Nature
b. Mind	b. Problem solving with reason	b. Body

FIGURE 9.4   Relationship of Realism, Idealism, and Pragmatism

were intermixed and could not easily be separated. Therefore, human thought affects the external world and vice versa. In the following excerpt, Peirce describes how human consciousness takes individual experiences and connects them in such a way that the experiences take on meaning:

> We observe two sorts of elements of consciousness, the distinction between which may best be made clear by means of an illustration. In a piece of music there are the separate notes, and there is the air. A single tone may be prolonged for an hour or a day, and it exists as perfectly in each second of that time as in the whole taken together; so that, as long as it is sounding, it might be present to a sense from which everything in the past was as completely absent as the future itself. But it is different with the air, the performance of which occupies a certain time, during the portions of which only portions of it are played. It consists in an orderliness in the succession of sounds which strike the ear at different times; and to perceive it there must be some continuity of consciousness which makes the events of a lapse of time present to us. We certainly only perceive the air by hearing the separate notes; yet we cannot be said to directly hear it, for we hear only what is present at the instant, and an orderliness of succession cannot exist in an instant. These two sorts of objects, what we are *immediately* conscious of and what we are *mediately* conscious of, are found in all consciousness. Some elements (the sensations) are completely present at every instant so long as they last, while others (like thought) are actions having beginning, middle, and end, and consist in a congruence in the succession of sensations which flow through the mind. They cannot be immediately present to us, but must cover some portion of the past or future. Thought is a thread of melody running through the succession of our sensations.[15]

Charles Sanders Peirce (1839–1914) believed that the purpose of thought is to produce action.

JOHN DEWEY

Early in his philosophical development, John Dewey (1859–1952) related pragmatism to evolution by explaining that human beings are creatures who have to adapt to one another and to their environments. Dewey viewed life as a series of overlapping and interpenetrating experiences and situations, each of which has its own complete identity. The primary unit of life is the individual experience.

Dewey wrote the following passage early in his career. In it he shows his zeal for education as a social force in human affairs.

> I believe that all education proceeds by the participation of the individual in the social consciousness of the race. This process begins unconsciously almost at birth, and is continually shaping the individual's powers, saturating his consciousness, forming his habits, training his ideas, and arousing his feelings and emotions. Through this unconscious education the individual gradually comes to share in the intellectual and moral resources which humanity has succeeded in getting together. . . .
>
> In sum, I believe that the individual is a social individual and that society is an organic union of individuals. If we eliminate the social factor from the child we are left only with an abstraction; if we eliminate the individual factor from society, we are left only with an inert and lifeless mass.[16]

RICHARD RORTY

Richard Rorty (1931–) is a contemporary pragmatist philosopher who has spent much of his life reinventing the work of John Dewey in light of the chaotic, ever-changing view of the world. Rorty contends that reality is not fixed, and it is the task of thinkers to come up with a procedure for correctly describing the nature of the real. He argues that reality is the outcome of inquiry, and as human inquiry shifts so too will shift the nature of what we call real. Rorty contends that different disciplines have different avenues for studying the world and therefore these avenues of inquiry create different realities. The way an artist looks at the world and creates a work of art and the way a chemist looks at the world and develops a new way of looking at molecules both affect the very nature of what is. Essential to this point of view is the understanding that disciplines such as science, mathematics, art, and history are not rooted in a fixed reality but are constructed by groups of people who are trying to make sense of the world. Hence, disciplines are arbitrary contrivances and one discipline is as good as another. Also, because disciplines are created by persons, they are subject to all the foibles, limitations, and prejudices of any human convention.

Although Rorty has not spoken directly to the field of education, his work provides a significant challenge to teachers. No longer can teachers represent expert knowledge as accurate or as true. Rather, expert knowledge is the current agreement of scholars at this point in time. Expert knowledge is simply a set of ideas and procedures that have been found to be useful. Rorty contends that a thinker should no longer be represented as a discoverer; rather, a thinker is more of a maker or cobbler who crafts meaning. People come together, agree on certain things, and then try to talk or reason their way to a sensible conclusion. The notion that expertise is more a matter of "usefulness" than truth spills over into the definition of critical thinking. In the following excerpt, Rorty presents his view of the nature of critical thinking. He contends that such thinking is not so much a quality of rationality and logic; rather, critical thinking is merely the act of trying to create useful meaning by suggesting alternatives.

> Liberality of mind and critical thought are not, on this view, matters of abstractness but of a sense of relativity, of alternative perspectives. Critical thinking is playing off alternatives against one another, rather than playing them off against criteria of rationality, much less against eternal verities.[17]

EXISTENTIALISM

In **existentialism,** reality is lived existence, and the final reality resides within the individual (metaphysics). Existentialists believe that we live an alien, meaningless existence on a small planet in an unimportant galaxy in an indifferent universe. There is no ultimate meaning. Whereas some people might be paralyzed by this view, existentialists find the definition of their lives in the quest for meaning (epistemology). The very meaninglessness of life compels them to instill life with meaning.

The only certainty for the existentialist is that we are free. However, this freedom is wrapped up in a search for meaning. We define ourselves; that is, we make meaning in our world by the choices we make. In effect we are what we choose (axiology).

EDUCATIONAL IMPLICATIONS OF EXISTENTIALISM

The existentialist believes that most schools, like other corporate symbols, deemphasize the individual and the relationship between the teacher and the student. Existentialists claim that when educators attempt to predict the behavior of students, they turn individuals into objects to be measured, quantified, and processed. Existentialists tend to feel that tracking, measurement, and standardization militate against the creation of opportunities for self-direction and personal choice. According to the existentialist, education ought to be a process of developing a free, self-actualizing person—a process centered on the feelings of the student. Therefore, proper education does not start with the nature of the world and with humankind, but with the human individual or self.

The existentialist educator would be a free personality engaged in projects that treat students as free personalities. The highest educational goal is to search for oneself. Teachers and students experience existential crises; each such crisis involves an examination of oneself and one's life purposes. Education helps to fill in the gaps with understanding that the student needs in order to fulfill those purposes; it is not a mold to which the student must be fitted. Students define themselves by their choices.

The existentialist student would have a questioning attitude and would be involved in a continuing search for self and for the reasons for existence. The existentialist teacher would help students become what they themselves want

existentialism

A school of philosophy that focuses on the importance of the individual rather than on external standards.

to become, not what outside forces such as society, other teachers, or parents want them to become.

Existentialist thinkers are as varied as the notions of individual thought and self-defined meaning would suggest. There are atheistic existentialists as represented by Jean-Paul Sartre, critical existentialists as exemplified by Friedrich Nietzsche, and humanistic existentialists such as Maxine Greene.

JEAN-PAUL SARTRE

Modern existentialism was born amidst the pain and disillusionment of World War II. Jean-Paul Sartre (1905–1980) broke with previous philosophers and asserted that existence (being) comes before essence (meaning).

Sartre saw no difference between being free and being human. This view opens great possibilities; yet it also creates feelings of dread and nausea as one recognizes the reality of nonbeing and death as well as the great responsibilities that accompany such radical freedom to shape oneself out of one's choices. The process of answering the question "Who are we?" begins at a crucial event in the lives of young people called the existential moment—that point somewhere toward the end of youth when individuals realize for the first time that they exist as independent agents.

In the following selection, Jean-Paul Sartre offers a defense of existentialism:

> What do we mean by saying that existence precedes essence? We mean that man first of all exists, encounters himself, surges up in the world—and defines himself afterwards. If man as the existentialist sees him is not definable, it is because to begin with he is nothing. He will not be anything until later, and then he will be what he makes of himself. Thus, there is no human nature, because there is no God to have a conception of it. Man simply is.[18]

FRIEDRICH NIETZSCHE

Friedrich Nietzsche (1844–1900) is an existential philosopher who stresses the importance of the individuality of persons. Throughout his writings, Nietzsche indicts the supremacy of herd values in modern democratic social systems. He criticizes the way social systems such as modern educational institutions foster a spirit of capitalistic greed. When Nietzsche turns his attention primarily to social systems, human beings are portrayed much more as victims of social dynamics than as inferior or superior beings.

Nietzsche sounds remarkably current when he criticizes the education of his times, denounces the "acroamatic" or declamatory method of teaching, and acknowledges oppressive structures that hinder the achievement of individual (human) good.[19] In Nietzsche's texts there is a strategy to liberate people from the oppression of feeling inferior within themselves, a teaching of how not to judge what one is in relation to what one should be. Although Nietzsche did not author a comprehensive teaching methodology, he teaches how to cultivate a healthy love of self-care, a taste for solitude, a perspective on perspective, literacy as a vital capacity, and an overall gratitude for one's existence.

Nietzsche observed that most teachers and parents

> hammer even into children that what matters is something quite different: the salvation of the soul, the service of the state, the advancement of science, or the accumulation of reputation and possessions, all as the means of doing service to mankind as a whole; while the requirements of the individual, his great and small needs within the twenty-four hours of the day, are to be regarded as something contemptible or a matter of indifference.[20]

MAXINE GREENE

A theme that permeates most of Maxine Greene's work is her unyielding faith in human beings' willingness to build and transcend their lived worlds. To Greene (1917–) philosophy is a deeply personal and aesthetic experience. Her

Philosopher Maxine Greene (1917–) contends that living is philosophy and that freedom means overcoming obstacles that obstruct our attempts to find ourselves and fulfill our potential.

Does Prepping for High-Stakes Tests Interfere with Teaching?

More and more states require students to pass tests in order to graduate or to receive a diploma. Some states offer different types of diplomas based on how well a student performs on a test. This type of testing is called high-stakes testing and it poses several philosophical questions. What do high-stakes tests say about the nature of knowledge? What does it mean to be educated in a high-stakes testing environment? What behaviors do high-stakes testing encourage? How do high-stakes tests influence teaching? The following debate raises these types of questions.

YES

Nancy Buell teaches fourth grade at the Lincoln School in Brookline, Massachusetts. She has taught for 32 years and serves on the state Board of Education's Advisory Council for Mathematics and Science.

NO

Charlotte Crawford teaches fourth grade at Coteau-Bayou Blue School in Houma, Louisiana. A 27-year teaching veteran, she helped set the cut scores for her state's high-stakes fourth-grade test and now serves on a state panel for staff development.

As I watch my students debate how much taller fourth graders are than first graders, I am struck by their intuitive use of significant features of the data. As in:

Lee: Fourth graders are 10" taller because the tallest fourth grader is 64" and the tallest first grader is 54".

Tamara: A first grader is about 5" shorter. I found the middle height for each and just subtracted. The middle for the fourth graders is 57" and the middle for the first graders is between 51" and 52".

Dana: 5" or 4", because the most common height for first graders is 53" and the most common height for fourth graders is 58" or 57".

These students are exploring ideas involving maximum, median, and mode. They are considering what features to use to tell what is typical of the two groups so they can be compared. Students support their ideas with information in the data itself. They are developing ways to think about data that will lead to deep understanding of more formal statistics.

The rich mathematical discussions in my class are an outgrowth of my participation in professional development that focused on inquiry-based teaching and the big ideas we should be teaching.

Preparing students to take high-stakes tests does not interfere with teaching. It enhances teaching. When used properly, high-stakes tests can focus attention on weaknesses in the curriculum and in the teaching of it, as well as furnish an assessment of student progress. Once identified, student weak areas can be strengthened.

When the new high-stakes tests and revised curriculum were introduced in Louisiana, along with new accountability standards, many teachers were bewildered at the prospect of being held accountable for teaching a new curriculum without being told how to teach it.

Yet many of these teachers were also open to the new ideas and began working to find ways to implement them. They were aided by funding from the state for additional reading materials and in-service training.

Teachers often feel overwhelmed by the changes involved in our state's rigorous new standards, but many Louisiana educators are beginning to take ownership of their new curriculum. They're growing confident when making scope and sequence decisions. They're consistently reevaluating what they have taught, and how they have taught it, so they can do better next time.

(continued)

writing blurs the distinction between philosophy and literature. This is appropriate because Greene contends that living is philosophy. Greene asserts that schools must be places that offer "an authentic public space where diverse human beings can appear before one another as best they know to be."[21]

YES

But since high-stakes testing arrived, professional development meetings often focus on how to improve test scores, not on how to improve learning.

Teaching that concentrates on improving test scores is very limited—by the nature of both testing and teaching. Testing involves sampling student knowledge. It is fragmented and only examines learning outcomes. It seldom looks at how well a student understands complex ideas.

A typical test item might give students a set of data and ask for the median. Students would not be asked to select the appropriate statistic to address a question and justify their choice. Yet knowing how to find the median, without knowing when to use it, is useless, except on tests.

If we teach facts and procedures likely to be on the test, without the deeper understanding behind them, we shortchange our students. We must not limit what we teach to what will be tested.

Many teachers feel pressured to choose teaching techniques that help with testing more than learning. They're urged to spend more time on information that mimics test items.

Students should, of course, know how to answer multiple choice, short answer, and open response questions, but teaching these test-taking skills should not be confused with teaching a subject. Some teachers spend a day a week using test-like items, not to sample what children know, but to try to teach the content.

Teaching should build on what students already know and help them develop a rich web of interconnected ideas. Real learning involves inquiry, hypothesis testing, exploration, and reflection.

Teaching to the test will not help my students think about how to use features of data sets to answer real questions. Teaching to the test is not teaching.

Source: "Does Prepping for High-Stakes Tests Interfere with Teaching?" *NEA Today* (January 2001), p. 11.

NO

These educators are revamping their classroom activities and their teacher-made tests to match them more closely to the format and tone of the state-mandated tests.

Helping students become familiar with the state-mandated test formats, by using them in the classroom, prevents having to spend valuable class time to "practice" for the high-stakes tests.

Learners, meanwhile, are reaping the benefits of having teachers who are determined that their students will be as prepared as possible to relate the skills they learn in school to real-life situations. They're becoming lifelong learners, besides performing well on standardized tests.

Some educators complain that they must "teach to the test."

But others consider this to be a weak objection since the state tests focus on information and skills students are expected to know at certain points in their schooling.

These educators say the curriculum objectives covered by the state tests should be taught before the tests are given, with the remaining objectives covered afterwards. This is a very workable arrangement when high-stakes tests are given early in the spring.

To be sure, some Louisiana educators are still resisting the changes that come with the state tests.

But most realize this is an idea whose time has come.

In 1998, my school helped pilot the fourth-grade language arts test. I was nervous about how my students would fare. When they finished, I asked for reactions.

Much to my surprise, students calmly informed me that the state test was "kind of hard, kind of easy, kind of fun."

That day, my students unwittingly reassured me that learners who are prepared for high-stakes tests need not fear them.

WHAT DO YOU THINK?
Does prepping for high-stakes tests interfere with teaching?

To give your opinion, go to Chapter 9 of the companion website (**www.ablongman.com/johnson13e**) and click on Debate.

Freedom means the overcoming of obstacles or barriers that impede or obstruct people's struggle to define themselves and fulfill their potential. Greene contends that the "obstacles" or "walls" individuals encounter are human constructs subject to removal. From this perspective, the educator has the formidable task of promoting freedom in each individual. But because embracing freedom is a matter of choice, it cannot be taught, only encouraged.

Through education, individuals

can be provoked to reach beyond themselves in this intersubjective space. It is through and by means of education that they may be empowered to think about what they are doing, to become mindful, to share meanings, to conceptualize, to make varied sense of their lived worlds.[22]

■ EASTERN WAYS OF KNOWING

Most studies of Western philosophy typically begin with the Greek philosophers. Yet there is evidence that Platonic philosophy owed much of its development to Eastern thinkers who emphasized the illusory quality of the physical world. Although there are many different philosophical writings among the Far Eastern, Middle Eastern, and Near Eastern philosophers, **Eastern ways of knowing** as a group stress inner peace, tranquillity, attitudinal development, and mysticism. Western philosophy has tended to emphasize logic and materialism; whereas Eastern ways of knowing, in general, stress the inner rather than the outer world, intuition rather than sense, and mysticism rather than scientific discoveries. This has differed from school to school, but overall Eastern ways of knowing begin with the inner world and then reach to the outer world of phenomena. Eastern ways of knowing emphasize order, regularity, and patience that is proportional to and in harmony with the laws of nature.

Eastern thinkers have always concerned themselves with education, which they view as a way of achieving wisdom, maintaining family structure, establishing law, and providing for social and economic concerns. Instruction includes the things that one must do to achieve the good life, and education is viewed as necessary not only for this life but also for achievement of the good life hereafter.

Eastern ways of knowing have not been as singular as has Western thought. One needs to study Eastern thinking system by system, culture by culture, and philosopher by philosopher. One good reason to study Eastern ways of knowing is that they offer vantage points from which to examine Western thought. Eastern ideas encourage one to question seriously the Western world's most basic commitments to science, materialism, and reason.

INDIAN THOUGHT

Far Eastern Indian thought has a long, complex history and is permeated by opposites. To Western philosophers, opposites need to be reconciled; but to the Eastern mind, this need for consistency is unimportant. For example, great emphasis is placed on a search for wisdom, but this does not mean a rejection of worldly pleasures. Though speculation is emphasized, it has a practical character. Far Eastern Indian thinkers insist that knowledge be used to improve both social and communal life and that people should live according to their ideals. In Far Eastern Indian thought, there is a prevailing sense of universal moral justice, according to which individuals are responsible for what they are and what they become.

Hinduism, Buddhism, and Jainism are three religions that provide different contexts for these Indian philosophical principles. Hinduism does not generally encourage asceticism or a renunciation of the world, but teaches that one should be able to control and regulate oneself. Fundamental truths include the concept that there is an ultimate reality that is all-pervading and is the final cause of the universe. This reality is uncreated and eternal. Meditation on this ultimate reality leads to a life of virtue and righteousness. Buddhism stresses nonattachment to material things and concern for humanity; it emphasizes a sense of harmony with the universe in which one is under no constraint to

When a man has pity on all living creatures, then only is he noble.

Buddha

Eastern ways of knowing

A varied set of ideas, beliefs, and values from the Far, Middle, and Near East that stress inner peace, tranquility, attitudinal development, and mysticism.

change forces within or without. Jainism is a religion that rejects systems as absolutes and affirms them only as partial truths or "maybes." Jains believe that the universe has existed from all eternity, undergoing an infinite number of revolutions produced by the powers of nature. Adherents of Jainism have great respect for all life and take vows to avoid injury to any form of life.[23]

CHINESE THOUGHT

The emphasis of Far Eastern Chinese philosophy is on harmony: Correct thinking should help one achieve harmony with life. This harmony of government, business, and family should then lead toward a higher synthesis. Confucianism and Taoism provide two major contexts for Chinese thought.

For more than two thousand years, Confucian thought has influenced education, government, and culture in China. Confucius (551–479 BCE) believed that people need standards for all of life, so rules were developed for a wide range of activities. Confucian thought gives education a high place but stresses building moral character more than merely teaching skills or imparting information. This moral approach has a practical component. Children should obey and defer to parents and respect the wisdom adults have gained in their journey through life. Following these principles enables children to become *chun-tzu,* persons distinguished by faithfulness, diligence, and modesty.

The central concept of Taoism is that of the "Tao," the Way or Path. The Tao is the way the universe moves, the way of perfection and harmony. It is conformity with nature. Perhaps the most significant aspect of the Tao is letting things alone, not forcing personal desires onto the natural course of events. It is a noncompetitive approach to life. Taoists believe that conflict and war represent basic failures in society, for they bring ruin to states and a disrespect for life.

JAPANESE THOUGHT

Japanese thought is rooted in Shinto, a way of thinking that recognizes the significance of the natural world. This respect for all nature permeates Japanese thought and life. Shinto accepts the phenomenal world (the world people apprehend through their senses) as absolute; this acceptance leads to a disposition to lay greater emphasis on intuitive, sensible, concrete events rather than on universal ideas. On the social level, Japanese express this focus on the natural world through many artifacts, including the patterns of traditional kimonos. Within the house, flowers are arranged in vases and dwarf trees placed in alcoves, flowers and birds are engraved on lintels, and nature scenes are painted on sliding screens. Seventeen-syllable poems, called haikus, cannot be disassociated from nature.

The Japanese perspective is one of acceptance, enjoyment of life, and kinship with nature. Intuition is often prized over intellectualism, and there is a strong feeling for loyalty, purity, and naturalness. Japanese philosophy has successfully fused Confucian, Buddhist, and Taoist beliefs and practices and has permeated them with a distinct Japanese perspective. One example of this is the development of Zen Buddhism. Zen emphasizes a dependence on oneself rather than on an outside source for answers and wisdom; it depends more on intuition than on intellectual discovery.

MIDDLE EASTERN THOUGHT

Many philosophies and religions (including Judaism, Christianity, and Islam) owe their origin to the Middle East. Historically, the Middle East has been a meeting ground between civilizations of the East and the West; partly because of this fact, Middle Eastern thought is more disjointed than that of the Far East. Judaism traces its origins to the call of Abraham (around 1750 BCE). Abraham believed in a God who had a special interest in humanity. Throughout the centuries, Judaic thought has included a belief in one God who created the world

Ancient Chinese philosopher Confucius (551–479 BCE) believed that people need standards for all of life so he developed rules for a wide range of activities.

Everything has beauty, but not everyone sees it. Wheresoever you go, go with all your heart.

Confucius

and who cares for the world and all its creatures. In earlier conceptions of Judaism, God was viewed as possessing human qualities but later became more idealized and incorporeal: "I am who I am."

Christianity grew out of Judaism through the words and deeds of Jesus of Nazareth, who proclaimed that he was the Messiah. The words and deeds of Jesus formed the basis of a New Testament that Christians believe is the fulfillment of Judaism. Christianity incorporates many of the Judaic beliefs, but it places greater emphasis on concepts of grace and redemption.

Islam is the most prominent religion in the contemporary Middle East. Mohammed (c. 571–632 CE) was born in Mecca. Through a revelation, Mohammed was called on to bring all people to worship Allah, the one true God. His mission was to restore to the Arabs the pure faith of their father, Abraham, and to free them from bondage and idolatry. Mohammed taught that Allah is a purposeful God who created things to reach certain desired goals. Those who follow the will of Allah will be eternally rewarded in paradise, an oasis of flowing waters. For those who do not follow the will of Allah, there is eternal suffering.

It is noteworthy that these three major religions that originated in the Middle East share striking similarities with one another. Judaism, Christianity, and Islam worship one God with different interpretations of the Law. They all share a belief that God cares for the world and that humans have a unique relationship with the divine.

EDUCATIONAL IMPLICATIONS OF EASTERN WAYS OF KNOWING

Eastern educational thought places great emphasis on the teacher–student relationship. Change springs from this relationship; that is, the student is changed as a result of contact with the guru, master, or prophet. Eastern educational thought emphasizes transformation: The individual must be transformed to face life. Attitude shaping is important because the attitude a person holds toward life will determine the individual's levels of goodness and wisdom.

A recurring educational aim in Eastern ways of knowing is to put humanity in tune with nature. There is great emphasis on observing nature and learning through wanderings and pilgrimages. The importance of achieving wisdom, satori, enlightenment, or nirvana is supreme. All paths must lead to this, and from this wisdom spring virtue, right living, and correct behavior.

GLOBAL PERSPECTIVES

The Fabric of Eastern Ways of Knowing

As you can see, Eastern thought is like a rich fabric of diverse ideas. It emphasizes sets of views that are quite different from the neat categorizations of Western thought. Eastern thought suggests that cohesive views can be achieved without the necessity of neat, hierarchically distinct categories. Although they are quite difficult to summarize, the philosophy and thought of the Far, Near, and Middle East suggest new ways of looking at long-accepted meanings and assumptions. As such, the study of Eastern thought is an important part of all future educators' preparation in an increasingly multicultural society.

In what ways do Eastern ways of knowing affect character education programs? What values would receive greater or lesser emphasis?

Native North American ways of knowing

A varied set of beliefs, philosophical positions, and customs that span different tribes in North America.

NATIVE NORTH AMERICAN WAYS OF KNOWING

Just as the rich past and diverse cultures make it difficult to summarize Eastern thought, Native North American ways of knowing are equally difficult to synthesize. **Native North American ways of knowing** include a varied set of beliefs, positions, and customs that span different tribes in North America. These beliefs, positions, and customs center on the relationship of humans to all of nature, including the earth, the sun, the sky, and beyond. Because Native North American ways of knowing center on the relationship of humans to all of nature, it is sometimes difficult to separate knowing from a way of life. In fact, to understand is to live and to develop an ever closer, more profound human-to-nature relationship. The types of relationships and the symbols that inform these human-to-nature relationships differ widely among tribes.

Although Native North American ways of knowing are as different as the four hundred—plus tribes in North America, these ways of knowing do have similar elements. They all include traditional stories and beliefs that dictate a way of knowing and living. All include a reverence for nature and a sense of humans' responsibility to nature. And all groups make reference to a supreme being—although the names are different, the relationships vary, and the expectations of some supreme beings are interpreted through natural elements. Thus, the Black Hills are sacred to the Lakota, the turtle is revered as Mother Earth by the Ojibwa, and so on. Native North American ways of knowing are orally developed rather than written. Hence, they change slightly from age to age. Additionally, the ways of knowing are subject to interpretation by the shaman, or holy one.

Traditionally, Native Americans view time as a flow of events with no beginning or end.

Lee Little Soldier, Native American educator

NAVAJO THOUGHT

The Navajo nation is the largest tribe in the United States. The Navajos' early history was nomadic, and their thoughts and customs are known for their unique ability to assimilate with and adapt to the thought and customs of other tribes. As with most Native North American cultures, the Navajo universe is an all-inclusive unity viewed as an orderly system of interrelated elements. At the basis of Navajo teachings and traditions is the value of a life lived in harmony with the natural world. Such a view enables one to "walk in beauty." To understand the Navajo worldview, one must note the teachings of the "inner forms" of things. These inner forms were set in place by First Man and First Woman. The concept of inner form is similar to the concept of a spirit or soul; without it, the Navajos say, the outer forms would be dead.[24]

LAKOTA THOUGHT

The Native American culture of the Great Plains, of which the Lakota form part, is based on mystical participation with the environment. All aspects of this ecosystem, including earth, sky, night, day, sun, and moon, are elements of the oneness within which life was undertaken. The Lakota celebrate the "sacred hoop of life" and observe seven sacred rites toward the goal of ultimate communion with Wakan-Tanka, the great Spirit.[25]

HOPI THOUGHT

The Hopi follow the path of peace, which they believe is a pure and perfect pattern of humankind's evolutionary journey. The Road of Life of the Hopi is represented as a journey through seven universes created at the beginning. At death the conduct of a person in accordance with the Creator's plan determines when and where the next step on the road will be taken. Each of the Hopi clans has a unique role to play, and each role is an essential part of the whole. Hopis must live in harmony with one another, with nature, and with the plan. Out of this complex interplay, then, the plan is both created and allowed to unfold.

We feel that the world is good. We are grateful to be alive. We are conscious that all men are brothers. We sense that we are related to other

Native North American ways of knowing provide a perspective that connects knowledge to the earth that surrounds us and of which we are a part.

creatures. Life is to be valued and preserved. If you see a grain of corn on the ground, pick it up and take care of it, because it has life inside. When you go out of your house in the morning and see the sun rising pause a moment to think about it. When you take water from a spring, be aware that it is a gift of nature. (Albert Yava, Big Falling Snow, Hopi)[25]

EDUCATIONAL IMPLICATIONS OF NATIVE NORTH AMERICAN WAYS OF KNOWING

Native North American educational thought emphasizes the importance of nature. The pursuit of knowledge and happiness must be subordinate to a respect for the whole universe. To know is to understand one's place in the natural order of things. To be is to celebrate through ritual and stories the spirit that informs all reality. These principles encourage educators to study the physical and social world by examining the natural relationships that exist among things, animals, and humans. Studying ideas in the abstract or as independent entities is not as important as understanding the relationships among ideas and the physical reality. Hands-on learning, making connections, holding discussions, and celebrating the moment are essential components of an educational experience.

SUMMARY

The study of philosophy permeates every aspect of the teacher's role and provides the underpinning for every decision. This chapter describes how philosophy is related to daily teaching decisions and actions, and it clarifies some of the major ideas that different philosophers have developed in their private quest for wisdom.

Philosophy revolves around three major types of questions: those that deal with the nature of reality (metaphysics), those that deal with knowledge and truth (epistemology), and those that deal with values (axiology). Successful teachers are those who are dedicated to and thoroughly understand their preferred beliefs. Decisions about the nature of the subject matter emphasized in the curriculum are metaphysical commitments to reality—what is real? Questions related to what is true and how we know are epistemological. Classroom methods are practices that aim to assist learners in acquiring knowledge and truth in the subject area. Classroom activities that deal with ethics (what is right or wrong), beauty, and character are in the realm of axiology (values). The task of the teacher is to identify a preferred style, understand that style as thoroughly as possible, and use that style with each unique group of learners.

Analytic and prophetic thinking provide two approaches to the process of philosophy. Analytic thinking provides clarity and precision, whereas prophetic thinking fosters breadth and sensitivity. Both thinking approaches are valuable and help educators understand the essential and critical features of situations or problems.

Four classical Western schools of philosophical thought (realism, idealism, pragmatism, and existentialism) were introduced. For each school of philosophy, representative philosophers and their ideas were provided to give prospective teachers a sense of how they might develop their own educational philosophy.

The chapter concluded with overviews of Eastern and Native North American ways of knowing. The Eastern and Native North American ways of knowing are varied and diverse. Despite such diversity, many of these ways of knowing share an underlying sensitivity to nature and an emphasis on wisdom, virtue, spirituality, and harmony within the larger universe. The educational implications of these ways of knowing include the importance of teaching respect for the earth and awareness of the interrelationships among all things.

DISCUSSION QUESTIONS

1. How would you describe philosophy to a young child?

2. In your opinion, which is the most important aspect of a given philosophy (for the teacher): the metaphysical component, the epistemological component, or the axiological component? State the rationale for your choice.

3. Early Greek philosophers suggest that all knowledge is based on experience. Discuss the implications of this statement for teaching methodology.

4. Describe the ways that Eastern and Native North American ways of knowing might influence what and how you teach.

JOURNAL ENTRIES

1. Classroom activities that deal with what is good or bad are in the realm of axiology (values). Prepare lists of the goods and the evils of the U.S. educational system. Then propose solutions to counteract as many of the evils as possible.

2. Consider the four components of prophetic thinking: discernment, empathy, tracking hypocrisy, and hope. Select one of these components and apply it to the educational controversy over school prayer. Record your thoughts, feelings, and observations.

PORTFOLIO DEVELOPMENT

1. According to idealistic philosophy, character education can be enhanced through study and imitation of exemplars/heroes in the historical record. Identify an exemplary educator from history and describe how you could teach character through that person's example. Place your essay in your folio as an example of your teaching methodology.

2. Assist a student as a mentor or tutor. Before beginning, gather samples of the student's thinking and schoolwork. Try to think like the student and by so doing uncover areas in which the student needs help. Develop a diagnosis that details what changes will be beneficial. Place these ideas in your folio as an example of your diagnostic and metacognitive skills.

PREPARING FOR CERTIFICATION

■ PHILOSOPHICAL THINKING

1. One of the topics in the Praxis II Principles of Teaching and Learning (PLT) test is using "teacher self-evaluation to enhance instructional effectiveness." In this chapter, you learned about two approaches to philosophical thinking—analytic and prophetic—that are useful tools to enhance instructional effectiveness. Review Figures 9.1 and 9.2. Think about a specific problem you might face in the subject or grade level you plan to teach. Analyze that problem using the two approaches. How does each approach contribute to your understanding of the problem?

2. Answer the following multiple-choice question, which is similar to items in Praxis and other state certification tests. If you are unsure of the answer, reread the section on Schools of Philosophy and Their Influence on Education in this chapter.

   Two middle school teachers are discussing their philosophical beliefs about teaching and learning. Jan says, "I think it is very important that all students master an essential body of knowledge; I would like to teach a unit in my subject area that focuses on specific content and make sure that all students master it." Lee says, "I disagree. I think it is more important that students are able to apply knowledge to solve problems. I would teach an interdisciplinary unit that focuses on real issues so students can see how what they are learning applies to the real world."

   Lee's position more closely resembles

   (A) realism
   (B) idealism
   (C) pragmatism
   (D) existentialism

3. Answer the following short-answer question, which is similar to items in Praxis and other state certification tests. After you've completed your written response, use the scoring guide in the *Test at a Glance* materials to assess your response. Can you revise your response to improve your score?

   Some school districts have established mandatory service-learning programs to encourage students to develop an ethic of caring, involvement in the community, and citizenship. Do you believe service-learning projects should be a requirement for graduation? What are the benefits of such a requirement? What are the arguments against such a requirement?

WEBSITES

webs.csu.edu/~big0ama/mpes/mpes. html The Midwest Philosophy of Education Society (MPES) comprises educators who are committed to the critical normative and interpretive aspects of education. The mission of MPES is to encourage scholarship in the field of philosophy of education; to dis-

cuss curricular, methodological, and institutional issues in the field; and to offer educators at large a forum for the philosophical analysis of educational issues. The site provides Internet resources, papers, and discussions that help teachers understand questions and concerns that flow from a philosophic perspective on education.

www.apped.org   The Association for Process Philosophy of Education (APPE) provides an opportunity to meet, discuss, share papers, and publish your thinking about and the connections between philosophy and educational theory and practice. The news, articles, essays, and announcements on these pages are influenced by the process philosophies of Henri Bergson, John Dewey, and Alfred North Whitehead, and by the work of contemporary philosophers and educators who have explored the relevance of these ideas for educational theory and practice. APPE members include those who teach at every level of school from kindergarten through the baccalaureate, those involved in adult learning, academic administrators, education theorists, and philosophers. The site offers educators an opportunity to meet, discuss, share papers, and publish their thinking about effective pedagogy and the connections between process philosophy and educational theory and practice.

www.pdcnet.org   The Philosophy Documentation Center (PDC) is a nonprofit organization dedicated to providing affordable access to the widest possible range of philosophical materials. Established in 1966, the PDC provides access to scholarly journals, reference materials, conference proceedings, and instructional software. This site provides easy access to the ideas and writings of a wide variety of philosophers of education.

busboy.sped.ukans.edu/~rreed/NAedPhilosophy.html   This is the Native American educational philosophy website maintained by the University of Kansas. This site emphasizes that Native American educational philosophy encompasses the education of the whole child with many types of learning styles and teaching styles.

FURTHER READING

Abel, Donald C. (1992). *Theories of Human Nature.* New York: McGraw-Hill. Describes different views of human nature and discusses the implications for teaching, working, and living in society.

Bahm, Archie J. (1995). *Comparative Philosophy: Western, Indian, and Chinese Philosophies Compared* (rev. ed.). Albuquerque, NM: World Book. Compares different thinkers, ideologies, and philosophies from both the West and the East.

Cromer, Alan H. (1997). *Connected Knowledge: Science, Philosophy, and Education.* New York: Oxford University Press. Written by a physicist, this text argues that students' understanding needs to be connected; it provides practical suggestions that advance students' understanding in an orderly manner.

Littleton, Scott C. (1996). *Eastern Wisdom.* New York: Henry Holt. Describes Eastern thought drawn from India, China, and Japan and shows how such ideas enhance life.

Nerburn, Kent, and Mengelkoch, Louise. (1991). *Native American Wisdom.* Novato, CA: The Classic Wisdom Collection. Describes the contributions of different Native American thinkers and suggests that their ideas need to be integrated into schools of learning.

Palmer, Parker. (1997). *To Know as We Are Known: Education as Spiritual Journey.* San Francisco: Harper. Shows the close relationship between learning and becoming a person. Provides both spiritual and practical suggestions that challenge views of knowledge.

Sassone, Leslie. (2002). *The Process of Becoming: A Democratic Nietzschean Philosophical Pedagogy for Individualization.* Chicago: Discovery Association. This book explores in detail the many Nietzschean perspectives on education. It also offers a democratic Nietzschean pedagogy supplemented by contemporary radical democratic education reformers Paulo Freire, Ivan Illich, Jonathan Kozol, and Neil Postman.

THEMES OF THE TIMES!

expect the world®
The New York Times
nytimes.com

Expand your knowledge of the concepts discussed in this chapter by reading current and historical articles from the *New York Times* by visiting the Themes of the Times! section of the companion website **(www.ablongman.com/johnson13e).**

NOTES

1. George F. Kneller, "The Relevance of Philosophy," in *Introduction to the Philosophy of Education.* Berrien Springs, MI: Andrews University Press, 1982, pp. 7–8.
2. Kneller, "Relevance of Philosophy," p. 31.
3. Herbert G. Alexander, *The Language and Logic of Philosophy.* Lanham, MD: University Press of America, 1987, pp. 107–108.
4. Cornel West, *Prophetic Thought in Postmodern Times.* Monroe, ME: Common Courage Press, 1993.

5. Nel Noddings, *The Challenge to Care in Schools.* New York: Teachers College Press, 1993, p. 2.

6. West, *Prophetic Thought,* p. 5.

7. West, *Prophetic Thought,* p. 6.

8. Plato, *The Republic,* trans. B. Jowett. New York: Dolphin Books, 1960, p. 208.

9. Immanuel Kant, *Critique of Pure Reason,* trans. J. M. D. Meiklejohn. New York: Wiley, 1855. Originally published 1781, Introduction, Part I.10.

10. Jane Roland Martin, "Reclaiming a Conversation," in *The Ideal of the Educated Woman.* New Haven, CT: Yale University Press, 1985, pp. 1–7.

11. Martin, "Reclaiming a Conversation, p. 178.

12. Aristotle, *Nicomachean Ethics,* trans. James E. C. Weldon. New York: Macmillan, 1897, Chapter 1.

13. John Locke, "Some Thoughts Concerning Education," in *The Works of John Locke,* Volume X. London: Printed for W. Otridge and Son et al., 1812, pp. 6–7.

14. Alfred North Whitehead, *The Aims of Education.* New York: Free Press, 1929/1957, pp. 1–2.

15. Charles S. Peirce, "How to Make Our Ideas Clear," *Popular Science Monthly 12* (January 1878), pp. 286–302.

16. John Dewey, "My Pedagogic Creed," *The School Journal 54*(3) (January 16, 1989), pp. 77–80. Reprinted with the permission of the Center for Dewey Studies, Southern Illinois University at Carbondale.

17. Richard Rorty, "Hermeneutics, General Studies, and Teaching," *Synergos 2* (Fall 1982), p. 11.

18. Jean-Paul Sartre, *Existentialism and Human Emotions.* New York: Philosophical Library, 1957, p. 17.

19. Friedrich Nietzsche, "On the Future of Our Educational Institutions," *The Complete Works of Friedrich Nietzsche,* ed. O. E. Levy, trans. J. M. Kennedy. Edinburgh: T. N. Foulis, 1910, p. 125. This work is a collection of five lectures delivered in 1871 at the University of Basel.

20. Friedrich Nietzsche, "The Wanderer and His Shadow," in *Human All Too Human,* trans. R. J. Hollingdale. Cambridge: Cambridge University Press, 1986, p. 6. This section on the writing of Nietzsche was developed by Dr. Leslie A. Sassone from the Foundations of Education faculty at Northern Illinois University.

21. Maxine Greene, *The Dialectic of Freedom.* New York: Teachers College Press, 1988.

22. Greene, *Dialectic of Freedom,* p. 12.

23. Howard A. Osman and Samuel M. Craven, *Philosophical Foundations of Education.* Columbus, OH: Merrill, 1986, pp. 66–85.

24. Terry P. Wilson, *Navajo: Walking in Beauty.* San Francisco: Chronicle Books, 1994.

25. Terry P. Wilson, *Lakota: Seeking the Great Spirit.* San Francisco: Chronicle Books, 1994.

26. Terry P. Wilson, *Hopi: Following the Path of Peace.* San Francisco: Chronicle Books, 1994.

Educational Theory in American Schools: Philosophy in Action

Education in the News

Know Thy Subject

Ronald A. Wolk, *Teacher Magazine,* November 2002

HOW STRANGE AND IRONIC IT IS THAT TEACHERS, WHO DISSEMinate knowledge, have so little time and opportunity to acquire it. Undergraduate teacher education is justifiably criticized—even by its recipients—for its lack of academic content and rigor. Many students exit colleges and universities insufficiently equipped to teach a specific subject. In a survey that asked teachers whether they felt prepared to teach basic mathematics, for example, the majority said no. Fewer than 20 percent of elementary school teachers and half of middle school teachers said they felt prepared. In fact, only three-fourths of high school math teachers said they know enough about the subject to teach it well—and, presumably, they majored, or at least minored, in it. This may be one of the reasons why fewer than 30 percent of American students score at a proficient level or better on the math portion of the National Assessment of Educational Progress.

The knowledge deficit that many teachers take to their first jobs is difficult to overcome. Once they begin their careers, they rarely have an opportunity to engage in the kind of professional development that will increase knowledge of their discipline and improve their practice.

"Professional development" is one of those "blah blah" terms that's shorthand for something that's actually very important: continuous learning that enriches one's knowledge and improves one's craft. Traditionally, it comprises college courses taken in the evenings or during the summer to move up the salary scale and the hit-and-run workshops schools hold once or twice a year, in which outside experts lecture to teachers. But these kinds of approaches do little, if anything, to improve teaching and, thus, student learning.

To be most effective, professional development needs to be integrated into the workday of the teacher and the culture of the school. That means finding more time for teachers to work together on problems, read and discuss relevant research, and analyze their practice. Finding time for those activities means reallocating (and probably increasing) funding, changing schedules, rethinking teacher roles, revising curricula, and even negotiating changes in union contracts.

States have invested heavily in standards-based reform, the nation's de facto strategy for improving public education. They have established standards and put in place accountability systems to monitor student performance. But they have done little to prepare faculty members to teach students what they are expected to know and be able to do. Unless those states realize the crucial importance of effective professional development and move with some urgency to mandate and support it, standards-based reform will fail.

Reprinted with permission from *Teacher Magazine,* November 2002.

Learning Outcomes

After reading and studying this chapter, you should be able to:

1. Identify the major tenets of authoritarian educational theories of perennialism, essentialism, behaviorism, and positivism. (INTASC 1: Subject Matter)

2. Identify the major tenets of nonauthoritarian educational theories of progressivism, reconstructivism, humanism, and constructivism. (INTASC 1: Subject Matter)

3. Compare authoritarian and nonauthoritarian educational theories. (INTASC 2: Development & Learning)

4. Relate educational theories to learning and curriculum development. (INTASC 2: Development & Learning)

5. State the relationship of progressivism to democracy and society. (INTASC 5: Motivation & Management; INTASC 9: Reflection)

6. Relate the tenets of critical pedagogy to societal change. (INTASC 3: Diversity; INTASC 9: Reflection)

School-Based Observations

You may see these learning outcomes in action during your visits to schools:

1. This chapter contains examples of classroom activities typically associated with various educational theories. As you work in the schools, take the class activity features with you and see whether you can determine which theories you observe in use. Then decide which educational theory you subscribe to and determine whether your own classroom activities are consistent with your personal educational philosophy.

2. Interview several teachers who organize their classrooms and teaching materials differently. Using probing questions, try to uncover the educational theory or theories that account for the differing teaching approaches.

This chapter introduces a number of significant educational theories that are based on various philosophies and ways of knowing. It offers a number of big ideas or key concepts that will help you identify underlying views about knowledge and learning that are implicit in the way classrooms are organized and subject matter is presented. Some of these big ideas include teacher-centered locus-of-control educational theories (such as perennialism, essentialism, behaviorism, and positivism) and student-centered locus-of-control educational theories (such as progressivism, reconstructionism, humanism, and constructivism). Other big ideas are drawn from educational practices that flow from the application of educational theory to the classroom; these include the Great Books program, socialization, problem-based learning, and reinforcement.

Educational theory can be analyzed as the application of philosophy to the classroom. The way curriculum is organized, the manner in which instruction is delivered, the character of school environments, and the processes used in testing and grading are informed by the philosophical views held by educators, parents, and legislators. Such views vary greatly among school districts and states. Table 10.1 describes the relationships between four schools of philosophy—idealism, realism, pragmatism, and existentialism—and education.

The four schools of philosophy described in Table 10.1 give rise to different, sometimes competing, learning foci, curricular goals, teaching methods, and approaches to character and aesthetic development. Educational theorists attempt to develop cohesive ideas about teaching and learning by drawing on one or more compatible philosophies. They also attempt to clarify how these different approaches to curriculum, instruction, and assessment work or do not work together. For example, a behaviorist educational theorist could focus on the mind, the physical world, or the social world. On the other hand, it would be inappro-

TABLE 10.1   Educational Implications of Philosophy

Educational Aspect	Teacher-Centered Locus-of-Control Philosophies		Student-Centered Locus-of-Control Philosophies	
	Idealism	Realism	Pragmatism	Existentialism
Learning focus	Subject matter of the mind: literature, intellectual history, philosophy, religion	Subject matter of the physical world: mathematics, science	Subject matter of social experience	Subject matter of personal choice
Curriculum goal	The same education for all	Mastery of laws of universe	Creation of a new social order	Personal freedom and development
Preferred teaching method	Teaching for the handling of ideas: lecture, discussion	Teaching for mastery of information and skills: demonstration, recitation	Problem solving: project method, product development	Individual exploration: discovery method, authentic pedagogy
Character development	Imitation of exemplars, heroes	Training in rules of conduct	Group decision making in light of consequences	Development of individual responsibility for decisions and preferences
Aesthetic development	Study of the masterworks; values of the past heritage	Study of design in nature	Participation in art projects based on cross-cultural and universal values	Development of a personal view of the world; self-initiated activities

Source: Adapted from Van Cleve Morris and Young Pai, *Philosophy and the American School* (2nd ed.). Boston: Houghton Mifflin, 1976. Copyright 1976 by Houghton Mifflin Company. Used with permission.

priate for the behaviorist to focus on personal choice because behaviorism essentially aims to control human behavior through teacher-directed reinforcement.

This chapter describes eight educational theories that draw on different philosophies. The educational theories are grouped according to the degree to which they rely on external (teacher-based) versus internal (student-based) authority. This distinction between a teacher-centered versus a student-centered locus of control can also be used to group schools of philosophy. As indicated in Table 10.1, the ideas and principles that surround idealism and realism imply that external authority is important to the attainment of truth and goodness, whereas pragmatism and existentialism focus more on the innate worth of the individual.

Many teachers hold the view that the purpose of education is to train pupils' minds so that they can deal better with the intellectual concepts of life. These teachers emphasize the mastery of facts and information. The general notion of this point of view—the idea that any child can learn any subject at any level if the subject matter is properly presented—remains a strong challenge to teachers to arouse motivation for subject mastery among pupils. Teacher-centered locus-of-control educational theories suggest that, except for the few children who have mental, emotional, or physical impairments, every child can master the entire curriculum of the school when adequate time and resources are provided. Continued attention to test scores, grade-level achievement, and other measures of subject matter competency reflect the importance that is still attached to the teacher-centered locus-of-control view of education. School boards, parents, and the general public increasingly demand that teachers provide concrete evidence that their pupils have made progress in mastering subject matter that has been deemed appropriate (by adults) for all students to learn.

In contrast, other teachers uphold John Dewey's view that the mind is not just a muscle to be developed. They accept the notion that human beings are problem solvers who profit from personal experience. These educators also give credence to the existential student-centered locus-of-control, position, which emphasizes the importance of the individual and of personal awareness. In light of the fact that Dewey's philosophical views have prevailed in U.S. teachers' colleges for the past half century, it is not surprising that many schools in the United States reflect this student-centered locus-of-control view more than do other schools throughout the world. When teaching techniques are focused on student interactions, teachers may find that some students appear to be aimless with regard to subject matter. In such instances, the teacher is challenged to arouse student interest through inquiry leading to subject content.

Educational theorists explain how teacher-centered locus-of-control teaching and learning principles differ from those of student-centered locus-of-control principles. They also help clarify how each set of teaching and learning principles forms a cohesive whole. The eight educational theories considered here are perennialism, essentialism, behaviorism, positivism, progressivism, reconstructionism, humanism, and constructivism. To varying degrees, each of these educational views is used by classroom teachers and applied to the way teachers organize their classroom, their instruction, and their assessments. As you study these different educational theories, you will find that one or more of them clearly meshes with your own views. Understanding your own position in terms of known theory will be an invaluable asset as you develop your personal philosophy of education.

TEACHER-CENTERED LOCUS-OF-CONTROL EDUCATIONAL THEORIES

Perennialism, essentialism, behaviorism, and positivism are educational theories that espouse a teacher-centered locus of control. Each theory's approach to subject matter, classroom organization, teaching methods, and assessment places most of the responsibility on the teacher, whose job it is to enable students to learn what is important. Although each educational theory forms a distinct cohesive whole, all four are rooted in an authoritarian principle—that is, that truth and goodness are entities best understood by the person with expertise who is in authority. The students' role is, then, to attempt to master and follow the directions of those in power who have experience and authority.

This chapter presents each educational theory's ideas on curriculum, teaching, and learning. In addition, for each theory we will describe a representative program along with an illustrative class activity. The class activity is further analyzed according to the nature of the learner (active or passive), the nature of the subject matter, the use of the subject matter, and the type of thinking that is emphasized (convergent or focused on right answers, or divergent or focused on developing multiple perspectives).

■ PERENNIALISM

perennialism

An educational theory that focuses on enduring principles of knowledge; nature, human nature, and the underlying principles of existence are considered constant, undergoing little change.

The basic educational view of **perennialism** is that the principles of knowledge are enduring. The term *perennial* may be defined as "everlasting," and the perennialist seeks everlasting truths. Although there are superficial differences from century to century, the perennialist views nature, human nature, and the underlying principles of existence as constant, undergoing little change. Because of its emphasis on ageless truth, perennialism is closely associated with idealism.

Perennialists stress the importance of time-honored ideas, the great works of past and present thinkers, and the ability to reason. To know reality, perennialists maintain, one must examine individual things and concepts so as to find their essence. To find the essence, one must discard the particulars and search for the unchanging underlying essentials. The essence of human beings lies in what they have in common: the ability to reason.

For the perennialist, the intellect does not develop merely by contact with relevant experiences. The intellect must be nourished by contact with ideas because truth ultimately resides in the nature of things rather than in the sensory aspects of things. Perennialists contend that instead of focusing on current events or student interests, educators should teach disciplined knowledge, with particular emphasis on students' mastery of established facts about the great ideas and works found in literature, the humanities, mathematics, science, and the arts. (See the Perennialist Class Activity.)

PERENNIALIST FOCUS OF LEARNING

The focus of learning in perennialism lies in activities designed to discipline the mind. Subject matter of a disciplinary and spiritual nature, such as mathematics, language, logic, great books, and doctrines, must be studied. The learner is assumed to be a rational and spiritual person. Difficult mental calisthenics such as reading, writing, drill, rote memory, and computations are important in training the intellect. Perennialism holds that learning to reason is also important—an ability attained by additional mental exercises in grammar, logic, and rhetoric, as well as through use of discussion methodologies. Reasoning about human matters and about moral principles that permeate the universe links perennialism to idealism. As the individual mind develops, the learner becomes more like a spiritual being. The learner is closer to ultimate knowledge when he or she gradually assumes the mind qualities of God. Idealism also harmonizes with some findings on the psychology of learning—findings suggesting that the mind can combine pieces of learning into whole concepts that have meaning.

PERENNIALIST CURRICULUM

Perennialists believe that early schooling is best directed toward preparing children for maturity, and they emphasize the three Rs in the elementary schools.

PERENNIALIST CLASS ACTIVITY

Ms. Rosemont's literature class had been studying the works of Henry David Thoreau. In the classroom session on "Reading" from *Walden,* discussion focused on the following questions:

- Do the classics embody truth? Why or why not?
- Have all our emotions and problems been written about by great authors?
- Are none of our experiences unique? Why or why not?
- What makes a book great?
- Does popular literature ever serve a noble purpose? Why or why not?
- With whom can one talk about the best book?
- Can only great poets read the works of great poets? Why or why not?
- Does dealing with truth help us become immortal? Why or why not?
- How can we get the most benefit from our reading?

This lesson followed the Great Books procedure for questioning and could, therefore, be considered a perennialist investigation of human nature.[1]

In this perennialist class activity, the nature of the learner is *active,* the nature of the subject matter is *structured,* the use of the subject matter is *cognitive,* and the thinking approach is *convergent.*

Perennialists focus learning on subject matter of a disciplinary and spiritual nature, such as mathematics, language, logic, great books, and doctrines.

Some lay and ecclesiastical perennialists consider character training, enhanced through Bible study, to be as important as the three Rs at the elementary level. A perennialist program for the secondary level is directed more toward educating the intellectually elite. Perennialism favors trade and skill training for students who are not engaged in the rigors of the general education program. Perennialists agree that the curriculum at the secondary level should provide a general educational program for the intellectually gifted and vocational training for the less gifted.

THE GREAT BOOKS: A PERENNIALIST PROGRAM

The Great Books program, associated with Robert M. Hutchins and Mortimer Adler, has brought attention to perennialism. Proponents of the Great Books program maintain that studying the works of the leading scholars of history is the best way to a general education. Perennialists debate the use of contemporary sources. Some contend that students can draw on modern sources to obtain knowledge and that the Great Books program should be flexible enough to include newer works of literature, science, and so forth.

■ ESSENTIALISM

Essentialism holds that there is a common core of information and skills that an educated person in a given culture must have. Schools should be organized to transmit this core of essential material as effectively as possible. There are three basic principles of essentialism: a core of information, hard work and mental discipline, and teacher-centered instruction. Essentialism seeks to educate by providing training in the fundamentals, developing sound habits of mind, and teaching respect for authority. The back-to-the-basics movement is a truncated form of essentialism because it focuses primarily on the three Rs and discipline.

Although essentialism shares many of the same principles as perennialism, there are several important differences. Essentialism draws equally from both idealism and realism. Essentialists are not so intent on transmitting underlying, basic truths; rather, they advocate the teaching of a basic core of information that will help a person live a productive life today. Hence, this core of information

essentialism

An educational theory that holds that there is a common core of information and skills that an educated person must have; schools should be organized to transmit this core of essential material.

Should Today's Education Be Relevant to Tomorrow's Job Market?

Educational theories hold competing views about the most valuable type of knowledge. Perennialism values underlying principles; positivism values clear, precise information that is verifiable in the physical world; and constructivism values the importance of personal meaning. The debate over how relevant knowledge should be to the job market rages in the midst of these educational theories.

YES

Norish Adams, coordinator of curriculum and research at the Florida A&M University Developmental Research School, has been a pioneer in the school-to-work movement in her area. A veteran teacher, preservice instructor, and NEA activist, Adams can be reached at nadams2@famu.edu.

NO

Janette Gerdes teaches English and literature at Signal Hill School in Illinois. She was nominated for a Golden Apple Award in 1997 and recognized in Who's Who Among American Teachers in 1998. A member of the Belleville Education Association, Gerdes can be reached at jgerdes@stclair.k12.il.us.

Over the course of my 30-year career, I've found no approach to teaching—and I've tried dozens—that has been as successful as one that ties subject knowledge to career development.

When students explore the future job market as an authentic component of learning, concepts take on more meaning than when introduced as abstract rules, definitions, and manipulations.

Here's what I've seen:

■ *Linking school and work enriches curriculum.* The beauty, creativity, and challenges of mathematics, for example, are richly revealed when viewed from the perspective of a doctor, master carpenter, quilter, astronaut, political analyst, or artist.

■ *Linking school and work motivates students.* Some of my students participate in a five-day career shadowing program at a nearby corporation. They learn firsthand about becoming a computer scientist, engineer, human resource director, and support employee with the space flight program.

Back in class, they write about their experiences and file their work in "course/career portfolios" that focus their thinking on school, work, and the connections between the two.

As one of my most reluctant students said, "The best part of keeping the portfolio is that it helps me see how all this required stuff fits into my life and helps to make it better."

■ *Linking school and work keeps options open for all students, without "tracks."* At the public high school in Tallahassee where I work, we don't have separate vocational and academic paths for students, relegating application to one and theory to the other.

Teachers should never allow the near-sacred mission of learning to be polluted by letting the public schools become the minor leagues for corporate America.

The goal of public schools should not be to train children to be worker drones. The goal should be to educate them so that they may enjoy full, happy, and productive lives.

If we educate kids to be thinkers, questioners, and problem-solvers, they'll do fine in the ever-changing, rarely predictable job market.

When I started teaching 10 years ago, the Internet was still used almost exclusively by scientists and government, a much smaller percentage of families owned home computers, and no one had even heard of anything called the World Wide Web.

Since then, we've seen huge changes in technology and the media, the Cold War has ended, and HMOs have overtaken American health care. What could we have taught the class of 1988 that would be relevant to today's job market anyway?

What we need to teach our students is how to read, write, think, question, and learn. Let the employers handle the specifics of job training.

Of course it's wholly appropriate to use technology to shape young minds. We should use whatever tools are available to turn kids on to learning, and kids love computers.

But a student with a well-rounded education—rather than one targeted for a job market that's likely to be obsolete by the time she's ready to enter it—has the advantage in the job market and, more importantly, will be better prepared to lead a full, satisfying life.

(continued)

YES

Students in academic classes need not ask, "When will I ever really use this?" Teachers will never have to say, "You'll understand next year when you go to college."

Instead, we're in the process of creating six career academies in the areas of business, health sciences, architecture and design, engineering, public policy, and education. These areas were selected based on job predictions in Florida and the nation, as well as surveyed student interests.

Our goal: to give all students a rigorous education in the basics, plus the skills they'll need in problem-solving, technology, business, and public policy to thrive in today's job market—and tomorrow's.

■ *Linking school and work helps students find their way with a minimum of struggle and cost.* Ninety percent of our students go on to postsecondary education. Many must work to help pay college costs, and they can't afford the luxury of taking six or seven years to graduate.

Our schoolwide career development program ensures that our graduates don't enter college unprepared to make wise, informed choices about their major, and that they don't flounder or drop out during the first year or two of college.

■ *Linking school and work is the best way to prepare students for whatever lies ahead.* Young people who understand the world they will work in will take the classes, engage in the activities, do the reading, join the organizations, and enter the competitions that will prepare them for the jobs of the 21st century—whatever they may be.

NO

NEA Today ran a cover story on the school-to-work movement last spring, which included anecdotes of students who became more motivated by participating in career-based learning.

But I suspect there are also kids who were turned off. And, worse, students focusing on math classes as a prelude to careers as pilots still might not see the point of studying literature or history.

This type of schooling sends such a terrible message to students—that learning is meaningful only when connected to a future job.

We have to be better than that, better than our money-obsessed culture. We have to show kids that there is more to life than a job, even a rewarding one.

There is the beauty of the natural world. There is freedom and the history of the struggle to achieve it. There is the tapestry of diverse cultures. There are great writers who speak to us from across the decades and centuries. And, yes, boys and girls, there is the immense pleasure of learning for its own sake.

I understand that people must have jobs to survive. But I will always teach my junior high English and literature students that life is about more than survival. . . .

Source: "Should Today's Education Be Relevant to Tomorrow's Job Market?" *NEA Today* (January 1999), p. 43.

WHAT DO YOU THINK?
Should today's education be relevant to tomorrow's job market?

To give your opinion, go to Chapter 10 of the companion website **(www.ablongman.com/johnson13e)** and click on Debate.

can and will change. This is an important difference in emphasis from the notions of everlasting truth that characterize the perennialist. In addition, essentialism stresses the disciplined development of basic skills rather than the perennialist goals of uncovering essences or underlying principles. (See the Essentialist Class Activity.)

ESSENTIALIST FOCUS OF LEARNING

Essentialism's goals are to transmit the cultural heritage and develop good citizens. It seeks to do this by emphasizing a core of fundamental knowledge and skills, developing sound habits of mental discipline, and demanding a respect for authority in a structured learning situation. The role of the student is that of a

ESSENTIALIST CLASS ACTIVITY

Mr. Jackson's second graders had just learned to count money. He decided to let them play several games of "musical envelopes." There was one envelope per student, each containing a different amount of paper "nickels," "dimes," "quarters," and "pennies." When the music stopped, students had to count the money in their envelopes. The one with the most money for each game got a special prize.[2]

In this essentialist class activity, the nature of the learner is *passive*, the nature of the subject matter is *structured*, the use of the subject matter is *cognitive*, and the thinking approach is *convergent*.

learner. School is a place where children come to learn what they need to know, and the teacher is the person who can best instruct students in essential matters.

ESSENTIALIST CURRICULUM

The essentialist curriculum focuses on subject matter that includes literature, history, foreign languages, and religion. Teaching methods require formal discipline and feature required reading, lectures, memorization, repetition, and examinations. Essentialists differ in their views on curriculum, but they generally agree about teaching the laws of nature and the accompanying universal truths of the physical world. Mathematics and the natural sciences are examples of subjects that contribute to the learners' knowledge of natural law. Activities that require mastering facts and information about the physical world are significant aspects of essentialist methodology. With truth defined as observable fact, instruction often includes field trips, laboratories, audiovisual materials, and nature study. Habits of intellectual discipline are considered ends in themselves.

Essentialism envisions subject matter as the core of education. Severe criticism has been leveled at U.S. education by essentialists who advocate an emphasis on basic education. Essentialism assigns to the schools the task of conserving the heritage and transmitting knowledge of the physical world. In a sense, the school is a curator of knowledge.

With the burgeoning of new knowledge in contemporary society, essentialism may be contributing to the slowness of educational change. In this context, essentialism has been criticized as obsolete in its authoritarian tendencies. Such criticism implies that essentialism does not satisfy the twenty-first-century needs of U.S. youth. Essentialist educators deny this criticism and claim to have incorporated modern influences in the system while maintaining academic standards.

> *The business of education is not to make the young perfect in any one of the sciences, but so to open and dispose their minds as may best make them capable of any, when they shall apply themselves to it.*
>
> **John Locke**

Essentialist teaching methods require formal discipline through emphasis on required reading, lectures, memorization, repetition, and examination.

ESSENTIAL SCHOOLS MOVEMENT

The Essential Schools movement is a contemporary school reform effort developed by Dr. Theodore Sizer. Sizer contends that students need to master a common core of information and skills, and he encourages schools to strip away the nonessentials and focus on having students "use their minds well." The Essential Schools movement does not specify what content is essential in a given culture at a given time. Rather, "essential schools" are required to analyze clearly what this core of information should be and to change the curriculum to emphasize this core.

The Coalition of Essential Schools (www.essentialschools.org) promotes a vision of schooling in which students engage in in-depth and rigorous learning. Essential schools select a small number of core skills and areas of knowledge that they expect all students to demonstrate and exercise broadly across content areas. Ten common principles have been developed by Dr. Sizer in collaboration with essential school participants to guide the efforts of the coalition. These principles include using the mind well; a focus on clear, essential learning goals; an attempt to apply these goals to all students; personalized teaching and learning; emphasis on student-as-worker; student performance on real tasks with multiple forms of evidence; values of un-anxious expectation; principal and teachers as generalists first and specialists second; budgets that do not exceed traditional schools by more than 10 percent; and nondiscriminatory policies and practices.

■ BEHAVIORISM

B. F. Skinner (1904–1990), the Harvard experimental psychologist and philosopher, is the recognized leader of the movement known as **behaviorism.** Skinner verified Pavlov's stimulus-response theory with animals and, from his research, suggested that human behavior could also be explained as responses to external stimuli. (See the Behaviorist Class Activity.) Because of its focus on the careful examination of environment, behaviors, and responses, behaviorism is closely linked to realism. Other behaviorists' research expanded on Skinner's work in illustrating the effect of the environment, particularly the interpersonal environment, on shaping individual behavior. In the words of Charles Wolfgang and Carl Glickman,

> Behaviorists share a common belief that a student's misbehavior can be changed and reshaped in a socially acceptable manner by directly changing the student's environment. The Behaviorist accepts the premise that students are motivated by the factor that all people will attempt to avoid experiences and stimuli that are not pleasing and will seek experiences that are pleasing and rewarding.[3]

BEHAVIORIST FOCUS OF LEARNING

Behaviorism is a psychological and educational theory that holds that one's behavior is determined by environment, not heredity. This suggests that education

behaviorism

A psychological theory that asserts that behaviors represent the essence of a person and that all behaviors can be explained as responses to stimuli.

BEHAVIORIST CLASS ACTIVITY

Students in Mr. Drucker's civics class were given merit tokens for coming into the room quietly, sitting at their desks, preparing notebooks and pencils for the day's lesson, and being ready to begin answering comprehension questions in their workbooks. On Fridays students were allowed to use their tokens at an auction to buy items that Mr. Drucker knew they wanted. Sometimes, however, students had to save tokens for more than two weeks to buy what they liked best.

In this behaviorist class activity, the nature of the learner is *passive,* the nature of the subject matter is *amorphous* (unstructured), the use of the subject matter is *affective* (having to do with feelings) or *cognitive,* and the thinking approach is *convergent.*

can contribute significantly to the shaping of the individual because the teacher can control the stimuli in a classroom and thereby influence student behavior. Behaviorists believe that the school environment must be highly organized and the curriculum based on behavioral objectives, and they hold that knowledge is best described as behaviors that are observable. They contend that empirical evidence is essential if students are to learn and that students must employ the scientific method to arrive at knowledge. The task of education is to develop learning environments that lead to desired behaviors in students.

REINFORCEMENT: A BEHAVIORIST PRACTICE

The concept of reinforcement is critical to teacher practices in behaviorism. The behav-

Behaviorists contend that learning takes place when approved behavior is observed and then positively reinforced.

iorist teacher endeavors to foster desired behaviors by using both positive reinforcers (things students like, such as praise, privileges, and good grades) and negative reinforcers (things students wish to avoid, such as reprimands, extra homework, and lower grades). The theory is that behavior that is not reinforced (whether positively or negatively) will eventually be "extinguished"—will cease to occur. In general, behaviorists contend that learning takes place when approved behavior is observed and then positively reinforced.

A teacher may provide nonverbal positive reinforcement (smiling, nodding approval) or negative reinforcement (frowning, shaking the head in disapproval). Similarly, nondirective statements, questions, and directive statements may be positive or negative. Both children and adults respond to the models other people (peers, adults, heroes) represent to them by imitating the model behavior. Behaviorists contend that students tend to emulate behaviors that are rewarded.

The behaviorists have supplied a wealth of empirical research that bears on the problems of attaining self-control, resisting temptation, and showing concern for others. Behaviorists do not attempt to learn about the causes of students' earlier problems. Rather, the teacher must ascertain what is happening in the classroom environment to perpetuate or extinguish students' behavior.

◼ POSITIVISM

The educational theory of positivism stems from what the social scientist Auguste Comte (1798–1857) described as "positive knowledge." Comte divided the thinking of humankind into three historical periods, each of which was characterized by a distinct way of thinking. The first was the theological era, in which people explained things by reference to spirits and gods. The second was the metaphysical era, in which people explained phenomena in terms of causes, essences, and inner principles. The third was the positive period, in which thinkers did not attempt to go beyond observable, measurable fact.

Positivism focuses learning on acquisition of facts based on careful empirical observation and measurement of the world.

The positivist position rejects essences, intuition, and inner causes that cannot be measured. Empirical verification is central to all proper thinking. This theory rejects beliefs about mind, spirit, and consciousness and holds that all reality can be explained by laws of matter and motion. In sum, **positivism** limits knowledge to statements of observable fact based on sense perceptions and the investigation of objective reality. Positivism became a rallying point for a group of scholars in Vienna. Because the group consisted largely of scientists, mathematicians, and symbolic logicians, positivism became known as logical positivism.

POSITIVIST FOCUS OF LEARNING

Practiced as an educational theory, positivism focuses learning on the acquisition of facts based on careful empirical observation and measurement of the world. Positivism requires schools to develop content standards that represent the best understandings of experts who have already uncovered important ideas based on their own observation and measurement. Students are encouraged both to master these expert understandings and to develop their own skills of observation, classification, and logical analysis.

OBJECTIVE FORCED-CHOICE TESTING: A POSITIVIST REQUIREMENT

Testing students' acquisition of content standards is a valued activity for the positivist educator. Creating objective tests that are free from bias is critical to education. Because empirical knowledge is proven by years of careful analysis, there is a set of truths that students should master and understand according to a clear set of criteria. The only way to ensure that such knowledge has been attained and understood is to test all students according to the same objective set of criteria. (See the Positivist Class Activity.)

DIRECT INSTRUCTION: A POSITIVIST APPROACH TO TEACHING AND LEARNING

What we have to learn to do, we learn by doing.

Aristotle

Direct instruction is a teaching and learning approach that requires teachers to clearly and precisely identify and state what a student needs to learn and master, as well as to restate this expectation through different media and assignments. It is a teaching and learning approach that places the responsibility for clear, precise expectations on the teacher. Once a teacher has identified precisely what students should know and be able to do, the teacher is expected to clearly describe to students exactly what they should know and be able to do. Teachers are encouraged to use repetition and have students practice and practice again, recite and recite again, what is to be learned. Teachers are further encouraged to have students repeat the main ideas of the instruction by using different media: oral recitation, writing, restating, drawing, and so forth. The

POSITIVIST CLASS ACTIVITY

Humberto Diaz introduced the meaning of surface tension to his junior high science students. During class he then distributed eyedroppers, water, and pennies to the students. He directed the students to determine how many drops of water could fit on the surface of the penny before spilling over. Students were to collect data and develop a data table and corresponding charts. At the end of the class, Mr. Diaz asked the students to discuss their findings and draw a conclusion.

In this positivist class activity, the nature of the learner is *active,* the nature of the subject matter is *structured,* the use of the subject matter is *cognitive,* and the thinking approach is *convergent.*

key ingredient for this approach is the use of clear, uncluttered statements and restatements about the focus of learning.

This approach to teaching and learning fits the positivist educational theory because in such an educational approach knowledge is considered something that is clear and precise. If all knowledge is clear, precise, and the same for all, then teachers can be expected to require all students to learn the same knowledge. Direct instruction is possible because all knowledge that is worthy is also clear and precise.

STUDENT-CENTERED LOCUS-OF-CONTROL EDUCATIONAL THEORIES

Progressivism, reconstructionism, humanism, and constructivism espouse a student-centered authority approach to subject matter, classroom organization, teaching methods, and assessment. Although each theory forms a distinct cohesive whole, all four are rooted in an internal locus-of-control principle, that is, the belief that truth and goodness belong to all persons no matter what their station. Teachers are learners and learners are teachers, and education is the process through which individuals help one another to clarify personal meaning.

As with the teacher-centered positions, we will present each student-centered locus-of-control theory's ideas on curriculum, teaching, and learning. In addition, for each theory we will describe a representative program along with an illustrative class activity. The class activity is further analyzed according to the nature of the learner (active or passive), the nature of the subject matter, the use of the subject matter, and the type of thinking that is emphasized (convergent or focused on right answers, or divergent or focused on developing multiple perspectives).

PROGRESSIVISM

In the late 1800s, with the rise of democracy, the expansion of modern science and technology, and the need for people to be able to adjust to change, people in Western societies had to have a new and different approach to acquiring knowledge in order to solve problems. A U.S. philosopher, Charles S. Peirce (1839–1914), founded the philosophical system called *pragmatism*. This philosophy held that the meaning and value of ideas could be found only in the practical results of these ideas. Later, William James (1842–1910) extended Peirce's theory of meaning into a theory of truth. James asserted that the satisfactory working of an idea constitutes its whole truth. Pragmatism was carried much further by John Dewey (1859–1952), who was a widely known and influential philosopher and educator. Dewey insisted that ideas must always be tested by experiment. His emphasis on experiment carried over into his educational philosophy, which became the basis for what was usually described as progressive education. **Progressivism** is an educational theory that emphasizes that ideas should be tested by experimentation and that learning is rooted in questions developed by learners.[4]

From its establishment in the mid-1920s through the mid-1950s, progressivism was the most influential educational view in the United States. Progressivists basically oppose authoritarianism and favor human experience as a basis for knowledge. Progressivism favors the scientific method of teaching and learning, allows for the beliefs of individuals, and stresses programs of student involvement that help students learn how to think. Progressivists believe that the school should actively prepare its students for change. Progressive schools emphasize learning *how* to think rather than *what* to think. Flexibility is important in the curriculum design, and the emphasis is on *experimentation,* with

Progressivism, the educational theory developed by philosopher John Dewey (1859–1952), emphasizes that ideas should be tested by experimentation and that learning is rooted in questions developed by the learners.

progressivism

An educational theory that emphasizes that ideas should be tested by experimentation and that learning is rooted in questions developed by the learner.

no single body of content stressed more than any other. This approach encourages *divergent thinking*—moving beyond conventional ideas to come up with novel interpretations or solutions. And because life experience determines curriculum content, all types of content must be permitted. Certain subjects regarded as traditional are recognized as desirable for study as well. Progressivist educators would organize scientific method-oriented learning activities around the traditional subjects. Such a curriculum is called experience-centered or student-centered; the essentialist and perennialist curricula are considered subject-centered. Experience-centered curricula stress the *process* of learning rather than the result.

Progressivism as a contemporary teaching style emphasizes the process of education in the classroom. It is more compatible with a core of problem areas across all academic disciplines than with a subject-centered approach to problem solving. It would be naive to suggest that memorization and rote practice should be ruled out. In progressive teaching, however, they are not stressed as primary learning techniques. The assertion is that interest in an intellectual activity will generate all the practice needed for learning. (See the Progressivist Class Activity.)

PROGRESSIVISM AND DEMOCRACY

A tenet of progressivism is that the school, to become an important social institution, must take on the task of improving society. To this end, progressivism is deemed a working model of democracy. Freedom is explicit in a democracy, so it must be explicit in schools. But freedom, rather than being a haphazard expression of free will, must be organized to have meaning. Organized freedom permits each member of the school society to take part in decisions, and all must share their experiences to ensure that the decisions are meaningful. Pupil–teacher planning is the key to democracy in classrooms and is the process that gives some freedom to students, as well as teachers, in decisions about what is studied. For example, the teacher might ask students to watch a film about an issue of interest and have them list questions about the issue that were not answered by the film but that they would like to investigate. Students and the teacher can then analyze the questions and refine them for research. Such questions can become the basis for an inquiry and problem-solving unit of study. However, even if pupil–teacher planning is not highlighted as a specific activity, any progressivist lesson allows students to give some of their own input in ways that influence the direction of the lesson. In that sense, progressivist lessons always involve pupil–teacher planning. For instance, asking students to make statements about life in 1908, using copies of pages from 1908 Sears and Roebuck catalogs as their information source, allows students to focus on any items *they* choose from the catalogs, not items determined by the teacher.

The one real object of education is to have a man in the condition of continually asking questions.

Bishop Mandell Creighton

PROGRESSIVIST CLASS ACTIVITY

Ms. Long's second graders read "Recipe for a Hippopotamus Sandwich" from *Where the Sidewalk Ends: Poems and Drawings of Shel Silverstein* (New York: Harper & Row, 1974). Ms. Long asked each student to draw a picture of the hippopotamus sandwich. For homework she instructed the children to read the poem to someone, show the picture, and then tell about the person's reaction on the following day.[5]

In this progressivist class activity, the nature of the learner is *active,* the nature of the subject matter is *structured,* the use of the subject matter is *cognitive,* and the thinking approach is *divergent.*

Progressivism views the learner as an experiencing, thinking, exploring individual. Its goal is to expose the learner to the subject matter of social experiences, social studies, projects, problems, and experiments that, when studied by the scientific method, will result in functional knowledge from all subjects. Progressivists regard books as tools to be used in learning rather than as sources of indisputable knowledge.

PROGRESSIVISM AND SOCIALIZATION

Many people believe that the socialization aspect of progressivism—the fact that it represents the leading edge of society and helps students learn how to manage change—is its most valuable aspect. However, progressivism is criticized for placing so much stress on the processes of education that the ends are neglected. Its severest critics contend that progressive educators have little personal commitment to anything, producing many graduates who are uncommitted and who are content to drift through life. Progressivists counter by stating that their educational view is relatively young and that therefore they expect criticism; after all, trial-and-error methods are a part of the scientific method. The advent of progressivism as a counterview to the more traditional educational views provided exciting discussions that continue among thinkers in education.

■ RECONSTRUCTIONISM

Reconstructionism emerged in the 1930s under the leadership of George S. Counts, Harold Rugg, and Theodore Brameld. Reconstructionism recognized that progressivism had made advances beyond essentialism in teacher–pupil relations and teaching methodology. However, progressivism fixated too heavily on the needs of the child and failed to develop long-range goals for society. Spurred by the Great Depression of the 1930s, reconstructionism called for a new social order that would fulfill basic democratic ideals. Advocates believe that people should control institutions and resources and that this could happen if there were an international democratic world government. Reconstructionism draws on both pragmatism (like progressivism) and existentialism.

CRITICAL PEDAGOGY: A RECONSTRUCTIONIST CURRICULUM

An education for a reconstructed society would require that students be taught to analyze world events, explore controversial issues, and develop a vision for a new and better world. Teachers would critically examine cultural heritages, explore controversial issues, provide a vision for a new and better world, and enlist students' efforts to promote programs of cultural renewal. Although teachers would attempt to convince students of the validity of such democratic goals, they would employ democratic procedures in doing so. (See the Reconstructionist Class Activity.)

A contemporary version of reconstructionism is rooted in the work of Henry Giroux, who views schools as vehicles for social change. He calls teachers to be transformative intellectuals and wants them to participate in creating a new society. Schools should practice "critical pedagogy," which unites theory and practice as it provides students with the critical thinking tools to be change agents.[6]

Reconstructionists teach students to critically analyze world events, explore controversial issues, and develop a vision for a new and better world.

RECONSTRUCTIONIST CLASS ACTIVITY

Mr. Brandese Powell asked his second graders to look at a cartoon that pictured a well-dressed man and woman in an automobile pulled by a team of two horses. The highway they were traveling along passed through rolling farmland with uncrowded meadows, trees, and clear skies in the background. He led a discussion based on the following questions:

1. What is happening in this picture?
2. Do you like what is happening in the picture? Why or why not?
3. What does it say about the way you may be living when you grow up?
4. Are you happy or unhappy about what you have described for your life as an adult?
5. How can we get people to use less gasoline now?
6. What if we could keep companies from making and selling cars that could not travel at least forty miles on one gallon of gasoline? How could we work to get a law passed to do this?

In this reconstructionist class activity, the nature of the learner is *active,* the nature of the subject matter is *structured,* the use of the subject matter is *affective,* and the thinking approach is *divergent.*

RECONSTRUCTIONISM AND WORLD REFORMATION

A persistent theme of reconstructionism is that public education should be the direct instrument of world reformation. Reconstructionism accepts the concept that the essence of learning is the actual experience of learning. Reconstructionism espouses a theory of social welfare designed to prepare learners to deal with great crises: war, inflation, rapid technological changes, depression. Based on the experiences of World War I, the Great Depression, and World War II, reconstructionist educators believe that the total educational effort must be seen within a social context.

As we indicated earlier, John Dewey had an immense influence on progressivism. Dewey also made major contributions to reconstructionist philosophy with his efforts to define the individual as an entity within a social context. Reconstructionists go further in urging that individuals, as entities within a social context, engage in specific reform activity. Reconstructionist classroom teachers tend to use affective (emotion-related) emphases and moral dilemmas in directing students' attention toward social reform.

Paulo Freire (1922–1997) was a contemporary social reconstructionist who dedicated his life to freeing society from an educational system that he saw as devised by the dominant class "for the purpose of keeping the masses submerged and contained in a culture of silence."[7] Having experienced hunger and poverty firsthand in the 1930s, Freire worked among the poor to assist them in improving their lot in life. He proposed a problem-posing approach to education, to replace what he called the "banking" method—in which one privileged class knows the truth and deposits it in the appropriate amounts into the empty and limited minds of the unwashed or dispossessed. Freire advocated an education that expands every human being's ability to understand and transform the world.

Paulo Freire (1922–1997) was a social reconstructionist who advocated educational reform that affirms the needs of all children, not just those from privileged families.

humanism

An educational theory that contends that humans are innately good—that they are born free but become enslaved by institutions.

▪ HUMANISM

Humanism is an educational approach that is rooted both in the writings of Jean-Jacques Rousseau and in the ideas of existentialism. Rousseau (1712–1778), the father of Romanticism, believed that the child entered the world not as a blank slate but with certain innate qualities and tendencies. In the opening sentence of *Émile,* Rousseau's famous treatise on education, he states that "God makes all things good; man meddles with them and they become evil."[8] Thus, Rousseau believed in basic goodness at birth. He also believed that humans are born free but become enslaved by institutions. Humanistic education mingles some of these ideas from Rousseau with the basic ideas of existentialism.

Humanistic educational theory is concerned with enhancing the innate goodness of the individual. It rejects a group-oriented educational system and seeks ways to enhance the individual development of the student. (See the Humanist Class Activity.)

Humanists believe that most schools de-emphasize the individual and the relationship between the teacher and the student. Humanists claim that as educators attempt to predict behavior of students, they turn individuals into objects to be measured. According to the humanist, education should be a process of developing a free, self-actualizing person—a process that is centered on the student's feelings. Therefore, education should not start with great ideas, the world, or humankind, but with the individual self.

Jean-Jacques Rousseau (1712–1778) is the father of Romanticism and believed that humans are born free but become enslaved by the structures of society.

HUMANISTIC CURRICULUM

Because the goal of humanism is a completely autonomous person, education should be without coercion or prescription. Students should be active and should be encouraged to make their own choices. The teacher who follows humanistic theory emphasizes instruction and assessment based on student interests, abilities, and needs. Students determine the rules that will govern classroom life, and they make choices about the books to read or exercises to complete.

Humanists honor divergent thinking so completely that they delay giving their own personal opinions and do not attempt to persuade students to particular points of view. Even though they emphasize the affective and thereby may make students feel a certain urgency about issues, it is always left to the individual student to decide when to take a stand, what kind of stand to take, whether a cause merits action, and, if so, what kind of action to engage in.

HUMANISTIC SCHOOL ENVIRONMENTS

Martin Buber's writings describe the heart of humanistic school environments. In *I and Thou,* Buber portrays two different ways in which individuals relate to the

HUMANIST CLASS ACTIVITY

Ms. Fenway wanted her ninth graders to think about the effectiveness of television and radio advertising. She asked students to write down any five slogans or jingles they could remember and the products advertised. Ms. Fenway selected from their items at random and tested the class. For each slogan, class members had to identify the product advertised. The test was corrected in class by the students, who were very surprised to find the grading scale reversed. Those who had all correct answers received Fs, and those who had only one correct answer received As. When asked why she had reversed the grades, Ms. Fenway responded, "Why do you think advertising is so effective?" She asked whether students resented some companies' selling tactics. Then she told students to help her make a list of questions to ask themselves in order to avoid spending money in ways they might later regret. She also asked for specific examples of spending money for items they later wished they had not bought.[9]

In this humanist class activity, the nature of the learner is *active,* the nature of the subject matter is *structured,* the use of the subject matter is *affective,* and the thinking approach is *divergent.*

Humanists believe that education should be without coercion or prescription and that students should be active learners and make their own choices.

outside world. In the I–It relationship, one views something outside oneself in a purely objective manner, as a thing to be used and manipulated for selfish ends. In contrast, I–Thou relationships are characterized by viewing other people as sacred entities who deserve profound respect. Such relationships focus on the importance of understanding and respecting diverse, subjective, personal meanings. Buber was deeply concerned that people were treated as objects (Its) rather than as Thous, especially in business, science, government, and education.[10]

Many students today believe that educators treat them as Social Security numbers stored in a computer. In college classes of 100 or more, it is difficult for teachers to remember students' names, let alone get to know them as individuals. Often teachers assign material, mark papers, and give grades without ever really conversing with students. When the semester ends, students leave class and are replaced by other, equally anonymous students. Buber did not believe that schools had to be this way. He contended that in a proper relationship between teacher and student, there is a mutual sensibility of feeling. There is empathy, not a subject–object relationship.

A humanistic school environment is one in which people (both teacher and student) share their thoughts, feelings, beliefs, fears, and aspirations with one another. Nel Noddings labels this *an environment of caring.* According to humanists, this kind of caring relationship should pervade the educational process at all levels as well as society at large.

In his book *Summerhill,* A. S. Neill provides a radical picture of a school environment that focuses on the development of caring, I–Thou relationships. Neill describes schools that treat teachers and students as individuals, allow students to create their own rules, make class attendance optional, and stress caring relationships over academic achievement. A number of schools in England and Canada were modeled after *Summerhill,* and some are still in existence.[11]

Inspired by humanism, many educators attempt to personalize education in less radical ways. Examples include individualizing instruction, open-access curriculum, nongraded instruction, and multi-age grouping. Each of these approaches attends to the uniqueness of the learner. Block scheduling permits flexibility for students to arrange classes of their choice. Free schools, storefront schools, schools without walls, and area vocational centers provide humanistic alternatives to traditional school environments.

Educational programs that address the needs of the individual are usually more costly per pupil than traditional group-centered programs. Consequently, as taxpayer demands for accountability mount, humanistic individualized programs are often brought under unit-cost scrutiny. Nonetheless, growing numbers of educators are willing to defend increased expenditures to meet the needs of the individual learner within the instructional programs of the schools.

◼ CONSTRUCTIVISM

constructivism

An educational theory that emphasizes hands-on, activity-based teaching and learning during which students develop their own frames of thought.

Constructivism is an educational theory that emphasizes hands-on, activity-based teaching and learning. Constructivism is closely associated with existentialism. The American Psychological Association (APA) has encouraged teachers to reconsider the manner in which they view teaching. The APA contends that students are active learners who should be given opportunities to construct their own frames of thought. Teaching techniques should include a variety of different learning activities during which students are free to infer and discover their own answers to important questions. Teachers need to spend time creating these learning situations rather than lecturing. Constructivist educators consider true learning to be the active framing of personal meaning (by the learner) rather than the framing of someone else's meaning (the teacher's).

Such a view of teaching and learning has profound ramifications for the school curriculum. If students are to be encouraged to answer their own questions and develop their own thinking frame, the curriculum needs to be reconceptualized. Constructivist theorists encourage the development of critical thinking and the understanding of big ideas rather than the mastery of factual information. They contend that students who have a sound understanding of important principles that were developed through their own critical thinking will be better prepared for the complex, technological world.

Few high school students look upon the language which they speak and write as an art, not merely a tool, yet it ought to be, the noblest of all arts, looked upon with respect, even with reverence, and used always with care, courtesy, and deepest respect.

Mary Ellen Chase

CONSTRUCTIVIST CURRICULUM

Constructivist ideas about curriculum stand in sharp contrast to the authoritarian approaches we described earlier. Traditionally, learning has been thought of as a mimic activity, a process that involves students repeating newly presented information. Constructivism, on the other hand, focuses on the personalized way a learner internalizes, shapes, or transforms information. Learning occurs through the construction of new, personalized understanding that results from the emergence of new cognitive structures. Teachers and parents can invite such transformed understandings, but neither can mandate them.

Increasing Student Achievement through Essential Schools

STUDY PURPOSE/QUESTIONS: The Coalition of Essential Schools (CES) completed a series of studies investigating the impact of an essential school approach on students' academic achievement. The study focuses on twenty-two schools in Ohio, Michigan, Massachusetts, and Maine that agreed to implement the ten essential schools principles and had received awards in 1998 to implement the tenets of essential schools. These schools typically serve students who start out with low standardized test scores, come from diverse ethnic and racial backgrounds, and live in poverty. All twenty-two schools received formal professional development and on-site coaching from the CES regional center in their states. The centers are the Center for Essential School Reform in Ohio; Michigan Coalition of Essential Schools; the Center for Collaborative Education in Boston; and the Southern Maine Partnership in Gorham, Maine.

STUDY DESIGN: Throughout 1999–2000 teachers used essential schools principles to redesign and implement their instructional approaches. The curriculum was reorganized to focus on essential concepts and skills. Students were provided a consistent approach with all teachers espousing the ten principles of essential schools. At the end of the academic year, students were tested on a variety of academic achievement measures including performance on standardized tests from the four states' Department of Education websites. Of the twenty-two schools, nineteen schools' scores were available on their states' websites.

STUDY FINDINGS: Student achievement data from these CES schools were compared to statewide averages and with averages from all other schools that received funding to improve their school's academic achievement beginning in 1999–2000, but which worked with other school reform organizations. The data from these two comparison groups allow the CES researchers to analyze student achievement in CES schools in the context of the achievement trends within their states. Achievement test score data were analyzed from a total of seventeen tests in the subjects of mathematics, reading, and writing. In some cases, the data were sufficient to make reasonable claims about the progress achieved by schools. In others, the data allowed the researchers to make initial observations but were insufficient to provide a complete picture. Here are the findings:

- The percentage of students in essential schools passing state achievement tests increased substantially from the initial year of testing.
- Essential schools are making significant progress in closing the gap between the percentage of their students who are passing and the state average of students passing the tests. On four tests in two states, CES schools not only narrowed the gap but also surpassed the state averages.

IMPLICATIONS: Based on the initial, positive findings in favor of essential schools approaches, it is reasonable to consider the essential schools approach as a legitimate method for enhancing student achievement. However, further research is needed to follow students' progress throughout a longer time period. Unexpected consequences would also need to be analyzed so that the full effect of such a program is understood.

Source: Coalition of Essential Schools, *Students Thrive in Schools That Promote Intellectual Rigor and Personalize Learning,* A Report on the Coalition of Essential Schools' Work with Comprehensive School Reform Demonstration (CSRD) Schools in Ohio, Maine, Massachusetts and Michigan, 2001.

Accepting this simple proposition—that students learn by shaping their own understandings about their world—makes the present structure of the school difficult. According to constructivist principles, educators should invite students to experience the world's richness and empower them to ask their own questions and seek their own answers. The constructivist teacher proposes situations that encourage students to think. Rather than leading students toward a particular answer, the constructivist teacher allows students to develop their own ideas and chart their own pathways. But schools infrequently operate in such a constructivist way. Typically, schools determine what students will learn and when they will learn it.

Schooling doesn't have to be this way, however. Schools can better reflect the constructivist point of view by allowing students to search for their own understanding. Nel Noddings writes:

> Having accepted the basic constructivist premise, there is no point in looking for foundations or using the language of absolute truth. The constructivist position is really post-epistemological and that is why it can be so powerful in inducing new methods of research and teaching. It recognizes the power of the environment to press for adaptation, the temporality of knowledge, the existence of multiple selves behaving in consonance with the rules of various subcultures.[12]

PROBLEM-BASED LEARNING: A CONSTRUCTIVIST PEDAGOGY

Problem-based learning has recently emerged as a student-centered teaching and learning approach that is in keeping with constructivist tenets. Based on Dewey's concept of teaching through student-centered problems, this educational methodology centers student activities on tackling authentic contemporary problems. Problem-based learning is a radical approach in that it challenges educators to focus curriculum on student interests and concerns rather than on content coverage. (See the Constructivist Class Activity.)

In a problem-based experience, students are presented with a "hook." The hook might be a letter from a civic group, a request from an environmental agency, or any other motivating beginning. The hook describes a contemporary dilemma and requests students to take on some real-life role to solve the problem. Problem-based learning usually requires students to spend time finding the core problem, clarifying the problem, assessing what is and is not known about the problem, gathering needed data to complement what has been uncovered, and finally presenting a position statement and/or suggesting a solution. Throughout the process, teachers act as guides or coaches and give great latitude to student interest. Students learn content and skills within the problem context. Teachers spend time selecting problems that are compatible with student maturity levels and curricular needs.

Constructivist educators invite students to experience the world's richness and empower them to ask their own questions and seek their own answers. Problem-based learning is an example of constructivist pedagogy.

CONSTRUCTIVIST CLASS ACTIVITY

Reiko Nishioka's sophomore biology class had just completed reading Michael Crichton's novel *Jurassic Park* when a letter from movie producer Steven Spielberg arrived addressed to each student in the class. The letter requested each student's assistance in Spielberg's effort to determine what aspects of the novel were or were not scientifically accurate with regard to dinosaurs. The letter asked students to prepare a written summary and to send the summary, along with proper documentation, to Spielberg's production company. Because time was limited, Spielberg requested that the summaries be completed within three weeks. Reiko provided time for her students to think about the letter and then asked them to determine what they would do next.

In this constructivist class activity, the nature of the learner is *active,* the nature of the subject matter is *unstructured,* the use of the subject matter is *authentic* to real life, and the thinking approach is *divergent.*

GLOBAL PERSPECTIVES
Looking beyond the Boundaries

Throughout this chapter, educational theories have been presented as consistent sets of ideas linked together logically. This kind of categorization is strongly related to the types of writings that were part and parcel of the work of European thinkers in the eighteenth and nineteenth centuries. It is no surprise that current educational theories in the United States tend to display a Western-style of thinking. Such thinking tends to create clear sets of distinctions. This also comes as no surprise, because in large part immigrants to this country during the eighteenth and nineteenth centuries and part of the twentieth century came primarily from Germany, Poland, Ireland, Scandinavia, England, France, Italy, and Switzerland.

This emphasis on Western-style, categorical thinking has begun to change. The last half of the twentieth century expanded the European focus. Faster and better communication, the opening of once-closed societies, and increased interdependence have permitted differing thinking schemes to intermesh and at times conflict with one another.

Such clashes, although uncomfortable, help educators break through or at least readjust the limitations of clear and neat categorical boundaries. The comfort of categories can cause stagnation or even imprison one's thinking. Neat sets of proven ideas provide sets of solutions, but these solutions are limited by the original thinking schemes that generated them. Calling into question these categories of thought is hard to do without the infusion of other types of thinking. The influx of Asian, African, and other types of Eastern thinking is especially helpful in breaking down the rigidity of thought boundaries. The thinking schemes from these Eastern cultures do not require such rigid boundary sets. Eastern thought is more concerned with the unification of ideas rather than the separation of ideas. The big ideas that are generated from a more encompassing way of thinking challenge the narrower ideas and categories. These bigger ideas provide more flexible thinking schemes and offer a type of cohesion different from that of strict logical distinctions. In what way does the idea of "harmony" influence the way you might study educational theories? In what way does the idea of "balance" influence the distinction between teacher-centered and student-centered loci of control? How does the concept of learner-centeredness challenge or cause you to reconsider the distinction between teacher-centeredness and student-centeredness?

SUMMARY

This chapter provided an overview of eight leading educational views that are held in part or entirely by teachers in U.S. schools. The teacher-centered locus-of-control educational theories include perennialism, essentialism, behaviorism, and positivism. Each of these theories emphasizes the importance of controlling the subject matter content, thinking processes, and discipline procedures within the classroom setting. Teachers are held responsible for controlling these areas of the school environment.

The student-centered locus-of-control educational theories include progressivism, reconstructionism, humanism, and constructivism. Each of these theories places less emphasis on the external control of the teacher and more emphasis on student control. Progressivism promotes individual student inquiry, whereas reconstructionism encourages critical thinking and promotes social activism. Humanism stresses student freedom, and constructivism emphasizes the importance of supporting personal meaning.

This chapter further illustrates the relationship of current educational views to the classical philosophies and describes the educational views in terms of the learner, subject matter orientation, and external versus internal locus-of-control tendencies.

Although your ultimate teaching style might not be completely committed to a single educational theory, the basic description of these views will help you to identify your personal preferences.

DISCUSSION QUESTIONS

1. What were the characteristics and behaviors of one of your favorite teachers who was authoritarian toward students? Of a favorite teacher who was focused on student-centered locus of control?

2. When might a teacher focus on personalized situations involving such things as death or injustice to stimulate student learning? How would such a strategy relate to the back-to-basics expectations of many U.S. schools?

3. The concept of reinforcement is influential on the teacher practices of behaviorists. How would you use positive reinforcers and negative reinforcers while teaching your subject area?

4. Experienced teachers often advise a beginning teacher: "Be firm with the students and let them know at the beginning how you intend to teach your classes." Is this advice good or bad? Discuss the pros and cons of such a procedure.

5. Constructivism rules out some of the conventional notions about educating youth. It emphasizes students' construction of personalized understandings of the world rather than an established curriculum. What implications does constructivism have for grouping students?

JOURNAL ENTRIES

1. Schools are being challenged to develop students who can achieve in a complex business world. Interview business executives from two different companies to determine the importance of ethics in the operations of the businesses. Determine the extent to which the executives' ethical values were influenced by teachers. In your journal, list recommendations for teachers made by the executives. Describe a teaching approach that responds to these recommendations.

2. Describe the teaching method and classroom environment that you believe has been most effective for you as a learner. Identify the educational theory or theories that would encourage the teaching method and environment you have selected. Create a graphic that visually represents your own theory of teaching and learning.

PORTFOLIO DEVELOPMENT

1. Develop a hands-on, activity-based lesson in a subject that you enjoy. Type up the entire lesson, with teacher and student directions and activity pages. Then write an introductory rationale that describes which educational theories are supported by the way you designed the lesson. Include this lesson in your portfolio as an example of your ability to analyze lessons in terms of theories.

2. Select one major concept from one of the national standards documents (available at your college library). Describe the teaching methods you would use to help students attain an understanding of that particular concept. Then annotate the teaching methods, explaining their theoretical foundations. Include this in your portfolio to illustrate your ability to apply theory to practice.

PREPARING FOR CERTIFICATION

■ EDUCATIONAL THEORIES

1. One of the topics in the Praxis II Principles of Teaching and Learning (PLT) test is "encouraging students to extend their thinking" through the use of a "repertoire

of flexible teaching and learning strategies" (for example, teacher-directed instruction, cooperative learning, independent study, laboratory/hands-on approaches). In this chapter, you learned about eight major educational theories and the various teaching and learning approaches, classroom practices, and educational programs of study related to each theory. Review each of the theories, paying particular attention to the relationship between how students learn and the teaching and learning strategies consistent with each theory. Which theory seems most compatible with your own beliefs and philosophy? Which theory seems least compatible?

2. Answer the following multiple-choice question, which is similar to items in Praxis and other state certification tests. If you are unsure of the answer, reread the chapter.

> Ms. Jones, a second-grade teacher, began a language arts lesson by reading the beginning and middle of a story to the children. Instead of reading the end of the story, however, she asked the students to create an ending of their own. The children wrote their own endings and then read them aloud. Ms. Jones then read the book's ending, and she and the class talked about the many ways a story can end. Which educational theory appears to guide Ms. Jones's lesson?

> (A) behaviorism
> (B) constructivism
> (C) positivism
> (D) reconstructionism

3. Answer the following short-answer question, which is similar to items in Praxis and other state certification tests. After you've completed your written response, use the scoring guide in the *Test at a Glance* materials to assess your response. Can you revise your response to improve your score?

> What is meant by the terms *teacher-centered locus of control* and *student-centered locus of control*? Give three examples of teaching practices or learning activities that you might observe in two classrooms—one dominated by teacher-centered locus of control and the other dominated by student-centered locus of control.

WEBSITES

Companion Website

www.ed.uiuc.edu/EPS/Educational-Theory/purpose.asp *Educational Theory* is a quarterly publication that fosters the continuing development of educational theory and encourages wide and effective discussion of theoretical problems within the education profession. You will find this journal filled with contemporary concerns that relate to teaching and learning.

www.funderstanding.com/constructivism.cfm Funderstanding contains a variety of theories on learning, instruction, assessment, influences, history of education, learning patterns, educational reforms, as well as additional links.

www.imsa.edu/team/cpbl/cpbl.html The Illinois Mathematics and Science Academy Center for Problem-Based Learning offers programs, ideas, examples of problem-based learning in classrooms, access to a problem-based learning teachers' network, and other resources that relate to the use of problem-based learning in contemporary schools.

www.summerhillschool.co.uk This is the official website for A. S. Neill's Summerhill School. The site presents the ideas of A. S. Neill and news about contemporary schools that follow a humanistic approach to education.

FURTHER READING

Joyce, B. R., Weil, M., and Calhoun, E. (2000). *Models of Teaching* (6th ed.). Boston: Allyn and Bacon. This book describes the relationship between different approaches to teaching and various educational theories. It shows that most teaching methods tend to draw from several related educational theories rather than a single educational theory.

Kohn, Afie. (1993). *Punished by Rewards: The Trouble with Gold Stars, Incentive Plans, A's, Praise, and Other Bribes.* Boston: Houghton Mifflin. Dr. Kohn describes the unexpected consequences of using reinforcement practices and cautions against the dangers of providing rewards to enhance good behavior.

Raines, Peggy, and Shadiav, Linda. (1995, May/June). "Reflection and Teaching: The Challenge of Thinking beyond the Doing." *The Clearing House, 68*(5), p. 271. This article describes how regular reflection about what has really occurred in the daily life of the classroom protects teachers from unexpected outcomes.

Strike, Kenneth A., and Soltis, Jonas F. (1985). *The Ethics of Teaching.* New York: Teachers College Press. A careful analysis of the ethics surrounding the life of a teacher. Drs. Strike and Soltis provide thoughtful questions and ideas that help teachers reassess their own ethical positions.

Torp, Linda, and Sage, Sara. (2002). *Problems and Possibilities: Problem-Based Learning for K–16 Education* (2nd ed.). Alexandria, VA: Association for Supervision and Curriculum Development. Provides a specific approach to the implementation of problem-based learning. The approach is supported by educational theories, and a clear set of steps for developing a problem-based learning unit is presented.

NOTES

1. Lloyd Duck, *Instructor's Manual for Teaching with Charisma.* Boston: Allyn and Bacon, 1981, Item 4, pp. 53–54.
2. Duck, *Instructor's Manual,* Item A, p. 40.
3. Charles H. Wolfgang and Carl D. Glickman, *Solving Discipline Problems: Strategies for Classroom Teachers.* Boston: Allyn and Bacon, 1980, p. 121.
4. John Dewey, *Democracy and Education.* New York: Macmillan, 1916, pp. 1–9.
5. Duck, *Instructor's Manual,* Item D, p. 41.
6. Henry A. Giroux, "Teachers as Transformative Intellectuals," *Social Education 49* (1985), pp. 376–379.
7. Paulo Freire, *Pedagogy of the Oppressed.* New York: Continuum Press, 1989.
8. Jean-Jacques Rousseau, *Émile,* trans. Alan Bloom. New York: Basic Books, 1979.
9. Duck, *Instructor's Manual,* Item C, pp. 50–51.
10. Martin Buber, *I and Thou,* trans. Ronald G. Smith. New York: Charles Scribner, 1958.
11. A. S. Neill, *Summerhill.* New York: Hart, 1960.
12. Robert B. Davi, Carolyn A. Maher, and Nel Noddings, "Constructivism Views on the Teaching and Learning of Mathematics," *Journal for Research in Mathematics Education,* Monograph No. 4 (1990), p. 27.

Building an Educational Philosophy

Education in the News

Scientists Explore the Molding of Children's Morals

By Susan Gilbert, *New York Times*, March 18, 2003

ALONG WITH THEIR ACADEMIC EDUCATION, STUDENTS IN kindergarten through 12th grade in the Metropolitan School District of Lawrence Township in Indianapolis have another field of study: character education.

Each school displays a poster listing what the district has identified as the "life skills for building character," including honesty, fairness and trustworthiness. Teachers look for ways to reinforce these traits each day.

Classroom discussions focus on the moral strengths and weaknesses of characters in the books that students have read. Students make quilts and write songs celebrating the life skills. They get buttons and other rewards for putting the skills into practice.

While the Lawrence Township schools are exceptional in the scope of their initiative, they are not alone in their effort to calibrate the moral compasses of their students. Over the last few years, schools in 48 states have introduced character education programs in the hope of bolstering students' resolve to resist the temptation to lie, cheat, bully, use drugs and behave immorally in other ways. The Department of Education has promoted these efforts by giving $27 million in character education grants since 1995.

Many of the programs draw on some recent research showing that although all children are born with the capacity to be moral, it needs to be nurtured by parents, schools and the community at large. Otherwise, its development is stunted.

Without a firm sense of right and wrong, some experts say, children tend to become cynical, alienated and extremely selfish. They cheat to get ahead, rationalizing that "everybody does it." They lack the social obligation to control their anger when they feel that they have been wronged. In the extreme, tragedies happen, like the massacre at Columbine.

Much of the impetus for character education in schools is a perception that the moral fiber of children as well as adults is unraveling. Two-thirds of Americans think that society is less honest and moral than it used to be, according to *Bowling Alone,* published in 2000, by Dr. Robert Putnam, a professor of public policy at Harvard.

Last year, a poll of 12,000 high school students by the Josephson Institute of Ethics, a nonprofit organization in Marina del Rey, Calif., found that 74 percent admitted cheating on a test in the previous year.

But some researchers—while not denying that there is considerable room for improvement—say children today are no less moral than their parents, grandparents and great-grandparents were as children.

Dr. Elliot Turiel, the author of *The Culture of Morality,* published last year, says cheating is just as common today as it was in the 1920's. He compared surveys of students done then with the findings of recent surveys like those of the Josephson Institute and found that the percentage of students who admitted to cheating was roughly the same.

"It may be that kids today are fresh and disobedient in fairly large numbers," said Dr. Turiel, a psychologist at the University of California at Berkeley, "but was it really different in the past? It wasn't with cheating."

Dr. Turiel and other researchers criticize many of the character education programs in schools for being superficial and ineffective. "Morality isn't traits of character but a complicated set of judgments," he said.

Dr. John M. Doris, a philosophy professor at the University of California at Santa Cruz, goes as far as to question whether there is such a thing as a moral character. He says that the existence of moral character, described by philosophers as far back as Aristotle, is not supported in the scientific literature today.

Learning Outcomes

After reading and studying this chapter, you should be able to:

1. Describe the influence of classroom practices on motivation. (INTASC 2: Development & Learning; INTASC 4: Teaching Methods; INTASC 5: Motivation & Management)

2. Analyze underlying differences among discipline practices. (INTASC 2: Development & Learning; INTASC 5: Motivation & Management)

3. List the characteristics of teachers as change agents. (INTASC 9: Reflection; INTASC 10: Collaboration)

4. Provide examples of teacher leadership behaviors. (INTASC 6: Communication & Technology; INTASC 9: Reflection; INTASC 10: Collaboration)

5. State the components of a personal philosophy of education. (INTASC 2: Development & Learning)

School-Based Observations

You may see these learning outcomes in action during your visits to schools:

1. While you are visiting different classrooms as part of your practicum experiences, record the various classroom planning and disciplinary activities that you observe. Next, classify the various styles you have observed and identify the classroom philosophies the teachers are employing. Seek out opportunities to discuss these findings with each teacher you observe.

2. Select a teacher who has a classroom organization approach that matches your own. Interview the teacher and use probing questions to clarify the underlying reasons why the teacher set up the classroom as he or she did.

This chapter helps you to clarify your role as a teacher in society and identify effective classroom practices. It offers a number of big ideas or key concepts that will challenge your image of what constitutes a good teacher. Ideas such as classroom environment or climate, voice and space, community of learners, and teacher as leader are presented to help you clarify your own approach to education. Which type of environment is best for today's students? How much teacher control is needed? Whose voices are predominant and whose voices are muted in today's classrooms? These questions are examined and shown to be important to the development of a classroom climate that is either open and authentic or directed and didactic.

The possibility of developing a community of learners in a world of standards-based education is also explored in this chapter. Should teachers be change agents, should they attempt to bring about a better society through their role as teacher, or should they help to emphasize the positive aspects of society and encourage students to be law-abiding citizens? What types of leadership qualities are implicit in today's teacher profession? These questions strike at the very heart of what it means to be a teacher, and this chapter helps you wrestle with them and assess your personal philosophy of education.

Extensive surveys of modern views of learning—as expressed in philosophy, psychology, and education journals and studies—reveal a seemingly endless and divergent range of views. Therefore, today's classroom teachers must identify their own beliefs about educating young people. Although labeling the classroom practice of any one teacher is not easy, we recommend that you, as a prospective teacher, carefully identify a personal set of operational principles with regard to classroom techniques.

Educational trends such as the back-to-basics movement and direct teaching are related to certain philosophies of education. The back-to-basics movement and direct teaching focus on clearly prescribed subject matter and are in the realms of essentialism and perennialism, whereas the concepts of free schools and problem-based learning are experience based and focus on student activity as identified in progressivism and constructivism. Figure 11.1 illustrates the association of these primary educational theories with teacher-centered authority,

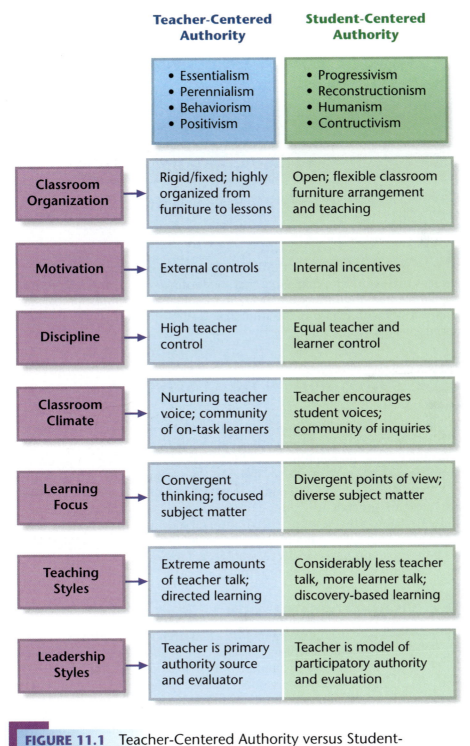

EDUCATIONAL THEORIES

	Teacher-Centered Authority	Student-Centered Authority
	• Essentialism • Perennialism • Behaviorism • Positivism	• Progressivism • Reconstructionism • Humanism • Contructivism
Classroom Organization	Rigid/fixed; highly organized from furniture to lessons	Open; flexible classroom furniture arrangement and teaching
Motivation	External controls	Internal incentives
Discipline	High teacher control	Equal teacher and learner control
Classroom Climate	Nurturing teacher voice; community of on-task learners	Teacher encourages student voices; community of inquiries
Learning Focus	Convergent thinking; focused subject matter	Divergent points of view; diverse subject matter
Teaching Styles	Extreme amounts of teacher talk; directed learning	Considerably less teacher talk, more learner talk; discovery-based learning
Leadership Styles	Teacher is primary authority source and evaluator	Teacher is model of participatory authority and evaluation

FIGURE 11.1 Teacher-Centered Authority versus Student-Centered Authority Classroom Approaches

A teacher's practices in the classroom reflect his or her personal philosophy.

which stresses convergent thinking, and student-centered authority, which stresses divergent thinking. Note that the terms *teacher-centered authority* and *student-centered authority* are meant to denote overall philosophical stances or perspectives with regard to the student and subject matter, not to imply strict or permissive classroom management.

USING PHILOSOPHY IN THE CLASSROOM

A philosophy of education is not a set of written words. It is a platform on which decisions are made and life is led. A teacher's practices in the classroom reflect his or her personal philosophy. The best goal for beginning educators is to become comfortable with a variety of classroom practices that address the needs of learners. It is not a matter of selecting one methodology over another but rather of understanding these different approaches and using them responsibly. We believe that a sound preparation for teaching addresses the need to develop a workable classroom philosophy—one that incorporates the larger role of teaching in a complex society as well as the microrole of the teacher working with students in the classroom setting.

CLASSROOM ORGANIZATION

classroom organization

A multifaceted dimension of teaching that includes the content, method, and values that infuse the classroom environment, planning, and discipline practices.

All teachers must be able to organize the classroom in such a way that it is conducive to teaching and learning. In fact, many school principals are quick to assert that the easiest way to predict the success of a beginning teacher is to evaluate his or her ability to organize the classroom. A common misconception is that good classroom organization means maintaining a controlled atmosphere and refusing to allow any behavior that even looks ungoverned or unplanned. Actually, **classroom organization** is a multifaceted dimension of teaching that includes the content, methods, and values that infuse the classroom environment. It is a dimension of teaching that requires analysis and selection similar to that used in the identification of a preferred teaching philosophy. Figure 11.1 shows how closely one's teaching philosophy affects the different components of classroom organization.

LESSON PLANNING

Careful lesson planning is mandatory if effective teaching and learning are to follow. If the learners are considered to be passive, the lesson plan might emphasize students' absorption of the factual content of the subject matter. Adherents of teaching styles that consider the learners to be active participants (student-centered authority) would tend to emphasize processes and skills to be mastered and view the factual content of the subject matter as important but variable.

Regardless of the expectation for the learner, active or passive, the teacher needs to plan sound lessons. Every lesson should be built from a basic set of general objectives that correspond to the overall goals of the school district. This is not to suggest that every third-grade classroom in a school district should have the same daily learning objectives for the students. Daily lesson objectives can vary from classroom to classroom depending on the particular needs of the students being served. However, if those daily teaching objectives are closely related to the overall objectives of the school district, then cross-district learning will reflect the school district's overall goals.

Lessons should be tied to some form of teaching units. These units should be planned in detail to include suggestions for teaching the lessons, types of materials to be used, and specific plans for evaluation. Initially, these are all philosophical questions for the classroom teacher. The way the teacher approaches these questions says a lot about his or her classroom philosophy.

THE PHYSICAL SETTING

The mere arrangement of classroom furniture and the use of classroom materials may be predicated on the teacher's perception of the learners as passive or active. Traditionally, the classroom has tended to be arranged in rows and columns at the elementary and secondary levels of schooling. This type of classroom arrangement has often been thought to be the best for classroom control and supervision. Often, however, the elementary teacher will rearrange the classroom into a series of small circles for special groupings in reading, mathematics, and other specific subjects.

Student-centered authority theories tend to support more open classrooms. The teacher intends learning for the students to be divergent in nature, and the student is expected to be more active in the learning process. This is not to suggest that one type of classroom arrangement is better than another or that one theory is superior to another; but we do suggest that the teacher in training examine classroom theory as it relates to the physical environment for learning.

STUDENT ASSESSMENT AND EVALUATION

In assessing student progress and assigning grades, most teachers use a variety of techniques including examinations, term papers, project reports, group discussions, performance assessments, and various other tools. If the subject matter is treated as a bundle of information, teacher-made tests will tend to seek certain facts and concepts as "right" answers, suggesting emphasis on

Teachers need to build sound lessons from a basic set of general objectives that correspond to the overall goals of the school district.

We not only want students to achieve, we want them to value the process of learning and the improvement of their skills, we want them to willingly put forth the necessary effort to develop and apply their skills and knowledge, and we want them to develop a long-term commitment to their learning.

Carole A. Ames

Are Uniforms a Good Way to Improve Student Discipline and Motivation?

Requiring students to wear uniforms is a practice that may or may not improve discipline and motivation. It also raises questions about student voice and school climate. Does restricting the way a student dresses also restrict individual expression? Your philosophy of education will help you determine your personal position concerning this debate.

YES

Pat Morse-McNeely retired two years ago after 26 years as a secondary school language arts, social studies, health, and special education teacher and guidance counselor in San Antonio, Stockdale, and Dallas, Texas. She also writes poetry.

NO

Dave Oland teaches social studies and is the peer coaching coordinator at Wyandotte High School in Kansas City, Kansas, where he has worked for ten years. He wrote this essay with Patty Kamper and Brian Dolezal, members of his teaching team.

In the late 1950s, South Houston Middle School instituted a very detailed dress code, although not exactly uniforms.

The kids could not come to school in their usual personal style. Girls wore dark skirts and light blouses. Hose and high heels were banned, as were extreme hairstyles like the beehives that were then becoming the big thing. Makeup was out except for light lipstick. Earrings had to be small and inconspicuous.

Boys wore dark pants and white shirts tucked in neatly, with loafers or lace-up shoes. No sneakers. No jewelry. Nothing to distract or compete for attention at the school.

Discipline improved drastically—fewer fights. Kids were not worrying about how they looked. They were on task 90 percent of the time. By the end of that year, the student body as a whole had jumped two grades, from Cs to As, Ds to Bs.

Since that time, I have read a lot of research both in favor of and against uniforms, and it appears to me that the preponderance of evidence is in favor. Catholic and other parochial schools have long used uniforms with success.

The American spirit is not about conformity. It is about allowing individuals the opportunity to think outside the box. The ingenuity of individual thought has made this country great, and public education has fostered this type of thinking.

As we work to change our schools, we must focus on real issues like building relationships with parents, students, and colleagues while improving the quality of instruction. Let's not resort to quick fixes and Band-aids like uniforms. We want to encourage our students to develop better attitudes on life, society, their future, and themselves. Let's engage them in a dialogue about what clothing is appropriate for school, rather than regulating what they must wear. Are we afraid to do the real work of changing the culture of our schools?

As our students come to the metal detectors in the morning, let's not greet them with, "Good morning. Do you have your uniform? No? Well, go home then. No education for you today."

Last year, our principal asked a committee to research this issue. We found no hard evidence that

(continued)

convergent thinking. However, if the subject matter is treated as big ideas that are applicable to problem solving, and if students are expected to engage in processes and develop skills to arrive at several "right" answers, teacher-made tests will tend to allow for divergent thinking.

How you develop your classroom philosophy will also dictate the emphasis you place on a student's academic performance. You must decide whether a student is to be compared with his or her peers or with a set of expectations based on individual needs and differences. Generally, teachers who support student-centered authority and look for divergence in learning will tend to place less emphasis on group norms. Teachers who favor teacher-centered au-

YES

Parents find that buying two or three uniforms is ultimately cheaper than buying clothes to follow the fads, and it stops arguments at home about what Johnny or Mary will wear to school on this day or that. Uniforms "level" the student body because one cannot tell the "haves" from the "have nots."

While kids say they hate uniforms, they can hardly wait to join some school group that wears one: ROTC, spirit club, band. They seek pins, necklaces, sashes, jackets—all uniforms—that state something about the person and identify them as "belonging to. . . ."

Uniforms build school spirit because they foster this sense of belonging. They enhance school loyalty and pride since the students are recognized wherever they go in the uniform as belonging to that particular school. They represent their whole student body.

In fact, I don't think it would hurt anybody if teachers were also required to wear uniforms! That would cut down on teachers' expenses and make them clearly identifiable to the student body.

Individualism does not depend on your hairdo or your dress, but upon your spirit, your personality, and your self-discipline. We are in real trouble if we depend on our mode of dress to express our individuality.

The only real freedom is freedom of thought. Conformity lives in rules and laws and all the other demands of living in large groups. Without conformity, there would be chaos.

When we adopt uniforms, we send a clear message: School is for learning, not showing off.

NO

uniforms had any significant impact on improving achievement, only scattered anecdotes. In all the educational conferences we have attended over the years, we have never seen one session touting the power of school transformation through uniforms.

We support our district's general clothing guidelines. But creating and maintaining a new uniform policy would reduce the time spent on instructional improvement and increase divisiveness, both among staff and between staff and students.

Do we choose to run our public schools in the manner of prisons, boot camps, and parochial schools? Should we in public education place such a premium on forced conformity? We should celebrate our students' individuality, which gives us the opportunity to open a significant port of entry into their lives and build deeper, more authentic relationships with them.

Since redesigning our school into "Small Learning Communities" four years ago, we have had fewer fights and discipline problems, higher scores, and a much higher graduation rate. We didn't need uniforms to accomplish this.

Some say it is more economical for families to buy uniforms. But kids who want nice clothes will want them regardless of a uniform policy, so parents may need to buy both uniforms and the clothes kids really want to wear.

Do we want to risk alienating kids who may already be on the edge? Are we okay with losing even one child who may quit school if uniforms are mandated? No.

Source: "Are Uniforms a Good Way to Improve Student Discipline and Motivation?" *NEA Today* (April 2002), p. 20.

WHAT DO YOU THINK?
Are uniforms a good way to improve student discipline and motivation?

To give your opinion, go to Chapter 11 of the companion website (**www.ablongman.com/johnson13e**) and click on Debate.

thority for the classroom with a stress on convergence in learning will be more apt to favor student evaluation strategies that are based on group norms.

◼ MOTIVATION

The concept of **motivation** is derived from the word *motive*, which means an emotion, desire, or impulse acting as an incitement to action. This definition of motive has two parts: First, the definition implies that motivation is internal because it relates to emotions, desires, or other internal drives; second, it implies that there is an accompanying external focus on action or behavior. Organizing

motivation

Internal emotion, desire, or impulse acting as an incitement to action.

The physical setting of the classroom tends to reflect whether the teacher follows a directive or nondirective theory of education.

a learning environment so that it relates to student needs and desires (internal) and also permits active participation in the learning process (external) is important to student motivation.

Teachers want students to be motivated to do many things: complete homework, be responsible, be lifelong learners, be on time, have fun, care about others, become independent. However, it is not always clear how one sets up a classroom environment that ultimately promotes these desired outcomes. For example, in a teacher-dominant orientation, control is primarily in the hands of the teacher. In such an authoritarian setting, motivation tends to come in the form of rules and regulations. Students are given clear

RELEVANT RESEARCH

The Three C's of Safe Schools: Cooperation, Conflict Resolution, and Civic Values

STUDY PURPOSE/QUESTIONS: Whether the school is urban, suburban, or rural, students report frequent problems involving physical aggression (being punched and kicked and seeing teachers being slapped or hit by students), property damage, and incivility (profanity, vulgarity, etc.). Highlands Elementary in Edina, Minnesota, chose to combat these problems by instituting a three-pronged program based on the three C's: cooperative community service, conflict resolution, and civic values. During the 1996–1997 academic year, David and Roger Johnson, Laurie Stevahn, and Peter Hodne conducted a study to determine the impact of the three C's program on Highlands Elementary.

STUDY DESIGN: The study focused on the program's impact on students, faculty, and community. The researchers employed three data collection methods: on-site observation of classrooms, analysis of instructional materials, and a review of journals and records related to the three C's program.

STUDY FINDINGS: The researchers reported positive findings. Almost 100 percent of students' parents were involved in establishing mutual goals, participating in a division of labor, and sharing resources. The school developed a strong sense of community in which members actively seek to resolve conflicts and solve problems together. All students learn to engage in problem-solving negotiations and how to mediate schoolmates' conflicts. Caring, respect, and responsibility values are posted in every classroom; and faculty and staff report that these values guide decision making about curriculum, instruction, and resources.

IMPLICATIONS: The positive results of this study imply that schools may need to incorporate cooperation, conflict resolution, and civic values into the regular instructional program. This notion challenges the extreme versions of realist philosophy and essentialist educational theory—for example, the argument that schools should focus solely on academic growth. To what degree schools should become involved in the direct instruction of values and attitudes is a difficult question. But research results such as these support this type of instruction.

Source: David W. Johnson, Roger T. Johnson, Laurie Stevahn, and Peter Hodne, "The Three C's of Safe Schools," *Educational Leadership* 55(2) (October 1997), pp. 8–13.

directions concerning their responsibilities; and they are expected to follow these directions because the teacher is in charge. For some students, this clarity of expectations and rules is comfortable. Students achieve because they must; in such a setting, the second half of motivation (external action) is achieved, but not the first (internal desire). The reason students' internal motivation may suffer is that they recognize that both the task of teaching and the responsibility for their learning belong primarily to the teacher.

Motivation of learners consists of two aspects: internal desire and action.

In a learner-dominant setting, the responsibility for learning is primarily borne by the students. The teacher attempts to produce a climate of warmth and mutual respect. Students are encouraged to achieve specific outcomes, but ultimately, they are free to select those that most interest them. In this type of setting, the first aspect of motivation (internal desire) is achieved, in that students select the learning outcomes and processes that interest them; however, the second aspect of motivation (external action) is not as clearly achieved, in that students act according to their personal desires and these desires do not always match those of the teacher.

As a teacher, you should arrange the classroom environment so that it matches your personal philosophy. Your task here is to consider carefully the "sources of power" that best reflect your philosophy of education. Figure 11.2 illustrates as many as five different power sources that relate to five different levels of motivation.[1] Power can be coercive when the motivation is "to obey." Power can take the form of rewards when the motivation is "to get." Power can be seen as legitimate when motivation is "to respect." Power can be in the form of charisma when the motivation is "to cooperate." Finally, power can be knowledge when the motivation is "to understand." Your philosophy of teaching could include all of these sources of power. All of them might be necessary at one time or another. On the other hand, it is important to assess how you set up your classroom rules and environment and make certain that they match your personal understanding of where power should lie in the teaching and learning process.

In every real man a child is hidden that wants to play.

Friedrich Nietzsche

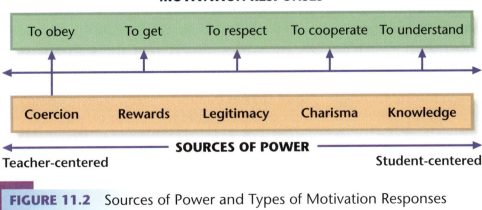

FIGURE 11.2 Sources of Power and Types of Motivation Responses

■ DISCIPLINE

The attention given by the national media to disruptive behavior in the classroom has rekindled conflicting views regarding discipline. Polls of parents and teachers alike list discipline among the top issues confronting the schools. The main source of dissatisfaction for nearly two-thirds of today's teachers is their inability to manage students effectively. Teachers also are concerned about the effect disruptive behavior has on learning. The discipline dilemma—how to achieve *more* teacher control in the classroom while adhering to a more open philosophy that advocates *less* teacher control—precludes the development of a school discipline policy that would satisfy both views. Depending on the school district's expectations, the teacher might be caught between conflicting demands. Whatever the personal philosophy of the teacher, he or she must address the wishes of the district when establishing classroom management schemes. The division of views on classroom discipline has inspired numerous books to assist teachers with discipline problems, and many special courses and workshops have been developed to deal with classroom discipline strategies. But because very few beginning teachers are given extensive exposure to discipline strategies in teacher preparation programs, the vast range of alternatives makes the choice of strategies difficult for teachers who have yet to develop their own styles.

Carl Glickman and Charles Wolfgang have identified three schools of thought along a teacher–student control continuum (Figure 11.3).[2] Noninterventionists hold the view that teachers should not impose their own rules; students are inherently capable of solving their own problems. Interactionists suggest that students must learn that the solution to misbehavior is a reciprocal relation between student and teacher. Interventionists believe that teachers must set classroom standards for conduct and give little attention to input from the students.

As you prepare to be a teacher, you need to identify your own beliefs regarding discipline in the classroom. The goal is to keep disruptive behavior at a minimum, thus enhancing the students' potential for learning as well as your own job satisfaction. Where maintenance of discipline is the primary concern, one might choose from among the entire range of possibilities along the Glickman–Wolfgang continuum regardless of one's own teaching style preference. Figure 11.4 illustrates how the major theories and behaviors of classroom management relate in terms of control issues along the teacher–student control continuum. It is the professional responsibility of each classroom teacher to understand how each behavior can be used to support his or her preferred teaching philosophy.

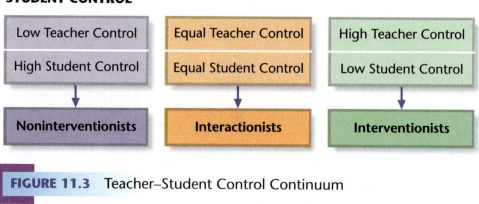

FIGURE 11.3 Teacher–Student Control Continuum

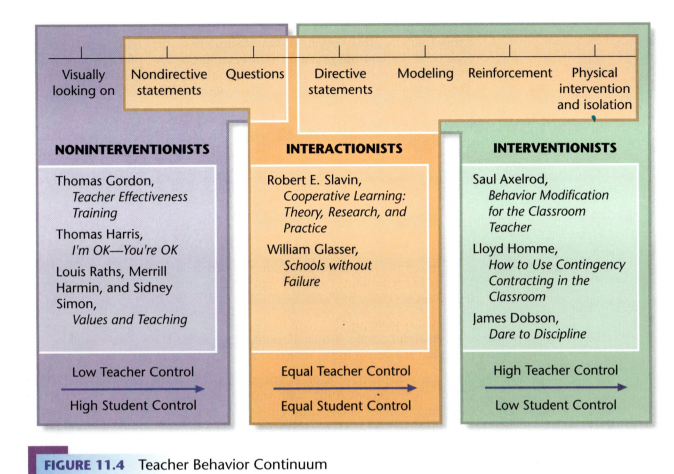

| Visually looking on | Nondirective statements | Questions | Directive statements | Modeling | Reinforcement | Physical intervention and isolation |

NONINTERVENTIONISTS

Thomas Gordon,
Teacher Effectiveness Training

Thomas Harris,
I'm OK—You're OK

Louis Raths, Merrill Harmin, and Sidney Simon,
Values and Teaching

Low Teacher Control

High Student Control

INTERACTIONISTS

Robert E. Slavin,
Cooperative Learning: Theory, Research, and Practice

William Glasser,
Schools without Failure

Equal Teacher Control

Equal Student Control

INTERVENTIONISTS

Saul Axelrod,
Behavior Modification for the Classroom Teacher

Lloyd Homme,
How to Use Contingency Contracting in the Classroom

James Dobson,
Dare to Discipline

High Teacher Control

Low Student Control

FIGURE 11.4   Teacher Behavior Continuum

CONTROL OR CHOICE THEORY

The psychiatrist William Glasser has advanced **control theory** as a requisite for classroom discipline practices. He suggests that a person's total behavior is composed of feelings, physiology, actions, and thoughts. How a person manages these aspects of behavior makes up an operational definition of control theory. Glasser asserts, "Control theory contends that we choose most of our total behaviors to try to gain control of people or ourselves."[3]

Over time, Glasser realized that the term *control theory* was subject to misinterpretation, so he retitled his theory *choice theory*. He felt that the term *choice* reflected a better understanding of his ideas. Glasser states that people are driven by six basic needs. All of our choices and behaviors are based on the urgency for survival, power, love, belonging, freedom, and fun. If there is an unbalance in any of these six basic needs, people act out.

As a beginning teacher thinking about classroom discipline, you will find that choice theory encourages you to realize that it is somewhat natural and human for students not to take responsibility for disrupting class or deviating from classroom norms. As a matter of fact, even teachers often find it difficult to take responsibility for some of their own behaviors that deviate from the norm. Choice theory requires teachers to consider the many factors that can account for problem behaviors: physiology, feelings, urges, and so forth. Finally, teachers are encouraged to seek the assistance of counselors, social workers, and parents to fully understand what is causing the problem behavior and only then design an appropriate response.

Choice theory is one of the most difficult management approaches for a new teacher to implement. The majority of discipline problems in the classroom

control theory

A theory of discipline that contends that people choose most of their behaviors to gain control of other people or of themselves.

derive from the misguided efforts of students to achieve control. Unfortunately, many teachers think they must have complete control over the classroom. This type of classroom management allows no room for other individuals to have their need for control met. Consequently, student acting out behaviors increase. The first challenge to a new teacher is to evaluate the inappropriate behavior exhibited by the student, determine which need the student thinks is being met by that behavior, and think of appropriate replacement behaviors. The next step, according to choice theory, is to help the student identify the inappropriate behavior and the natural consequences of that behavior. This is done through a series of questions:

- What are you doing?
- What are you supposed to be doing?
- What is the rule?
- Are you making the best choices?

It is important for teachers not to impose artificial consequences. The final challenge is to get students to design a plan on their own. This can be accomplished by follow-up questions such as:

- What is your plan?
- What choices do you need to make?
- What are you going to do to bring your plan into action?

As a prospective teacher, you will need to evaluate whether control or choice theory is compatible with your view of human nature. If you believe that problem behavior is a natural consequence of our need to balance and fulfill natural urges for survival, power, love, belonging, freedom, and fun, then control theory will fit your philosophy of education. If, however, you believe that humans are blank tablets who simply need to be directly taught the proper ways of acting, this approach probably won't be for you. You may find the next discipline approach more conducive to your beliefs.

ASSERTIVE DISCIPLINE

Assertive discipline is a teacher-in-charge, structured classroom management approach designed to encourage students to choose responsible behavior. Developed by Lee Canter over twenty years ago, this discipline approach is based on consistency, follow-through, and positive relationship building. The underlying tenet of this approach is that teachers have a right to teach and pupils have a right to learn.

Assertive discipline contends that the teacher has the right to determine what is best for students and to expect compliance. No pupil should prevent the teacher from teaching or keep another student from learning. Student compliance is imperative in creating and maintaining an effective and efficient learning environment. To accomplish this goal, teachers must react assertively, as opposed to aggressively or nonassertively.

Assertive discipline requires teachers to develop a clear classroom discipline plan. The classroom plan must clarify behaviors that are expected of students and clarify what students can expect from the teacher in return. The aim of the plan is to have a fair and consistent way to establish a safe, orderly, positive classroom in which teachers teach and pupils learn. The plan consists of three parts:

- *rules* that students must follow at all times
- *positive recognition* that students will receive for following the rules
- *consequences* that result when students choose not to follow the rules

According to assertive discipline, students cannot be expected to guess how a teacher wants them to behave in all situations. If students are to succeed in the classroom, they need to know, without doubt, what is expected of them. When students are not given the limits they need, they will act up in order to make the adults around them take notice. A student's disruptive behavior is often a plea for someone to care enough to make him or her stop.

Assertive discipline is not without critics. Some contend that assertive discipline is undemocratic. It conveys a message that only those with power have the right to make rules. Some teachers have responded to this criticism by allowing students to enter into the rule-making process. However, in the end, the assertive discipline teacher makes the final decision.

Other critics of assertive discipline claim that it is simplistic. Assertive discipline does not get at the root of some discipline problems. It assumes that by simply setting up clear rules and consequences along with providing positive feedback, all problem behaviors can be expunged.

In addition, some critics contend that children should obey rules because that is the right thing to do, not because there is some reward associated with obeying or some punishment for not obeying. The long-term implications of rewarding behavior as suggested by the assertive discipline model is that children obey because of positive feedback or because they are told to obey by an authority figure. Real discipline, according to the critics of assertive discipline, should be internal. Responsible behavior should be based on doing what is right.

As a prospective teacher, you will need to assess to what degree assertive discipline fits your philosophy of education. If your philosophy tends to be focused on the teacher's responsibility to control students, assertive discipline is compatible. If your philosophy is focused on students' authority, you would need to modify some of the assertive discipline tenets or not use this discipline.

The mediocre teacher tells. The good teacher explains. The superior teacher demonstrates. The great teacher inspires.

William Arthur Ward

DISCIPLINE WITH DIGNITY

Richard Curwin and Allen Mendler suggest that it is not enough to simply "control" students. Educators on all levels must help students learn to become decision makers and critical thinkers about their own actions. Their approach, a program called Discipline with Dignity, provides a method for teaching students to take responsibility for their own behavior. The approach offers essential skills and strategies for dealing with angry, disruptive behavior while positively affecting the lives of students. The students learn to manage themselves as stress and pressures mount. The program emphasizes prevention by fostering a positive classroom environment and sensitive communication. Students are viewed as partners in the process of ensuring positive, productive classroom environments.

CONFLICT RESOLUTION

Another approach to discipline, conflict resolution focuses on the process of teaching students how to recognize problems and then solve them constructively. Students are taught to be conflict managers and are trained to deal with difficulties on the playground, in the hallways, and in the classroom. The student "managers" learn specific skills that enable them, for example, to guide a discussion about a problem between two people who are fighting. There are a variety of ways to train the students, but the underlying benefit is that the students solve their own problems with minimal assistance of adults. Advocates of conflict resolution contend that permitting students to share in the structure and even the enforcement of discipline policies helps them learn to contribute to the school and to society as a whole.

PEER MEDIATION

Peer mediation programs are closely associated with conflict resolution approaches. The focus of peer mediation is not so much the resolution of conflict but rather the proactive cultivation of a climate of peace. In these programs, students receive training in empathy development, social skills, and bias awareness.

The overall goal of peer mediation training is to help students develop a social perspective wherein joint benefit is considered over personal gain.

RULES FOR DISCIPLINE

There is no cookbook formula for classroom discipline rules and procedures. There are, however, some general guidelines that will help the beginning teacher to establish some operating rules that will be accepted and practiced by students. These guidelines are as follows:

1. Students and teachers need to learn the importance of considerate behavior and communication.
2. Students need to be treated with respect. Students who are treated with respect develop strong self-esteem.
3. Teachers need to apply critical thinking skills when creating disciplinary rules or analyzing needed disciplinary action.
4. Teachers need to examine how their actions of a social or instructional nature may have helped trigger misbehavior.

The way the teacher introduces and uses these general principles for establishing rules for discipline will set the tone for classroom interactions, creating an environment that is conducive to learning and that minimizes classroom interruptions.

Classroom discipline strongly reflects the teacher's operating classroom philosophy. As you examine the educational philosophy that wins your interest and support, search for its applications to discipline in your classroom.

■ CLASSROOM CLIMATE

John Goodlad, in his observation of more than one thousand classrooms, found that differences in the quality of schools have little to do with teaching practices. Differences come from what Goodlad called an overall **classroom climate.**[4] Classroom climate is not a simple set of rules or ways of acting; it is a holistic concept, one that involves a set of underlying relationships and an underlying tone or sense of being and feeling.

Different types of classroom climate have been found to be successful. Goodlad's research showed that successful schools are ones with favorable conditions for learning, parent interest in and knowledge of the schools, and positive relationships between principals and teachers and teachers and students. S. M. Johnson identified school climate as one of the most important components contributing to effective learning and high levels of student motivation.[5] In *The Schools We Deserve,* Diane Ravitch defined a positive school climate as relaxed and tension-free. Teachers and students alike know that they are in a good school, and this sense of being special contributes to high morale.[6]

Vito Perrone set out to uncover the underlying characteristics of a classroom climate that could be linked to increased student achievement. After examining hundreds of studies, Perrone determined that a successful learning climate was one in which (1) students have time to wonder and find a direction that interests them; (2) topics have an "intriguing" quality, something common seen in a new way; (3) teachers permit—even encourage—different forms of expression and respect students' views; (4) teachers are passionate about their work; (5) students create original or personal products; (6) students do something—they participate in activities that matter; and (7) students sense that the results of their work are not predetermined.[7]

The problem with establishing a certain type of school climate is that climate is not something that can be developed artificially. Climate arises from the interactions of all the things that teachers do in the classroom. There are two concepts, however, that can help you examine climate a little more closely: voice and space.

classroom climate

A holistic concept that involves a set of underlying relationships and a tone or sense of being and feeling in the classroom.

VOICE

Voice is a term brought to education by Henry Giroux.[8] Giroux's concept of **voice** refers to the multifaceted and interlocking set of meanings through which students and teachers actively engage in dialogue with one another. Each individual voice is shaped by its owner's particular cultural history and prior experience. Voice, then, is the means that students have at their disposal to make themselves "heard" and to define themselves as active participants in the world. Voice is an important pedagogical concept because it alerts teachers to the fact that all learning is situated historically and mediated culturally and derives part of its meaning from interaction with others.

Teacher voice reflects the values, ideologies, and structuring principles teachers use to understand and mediate the histories, cultures, and subjectivities of their students. For instance, teachers often use the voice of common sense to frame their classroom instruction. It is often through the mediation of teacher voice that the very nature of the schooling process is either sustained or challenged. The power of teacher voice to shape schooling is inextricably related not only to a high degree of teacher self-understanding but also to the possibility for teachers to join together in a collective voice for social betterment. Thus, teacher voice is significant in terms of its own values as well as in relation to the ways it functions to shape and mediate school and student voices.

Teachers need to be aware of the voices of their students as well as their own voice. Too often the teacher's voice is the only voice that counts in a classroom. Teachers must analyze the interests that different voices represent less as

You can teach a student a lesson for a day; but if you can teach him to learn by creating curiosity, he will continue the learning process as long as he lives.

Clay P. Bedford

voice

The multifaceted interlocking set of meanings through which students and teachers actively engage with one another.

Each individual voice is shaped by its owner's particular cultural history and prior experience. Voice is the means students have to make themselves "heard" and to define themselves as participants in the world.

oppositional components and more as a medley that shapes the individual meanings of all participants in the learning process.

SPACE

"Authentic public space" is a concept developed by Maxine Greene.[9] She contends that a climate consists of spaces between and among people. The manner in which this space is maintained and the type of space that is created determine the climate. Space that permits students to explore, take risks, make mistakes, and take corrective action is an authentic space—one in which people do not have to engage in pretense. Space that requires perfection, does not tolerate divergent responses, and is limited is a space that restricts freedom.

As Greene sees it, educators must attempt to climb into the consciousness of the learner and see the world as it is presented to and experienced by the learner. By trying to understand the world through learners' eyes, teachers are enabled to intuit the kinds of experiences and explanations that will help the students in their current developmental stage. Ultimately, such an approach creates authentic public space in which students "may be empowered to think about what they are doing, to become mindful, to share meanings, to conceptualize, to make varied sense of their lived worlds."[10]

Another way of creating space is by developing a "community of inquiry." This phrase, coined by Charles Sanders Peirce, has come to mean an environment in which students listen to one another with respect, build on one another's ideas, challenge one another to supply reasons for their opinions, assist one another in drawing inferences, and seek to identify one another's assumptions.[11] Teachers ask questions and students answer them without either party's feeling the least

By creating an environment in which students listen to each other with respect and build on one another's ideas, a teacher helps students build a community of inquiry.

twinge of embarrassment, because the process of such thinking and rethinking is natural. An ongoing dialogue ensues and a community of inquiry forms.

Ultimately, classroom climate arises from the beliefs and values held by teachers and students. Your understanding of your own views and beliefs is critical to the climate that will ultimately emerge in your classroom. Your clarity about your most deeply held views on the nature of knowledge, the nature of reality, and the importance of teacher-led versus student-led actions will ensure that your classroom climate authentically represents you.

■ LEARNING FOCUS

As you consider the components of your personal philosophy of education, you will face the question of student learning. What constitutes your vision for a learned person? Is it learning about the acquisition of knowledge?

Is it concerned with good thinking? Or is it concerned with good character? An easy answer, of course, is that learning includes all these things: knowledge, thinking, and dispositions. However, as a teacher you will need to determine what is the proper mix: how much learning time should be spent on knowledge acquisition, how much time should be devoted to practicing skills, and how much time should be spent on the development of character traits or values. To make this question even more difficult, you will need to consider what types of knowledge, skills, and dispositions are appropriate. Unfortunately, you will not find easy answers to these questions in your district's curriculum guide or text-books. These tools provide only a set of opportunities for learning; your philosophy of education will be the force that guides you in determining which of all these things you wish to emphasize in your teaching.

USING PHILOSOPHY BEYOND THE CLASSROOM

The way you manage your classroom and the content, teaching methods, and values you stress will be based on your personal view of the proper role of the teacher in society. A classroom philosophy must incorporate this larger societal view into other views that relate to student learning and behavior in the classroom.

Schools play a role within the larger society. This role is determined by a number of factors: the expectations of society's leaders, economic conditions, the ideologies of powerful lobbying groups, and the philosophies of teachers. It is especially important for educators to examine the role of the school in terms of the larger society—because if such reflection does not occur, schools will merely reflect the status quo or the needs and desires of a single powerful group.

TEACHERS AS CHANGE AGENTS

An age-old question about the role of schools in society concerns the proper role of the school and the teacher in relation to change. Should teachers be **change agents,** actively working for changes in the existing scheme of things? Or should they reemphasize eternal truths and cultural positions? This question of change versus transmission of ongoing values has been articulated in a variety or ways.

CHANGE AS ADAPTATION

Isaac L. Kandel (1881–1965) was a leader in the essentialist movement who advocated change as a process of **adaptation.** The adaptation approach emphasized the importance of promoting stability in schools and enabling the individual to adapt to the larger environment. The school should provide students with an unbiased picture of the changes that occur in society. But schools cannot educate for a new social order, nor should teachers use the classroom to promote doctrine. Change occurs first in society. Schools follow the lead.[12]

CHANGE AS RATIONAL PROCESS

John Dewey believed that schools have a part in social change. He contended that change continually occurs, often without a clearly defined direction. Schools need to assume a leadership role in this change because

change agent
A person who actively endeavors to mobilize change in a group, institution, or society.

adaptation
In the context of social change, an educational approach that favors the promotion of a stable climate in schools to enable students to obtain an unbiased picture of changes that are occurring in society and thus to adapt to those changes.

Teachers make their decisions about student outcomes, discipline procedures, instructional methodologies, and assessment methods based on how they view themselves as change agents in the school.

educators have the time to study newer scientific and cultural forces, estimate the direction and outcome, and determine which changes may or may not be beneficial. Schools need to provide an environment in which students can learn these analytic skills and participate in helping society determine the direction that is of most worth.[13]

CHANGE AS RECONSTRUCTION

The reconstructionist Theodore Brameld contended that every educational system should help diagnose the causes of world problems. Schools need to do more than assess scientific and technological change; they should be places where teachers and students alike can reconsider the very purpose of schooling and study new ways of formulating goals and organizing subject matter. Schools and society alike need to be reconstructed according to a set of human goals based on cross-cultural, universal values.[14]

CHANGE AS DIALECTIC

Samuel Bowles and Herbert Gintis[15] call for a dialectical humanism through which teachers can help students explore the tension between the individual and society. They identify a conflict, or **dialectic,** between the reproductive needs of society and the self-actualizing needs of the individual. Bowles and Gintis claim that entities such as schools, churches, peer groups, and town meetings attempt to mediate this tension between individual freedom and responsibility for the community. The problem schools face is that they are often unaware that they are mediating this underlying tension, and teachers are often caught in the middle of the dilemma. Teachers are asked to respond to the unique needs of the individual while simultaneously answering to the conflicting needs of society. Bowles and Gintis call on teachers to develop a participatory democracy in which all interested parties learn both to pursue their interests and to resolve conflicts rationally. Educators must develop a dialectical educational philosophy that seeks a new synthesis between the individual and the community.

As a teacher, you will become part of the educational system. As part of this system, you will be asked to make decisions about student outcomes, discipline procedures, instructional methodologies, and assessment methods. Your decisions regarding these educational issues will be greatly influenced by how you perceive teachers as change agents. You will make different decisions depending on whether you determine that teachers need to help schools adapt, rationally change the social order, reconstruct, or participate in a dialectic. Your task is to consider carefully each of these change paradigms and select the one that matches your personal system of beliefs.

■ TEACHERS AS LEADERS

Teachers serve as leaders for their students. Evidence of this can be found in the testimonials that are offered by former students when they have become adults. Most students, whether they have achieved graduate degrees or have followed vocational pursuits immediately after high school, report remembering teachers who had a personal impact on their lives. These students will usually discuss the leadership and modeling behaviors of the teachers they remember.

The idea of teachers as leaders suggests that the new teacher should be aware of the need to develop a beginning repertoire of leadership qualities to which students can look for guidance during their developmental years. These leadership qualities—and the practice of them—are highly dependent on the classroom philosophy that the new teacher puts into practice. Some beginning concepts for teacher leadership are vision, modeling behaviors, and use of power.

A good teacher is first of all a good human being—someone who in personality, character, and attitude exercises a wholesome and inspiring influence on young people.

Norman Cousins

dialectic

A conflict between opposing forces or ideas; in change theory, this conflict is the one between individual needs and the needs of society.

VISION

Classroom leadership behaviors begin when a teacher possesses both a vision and the intent to actualize that vision for the students. How a teacher actually puts his or her vision into practice depends wholly on the teacher's philosophical convictions. A **vision** is a mental construct that synthesizes and clarifies what you value or consider to be of highest worth. The clearer the vision or mental picture, the easier it is for a leader to make decisions or persuade or influence others. Formulating a vision requires reflection concerning what you believe about truth, beauty, justice, and equality. It is important to consider these issues and formulate a vision about how schools and classrooms should be organized and what ideas should be implemented.

Linda Sheive and Marian Schoenbeit offer five steps to help leaders put their visions into action:[16]

1. Value your vision.
2. Be reflective and plan a course of action.
3. Articulate the vision to colleagues.
4. Develop a planning stage and an action stage.
5. Have students become partners in the vision.

If teachers reflect on their vision, they can plan the course of action they need to use with their learners. Articulation provides teachers with an opportunity to share their vision with colleagues. Inservice or staff development sessions are excellent times to articulate a classroom vision. Visions require a planning stage and an action stage if they are to become reality. Planning and action stages should involve the students who are intended to be the receivers of this vision. For example, if a teacher wishes students to be reflective in their learning environment, then the teacher needs to help the students understand the benefits of reflectiveness and become partners in the planning. The teacher might engage the students in free and open discussions of the vision and its importance to the learning environment in the classroom.

MODELING

If teachers hold certain expectations of learner behaviors in the classroom, it is imperative that they model those behaviors with the students. If the classroom teacher is rigid and fixed in his or her classroom practices and creates an authoritarian atmosphere, then the students will probably respond accordingly. On the other hand, if the teacher provides a more democratic classroom, the students will respond similarly in their classroom encounters. We would caution that a laissez-faire environment will probably produce a classroom where learners have little or no direction. Teachers should consider the modeling effect on the classroom environment and exhibit behaviors consistent with their philosophy of education.

EMPOWERMENT

The concept of power in the classroom should not be considered good or bad; power in itself has no value structure. The use of power, however, gives it a good, poor, or bad image. All leaders have power that is associated with their position, but the successful leader is judicious in its use. The

vision
A mental construction that synthesizes and clarifies what a person values or considers to be of highest worth.

Teaching can be looked at in a variety of ways, ranging from helping students create their own meaning to taking a deliberate stand and arguing for social change.

nature of the teaching position entrusts a teacher with power both within and outside the classroom. How a teacher uses power in the classroom or in the school building is wholly determined by the classroom philosophy the teacher wants to project.

Teachers' use of power can be classified into two different styles: teacher-dominant and learner-supportive. Past and present practices in schools tend to lean heavily on the teacher-dominant style. Therefore, although many teachers in training study both categories of teaching styles, they tend to see only one major type in practice when they visit schools. We suggest that you continually study both major styles so that you can apply either one as needed on the basis of your classroom objectives for students and your classroom philosophy.

A teacher-dominant power style is based on an authoritarian construct for the classroom. Learners are not expected to be active verbally in the learning process but are generally expected to be receivers and practicing users of teacher-given information. Learning is very convergent. It is selected and given to the learner in the particular way in which the teacher wishes the student to acquire it.

A learner-supportive power style views the learner as someone who is verbally active and who seeks divergence in learning. Learner-supportive power styles encourage the active participation of the learner in exploring learning and helping to determine the extent to which he or she will engage in alternative approaches. Learning is very divergent. These power styles tend to recognize differences in learning, individual interests, and higher-order learning.

Teachers' use of power extends beyond the classroom. Teachers, by their very occupation, are empowered with both rights and responsibilities. They have a unique obligation to advocate for the needs of children, to remind society of its obligations to coming generations, to look beyond material wealth, and to consider the spiritual wealth of knowledge. Teachers, by virtue of their occupation, are given certain rights to speak and be heard. The greater society looks to teachers for guidance concerning the future health of the world.

GLOBAL PERSPECTIVES
The World as a Classroom

This chapter encourages you to examine your beliefs and assumptions in an effort to develop a personal philosophy of education. It is also important, however, to consider the limitations that such a philosophy can impose. For example, to what degree does your philosophy of education incorporate the larger world of thinkers? Does your philosophy affirm or disaffirm varied thinking schemes, varied beliefs, and varied ways of arriving at answers? Relating to global neighbors is no longer a matter of respecting differences. If educators are truly to relate and work collaboratively, their thinking schemes need to intermingle with those of other educators, educators who may have vastly different ways of thinking. Yet a personal philosophy implies the development of a cohesive set of views about knowledge and the nature of the world. Teachers must balance this need to intermix against the importance of clarifying an individual point of view; this is the challenge the world classroom presents to every teacher. How might you present you own views about what knowledge is of most worth to another teacher? What can you do if you are asked to team teach with another educator who views knowledge differently than you do?

SUMMARY

The characteristics of classroom philosophy discussed in this chapter help you become comfortable with your own preferences for teaching. Prospective teachers, whether or not they have had educational philosophy coursework in their preparation programs, should find this practical classroom philosophy treatment a useful way to examine teaching behaviors and to identify trends and preferences related to a teaching style or philosophy of education. The types of philosophies that infuse different approaches to classroom organization, student motivation, and discipline were described so that you can select those approaches that best match your own philosophy of education. Remember that there are no perfect teaching styles or teaching methodologies. For this reason, we encourage an eclectic approach—an approach that draws on many different sets of ideas.

As a new teacher, you need to know how to minimize the negative effects and weaknesses associated with any particular teaching style. The styles that emphasize convergent thinking, for example, tend to reward students for giving an answer that is the exact phrase the teacher wants. These teaching styles also affect student voice and classroom climate. Teachers using such methods must be careful with their responses to students, or students will not risk participating in discussion unless they are absolutely certain they have the exact answer. This can limit classroom climate and student voice.

Divergent types of teaching styles may, in contrast, require students to participate in interesting activities but not make them fully aware of why they are participating or what they are learning. If students are not required to justify the generalizations they make and are not made to see that they are learning many facts and skills, they may end up feeling that all answers are so relative that problem-solving processes are not worthwhile. Teachers who know enough about themselves and their teaching styles to show students how to succeed with both convergent thinking and divergent thinking are well on their way to reaching the ideal of being healthy eclectics.

Finally, to perceive a philosophy is one thing; to live according to the philosophy is another. In teaching, one must exhibit behavior that is compatible with a personal educational philosophy. In life, one must consider the implications of a philosophy of education for acting responsibly in society. What types of societal change match your philosophy of education, and what type of responsible leadership does your philosophy compel you to assume?

DISCUSSION QUESTIONS

1. What is your vision of democracy in the classroom? To what degree should students be permitted to decide what they will study, when they will study, and how they will study? Why?

2. What characteristics or practices can you identify in a former teacher whom you would label your favorite?

3. Teachers must be able to manage the classroom in such a way that the environment created is conducive to teaching and learning. How do you plan to organize your classroom to set up such an environment?

4. Identify some significant beginning classroom practices that a new teacher should try to develop if he or she wants to be judged a successful teacher.

JOURNAL ENTRIES

1. Think about the different student seating arrangements in various classrooms. Sketch each seating arrangement and describe the types of student interaction and the types of learning that each seating arrangement supports. Draw the seating arrangement that you prefer, and describe the types of student interaction and learning that it encourages.

2. Choose and write down a metaphor for each of the educational theories you have studied; for example, "constructivism is a shared voyage into new and uncharted territory." Then design a metaphor for your personal educational theory and clarify how it compares to the other educational theory metaphors.

PORTFOLIO DEVELOPMENT

1. Prepare a synopsis of your overall philosophical perspective. Include your views about classroom organization, motivation, discipline, and climate. Try to develop a graphic that clearly shows how all these components connect and are consistent to your overall perspective.

2. Develop a statement that depicts how you intend to function as a teacher/leader within the larger society. Describe one position you support related to a political action.

PREPARING FOR CERTIFICATION

■ TEACHING AND LEARNING CLIMATES

1. Several topics in the Praxis II Principles of Teaching and Learning (PLT) test relate to the contents of this chapter, including "structuring a climate for learning," developing "strategies to maintain discipline to promote student learning," and becoming skilled in "allocation of time for instructional activities, including transition time." Review the Classroom Climate section of this chapter. How will you build on John Goodlad's findings about positive classroom climate, Henry Giroux's conception of voice, and Maxine Greene's conception of space in your own classroom?

2. Answer the following multiple-choice question, which is similar to items in Praxis and other state certification tests. If you are unsure of the answer, review the opening section of this chapter and Figure 11.1.

   Which of the following activities would most clearly be an inappropriate activity to encourage divergent thinking in a mathematics lesson on patterns and shapes?

   (A) Children will identify and match pictures of three-dimensional shapes while playing a board game with peers.

   (B) Children will create patterns using different shapes of pasta noodles and write how many pieces are in their designs.
   (C) Children will use an online program in which they correctly identify shapes.
   (D) Children will search for shapes in the classroom and make a chart listing the types and numbers of shapes found.

3. Answer the following short-answer question, which is similar to items in Praxis and other state certification tests. After you've completed your written response, use the scoring guide in the *Test at a Glance* materials to assess your response. Can you revise your response to improve your score?

   The Jefferson Elementary School staff is debating the merits of the assertive discipline program developed by Lee Canter. One of the teachers, Leslie Brown, is strongly in favor of the program. Another teacher, Robin James, strongly opposes the program. What arguments might Leslie make in favor of the assertive discipline program? What arguments might Robin make against the program?

WEBSITES

 www.criticalthinking.org/university/default.html The Foundation for Critical Thinking is dedicated to providing educators, students, and the general public with access to information about critical thinking, theory and practice, concepts, techniques for learning and teaching, and classroom exercises.

www.theteachersguide.com The Teachers Guide is a web-based company that provides information, professional articles, resources, books, virtual field trips, and educational software related to classroom management, educational psychology, special education, and so on. Click on Class Management for more information.

www.aft.org/lessons/two/elements.html The American Federation of Teachers website offers an overview of classroom management with details about discipline codes and practices. The site also discusses the importance of parental involvement.

teacher2b.com/discipline/discistr.htm The English Teacher website details philosophies underlying discipline, the cause of discipline problems, and useful strategies for dealing with discipline problems.

falcon.jmu.edu/~ramseyil/disciplinebib.htm School Discipline Classroom Management: A Bibliography covers the publications of authors of some of the major discipline programs. The Internet School Library Media Center is a meta-site for librarians, teachers, and parents.

www.nwrel.org/scpd/sirs/5/cu9.html The School Improvement Research Series website provides introductions, definitions, and research on discipline practices. Discussions include research findings, teacher training in classroom management, discipline of multicultural students, specific discipline programs, and ineffective discipline practices. The site also includes a summary of research perspectives on improving school and classroom discipline.

FURTHER READING

Campbell, D. M., Cignetti, P. B., Melenyzer, B. J., Nettles, D. H., and Wyman, R. M. Jr. (1997). *How to Develop a Professional Portfolio: A Manual for Teachers.* Boston: Allyn and Bacon. This booklet provides a comprehensive look at what is needed to develop a professional portfolio for education professionals.

Carlson, Richard. (2003). *The Don't Sweat Guide for Teachers: Cutting through the Clutter so That Every Day Counts.* New York: Hyperion. How to deal with the demands of teaching and still enjoy the job. Gives strategies for creating surprise, modeling respect, and being a talent scout.

Clark, Ron. (2003). *The Essential 55: An Award-Winning Educator's Rules for Discovering the Success in Every Child,* New York: Hyperion. The winner of the 2001 Disney Teacher of the Year Award presents some revolutionary ideas for classroom industriousness and accountability.

Ladson-Billings, G. (1994). *The Dreamkeepers: Successful Teachers of African American Children.* San Francisco: Jossey-Bass. A reflective look at different teaching strategies in terms of their effectiveness with African American students.

MacKenzie, Robert J. (2003). *Setting Limits in the Classroom.* Roseville, CA: Prima. Offers up-to-date alternatives to punishment and permissiveness beyond the usual methods. Also offers special tools for handling the "strong-willed" student.

Martin, Jane Roland. (1995, January). "A Philosophy of Education for the Year 2000." *Phi Delta Kappan, 77*(1), pp. 21–27. This article describes the work of an existentialist and how to develop a philosophy of education that is consistent with existential principles.

NOTES

1. R. Schmuck and P. A. Schmuck, *Group Processes in the Classrooms.* Dubuque, IA: Wm. C. Brown, 1983.

2. Carl D. Glickman and Charles H. Wolfgang, "Conflict in the Classroom: An Eclectic Model of Teacher–Child Interaction," *Elementary School Guidance and Counseling 13* (December 1978), pp. 82–87.

3. William Glasser, *Control Theory in the Classroom.* New York: Harper & Row, 1986, p. 47.

4. John Goodlad, *A Place Called School: Prospects for the Future.* New York: McGraw-Hill, 1984.

5. S. M. Johnson, *Teachers at Work: Achieving Success in Our Schools.* New York: Basic Books, 1990, pp. xvii–xix.

6. Diane Ravitch, *The Schools We Deserve: Reflections on the Educational Crisis of Our Times.* New York: Basic Books, 1985, p. 303.

7. Vito Perrone, ed., *Expanded Student Assessment for Supervision and Curriculum Development.* Alexandria, VA: Association for Supervision and Curriculum Development, 1991.

8. Henry Giroux, *Ideology, Culture and the Process of Schooling.* Philadelphia: Temple University Press, 1981.

9. Maxine Greene, *The Dialectic of Freedom.* New York: Teachers College Press, 1988.

10. Maxine Greene, "Curriculum and Consciousness," in William Pinar, ed., *Curriculum Theorizing: The Reconceptualists.* Berkeley, CA: McCutchan, 1975, p. 12.

11. C. S. Peirce, "The Fixation of Belief," in Justus Buchler, ed., *Philosophical Writings of Peirce.* New York: Dover, 1955, pp. 5–22.

12. Isaac L. Kandel, *Conflicting Theories of Education.* New York: Macmillan, 1938, pp. 77–88.

13. John Dewey, "Education and Social Change," *The School Frontier III* (1937), pp. 235–238.

14. Theodore Brameld, "Imperatives for a Reconstructed Philosophy of Education," *School and Society 87* (1959), pp. 18–20.

15. Samuel Bowles and Herbert Gintis, *Schooling in Capitalistic America.* New York: Basic Books, 1975, pp. 18–20.

16. Linda Tinelli Sheive and Marian Beauchamp Schoenbeit, "Vision and the Worklife of Educational Leaders," in *Leadership: Examining the Elusive.* Alexandria, VA: Association for Supervision and Curriculum Development, 1987, p. 99.

Curricular Foundations of Education

Viewing Education through a Curricular Lens

The curricular lens provides a way to examine what students should know and be able to do as a result of attending school. It allows us to explore the most effective ways to help students learn the content through the instructional strategies of teachers. However, it is not enough to teach the subject matter. Parents and others expect their children to learn the core knowledge and skills they will need for the future. Thus, assessments are essential tools for helping teachers determine whether students are learning. Effective assessments can help teachers adjust their instruction to help all students learn.

The curricular lens focuses on the relationship between teaching and learning. Deciding what to teach and how to teach it is central to the work of a teacher. Continuous learning is a lifelong pursuit for teachers as new standards are adopted, the curriculum changes, new teaching strategies evolve, new technology is introduced, and different types of assessments are imposed. The filters through which we will examine curricula in this section include standards, assessments, accountability, instruction, technology, and continuous learning and development on the part of teachers.

Focus Questions

The following questions will help you focus your learning as you read Part VI:

1. What are standards and why are they so important in today's schools?
2. What are authentic assessments and why do educators find them more helpful in the classroom than most standardized tests?
3. What is the relationship of standards and assessments to student learning?
4. How are teachers and schools held accountable for student performance?
5. Who is involved in determining the curriculum in schools and what role do teachers have in deciding what is taught in their classrooms?
6. What instructional or teaching strategies guide the work of teachers?
7. How should technology relate to and interact with curriculum and instruction to help students learn?
8. How can teachers work effectively with parents to support student learning?
9. What is a teacher's responsibility for participating in professional organizations and developing a plan for continuous learning?

Standards-Based Education and Assessment

Education in the News

Most Students Who Repeat Grades Fail MCAS, Boston School Records Show

By Michele Kurtz, *Boston Globe,* June 1, 2003

IT BEGAN IN 1998, JUST BEFORE STUDENTS HAD TO START passing MCAS to graduate. Districts around the state [Massachusetts] began holding back more ninth-graders than usual, believing that it is better to flunk students than to force them to take the high-stakes test and classes they're not ready for.

But a *Globe* analysis of Boston student records suggests that it is an experiment that merits further review. Only about a third of the students in the class of 2003 who repeated ninth grade and took the MCAS passed it.

And nearly half of those ninth-grade repeaters are no longer attending Boston schools. Of the 661 who have left, nearly two-thirds either dropped out, entered GED programs, or have vanished—the district has no record of why they left.

Another 800 or so of the repeaters still attend Boston schools, but only two out of five have caught up with their peers and are seniors this year, according to the student records. The numbers—particularly the MCAS passing rate of the ninth-graders held back—drew an expression of concern from the state's top education official who has defended the practice. "I would have thought the numbers would have been higher," state education commissioner David P. Driscoll said of the 37 percent MCAS passing rate among the Boston repeaters. "That's a discouraging statistic."

Driscoll cautioned against drawing conclusions from the passing rate but said it's worth studying. The city records the *Globe* analyzed covered only the class of 2003, so comparisons could not be made to passing rates among students held back in previous classes when the MCAS was not a graduation requirement.

Boston Globe, June 1, 2003. Reprinted with permission.

INTASC Learning Outcomes

After reading and studying this chapter, you should be able to:

1. Identify different conceptions of standards and analyze the consequences that these conceptions have for teaching and learning.

2. Compare different sources of standards and describe the conflicts that result from the varied interests of these sources.

3. Identify problems that surround standards-based assessment practices and predict their influence on teachers and classroom practices. (INTASC 8: Assessment)

4. Define accountability for student learning and describe how the No Child Left Behind Act is holding schools, school districts, and states accountable for student achievement.

5. Understand the meaning of "helping all students learn" and explain how standards

and assessments may increase or limit the chances of schools to meet this goal. (INTASC 8: Assessment)

School-Based Observations

You may see these learning outcomes in action during your visits to schools:

1. Talk with teachers in the schools that you are observing and review the school district's website; then identify the standards that teachers are supposed to use. During your observations, record the evidence that convinces you that standards are (or are not) integrated into classroom instruction. Also indicate how the school is (or is not) supporting teachers in preparing students to meet the standards.

2. Identify the assessments that a school you are observing requires at the grade level and for the subject you plan to teach. Compile data on the length of time these assessments have been used, student performance on the assessments, and areas in which students are not performing as well as expected. Write your conclusions about the quality of instruction for that subject and grade level.

3. Interview several teachers who are required to administer state assessments that reflect standards. Ask the teachers to identify what they do to help students prepare for the assessments. Record the results of your interviews and then write your own stance (from an educator's perspective) with regard to the value of statewide and high-stakes assessment.

Standards are a popular topic of debate in both the business and education worlds. Policymakers at the state and federal levels are concerned about standards, their rigor, and student achievement as measured against them. School administrators, teachers, curriculum developers, and education reformers are expected to implement the standards and show evidence that students meet them. Interestingly, even though people are using the term *standards,* their definitions of the term can be quite different. Some people view standards as synonymous with rigor and the setting of high expectations for schools, teachers, and students. Others focus on the specification of learner outcomes or use the term in relation to a particular approach to instruction. Still others equate standards with high-stakes tests.

Four big ideas surround and inform the standards movement. First is the articulation of rigorous standards for student achievement. A second is the increased demand from policymakers and the public for accountability—that students meet these standards. A third big idea is an emphasis on the importance of authentically assessing what students have learned. Fourth, standards require a major change in the curriculum and the way teachers and students think and work in classrooms. In total, the emphasis on standards-based education represents a major shift in thinking about accountability, teaching, and learning.

A number of important challenges and critical issues have emerged around the standards and assessment movement. Some of the questions that will be explored in this chapter include:

- What type of standards and assessments are appropriate for today's schools?
- Who determines the content of standards and assessments?
- How fair is a common set of standards and assessments for a diverse population?
- How can assessments be made authentic to the contexts of the community and the world of work?
- When should assessments be tailored to individual development and when should they be standardized?

- What is the role of the teacher in today's standards and assessment environment?
- What is the role of students and parents in today's standards and assessment environment?

The dimensions that make up a standards-based curriculum as well as the implications for assessment practices are discussed in this chapter. We will also tackle issues and questions that surround standards-based education and assessment. At every turn, we place the emphasis on what teachers need to know and understand about this important education movement.

STANDARDS-BASED EDUCATION

Before 1987 most standards focused on the curriculum, identifying the content that teachers should teach. Many of today's standards no longer describe what teachers and professors should teach. They identify what students and teachers should know and be able to do when they finish a course, a grade, or a program. Most of the standards-setting efforts are grounded in a constructivist approach to teaching and learning, encouraging "*all* students to construct, integrate, and apply their knowledge; to think critically and invent solutions to problems; and to respond creatively to unforeseeable issues that will confront them in the complex world of tomorrow."[1]

The accountability theme is heard in the repeated calls for schools to set rigorous educational standards that are measured by student performance on standardized tests. In many states, testing has become high stakes, determining who is permitted to move to the next grade, graduate from high school, be admitted to higher education, or be allowed to teach. In a growing number of states, accountability has taken the form of legislation that establishes statewide standards and assessments, with test scores being used to rank schools and label some schools as low performing or failing. These state report cards become headline stories in local and state newspapers, celebrating high test scores or decrying the poor state of education in communities where test scores are below a proficient level.

proficiencies

Knowledge, skills, or dispositions that students are expected to acquire in order to meet a set of standards.

Many teachers are developing and using new forms of assessments that focus on student **proficiencies** identified in standards. Learning is measured through a variety of assessments throughout a school year rather than depending on a single test. Within the classroom there are three related themes: the use of standards to determine curriculum, the use of multiple assessments of student learning, and the development of a new model, or paradigm, of teaching and learning called standards-based education.

Standards-based education is a systemic approach to the entire teaching and learning process. Systemic implies that the entire school system (including the curriculum, instruction, assessments, and professional development) is driven and linked by

Students must meet high standards before they can graduate from high school. A growing number of states are requiring students to pass a test before they receive a diploma.

In order to ensure that our children receive a better education, higher standards need to be set for all students—not just the academic elite—and schools need to be held accountable for helping their students meet those standards.

Achieve, Inc. (an organization committed to raising standards)

a set of standards that the community of teachers, administrators, parents, and learners endorse. As an instructional approach, standards-based education places student learning at the center. Achievement of the standards is paramount and increasingly linked to a student being promoted or receiving a diploma. Student achievement of the standards, which is often measured by performance on standardized tests, sometimes determines the jobs and salaries of teachers and principals.

■ DIFFERING CONCEPTIONS OF STANDARDS

Standards are statements that describe an expected level of attainment or performance. However, they can have quite different meanings for different people. For some, a standard is noteworthy accomplishment by a great performer. Such world-class standards are very high levels of learning and performance that are generally out of reach for most individuals. For others, a standard is the norm; it is a statement of what most people should be able to achieve. As such, this type of standard can be considered the bottom line, one that is reachable by most. Others describe standards in terms of desired student learning in a discipline or content area. At the same time, not everyone believes that the standards movement is desirable. They worry that standards will lead to a national curriculum, which they find problematic, or become overly prescriptive in their requirements for curriculum and instruction.

WORLD-CLASS STANDARDS

Some educators and policymakers think of standards as world-class goals based on the performances of outstanding individuals, such as successful mathematicians, scientists, authors, and Olympic athletes. Schools such as Julliard or the

World-class standards describe the high levels of performance necessary to be competitive at national and international levels.

Rhode Island School of Design have as their goal assisting artists in reaching world-class standards. These standards cannot be met in an elementary or secondary school setting. Rather, they are statements of accomplishment to be used for admiration and as models of excellence. Standards in this context are meant to inspire students to do better over time; they are not intended to be met within a single school year. Educators who adopt world-class standards tend to look at their curriculum as a developmental process. The purpose of each year in school is to show individual student improvement toward the high standard. Common sets of specific proficiencies that all students are expected to master are not seen to be as important as showing improvement in multiple and diverse ways over time.

REAL-WORLD STANDARDS

Another segment of the public believes that standards should be real-world goals. This conception of standards places primary emphasis on the necessary knowledge and skills that will make students employable and enable them to live independent lives. Assessments of reading, writing, and computing skills show that too many high school graduates lack these skills. Major U.S. firms report that 34 percent of tested job applicants lack the basic skills necessary for the job.[2] In contrast to world-class standards, real-world standards are seen as being achievable in schools. Real-world standards set the expectation that students learn the basic skills of reading, writing, and computing that allow them to balance checkbooks, prepare for job interviews, manage their daily lives, and maintain employment.

DISCIPLINE-BASED OR CONTENT STANDARDS

Other people think of standards as discipline based. These standards describe what teachers and students should know and be able to do in various subject areas such as science, mathematics, history, geography, social studies, physical education, and the arts. Usually, these **content standards** emphasize the core components or big ideas of the discipline that should be known at a specific age or grade level. They are often accompanied by standards for what teachers should know about the content or subject to teach at the preschool, elementary, middle, or secondary level.

At a meeting of the U.S. state governors in 1989, President George Bush supported the development of content standards to ensure that the nation's students would be first in international academic competitions. The first set of student standards was released in 1989 by the National Council of Teachers of Mathematics (NCTM). With federal support, standards for P–12 students were developed by professional associations and other groups such as the National Research Council in subsequent years. Many states followed suit, developing their own content standards or adapting the national standards to their own state contexts.

NO CHILD LEFT BEHIND AND STANDARDS To help ensure that all students will learn at acceptable levels, Congress enacted legislation entitled No Child Left Behind (NCLB) in 2001. This act required all states to set standards for what a child should know and learn for all grades in mathematics, reading, and science. In addition, the states were required to set a level of proficiency for determining whether the standards are met by students. Schools are expected to make adequate yearly progress (AYP) as shown by their students achieving at the state's proficiency level or above on the state test. Federal expectations are that low-income students, students with disabilities, English language learners, and students from different racial and ethnic backgrounds will meet state proficiencies. If AYP is not achieved by one or more of these groups for more than two years, the school will be identified as needing improvement. Student performance will be publicly reported for schools in district report cards. By 2013 all students are expected to be at the proficiency level for their grade level.

WHY STANDARDS DIFFER

These diverse conceptions of standards stem from differing expectations people have for education. Business leaders tend to want high school graduates who are ready for work by being able to read, write, and compute. They expect schools to prepare a supply of future workers. Businesses are willing to provide specific job training, but they do not want to teach what they consider basic skills that all students should have before entering the world of work.

Policymakers think about the larger, long-term needs of society. They promote more rigorous academic standards that will ensure that students perform at high levels on international comparisons, maintaining world-class status for the United States. They want students to know more science, history, mathematics, literature, and geography than students in other countries.

Parents choose standards based on their own personal goals and family histories. Some parents want their children to go to prestigious colleges; others want their children

content standards
Standards that specify learning outcomes in a subject or discipline (for example, mathematics or social studies).

The purpose of this title is to ensure that all children have a fair, equal, and significant opportunity to obtain a high-quality education and reach, at a minimum, proficiency on challenging state academic achievement standards and state academic assessments.

No Child Left Behind Act

CROSS-REFERENCE
Chapters 1, 5, and 12 also include references to No Child Left Behind.

The setting of standards requires understanding different expectations, learning new things, and extensive discussions about the content.

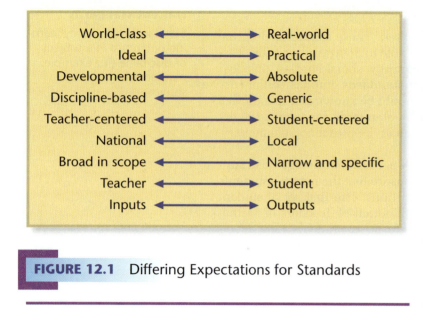

World-class ←→ Real-world
Ideal ←→ Practical
Developmental ←→ Absolute
Discipline-based ←→ Generic
Teacher-centered ←→ Student-centered
National ←→ Local
Broad in scope ←→ Narrow and specific
Teacher ←→ Student
Inputs ←→ Outputs

FIGURE 12.1 Differing Expectations for Standards

to obtain a job immediately after high school; still others want their offspring to prepare for a professional career such as a medical doctor, lawyer, or engineer. These expectations influence the type of standards that parents support.

Figure 12.1 is a summary of the different dimensions and tensions that those who develop standards must consider. School districts wrestle with these differing expectations for schools when they adopt a set of learning standards. It is not easy to have a clearly articulated, coordinated set of standards that meets the expectations of all members of a community. The process of setting standards is not a simple one, and those who write standards often receive criticism from various dissatisfied community members. Despite these difficulties, the development of clear standards enables different constituencies within the school community to clarify their needs and their aspirations. The process of selecting and adapting standards also provides a forum for conducting dialogues and negotiating what schools should do and for what schools, teachers, and students should be held accountable.

USES OF STANDARDS

Just as standards differ conceptually, they can also be used for different purposes. Standards can be used to make school curricula across a district or state more alike. They can provide a set of uniform expectations by grade level that must be met by all students before they can progress to the next grade. When standards are used in this way, all teachers are focused on the same set of knowledge and skills, and they are aware of the relationship of their work to other grade-level expectations.

Standards can also be used as guidelines for improving student learning, as Congress expects under No Child Left Behind. These standards clearly articulate what students should know and be able to do by the time they finish a grade, finish high school, or complete a professional program. They generally enable schools to show that all students have attained specific types of knowledge and skill development. Curriculum, instruction, and assessments must be aligned to support students in meeting the standards at a specified level of proficiency. On the other hand, standards do not always clearly meet the diverse needs of students. The uniqueness of individual students can be neglected in the push to make clear what most students should learn.

SOURCES FOR STANDARDS

The sources of educational standards seem as plentiful as stars in a clear night sky. In fact, within the past fifteen years many groups have set standards for students and educators alike. The authors of the standards released in 1989 by the National Council of Teachers of Mathematics had researched, developed, sought feedback, and refined their student standards over a ten-year period. The process had involved both mathematics teachers and mathematicians. The NCTM standards became the benchmark for other standard-setting projects at the state and national levels.

During the 1990s, the U.S. Department of Education funded subject-area groups and coalitions to prepare standards similar to the mathematics standards in disciplines such as science, history, civics, language arts, geography, the fine arts, and foreign language. Standards continue to be developed and refined by many different groups. For example, the National Council for the Social Studies (NCSS), the American Association for the Advancement of Science (AAAS), and the National Association for Sports and Physical Education (NASPE) have all published sets of standards that represent what they believe students should know and be able to do throughout primary, elementary, middle, and secondary school. These national content standards have been translated into different sets of state standards. Individual school districts have also developed district learning standards based on their interpretations of state standards.

Although all of these student standards are worth examining, it is not easy for individual teachers to determine which set is best suited for their individual contexts, philosophies, and teaching styles. The challenge for teachers is to have a clear understanding of each group's rationale for developing a set of standards and be able to articulate a clear set of professional reasons for endorsing one set of standards rather than another.

In addition to the work of discipline-specific groups that have developed standards for student achievement at the P–12 level, professional education associations have developed standards for teachers and other professional school personnel. These professional standards outline what educators should know and be able to do to teach or work as a school library media specialist, school counselor, principal, or other professional in a school. You are probably expected to demonstrate the knowledge, skills, and **dispositions** of one or more sets of these standards before you obtain a license to teach.

■ TYPES OF STANDARDS

At least three types of standards have emerged from the different conceptions and uses of standards. Content standards focus on knowing the subject matter. Performance standards focus on teacher and student accomplishments. Opportunity-to-learn standards focus on the resources and support necessary to ensure that students can meet content and performance standards. Each type ultimately focuses on developing student achievement. For example, if teachers attain a certain level of professional expertise (performance standards) and schools meet stringent opportunity-to-learn standards by providing resources that relate to student achievement, all students will benefit from such a concerted effort to support learning.

CROSS-REFERENCE
Assessments for teachers and teacher candidates are discussed in greater detail in Chapter 1.

CONTENT STANDARDS

Content standards establish the knowledge that should be learned in various subject areas. These standards are often linked to big ideas, themes, or conceptual strands that should be nurtured throughout a student's education. For example, in the national science standards, the big ideas of evolution and equilibrium, form and function, systems, and the nature of science are explicitly described, along with specific grade-level **benchmarks** that are linked to these bigger ideas. The same is true in the standards for social studies; the big ideas of community, scarcity of resources, and democracy are specified in statements concerning what students should know in primary, elementary, middle, and secondary schools. The NCTM standards, furthermore, state that students should be able to understand and use numbers and operations; specifically, they should

- *understand numbers,* ways of representing numbers, relationships among numbers, and number systems;
- *understand meanings* of operations and how they relate to one to another;
- *compute fluently* and make reasonable estimates.[3]

dispositions

A habitual tendency or inclination to behave in a specific way.

benchmarks

A level of performance at which a standard is met. Examples of levels include "proficient" and "correct response on 80% of questions or performances."

In addition to knowledge acquisition statements, content standards often specify what thinking and process skills and strategies students and/or teachers should acquire. These skills and strategies might include developing a plan and hypothesis; interpreting, extrapolating, drawing conclusions; and communicating results. Standards may also include statements about the habits or dispositions that should be nurtured in students. These habits or dispositions include curiosity, perseverance, tenacity, caring, and open-mindedness. For instance, the INTASC standards for state licensure expect new teachers to demonstrate the following dispositions related to individual and group motivation and behavior:

- The teacher takes responsibility for establishing a positive climate in the classroom and participates in maintaining such a climate in the school as a whole.
- The teacher understands how participation supports commitment, and is committed to the expression and use of democratic values in the classroom.
- The teacher values the role of students in promoting each other's learning and recognizes the importance of peer relationships in establishing a climate of learning.
- The teacher recognizes the value of intrinsic motivation to students' lifelong growth and learning.
- The teacher is committed to the continuous development of individual students' abilities and considers how different motivational strategies are likely to encourage this development for each student.[4]

PERFORMANCE STANDARDS

Performance standards are statements about what a student or a teacher should be able to do. These performance statements are not a list of discrete facts or skills; rather, they encompass combinations of knowledge and skills. The development of performance standards is the next logical step after determining a content standard. For example, once we know that we want students to understand the events of the Revolutionary War, the next logical question is, "How will we know they understand?" This is where performance standards come into play. Performance standards are used in specifying both student learning and teacher development.

Performance standards differ from district to district, even though many lists of performance standards have been developed by state and national groups. Some educators contend that one set of uniform performance standards for P–12 students should be developed across the nation to guarantee a minimum level of achievement. A collaboration of the Learning Research and Development Center of the University of Pittsburgh and the National Center on Education and the Economy in partnership with state boards of education, New Standards has developed and disseminated a national set of student performance benchmarks that try to answer the question "How good is good enough?" These performance standards were derived from the various content standards and consist of two parts:

Performance descriptions: Descriptions of what students should know and the ways they should demonstrate the knowledge and skills they have acquired in the four areas assessed by New Standards—English language arts, mathematics, science, and applied learning—at the elementary, middle, and high school levels.

Work samples and commentaries: Samples of student work that illustrate standard-setting performances, each accompanied by commentary that shows how the performance descriptions are reflected in the work sample.[5]

One example from the New Standards performance description for reading clearly states the performance expectations for students:

Students read at least twenty-five books or book equivalents each year. The materials should include traditional and contemporary literature as well as magazines, newspapers, textbooks, and on-line materials. Examples of activities through which students might produce evidence of reading include:

- Maintain an annotated list of works read.
- Generate a reading log or journal.
- Participate in formal and informal book talks.[6]

An example of a performance task in elementary mathematics requires students to show how many different ways nine fish can be put into two bowls. Students are required to show all their work and at the end explain why they made the decisions they did as they solved the problem.[7] A performance task in elementary science requires students to complete a laboratory activity in which they adjust the mass and/or volume of an object so that the object does not float on top of water or sink. This task calls for students to explore the range of available floating and sinking objects. To accomplish the task, it is necessary to combine floating and sinking objects to construct one of the correct density.[8] These examples of performance standards provide a set of benchmarks against which teachers and students can determine how well they are doing in moving toward the full achievement of a standard.

OPPORTUNITY-TO-LEARN STANDARDS

Teachers' and students' awareness of content and performance standards will do little to ensure achievement unless supports and resources are provided by the district and the community. Hence, some experts have advocated for opportunity-to-learn standards, which are sometimes called input or delivery standards. These standards address the need for the provision of adequate and appropriate instructional resources, assessments, and system structures to create the proper conditions for students to achieve the standards. Examples include guaranteeing that students have sufficient opportunities to relearn when a standard is not achieved, ensuring that sufficient time is offered to students so that they can achieve various standards at their own pace, offering alternative ways to achieve a standard based on individual needs, specifying the types of technology to be available in schools and classrooms, and regularly providing staff inservice that helps teachers fine-tune instructional techniques that lead to student achievement of specific standards. Students with disabilities and English language learners should be provided appropriate accommodations to support their learning of the proficiencies outlined in standards.

CROSS-REFERENCE

See Chapter 3 for more information on accommodations for students with disabilities.

■ DEBATES OVER SETTING STANDARDS

Sometimes conflict exists among stakeholders regarding setting standards at the national, state, and local levels. For example, the National Council of Teachers of English, the International Reading Association, and the Center for the Study of Reading at the University of Illinois received funding from the U.S. Department of Education (USDE) to draft content standards in the English language arts. However, the USDE rejected the standards proposed by this coalition and terminated its funding. One reason for the rejection of the standards was the perceived excessive emphasis on process rather than knowledge.

Standards are influenced by one's perspective along a continuum, with pluralists who support multiple perspectives at one

Opportunity-to-learn standards identify the resources and support needed to ensure all students can meet content and performance standards.

end and fundamentalists who believe in the existence of one correct perspective at the other. These differences led to conflict in the acceptance of the proposed American history standards. Critics objected to the absence of certain American heroes in the secondary standards proposed by the National History Standards Project. They argued that the attempt to make the standards inclusive of the numerous ethnic and cultural groups in the United States would be divisive rather than unifying. As a result, these standards were the focus of a full-scale debate in the U.S. Congress in January 1995. Some members objected to the absence of Robert E. Lee and the Wright Brothers; others noted that Senator Joseph McCarthy was mentioned nineteen times, but Albert Einstein was not mentioned at all. Such criticism led to a ninety-nine-to-one vote in the Senate for a resolution condemning the standards.[9] Similar debates have occurred at the state and local levels about the use of phonics versus whole language in the English language arts and reading, the importance of teaching historical facts in social studies, teaching of creationism versus evolution in science, and the use of calculators to teach mathematics.

A third type of conflict over standards occurs when two groups attempt to develop standards for the same area, as occurred in science when the National Science Standards were developed through federal funds by the National Research Council and Benchmarks for Science Literacy were developed by the Association for the Advancement of Science. These two sets of national standards exist as independent sources for teaching science. Some argue that having different sets of national standards is positive and provides a necessary dialectic for selecting standards. Such healthy conflict allows for change and guards against developing a rigid, inflexible set of standards. Others note that in the absence of a single set of national standards, schools and teachers are left in the precarious position of having to choose their own unique sets of standards, and once again there is little guarantee of uniformity in the content that all students are expected to know and be able to do at the end of their schooling experience.

THE FUTURE OF STANDARDS-BASED EDUCATION

There is no escaping standards in schools today. They are not abstract statements of ideals that teachers can simply ignore. They are now driving what teachers teach and, in many districts, how schools—and in some cases teachers—are evaluated. Moving from a traditional to standards-based education requires a great deal of time, the involvement of all constituencies (teachers, administrators, parents, and community members), and good communications among the stakeholders.

Standards-based education is a complex and sophisticated approach to teaching and learning. It is a professional challenge for beginning teachers, as well as experienced teachers, to learn to teach this way. The teacher's role shifts from conveyor of knowledge and dispenser of grades to coach and facilitator of students as they engage in learning. The expectations and checkpoints are stated and known by the teacher and students before instruction begins. Students not only know beforehand what is to be learned, but they also know what the assessment tasks will be like—that is, the types of performances described in the expectations.

Many questions color the future of standards. How will school organization, use of time, graduation requirements, and power relationships change because of the standards movement? Can the same standards really be put in place everywhere without also bringing opportunity-to-learn standards to the front and center? How can the plethora of standards be managed by teachers and still be integrated with the move toward thematic and interdisciplinary instruction? If the standards movement is to be worth the upheaval it has generated, such questions must be answered by thoughtful, knowledgeable participants who are engaged in the process of changing what students learn and how they learn. One important step is the compilation of data about student learning related to standards. Therefore, one of the early efforts in the standards movement has been significantly increased attention to methods for assessing student learning.

ASSESSMENT: THE OTHER SIDE OF STANDARDS

Standards are not an end unto themselves. Simply listing standards in a school brochure will make little difference in the way students learn and achieve. If standards are to have any real effect on schools and on student achievement, they need to be supported by other elements in a school's structure: an articulated curriculum, professional development sessions focused on improving student achievement, and a well-thought-out array of assessments that match the standards.

When assessments are linked to standards, changes will occur in the types of assessments used, the kinds of data collected, and the ways in which assessment results are used to enhance student achievement. These changes in the assessment process can be quite dramatic, since assessment in the past has often meant little more than teachers producing grades or students doing well on paper-and-pencil achievement tests. When assessments are interwoven into standards-based frameworks, they become much more varied and meaningful to teachers and students alike. The following section examines the changing face of assessment and the ways in which it should enhance the teaching and learning process.

■ WHAT IS ASSESSMENT?

Assessment in education implies many things: evaluation, grades, tests, performances, criteria, **rubrics,** and more. To adequately encompass its many dimensions, it is helpful to examine assessment in a broader sense by analyzing its root meanings. The term *assessment* is derived from the Latin word *assessio,* which means "to sit beside." This image provides an excellent metaphor. Ultimately, assessment can be thought of as the act of sitting beside oneself and analyzing what one observes. In a sense, all assessment is based on this image: the examination of oneself through the perception of an examiner who sits beside you and provides feedback. Some theorists contend that all true assessment is ultimately self-assessment. Assessors can provide information, but in the end it is the person being assessed who accepts the information or rejects it, using the information to further his or her development or setting aside the information as unimportant.

The image of an assessor sitting beside a learner also implies the use of tools or measuring devices that enable the assessor to gather different types of information. Paper-and-pencil tests, performance assessments, portfolios, journals, and observation checklists are examples of different assessment measures. Often these tools are labeled assessments, but in fact they are merely measures that assessors use to provide feedback. Keep in mind that assessment is really the larger process of gathering information, interpreting the information, providing feedback, and ultimately using or rejecting the feedback.

■ PURPOSES FOR ASSESSMENT

The ultimate reason for assessment in the classroom is to help students learn. However, assessments of students and teachers today are being used for a number of other purposes as well. It is important to clarify these different purposes before attempting to interpret assessment results.

STUDENT LEARNING

Put simply, for teachers and students, assessing in classrooms is done for two purposes. The first is a **formative assessment** to determine what the student

rubric

Scoring guides that describe what learners should know and be able to do at different levels of competence.

formative assessment

Collection of data to show what a student has learned in order to determine instruction required next.

summative assessment

Data about student performance that are used to make a judgment about a grade, promotion to the next grade, graduation, college entrance, etc.

has learned and provide feedback to the learner so that both the teacher and the student can understand where to next focus their energies. The second is a **summative assessment** to make a final judgment about whether a certain level of accomplishment has been attained, such as passing a course. Most assessments for these purposes have been developed by teachers for use in their own classrooms. In standards-based education, teachers are checking throughout the year for evidence that students are meeting the standards through tests and a variety of other sources.

Student essays, projects, and portfolios are also valuable resources for knowing how deeply students understand the content of a subject. Observing students as they conduct experiments, demonstrate how to solve a mathematics problem, or interact with other students on a group project provides additional information about student learning. More and more teachers are recording their observations of student learning throughout the school year in journals that can show growth over time. These formative assessments help teachers know which students know the content at the expected level and which students need additional assistance.

DIAGNOSIS

Diagnostic assessments are used to determine at what level a student is functioning as compared to the level at which he or she should be able to function developmentally. Tests and other assessments can be used to help determine whether students are performing at grade level. The feedback from these sources should help teachers design new or different instructional strategies that will assist students who are having difficulty. These types of assessments provide an array of questions and tasks for a student to perform in a specific area such as reading, writing, mathematics, or motor skills. In such assessments, the questions and tasks might be organized by difficulty. As the student performs each task successfully, she or he is given another, more difficult question. Eventually, the student will be unable to answer or perform any tasks successfully.

Diagnostic assessments are also used to determine the need for special services or accommodations and are usually conducted by a special education teacher, school psychologist, speech/language pathologist, occupational therapist, or regular teacher trained to administer a specific test. Most school districts require these tests of students who have been referred by teachers or parents for special education or gifted and talented services. If a student is identified as needing special education services, an individualized education plan (IEP) is developed collaboratively by the regular teacher, a special education teacher, parents, and appropriate specialists such as a reading specialist or speech/language pathologist. The goal of the IEP is to identify appropriate instruction to support student learning at a level and pace that is appropriate to a student's specific needs.

CROSS-REFERENCE

An application of the IEP is presented in Chapter 3.

GATEKEEPING

Assessments are often used as gatekeepers to determine who moves to the next grade or is admitted to a profession. For example, college admissions offices have a long history of using students' performance on standardized tests such as the ACT and SAT to determine who can be admitted. Professions such as law, medicine, nursing, physical therapy, certified public accountancy, and architecture require persons to pass a standardized test before they are admitted to the profession and allowed to work in a specific state. Most state departments of education require new teachers to pass a standardized test to be eligible for a license to teach. The use of standards for gatekeeping purposes is also becoming a way of life at the P–12 level. One of the first steps for children entering some of the prestigious preschools in a number of metropolitan areas is passing a test. A growing number of states require students to pass a test before a diploma of graduation is granted. Some school districts expect students to pass a test to move to the next grade.

■ TRADITIONAL ASSESSMENTS

Educators use different types of assessments depending on the purpose of the assessments. The types described next are among the most common. Many are manifested in paper-and-pencil formats; others take the form of a demonstration of skills. Educators and parents should know the type of assessments being administered to their students and children. Are the assessments designed to compare students across the state, or to determine if students have developed the core knowledge and skills expected in standards? The second design could be very helpful to a teacher and parents in knowing whether students are learning.

COMPETENCY-BASED ASSESSMENTS

These assessments can be used to demonstrate a specific competence. For example, if students have been taught a specific method for using a piece of science equipment, such as a gram balance, a competency-based assessment would include having the learner weigh several objects on a balance. The teacher would typically observe the learner to see whether all the specific techniques in accurately weighing a sample were used. Assessments of specific competencies in schools include many teacher-made assessments that focus on the specific things a learner has studied. An example of a competency-based assessment outside the classroom is the road test employed in most states as a prerequisite to receive a driver's license. The critical characteristic of such an assessment is that the assessment is closely related to something the learner must be able to do. Hence, in the road test, a person drives a car in situations that the driver will typically experience: turning left or right, backing up, parking, and so forth. The person is usually scored through an observation checklist that the assessor uses.

Paper-and-pencil tests remain the major type of standardized assessments used to measure student achievement.

NORM-REFERENCED ASSESSMENTS

Sometimes assessments are used to demonstrate who is best in some area. In a norm-referenced assessment, the individual's performance is compared with that of a norm group of similar individuals. After these types of assessments are developed, they are carefully revised on a regular basis to ensure that the tests yield varied test scores from low to high. These types of assessment do not reveal all that an individual child knows or is able to do. They are not the appropriate assessment to use to determine whether students meet proficiencies outlined in standards. In some ways, norm-referenced assessments are like a contest, and it is expected that some students will excel and others fail.

Norm-referenced assessments are misused more often than most other assessments. Teachers must be cautious in concluding that individual students who score low are not doing well. Norm-referenced tests typically sample only a portion of what students in a particular class are expected to know and do. Therefore, the student might not be performing well in those areas assessed by the tests but be doing better in other areas that were not tested.

Sometimes state authorities penalize a school district or school whose students as a group perform below a specific level on a norm-referenced test. This is a flawed practice because norm-referenced tests are designed such that 50 percent will score below the fiftieth percentile. In fact, when schools begin to score regularly above this percentile, the test is made more difficult. A related problem is that the nature of the test prevents the inclusion of questions on some of the core, most important concepts in content standards. Too many students select the correct answer because their teachers focused on this key concept in their teaching to ensure that students learned it. If a large number of students select the correct answer, the test question is revised. As a result, many of the items on the test address peripheral areas of the standards, avoiding the important knowledge and skills at the heart of the standards. The goal is not to determine if most students meet standards but to make sure there is an appropriate distribution of scores.

CRITERION-REFERENCED ASSESSMENTS

Instead of comparing a student's performance with that of a group of students, criterion-referenced assessments compare a student's performance with a specific type of accomplishment or criterion. For instance, one can assess whether students can add two-digit numbers without regrouping. To measure this skill, a student could be asked to answer ten different questions. If a child successfully answers all ten, or nine or even eight of the ten questions, a teacher can state with some degree of confidence that the child knows how to add two-digit numbers without regrouping. This type of assessment is similar to a competency-based assessment; the major difference is that the criterion may be a very narrow competency, such as adding two-digit numbers, in contrast to a competency such as driving a car.

Most classroom tests should measure students' knowledge in a criterion-referenced manner; that is, a student should be asked to answer questions a number of times that measure the same learning. Then, instead of scoring the test by using some sort of A through F range, the teacher sets an acceptable score that determines that the student really understands a concept at an acceptable level.

CAPSTONE/SUMMATIVE ASSESSMENTS

Summative or capstone assessments can be developed to celebrate a milestone accomplishment or to demonstrate how well a person has mastered something. These types of assessments are used near the end of some major accomplishment such as recitals or graduation. For instance, after completing courses in education, a teacher candidate student teaches to show that he or she can help students learn the subject matter. Hence, student teaching is a capstone-type assessment. This capstone assessment is evaluated by a master teacher who notes all the accomplishments that are shown by the student teacher throughout the performance. In such an assessment, deficiencies can also be identified, but the major focus is to uncover what a teacher candidate has mastered throughout a program of study.

At the school level, a capstone assessment can be used at the end of a school year. Students can be asked to apply all they have learned in science by completing a science project or in language by writing a short story or a research paper. Some schools require a comprehensive test, presentation of student work in a portfolio, or essay as the capstone experience for graduation.

■ PERFORMANCE ASSESSMENT

The notion of assessment is changing. For decades, educators have called for better testing, but the response was the proliferation of a number of different kinds of tests with different emphases. Tests of achievement, basic skills tests, criterion-referenced tests related to specific objectives, tests of cognitive ability, tests of flexibility, and tests of critical thinking were developed. Despite these worthy attempts, these tests provided a limited view of what students know. Many educators viewed these paper-and-pencil instruments as an intrusion and not directly related to what was really happening in the classroom.

Instead, educators wanted performance assessments that would allow students to demonstrate in a number of ways that they met standards in real-world or authentic settings. The best performance assessments are designed to promote student understanding, learning, and engagement rather than simply the recall of facts.

I hear and I forget. I see and I remember. I do and I understand.

Chinese proverb

These performance assessments are examples of an **authentic assessment,** which clearly examines student performance on a learned task. Generally, this is accomplished by using a context or situation that directly relates to what the student has learned.

TYPES OF PERFORMANCE ASSESSMENTS

To provide opportunities for students to show what they know and can do, multiple assessment methods must be used. At the basis of these tools or methods is the notion of performance. Thinking of assessments as performances in which the student is given opportunities to display some sort of learning task is critical to the design of an authentic performance assessment method. To be authentic, educators employ a wide variety of assessment opportunities to evaluate student success.

LEARNING LOGS AND JOURNALS   Learning logs are notebooks or journals that contain written descriptions, drawings, reminders, data, charts, conclusions, inferences, generalizations, and any number of other notes developed by the student during the learning process. The teacher's role in the development of these learning logs is to generate questions for the student to ponder and respond to during the learning task. The more varied the questions, the better the assessment. For example, during a learning task, students can be asked to relate what they are studying to their real lives. They can be asked to make a generalization based on what they are doing or to communicate through a mind map, drawing how what they are learning relates to something else. The most important element of using learning logs is the development of a rich bank of questions so that the student practices and records different modes of learning.

Assessment is an ongoing process in which teachers collect data on student progress toward meeting standards as they interact with, listen to, and observe students on a regular basis.

FOLIOS AND PORTFOLIOS   Students can use learning logs to develop a portfolio as well. Samples of student work can be organized and stored in a folio, which is similar to a file cabinet drawer in which all sorts of examples are kept for later use. Samples of student work might show growth over time. Samples can be self-selected by students or with assistance from others. Students can be asked to annotate their work samples by describing the characteristics that make their work noteworthy. The process promotes self-assessment and encourages students to develop skills for defending and describing their work.

Students' best work can be compiled into a portfolio to show that they are meeting standards. For example, they can be asked to examine their folio and select their best science and social science diagrams and write down the characteristics that make each example a good diagram. Teachers can also have students select their most accurate drawing or their best graph. In all cases, the student should articulate why they chose the items they did. Including elements of a student's log permits the student to display learning in yet another way. Portfolios don't have to be in the more traditional hard-copy format. Portfolios can be electronic, including voice, video, CD-ROM, and an archive of written documents.

The important point is that a collection of work is not an assessment unless the student and/or teacher does something with it. Portfolios can have several goals: to show growth over time, to show the breadth of achievements, and to showcase the student's best work. Students and their teacher should formulate a shared goal, students should select entries from their folio that reflect learning related to the goal, students (and possibly the teacher) should include written self-assessment about the student's progress, the teacher should provide feedback, and both should discuss the portfolio, possibly in relation to a rubric they developed for evaluating the portfolio.

CROSS-REFERENCE
Portfolios for teacher candidates are described in Chapter 1.

authentic assessment
A multifaceted performance task that is based in the context of the learner and allows the learner to construct a response that demonstrates what he or she has learned.

Observing students at work is a very useful form of assessment.

INTERVIEWS Students can also indicate what they have learned by being interviewed, either by another student or by the teacher. Face-to-face discussion that includes probing questions is one way in which teachers and students can determine whether something has been learned. Once again, interview questions need to be varied to allow a full range of responses from the student.

OBSERVATION AND ANECDOTAL RECORDS Classroom observation has been a tool used for many years. Within the realm of authentic assessment, observation means using day-to-day classroom activities to determine whether understanding and skills are being demonstrated. To accomplish this properly, teachers need to keep observation notes or checklists, regularly recording what they see and the type of learning being exhibited. These daily observations can be a powerful resource in assessing learning.

In addition to formal observations, keeping anecdotal records is an excellent assessment technique. Teachers who keep a diary and jot down any relevant information about the child's learning progress, accomplishments, and other relevant information will find that their understanding of the whole child is increased. One important caution in using anecdotal records is to be careful in distinguishing between what has been observed (the objective facts) and interpretations of the meaning (judgments).

STUDENT PRODUCTS AND PROJECTS Teachers can have students achieve closure for their learning by completing a project. Sometimes this project can take the form of a specific product. Products include writing a eulogy for a famous person, developing a room layout, designing a complex machine composed of simple machines, creating a proposal for a new park facility, organizing a senior trip, writing a proposal for improving school safety on the playground, or writing a morning radio news report for the school. Displaying these products and using them to note the content and the skill acquisition implicit within each product is another excellent assessment device.

VIDEOTAPES/AUDIOTAPES Teachers can use audiotapes and videotapes to record a student's abilities in areas hard to document other ways. Teachers can also use video to record the process students use as they develop individual products. These tapes are excellent assessment tools that teachers can show to students and parents alike to exhibit what students know and can do. Tapes can provide a record of growth over time, such as a student giving a speech at the beginning and at the end of a year. The tapes can also show what students still need to learn.

RUBRICS

In its simplest and most basic sense, a rubric is a scoring guide. Rubrics are often associated with performance assessments because, in evaluating a performance, it is important to clarify what aspects of the performance are expected at different levels. Rubrics enable assessors to focus on the important components of a performance. They also provide guidance to ensure that different assessors score in the same manner.

Rubrics can be analytic or holistic measures. *Analytic* means looking at each dimension of the performance and scoring each. *Holistic* refers to considering all

A Case Study of Alternative Assessment: Student, Teacher, and Observer Perceptions in a Ninth-Grade Biology Classroom

STUDY PURPOSE/QUESTIONS: This single-site phenomenological case study at a suburban high school examined the perceptions of one teacher (Len) as well as his students, colleagues, and principal about alternative assessment strategies and associated phenomena in Len's ninth-grade biology classroom. Researcher perceptions are also included. The primary focus of the research was to understand and make sense of the world in which Len existed and where he viewed what he considered more meaningful assessment activities as alternative assessments. The study's intent was to contribute to the understanding of alternative assessment by providing detailed, in-depth analysis of how Len, a thirty-year biology teacher, implemented and perceived assessment.

STUDY DESIGN: This study was a qualitative descriptive case study using a phenomenological perspective that describes the world experienced by the participants in their own terms. Questions guiding the study were: (1) What happened in Len's biology classroom as he used alternative assessment? (2) What were Len's perceptions of alternative assessments? (3) How did students view Len's assessment strategies? (4) What did students think were the primary determinants of their grades?

STUDY FINDINGS: Data were reduced from interview transcripts, observations, and documents into thematic perception generalizations of Len and the other participants toward alternative assessment. The resulting generalizations were as follows:

- Len's early and ongoing informal assessments of students' abilities and attitudes played a key role in his perceptions of individual students' work ethic.
- Len's involvement with professional development experiences had a direct impact on what assessments were used in his classroom.
- Arriving early to school, staying late after school, working weekends, and expending large amounts of physical energy facilitated Len's use of alternative assessments within his standard fifty-minute class period.
- Len felt that he was a "Lone Ranger" in his use of alternative assessments.
- Students worked toward learning goals only if an extrinsic reward existed in the form of either points or grades.

- Students felt that they did best when they worked in cooperative groups, took fewer tests, did projects, were active in class, and experienced less teacher talk.
- Students were more comfortable when the teacher evaluated them than when they evaluated themselves or each other.
- Len's colleagues perceived alternative assessments as requiring too much time for the number of students they taught.
- Len's principal had only limited knowledge about alternative science assessment but thought that her science teachers were "moving in the right direction."

IMPLICATIONS: This study uncovered several problems inherent in alternative assessment. Len discovered that using interviews, observations, and projects as assessment tools required a great deal of extra time and energy. His colleagues remained skeptical about the value of alternative assessments; they were concerned about the time needed to implement and interpret them. Len also found that students did not appreciate the value of self-assessment techniques, which are at the heart of alternative assessment approaches.

The study also clarified positive elements in alternative assessments. Students noted that the collaboration activities that Len used throughout the assessment projects developed their personal understandings of the content. Len felt that he had a clearer, more detailed understanding of individual students' achievement; he also noted that alternative assessment techniques provided insight into students' dispositions and work ethic (aspects that national learning standards emphasize).

This study elucidates questions about the feasibility and use of alternative assessments. Given the heavy investment of time both during the school period and outside of school, is alternative assessment worth the cost? How do teachers who want to use alternative assessments deal with student resistance to self-assessment? Because alternative assessment is focused on clarifying what precisely students know and do not know, how can this descriptive information be translated into letter grades?

Source: Peter D. Veronesi, "A Case Study of Alternative Assessment: Student, Teacher, and Observer Perception in a Ninth Grade Biology Classroom." Paper presented at the Association of Educators of Teachers in Science, January 2–4, p. 2000.

criteria simultaneously and making one overall evaluation. You might sum all the analytic scores for a total score, or you might have one holistic dimension within an analytic rubric to provide an overall impression score. By doing this, assessors can access the benefits of both analytic and holistic scoring procedures. Analytic scoring, of course, provides the most specific data for use as a diagnostic assessment; it also limits flexibility because the dimensions are prescribed ahead of time. Holistic scoring does not require specific dimensions to be assessed; as such, it provides more flexibility and allows an assessor to give credit for unexpected dimensions that may contribute to the overall success of a performance. However, holistic scoring provides less direction for students than analytic scoring does. Tables 12.1 and 12.2 are examples of analytic and holistic scoring rubrics.

DESIGNING AUTHENTIC PERFORMANCE ASSESSMENTS

There are three major areas to consider in developing authentic assessments for standards. First, a rich context needs to be designed, one that permits inquiry to occur. Second, it is important to fill the context with a wide variety of questions so that different types of thinking can occur. Finally, the critical indicators for learning need to be identified.

SELECTING A PROPER CONTEXT   The first and most important step in developing authentic assessments is to structure some task that is complex enough to permit students to show important learning, that is motivating enough to en-

TABLE 12.1   Analytic Trait Rubrics for Fifth-Grade Science Experiments

The rubric below uses a scale of one to four. Level 1 is a beginning or low level of performance; level 4 is a high level of performance.

Experiment Design	Scientific Results
4 Design shows student has analyzed the problem and has independently designed and conducted a thoughtful experiment.	4 Pamphlet explained with convincing clarity the solution to the problem. Information from other sources or other experiments was used in explaining.
3 Design shows student grasps the basic idea of the scientific process by conducting experiment that controlled obvious variables.	3 Pamphlet showed that student understands the results and knows how to explain them.
2 Design shows student grasps basic idea of scientific process but needs some help in controlling obvious variables.	2 Pamphlet showed results of experiment. Conclusions reached were incomplete or were explained only after questioning.
1 Design shows student can conduct an experiment when given considerable help by the teacher.	1 Pamphlet showed results of the experiment. Conclusions drawn were lacking, incomplete, or confused.

Data Collection	Verbal Expression
4 Data were collected and recorded in an orderly manner that accurately reflects the results of the experiment.	4 Speech presented a clearly defined point of view that can be supported by research. Audience interest was considered, as were gestures, voice, and eye contact.
3 Data were recorded in a manner that probably represents the results of the experiment.	3 Speech was prepared with some adult help but uses experiment's result. Speech was logical and used gestures, voice, and eye contact to clarify meaning.
2 Data were recorded in a disorganized manner or only with teacher assistance.	2 Speech was given after active instruction from an adult. Some consideration was given to gestures, voice, and eye contact.
1 Data were recorded in an incomplete, haphazard manner or only after considerable teacher assistance.	1 Speech was given only after active instruction from an adult.

Source: From G. Wiggins, *Educative Assessment.* San Francisco: Jossey-Bass, 1998, p. 167. Copyright © 1998 Jossey-Bass. This material is used by permission of John Wiley & Sons, Inc.

TABLE 12.2 Holistic Oral Presentation Rubric

5—Excellent	The student clearly describes the question studied and provides strong reasons for its importance. Specific information is given to support the conclusions that are drawn and described. The delivery is engaging and sentence structure is consistently correct. Eye contact is made and sustained throughout the presentation. There is strong evidence of preparation, organization, and enthusiasm for the topic. The visual aid is used to make the presentation more effective. Questions from the audience are clearly answered with specific and appropriate information.
4—Very Good	The student describes the question studied and provides reasons for its importance. An adequate amount of information is given to support the conclusions that are drawn and described. The delivery and sentence structure are generally correct. There is evidence of preparation, organization, and enthusiasm for the topic. The visual aid is mentioned and used. Questions from the audience are answered clearly.
3—Good	The student describes the question studied and conclusions are stated, but supporting information is not as strong as a 4 or 5. The delivery and sentence structure are generally correct. There is some indication of preparation and organization. The visual aid is mentioned. Questions from the audience are answered.
2—Limited	The student states the question studied but fails to describe it fully. No conclusions are given to answer the question. The delivery and sentence structure are understandable, but with some errors. Evidence of preparation and organization is lacking. The visual aid may or may not be mentioned. Questions from the audience are answered with only the most basic response.
1—Poor	The student makes a presentation without stating the question or its importance. The topic is unclear, and no adequate conclusions are stated. The delivery is difficult to follow. There is no indication of preparation or organization. Questions from the audience receive only the most basic or no response.
0	No oral presentation is attempted.

Source: From G. Wiggins, *Educative Assessment.* San Francisco: Jossey-Bass, 1998, p. 166. Copyright © 1998 Jossey-Bass. This material is used by permission of John Wiley & Sons, Inc.

courage students to think, and that is rich enough with multiple opportunities to show how and what students have shaped into an understanding. Some writers call the structure of such a task the context. By context they mean the various activities, hands-on experiences, and questions that encourage learners to think and to show what they know.

Selecting the context for a performance of worth begins by considering the learning goals, standards, and outcomes of current and past instruction. It is critical that students be assessed on the intended goals and outcomes of their instruction and that the assessments are authentic—that is, that they match the instruction. Too often teachers assess one way but teach in another. Assessing by using paper-and-pencil, single-answer questions when instruction has been emphasizing inquiry is inappropriate. The reverse is also true. Assessing students in a hands-on inquiry mode when all instruction was lecture and reading/writing is equally improper.

In addition, the teacher needs to consider how the learning goals and standards relate to the lives and actions of scientists, writers, historians, and mathematicians. Consider what professionals do and how they use their different ways of knowing. Together, these considerations will often trigger ideas for the performance context.

To illustrate this way of determining a context, consider a curriculum that is filled with learning experiences focused on food chains, prey and predator relationships, and the balance of nature. How does this translate into a real-world context? Having students dissect owl pellets and analyze findings in light of the previous concepts provides one such context that is closely tied to the real world and to environmental issues. Like practicing scientists, students could be asked to investigate a set of owl pellets that have been collected from a specific area of the country. Students can apply what they know and use skills and thinking processes throughout the investigation. The assessment should provide students with opportunities to take measurements, make observations, and record observations about the owl pellets. Students can be asked to create data tables that summarize the types of prey that were consumed, make inferences and draw conclusions about food availability, and finally even answer direct questions about food chains.

STUFFING THE CONTEXT WITH MULTIPLE OPPORTUNITIES   Once a context has been selected, it needs to be structured and filled with opportunities to show how and what students have learned. Asking students to display their cognitive abilities in as many ways as possible enhances the teacher's understanding of students' unique ways of knowing. This is where assessment tools are helpful. Observing students in action and recording these observations in a variety of ways are critical.

ASKING DIFFERENT TYPES OF QUESTIONS   Teachers have long been aware that questioning is an important way to cue students to display their understanding. Research indicates that the types of questions students are asked determine the academic culture of a classroom. Questions that focus on a single aspect of knowing (knowledge or skills) limit the opportunities for showing understanding (the interactions of knowledge, skills, and habits of mind). Having a clearer picture of the multidimensionality of understanding (ways of knowing) directs teachers to ask a wide variety of questions. This is especially true during an assessment experience. Students should be asked many different types of questions within a rich, hands-on context. Table 12.3 presents examples of the variety of question types that allow students multiple opportunities to show their various ways of knowing.

ASSESSING THE IMPORTANT ELEMENTS   Once students are engaged in a motivating inquiry, they will be better able to exhibit learning development. It is important that teachers focus on all aspects of learning when they examine student performance and not simply focus on those aspects that are easy to assess. If a

---

TABLE 12.3   Examples of the Types of Questions That Encourage Students to Show Different Ways of Knowing

- Analysis Questions: What are the key parts? Which parts are essential and why?
- Comparison Questions: How are these alike? What specific characteristics are similar? How are these different? In what way(s) are they different?
- Classification Questions: Into what groups could you organize these things? What are the rules for membership in each group? What are the defining characteristics of each group?
- Connections Clarification Questions: What does this remind you of in another context? To what is this connected?
- Constructing Support Questions: What data can you cite that support this conclusion? What is an argument that would support this claim?
- Deduction Questions: On the basis of this rule, what would you deduce? What are the conditions that make this inevitable?
- Inferring and Concluding Questions: On the basis of these data, what would you conclude? How likely is it that this will occur?
- Abstracting Questions: What pattern underlies all these situations? What are the essential characteristics of this thing?
- Error Analysis: How is this conclusion misleading? What does not match?

context is truly authentic, there should be ample opportunities for students to display what they know and can do across a variety of different standards:

- Knowledge and comprehension of concepts, application of concepts, and connection of concepts to real-world contexts
- Ability to solve problems and exercise thinking skills
- Ability to perform and apply process skills
- Ability to structure thinking
- Collaboration and other dispositions
- Communication and ability to modify ideas on the basis of new evidence

A rich assessment context allows students to display many of these components of understanding and skill. The art of assessing well includes identifying indicators—things that can be observed that relate to different aspects of some important standard. Identifying indicators in a performance task is much like acting as an X ray; teachers need to notice what behaviors count and how successful ways of doing and knowing look. To do this, teachers need to step back from the performance, much like a physician, and identify those actions that are meaningful and, more important, the learning that those actions indicate. Once teachers develop lists of indicators, they can easily assess what a child knows and does not know. These lists can form the basis for assigning grades, discussing student progress, and making decisions about student needs.

Authentic assessment is both an art and a science. As an art, assessment is like the world of a play. Placing students in the proper context is like situating characters to play a particular role; once in this context, students cannot help but display the knowledge, thinking, and habits of mind they have developed. On the other hand, authentic assessment is also like a science in that the educator needs to meticulously identify and examine the important questions and other types of learning indicators that are important to the task.

As can be seen, authentic assessment is an attempt to make testing both in and out of the classroom more closely grounded in the context of student learning and less narrowly focused on a few aspects of what has been learned. Its very name implies trying to better determine what children have really learned.

PROFESSIONAL ASPECTS OF GOOD ASSESSMENTS

Thus far, we have examined the purposes and described a variety of the methods being applied to performance assessment. However, assessing student learning has more to it than the mechanics of constructing authentic tasks. Assessing student learning is an activity that influences and affects many people. Therefore, there are professional and ethical considerations. A number of very technical issues are also related to whether each assessment task is fair and truly assesses what was intended.

PRINCIPLES FOR HIGH-QUALITY ASSESSMENTS

Like other professionals who have knowledge that their clients do not have and whose actions and judgments affect their clients, classroom teachers are responsible for conducting themselves in an ethical manner. This responsibility is particularly important in education because, unlike other professions, students have no choice about whether they will or will not attend school. The following principles are keys to developing and using powerful and responsible assessments:

- Base assessments on standards for learning.
- Represent performances of understanding in authentic ways.
- Embed assessments in curriculum and instruction.
- Provide multiple forms of evidence about student learning.
- Evaluate standards without unnecessary standardization.

- Involve local educators in designing and scoring assessments.
- Let the innovators of the system lead.
- Provide professional development that builds the capacity of teachers and schools to enact new teaching and assessment practices.
- Judge school performance based on practices as well as longitudinal performance data for individuals.[10]

In addition, parents, students, and members of the community should join a variety of experts, teachers, and other educators in shaping the assessment system. Discussion of assessment purposes and methods should involve a wide range of people interested in education. Educators, schools, districts, and states should clearly and regularly discuss assessment system practices and student and program progress with students and their families. Examples of assessments and student work should be made available to parents and the community. Finally, assessment systems should be regularly evaluated and improved to ensure that they are beneficial to all students. Reviewers should include stakeholders in the education system and independent experts.

FAIRNESS

Some of the attractions of state tests are that they are standardized, perceived as objective, and inexpensive in comparison to performance assessments. One of the problems is that they ignore the lived experiences of many test takers, resulting in biases that give students from one group an advantage over another. Analyses of test items show that many of them are biased against students from low-income families. Basing assessments on a set of standards provides appropriate standardization. Performance assessments, unlike standardized tests, can take into account the variations in students' learning contexts while still holding to the levels of achievement expected to meet standards.[11]

RELIABILITY AND VALIDITY OF ASSESSMENTS

Two critical aspects of any effort to assess student learning, whether the assessment items have been developed by an individual teacher or a national testing company, are reliability and validity. Each of these terms is regularly used in professional discussions; however, their meaning and implications might not be appreciated. The only way in which any assessment of student learning can be counted on to be fair is if each and every item is both valid and reliable.

Communicating with all constituencies, including taxpayers, parents, and students, is an essential part of developing standards and having a shared understanding about assessment methods and the meaning of results.

Validity refers to whether the assessment item measures what it is intended to measure. All too frequently, test items do not measure what the test maker had in mind. For example, a history teacher could have a learning objective related to students being able to describe key social, economic, and political causes of the Civil War. If the teacher then uses a test item that asks students to describe the results of key battles during the Civil War, the test item would not be valid. It did not ask students to demonstrate what they had learned in relation to the stated learning objective. This is a simple and obvious example of an assessment item that is not valid. Problems related to validity are many and can be extremely complex. Still, it is essential that teachers make every effort in the construction of assessment items to make sure that what students are being asked to do is closely aligned with the statement of standards and learning objectives.

Reliability is an equally important technical aspect of having high-quality assessments. Reliability has to do with the consistency of information about student learning that results from repeated use of each assessment item or task. If two students who have learned the same amount complete the same assessment, do they receive identical scores? If they do, then the item has high reliability. If two students with the same level of learning receive discrepant scores, then the item is not consistent or reliable. Test makers often check for reliability of their items in another way, called test–retest. In this approach to checking reliability, the same student responds to the same test item after a carefully selected time interval, typically a week or two. Here too the reliability question is "How consistent are the results from both administrations of the assessment?" If both assessments have similar results, then the assessment is considered to be reliable.

ACCOUNTABILITY

Parents and policymakers in many areas of the country are holding their teachers, schools, and school districts accountable for student learning as measured on standardized tests. The federal legislation No Child Left Behind requires schools to annually test all students in grades 3 through 8 on their achievement of standards in math, reading, and science by 2008. Secondary students must be tested at least once. One of the purposes is to provide feedback on student learning to students, parents, and teachers. Data are publicly reported in district and state report cards that show how students in local schools perform in comparison to students in other schools. The legislation allows parents to remove their children from a local school that has been found in need of improvement for two consecutive years and send them to a school at which students are achieving at a higher level.

Student assessments can provide important information on whether school programs are effective. One way of assessing the success of a school program is through norm-referenced assessments, but these assessments are quite limited. They measure only how well a group of students does on a standardized paper-and-pencil task in comparison to other groups of students across the country. To determine how well a program is doing, it is important to use multiple assessments. For example, one additional way to assess a school program would be to regularly gather information about how graduates are performing in the real world. Information about how many students successfully graduate without being retained could be another useful indicator. Having a broad array of assessment data can enable school districts to take stock and redirect efforts such as changing the types of instruction being used and the types of learning being emphasized.

■ TESTING UPS AND DOWNS

The nationwide movement toward standards, performance, and a variety of assessment strategies is a good one, especially for teachers and their students. The goals of teaching and learning are made clear, which then makes it easier for teachers to know what to teach and how. Having standards certainly aids students in understanding what is most important to learn. And having standards helps teachers, schools, school districts, and states in determining the learning outcomes that should be assessed. Still, as with any education initiative, the standards movement has had a number of unintended consequences that need to be considered. Several of the more important of these consequences with direct impact on teachers and students in classrooms are discussed next.

Schools will be responsible for improving the academic performance of all students, and there will be real consequences for districts and schools that fail to make progress.

No Child Left Behind Act

I believe that we should get away altogether from tests and correlations among tests, and look instead at more naturalistic sources of information about how people around the world develop skills important to their way of life.

Howard Gardner

TABLE 12.4   Criteria for High-Stakes Testing Practices

The American Educational Research Association's (AERA) *Public Policy Statement on High-Stakes Testing in PreK–12 Education,* adopted in July 2000, provides twelve criteria, based on solid research, that state education leaders, local school leaders, parents, and others can use to assess the assessments. AERA states that every high-stakes testing program should ensure:

- Protection against high-stakes decisions based on a single test
- Adequate resources and opportunity to learn
- Validation for each separate intended use
- Full disclosure of likely negative consequences of high-stakes testing programs
- Alignment between the test and the curriculum
- Validity of passing scores and achievement levels
- Opportunities for meaningful remediation for examinees who fail high-stakes tests
- Appropriate attention to language differences among examinees
- Appropriate attention to students with disabilities
- Careful adherence to explicit rules for determining which students are to be tested
- Sufficient reliability for each intended use
- Ongoing evaluation of intended and unintended effects of high-stakes testing

For more information, visit AERA's website at www.aera.net.

Source: Denise McKeon, Marcella Dianda, and Ann McLaren, *Advancing Standards: A National Call for Midcourse Corrections and Next Steps.* Washington, DC: National Education Association, 2001, p. 8.

HIGH-STAKES TESTING

As the focus on student performance has intensified, policymakers have mandated that students be tested annually. Testing of this type is called high stakes because of the consequences for the test taker or school once the test results are known. At a minimum, the student test results are compiled by schools and reported to the public. Schools are named and ranked in the newspaper, and sharp questions are asked about those schools that are not meeting adequate yearly progress.

Another way in which testing can be high stakes is through the assignment of rewards and sanctions. In a few states, "high-performing" schools receive additional funds. In some districts, teachers and/or principals receive salary bonuses if test scores improve. Some states provide rewards to high-performing schools, but much more likely is some sort of sanctioning of the low-performing schools. Over half the states and the District of Columbia identify schools as low performing.[12] On the positive side, Kentucky and North Carolina provide assistance to schools that are "in need of improvement" by assigning an experienced master teacher or principal to work with the schools. In other cases, principals are reassigned and entire school staffs replaced. In states such as New Jersey, Massachusetts, and Ohio, an entire school district that is designated low performing can be taken over by the state. Criteria for high-stakes testing are listed in Table 12.4.

Tests can be high stakes for students and their future as well. Nineteen states now use standardized exams to determine graduation from high school, and five states use tests to decide student promotions.[13] Nearly half the population thinks that about the right amount of testing is occurring in schools, as compared to 31 percent who think there is too much testing.[14] Over half the public supports the use of high-stakes testing, as shown in Figure 12.2.

PRESSURES TO CHEAT

In high-stakes conditions, we can expect teachers and principals to invest concerted effort in helping their students do well on the tests. In nearly every school and classroom, teachers stop their regular instruction for a week or more to help students prepare for the test. These preparations can be as practical as practicing answering multiple-choice questions and reviewing what has been taught during the year. The problem arises when teachers—and in some cases principals—help their students cheat. Cheating ranges from telling students how to answer specific test items to teachers, principals, and school district administrators actually changing students' responses on individual tests. In other instances, schools have encouraged some students, such as those with learning disabilities, to stay at home on the day of testing.

TEACHING TO THE TEST

A related issue has to do with balancing the time teachers spend on topics that are likely to be on the test versus instructional time spent on the rest of the curriculum. About two-thirds of teachers indicate that their instruction is too focused on content that will be tested, to the detriment of covering other material. Almost 80 percent of teachers report that they teach test-taking skills to students,[15] reducing the amount of time to teach the content itself.

Any single test is bound to sample a very limited part of what students learn. Also, state tests might have little overlap with the various sets of content standards and the emphasis in district curriculum materials. Time spent on preparing for high-stakes tests reduces the time available to teach related material and other subjects, such as the performing arts, that are not being tested or for which the stakes are not as high. Teaching to the test also often means that the development of critical-thinking and higher-order thinking skills is neglected. If the whole of the district curriculum is aligned with state standards, then those students whose instruction covers more of the standards should perform better on the tests.

ONE-SIZE-FITS-ALL

Another critical issue related to the heavy focus on testing is the assumption that the same test is appropriate for all students, schools, and states. Historically, in the U.S. system of education heavy emphasis has been placed on the importance of attending to individual differences and emphasizing that all students do not develop at the same rate. Now policymakers are mandating that one test be given to all students at a certain grade level at a specified time—in other words, one-size-fits-all. No matter what the uniqueness of individuals might be, all are to take the same relatively narrow test, and major decisions about individual students and/or schools are based on the test results. Academically able students take the same test that poor urban students take. This practice undermines the credibility of the test and its results and clearly disadvantages some students and schools.

THE THREAT OF A NATIONAL EXAM

A growing concern of some people is that the practice of many states using the same tests is just one step away from a national exam, which will lead shortly thereafter to a national curriculum. This is the one-size-fits-all concern taken to the extreme. Others believe that there already is a national curriculum and that national requirements are appropriate. A key target of this perspective is the National Assessment of Educational Progress (NAEP), which is administered each year to students in a sample of schools in each state. One of its purposes is to make it possible for policymakers and educators to view nationally how well students are doing. Comparisons then are made with student achievement in other countries, and most assuredly comparisons are made from state to state in this country. NAEP is designed to make inferences about student achievement

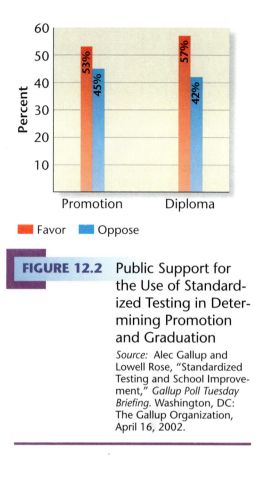

FIGURE 12.2 Public Support for the Use of Standardized Testing in Determining Promotion and Graduation

Source: Alec Gallup and Lowell Rose, "Standardized Testing and School Improvement," *Gallup Poll Tuesday Briefing.* Washington, DC: The Gallup Organization, April 16, 2002.

What Is the Proper Way to Prepare for High-Stakes, State-Mandated Tests?

Schools across the country are now required to administer state assessments linked to learning standards. The assessments tend to be paper-and-pencil, multiple-choice examinations of reading, mathematics, science, social studies, and writing. The assessments are given annually to students in grades 3–8. Teachers within these targeted grade levels are required to interrupt their regular school instruction to administer these state examinations.

The state-mandated assessments are comprehensive in nature; that is, they cover a wide variety of topics that relate to the state standards. This often poses a dilemma for teachers who instruct at one of the targeted grade levels. Students in their classrooms might show that they have not had proper instruction in one or more aspects of the state content. This can and does occur because the district curriculum might not fully represent state standards, because individual students do not develop at the same pace, or because students transfer from school districts that have diverse curricula.

What can or should a teacher at a targeted grade level do to assist students on these state examinations? Some teachers attempt to teach to the test. That is, they try to get sample test items, and they clarify what was on the prior year's examination. These teachers may even develop teacher-made test questions that mimic the state examination and require students to practice taking these preparation tests. In some states,

practice tests can be purchased from private publishing companies. Teachers who teach to the test in this way are sometimes criticized because they take time out of the regular school curriculum. They are also criticized because some educators consider teaching to the test to be improper.

Other teachers do not try to teach to the test, but they do have students practice test-taking techniques. They teach students strategies that could assist them in taking any standardized multiple-choice examination. They too take time out of the normal curriculum, but these teachers contend that the acquisition of such test-taking skills assists in all areas of learning.

A third group of educators refuse to do any test preparation other than to teach the required curriculum for their grade level. These educators believe that state tests should not affect the normal instructional process. If students do not perform well, then the curriculum should be officially changed.

- What will you do if you are teaching in one of these target grade levels?
- Should you teach to the test?
- Should you teach test-taking techniques?
- Should you ignore the test and simply follow the normal curriculum?
- What approach can you defend as the proper one?

To answer these questions on-line and e-mail your answers to your professor, go to Chapter 12 of the companion website (**www.ablongman.com/johnson13e**) and click on Professional Dilemma.

---

within states. It is not designed to make judgments about individual students or schools. Unfortunately, although NAEP has existed for several decades and its findings are very useful, school districts and schools are increasingly unwilling to participate owing to the mounting pressure and time demands of the many other required tests.

GLOBAL PERSPECTIVES

Assessment of Student Learning across Nations

National assessment is not limited to the United States; it is a worldwide phenomenon that has blossomed over the past decade. Participants in the World Education Forum adopted a World Declaration on Education for All in Jomtien, Thailand, in 1990 and ratified the declaration in Dakar, Senegal, in 2000. The declaration recognized that periodic student assessments make a valuable contribution toward the improvement of educational quality. Many countries consider academic achievement as pivotal in establishing a highly qualified labor force that attracts foreign capital and allows them to be competitive in the global martketplace.[16] To promote these efforts, the World Bank, Inter-American Development Bank, United Nations Educational, Scientific, and Cultural Organization (UNESCO), and the U.S. Agency for International Development (AID) have invested in the design and implementation of national assessments.

What assessments are required in other countries? England has a national examination for students at ages seven, eleven, fourteen, and sixteen that measures the effectiveness of schools in delivering the national curriculum. Schools in England set targets for student growth. France conducts national assessments at grades 3, 6, and 9 for diagnostic and planning purposes. The tests at the end of grade 9 and the end of high school measure student achievement.[17]

National examinations in Hong Kong dictate instruction in schools. China views its National College Entrance Examination as critical to the nation's development. Much of the population sees the national test as providing opportunities for the oppressed to achieve an elite education. The only national test in Japan is for college entrance. However, Japanese students take other high-stakes tests to gain admission to high schools.[18]

Students in Argentina are tested annually in grades 3, 6, 7, 9, and 12 in mathematics, language, science, and social studies. All twelfth graders are tested, but testing at the other grades is conducted through a sampling process. Chile assesses all students in grades 4 and 8 in language and mathematics, and samples 10 percent of the students in natural sciences, history, and geography. Uruguay tests students in mathematics and language in grades 3, 6, and 9. Each of these three South American countries compiles data on the school and family socioeconomic conditions of test takers and develops individualized school reports. Argentina and Chile have disseminated test results publicly for nearly a decade.[19]

INCREASED TEACHER BURDEN

As exciting and important as the new approaches to assessment are, one of the downsides is the increased work for teachers. Developing more authentic tasks takes more time than does constructing multiple-choice and true/false test items. Deriving scoring devices for authentic tasks is added work too. Holistic scoring entails first developing a scoring rubric and then examining each student's response in sufficient detail to be able to determine a total score. The load on teachers becomes even heavier in secondary schools because each teacher has contact with more students. One of the important solutions to the risk of an increased burden is for teachers within a school or school district to collaborate in the development of assessment tasks. There also is national sharing of assessment items through discipline-based professional associations and various chat rooms on the web. A related key for individual teachers is to keep in mind that many of the traditional activities that teachers have been doing to assess student learning, such as noting their performance in laboratories and in the field, have become more legitimate with the move to authentic assessment.

▪ EQUITY WITHIN ACCOUNTABILITY

No Child Left Behind expects schools to help all students meet standards at defined proficiency levels regardless of their socioeconomic status, ethnicity, race, first language, disability, migrant status, or gender. In fact, performance by students from each of these groups must be reported on the school's and district's annual report card. Thus, teachers are held responsible for helping all students learn as reflected on a single assessment—the state content test. Meeting this goal will be more difficult in some settings than others, especially when resources are limited or nonexistent for providing students with the facilities and support

There's something wrong with imposing universal standards on a state or nation until, prior to that time, we have given the children genuinely equal resources. The way it is being done today is invidious, punitive, and humiliating.

Jonathan Kozol

Should Special Needs Students Be Exempt from Graduation Tests?

Students with disabilities, their parents, and their advocates have been fighting for years for inclusion in classrooms and fairness in all aspects of the educational process. One area that continues to be debated is the treatment of students with disabilities in a high-stakes environment. This debate explores the question of whether students with disabilities should be exempted from the graduation tests, which may give them access to jobs and higher education.

YES

Timothy Bush teaches special education at Seaford Senior High School in Delaware. Currently a member of the Delaware State Education Association executive board, he's also a lead teacher for his district's New Teacher Mentoring Program.

NO

Ed Amundson is a special education teacher at C. K. McClatchy High School in Sacramento, California. Chair of NEA's Caucus of Educators for Exceptional Children, he is a national presenter and staff trainer on special education issues.

Special educators are trained to look at the whole child and make decisions based on individual needs. I feel that I must qualify my "yes" answer by rephrasing the question to read, "Should some special needs students be exempt from taking graduation tests?"

I don't believe students should be routinely exempted, but I do believe that only the experts who participate on a student's Child Study Team should make that decision. As long as bureaucrats and politicians can mandate that all students take a single test to graduate, a team's ability to exempt a student from such testing is compromised.

If special needs students are lumped together with nondisabled peers and required to take high-stakes tests without procedural safeguards, I have grave concerns about fairness.

These concerns center around how special needs students are identified and tracked, what accommodations for them are made, and whether a single indicator is relied on for an assessment.

The referral process for identifying special education students always involves the use of multiple indicators. Tests, observations, psychological reports, student work samples, parent and teacher interviews, and many other tools are used to identify, describe, and provide

The question is not whether special needs students should be exempt from taking graduation tests. The real question is whether students should be required to take tests that do not include appropriate accommodations. The answer is no.

As states and locals move toward higher standards and expectations, it's critical to include students with special needs. For many years special ed was viewed as an adjunct program that was trying to "mainstream" such students into the general ed environment. Access to the curriculum was an afterthought.

Under IDEA '97, the emphasis is not just on access to the school but access to the curriculum as well, and, with it, recognition of student effort. We now expect that, with appropriate accommodations, students can complete the core curriculum.

Many states and locals currently acknowledge the different learning needs of all students and make accommodations through the IEP process. Schools recognize student strengths and weaknesses and allow for measures of what a student knows and not what they do not. Should a standard exit exam do the same?

I posed this question to a group of secondary learning disabled students to get their impressions. Their re-

(continued)

necessary to promote learning at a high level and providing teachers the necessary professional development. Nevertheless, it is a goal worth achieving.

A continuing point of criticism about these traditional tests is that they do not address or accommodate the diversity of students in today's classrooms. Each student brings a unique set of background experiences, prior knowledge, and cultural perspectives to learning. Asking all students to show what they know on a narrow standardized test is a very real problem.

YES

information about disabilities that may be affecting a student's performance.

After identification, appropriate individual accommodations, supports, and adaptations are developed to modify instruction, allowing for as much success as possible. When tests are used in the classroom, they are often modified in ways consistent with a student's IEP and list of appropriate accommodations.

It's understood that the nature of a student's disability might not allow that student to demonstrate mastery of concepts the way other students do. Why isn't it understood that graduation tests require the same modification?

I believe that holding all students accountable to high graduation standards is certainly important and necessary. But test designers often fail to consider the possible disabilities of students taking the graduation tests. They construct the test items with standards in mind, but do they think about what kinds of students must take the test?

What about students who have visual or motor problems that interfere with their ability to quickly process and respond to information? Will the test come in a format that allows it to be untimed for these students?

Can the test be broken into segments or must it be taken in one massive block? Will there be enlarged print or Braille versions?

It's extremely difficult for test makers to anticipate the wide variety of accommodations that may be required, which returns us to the concept of considering special needs students on an individual, case-by-case basis.

Ultimately, I think, we may need to develop criteria for creating a "body of evidence" that assesses student mastery. My overriding concern is that special needs students be treated fairly. To do anything less is simply discriminatory and unfair.

NO

sponse was intriguing. The feeling was unanimous that they should be required to take an exit exam. They are eager to show what they have accomplished.

But these students were perplexed about why the core classes required to graduate could be modified but not the tests that would measure their success.

As one student put it: "I am good at some things and not others, but how would anyone know?"

The question is valid. What other people may know or perceive is extremely important. If students are not awarded diplomas, what do they receive?

If the purpose of a diploma is to demonstrate a student has successfully completed the required course of study, anything less sends a message of failure the student will carry for life.

"All potential employers are going to think is that I did not make the grade," one student told me. "They won't know how hard I worked, what I did learn, or what I can still learn. For the rest of my life, my application will say I couldn't do it. That just isn't fair."

Many would argue that making accommodations creates an unequal playing field. But equal is not the issue. Equal is when every student gets the same thing. Fair is when all students get what they need.

The national demand for high standards and accountability is appropriate for all students. But it's patently unfair not to make the accommodations that will enable students with special needs to demonstrate their abilities.

Would we not make accommodations for a student in a wheel-chair? A disability is a disability.

For many students, gaining a high school diploma is a major life goal. As educators, we are the keys that open doors to opportunity and dreams. We must leave the door open for all students.

Source: "Should Special Needs Students Be Exempt from Graduation Tests?" *NEA Today* (November 2000), p. 11.

WHAT DO YOU THINK?
Should special needs students be exempt from graduation tests?

Companion Website

To give your opinion, go to Chapter 12 of the companion website (**www.ablongman.com/johnson13e**) and click on Debate.

The gap between the test scores of white students and most students of color remains wide. The data collected from the fifty states and the District of Columbia for *Education Week's Annual Quality Counts 2003* showed that the achievement gap between white and black or Latino students in twenty-five states on the NAEP eighth-grade math test was 20 percentage points or more.[20] Ironically, many researchers have found that state tests are much better determiners of the family's socioeconomic level than of academic ability. Students who perform poorly on these tests are disproportionately from low-income families.

Supporters of NCLB argue that black and Latino students will perform at a more equal level over time because schools will be able to raise their test scores by hiring only **highly qualified teachers,** teaching reading more effectively, basing instruction on what is known to work from "scientifically based research," and allowing parents to remove their children from low-performing schools and place them in higher-performing schools. Critics also believe that all students can learn and that highly qualified teachers are essential, but they worry about the use of a single standardized test rather than multiple assessments to determine whether a student can be promoted or graduate. They also question the ability of schools, especially in high-poverty areas, to raise test scores without intensive professional development of teachers, reduction of student-to-teacher ratios, greater involvement of parents, and more stimulating curriculum and instruction—all areas that require financial resources that are not usually available in communities with the greatest need.

These issues become even more glaring for students who are English language learners and those with special needs and learning disabilities. State assessments usually allow for exemptions from taking the test for some students and require appropriate accommodations for others. Often, simply changing the way in which learning is assessed can provide significant new opportunities for these students to demonstrate their knowledge and skills against a set of standards.

SUMMARY

Standards, assessments, and standards-based education are core components of the standards movement and are affecting everyone who has a stake in education. One of the dilemmas related to standards includes the varying conceptions of standards endorsed by different groups. Standards can be used to make school curricula more alike. They can provide a set of uniform expectations by grade level that all students must meet before progressing to the next grade. They can also be used to compare the performance of students across schools and groups of students.

Three types of standards have emerged based on the different conceptions and uses of standards: content standards, which focus on student achievement of subject matter and school curricula; performance standards, which focus on teacher and student accomplishments; and delivery or opportunity-to-learn standards, which focus on resources and support for schools. Each of these types of standards ultimately focuses on developing student achievement.

Standards and assessments are being used to hold schools and school districts accountable for student learning. Assessments that are integrated into a standards-based program need to be multiple and varied. Authentic contextualized assessments provide opportunities for students to show what they know and are able to do within and across a number of different disciplines. However, standardized tests are the most prominent assessment used by states and the federal government to make public the performance of students within a school.

DISCUSSION QUESTIONS

1. Standards have now been developed for the subjects taught in P–12 schools. What are the core knowledge, performances, and dispositions in the standards that you will be expected to implement in the subject(s) that you plan to teach at the grade level in which you plan to work (for example, early childhood, elementary, middle level, or high school)? How reasonable is it to expect you to ensure that students meet these standards by the time they finish a school year?

2. States are being required by No Child Left Behind to develop standards for different grade levels. What benefits and problems are inherent in developing a common set of standards for all students across a state?

3. Standards-based education calls for the use of performance assessments in determining whether students meet standards. How could student portfolios be used to show what students have learned? What problems might such assessments cause?

4. How fair is it to demand that all students, no matter what their ability or socioeconomic status, master a common set of learning standards before obtaining a diploma? In what cases do you think students should be exempt from testing requirements for graduation?

5. What do you see as your role as a teacher in a standards-based education classroom? What professional development will you need as a new teacher in order to implement standards-based curriculum and performance assessments in your classroom?

JOURNAL ENTRIES

1. Consider the types of assessments that have been used throughout your college studies. Select one assessment experience that you have found to be especially helpful in displaying what you believe you really know and can do. Describe the assessment, and then list what characteristics of the assessment enabled you to express your understanding.

2. Obtain a copy of your state's learning standards for one discipline. Examine the framework in which the standards are described. Do they have related goals, benchmarks, or other dimensions? Focus on one standard and identify all of the components that relate to that learning standard. In your journal, draw a diagram or create a mind map or concept map that shows the interrelationships of all the supporting pieces that surround the standard.

3. Standards-based education and new approaches to assessing learning are being applied in higher education, especially in teacher education programs. The same ideas apply in both P–12 and higher education settings. In what courses have you seen standards-based education reflected? In what ways? How would you compare the effectiveness of a standards-based approach to a traditional approach to teaching and learning?

PORTFOLIO DEVELOPMENT

1. Authentic assessments attempt to provide students with opportunities to show what they know and can do within a real-world setting. Within your major subject area, develop an authentic assessment that would enable students to demonstrate what they have learned in relation to one of the national standards.

2. Use the library, the web, or a faculty member to search out information about the activities in one school district regarding their use of standards and their assessment of learning related to those standards. Look closely at the standards and assessments for your planned teaching area. Develop a page of notes about what you would say in a job interview related to their use of standards-based education. Also note three or four questions for which you would need to find additional information or develop better understanding before you went to the interview.

PREPARING FOR CERTIFICATION

■ STANDARDS AND ASSESSMENT

1. Two topics in the Praxis II Principles of Teaching and Learning (PLT) test relate to this chapter: "monitoring students' understanding of content through a variety of means" and "reflecting on the extent to which learning goals were met." In this chapter, you learned about the importance of the standards movement in establishing curriculum goals and assessing student learning. Learn more about the national standards for the subjects and grade levels you plan to teach. What goals for learning are contained in those standards? What are a variety of ways in which you might assess those goals?

2. Answer the following multiple-choice question, which is similar to items in Praxis and other state certification tests. If you are unsure of the answer, reread the Assessments: The Other Side of Standards section of this chapter.

> Mr. Harding has just completed a unit on sonnets. To assess students' understanding of the structure of sonnets, he constructed a quiz of ten poems and asked students which poems were sonnets. He expected students to be able to classify the poems with at least 80 percent accuracy.
>
> This assessment is an example of
>
> (A) norm-referenced assessment
> (B) criterion-referenced assessment
> (C) authentic assessment
> (D) summative assessment

3. Answer the following short-answer question, which is similar to items in Praxis and other state certification tests. After you've completed your written response,

use the scoring guide in the *Test at a Glance* materials to assess your response. Can you revise your response to improve your score?

Reread the Education in the News feature at the beginning of the chapter, which reports that some school districts in Massachusetts are holding back more ninth-grade students to better prepare them to pass the state's MCAS test, a requirement for graduation. Next, complete the following task.

You are a ninth-grade teacher in a school district that is proposing a policy to retain students at the ninth-grade level if they clearly will be unable to pass the state test in the tenth grade. Your school principal is interviewing all the ninth-grade teachers to get their opinions of this proposed policy. What will you tell the principal? Take a position for or against the policy and provide your reasons for the position you take.

WEBSITES

www2.edtrust.org/edtrust The Education Trust website provides data, policies, and recommendations related to students' academic achievement with an emphasis on students who have not been served well in the educational system.

www.nces.ed.gov/nationsreportcard The National Assessment of Educational Progress website provides information about the national testing programs and national report card.

www.nctm.org Information about the National Council of Teachers of Mathematics and its standards can be found at this website.

www.relearning.org This site for Relearning by Design provides information on standards and authentic assessment and is hosted by the Coalition for Curriculum and Assessment (CCA).

www.ncss.org The website for the National Council for the Social Studies includes the council's standards, background papers, and description of its many other professional activities.

www.project2061.org The website for the American Association for the Advancement of Science's Project 2061 supports a national initiative to improve K–12 science, mathematics, and technology education.

FURTHER READING

Goodwin, A. Lin. (Ed.). (1999). *Assessment for Equity and Inclusion: Embracing All Our Children*. New York: Routledge. A discussion of the debates about standardized testing and alternative assessment methods with suggestions for including, rather than excluding, students to create a diverse community of learners.

Kohn, Alfie. (1999). *Schools Children Deserve: Moving beyond Traditional Classrooms and "Tougher Standards."* Boston: Houghton Mifflin. A discussion of the overemphasis on achievement and standardized testing. The author calls for intellectually stimulating classrooms and provides examples from classrooms.

Popham, W. James. (2001). *The Truth about Testing: An Educator's Call to Action*. Alexandria, VA: Association for Supervision and Curriculum Development. A critique of the tests being used by states for high-stakes

testing programs. Guidelines are included to help teachers use tests for instructional benefits.

Sacks, Peter. (1999). *Standardized Minds: The High Price of America's Testing Culture and What We Can Do to Change It*. Cambridge, MA: Perseus Books. A critique of standardized testing and its negative impact on teaching and learning, especially for students from low-income families.

Symcox, Linda. (2002). *Whose History? The Struggle for National Standards in American Classrooms*. New York: Teachers College Press. A discussion and analysis of the drafting of the history standards, the controversy, and their subsequent rejection by Congress. The analysis provides valuable insights into how decisions are made about the history to be taught in schools and about developing national content standards.

THEMES OF THE TIMES!

expect the world®

The New York Times

nytimes.com

Expand your knowledge of the concepts discussed in this chapter by reading current and historical articles from the *New York Times* by visiting the Themes of the Times! section of the companion website (**www.ablongman.com/johnson13e**).

NOTES

1. Linda Darling-Hammond and Beverly Falk, "Supporting Teaching and Learning for All Students: Policies for Authentic Assessment Systems," in A. Lin Goodwin, ed., *Assessment for Equity and Inclusion: Embracing All Our Children.* New York: Routledge, 1997, p. 51.

2. American Management Association, *AMA Survey on Workplace Testing: Basic Skills, Job Skills, Psychological Measurement.* New York: Author, 2001.

3. National Council of Teachers of Mathematics, *Principles and Standards for School Mathematics.* Reston, VA: Author, 2000, p. 29. The standards are available electronically at standards.nctm.org.

4. Interstate New Teacher Assessment and Support Consortium, *Model Standards for Beginning Teacher Licensing, Assessment, and Development: Resource for State Dialogue.* Washington, DC: Author, 1992.

5. Standards Development Staff, *New Standards Performance Standards,* vol. 2. Pittsburgh, PA: National Center on Education and the Economy, 1997, p. 22. For information on these standards, visit www.newstandards.org.

6. Ibid.

7. Ibid.

8. Ibid.

9. Linda Symcox, *Whose History? The Struggle for National Standards in American Classrooms.* New York: Teachers College Press, 2002.

10. Darling-Hammond and Falk, "Supporting Teaching and Learning."

11. Ibid.

12. Kathryn M. Doherty and Ronald A. Skinner, "State of the States," *Quality Counts 2003: "If I Can't Learn from You . . . ," Education Week, 22*(17) (January 9, 2003), pp. 75–78.

13. Ibid., p. 76.

14. Lowell C. Rose and Alec M. Gallup, "The 34th Annual Phi Delta Kappa/Gallup Poll of the Public's Attitudes toward the Public Schools," *Phi Delta Kappan, 84*(1) (September 2002), pp. 41–56.

15. Lynn Olson, "Overboard on Testing?" *Quality Counts 2001: A Better Balance, Education Week, 20*(7) (January 22, 2001), available at www.edweek.org/sreports/qcol/articles/qcolstory.cfm?slug=17test.h20.

16. Luis Benveniste, "The Political Structuration of Assessment: Negotiating State Power and Legitimacy," *Comparative Education Review, 46*(2) (February 2002), pp. 89–118.

17. John A. Holloway, "A Global Perspective on Student Accountability," *Educational Leadership, 60*(5) (February 2003), p. 74, 76.

18. Ibid.

19. Benveniste, "Political Structuration."

20. Doherty and Skinner, "State of the States."

Designing Programs for Learners: Curriculum, Instruction, and Technology

Education in the News

Texas Board Adopts Scores of New Textbooks

By Kathleen Kennedy Manzo, *Education Week,* November 27, 2002

TEXAS SCHOOL CHILDREN WILL LEARN ABOUT AFRICAN INvolvement in slavery, the contributions Hispanics made throughout state history, and a religiously correct time frame of glacial movement when newly adopted history and social studies textbooks hit classrooms next school year.

They will not, however, encounter some original textbook passages that emphasized positive aspects of Islam and Communism, or those that presented the problems of global warming and acid rain as undisputed fact.

As has been a long-standing tradition in the Lone Star State, the selection of history and social studies textbooks, which will be used in classrooms for the next seven years, fueled a vigorous debate over content details large and small. (See *Education Week,* Aug. 7, 2002.) And in the weeks leading up to the Nov. 15 adoption by the state board of education, publishers anxious to tap the nearly $250 million the state has earmarked for texts in the subjects made hundreds of changes. Alterations came after board members, interest groups, and citizens highlighted what they saw as inaccuracies or bias.

Outside Influence

The board approved dozens of textbooks for use in the state's classrooms to teach history, civics, geography, and economics beginning in the 2003–04 school year. As the second-largest state to adopt textbooks behind California, Texas is bound to influence the choices offered to other states whenever it approves a list of textbooks that its districts can buy with state money.

Reprinted with permission from *Education Week,* November 27, 2002.

INTASC — Learning Outcomes

After reading and studying this chapter, you should be able to:

1. Analyze the effects of different influences on the selection and design of curricula in your state. (INTASC 10: Collaboration)

2. Describe and compare different curriculum designs. (INTASC 1: Subject Matter; INTASC 4: Teaching Methods; INTASC 7: Planning; INTASC 8: Assessment)

3. Identify and apply different types and forms of learning objectives to instruction. (INTASC 4: Teaching Methods; INTASC 7: Planning)

4. Describe and analyze characteristics of direct and indirect teaching strategies. (INTASC 4: Teaching Methods)

5. Compare the learning needs of different types of learners and the relative effectiveness of different teaching strategies. (INTASC 2: Development & Learning; INTASC 4: Teaching Methods)

6. Describe indicators and examples of opportunities for integrated use of technology in instruction. (INTASC 2: Development & Learning; INTASC 4: Teaching Methods; INTASC 6: Communication & Technology)

The content taught, the materials selected, the teaching strategies used, and the activities in which children engage are elements of the curriculum. Deciding on these elements is a complex process. Most major decisions about the curriculum are made a long way from the classroom. As a result, contrary to what you might expect, today's teachers have a limited say in selection of the curriculum. Many citizens—including policymakers, parents, advocacy groups, and publishers—are involved in determining the curriculum.

However, teachers continue to have major responsibility for and autonomy in the *delivery* of the curriculum. Which content is taught, how much time it receives, and student perceptions of the importance of particular subject areas are determined by the classroom teacher. The real-time delivery of a lesson, how the classroom is managed, the responses made to student statements, and the day-to-day assessment of student work are also in the hands of the teacher. Determining which students respond to questions, whose work is displayed, and which students are selected to be group leaders are key elements of instruction and primarily, if not solely, the responsibility of the teacher. All of these instruction decisions and actions are elements of the curriculum. Likewise, the teacher decides how much of the textbook to use and the extent to which the teacher, or the students, touch the manipulative materials. Because teachers control the delivery of the curriculum in the classroom, also known as *instruction,* the role of the teacher is probably more significant than ever.

Technology is a related component of the curriculum that has become very important. The types and quantities of technological resources available to teachers and students continue to increase at exponential rates. As with other components of the curriculum, many key decisions about technology begin far from the classroom. For example, if a particular state or school district does not purchase particular technologies, or invest in the necessary infrastructure such as high-speed Internet access, then what teachers can do becomes limited. Still, as with other components of the curriculum, the teacher determines what, when, how, and who will use each type of technology in the classroom.

This chapter is organized around these three major topics—curriculum, instruction, and technology. One big idea addressed has to do with diagramming the many constituents and interest groups that have a hand in determining the curriculum. A second has to do with the fact that much of the curriculum is not readily visible or even understood by teachers, parents, and community members. Of course, the important responsibilities and role of the teacher in planning, delivery, and assessing instruction are covered. What teachers decide to do and not do makes significant differences in what students learn. A big idea related to technology is that its uses in the classroom need to be tied to the curriculum and instruction. Rarely should technology itself be the purpose of a lesson. Instead, technology should be seen as a tool to support teachers, teaching, and student learning.

When technology is used, it is important that its purpose be directly tied to the lesson

CURRICULUM: RELATING EXPECTATIONS FOR LEARNING TO WHAT IS TAUGHT

The **curriculum** is anything and everything that supports student learning. Certainly, curriculum includes the materials and teaching processes that are described in various documents such as curriculum guides and textbooks. The curriculum also includes statements for student learning and the methods used to assess student learning. It includes the informal and less visible parts of the school day. Deciding on the curriculum is an important beginning. However, choosing certain learning outcomes—in other words, standards—and describing the particular subject content and perhaps some of the teaching activities are only the beginning. An important next step is curriculum development. In developing curriculum, there are a number of basic designs to choose from. Once selected and developed, the whole of the curriculum for each state and each school district must be managed and evaluated. Each of these steps and processes is of critical importance, and each must be done well in order for teachers to do the most they can to help all of the students in their classrooms learn. Over the next several pages, we describe each of the steps in the curriculum development process along with direct implications for classrooms, teachers, and their students.

■ CURRICULUM RESOURCES AND SELECTION

The curriculum delivered in each classroom has a rich and complex foundation. The tangible items for the teacher and the students include curriculum guides, textbooks, student workbooks, available technologies, and manipulative materials and lab supplies. However, the curriculum is more than printed documents. It also encompasses schoolwide resources and special-purpose facilities such as the media/resource center, playground and athletic facilities, cafeteria, auditorium, band practice hall, and arts and crafts classroom. As stated previously, the curriculum also includes the expectations for student learning. Each of these curriculum resources is important for teachers to understand, carefully examine, and use wisely.

TEXTBOOKS

For teachers, one of the primary sources of information about the curriculum is the commercially published textbook. Textbook publishers employ expert author

Curriculum is the substance of schooling—the primary reason why people attend school.

M. Francis Klein

curriculum

Standards, teacher resources, classroom materials, and teaching processes that in combination support student learning.

teams and invest large sums of money to provide students and teachers with up-to-date and well-designed materials. In U.S. schools, for most subjects textbook packages provide the bulk of the content, lesson objectives, and audiovisual resources, as well as student assignments. Most textbooks have an accompanying instructor's guide that provides the teacher with additional background subject information, lesson plans, suggestions for extensions and special assignments, and test items. A number of additional resources exist for teachers who use textbooks in the major subject areas such as science, mathematics, and English. These additional resources include training workshops, access to supporting websites, and perhaps videos of classroom lessons in which the textbook is used.

CURRICULUM GUIDES AND COURSE SYLLABI

Another important curriculum resource consists of the support materials for the teacher prepared by the school district and state. These include syllabi and curriculum guides for each subject area and grade level. Curriculum guides and syllabi draw the connections between what is to be taught at each grade level and the expectations for student learning in state and district standards. These guides also provide a vertical view of how the subject is to be covered from grade level to grade level. This is important because students experience school one year at a time, but their learning needs to be cumulative across the years. Teachers need to see how what they are teaching this year relates to what students learned last year and what they will be expected to learn next year. District and state curriculum guides are very useful for teachers as they plan daily lessons, especially when information is provided about the specific benchmarks for student learning that must be addressed and assessed at each grade level and for each subject. In some cases, such as in California, instead of having guides the state curriculum is organized around the **big ideas** for each subject area and published as Curriculum Frameworks. For example, in describing the nature of science, three broad assumptions are stated:

> The scientific method is a process for predicting, on the basis of a handful of scientific principles, what will happen next in a natural sequence of events. Because of its success, this invention of the human mind is used in many fields of study. The scientific method is a flexible, highly creative process built on the broad assumptions:

> - Change occurs in observable patterns that can be extended by logic to predict what will happen next.
> - Anyone can observe something and apply logic.
> - Scientific discoveries are replicable.[1]

TESTS

How often in your career as a student have you thought about asking or heard someone else ask the teacher, "Will this be on the test?" An important indicator of which elements of the curriculum are seen as most important is what is actually tested. With the continuing emphasis on high-stakes testing, teachers and their students must be knowledgeable about what is tested. A core assumption in some school districts and states, such as Texas, that have "no-pass-no-play" rules is that students will work harder to learn the material if they are tested and experience the direct consequences of the results.

For you as a teacher, understanding what is on the test is important for at least two reasons: (1) Your students will be highly motivated to learn what will be on the test; and (2) you will quickly discover that for your grade level or subject, some critical topics are not covered on the high-stakes test. Both of these reasons illustrate an important aspect of the curriculum: The curriculum is not just what is in the textbook, nor just what is in the classroom lessons; it also is embedded in the expectations for learning and related assessments.

big ideas

The organization of content around major themes and principles.

COCURRICULUM AND EXTRA-CURRICULUM

When most teachers, parents, and the public think about curriculum, they think about the core academic subjects of language arts, science, mathematics, and social studies. However, school includes other subjects, such as world languages, physical education, and, especially in secondary schools, athletics, band, drama, choir, and many clubs. These other subjects, after-school activities, and clubs make up the **cocurriculum,** which sometimes is called the **extra-curriculum.** In many ways, it can be argued that the cocurriculum is of equal importance as the basic subject areas. The cocurriculum is especially important in high schools. Unfortunately, during times of budget cuts, various pieces of the cocurriculum are targeted. For example, driver education used to be a free component of the cocurriculum in most public high

Student participation in the cocurriculum/extra-curriculum can provide important opportunities for learning, as well as encouragement for staying in school.

schools. Now, if it is offered through the school at all, it requires a fee. This is unfortunate because for many students participation in the cocurriculum is a prime reason for staying in school. Cocurriculum teachers are excited about their programs and spend long hours after school, at night, and on weekends working with students to publish the student newspaper or yearbook, or to prepare the team or band for the next competition. These highly dedicated teachers and their programs provide students with experiences and skills they will carry with them throughout their adult lives.

SELECTING CURRICULUM IS A COMPLEX BUSINESS

At the beginning of this chapter, we observed that in today's schools teachers play a limited role in selecting the curriculum. In the past, teachers could teach their favorite lessons without worrying that there would be dire consequences for them or their students as a result of not following the guide or syllabus. Today, teachers do not have this flexibility; they are responsible for helping all students achieve in terms of the published standards and benchmarks. So, then, who does select the curriculum?

DIFFERENT LEVELS OF INFLUENCE

In true American fashion, many people and groups have a say in selecting the curriculum for public schools. Figure 13.1 illustrates the many different actors and forces involved in determining the curriculum. Around the outer circle is the array of forces and interest groups that represent the macro view. The middle ring summarizes many of the local factors and conditions that influence curriculum decisions. The inner ring shows the school context and influences. The product of this array of forces and interests is the curriculum that is selected and implemented in each classroom.

LARGE SCALE INFLUENCES ON CURRICULUM SELECTION   The primary effect of the various elements that form the outer ring in Figure 13.1 is to influence what will be common for curriculum for all states and school districts. Court cases, state and federal legislation, national reports, and educational research, as well as textbook publishers, determine much of what will be taught and learned in

cocurriculum/ extra-curriculum

School activities and programs, before, during, and after regular school class hours, that enrich the curriculum and provide extended opportunities for student participation.

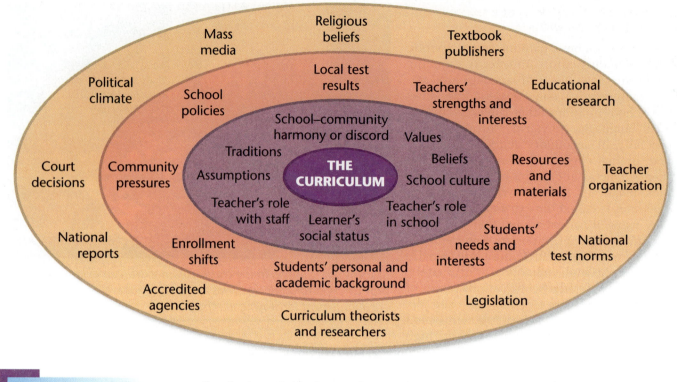

FIGURE 13.1 Influences on Curriculum Selection and Development

Source: F. W. Parkay and B. H. Stanford, *Becoming a Teacher* (5th ed.) p. 378. © 2001. Published by Allyn and Bacon, Boston, MA. Copyright © 2001 by Pearson Education. Reprinted by permission of the publisher.

CROSS-REFERENCE
Local control is described in Chapter 6.

interest groups

Informal and formal organizations of individuals who hold a common interest and shared agenda in regard to a particular topic or policy.

unfunded mandates

Policies that are required to be implemented for which no financial support is forthcoming.

school improvement process (SIP)

A plan for future action that results from a school leadership team review of current successes and needs.

all schools and classrooms. In fact, this set of influences works against local control of schools. Instead of local control, there is a steadily growing movement toward the establishment of a statewide and even national curriculum.

Another macro-level influence on the curriculum is the various **interest groups,** such as teacher and administrator organizations, political parties, and religious advocacy groups. The membership of each of these groups pays close attention to the work of committees charged with developing standards, curriculum guides, and test items. Each group is likely to have its own unique perspective and agenda. For example, teacher associations tend to resist any accountability moves that would link student performance on tests with the identity of the teachers who taught them. Many religious groups advocate that their positions, such as creationism, be included and that contrary positions, such as evolution, receive less emphasis. A different perspective might be represented by administrator associations, which are concerned more about the costs and being asked to implement **unfunded mandates.**

The various accrediting bodies, such as Southern Association of Colleges and Schools (SACS) and the New England Association of Schools and Colleges (NEASC), influence the curriculum through their standards for all schools they accredit. These standards in some ways set a common curriculum for all schools. For example, school accrediting bodies require each school to have a **school improvement process (SIP).** An SIP usually is written by a school committee and the principal during the spring of the year. The plans include analyses of data about student learning, reports about the year's efforts to improve the school, and specific plans for the next year. Key expectations for these plans include analyses of student success on state tests such as those in mathematics, literacy, and, in some states, writing. The accrediting body expects improved student performance on state tests; a direct consequence of this expectation is that each school and teacher is expected to provide curriculum and instruction designed to enhance student achievement on the prescribed test. In ways such as this, a common curriculum is defined and implemented for all accredited schools.

INTERMEDIATE INFLUENCES ON CURRICULUM SELECTION   At the local school district level, many additional factors influence the curriculum. Clearly, community interests and priorities are an influence. If the community values high school football and marching band, these two program areas will be an integral part of the cocurriculum. The personal background of students also influences the curriculum. For example, in most school districts a significant proportion of the students might be **English language learners (ELLs).** ELL students are in middle and high school classrooms as well as elementary school classrooms. Curriculum influences of this population are many. There is more demand for teachers who speak their native languages. ELL students also need more assistance in learning academic subjects because they are learning English at the same time. One likely consequence is that ELL students do less well on high-stakes tests, especially if they are expected to read and respond in English. The overall result is that the curriculum in the classroom needs to be adjusted in response to these influences.

Special interest groups are a powerful influence on the selection of curriculum.

SCHOOL SITE INFLUENCES   The inner circle of Figure 13.1 summarizes some of the school's influences on the curriculum. Assumptions about learning, for example, make a significant difference in which subjects are emphasized, what is taught, and how. For example, if teachers in a particular school truly believe that all students can learn, then the curriculum is organized and delivered in ways that support all students learning: Students are grouped according to their needs; regular classrooms include students with special needs; and most group activities are organized to take advantage of the diverse talents and interests of students rather than having like students grouped together. In comparison, if teachers in a particular school believe that some of the children can't learn, then "those" children are given less opportunity and more limited access to the curriculum. The result confirms the teacher's beliefs: Those students do less well.

The reason for introducing the many influences on curriculum selection, its development, and its implementation is to make it clear that in the end the curriculum is delivered in classrooms. However, there are two important implications. The first is that the role of the teacher in implementing today's curriculum is enormous. Although teachers have relatively little say in curriculum selection, they have the primary responsibility for helping students learn and achieve the desired outcomes. The second implication is that teachers have a plethora of curriculum resources to work with: curriculum guides, teacher-training sessions, and textbooks, as well as standards and benchmarks. All of these curriculum resources assist teachers in understanding what they should be teaching, and they help them see what came before and what will happen next year with the students they teach this year.

CURRICULUM DESIGNS

Several basic designs for curricula exist. Each design has particular strengths, weaknesses, and implications for teachers. Some designs are typically found in U.S. schools, whereas others are more apt to be seen in schools in other countries. Each design is based on assumptions about what is important for students to

English language learners (ELLs)

Students whose first language is other than English and who therefore are learning English at the same time they are learning the content specified in the curriculum standards.

Teachers in today's schools meet face-to-face with increasing attitude problems of learners. These problems are manifested in a lack of respect for teachers, visual boredom in learning, and a lack of work ethic for career. The lack of respect comes from the societal image of teachers, who experience criticisms such as "Those who can't, teach!" Additionally, whatever is wrong in society tends to be blamed on the teacher and the school program. Teacher authority is usurped by parents and the society, which challenge the teacher's right to discipline students, even the unruly ones. Students call into question the worthiness of professional teachers, who are considered to have lower status when compared with other professions. The fact that teachers tend to be grossly underpaid for the type of workload they face does not offer a positive image for teaching as a career.

Students exhibit boredom and are not motivated to learn because they do not see the relevance of what they are studying. To them, much of what they study seems to be important only for the tests they take and has no relevance to their lives. They yearn for assurance that teachers not only are competent but also care. The lack of a work ethic may be attributable to an environment that provides everything material they need and want. This student problem is probably related to the "good life" quality of a society that tends to have everything it needs. Most students have economically secure homes, are provided with an overabundance of goods and services, and are not held accountable for responsible activities in the family.

This dilemma does not paint a glowing picture of what is waiting for the teacher when she or he enters the classroom. If this picture is accurate and is to be altered, then the teacher needs to actively pursue the following:

- Develop with the students a common ground for the establishment of respect for each other. How can the teacher show respect for the students and have the students show respect for the teacher?
- How does the teacher prepare a learning environment that has meaning to the everyday life of the learner?
- How does the teacher work with the home and community in providing a learning atmosphere in which students develop a work ethic and recognize its value?

To answer these questions on-line and e-mail your answers to your professor, go to Chapter 13 of the companion website (**www.ablongman.com/johnson13e**) and click on Professional Dilemma.

---

learn as well as particular philosophies about teaching and how students learn best. Summaries of common designs are presented in Table 13.1

The earliest schools in America were **subject-centered.** There were three subjects: religion, Latin, and Greek. The only teaching style was lecture. The students were expected to learn—in other words, memorize—the content. Since that time, a series of evolutions in curriculum design have occurred. One theme to the changes is an increase in the number of content areas taught. A second theme is developing curriculum designs that are of more interest to students. The move toward various types of integrated and problem-centered curricula is a reflection of the first theme, whereas the decreasing popularity of teacher lecture is seen as an effective way to increase student motivation.

■ MANAGING CURRICULUM

Clearly, many levels of interest and many perspectives directly influence the selection of a curriculum. This large and diverse set of influences also affects the processes for designing curricula. Without some sort of control mechanisms or an organized authority, it would be impossible for each teacher to choose what to teach and how to teach in ways that satisfy a majority of the influences. Without some sort of overall authority, there would be no continuity in the curriculum from teacher to teacher, grade level to grade level, or school to school.

subject-centered

Curriculum that is organized around a finite and limited set of core subjects.

TABLE 13.1 The Variety of Curriculum Designs

Curriculum Design Name	Design	Role of the Teacher	Role of the Student
Subject-Centered	Selected subjects are identified. Organization is tight and narrow, and the sequence is specified.	Primary strategy is lecture. Teachers are expected to teach to the prescribed sequence and use the prescribed materials.	Students learn the content. The narrow focus allows students to learn more content in less time.
Broad Fields	A number of subjects are integrated and theme generalizations from each subject become the big ideas.	Teachers may lecture. Focus is on the broad generalizations instead of depth in a particular content.	Students are expected to develop a broad understanding across a number of contents. Students may not understand the broad themes and simply memorize them.
Core	Includes some contents all students should know. Depending on the philosophical perspective, a set of subjects is selected to be the center of the curriculum.	Rather than discrete content courses, integrated blocks may be offered. The content is taught in relation to problems or topics Each problem uses each of the content areas. Typically, teachers teach as interdisciplinary teams.	Students learn through the study of interdisciplinary problems. Accompanying this learning is learning in related subjects.
Spiral	The curriculum is viewed across the P–12 continuum, the assumption being that key content will be taught more than once. In an early grade, a particular topic will be introduced in a general way. Several years later, the subject will be taught a second time with more depth. Then in the high school years, the topic will be taught again with even greater depth.	Teachers will use a variety of teaching strategies. The key is that teachers must have sufficient depth of knowledge to offer more content depth with each cycle in the spiral. Teachers also must make a concerted effort to add depth to student understanding with each subsequent pass.	Students are expected to learn the content at the depth taught each time. The risk is that they will not retain the knowledge and understanding developed in the previous cycle.
Problem-Based	Students work in groups and are presented with a problem. Solving the problem requires that they learn new content.	The teacher is guide and coach rather than dispenser of content. Only when the need arises does the teacher present content.	Students are expected to be able to work cooperatively as members of problem-solving teams. They must be self-starters and motivated to study the problem.
Mastery	Levels of learning that all students are to reach are identified. Students are given as much time as they need and a variety of activities to aid their reaching mastery.	Teachers must be able to provide a variety of activities and ways for students to reach mastery. Teachers also must be skilled at assessing what students do and do not know.	Once students have met the criterion for a particular learning, they move on to addressing the next learning target.
Standards-Based	The standards of learning become the content.	Student learning is placed at the center rather than the topic being taught. Teachers use a wide variety of lessons and assessment strategies, all of which are aimed at assisting students in constructing their own understanding.	Students know the standards and specific benchmarks they are studying. They self-assess in relation to these.

In the United States, the legal responsibility for schools, and therefore for the curriculum, lies with each state. In large part, state legislatures and state boards of education determine the curriculum. Additional structures exist to set and support the curriculum at the school district level. In addition, even with the centralizing roles of the state and district, schools and teachers retain a number of important roles and responsibilities.

THE STATE ROLE IN MANAGING CURRICULUM

Because each state has the primary responsibility for setting the curriculum for schools within that state, teachers need to know how this is done and what they can do to contribute to the process. The states have assumed two major areas of responsibility for curricula. The first is establishing what students are expected to learn, and the second is determining the instructional materials that can be used.

STATES SET STANDARDS   The statements of expectation for student learning are determined at the state level. However, the statements of content standards that have been developed by the various national associations, such as the National Council of Teachers of Mathematics (NCTM), are a major resource for the states. The typical process is to establish a statewide committee comprising teachers, school administrators, higher education faculty, and state policymakers, such as a representative state board of education member or a legislator, such as chair of the House Education Committee. Standards committees with similar composition are established for each content area. Each committee reviews the national curriculum standards for its content area. These committees hold public hearings around their state so that the various interest groups (remember the different circles in Figure 13.1) can present their positions. When each of these committees completes its work, members recommend a set of state standards to the state board of education. Once the state board approves them, all districts, schools, and classrooms in the state are required to teach to those standards.

STATES MAY CHOOSE CURRICULUM MATERIALS   There is some variation from state to state in the extent of state-level involvement in selecting curriculum materials. The main area of involvement is in selecting textbooks. States have either **open adoption** or **state adoption** policies. Most southeastern states as well as Texas and California have formal state-level processes for adopting textbooks; these are state adoptions. In these states, a committee is charged with reviewing the various available textbooks and establishing an adoption list. School districts and schools then select the textbooks they will use from this list of approved materials. If schools wish to select curriculum materials from the adoption list, they receive state funding to support the purchase. If a district or school decides to select materials not on the state's adoption list, it will have to pay the full cost. In open states, the adoption of textbooks is a matter of local choice; the state leaves responsibility for the selection of curriculum materials to each school district, even when there is state funding for their purchase.

THE DISTRICT'S ROLE IN MANAGING CURRICULUM

Regardless of whether a school district is located in an adoption state or an open state, major curriculum-related tasks and responsibilities are assumed by each school district.

DISTRICT TEXTBOOK SELECTION   One obvious district task is to select the textbooks and related curriculum materials to be purchased and used within the district. Typically, a district will use a process similar to that used at the state level. A curriculum committee is established that includes teachers, principals, parents, and perhaps higher education faculty. The committee reviews the current status of the subject area, including how well students are doing on tests.

open adoption
A state text adoption policy that allows each school district the autonomy to review and select whichever textbooks it chooses.

state adoption
A state textbook adoption policy that limits financial support and selections to those that are included on a state-approved list.

The committee examines available text and materials options, and then recommends to the district superintendent and school board which materials should be purchased. Teacher participation on these committees is important. Teachers are concerned about the textbooks and other curriculum materials they will have to use. Therefore, they have a strong interest in and pay close attention to what the district curriculum selection committee does.

DISTRICT OFFICE CURRICULUM SPECIALISTS School districts also employ a number of professional specialists whose responsibility it is to see that each curriculum area is supported and that teachers are prepared. One important role is that of curriculum coordinator/liaison/specialist. Typically, earlier in their careers these individuals were master teachers. Now their role is to guide, support, and champion their subject areas. In smaller districts, an individual might have responsibility for a number of content areas, such as language arts and social studies. Larger school districts have curriculum specialists assigned for at least each of the "big four" areas: reading, mathematics, science, and social studies. There are also specialists for special education, bilingual/ELL education, compensatory education, and other need areas.

DISTRICT OFFICE TEACHER DEVELOPMENT SPECIALISTS In addition to the subject-specific specialists, most school district office staffs include **generalists.** Instead of being experts in a particular content area, these individuals are experts in helping teachers learn and apply different teaching strategies, assessment procedures, and use of technology. District office generalists include:

- Experts in general teaching strategies, such as cooperative grouping and assessment methods, that can be used in most content areas.
- Induction specialists, who are responsible for offering workshops, mentoring, and other supports for beginning teachers.
- Staff developers, who coordinate and present teacher inservice workshops, including those offered districtwide at the beginning of each school year.
- **Teachers on special assignment (TOSAs)** are expert teachers who leave the classroom for one to three years to participate in a curriculum review, including selection of new materials, and to support teachers during the implementation phase. These teachers then return to the classroom, although some move on to other leadership positions, such as department head and assistant principal.

MANAGING THE CURRICULUM WITHIN THE SCHOOL Even with all of the activities done at the national, state, and district levels, each school has major tasks and responsibilities for managing the curriculum. It still is up to each school and teacher to bring the curriculum alive in each and every classroom. Each teacher must do his or her part by being informed about the state standards and the benchmarks for their students' grade level, and they must teach with the materials and strategies that will help all students learn. In secondary schools, an important curriculum management structure is the department. When teachers for one subject are organized as a department, they can easily seek ideas from colleagues who know the content, and they can coordinate across grade levels what is taught in each course. The same ends are obtained in elementary schools by having grade-level teams and in larger schools by establishing content-specific curriculum committees.

■ EVALUATING CURRICULA

How do we know if the selected and implemented curriculum is making any difference? The obvious answer is that without systematic and well-organized evaluation studies, we cannot know. Evaluation of the curriculum has to be done carefully and at all levels, from teachers in classrooms, to school- and

generalists
Professional educators housed in the district office who provide classroom support across a number of content areas.

teachers on special assignment (TOSAs)
Teachers who are assigned to the district office for a limited time in order to accomplish a specified curriculum support task.

district-level evaluation, to statewide evaluation. In addition, national and international curriculum evaluation studies are conducted.

CLASSROOM-BASED CURRICULUM EVALUATION

Curriculum evaluation is based on what occurs in the classroom. Until the curriculum is implemented and student learning is assessed, direct evidence of effectiveness cannot be obtained.

TEACHER EVALUATION OF THE CURRICULUM   The first evaluation step is done by each teacher who implements the curriculum. Teachers' informal assessments of how easy it is to teach, the effectiveness of textbooks and materials, and the amount of student interest and motivation are early indicators of how effective any curriculum will be. Another early indicator is teacher assessments of the extent of student learning. Through informal teacher assessments and the formal testing done in the classroom, teachers and curriculum specialists can obtain early evidence of how well a curriculum is working.

CLASSROOM IMPLEMENTATION STUDIES   Researchers and curriculum evaluators also focus on classrooms to determine curriculum effectiveness. Whereas the teacher examines only his or her classroom, researchers systematically document use of the curriculum and related student learning in a large number of classrooms. For example, in a study of teaching and learning mathematics with a curriculum designed around the NCTM standards, the researchers documented classroom processes and student learning in over one hundred classrooms. The results of their study included the following findings: (1) Classrooms where the teaching most closely approximated the best practices as outlined in the NCTM standards had the highest levels of student performance, the corollary being that in classrooms with less use of the new curriculum, students achieved less; (2) students in classrooms with teachers who were collaborating with other teachers in teaching the new curriculum had higher levels of achievement.[2]

DISTRICT AND STATE CURRICULUM EVALUATION PRACTICES   In today's high-stakes testing environment, school districts and states are focusing on student performance on standardized tests. Unfortunately, there is little examination of what goes on in classrooms. Instead, schools and school districts are being judged and labeled based on overall test score results. In an increasing number of states, the test scores for each school are published in the local newspaper. In extreme situations, when test scores are at the bottom year in and year out, (such as in Hartford, Connecticut; Compton, California; and Trenton, New Jersey), the state may "take over" operation of the school district. The results of these state takeovers are mixed, at best. In some districts, such as Hartford Public Schools, student test scores have gone up. In other districts, they have remained low.

NATIONAL CURRICULUM STUDIES   Two important national approaches to curriculum evaluation are the National Assessment of Educational Progress (NAEP) and the testing at most grade levels mandated in the federal 2002 No Child Left Behind Act (NCLB). These approaches reflect two very different philosophies about curriculum evaluation. In NAEP a random sample of students is selected from across each state. The sample is drawn from all students in the state but does not include all of the students in one school or from one classroom. Therefore, the findings from NAEP indicate how well students are doing in reading, science, or mathematics by state. NAEP cannot make judgments about the effectiveness of particular schools or school districts.

In No Child Left Behind, Congress has mandated that all public school students be tested each year in grades 3 through 8 and in one year of high school. Each state can select the test, but the major content areas must be tested. These data will allow the labeling of schools and districts, even ranking each in terms of student performance on the selected tests.

CROSS-REFERENCE
Key requirements of NCLB are described in Chapter 5.

INTERNATIONAL CURRICULUM EVALUATION STUDIES   In the last decades, there has been escalating concern about how well American students do in comparison with students from other developed countries. Here again, student performance on standardized tests is the benchmark. The most widely reported study is the Third International Math Science Study (TIMSS) (see http://nces.ed.gov/timss), which was first administered in 1995 and again in 1999 and 2003. In 1995, data were collected in forty-two countries on student achievement in math and science at the fourth-, eighth-, and twelfth-grade levels.

■ SUMMARY OF CURRICULUM

In this section, we have introduced key ideas and themes about curricula. One of the first points is that teachers do not have the responsibility, or the authority, for determining the curriculum. In fact, as it should be in the United States, many groups and interests contribute to the content and organization of the curriculum. This process begins at the state and, increasingly, national levels. Once standards and the big ideas are agreed on, state and local selection committees determine which texts and related materials will be purchased for use in schools and classrooms. Another important point is that once selected and implemented, curricula need to be evaluated. The most important variable in curriculum evaluation is student learning. The intent of all curriculum development efforts is to identify content and materials that will allow all students to achieve. In this time of global economy and international competition, one of the important ways to evaluate curricula in U.S. schools is through international comparisons. In these studies, such as TIMSS, the key question is, how well do U.S. students do in comparison with their peers in other countries? Once standards for learning are identified and the content and curriculum resources have been purchased, it is time for teachers to bring the curriculum alive in the classroom—this is what instruction is about.

INSTRUCTION: TURNING CURRICULUM INTO CLASSROOM ACTIVITIES

Once the influences and committees have converged and a curriculum has been selected, teachers have the responsibility to bring it to life in classrooms. This is extremely important work. If teachers fail in the delivery of the curriculum, students cannot learn material required in the stated benchmarks and standards. One dire consequence of students not learning is failure—failure for the students and the teacher, as well as for the school and community that have supported development of the curriculum.

Thus, as is true for curriculum development, instruction begins with consideration of what students need to learn. Teachers need to think about student learning in relation to each lesson and how lessons will unfold across days and weeks. Based on the expectations for learning and the characteristics and interests of the students, particular teaching strategies can be selected. Another important influence on instruction is the schoolwide effort to improve learning that includes components that are expected to be implemented in all classrooms. For example, all elementary teachers in a school or school district may be expected to use the same instructional approach in teaching reading. Fortunately, many instructional resources are available for teachers.

■ INSTRUCTIONAL OBJECTIVES FOR STUDENT LEARNING

Standards and benchmarks are descriptions of expected student learning that represent relatively long-term steps. Teachers and their students need more focused and short-term statements in order to focus individual lessons and the accumulation of several weeks of lessons. The instructional tools for creating this focus are called **objectives;** these are the statements of expected student learning for each lesson. The difference between objectives and standards is the size and scope of learning described. Standards represent the broad learning outcomes that students are expected to achieve across a year or two. Benchmarks address parts of standards, but they still are quite broad and can describe learning accomplishments that can take months. Instructional objectives, on the other hand, are the teacher's tool to help them identify each lesson's focus.

AIMS, GOALS, AND OBJECTIVES

Before the term *standards* was applied to student learning, three kinds of outcomes for education were used: aims, goals, and objectives. **Aims** are general, long-term aspirations for education. In fact, they are so general and long term that they are not seen as direct outcomes of attending school. Instead, these are statements that apply to lifelong aspirations. Aims also tend to be thought of as something that a group, rather than an individual, can accomplish. For example, an aim for many people is to complete high school and be the first in their family to graduate from college.

Goals are statements of educational aspirations, again related to group accomplishment but somewhat narrower in scope and with a shorter timeline. Goals typically cover two to four years and address a major area of educational accomplishment. For example, many school districts and states set a goal to reduce the dropout rate by 10 percent. Or they may establish a goal to increase the high school graduation rate from 87 percent to 97 percent. Accomplishing these goals takes several years, and not everyone accomplishes them.

Objectives address the daily learning expectations for students. Tests, daily lessons, and classroom activities need to be clearly tied to the important expectations for learning. Contrary to what some teachers practice, objectives for instruction should be known and understood by *both* the teacher and the students.

OBJECTIVES ARE ABOUT STUDENT LEARNING

One of the important elements of writing objectives is understanding their purpose. Frequently, when teacher education candidates first write objectives they write them as *input statements,* which describe what the teacher will do and what will happen in the lesson. The following objective is incorrect in instruction today: "The students will be assigned to groups and they will read the chapter in the text."

Objectives should be written as *output statements,* or descriptions of what students are to learn as a result of experiencing the lesson or lessons. For example, "As a result of this lesson, students will be able to compare and contrast the reasoning behind the economic and political arguments for and against sending troops into Iraq."

The difference between thinking in terms of inputs and outputs is crucial to your becoming a successful teacher (see Figure 13.2). The natural tendency of teachers and professors is to think in terms of "what I am teaching." They may even say things such as "I teach English." In the past, this way of thinking about instruction was acceptable; however, in today's schools teachers need to be thinking and talking in terms of what their students are learning. "My students have been learning about the Civil War and the terrible cost of life that occurred." Fortunately, the use of instructional objectives can help teachers make this important shift in thinking.

◼ DIFFERENT KINDS OF INSTRUCTIONAL OBJECTIVES

As an additional support for teachers, scholars have identified different ways of describing learning outcomes. The development and refinement of these typologies has occurred over the last thirty to forty years. Each type addresses a different kind of learning, and assessing student learning requires different

objectives

Statements of learning outcomes for a lesson or several weeks of lessons.

aims

General, long-term aspirations for education.

goals

Expectations for education that typically cover two to four years of accomplishments.

behavioral objectives

Expectations for student learning that are stated in terms of observable behaviors.

task analysis

The process of systematically identifying and sequencing the small learnings that must be accomplished in order for students to demonstrate mastery of a particular task or benchmark.

methods, depending on the type of objective. For most lessons, teachers will likely have at least two kinds of learning objectives, which also means that careful thought has to be given to how the learning outcomes will be assessed.

BEHAVIORAL OBJECTIVES

Behavioral objectives, as the name implies, focus on observable performance. In fact, the proponents of behavioral objectives advocate that if the learning cannot be described in terms of observable behaviors, then there is no way to tell if learning took place. From this point of view, student learning is to be described in terms of behaviors. This means that in behavioral objectives, the verb, or action word, is key. The objective needs to focus on a behavior, such as to observe, classify, name, or interpret, and not on words, such as *appreciate* and *understand*.

Behavioral objectives are a useful instructional tool for teachers in planning, teaching, and assessing student learning. A useful approach to identifying student behaviors is to perform a **task analysis,** which is the systematic identification of the key skills that someone needs to be able to do to complete a task or satisfy a benchmark. The typical steps for a teacher in doing a task analysis include:

- Examine the related standards and benchmarks in order to identify the observable skills that students must demonstrate.
- Identify the small learning steps that in combination would result in students being able to do the whole task.
- Describe each behavior in terms of behaviors that can be observed.
- Determine the sequence in which students will need to learn the behaviors.
- Write behavioral objectives for the most central and important of these behaviors.
- Be attentive as the lesson unfolds to facilitating students acquiring those behaviors.
- Create an end-of-lesson, or unit, test that focuses on whether the students can exhibit the behaviors described in the behavioral objectives.

This approach to thinking about learning and teaching has been criticized as too linear and rational. Still, it is a useful way for teachers and students to maintain a focus on the key elements of a lesson. The real risk with behavioral objectives is having too many objectives and objectives that are so specific and narrow that they are trivial. It is one thing to write a behavioral objective that describes what both hands are doing when a person is touch typing, but it's another thing—and on a much more micro level of task analysis—to have an individual objective for the placement of each finger on the keyboard.

LEARNING OBJECTIVES FOR THE COGNITIVE DOMAIN

In 1956 a significant small book was published titled *Taxonomy of Educational Objectives: The Classification of Educational Goals*

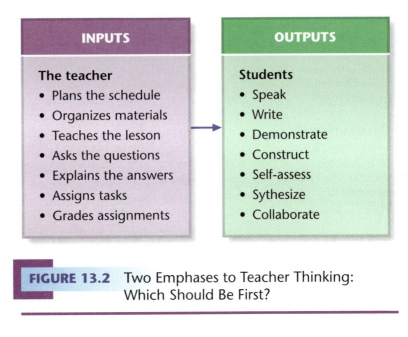

INPUTS	OUTPUTS
The teacher • Plans the schedule • Organizes materials • Teaches the lesson • Asks the questions • Explains the answers • Assigns tasks • Grades assignments	**Students** • Speak • Write • Demonstrate • Construct • Self-assess • Sythesize • Collaborate

FIGURE 13.2 Two Emphases to Teacher Thinking: Which Should Be First?

Analysis of the various skills that students are to learn is an important early step in planning instruction.

Bloom's Taxonomy
A system for classifying knowledge learning outcomes in terms of the complexity of mental activity required.

affective domain
A system for classifying learning outcomes in the area of human reactions and responses.

Handbook 1: Cognitive Domain.[3] The lead author of this book was a scholar named Benjamin Bloom. He and his coauthors had developed a typology of different types of learning objectives in the area of knowledge. The basic premise was that educational objectives should be classified according to the type of knowledge the learner was acquiring. This book and the classification system it introduced has become a cornerstone of curriculum and instruction; the classification system is known as **Bloom's Taxonomy.** Rather than treating all knowledge that is learned as being the same, Bloom and his colleagues identified six different levels of learning and therefore educational objectives. These six levels are summarized in Table 13.2.

In Bloom's Taxonomy, each of the six levels of the cognitive domain represent different amounts of complexity of knowledge and different extents of knowledge use. Teachers require different types of learning of students, depending on which level of the taxonomy is being addressed. In addition, teachers must keep in mind that this taxonomy is also a learning hierarchy. Students cannot perform at the higher levels unless they have already learned the necessary knowledge at the lower levels. The level of learning must be reflected in the way the learning objective is written. Simple memory and recall is a very different level of learning than is Application or Analysis.

LEARNING OBJECTIVES FOR THE AFFECTIVE DOMAIN

The **affective domain** of student learning also is important for teachers to consider as they plan instruction, teach lessons, and assess student learning. The affective domain addresses human reactions and responses to the content and subject matter. Student attitudes, feelings, and dispositions are a key compo-

---

TABLE 13.2   The Six Levels of Bloom's Taxonomy of the Cognitive Domain

1.00 Knowledge:	Knowledge and behaviors that emphasize remembering and recall. This could be relatively simple memorization such as facts, word spelling, and the multiplication tables. This domain also includes knowledge of criteria, rules, principles, methods, and theories.
2.00 Comprehension:	Students being able to understand communication and making some use of the idea. The communication may be oral, written, or an equation or some other symbolic form. Three types of comprehension are translation, interpretation, and extrapolation. Translation entails the ability to understand an idea presented in one form, such as a graph, and be able to describe its meaning in another form, such as a written paragraph. Interpretation moves beyond translation to being able to weigh the different parts of a communication and to identify and understand the major ideas as well as the interrelationships. Extrapolation is extending beyond the presented communication by predicting consequences or likely next steps.
3.00 Application:	The student is able to apply learning to a new situation. Further, the student is able to select the correct application without coaching by the teacher or other students. Using a principle to predict what will happen when a certain factor is changed is application.
4.00 Analysis:	Analysis addresses the ability to break something down into its parts or pieces. Analysis also deals with detection of the relationships between the parts and how the whole is organized. Analysis begins with identifying the elements and then the relationships and interactions between the elements. Analysis goes beyond the stated and also includes recognition of the implicit.
5.00 Synthesis:	This is the process of putting together the parts to make a whole. Bloom points out that this is the level of the taxonomy that addresses creative behavior. This does not mean completely free creative effort, as there are likely lesson and problem contexts that set outside limits. At this level, the learner is working with a given situation. The product of synthesis might be an original idea.
6.00 Evaluation:	Evaluation is about making judgments about the value or worth of ideas, products, or problem solutions. Although evaluation is presented as the last level, Bloom emphasizes that some effort at evaluation is a component of most of the other levels as well. At this level, evaluation is seen as a considered process based on criteria. It is not a simplistic rush to opinion. Instead, there is a reasoned analysis of all facts and weighing of alternatives and the consequences of each.

nent of instruction. Shortly after the development of the cognitive domain taxonomy, a parallel effort was underway to develop a taxonomy of educational objectives in the affective domain. The leader of this team was David Krathwohl.[4]

An unavoidable part of instruction is consideration of students' attitudes and beliefs, because these affective elements are related to classroom behaviors. Krathwohl's Affective Domain Taxonomy provides an analytical tool for planning instruction and an aid for teachers to think about different levels of student learning in terms of values and beliefs (see Table 13.3). In planning instruction and during teaching, the affective domain can be used to assess the openness to and interest of students in learning about a particular topic. If certain students are at level 1.0, Receiving (Attending), the lesson will need to be

The level and complexity of student learning that are stated in learning objectives should be reflected in the assessment method.

aimed at having students become more engaged with the topic and opening a willingness to move toward level 2.0, Responding, and level 3.0, Valuing. If students are already at level 4.0, Organization, then the learning objectives can ask students to weigh, compare, and form judgments. Values and beliefs, as well as motivation and interests, are a core component of learning. Students of teachers who continually attend to the affective domain will have greater learning success in the cognitive domain. When students are interested in learning and see the

TABLE 13.3	The Five Levels of Krathwohl's Taxonomy of Affective Domain
1.0 Receiving (Attending):	The learner is sensitized to the condition, phenomenon, or stimulus that is the aim of the lesson or topic of study. At the most basic level, the learner is *aware* of the object or phenomenon. For example, in music students are aware of differences in mood or rhythm. Another component of this level is the *willingness to receive* or to attend to the topic of study. If there is not openness to learning more, then higher levels of the affective domain cannot be reached.
2.0 Responding:	At this level, the learner is motivated beyond simply attending and is actively attending. At the lowest level of responding, there is acquiescence *in responding;* in other words, the learner is willing to go along. Slightly higher is the *willingness to respond,* in which the student looks for additional information or experience. A higher level of responding is indicated when the student shows *satisfaction in response.*
3.0 Valuing:	At this level, the student is behaving in ways that reflect a sense of belief or attitude. Within this level, there is the range of behavior from *testing for acceptance of a value* to *commitment.* Actions of reaching out to learn more about a new topic, such as asking questions or searching out the topic on the web, are indicative of acceptance. With commitment there is a conviction and loyalty to the topic, position, or group.
4.0 Organization:	As more than one value becomes relevant, there is a need to develop an internal system of organization of values. Organization begins with *conceptualization* of particular values and beliefs. This does not necessarily require verbal expression, but the learner is able to compare one value or belief to another. This process leads to *organization of a value system,* which brings together a number of values and their relationships.
5.0 Characterization by a Value or Value Complex:	At this level, the learner has a set of values in place, the values are organized into some kind of internal system, and behaviors are consistent over time in relation to these values. The values represent a *generalized set,* and there is a *characterization* of the person in terms of the internal consistency of thought and an external consistency of action that is characteristic of the person.

value of learning certain content, they will more intensely engage with the curriculum, which makes instruction more interesting and successful.

LEARNING OBJECTIVES FOR THE PSYCHOMOTOR DOMAIN

Another domain, which has received much less attention, is related to learning physical skills, which require the mind and body to work together. Music, art, drama, industrial arts, and other vocational courses require students to perform tasks physically. The corresponding taxonomy, the **psychomotor domain,** has received attention from curriculum theorists and was developed by E. J. Simpson.[5] The first two levels are Perception and Set, which address the learner becoming aware of a particular stimulus and becoming ready to act. For example, the band director raises the baton and all members prepare to play the first note. Levels 3 and 4 of Simpson's psychomotor domain taxonomy address Guided Response and Mechanisms. When trying something for the first time, it helps to have suggestions and directions as a guide. With time the steps become automatic. At Level 5, Complex Overt Response, the learner can accomplish more complex tasks and movements. At the still higher level, Adaptation, the learner is able to adjust his or her behavior and accommodate its application in different settings or under different conditions. At the highest level, Origination, creativity is demonstrated. For example, the trumpet student moves beyond playing the written music to improvisation.

■ TEACHING STRATEGIES

Once the curriculum has been established and instructional objectives have been written, it is time to plan for and teach lessons that will help students learn the knowledge, dispositions, and skills identified in the objectives, benchmarks, and standards. Two hundred years ago, there was only one teaching strategy—lecture; the teacher talked and the students memorized. Today this "stand and deliver" strategy has fallen into disrespect. Students are not willing to sit through continuous lectures, and a variety of teaching strategies have been demonstrated to be significantly more effective in engaging students and having students achieve at higher levels.

DIRECT INSTRUCTION

Although the lecture method continues to receive criticism, there is an appropriate time for teachers to impart information directly. Over the last thirty years, extensive research has been done on the behaviors of the teacher and the effectiveness of direct instruction.[6] When direct instruction is done well and with appropriate learning objectives, students learn. A basic, underlying assumption of this teaching strategy is that the teacher knows the content and the easiest way for students to learn it is for the teacher to directly communicate it to them.

Although with direct instruction information is passed from teacher to students, additional ways to communicate information exist besides teacher lecture. Reading the textbook, questions and answers, as well as different applications of technology such as videos, television programs, and information searches on the web are ways to impart information and to make direct instruction more interesting and motivating for students.

To be most effective in using direct instruction, the teacher must manage a number of important steps (see Table 13.4). With direct instruction, the teacher is at the center and maintains full control of the lesson. The teacher must control the flow and keep all talk focused. Sidebars and off-topic discussion are discouraged. A primary purpose of direct instruction is to maintain a high amount of on-task learning time, or **active learning time (ALT).** Higher proportions of class time in which students are engaged will yield higher levels of student learning.

Children engaged in daily physical education show superior motor fitness, academic performance, and attitude toward school as compared to their counterparts who do not participate in daily physical education.

James Pollalschele and Frank Hagen

psychomotor domain

A system for classifying learning outcomes that require physical activity and performance.

active learning time (ALT)

The proportion of time within a lesson that students are actively engaged with the task of learning the objectives.

TABLE 13.4 Key Characteristics of Effective Direct Instruction

1. Direct instruction works best when the learning objectives are clear and narrow in scope.
2. Information and/or tasks should be presented in sequence and one step at a time.
3. The teacher should check carefully for student understanding as the presentation unfolds.
4. Build in student practice with corrective feedback.
5. Avoid negative criticism.
6. Include review at key points.
7. Tasks and assignments should be clearly structured.

INDIRECT INSTRUCTION

The opposite approach to direct instruction is indirect instruction, which covers a large number of teaching strategies in which students have greater responsibility for structuring tasks and managing their own learning. The teacher still has overall responsibility, but students have to initiate more, to organize more of the tasks and their thinking, and in the end be able to construct their own product or way of demonstrating what they have learned. Key characteristics of indirect instruction are presented in Table 13.5.

INQUIRY   Inquiry lessons begin with a problem or puzzle being posed by either the teacher or students. Then the students initiate investigations or problem-solving strategies in an effort to construct an answer. *Problem solving* is another name for this general approach. Students assume major responsibility for their learning with this approach. In an inquiry lesson, the first phase is to define the problem. The teacher might pose a dilemma, or in a science lesson do a demonstration, for which the answer is not obvious. The students then have to define the specific question or problem. The second major phase in inquiry lessons is discovery of the solution. The discovery phase might include conducting an experiment, seeking out information from reading or on the web, or, in a mathematics lesson, using manipulative materials. In the end, the students will have constructed new understanding and have learned new concepts and principles.

PROBLEM-BASED LEARNING   One innovative adaptation of the inquiry approach, which was first used in medical education, is problem-based learning (PBL). In this approach, a real or simulated problem is posed, and students work in groups to develop a solution. The problem does not have a quick or obvious answer, nor is it one about which the students will already have sufficient knowledge. The purpose of PBL is to engage a team of four to six students in

TABLE 13.5 Key Characteristics of Effective Indirect Instruction

1. The teacher or students pose a problem or puzzle.
2. The problem or puzzle is one that stimulates student interest and inquisitiveness.
3. The teacher does not provide the answer or problem solution.
4. Students initiate activities and investigations to analyze the problem or puzzle.
5. The teacher serves as a guide or coach only when students are stymied.
6. All possible solutions/answers are given open consideration.
7. Students articulate orally, in writing, and/or through presenting the reasoning behind their answer/solution.

systematic inquiry, decision making, and problem solving. The result is deeper understanding of the subject as well as the development of skills in inquiry and collaborative work. In medical education, the students will need to seek out information in journals, attend lectures by professors, meet in their group to analyze the problem, and pool their developing understanding. Many medical schools have small seminar rooms reserved for PBL teams to study the problem and concentrate their efforts for weeks. The evaluations of the use of PBL in medical education have demonstrated that the future MDs do just as well on the standardized licensure exams and they are better at information retrieval and problem solving.

MODEL-CENTERED INSTRUCTION   Models are an important device for organizing and explaining knowledge, and they are used widely in science. In the model-centered approach to teaching, a twelve- to fourteen-week curriculum allows the students to explore and evaluate models and to create their own models for explaining and predicting phenomena (such as force and motion in astronomy). Research on this approach shows improvements in student content knowledge.[7]

STUDENT GROUPING

One important component of all teaching strategies has to do with how students are grouped. Should students be taught as a whole class? When should students be divided into groups? What should be the size of the groups? Should the groups be kept the same? What should be done about the different ability levels and skills of students? All of these questions must be answered in relation to student grouping.

HOMOGENEOUS OR HETEROGENEOUS GROUPING   Grouping together students who have similar levels of achievement and abilities is called **homogeneous grouping.** Grouping together students with different levels of achievement and different abilities is called **heterogeneous grouping.** The best way to group depends to some extent on the task. The decision has a philosophical component also. Deciding on which way to group students is philosophical too. Proponents of heterogeneous grouping point out that high-achieving students help the lower-achieving ones and that everyone learns. On the other hand, the proponents of homogeneous grouping believe that mixed-ability grouping slows down the fast learners. Note that the unstated assumption in this debate is that the only learning that counts is that of each student individually. The accomplishment of the group is not considered.

homogeneous grouping
Grouping together students who are alike in terms of their ability to learn or interests.

heterogeneous grouping
Grouping together students who are diverse in their interests and ability to learn.

cooperative learning
A strategy for grouping that provides specific roles and responsibilities for each member.

COOPERATIVE LEARNING   A widely used approach to grouping is **cooperative learning,** in which students are expected to work together to accomplish tasks and are held accountable for both individual and group achievement. In this approach, the general plan is to have a mix of students, so that each group will include students with high, middle, and lower abilities. An alternative is to have students grouped according to interest and assign them activities according to those interests. Typically, cooperative learning groups work together for several weeks or longer. Each group member has an assigned role, including group leader, monitor, resource manager, recorder, and reporter. In this way, leadership and task responsibilities are shared. Extensive research has been done on this approach to grouping. Some of the outcomes are improvement in understanding of content, development, and support of using acceptable social skills; opportunities for student decision making; and encouragement of student responsibility.[8] Criticisms of cooperative learning include the arguments against homogeneous grouping cited previously. Other critics, including many parents, object to grading students based on group accomplishments.

Education programs in the United States always suffer in comparisons with other schools of the world, particularly those in Europe. A recent comparison of German and American schools, however, gives a more accurate analysis of the two systems and what they produce. Before comparing the two systems, the analysis places the systems on the same playing field. For example, U.S. schools, in addition to the major charges of teaching the three Rs, must provide social education, including understanding and appreciating differences in ethnicities, races, creeds, and cultures; recreation; avocational education; vocational education; art; music; and theater—and the list goes on. German schools have a much narrower mission. Their focus is on the three Rs, special education, and socialization. Extracurricular activities, from music to sports, are the responsibility of the communities, churches, and amateur athletic associations. Vocational education is the primary responsibility of business and industry. Health and safety are the responsibility of health maintenance organizations (HMOs), government, churches, private institutions, and the home.

After the sixth grade, German students elect, by choice and examination, the main school, *Hauptschule* (about a third of the students), the *Realschule* (about one-fourth of the students), or the *Gymnasium* (about one-third of the students). Whereas the *Hauptschule* and *Realschule* prepare students for vocational education and apprenticeship programs, the *Gymnasium* is the academic school for the development of the mind and preparation for college attendance for professional careers. Special education students, about 10 percent of the student body, attend well-supported special schools called *Sonderschule.* Although a comprehensive-type high school, *Gesamtschule,* which is patterned after the American comprehensive high school, has been started, fewer than 10 percent of the students attend it.

There is little or no heterogeneous grouping in German schools, and teachers are firmly supportive of ability grouping. In the college preparatory schools, students can shift programs on the basis of interest and societal need, but the longer they wait to do that, the longer it takes them to complete their education because they must make up deficient prerequisites. Classes are spread over twelve months of the year and meet six days a week. However, with time allowed for vacations and holidays, German schools are open about 180 days a year, much like those in the United States. College-bound high school students experience a program that is closer to that of the U.S. college than of the U.S. high school.

Teachers in Germany are better paid and more respected than their U.S. counterparts. Recently, a German poll ranked teachers second behind judges in the list of most respected professionals. As a profession, teaching maintains a type of guild that is somewhat similar to the teaching ranks in U.S. colleges. Most master teachers in the *Gymnasium* have earned a doctorate along the way up their career ladder. The state, Germany, pays teacher salaries, but the communities are responsible for the construction, care, and maintenance of the various schools in their community. Businesses and industries provide the financial support for vocational education.

To compare the students of these two countries requires that similar students be compared. The best of the U.S. academically talented students compare most favorably with the students of the *Gymnasium.* German students who are not in that school are not used for comparison purposes with American students, but all American students of the U.S. comprehensive high schools become data for comparison with foreign students. Therefore, most comparisons are not apples to apples, but rather apples to sauerkraut.

CROSS REFERENCE

Language diversity and special needs are discussed further in Chapter 2.

■ TEACHING STRATEGIES FOR ADDRESSING STUDENTS WITH EXCEPTIONALITIES

A central consideration in selecting teaching strategies is how well they match up with the learning needs of diverse students. In many ways, each student in a classroom is unique. Effective teachers use strategies that take advantage of each student's strengths and that accommodate areas of need. Students will vary in their ability to read and calculate. They will vary in their ability to use English and in how well they can communicate orally and through writing. Some will be exceptionally fast at learning, and others will be slow.

One important component of instruction that teachers must examine and understand is how best to address the array of students with special needs and those who are English language learners. For example, students with learning disabilities are apt to have difficulty with direct instruction strategies, especially lecture. However, they benefit from having clear and concrete teacher directions and activities that are well structured and sequenced. ELL students can be very successful with strategies that facilitate their interaction with other students and that provide ample time for processing what is happening. ELLs also benefit from indirect instruction strategies, because their learning is less dependent on understanding everything the teacher says. ELL students in secondary school classes in particular do not benefit from direct instruction. Fortunately, a number of well-developed approaches exist for accommodating the needs of diverse learners.

WHICH APPROACH IS BEST—TRANSITIONAL OR IMMERSION? A seemingly never-ending debate has to do with selecting the best instructional approach for ELL students. Some advocate **immersion** programs, or English as a second language (ESL), in which students are taught primarily in English, and their native language is limited and used only on a case-by-case basis to clarify instructions. Other experts advocate that ELL students be placed in **transitional** programs, also called **bilingual** education, in which their native language is used along with English to ensure content understanding, but only until the student can make the full transition to all-English instruction. The Institute for Education Sciences (IES) of the U.S. Department of Education is currently funding a major research study related to this debate. Table 13.6 was developed by IES as a summary of distinctions between these two program models.

RESOURCES FOR TEACHING ELL STUDENTS Among the many resources for teachers who have ELL students are several federally funded centers. One of these is the National Clearinghouse for English Language Acquisition (www.ncela.gwu.edu). The NCELA is a repository for best practices, research, and related information for teachers who work with ELL, dual language, and migrant education. Subjects on the NCELA website include assessment and accountability, curriculum and instruction, and parent and community involvement. The website also includes links to legislation and regulations related to the No Child Left Behind Act, searchable databases, and strategies and activities for ELL teachers.

In practice, teachers of ELL students should include two kinds of objectives: language and content. Content objectives are established for all students. For the ELL students, adding a language objective helps with their language development. For example, a language objective could be that the ELL students will be able to identify and say vocabulary words when shown a picture.

During an elementary school lesson, the teacher could speak the key words while pointing to them in a Big Book or writing them on the whiteboard. In a secondary classroom, the teacher could use a worksheet that has sentences with blanks where the key vocabulary words should go. This task will help the ELL student focus on the key words and concepts. Another useful technique in both elementary and secondary classrooms is to have one or two of the students

immersion

A program approach in which ELL students are taught primarily in English, with use of their native language only on a case-by-case basis.

transitional/bilingual

A program approach in which ELL students are taught in their native language along with English.

TABLE 13.6 Comparison of English Immersion and Transition Programs

	Structured English Immersion	Transitional
Content Instruction	Instruction is in English with adjustments to proficiency level so that subject matter is comprehensible. Instruction is supplemented by visual aids and gestures.	Literacy and academic content areas begin in Spanish and continue to grade-level mastery of academic content. As proficiency in oral English develops, the language gradually shifts to English. The transition usually begins with math computation, followed by reading and writing, then science, and finally social studies. Students transition to mainstream classes in which all academic instruction is in English once they acquire sufficient English proficiency.
Language Arts Instruction	English is taught through content areas. Subject matter knowledge and English are taught together by teaching content through learner-appropriate English. A strong language development component is included in each content lesson.	Begins in student's primary language with instruction in English oral language development. The goal is to achieve both basic oral English proficiency and content knowledge, mainstreaming to an all-English program by the end of grade 3.
Language Goals	English acquisition and content knowledge by grade 3.	English acquisition and content knowledge by grade 3.
How Spanish Is Used	Spanish is limited to use on a case-by-case basis, primarily to clarify English instruction.	Spanish is used to ensure grade-level mastery of academic content but only until the student can make a full transition to all-English instruction.
How English Is Used	To teach content instruction, adjusted to proficiency level.	Shifts from Spanish to English as proficiency in oral English develops. English is frequently used in nonacademic subjects such as art, music, and physical education.

Source: U.S. Department of Education, Institute of Education Sciences.

model the task before the whole class begins individual or group work. ELLs, as well as all the other students, are able to see what is expected of them. Table 13.7 presents another useful set of tips for assisting ELL students.

ACCOMMODATING STUDENTS WITH SPECIAL NEEDS

There is a wide range of variability in student needs and the resources that teachers have to address them. In the past, most students with special needs were isolated and placed in "special education" classrooms. This self-contained model came under heavy criticism for a number of reasons, including the absence of contact with general education student role models and special education students losing out on many school activities and events. One consequence of P.L. 94-142 was establishment of the resource room and a major change in philosophy. Now there is an expectation that special-needs students are members of the general education classroom and go to the resource room only for special instruction—in other words, inclusion.

DISPOSITIONS ARE IMPORTANT The first step in addressing teaching and learning for special-needs students is appropriate attitude. There is a strong tendency on the part of all students to look for differences and to prefer to interact with peers who are like themselves. Rather than accepting and valuing diversity (here is a hint of the need for affective learning objectives), students may have a predisposition to reject and isolate peers who are different in gender, race, socioeconomic class, or ability to learn. The expectations that students in any classroom hold and act on in regard to students with special needs begins with

CROSS REFERENCE
P.L. 94-142 and other federal statutes related to special education are described in Chapter 6.

TABLE 13.7 Entrees to English: Tips for Assisting Language Learners

- **Engage cooperative groups of English language learners (ELLs) and English speakers in common tasks.** This gives students a meaningful context for using English.

- **Develop content around a theme.** The repetition of vocabulary and concepts reinforces language and ideas and gives ELLs better access to content.

- **Allow student nonverbal ways to demonstrate knowledge and comprehension.** For example, one teacher has early primary students hold up cardboard "lollipops" (green or red side forward) to indicate "Yes" or "No" to questions.

- **Don't constantly correct students' departure from Standard English.** It's better to get students talking; they acquire accepted forms through regular use and practice. A teacher can always paraphrase a student's answer to model standard English.

- **Consider using visual aids and hands activities to deliver content.** Information is better retained when a variety of senses are called upon.

- **Use routines as way to reinforce language.** This practice increases the comfort level of second language learners; they then know what to expect and associate the routine with language.

Source: Reprinted from "Entrees to English: Tips for Assisting Language Learners" by Judith Lessow-Hurley, *Curriculum Update,* Fall 2002. Alexandria, VA: Association of Supervision and Curriculum Development. Copyright © 2002 ASCD. Reprinted by permission. All rights reserved.

the attitudes and behaviors of the teacher. There is no escaping the fact that how well students in a classroom value and respect diversity is in large part related to the values and behaviors of the teacher. This is true for each school as a whole. In schools where the principal and teachers all share the belief that all students can learn and there is a shared responsibility for helping all students learn, all students do learn more. This is a matter of disposition and begins with the adults in the school. A useful set of questions for assessing how well students are doing to promote a sense of community and social acceptance is presented in Table 13.8.

Often, determining students' dispositions is as easy as looking at each student individually. Deciding what to do is more complex.

TABLE 13.8 Questions for Determining the Extent to Which a School/Classroom Is Promoting a Sense of Community and Social Acceptance

- Are students with disabilities disproportionately teased by other students?
- Do students with disabilities seem to enjoy being in the general education classroom?
- Do students without disabilities voluntarily include students with disabilities in various activities?
- Do students without disabilities seem to value the ideas and opinions of students with disabilities? Do students with disabilities seem to value the ideas and opinions of nondisabled students?
- Do students with disabilities consider the general education classroom to be their "real class"? Do they consider the general education teacher to be one of their "real teachers"? (p. 25).

Source: D. Voltz, N. Brazil, and A. Ford, "What Matters Most in Inclusive Education: A Practical Guide for Moving Forward." *Intervention in School and Clinic, 37,* (2001), pp. 23–30.

CLASSROOM MANAGEMENT

A critical component of instruction for all students is managing materials, organizing of tasks, scheduling, monitoring the flow of activities, and setting rules of behavior. Classroom management is even more important when addressing the needs of special students, whether they are gifted or have a disability. The following are some useful tips:

- Involve the students in setting classroom rules and expectations.
- Be careful not to have too many or too few general rules. A total of six to eight seems to be about right.
- Post the general rules and always refer to them when correcting behavior.
- Create a safe, supportive, and welcoming environment.
- Strive to have the students assume responsibility for their own behavior and do their part to establish and maintain the general norms of the classroom.
- Seat students who tend to be disruptive close to you.
- Keep in mind that students with hearing and vision impairments need to be seated where they can see and hear.
- Regularly evaluate classroom arrangements to be sure there are no hazards and that any students with disabilities have ready access to instruction, materials, and activities.
- Use a variety of techniques to reinforce positive behaviors. Be sure that your reinforcers are meaningful to individual students.
- When there are behavior problems, think about what is going on in the classroom that is encouraging the student to do the behavior.
- Strive to have all students become self-managers of appropriate behaviors.
- Keep the teacher's desk organized, as well as all of the classroom materials and supplies. High and tilting stacks of paper are a temptation.

This list of classroom management tips is just a beginning. In order for all students to learn, there first has to be organization, order, and predictability in the rules of behavior, schedule of activities, location and access to manipulative materials, and sanctions for misbehaviors.

MODELS FOR SCHOOL REFORM

Over the last three decades, there has been continuing and ever-increasing frustration with U.S. schools. National, state, and local policymakers frequently use criticism of schools in their campaigns for political office. Education researchers and leading educators also regularly express concern about the quality of schools and the readiness of high school graduates to enter the workforce. In response, educators have developed a number of **school reform** models. These are comprehensive schoolwide efforts to change curriculum and instruction with the expressed intent of increasing student test scores. School reforms are systematic, multiyear, involve all school staff and all subject areas, and are organized to focus all efforts on curriculum and instruction in order to increase student learning. The most widespread approach is generally called school improvement. Ten or more different reform models are based on particular philosophies of education, research findings, and specialized processes that the school staff must move through. Each of these reform models is led by a university scholar, and the participating schools will belong to a regional or national network of schools that are engaged with the same approach. Teachers will receive special training and they will be expected to use certain instructional approaches. Each approach involves a number of schoolwide elements including acceptance of certain beliefs about students and learning, use of specified curriculum and teaching strategies, and a special vocabulary that draws attention to the core philosophy and principles of the reform model. For most models, there is a leading scholar of national prominence who originated the basic principles for the reform approach and is the national spokesperson for the model. Many of these school reform models have been designed especially to serve urban schools and schools with a high proportion of at-risk students. Most of the models have been designed to be used in elementary schools, although several can be applied in secondary schools and at least one was designed explicitly for high schools. A sampling of these models is described briefly in the next few paragraphs.

SCHOOL IMPROVEMENT

The most widespread approach for gradual improvement of schools is generally the SIP. An example of an organizing framework for school improvement is presented in Figure 13.3. Note what is placed at the center of this framework, as well as how arrows are used to indicate the importance of drawing connections between goals, data about past performance, and action plans for next steps. The typical SIP requires a number of steps, including principal leadership, and the establishment of a school SIP team composed of teachers, department chairs or grade-level team leaders, and parents. School improvement processes have an annual rhythm to them. During spring the SIP team will hold meetings and examine test scores and other data about how well students are performing. The SIP team produces a school improvement plan that identifies specific targets that everyone in the school will work on during the next year. The intention behind the selection of the targets is to identify specific areas, such as writing, algebraic reasoning, or SAT vocabulary, in which a schoolwide effort should be able to lead to increases in student learning. The SIP plan will be reviewed and approved by district office staff. As schools open in August, the school staff may receive related professional development, and during the entire school year the specific objectives stated in the SIP plan will be monitored. The following spring the SIP team will meet and start the school improvement process cycle all over again. Ideally, there will be data documenting gains in the target areas, and for the next year a different set of specific targets will become the focus of improvement efforts.

ACCELERATED SCHOOLS

SIP is a widespread generalized approach to improving schools. The various reform models are more customized. Each reform model is based on a particular philosophy of teaching and learning. Each reform model is also based on a particular line of research, which was directed by the lead proponent of the re-

school reform

The use of comprehensive programs that are intended to bring about schoolwide changes in curriculum and instruction and thereby increase learning outcomes for all students.

form model. For example, Henry Levin, formerly of Stanford University and more recently Teachers College of Columbia University, is the founder and conceptual leader for the Accelerated Schools approach to school reform. Professor Levin proposed that rather than slowing down instruction for low-achieving students, teachers should *accelerate* their expectations for students as well as the way they teach. For more information and print materials related to Accelerated Schools, see the website www.creativelearningpress.com.

SUCCESS FOR ALL (SFA)

The leading scholar for the Success For All (SFA) school reform model is Robert Slavin of Johns Hopkins University.[9] The foundations for SFA demonstrate another important feature of school reform models—they are based on the findings from classroom research. In the case of SFA, much of the research was done in inner-city schools with children who were truly at risk of failure and in schools with track records of failure. As a result, SFA was developed around the

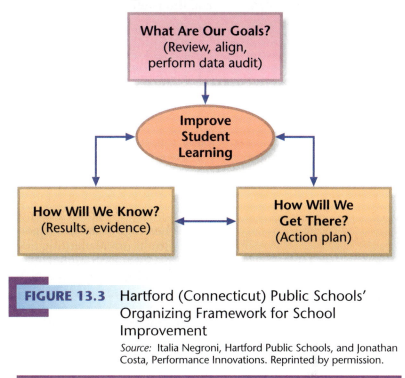

THREE BASIC QUESTIONS OF SCHOOL IMPROVEMENT

FIGURE 13.3 Hartford (Connecticut) Public Schools' Organizing Framework for School Improvement

Source: Italia Negroni, Hartford Public Schools, and Jonathan Costa, Performance Innovations. Reprinted by permission.

core assumption that every child can read. Implementation of SFA begins with implementation of a structured approach to the curriculum and support for children as they learn to read. For example, the first step is *prevention,* which requires strong preschool and kindergarten reading readiness programs. Curriculum instruction and classroom management are addressed through training for all teachers. The approach includes specific reading books, the use of reading tutors, and eight-week reading assessments. All reading teachers employ a prescribed strategy. For example, reading time begins by having the teacher read children's literature to the students and engage them in a discussion of the story. Another component is Story Telling and Retelling (STaR), which engages the students in listening, retelling, and dramatizing literature. Each of these components has been derived from earlier research studies, and SFA is regularly evaluated to assess how well it is working in terms of increasing student achievement.

INSTITUTE FOR LEARNING

The Institute for Learning (IFL), which is housed at the University of Pittsburgh, is directed by Lauren Resnik. As with SFA, the IFL approach is based on decades of research in classrooms. The IFL model is grounded in a set of Principles of Learning, which have been derived from the many research studies. In the IFL model, there are clear and high expectations for student work. Curriculum and instruction are tied to standards, as are evaluations. There is an expectation of academic rigor and a thinking curriculum. The curriculum is to focus on a Knowledge Core that is to "progressively deepen" understanding of core concepts. This approach also expects students to self-manage their learning.

SCHOOL REFORM MODELS FOR HIGH SCHOOLS

School reform models for high schools are fewer in number but equally challenging for teachers and students. One of the most extensively applied models was developed by Theodore Sizer.[10] The participating high schools belong to a

CROSS-REFERENCE
The Essential Schools movement is also discussed in Chapter 10.

national network called the Coalition of Essential Schools. Members of this coalition subscribe to a set of common principles:

1. Learning to use one's mind well
2. Less is more, depth over coverage
3. Goals apply to all students
4. Personalization
5. Student-as-worker, teacher-as-coach
6. Demonstration of mastery
7. A tone of decency and trust
8. Commitment to the entire school
9. Resources dedicated to teaching and learning
10. Democracy and equity

Another approach to reform in high schools is the International Baccalaureate Diploma Program. This program is a comprehensive two-year curriculum, which has high academic rigor. The curriculum emphasizes critical thinking, intercultural understanding, and exposure to a variety of points of view. Typically, this program will be offered as an option within a high school rather than instituted as the only route for all students. High school students who have an IB diploma are readily accepted at universities around the world.

MULTIPLE INTELLIGENCES

Another approach to school reform and thinking differently about instruction is based on Howard Gardner's theory of multiple intelligences (MI).[11] Gardner argues that there is not a single form of intelligence such as that measured in traditional IQ tests. In other words, there are many ways to be "smart." In his most recent works, Gardner identifies eight different intelligences (see Table 13.9). Each of these represents a unique way that students, and adults, can excel. Gardner's theory at a minimum should be a cautionary reminder to teachers not to oversimplify examination of the intelligence of students. If there are many ways to be smart, or at least multiple dimensions to intelligence, then one clear implication is that classrooms and schools can be organized to help students learn in relation to each form of intelligence.

CROSS-REFERENCE
Additional information about school reform can be found in Chapter 8.

An important implication of Gardner's model is the importance of appreciating how assessment of learning changes in an MI classroom or school. Tests of

---

TABLE 13.9 Howard Gardner's Multiple Intelligences

Linguistic Intelligence uses language to communicate and make sense of the world.

Musical Intelligence involves creation, communication, and understanding of sound.

Logical-Mathematical Intelligence uses abstract relations.

Spatial Intelligence addresses perceiving visual and spatial information, transforming this information, and recreating visual images from memory.

Bodily-Kinesthetic Intelligence uses all or part of the body to create products and solve problems.

Interpersonal Intelligence entails recognizing and making distinctions about others' feelings and intentions.

Intrapersonal Intelligence entails recognizing and making distinctions about ones own feelings.

Naturalist Intelligence includes distinguishing, classifying, and using features of the environment.

Source: Project SUMIT (Schools Using Multiple Intelligence Theory), "Theory of Multiple Intelligences."

reading, writing, and calculations are no longer sufficient. Student performance in athletics, music, communication with others, and self-assessment of feelings will be equally important forms of assessment. Each classroom and the school will be striving to help students learn in relation to each of the eight intelligences.

SUMMARY OF INSTRUCTION

Teachers have primary responsibility for translating the standards for learning and the curriculum into minute-to-minute and day-to-day learning experiences for students—in other words, instruction. The beginning point for teachers must be the standards for learning and the grade-level and subject-area benchmarks. Following careful study of the standards and benchmarks, teachers need to identify the specific learning objectives for a lesson, the day, the week, and the month. There are several forms and kinds of objectives, including behavioral, cognitive, affective, and psychomotor. In any classroom, there is likely to be a wide diversity of learners. In writing objectives and selecting teaching strategies, then, teachers need to examine how well a particular instructional approach will facilitate each student's learning. Direct instruction is teacher-centered and works well in certain situations. In other situations, indirect instruction will work better. In all cases, teachers must be sure that the instructional strategies employed will address the needs of all learners, especially ELLs and students with disabilities. An important additional influence on instruction is the school reform movement. Teachers in schools that have adopted one of the school reform models will have additional support and expectations about the shape of instruction. A useful reminder of the uniqueness of each student is offered in the multiple intelligences theory of Howard Gardner. At its simplest, Gardner's theory points out that students can be smart in many different ways, which means that in order for students to learn the most, instruction needs to be designed and delivered in a variety ways.

TECHNOLOGY: INTEGRATED USES FOR CURRICULUM AND INSTRUCTION

In today's world, it is difficult to imagine U.S. public schools and classrooms without technology. An expectation exists that nearly all schools and classrooms will have access to some form of computers. Other forms of technology such as videotapes, DVDs, television, calculators, digital cameras, and overhead projectors are found in most schools and available to most classrooms. We are teaching and learning in a technology-rich environment.

It is much more difficult to imagine what teachers and students are actually doing with the available technology resources. Teachers and students may be limited by what technology is available, but an even bigger limitation is their imaginations about what can be done with technology. In far too many classrooms, technology resources are mainly on display rather than in use. In other classrooms, a particular type of technology can become the content instead of a tool for teaching established goals, standards, and curriculum. All too frequently, teachers and their students become specialists in one or another technology or a narrow set of applications. Names for such classrooms include "the handheld calculator classroom" or "the web for everything classroom." As these examples illustrate, the purposes of having technology in schools and classrooms easily can be lost in the moment and excitement of manipulating the technology.

Teachers have the major responsibility for seeing that all forms of technology are used for enhancing teaching and learning. The vision of how best to use technology begins with the expertise of the teacher.

EXPECTATIONS FOR TEACHERS AND INTEGRATED USE OF TECHNOLOGY

The ways in which technology is or is not used in classrooms in large part depends on the teacher. If certain technologies are not available, then it would be unreasonable to expect teachers to use them. However, the implementation of available technologies is directly related to the skills, interests, and expectations of the teacher. One guide to the expectations for teachers is a set of national standards.

TECHNOLOGY STANDARDS FOR TEACHERS

As with other standards, a national committee of educators identified a set of technology standards and performance indicators for teachers. In this case, the committee was established by the International Society for Technology in Education, or ISTE (www.iste.org). The standards are presented in Table 13.10. Examine these standards closely.

The first standard sets an expectation that teachers will know about technology, have skill in operating a variety of technologies, and continue to learn about concepts, technologies, and applications. The remaining standards make it clear that the expectations for teachers go far beyond having some knowledge and skill in operating various technologies.

Notice standards III and IV. As emphasized in the earlier sections of this chapter, curriculum, instruction, and now uses of technology need to be planned for, implemented, and evaluated in terms of effects on student learning. The fifth standard addresses teachers' use of technology for planning and improving their own productivity, whereas the sixth standard addresses the importance of teachers being aware of and thinking about the many value issues, including ethics and access. In combination, this set of standards sets high yet reasonable expectations for teachers and their uses of technology in instruction.

INTEGRATED USES OF TECHNOLOGY

Given the ever-expanding forms and types of technologies that can be used in classrooms, teachers face a daily challenge of considering the many possibilities

---

TABLE 13.10   ISTE National Educational Technology Standards (NETS) for Teachers

I. Technology Operations and Concepts
Teachers demonstrate a sound understanding of technology operations and concepts.

II. Planning and Designing Learning Environments and Experiences
Teachers plan and design effective learning environments and experiences supported by technology.

III. Teaching, Learning, and the Curriculum
Teachers implement curriculum plans that include methods and strategies for applying technology to maximize student learning.

IV. Assessment and Evaluation
Teachers apply technology to facilitate a variety of effective assessment and evaluation strategies.

V. Productivity and Professional Practice
Teachers use technology to enhance their productivity and professional practice.

VI. Social, Ethical, Legal, and Human Issues
Teachers understand the social, ethical, legal, and human issues surrounding the use of technology in PK–12 schools and apply that understanding in practice.

Source: Reprinted with permission from *National Education Technology Standards for Teachers Preparing Teachers to Use Technology,* copyright © 2002, International Society for Technology in Education. All rights reserved.

and matching their applications with the most appropriate needs. A core principle for educational technology experts is that technology needs to be seen and used as a tool. Technology should not be the end of instruction; rather, it should be another means to achieving greater learning. This means **integrating technology** into curriculum and instruction rather than having technology become the curriculum. Educational technology also expects teachers and students to take full advantage of the potential of each technology rather than limiting its application to the simple, the tried and true, and the basic.

A recent summary of the research related to uses of technology in education places heavy emphasis on the importance of integrating uses:

> The overriding message from most current research on computer-based technology in K–12 education is that technology is a means, not an end; a tool for achieving learning goals, not a goal in itself. Yet many schools and districts make their investments before establishing clear plans for technology use.
>
> A key issue in implementing a plan for technology use is determining purpose. Will students be learning "from" computers or "with" them? In other words, will computers essentially be tutors, used to increase basic skills and knowledge? Or will technology be a resource helping students develop such abilities as higher-order thinking, creativity, and research skills.[12]

This quote directly addresses the importance of student uses of technology, but teachers also use technology. They can use technology in teaching lessons and also in preparing lessons, managing records and grades, and finding sources of information. Integrated use of technology means having teachers, as well as students, using technology in a variety of ways. Figure 13.4 is a useful representation of key ways in which technology can be used by students and teachers. Integrated use occurs when a number of these forms and applications are used in combinations with the intent of increasing student learning. Note that a number of the groupings in Figure 13.4 address teacher uses of technology. For example, the personal productivity cluster of applications applies to the teacher, as well as to students. In fact, all of the clusters include technologies and potential applications that can be of help to both teachers and students.

THE PLETHORA OF TECHNOLOGIES

One of the most significant attributes of educational technology is that there is always something new. Whatever was "hot" last year is being replaced this year with an alternative or more advanced configuration. Entirely new devices are being created and everything is being done faster. This means that teachers have to continually work to keep abreast of what is new, as well as consider what really works best with students. A sample of educational technologies is presented next to illustrate the range of possibilities.

PERSONAL COMPUTERS (PCS)   An obvious place to begin exploring educational technologies is with the personal computer. The evolution of the PC clearly illustrates the ever-expanding application possibilities and the exponential increases in speed and size. The first PC used widely in schools was the Apple I, which was introduced in the early 1980s. Curiously, the term *personal computer* was coined after the introduction of the Apple and originally referred to the IBM versions. Apple I's were useful for basic word processing as long as the document wasn't too big, and they had a calculator. As innovative teachers adopted Apples, they quickly started creating new programs and even establishing classes to teach students programming in Basic (a computer language) so that special applications could be done by computer. Almost as quickly as the PC was introduced, educators were confronted with the age-old question about applying a new technology in the classroom: Is the primary purpose of this new educational technology to learn *about* computers or to use computers *to learn?* Fortunately, classes in writing programming code did not last long. Today, PCs are the

integrating technology
Incorporating technology into lessons as an aid to teaching and learning, rather than technology being the content.

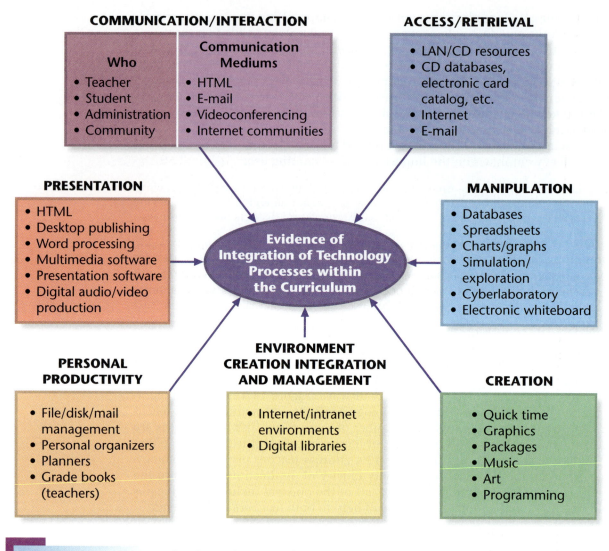

COMMUNICATION/INTERACTION

Who
- Teacher
- Student
- Administration
- Community

Communication Mediums
- HTML
- E-mail
- Videoconferencing
- Internet communities

ACCESS/RETRIEVAL
- LAN/CD resources
- CD databases, electronic card catalog, etc.
- Internet
- E-mail

PRESENTATION
- HTML
- Desktop publishing
- Word processing
- Multimedia software
- Presentation software
- Digital audio/video production

Evidence of Integration of Technology Processes within the Curriculum

MANIPULATION
- Databases
- Spreadsheets
- Charts/graphs
- Simulation/ exploration
- Cyberlaboratory
- Electronic whiteboard

PERSONAL PRODUCTIVITY
- File/disk/mail management
- Personal organizers
- Planners
- Grade books (teachers)

ENVIRONMENT CREATION INTEGRATION AND MANAGEMENT
- Internet/intranet environments
- Digital libraries

CREATION
- Quick time
- Graphics
- Packages
- Music
- Art
- Programming

FIGURE 13.4 Schema for Organizing Evidence of Integrating Uses of Technology in Classrooms

Source: Adapted from an Innovation Configuration Cluster Map developed by a Department of Defense Dependents' School (DoDDS) team of educators at RAF Lakenheath, England.

same physical size, but now they can store enormous amounts of information in digital form and are faster each year. Given the current capacity and speed of PCs, it is of concern to see them lined up along the side wall of classrooms being used only for drill, practice, and some word processing. The potential of PCs in today's classrooms is amazing. Nearly all of the applications shown in Figure 13.4 begin with the PC and the tools that have been built into them.

PC TOOLS Today's desktop computers can do amazing things that were hard to imagine ten years ago. Many of the "tools" are so frequently used that they are taken for granted. Some have been available from the beginning, such as word processing. However, today's word-processing programs can do more. The ability to select font size and style and insert bold lettering, underlining, and italics is a routine feature. Each of the drop-down icon menus unveils another tool, such as PowerPoint for presentations, graphics for art, and clip art. Other tools such as spreadsheets, tables, drawing aids, and calendar organizers have become routine features of PCs as well. Saving digitized files in memory, on CDs, or on Sony's Memory Sticks means that the storage capacity of today's PC is so large that teachers and students can save nearly unlimited amounts of text, photos, video, and audio. The PC really has the potential to become the mainstay classroom workstation for the teacher and for students.

THE INTERNET   No longer are teachers and students limited to the information found in the school library. The Internet makes it possible to be connected to most parts of the world and to access information wherever it may be located. Teachers and students can use search engines and web browsers such as Netscape, Yahoo!, and Google to seek out information and to publish their own works. The Internet can also be used to make information available to others. Teachers and students can construct reports or descriptions of their projects, community, or even the local weather and make these available to anyone who is interested, assuming they also have Internet access.

E-MAIL   Through e-mail it is possible for individuals to send and receive information almost as quickly as it can be typed. The receiver of e-mail can respond as soon as the message arrives or any time thereafter. Currently, the home is where the highest use of e-mail occurs. However, as schools and classrooms around the world become "wired," there will be ever-increasing opportunities to use e-mail for instruction. In classrooms that have e-mail capability, teachers and students are able to correspond with their counterparts in other classrooms in their home state, across the United States, or almost anywhere around the world. The exchange of information, both academic and personal, that e-mail makes possible is a clear example of how technology is contributing directly to the development of a global community.

MOBILE DIGITAL DEVICES   The ability to unplug the PC and take it around the classroom, as well as outside, has resulted in the creation of a number of new devices and innovative ways in which digital technologies can be used in instruction. One of the first devices was the handheld calculator. A related device is the graphing calculator. These allow teachers and students to perform calculations that were impossible in the past.

Technology manufacturers are continually improving each mobile device and adding additional features and tools. For example, battery life keeps getting longer, and laptops now can be purchased with a notepad screen that responds to pen and touch. The user can write or draw on the screen and the laptop converts the writing or drawing into a digital file that can be stored, transferred, and printed.

Another handheld device is the cellular telephone, or cell phone, which in other countries actually is called "the mobile." The application of the cell phone for instruction seems to be somewhat limited, but as it is combined with the rapidly developing technology of the handheld personal digital assistant (PDA), greater applications in classrooms will follow. Until recently, the most widely used PDA was that manufactured by Palm. Today, more manufactures are creating PDAs, including Compaq, Dell, Nokia, Handspring, and BlackBerry. The first Palm Pilots stored addresses, a calendar, and notes and had a calculator. By touching the screen with a stylus, the user could touch-type or use a form of shorthand to add or delete information.

Now PDAs come with full keyboards and greater computing capacity and can be combined with cell phone and digital camera technology. The size of file storage in PDAs is now so large that presentations including visuals and large amounts of text can be stored in them and shown on demand. Looking ahead, the array of mobile digital devices is likely to merge into one handheld technology that combines the operations of the PC, cell phone, fax, e-mail, digital camera, and notepad that operates anywhere and can store large amounts of data.

GOING WIRELESS   Wireless is a developing technology that makes it possible to use PCs and PDAs nearly anywhere. Instead of having to hardwire classrooms, offices, and homes, it now is possible to set up a tower, which is a small digital device, that exchanges electronic signals with technologies such as PDAs and laptops. For example, for relatively little cost and no new wiring it is possible to make any room in your home a workstation. You can simply plug in and turn on the tower, have the appropriate antenna/receiver card in your laptop, go anywhere inside and nearby outside, open your computer, and browse the web. You can catch up on the news by pulling up the most recent edition of the *Washington Post* or the *Economist*, or check e-mail without having to go to a fixed, hardwired station.

AUDIO, PHOTO, AND VIDEO   Curriculum, instruction, and student learning also can benefit from uses of new technologies for recording and reproducing sound and visual images. In recent years, the digital recording of sound has moved vinyl records and audiotape off the shelves. With the advent of affordable CD burners, it is possible to record audio, photos, and videos on CD. Small, affordable, and portable digital devices for recording sound and still and motion images increasingly are being used in classrooms. This means that teachers can record samples of their teaching and of their students' works. Students also can develop audio and visual productions using digital cameras and "produce" reports that are stored on CD or, increasingly, on Memory Sticks.

MULTIMEDIA   **Multimedia,** in the context of education, refers to the concurrent use of a number of technologies for teaching and learning. A basic principle is that teachers and students should be using a variety of technologies and that each should be appropriate to the task at hand. Using only PCs, for example, and even worse, using them only for drill and practice does students a disservice. It is a disservice to students because it restricts their opportunity to learn, and it is a disservice to the potential of each technology. When a variety of technologies is used and each technology is used in more advanced ways, the effectiveness of teaching and student learning improves.

DISTANCE LEARNING   An implicit assumption in the descriptions of educational technologies up to this point has been that the teacher and students are in the same place—their classroom. Technology opens up another possibility: The teacher and students are scattered. In its early days, a widely used form of distance education was correspondence courses, which were delivered by the postal service. Study packets would be sent to the student, and the student would do the work and then mail back his or her products. A subsequent form of distance education, which is still used in remote parts of the world including the Outback of Australia, is two-way radio. Students are at home, probably with one room in the house dedicated to school. Curriculum materials, textbooks, and worksheets are on hand, and the teacher and students communicate about the lessons by two-way radio. Today's newer distance education technologies use optical fiber phone lines or communication satellites to have two-way simultaneous delivery of audio and video. There also are web-based courses in which students receive instruction via the Internet, interact with other students and the instructor using e-mail chat rooms, and submit their assignments over the web. A distinct advantage of distance education is that for many of the applications neither the students nor the teacher has to be online at the same time.

One important use of distance education in high schools is to increase the variety of course offerings. For example, a small rural high school might have only two or three students in any year who desire a physics course or instruction in a particular foreign language. Through distance education, the students can access the course and the school district does not need to find and employ an additional teacher.

multimedia

The concurrent use of a number of technologies for teaching and learning.

TECHNOLOGIES FOR TEACHER PRODUCTIVITY

Most of the presentation up to this point has addressed the uses of technology in teaching with the expectation that both the teacher and the students have access to the technology. As identified in Figure 13.4, the personal productivity of teachers can be dramatically enhanced with technology. The most obvious advantage, certainly, is the use of the PC for word processing and the preparation of visuals for lessons. Another obvious resource is the Internet. Teachers can search for information about a topic. Teachers are also great at sharing, so many sources for lesson plans are on the Internet.

Some relatively new web-based systems help teachers prepare lesson plans, organize student records, and even provide test items. One such resource is TaskStream: The Tools of Engagement (www.taskstream.com). This system provides teachers with PC-based tools for designing unit and lesson plans. Teachers can begin their planning by pulling up and copying the relevant state and national standards. Guides and resources for developing standards-based learning activities and templates for making sure that they are aligned with the curriculum standards are available. There is even a tool to assist teachers in developing assessments that are parallel with the standards and aligned with the lesson and the specific learning objectives.

Another example of a technology-based teacher productivity tool has been developed by Edusoft (www.edusoft.com). Their system provides software to help teachers and schools organize assessments and assessment data. If a school or school district has adopted this system, it provides a device for scanning and scoring tests. Another useful tool is an online gradebook that facilitates teachers' ability to see how students are doing across time. The tool will develop tables and graphs, which are useful in visualizing trends in student test scores.

EMERGING TECHNOLOGIES

One of the interesting attributes of technology is how fast it keeps changing. Still, some emerging technologies are important for future teachers to know about.

INTERACTIVE WHITEBOARDS One technology that has great promise is the interactive whiteboard, which is not a chalkboard. This is a new digital technology

The proper artistic response to digital technology is to embrace it as a new window on everything that's eternally human, and to use it with passion, wisdom, fearlessness and joy.

Philip Greenspun

Today's students with special needs and their teachers have a number of effective technologies to support learning.

Should School Computer Labs Be Phased Out?

As technologies develop and their applications expand, educators try to determine the best way to integrate them into daily teaching and learning. This debate focuses on one question that arises from such attempts to use technology effectively in education.

YES

Barbara Barr is a K–1 teacher at Brookside Elementary School in Nicholasville, Kentucky. This twenty-four-year teaching veteran teaches nearly all lessons using classroom computers. In the fall, Barr will work in her district's technology office training teachers how to integrate computers into the curriculum.

NO

Ferdi Serim taught computer lab at John Witherspoon Middle School in Princeton, New Jersey, until his recent move to New Mexico. Serim is coauthor of the book NetLearning: Why Teachers Use the Internet *and editor of* MultiMedia Schools *Magazine.*

Computers belong in all classrooms, not held captive in the computer lab and taught as a specialized subject area at a scheduled time.

All staff and students need to learn how to effectively use this instrument. This can most realistically happen when computers are conveniently accessible in a classroom.

Computer labs have a number of drawbacks. In a lab setting, the computer is learned apart from other subjects and activities. It is much more difficult to integrate technology into other areas of the curriculum within the lab setting. The computer becomes a separate course or activity, rather than a tool used to enhance learning in other areas.

Time limits are another disadvantage to computer labs. Most educators have an assigned time to use the lab. This restricted access limits activities a teacher can conduct with students.

The time limits affect students, too. For example, a student doing a research project on World War II using computers in the classroom has instant access to major databases and can use the Internet to get resources. Research can be performed instantly and on an ongoing basis.

Scheduled time to conduct research in a lab a few times a week doesn't allow ample time to work on projects like this.

I call this the "right shoe vs. left shoe" debate. You need both kinds of shoes to get anywhere. In an ideal world, computers belong on every student's lap. But rather than focusing on where we put them, we need to focus on how the computers will be used. Once we know that, we can make better decisions about how they'll be deployed.

For the past ten years, I've worked as an educator in computer labs, in two different districts. I've seen labs used well, and I've seen them used in ways that make me cringe. There is indeed a push by some to get rid of labs. Computer labs should not be phased out. Rather, they should be used in ways that make educational sense.

There is great value in having spaces where entire classes can use technology at the same time, whether it's a computer lab or a library/media center.

Computer labs are effective places to give all students adequate access to technology to perform meaningful work.

A good example of this is when Shannon Dahl, an eighth-grade language arts teacher at my school, had her kids create books using the computer. Students gathered autobiographical information, pictures, and relics. They used a range of desktop publishing technologies to print, bind, and produce these one-of-a-kind

(continued)

that is being used more in England than in the United States but is catching on here as well. A digital whiteboard is either built into the wall of the classroom or on wheels and is the size of a chalkboard. When the teacher turns on the interactive whiteboard, it becomes a computer screen, with icons at the bottom and toolbars at the top, and it has a wireless connection to the Internet. The teacher and students can walk up to the board and touch an icon or toolbar, and the func-

YES

Even the physical location of computer labs causes problems in many schools. It is just too inconvenient to have educators take away from their classroom time to shuttle students down the hall or to another part of the school building. Once they get to the lab, there is no access to regular classroom materials.

Having computers located within an educator's classroom setting has a number of advantages. With just one computer in the classroom, we can:

- Create a spreadsheet of students' names and have each student enter data for daily attendance, lunch count, and records of monies received.
- Use a scrolling marquee screen saver for spelling words, new vocabulary, announcements, or information.
- Replace messy chalk boards or overheads with PowerPoint presentations or a simple text program using enlarged fonts.
- Instantly access encyclopedia programs, museums, libraries, and universities.

Not only are computers convenient, they are the only teaching instrument that can handle all subjects on every developmental level and still keep up with the latest information. When the student is ready to learn, the classroom computer is there!

Teachers must become comfortable with computers in order to use them effectively. This will happen when computers are available in the classroom on a consistent daily basis.

In my 24 years teaching, I've seen programs come and go with varying degrees of success. Never have I found one simple item that added so much to instruction, while instilling a passion for knowledge in students. Why limit this tremendous tool to scheduled sessions in a room at the other end of the building?

NO

heirlooms. The project ended in an "author's breakfast" for 125 kids, their families, and the community.

It took Shannon Dahl three weeks to complete the project using the computer lab. If she had only two computers in her room, the project would take all year. Having six machines would have allowed her to complete it in 15 weeks. That doesn't make educational sense.

Before getting rid of labs and putting more computers in classrooms, educators should consider these additional benefits of computer labs:

- Most classroom computers are not networked to other school computers. Computer labs allow teachers and students to make projects and information available for collaboration via the school network.
- Classroom computers don't often allow for projection devices to support group activity.

When teachers used my lab, I'd make "housecalls" to other computers with my laptop and an LCD panel for wider viewing by groups of students. The teachers I worked with would rather have a machine that let "everybody" observe a demonstration than five or six machines that only served a fraction of their class.

I will say that simply having a computer lab within a school is not enough. The spectre of the empty, locked lab is responsible for much of the impulse to do away with labs and put the machines back into the classroom.

The lab must be viewed as a shared resource for both the classroom teacher and the computer lab teacher. Computer labs will only work when there are people who know how to use them, and who are empowered to make them serve educators' needs.

Source: "Should School Computer Labs Be Phased Out?" *NEA Today* (September 1999), p. 11.

WHAT DO YOU THINK?
Should school computer labs be phased out?

To give your opinion, go to Chapter 13 of the companion website (**www.ablongman.com/johnson13e**) and click on Debate.

tions of a typical PC operate. You can write on the whiteboard too. If something is written or an image is called up that you would like to save, touch the appropriate icons and it is saved. You can even make copies if you like.

VOICE RECOGNITION Another slowly emerging technology that has significant potential for schools is voice recognition. Each year the computer programs that recognize speech are improving in accuracy and becoming more affordable. Commercially available programs can turn the spoken word into text. The current programs require that the speaker practice for quite some time so that the computer can "learn" the speaker's pronunciations. One area of application of this technology would be in language arts instruction as an aid to linking speech with writing. Take a moment to think about how exciting voice recognition technology can be for teachers and students. The potential applications seem limitless.

INTEGRATING TECHNOLOGY WITH CURRICULUM AND INSTRUCTION

In this section, a brief example of how several technologies could be integrated to support curriculum and instruction is presented. This is a hypothetical example, although it is not too far removed from what happens in many classrooms. The description begins by addressing the use of one technology, but notice that other technologies are drawn in quickly.

As you review this brief description of integrated uses of technology, observe in classrooms, and read and study further, you will discover many examples and interesting applications of technology. In each case, think about four questions:

1. What student learning needs are being addressed with this application of technology?
2. Why are these technologies and their applications appropriate?
3. Who is doing what, and why?
4. How is student learning being assessed during each lesson and at the end of the unit?

POSING THE PROBLEM Assume that in a particular state there is a learning expectation that students will be knowledgeable about schooling in other countries. This is a component of a social studies standard about knowledge of world geography and life in other places. There are benchmarks at each grade level related to this standard. Although the state-adopted curriculum outlines the general expectations and some suggested teaching activities, teachers are able to create a number of lessons on their own as long as they will help students attain the benchmarks and ultimately satisfy the standard. A beginning strategy in this case would be to use indirect instruction. Teachers could pose a problem or open-ended question that cannot be answered by students simply or quickly. For example, in an elementary school classroom the teacher asks students if they think that students in other countries study the same subjects. In a middle school social studies classroom, students could be asked to learn more about schools in other countries and whether students there also have to pass high-stakes tests. In a high school class, students could be asked to compare and contrast what they are learning with what students in other countries are learning in mathematics and whether the types of tests students take in other countries are the same or different. Note that in this simple example the cognitive level (remember Bloom's Taxonomy?) of the learning increases as the grade level goes up.

USING THE INTERNET One immediate consequence of the questions posed by each teacher is that students would likely turn to the Internet as a source of information. They would use a browser to search across a number of countries for sources that might contain information related to the posed questions. More than likely, it will take students several days or even weeks to obtain sufficient relevant information. This will be especially true for students who are inexperienced in the mechanics of Internet navigation. An important reminder is to be sure that instructions really do relate back to the expectations for student learning. Rather than training in Internet navigation, the purpose should be related

Small Groups and Individual Learning with Technology

STUDY PURPOSE/QUESTION: When computer technology (CT) is used for instruction, which has the higher learning outcomes, students working individually or students working in small groups? And does group size make a difference?

STUDY DESIGN: This study used a special research method called meta-analysis. Instead of analyzing the data from a single study, with meta-analysis it is possible to summarize the findings of many different studies. In this case, 122 studies involving 11,317 learners were analyzed.

STUDY FINDINGS: The first finding was that social context played an important role when students learn with CT. In other words, students who worked in small groups learned more than those students who worked alone. "In general, small group learning with CT had more favorable effects than individual learning with CT on student cognitive, process and affective outcomes" (p. 476).

The results from working in small groups were positive across several types of learning outcomes. "These positive results indicate that when working with CT in small groups, students in general produced substantially better group products than individual products and they also gained more individual knowledge than those learning with CT individually" (p. 476).

There were a number of instructional features that made a positive difference: (a) students had experience in working in groups, (b) students were instructed in specific cooperative learning strategies, (c) the group size was small, and (d) the content was tutorials, practice software, learning computer skills, or social sciences. However, there was a small negative effect when the subject matter involved mathematics, science, or language arts. Also the best group size is two, which probably is as many as can easily see the CT screen at one time.

IMPLICATIONS: The findings from this meta-analysis indicate that teachers should plan carefully and organize instruction differently depending on the number of students, the number of CT stations, and the subject area. Ideally there should be no more than two students per station, and the students should have had prior instruction and experience with doing group work. The subject area being taught could make a difference; however, the meta-analyses seemed to indicate that the negative effects from small group versus individual work was quite small and probably could be offset by better organization and structuring of the tasks. Preparing students to use cooperative learning strategies would appear to be important for a number of different teaching strategies and subject areas, as well as with small group work at CT stations. It probably is worthwhile to teach children skills for cooperative grouping early in the school year.

Source: Yiping Lou, Philip C. Abrami, and Sylvia d' Apollonia, "Small Group and Individual Learning with Technology: A Meta-Analysis," *Review of Educational Research, 71*(3) (Fall 2001), pp. 449–521.

---

to using the Internet to learn more about the topic at hand. Note that in this example the Internet is being used first as an information resource.

E-MAIL E-mail is another technology that should be integrated quickly as this unit unfolds. Students could use e-mail to contact schools, teachers, and students in other countries. Then they would be able to collect firsthand reports and specific examples.

INSTRUCTION POSSIBILITIES A number of elements of this lesson have not been addressed; they should be part of the original planning that each teacher does. For example, how are students grouped for this unit? Cooperative grouping would work well. Another possibility has to do with monitoring student progress. How will each teacher know and keep track of what each group and student is doing? Teacher productivity tools available from TaskStream would be of help. Also, what type of final product are the students to produce? Multimedia presentations might be perfect.

MULTIMEDIA PRESENTATIONS   Having the students work in cooperative groups supports having their final report in a multimedia format. The presentations could use a combination of text, photos of classrooms in other countries, and audio and video segments of students and classrooms that were filmed by new-found friends in other countries. For those students who do not understand the language, a voice recognition program could be used. There also could be maps with names of cities and physical geography for each country. Whereas the elementary students' presentations would be mainly descriptive, the higher cognitive level target for the high school students would mean that they should compare and contrast in their multimedia presentations. By asking students to seek out information from students in a number of countries, another important learning outcome would be built in—an increasing understanding of people in other cultures.

SUMMARY

The big ideas in this chapter were organized around the topics of curriculum, instruction, and integrated use of technology. Explicit throughout was an additional big idea: Teachers need to always have in mind the expectations for student learning.

Contrary to what many beginning teachers may assume, today's teachers have little influence over the selection of the curriculum. These decisions are made by others who generally are far removed from the classroom. A clear example is that the expectations for student learning—standards—are set first by national and state committees. The curriculum for each school district and classroom has to follow the expectations set by the state.

Teachers' major responsibility is instruction, which brings the curriculum to life in classrooms. Teachers plan for and implement teaching strategies, and they assess student learning daily, weekly, and monthly. In most schools, teachers have a great deal of latitude in determining the

way the curriculum will be taught. However, in some settings, especially in schools that are adopting one of the reform models, even the teaching strategies may be dictated from outside the classroom.

Technology is one of the important resources that today's teachers have. The particular types and the quantity may vary, but most classrooms are supplied with a variety of technologies. The teacher has the major responsibility for seeing that each technology is used effectively and that most lessons have integrated uses.

Success at translating the curriculum into instruction and skill at integrating different technologies are big challenges. Teachers must have a vast range of knowledge and skills. They also adjust and adapt instruction and the uses of technology so that every student in their classroom has maximum opportunities to learn. After all, that is what curriculum and instruction is about—helping all students learn.

DISCUSSION QUESTIONS

1. A basic premise in this chapter is that how much and how well students learn about particular content is directly related to the level of knowledge, skill in teaching, and dispositions of the teacher. At the same time, standards of learning, curriculum, and, in many situations, even the instructional strategies are determined for the teacher. Given this situation, what are the most significant ways in which teachers can make a difference in the learning of *all* the students in the class?

2. Over the last twenty years, the state and federal governments have become more directive about curriculum and instruction. In the past, most community leaders believed in *local control;* those closest to the classroom should know the most about what is needed. What do you see as the pros and cons of the trend toward centralized direction and the emergence of a national curriculum?

3. As the variety of technologies available for instruction continues to increase, is there a point at which teachers will no longer be needed?

JOURNAL ENTRIES

1. Examine the ISTE technology standards for teachers that are presented in Table 13.10. Conduct a self-assessment. How skilled are you? Develop a table that summarizes your level of proficiency in relation to each standard. In one column of the table, identify steps that you will take to increase your ability to use various classroom technologies.

2. Most schools and classrooms in the United States have ELL students. Now is the time for you to begin thinking and planning for what you will do to make sure ELL students in your classes are successful learners. Make your top ten list of steps to take to ensure ELL student success.

PORTFOLIO DEVELOPMENT

1. At the library, or when visiting a school curriculum resource room, examine the curriculum materials for a subject that you plan to teach. For one lesson, use Bloom's Taxonomy as a guide and write a set of learning objectives. This task will provide you with experience and a sample product that you can use as you are planning lessons in the future.

2. Teachers need to have skill in using a variety of technologies. Learn to use a technology that you have not used before, or learn a new application of a technology you have used before. Use the technology to develop a teaching product that you might be able to use in student teaching or in your first year of teaching.

PREPARING FOR CERTIFICATION

■ CURRICULUM AND INSTRUCTION

1. A topic in the Praxis II Principles of Teaching and Learning (PLT) test related to curriculum and instruction is "creating or selecting teaching methods, learning activities, and instructional materials or other resources that are appropriate for the students and are aligned with the goals of the lesson." Praxis II also has tests in academic disciplines; most states require prospective teachers to take the appropriate subject matter tests as well as the PLT. Go to the Praxis website (www.ets.org/praxis) and review the *Tests at a Glance* materials for the test in your subject area or teaching field. What is the structure of the test (e.g., multiple-choice, essay, or both)? What topics does the test cover? Can you answer the sample questions?

2. Answer the following multiple-choice question, which is similar to items in Praxis and other state certification tests. If you are unsure of the answer, reread the Teaching Strategies and Student Grouping sections of this chapter.

> Ms. Sanchez, a second-grade teacher, after assessing the reading levels of students in her classroom, brought a group of five low-achieving students to work with her on the \ea\ sounds. She asked students to brainstorm words that contained \ea\ and recorded students' responses on the board. She then asked, "Does the \ea\ in all of these words have the same sound? How many sounds do you think \ea\ makes in English? To-

day you will find out how many different sounds \ea\ can make." After working with students on the concept, she showed a series of flashcards with words containing \ea\ and asked students to read the words. She recorded the number of correct responses each child made on an informal assessment sheet.

This assessment is an example of

(A) homogeneous grouping and direct instruction
(B) heterogeneous grouping and indirect instruction
(C) homogeneous grouping and direct instruction
(D) heterogeneous grouping and indirect instruction

3. Answer the following short-answer question, which is similar to items in Praxis and other state certification tests. After you've completed your written response, use the scoring guide in the *Test at a Glance* materials to assess your response. Can you revise your response to improve your score?

> Some states have passed legislation requiring that all schools use immersion programs rather than bilingual programs for English as a second language (ESL) students. Define the immersion and bilingual approaches to teaching students who are not proficient speakers of English. What are the arguments for and against each approach? Which position do you support, given your current level of knowledge?

WEBSITES

www.nea.org/neatoday/9903/gardner. html This *NEA Today* article is an interesting interview with Howard Gardner. He reflects on his theory of multiple intelligences, responds to some of the criticisms, and offers suggestions for instruction.

www.iste.org The website of the International Society for Technology in Education gives information about the society's mission and projects, including technology standards for students and teachers.

www.ncela.gwu.edu The website of the National Clearinghouse for English Language Acquisition, spon-

sored by the U.S. Department of Education, is a great resource for information about teaching ELL learners.

www.creativelearningpress.com This publisher's website provides information and print materials related to Accelerated Schools.

www.successforall.com The website of the Success For All program provides ample information about this successful school reform model.

FURTHER READING

Educational Leadership, the journal of the Association for Supervision and Curriculum Development. This periodical is designed for teachers who are interested in learning about the latest curriculum and instruction ideas, approaches, and issues.

Grabe, Mark, and Grabe, Cindy. (2004). *Integrating Technology for Meaningful Learning* (4th ed.). Boston: Houghton Mifflin. An informative text with practical examples of integrated applications of technology.

Joyce, Bruce, Weil, Marsha, and Calhoun, Emily. (2000). *Models of Teaching* (6th ed.). Boston: Allyn and Bacon. An entire book devoted to description and analysis of different teaching strategies and how to use them in instruction.

Leu, Donald J., and Leu, Deborah Diadiun. (2000). *Teaching with the Internet Lessons from the Classroom* (3rd ed.). Norwood, MA: Christopher-Gordon. This book is filled with interesting ways to use the Internet in instruction. Chapters provide examples of activities to use in different subject areas and applications that work well with students who have special needs.

Smith, Tom E., Polloway, Edward, Patton, James R., and Dowdy, Carol A. (2004). *Teaching Students with Special Needs in Inclusive Settings* (4th ed.). Boston: Allyn and Bacon. This text is a useful resource for teaching students with special needs. There are chapters devoted to suggestions for each type of disability as well as chapters on teaching in elementary and secondary school classrooms.

THEMES OF THE TIMES!

expect the world®

The New York Times
nytimes.com

Expand your knowledge of the concepts discussed in this chapter by reading current and historical articles from the *New York Times* by visiting the Themes of the Times! section of the companion website **(www.ablongman.com/johnson13e).**

NOTES

1. California Department of Education, *The Nature of Science and Technology.* Sacramento, CA: Author, 2003, p. 9.
2. Archie A. George, Gene E. Hall, and Kay Uchiyama, "Extent of Implementation of a Standards-Based Approach to Teaching Mathematics and Student Outcomes," *Journal of Classroom Interaction,* 35(1) (Spring 2000), pp. 8–25.
3. Benjamin S. Bloom, ed., *Taxonomy of Educational Objectives: The Classification of Educational Goals Handbook 1: Cognitive Domain.* New York: David McKay, 1956.
4. David R. Krathwohl, Benjamin S. Bloom, and Bertram B. Masia, *Taxonomy of Educational Objectives: The Classification of Educational Goals Handbook II: Affective Domain.* New York: David McKay, 1964.

5. E. J. Simpson, *The Classification of Educational Objectives in the Psychomotor Domain: The Psychomotor Domain,* Vol 3. Washington, DC: Gryphon House, 1972.

6. Barak Rosenshine and R. Stevens, "Teaching Functions," in M. C. Wittrock, ed., *Handbook of Research on Teaching* (3rd ed.). New York: Macmillan, 1986, pp. 376–391

7. Christina V. Schwarz, Using Model-Centered Science Instruction to Foster Students' Epistemologies in Learning with Models. Paper presented at the annual meeting of the American Educational Research Association, New Orleans, April 2002.

8. David W. Johnson and Roger T. Johnson, *Learning Together and Alone: Cooperative, Competitive and Individualistic Learning* (5th ed.). Boston: Allyn and Bacon, 1999.

9. Robert Slavin, *Education for All.* Exton, PA: Swets & Zeitlinger, 1996.

10. Theodore R. Sizer, *Horace's Hope: What Works for the American High School.* Boston: Houghton Mifflin, 1997.

11. Howard Gardner, *The Disciplined Mind: What All Students Should Understand.* New York: Simon & Schuster, 1999.

12. *WestEd Policy Brief,* San Francisco: West Ed, 2002, p. 1.

Education in the Twenty-First Century

CHAPTER 14

Education in the News

Linking Their Thinking

By Andrew Trotter, *Education Week*, January 30, 2002

CAMBRIDGE, MASS.—PRETEND YOU KNOW HOW TO DO THIS: Take a digital camera and wire it to a global positioning satellite receiver, and, for good measure, stick on a digital compass.

Could such a contraption—if you could make it—help kids learn?

Well, Brian Smith thinks so.

The faculty researcher at the Massachusetts Institute of Technology's Media Lab plans to give a bunch of the devices, as yet tested only with undergraduates, to an 8th-grade social studies class. The students will walk between MIT's campus here and nearby Harvard Square, snapping away at views that interest them. The students will compare their digital photos—which Smith's gadgets have tagged with the precise location and the compass orientation of the camera when the picture was taken—to photos of the same route taken throughout the 20th century. The matching process uses a high-end software program called a geographic information system and an archive of more than 1,000 historical images donated by the Cambridge Historical Commission.

The next step is key: Students and teachers discuss how, and why, this urban landscape has changed over the past century, and whether the changes have been for better or worse.

Smith's multi-tasking camera is just one of the many gadgets developed by the Media Lab, a place where ideas about how to link new technologies to education are percolating round-the-clock. Housed in a five-story modernist box near the center of the MIT campus, the Media Lab can point to many successes in its now-16-year-old mission to explore the possibilities—in education and in other areas of life—of the digital age.

"They're on the cutting edge, and as with any kind of high-end institution, they have the luxury of doing very innovative and creative things," says Tracy Gray, the vice president of youth services at the Morino Institute, a Washington-based philanthropy that recently published a guide to using technology in after-school programs. "Really, their challenge is taking their learning approaches and getting them in the hands of those who could use them."

Smith's goal of putting novel technologies into the hands of young people—and have them pursue realistic experiences with academic payoffs—is shared by all the education researchers at the lab. The researchers are steeped in the philosophy that children learn by doing, and especially by designing and building things themselves. It's the familiar idea of project-based learning, yet the Media Lab applies such thinking to the new vistas that advances in computing are making possible.

To the casually dressed, intense, and sometimes scruffy faculty and graduate students who inhabit the lab at all hours, computing has the same role as clay to a guild of potters. Some of the "computational environments," as they call them, are familiar personal computers and handheld devices, along with standard software and Web sites. But others seem far out: computers that are built into robots, name tags, clothing, stacking blocks, and musical instruments—and, of course, Smith's camera-plus-GPS system.

And why would you want a programmable brick in the form of a name tag or stacking blocks?

In the case of the name tags, the researchers say those devices can detect other name tags worn by people in a school or at a conference, and display or transfer information.

A computing device in the form of stacking blocks, meanwhile, could enable children who can't yet read to learn how to program a computer. The youngsters would select blocks and place them in an order that would provide instructions to the computer, according to the researchers.

David Cavallo, who leads the lab's Future of Computing group, explains that robotics and other forms of computing "off the screen" give children a different and concrete learning experience that complements their use of desktop computers.

"By being a physical material off the screen," he says, a robot "lets you do different types of explo- rations that are still computational but have a differ- ent feel from when they happen on the screen."

Reprinted with permission from *Education Week*, January 30, 2002.

(INTASC) Learning Outcomes

After reading and studying this chapter, you should be able to:

1. Identify the characteristics of twenty-first-century change and articulate how these change characteristics affect schools, teachers, and students. (INTASC 2: Development & Learning; INTASC 3: Diversity; INTASC 4: Teaching Methods)

2. Describe the ways that futurism anticipates contemporary trends in education. (INTASC 4: Teaching Methods)

3. Analyze contemporary educational reform initiatives and distinguish those reforms that are transforming from those that merely extend existing school structures. (INTASC 7: Planning)

4. Conceptualize a professional development profile for yourself as educator. (INTASC 2: Development & Learning)

5. Develop a personal, preferable vision for twenty-first-century schools that is based on contemporary trends. (INTASC 9: Reflection)

School-Based Observations

You may see these learning outcomes in action during your visits to schools:

1. Ask teachers to describe educational initia- tives that are being implemented in the school. Ask if they think any of these initia- tives affect their role, how they teach, or how they relate to students. Based on the teachers' responses, determine if any of the educational initiatives are transformational.

2. Check the teachers' lounge for publications or announcements from professional organiza- tions. If so, read through those that relate to your area of study and summarize current key issues.

The new millennium has ushered in major shifts, changes, and a reexamina- tion of values in the United States and the world. All professions are now caught up in this confusing, fast-paced time of change. The Education in the News feature describes how computers can be used in developing firsthand ex- periences for students beyond those simulated on flat computer screens. Ro- botics and handheld computer devices may abound in schools of the future. Information and technology are growing at exponential rates, and access to in- formation is as immediate as the World Wide Web. Relativity governs the ac- tions of society.

This text explores and reflects on schools, students, teaching, and assess- ment because the teachers of this new millennium must be able to anticipate, un- derstand, and manage change throughout their careers. As one of these teachers, you will become the agent of change. Not only will the complexity and makeup of U.S. society change ethnographically, but so also will society across the globe, where, despite differences, we interact more and more. Schools, which once had the primary purpose of educating the masses in the fundamentals of learn- ing—namely, the three Rs—now additionally must focus on how to live in and protect our world. What values will enhance all peoples' lives? What ecological issues and practices must we adopt if the planet is to survive?

Teachers are prepared better than ever before for their careers. Students are more capable and demanding than ever before. And the school, despite constant attacks on it by critics, is better prepared to respond to the demands of a fast-paced society. The system is not perfect, but it has proven to be resilient and has carefully survived and adjusted to become what society wants. However, schools still face tremendous difficulties associated with their readiness and continuing ability to identify and conceptualize just what it is we want for society and the schools.

This final chapter examines the possibilities for schools as they move forward into the twenty-first century. As such, it is a chapter of intelligent predictions, predictions that are by no means certainties but that provide a reasonable set of possibilities for the students and teachers of the immediate tomorrow. The big ideas of change, transformation, reform, futurism, and twenty-first-century professionalism provide the framework for this chapter. These ideas also provide an exciting set of challenges that we believe you and other professionals will respond to and in the process of your responses create exciting new visions for schools, students, learning, and ultimately society.

THE NATURE OF CHANGE IN THE TWENTY-FIRST CENTURY

CROSS-REFERENCE
The various roles that teachers play as change agents in contemporary society are discussed in Chapter 11.

There is no escaping change in today's world. In the first few years of this new century, we have witnessed horrors and amazing acts of courage. As a nation of free and independent thinkers, we have had to consider the proper, human response to the events of September 11, 2001. We have had to determine our own thinking with regard to a war in Iraq, and we have had to cope with a struggling economy that has put enormous limitations on school programs.

One of the biggest challenges for twenty-first-century teachers is to respond to societal change intelligently. Information continues to increase in both amount and speed. Instant messaging, Internet news, and satellite communications have made global consciousness a reality. Embedded reporters provide instant reports about happenings around the world as they occur. Distinctions have begun to fade. The home is the workplace; what happens in one nation instantly affects another; national banks are giving way to world banks. Yet, despite the blurring of borders and time, there exists greater diversity than ever. What we once considered to be a single nation with an ethnic identity has given way to multiple identities working with and against other identities. We no longer think of a country as a nation-state of similar peoples; rather, we see nations as a complex of interconnecting groups with divergent identities, values, and histories.

Innovative ideas, reforms, and practices abound, and teachers are constantly being asked to make them work for the betterment of students. This section provides a perspective on twenty-first-century change, a perspective that helps you determine what type of change is being proposed and how to cope with change requests.

Be the change you want to see in the world.
Mahatma Gandhi

CHARACTERISTICS OF CHANGE

Changes come in various sizes. As with business and industry, change in schools can be vast and sweeping or small and insignificant. Another aspect of change is that, in many instances, planned changes are not actually implemented; there is a great deal of talk, but the change itself is never put into practice. In other cases, small changes occur that do not make a major difference in what students learn. Therefore, a distinction can be made between talking about change and tinkering with relatively small changes.

Changes that provide a different way of thinking or acting—changes that really make a difference—are called transformational. **Transformational changes** are those that dramatically influence the shape, structure, and operations of schools and classrooms.

■ SIZE OF EDUCATIONAL CHANGE

One way to view the different magnitudes of change is illustrated in Figure 14.1. This ten-point scale goes from "talking" to "thinking" to "transforming." At the talking end of the scale are speeches, press announcements, and published com-

	LEVEL	NAME	EXAMPLES
Talking	0	Cruise control	• 1950s • Teacher in same classroom for many years
	1	Whisper	• Pronouncements by officials • Commission reports
	2	Tell	New rules and more regulations of old practices
	3	Yell	Prescriptive policy mandates
Thinking	4	Shake	• New texts • Revised curriculum
	5	Rattle	• Changing principal • Team teaching
	6	Roll	• Change teacher's classroom • Change grade configurations
	7	Redesign	• Evening kindergarten • Integrated curriculum
Transforming	8	Restructure	• Site-based decision making • Differentiated staffing
	9	Mutation	• Teacher and principal belong to the same union • Changing the role of school boards • Coordinated services
	10	Reconstitution	• Local constitutional convention • Glasnost

FIGURE 14.1 Hall's Innovation Category Scale (HICs)

Source: G. E. Hall, *"Examining the Relative Size of Innovations: A Scale and Implications."* Greeley, CO: College of Education, University of Northern Colorado, 1993.

transformational changes

Changes that influence the shape, structure, and operations of schools and classrooms.

mission reports; these result in little if any change in classrooms. As one moves toward the thinking section, changes take place in schools and in classrooms; however, the changes are of modest impact. These changes do not affect the structures of the school or its essential orientation. The categories of change at the transforming end represent major, wide-ranging restructurings, redesigns, and alternative configurations of what schools and school practices can be like.

Think about the changes in schools that you are aware of and the ones you have read about in this text. How many of the ideas have been put into practice? Often good ideas are never implemented in schools. This is because change is difficult, and large-scale change is personally uncomfortable. Also, the truly transforming changes tend to be seen as reckless. Ideas such as having schools replaced by large, open centers for learning or schools embedded into the life of the community with students, businesses, and community centers working collaboratively represent major shifts from schools as we know them. Transforming ideas, such as having public schools begin with children at birth or having a high school student take two months to do an independent project away from the school, are hard to accept as realistic. Yet an increasing number of transforming innovations are being tried.

The remainder of this chapter describes futurism, the teaching profession, and various transforming types of educational innovations. The purpose is to stretch your thinking and to increase your awareness of the vast variety of major

Never let the future disturb you. You will meet it, if you have to, with the same weapons of reason which today arm you against the present.

Marcus Aurelius

Involving students in solving real-world problems such as dealing with waste enables them to apply school content to their lives and the world around them.

changes that already exist in some U.S. schools. As the 2000s continue to unfold, more of these transforming innovations will take place, and in your career as a teacher you will have the opportunity to participate in the implementation of many of them. At the very least, you will likely experience working in a school district where one or more schools will be incorporating some of these practices. Perhaps, as your career unfolds, you will have the opportunity to create additional innovations in teaching, curriculum, and classroom school operations.

FUTURISM AND TRANSFORMATIONAL TRENDS IN TWENTY-FIRST-CENTURY EDUCATION

Futurism is the science of strategically analyzing trends, ideas, and movements to bring about futures that are preferable for the welfare of society. Futurists identify and study trends, interpret the trends, attempt to forecast their future effects on society, and generate alternative courses of action that might achieve the desired effects. Alvin Toffler notes the importance of futuristic thinking when he states:

> Every society faces not merely a succession of probable futures, but an array of possible futures, and a conflict over preferable futures. The management of change is the effort to convert certain possibles into probables, in pursuit of agreed-on preferables. Determining the probable call for a science of futurism. Delineating the possible calls for an art of futurism. Defining the preferable calls for a politics of futurism.[1]

Futuristic thinking, therefore, includes not only studying and considering the knowledge of the past and present but also conjuring up alternative futures. It further involves using values in choosing a desired alternative and then planning and acting to create the preferred alternative.

Our ability to forecast the future of schools is limited, like our ability to generate possible alternative futures. Furthermore, choosing preferred alternatives from possible alternatives is likely to be challenging; and finally, creating the desired state of the future may be impossible. Yet a basic assumption is that the future will be different from the past and the present, and we have a responsibility to try to shape it. As a member of the teaching profession, you cannot escape the responsibility to enter into discussions about changes that will bring about a better future. Whether you do so by active discussion and engagement or by passive acceptance of the trends of the day, you do influence the future of schools. The following sections discuss possible future trends in education that may or may not materialize. No matter what your response to the pressures that surround these trends, you will help determine if the trends come to be and do or do not provide a preferable future.

■ INCREASED ACCOUNTABILITY FOCUSED ON STUDENT LEARNING

futurism

The science of strategically analyzing trends, ideas, and movements to bring about futures that are preferable for the welfare of society.

A contemporary trend is the expectation of data-driven results. This expectation permeates much of today's school legislation. Teachers are increasingly held accountable for their students' development. Teachers are challenged to show evidence that students have achieved specific learning outcomes. There is less interest in what teaching skills were employed and more interest in whether the teaching techniques actually improved student learning.

Some states reward teachers whose students show improvement on state tests and other learning performance measures. Schools are required to publish annual reports that describe students' performance on various tests. Schools can be punished for low performance by allowing parents to remove their children from a low-performing school. Sometimes schools are taken over by the state department of education if they continue to show low student achievement.

Along with the increased focus on student achievement results, teachers are required to collect supporting evidence of student growth. To collect this evidence, they may develop pre- and postassessments that show students have achieved specific learning outcomes based on their participation in classroom activities. Student logs, portfolios, observation checklists, and test results are increasingly important aspects of a teacher's evidence repertoire.

CROSS-REFERENCE
The roots and importance of accountability as well as school district report cards are discussed in Chapter 5.

■ SCHOOLS AS THE CENTER FOR DELIVERY OF COORDINATED SERVICE

Twenty-first-century schools will be transformed from single-purpose to full-service centers. Increasingly, schools will be the center for access to many types of services including emotional, health, welfare, education, criminal justice, and dental. Instead of attempting to address the educational needs of children and families in isolation from other needs, some schools have already become such holistic family resource centers.

This approach is a dramatic move away from the array of individual agencies that have dealt with distinct parts of the child. Each of these agencies may have been performing well, but none dealt with the child as a whole person. In fact, it is not uncommon to have an average of five different social service agencies addressing the needs of one child who is at risk. Typically, none of these agencies communicates with the others concerning their knowledge of the child or the child's family, nor do they communicate about the interventions implemented. In addition, the various levels of federal, state, and local human service agencies complicate the delivery of services. For example, in the California state government, 160 different programs and thirty-five state agencies deal with services to children. The whole child is not seen by one agency, as each agency specializes in the delivery of its specific service.

■ EMPHASIS ON CHARACTER DEVELOPMENT

Since the origin of the common school, character development has been an important aspect of a child's education. Throughout the last century, this emphasis declined in favor of academic achievement. However, the tragic events of 9/11 coupled with increased school violence have brought character development to the forefront of American consciousness. A recent poll found that violence, fighting, gangs, and drugs ranked in the top five problems faced by schools.[2] Whereas society's typical responses to student violence are increased restrictions and law enforcement measures, character development advocates call for smaller classes and mutual respect among all school constituents, reciprocity among students, and the development of reverence for others.[3]

CROSS-REFERENCE
Developing character in students is discussed as part of a humanistic educational theory in Chapter 10 and as part of discipline in Chapter 11.

In response to these issues, character education programs have emerged with great support. A Forest of Virtues, Character Counts, and many other programs claim that by incorporating character education lessons in the curriculum, students' character will be enhanced. Unfortunately, little research has yet been completed to support these claims. Additionally, critics have raised serious concerns about character education, citing the problem of superficial obedience to rules of conduct versus the development of authentic character traits.[4]

Despite the debate that surrounds the proper conduct of character education, the importance of including moral development or some sort of character development in the school curriculum remains strong in the United States. Most experts advocate a comprehensive approach to the development of character in educational settings. Such an approach goes beyond direct instruction to incorporate the development of democratic classroom practices, cooperative learning, conflict resolution, moral reflection, caring, altruistic behavior, and the inclusion of ethical concerns within science, social studies, and other academic disciplines.

More and more educators are aware that the character development domain is embedded in the academic or intellectual domain and that there is no real way to separate the two. Theodore Sizer and Nancy Sizer call for educators to grapple in an informed and careful discussion with how morality relates to the full curriculum. They note that character education is neither a discrete curriculum added as an afterthought nor an unreflective activity, such as required community service. True moral education is an intellectual undertaking that must infuse the entire school; it assumes that a good person has both passion and restraint, respect for evidence, and patience when evidence is not readily at hand. More important, "character education must be led by adults who know things, who themselves are regular grapplers with all the work and messiness and confusion that rich content entails."[5]

■ INCREASED COMPETITION AMONG SCHOOLS

Schools are increasingly feeling the pressures of a competitive environment. Public displays of school and district report cards, annual comparisons of state test results in newspapers, and legislation that permits students to transfer from low-performing schools are changing the vision of stable neighborhood school settings. Schools are slowly feeling the effects of a results-oriented workplace with competitive vendors vying for customers.

Examples of school choice include open-enrollment options, privately and government-funded vouchers, tax credits, and charter schools. Philanthropists in many locations provide vouchers to enable students to attend nonpublic schools. The most notable examples of these privately funded choice ventures can be found in New York City and Chicago. In New York, a group of business executives provided funding for scholarships that enabled 2,200 students to attend nonpublic schools, while another group of citizens raised millions of dollars for a national program to provide inner-city students with similar scholarships.

Another trend that ultimately increases competition in public schools is privatization. Privatization occurs when the operation of public schools is contracted out to business corporations. A well-known, controversial privatization initiative is the Edison School Corporation. In 1995, Edison won contracts to operate four schools. The company has since contracted with school districts to operate more than a hundred public schools. Although the success of Edison has not yet been established, private contractors are increasingly taking over all or some of school operations. Sylvan Learning Corporation and other private companies provide tutoring assistance to at-risk students in public schools across the country. Private firms have also taken over the financial operations of some school districts.

THE CHANGING PROFESSION OF EDUCATION

CROSS-REFERENCE
The many responsibilities that accompany the profession of teaching are discussed in Chapter 1.

The profession of education is changing. There is no longer a single path or description of the twenty-first-century educator. Rather, a career in education involves a wide variety of possibilities and develops with increased responsibilities that range far beyond the presentation of content or developing discipline approaches.

Will Public Education Survive the Next Century?

As the pace of change escalates and the future becomes more and more uncertain, the relevance of public schools is called into question. Has society so changed that requiring students to come to a specific place called school and earn elementary, middle school, and high school degrees is unnecessary? Ivan Illich thought that society would be better if it were de-schooled.

YES

Dr. Barbara Smith Palmer is an elected member of the United Teachers of Los Angeles House of Representatives and Political Action Committee, the California Teachers Association State Council, and a UTLA delegate to the NEA Representative Assembly.

NO

Cynthia Russ is a curriculum coach for Residence Park Latin Grammar Classical Studies Magnet School in Dayton, Ohio. A teacher for more than 26 years, Russ is an alternate member of the Resolutions Committee for both the Ohio Education Association and the NEA.

I'm excited about the prospects for teaching and learning in the 21st Century. But for public education to truly survive in the 21st Century, we will need to make some adjustments in our efforts at reform, in our philosophy, and in our teaching.

■ **Reform.** How schools are structured has complicated our attempts at innovation. The relationship between knowledge and power, within the social and political contexts for our schools, has placed burdensome external controls on teachers and students, controls ranging from excessive regulation to massive testing.

Current policies that focus on national testing and national standards are too narrow. There is no one approach that can work for all kids. Our testing and standards policies must take into account the many diverse learning styles in our student population.

■ **Learning Approaches.** Our presuppositions commonly prevent us from thinking effectively about education issues—and from committing ourselves to equity and excellence for all. We must put an end to deficit terminology and labeling. Terms like "at-risk" marginalize kids into categories and make assumptions about their learning capabilities that aren't true. Children are capable of much more than teachers and parents generally realize.

■ **Teaching.** In the school of the 21st Century, teachers will have to challenge traditional approaches to teaching and learning by modeling a collaborative form of practitioner inquiry.

Teachers need to encourage students to question answers and to express their own viewpoints. They have to provide ways for students to participate in the discourse that shapes their lives. Curiosity, industry, and imagination should be encouraged and rewarded.

As I look ahead to the next century and think about the fate of our public education system, I feel discouraged. I do not think public education will, in fact, survive the next century.

Public schools, to be sure, have always faced challenges. As public educators, we've always had to battle to make sure all children have the rights and opportunities they deserve. We had to fight to end segregation, fight for equity for Native American children schooled on reservations, and fight to get adequate funding for inner-city schools.

But the opponents we face now seem tougher than ever, and we find ourselves battling on so many different fronts.

■ **Vouchers.** The increasing clamor for private-school tuition vouchers is a direct threat to public education's survival in the next century.

Vouchers siphon off much needed funding from public schools. In a voucher-friendly America, those who remain in an underfunded public system will face a vicious downward spiral of deteriorating buildings, out-of-date materials, overcrowded classrooms, and uncertified teachers. This downward spiral will only create pressure for more vouchers.

■ **Charter Schools.** Charters today are too often run by businesses out to make a buck, not educators with visions they want to try to realize. The results are predictable. Children become mere moneymakers for the companies involved. But what happens when the money runs out?

If charters continue, with little public oversight, we won't have much in our education budgets left in the next century for children to receive the education they deserve.

(continued)

YES

Teachers need more autonomy and the ability to create exciting educational experiences for students. By encouraging democratic dialogue among educators, we can empower teachers.

We can excel in the new century if teachers function as a community of scholars, engaging in collaborative diagnostic and problem-solving work to create alternative approaches for designing tasks and assessing activities.

In the classroom of the 21st Century, teachers need to involve students in interesting project-based assignments so that they can learn by doing.

Students should become more engaged readers. Activities like peer-assisted reading, classroom discussions about texts, and book club projects can allow students to become leaders on their own terms.

Students will reach their personal goals through the gentle guidance of teachers, who hold themselves and their students accountable to high standards for all.

Educators joining with each other and with their students to explore a critical pedagogy of group work, collaboration, and serious individualized attention will create a revolutionary classroom where all children learn at the highest levels.

If that happens, public education will not only survive through the 21st Century, it will thrive!

NO

■ **Lack of Parental Involvement.** The absence of parents in our schools is another factor that leads me to believe that public education may not survive.

Parental support has always been the backbone for public education. With dwindling parental support, lines of communication tend to close. Schools are then left subject to gossip, innuendo, misconceptions, and bad feelings.

Schools that do not have a strong communication link with parents will not survive. We cannot survive in the next century if parents and the community do not understand what is really happening in our schools today.

If public education is to survive into the next century, we need to rebuild general public support. We must not let vouchers and other schemes take away the resources we need to help our public schools thrive.

There are problems, of course, in our public school system. But American public education—available to everyone, without regard to race, color, creed, economic status, or physical and mental ability—remains our nation's greatest contribution to democracy.

Society needs to understand that our children are our future. If we continue diluting public education, we will no longer have a viable method to educate all children. And without a focus on all children, public education will cease to exist.

Source: "Will Public Education Survive the Next Century?" *NEA Today* (January 2000), p. 11.

WHAT DO YOU THINK?
Will public education survive the next century?

To give your opinion, go to Chapter 14 of the companion website **(www.ablongman.com/johnson13e)** and click on Debate.

Companion Website

■ CAREER DEVELOPMENT CONTINUUM

The notion that becoming a teacher involves obtaining a degree in education followed by state licensure is obsolete. As in the medical profession, teachers grow into their profession and gradually develop their skills along a novice-to-master career continuum. For example, beginning teachers focus on fine-tuning their skills in the classroom. This developmental opportunity involves personal assessment of daily interventions with students, journaling, and discussing classroom events with other teachers. Mentoring is also a major component of the novice teacher's professional life. As you move from the novice teacher stage to the experienced teacher stage, you will find yourself involved in more and more activities that go beyond the classroom. You will likely be a member of various school program committees and take on leadership roles that provide direction for the larger school program.

As teaching careers evolve, some teachers find it interesting to complete an administrative internship. This provides teachers an opportunity to see school through the eyes of administration. Other teachers explore a curricular internship that allows them to provide leadership in the development of different curricular projects such as designing a scope and sequence for the science program or developing a school mission statement. These experiences provide veteran teachers an opportunity to see school life outside the classroom.

As teachers develop into master teachers, they often take on the role of mentors. Some master teachers spend time in other teachers' classrooms providing expert advice and modeling sophisticated teaching approaches. Other master teachers do not even have their own classrooms but spend their entire day working in the classrooms of other teachers and providing leadership in various school program initiatives. Master teachers also develop ideas for grants and spend time working with local businesses and other community groups helping to develop meaningful partnerships.

Developing professional learning communities provides personal growth and enhances the quality of projects.

During this advanced developmental phase, teachers often seek National Board certification and complete advanced degree programs. These external awards and certifications provide further evidence of professional career standing.

■ PROFESSIONAL COLLABORATION

Teaching today requires working with colleagues in a number of activities. In the classroom, teachers may team teach or plan with other teachers who are teaching the same grade or subject. Teams work together to plan curriculum and assessment activities. Teachers support one another through professional development activities and peer evaluations in a number of schools. Special educators, bilingual educators, school psychologists, and other professionals serve as resources for teachers who are planning for individualized student learning as well as physical and emotional development. Support personnel in schools include custodians, secretaries, principals, other administrators, and parent or community liaison people. These support personnel can be helpful to teachers in maintaining a positive learning environment, understanding the community, and contacting families. They can serve as resources in planning events and making appropriate contacts in the community.

Teachers are also expected to work with families in support of student learning. Parental involvement is no longer limited to parent–teacher conferences scheduled periodically during the school year. Teachers and other school officials contact parents to confer about students and to prevent potential problems that could interfere with learning.

■ PARTICIPATING IN THE PROFESSION

One of the rewarding aspects of becoming a teacher is the opportunity to work with other well-educated and highly dedicated professionals. There are many types of professional organizations and associations that teachers can join. In most school districts, teachers are represented by a teachers' organization or

Progress is impossible without change, and those who can change their minds can change anything.

George Bernard Shaw

union that is responsible for negotiating contracts and setting working conditions. These organizations and associations have had a major influence on the development of national education policy; in the determination of state policies, laws, rules, and regulations related to schooling; and (at the local level) in curriculum decisions and labor contract negotiations. At all of these levels, teachers are actively involved and are responsible participants as well as part of the membership that works with the resultant policy decisions and curriculum products.

Teachers have opportunities to become involved in professional or specialty associations as well. These associations deal directly with issues such as the development of student and teacher standards, the design of curriculum, innovation in teaching, improving instructional processes, and so forth. They provide teachers with the opportunity to collaborate with other teachers who have like concerns and interests; they also enable teachers to participate in various professional leadership activities. Some specialty organizations focus on teaching specific subjects, such as science, math, literature, and reading, or specific grade levels, such as middle school and early childhood education. These associations usually have national, state, and local chapters. Clearly, teachers can profit from membership and participation in both professional organizations and professional or specialty associations.

TEACHER UNIONS

Teacher unions were organized to improve working conditions. The National Education Association (NEA) and the American Federation of Teachers (AFT) are the two major unions for teachers in the United States. Some teachers have chosen to join other state or local organizations that are not affiliated with the NEA or the AFT but operate similarly to a union. The unions provide a number of services for their members, leadership on a number of professional issues, and a political presence at the local, state, and national levels.

NATIONAL EDUCATION ASSOCIATION (NEA)   The National Education Association is by far the largest teachers' organization, with 2.5 million members, including teachers, administrators, clerical and custodial employees, higher education faculty, and other school personnel. Teacher education candidates can join the NEA's Student Program. More than a million teacher education candidates have joined the student group since it was formed in 1937. You might wish to explore the advantages of joining this organization on your campus.

The NEA is committed to advancing public education. The organization was founded in 1857 as the National Teachers' Association (NTA). In 1870 the NTA united with the National Association of School Superintendents, organized in 1865, and the American Normal School Association, organized in 1858, to form the National Education Association. The organization was incorporated in 1886 in the District of Columbia as the National Education Association and was chartered in 1906 by an act of Congress. The charter was officially adopted at the association's annual meeting of 1907, with the name National Education Association of the United States.

The Representative Assembly (RA) is the primary legislative and policy-making body of the NEA. NEA members of state and local affiliates elect the 9,000 RA delegates who meet annually in early July to debate issues and set policies. The president, vice president, and secretary-treasurer are elected at the annual RA. The top decision-making bodies are the Board of Directors and the Executive Committee. An executive director has the primary responsibility for implementing the policies of the association, and standing committees and ad hoc committees carry out much of the work.

Given its long history of advocacy of teaching as a profession, it should not be surprising to learn that the NEA sponsors many professional initiatives designed to disseminate best practices, facilitate teacher leadership, and empower teachers to reform schools. The NEA has organized to provide professional help in student assessment and accountability; professional preparation, state licensure, and national certification; and governance and member activities. The NEA also initiated in 1954, along with four other associations, the accrediting body for teacher education, NCATE, and continues today to provide leadership through appointments to NCATE's governance board and board of examiners, the practitioners who visit college campuses to apply the standards. These and other program areas offer an array of activities and initiatives to further advance teacher professionalism.

Members of the NEA receive its newsletter, *NEA Today,* and have access to numerous other publications and products, including publications that are available online through its professional library. Recent reports from the association address diversity, portfolios, student assessment, school safety, cooperative learning, discipline, gender, inclusion, reading and writing, and parent involvement. Handbooks published by the NEA and written by experienced teachers are helpful resources for new teachers.

AMERICAN FEDERATION OF TEACHERS (AFT) The second largest teachers' union is the American Federation of Teachers, with national headquarters in Washington, D.C. It was organized in 1916 by teachers in Winnetka, Illinois, to establish an organization to meet their needs and to create a strong union affiliation. The Chicago Teachers' Federation preceded the AFT, having been established in 1897 and affiliating with the American Federation of Labor (AFL) in 1902. Since 1916, AFT membership has grown steadily. The late Albert Shanker, who was AFT president from 1964 until his death in 1997, is given much of the credit for the growth and success of the AFT, including its national involvement in political discussions related to education. In 1965, membership was at 110,500; by 2000, membership exceeded one million. The organization of the AFT includes a president, numerous vice presidents, a secretary-treasurer, and administrative staff. The membership serves on standing committees and council committees.

Since its inception, the AFT has boasted of its affiliation with the AFL, and later the AFL-CIO. AFT has stressed that organized labor was an important force in establishing our system of free public schools and that it has actively supported school improvement programs. Affiliation with organized labor gives the AFT the support of the more than 15 million members of the AFL-CIO. Support from local labor unions has often worked to the advantage of local AFT unions in their efforts to gain better salaries and improved fringe benefits from local boards of education.

The AFT has diverse resources available to its members. Its lobbying and political action activities support a number of professional issues, in addition to bargaining issues at the local, state, and national levels. Its publications include the journal *American Educator.* Jointly with the NEA, the AFT conducts the annual QUEST conference to convene the leadership of both organizations to discuss professional issues. The Educational Research and Dissemination Program helps make selected findings from recent research on classroom management and effective teaching available to teachers.

STATE AND LOCAL TEACHER ORGANIZATIONS The state and local affiliates of the NEA and the AFT are the power bases of the organizations. Although the local association of teachers has the highest priority in the organization, its strength lies in the solidarity of numbers, services, and resources provided by the state and its regional administrative offices. For the most part, teachers participate directly in the affairs of local organizations. Solutions to the problems at hand are primarily the concern of local teachers' organizations. Still, the influence of these groups could be weakened without the support and resources of strong state and national parent organizations. At the same time, local organizations sometimes become indifferent about their national and state affiliations.

Leadership at the national level views the problems and differences in beliefs among local organizations as a viable part of the democratic process rather than as divisive. From the many geographic locations, issues identified by grassroots local teacher organizations may rise through the state associations to the national level or from the local organizations directly to the national level. Decisions related to national policy are then made by majority vote, with attention paid to input from all levels—local, state, and national. In some instances, local organizations have severed relations with their state and national affiliates when the members felt that their particular needs were not well met. Because the power of the state and national organizations is reduced somewhat each time a local organization withdraws its affiliation, these state organizations are compelled to pay careful attention to the particular needs of local teachers' association affiliates.

POLITICAL ACTION   Both the NEA and AFT have political action committees and government relations departments. **Political action committees** are engaged in action to elect political candidates who are sympathetic to education and teachers' issues. They monitor elected officials' voting records on education bills and analyze the platforms of new candidates. They actively participate in the election campaigns of the president, governors, and key legislators. Although the unions have traditionally supported Democratic candidates, they now are somewhat less partisan, endorsing candidates who support education and teacher issues that the association values, regardless of the candidates' political affiliation.

The state and national political action committees of the NEA and AFT have a common aim: to promote education by encouraging teachers to participate in the political life of their local, state, and national communities. These committees throughout the states are responsible for recommending political endorsements to their respective boards of directors. Union leaders believe that their political clout pays off for education. In terms of support of future political candidates, teachers' unions remain consistent in their claims that they will support those who seem to favor public education.

PROFESSIONAL ASSOCIATIONS

Teachers can join, participate in, and provide leadership for many professional associations that focus on their chosen professional interests. These associations are organized around academic disciplines and specific job assignments, such as science teaching, mathematics teaching, special education, school psychology, reading, cooperative learning, and multicultural education. Over 500 organizations focusing on some aspect of education exist in the United States. A selected list of professional organizations with website addresses is found in Appendix E at the end of this book.

PHI DELTA KAPPA INTERNATIONAL   The professional organization Phi Delta Kappa International (PDK) is one of the largest and most highly regarded organizations for educators in the world. Today it is open to all educators, although in its earlier years women were not allowed to join. It publishes excellent professional material, including the journal *Phi Delta Kappan,* a newsletter, *Fastback* booklets on timely educational topics, research reports, books, and various instructional materials. The organization also sponsors many surveys, research projects, grants, awards, conferences, training programs, and trips. Local PDK chapters bring together teacher candidates, higher education faculty, and local teachers and administrators. You might want to consider a student membership and become involved in your local chapter.

RELIGIOUS EDUCATION ASSOCIATIONS   National and regional religious education associations are under denominational or interdenominational control. These organizations might represent sectarian schools attended by students

political action committees

Committees focused on electing political candidates who are sympathetic to education and teachers' issues.

whose families prefer them to public schools or secular private schools. Some religious groups or clubs supplement the public or private school program by offering educational activities for youth and adults. Examples of religious organizations include the Association of Seventh-Day Adventists Educators, Catholic Biblical Association of America, Council for Jewish Education, National Association of Episcopal Schools, Association of Christian Schools International, and Religious Education Association.

GLOBAL PERSPECTIVES
Education International

In January 1993, Education International (EI) officially replaced the World Confederation of Organizations of the Teaching Profession (WCOTP), which had worked vigorously to improve the teaching profession and educational programs around the world. EI has united more than 240 national educator unions and professional associations from around the world. This new organization brings together more than 20 million elementary, secondary, and higher education professionals. In the United States, this merger brings the NEA and the AFT together under a world umbrella. The EI is focusing its efforts on improving the quality of education throughout the world, upgrading education employee working conditions and compensation, fighting for adequate educational funding, sharing curricula, safeguarding human rights, fighting for gender equality, and building stronger educational organizations. To what degree do you think the working conditions of public school teaching in the United States should provide a model for working conditions in schools in other countries?

A VISION FOR TWENTY-FIRST-CENTURY SCHOOLS

This last section posits a possible and preferable future for schools. It is by no means presented as a certainty, but using the tools of futurism, it presents a possible and preferable vision for twenty-first-century schools.

PROFESSIONAL LEARNING COMMUNITIES

Professional learning communities is a concept that positions teachers as inquirers. The distinction between teacher and learner is blurred in this vision of a teacher. A professional learning community is characterized by collaboration, a commitment to a shared vision and mission, a focus on learning, shared leadership, continuous school improvement, celebration, and persistence.[6] In this culture, teachers and administrators work together to enhance learning across the entire school community. Inquiry is at the center of everyone's life. Teachers collaborate in advancing new ideas, actualizing these ideas and collecting evidence to determine if the ideas are helping students learn. Principals collaborate with teachers and other principals in the same endeavor. Celebrations occur as the results of ongoing inquiries are shared. Such celebrations enable others to know what has or has not been fruitful, and thus new ideas are generated. School improvement occurs naturally through this process of shared inquiry.

In such a culture, teachers are in one anothers' classrooms on a regular basis. No longer is the classroom an isolated community. Rather, teachers work together as part of the larger learning community. Change occurs because of this collaboration.

Coming together is a beginning, staying together is progress, and working together is success.

Henry Ford

Can Groups Learn?

STUDY PURPOSE/QUESTIONS: Learning in groups can encourage student creativity and imaginative problem solving; it also provides a productive exchange of ideas. However, groups with assigned tasks often have only a vague idea about the criteria that will be used to assess their group projects. The researchers contended that lack of clarity about the group project criteria diminished the quality of group learning and the quality of the final project. This study sought to answer the proposition that providing students with specific guidelines as to what makes an exemplary group product improves the character of group discussion as well as the quality of the group project.

STUDY DESIGN: This was an experimental study of five sixth-grade classrooms located in California's Central Valley. All five participating teachers were skilled in using complex instruction, a special set of instructional strategies enabling heterogeneous classrooms to work at a high intellectual level. Groups in the different classrooms carried out the same tasks using the same curricular material. The researchers assessed the work of creative problem-solving groups who were studying the same social studies unit on ancient Egypt. The measures for creative problem solving focused on the nature of the group discussion, the quality of the group product, and essays written by the students upon completing the unit.

After careful preparation and practice on three prior instruction units, the focal unit on ancient Egypt required five days of implementation. Each group worked on five different tasks, gave a presentation on their group product, and received feedback from the teacher and their classmates. In three of the five classrooms, groups worked with explicit evaluation criteria provided with their instructions and resource materials. With this one exception, the instructions to groups in the other two classrooms were the same. Following the completion of the learning tasks, all students wrote essays on the relationship of specific group activities and products to the central idea of the unit.

STUDY FINDINGS: The researchers found that groups that used evaluation criteria were more self-critical, more task focused, had better quality group products, and had higher essay scores. The amount of evaluative and task-focused talk and the quality of the group products were independent predictors of the group's aggregate score on the essays. When groups were more focused on the content of the product, they created a better group product. This assisted their understanding and grasp of academic content as measured by the essays. In addition, the more the group evaluated their product and performance, the higher their essay scores.

IMPLICATIONS: Providing evaluative criteria helps groups to become more self-critical and to increase their effort. Such increased effort leads to superior group products, thereby strengthening students' written performance. By holding groups accountable for their products, the teacher can do much to ensure the kind of group performance that will lead to individual learning. Teachers can and should assess group products and provide feedback based on the evaluation criteria clearly presented to the groups prior to their activity.

Source: Elizabeth G. Cohen, Rachel Lotan, Beth Scarloss, Susan E. Shultz, and Percy Abram, "Can Groups Learn?" *Teachers College Record 104*(6) (2002), pp. 1045–1068.

■ CLASSROOMS AS DYNAMIC CENTERS OF LEARNING

If you want to know your past, look into your present conditions. If you want to know your future, look into your present actions.

Buddhist saying

In this vision of a preferable future, the walls of individual classrooms disappear. Classrooms are merely centers for learning—places where information is shared and assessed. Learning occurs beyond the classroom in laboratories, in the community, in businesses, and in technology centers. Learning is authentic, and students construct their own meaning as they attain new knowledge, solve real-world problems, gather data, make inferences, and draw conclusions. These conclusions are shared in the classroom. Through this sharing, conclusions are challenged and students learn to shift their thinking in response to legitimate criticism and questions.

Mentoring is the primary teaching technique in such a vision. Teachers mentor other teachers, teachers mentor students, students mentor other students, and parents and community members mentor as well. Dialogue across the community occurs on a regular basis because so many constituents of the community are involved with students.

Yearlong schools are the norm. The school schedule closely relates to the calendar of the community. Breaks in the school year correspond to the holidays and work schedule of community members. Schooling also occurs outside the school. Computers provide access to learning opportunities at home, at church, and at community centers. There is no need to stop learning just because the school has closed its doors for vacation.

The curriculum is integrated. Ideas interrelate as they are studied in different problems and contexts. Thinking strategies, content acquisition, the practice of dispositions, the moral component, play, exercise, sports, the environment, and community service are part of the school day. More important, learning is viewed as natural and lifelong.

SUMMARY

The vision for education described in this chapter is by no means certain. But it does provide a preferable future for us to discuss, debate, and ultimately aim to achieve. A variety of twenty-first-century trends are cited throughout the chapter, including increased accountability for student achievement, schools as centers for integrated services, character development, and increased competition.

The big ideas of change, transformation, reform, futurism, and twenty-first-century professionalism provided the framework for this final chapter. Change was described as continual and complex. Distinctions among "talking," "thinking," and "transforming" types of change are described. Futuristic thinking is shown to be a necessary in-

gredient to coping with the many demands for reform and school change. The teacher as a professional is described as a developing process moving from novice to expert. Professional leadership in education is exemplified by involvement in a wide variety of organizations. These ideas provide an exciting set of challenges that we believe you and other professionals will respond to and, in the process of your responses, will create exciting new visions for schools, students, learning, and ultimately society. We wish you the best in such a future and look for your leadership in making the twenty-first century an exciting world of peace, justice, and learning.

DISCUSSION QUESTIONS

1. What types of change do you observe in your college or university? Are they talking, thinking, or transforming?

2. Consider a transforming change that you believe would be good for your college. Why do you think this transforming change would be difficult to implement?

3. Recall a character education learning experience from your high school. Describe the experience and explain why it was worthwhile or not.

4. List the reasons you intend to join or not join a specific professional organization.

5. What vision for schools do you have for the future? What obstacles might inhibit your vision from materializing?

JOURNAL ENTRIES

1. Record your vision of an ideal school.

2. Analyze a character development program that you believe has potential for developing students. In your journal, record the reasons such a program would be effective.

3. Investigate a professional organization that is of interest to you. Record the ways that you could be involved in the organization.

4. Find out if any aspect of your college is operated by a private firm. Jot down the reasons that your college chose to employ an external agency to run the service.

PORTFOLIO DEVELOPMENT

1. Visit a school setting that you believe exhibits a teacher-friendly culture. Describe what constitutes this culture and what variables make this culture possible.

2. Develop a sample lesson that incorporates some sort of character development activity embedded in an academic subject.

3. Develop a research project about your future students. Provide a rationale for your research question and outline the types of data you would collect in order to answer the question.

PREPARING FOR CERTIFICATION

PROFESSIONAL RELATIONSHIPS AND STANDARDS

1. One of the topics in the Praxis II Principles of Teaching and Learning (PLT) test is "building professional relationships with colleagues to share teaching insights and coordinate learning activities for students." Think about people you have worked with so far in your teacher preparation program—fellow students, teachers, professors, and others in the field of education. How has each contributed to your insights about teaching and learning? Can you build on those relationships and interactions to make them even more professionally beneficial for you and for them?

2. One of the themes of this book has been the importance of understanding the role of standards, assessment, and accountability in education today. When used well, standards provide a common language for teachers, students, parents, and the community in the shared goal of students' learning and growth. Standards for teachers, such as the INTASC standards and the principles underlying Praxis and other state-mandated teacher licensure tests, serve a similar purpose. When used well, INTASC standards, Praxis, and other tests provide a common language for prospective teachers' learning and growth.

As stated in Chapter 1, the best way to prepare for Praxis or any other standardized certification test is to understand the concepts covered in the test and how they relate to the content in each of your courses and field experiences. At the end of each chapter, you were encouraged to relate what you learned to concepts in the Praxis test and to try a few sample questions. As a final reflective activity, return to the ETS *Test at a Glance* materials for the PLT test. Read through the topics covered and think about how they relate to the ideas in this book. Are you now better prepared to address some of those topics? Think ahead to future courses and experiences in your teacher preparation program. Which topics do you need to learn more about? Make a plan for how you will continue to relate the content of future courses and field experiences to the test you will eventually take.

WEBSITES

www.ilt.columbia.edu/publications/index.html   The Institute for Learning Technologies website hosted at Columbia University provide papers, ideas, and visions of an idealized system of U.S. twenty-first-century schools.

www.ratical.org/many_worlds/PoL.html   The Paths of Learning Resource Center provides a free online tool that can assist in your educational explorations. You can now search over 500 indexed books, magazines, and journal.

www.rethinkingschools.org   Rethinking Schools began as a local effort led by classroom teachers dedicated to equity in public education. It is now a prominent organization and publisher focused on providing new visions for public education and the creation of a humane, caring, and multiracial democracy. The site provides provocative articles, innovative projects, and its own search engine.

www.pdkintl.org   The Phi Delta Kappa International website provides educational resources, papers, and discussions about best practices in education.

www.ei-ie.org   Education International is an international federation of educators. Its website provides ideas, projects, and visions for education across the globe and is an excellent resource for viewing education in a broader context.

FURTHER READING

Fullan, Michael. (1991). *The New Meaning of Educational Change.* New York: Teachers College Press. Excellent analysis of both the theoretical basis and the practical implications of research on the school change process.

Palmer, P. J. (1998). *The Courage to Teach: Exploring the Inner Landscape of a Teacher's Life.* San Francisco: Jossey-Bass. A reflective look at the life of a teacher from the inside out.

Scapp, Ron. (2003). *Teaching Values: Critical Perspectives on Education, Politics, and Culture.* New York: Routledge and Farmer Press. A provocative text that raises questions about values and morality embedded in our curriculum but often hidden from discussion.

Witte, John F. (2000). *The Market Approach to Education. Princeton,* NJ: Princeton University Press. Concentrating on but not limiting his attention to the Milwaukee voucher program, Witte assesses both the promises and dangers of vouchers, open enrollment, and other choice mechanisms.

THEMES OF THE TIMES!

expect the world®

The New York Times

nytimes.com

Companion Website

Expand your knowledge of the concepts discussed in this chapter by reading current and historical articles from the *New York Times* by visiting the Themes of the Times! section of the companion website **(www.ablongman.com/johnson13e).**

NOTES

1. Alvin Toffler, *Future Shock.* New York: Bantam, 1971, p. 460.
2. Lowell D. Rose and Alec M. Gallup, "The 34th Annual Phi Delta Kappa/Gallup Poll of the Public's Attitudes toward the Public School," *Phi Delta Kappan, 83* (September 2002), p. 52.
3. Mary Anne Raywid and Libby Oshiymam, "Musing in the Wake of Columbine," *Phi Delta Kappan, 81* (February 2000), p. 449.
4. Alfie Kohn, "How Not to Teach Values: A Critical Look at Character Education," *Phi Delta Kappan, 78* (February 1997), pp. 428–439.
5. Theodore R. Sizer and Nancy Faust Sizer, "Grappling," *Phi Delta Kappan, 80* (November 1999), p. 190.
6. Robert Eaker, Echard Dufour, and Rebecca DuFour, *Getting Started: Restructuring Schools to Become Professional Learning Communities.* Bloomington, IN: National Educational Service, 2003, pp. 9–29.

State Certification and Licensure Offices throughout the United States

A teaching certificate or license is valid only in the state for which it is issued. Certification and testing requirements are never static. States are changing requirements constantly. If you are planning to move to another state, you should contact that state's certification/licensure office as the first step. Below are websites to guide you.

When you contact a state office, indicate the type of certificate you are receiving, your state, and the tests you have taken. You may also find information at www.nasdtec.org, and click on the Interstate Agreement to look at states that cooperate with licensure transfer. School districts that want to employ you may also have methods of hiring you on a temporary license for 1–2 years.

Alabama
www.alsde.edu/html/sections/section_detail.asp?section=66&

Alaska
www.educ.state.ak.us/teachercertification

Arizona
www.ade.state.az.us/certification

Arkansas
http://arkedu.state.ar.us/teachers/index.html

California
www.ctc.ca.gov or http://www.calteach.com

Colorado
www.cde.state.co.us/index_license.htm

Connecticut
www.state.ct.us/sde/dtl/cert/index.htm

Delaware
www.doe.state.de.us

District of Columbia
www.k12.dc.us/dcps/teachdc/certification.html

Florida
www.fldoe.org/edcert

Georgia
www.gapsc.com/TeacherCertification.asp

Hawaii
http://doe.k12.hi.us/teacher/index.htm

Idaho
www.sde.state.id.us/certification

Illinois
www.isbe.net/teachers.htm

Indiana
www.in.gov/psb

Iowa
www.state.ia.us/educate/programs/boee/index.html

Kansas
www.ksbe.state.ks.us/cert/cert.html

Kentucky
www.kyepsb.net/certinfo.html

Louisiana
www.louisianaschools.net/lde/index.html

Maine
www.usm.maine.edu/cehd/etep/certify.htm

Maryland
http://certification.msde.state.md.us

Massachusetts
www.doe.mass.edu/educators/e_license.html

Michigan
www.michigan.gov/mde

Minnesota
www.education.state.mn.us/html/intro_licensure.htm

Mississippi
www.academploy.com/cert/certms.htm

Missouri
www.dese.mo.gov/divteachqual/teachcert/index.html

Montana
www.opi.state.mt.us/index.html

Nebraska
www.nde.state.ne.us/tcert/tcmain.html

Nevada
www.academploy.com/cert/certnv.htm

New Hampshire
www.academploy.com/cert/certnh.htm

New Jersey
www.state.nj.us/njded/educators/license/index.html

New Mexico
www.sde.state.nm.us/div/ais/lic/index.html

New York
http://usny.nysed.gov/teachers/teachercertlic.html

North Carolina
www.ncpublicschools.org/employment.html

North Dakota
www.state.nd.us/espb/

Ohio
www.ode.state.oh.us/teaching-profession/
teacher/certification_licensure

Oklahoma
www.octp.org/octp/index.html

Oregon
www.ode.state.or.us/supportservices/careers.htm

Pennsylvania
www.pde.state.pa.us/pde_internet/site/default.asp

Rhode Island
www.ridoe.net

South Carolina
www.scteachers.org/index.cfm

South Dakota
www.state.sd.us/deca/account/opa

Tennessee
www.state.tn.us/education/lic_home.htm

Texas
www.sbec.state.tx.us/SBECOnline/default.asp

Utah
www.usoe.k12.ut.us/cert/require/reqs.htm

Vermont
www.state.vt.us/educ/new/html/maincert.html

Virginia
www.pen.k12.va.us/VDOE/newvdoe/teached.html

Washington
www.k12.wa.us/certification

West Virginia
http://wvde.state.wv.us/certification

Wisconsin
www.dpi.state.wi.us/dpi/dlsis/tel/index.html

Wyoming
www.k12.wy.us/ptsb

United States Department of Defense Dependents Schools
www.odedodea.edu/pers

Source: Locating U.S. State Certification Offices. 2004 AAEE Job Search Handbook, American Association for Employment in Education, Inc.

Code of Ethics of the Education Profession

PREAMBLE

The educator, believing in the worth and dignity of each human being, recognizes the supreme importance of the pursuit of the truth, devotion to excellence, and the nurture of the democratic principles. Essential to these goals is the protection of freedom to learn and to teach and the guarantee of equal educational opportunity for all. The educator accepts the responsibility to adhere to the highest ethical standards.

The educator recognizes the magnitude of the responsibility inherent in the teaching process. The desire for the respect and confidence of one's colleagues, of students, of parents, and of the members of the community provides the incentive to attain and maintain the highest possible degree of ethical conduct. The code of Ethics of the Education Profession indicates the aspiration of all educators and provides standards by which to judge conduct.

The remedies specified by the NEA and/or its affiliates for the violation of any provision of this Code shall be exclusive and no such provision shall be enforceable in any form other than the one specifically designated by the NEA and/or its affiliates.

PRINCIPLE I

COMMITMENT TO THE STUDENT

The educator strives to help each student realize his or her potential as a worthy and effective member of society. The educator therefore works to stimulate the spirit of inquiry, the acquisition of knowledge and understanding, and the thoughtful formulation of worthy goals.

In fulfillment of the obligation to the student, the educator—

1. Shall not unreasonably restrain the student from independent action in the pursuit of learning.
2. Shall not unreasonably deny the student's access to varying points of view.
3. Shall not deliberately suppress or distort subject matter relevant to the student's progress.
4. Shall make reasonable effort to protect the student from conditions harmful to learning or to health and safety.
5. Shall not intentionally expose the student to embarrassment or disparagement.

6. Shall not on the basis of race, color, creed, sex, national origin, marital status, political or religious beliefs, family, social or cultural background, or sexual orientation, unfairly—
   a. Exclude any student from participation in any program
   b. Deny benefits to any student
   c. Grant any advantage to any student
7. Shall not use professional relationships with students for private advantage.
8. Shall not disclose information about students obtained in the course of professional service unless disclosure serves a compelling professional purpose or is required by law.

PRINCIPLE II

▪ COMMITMENT TO THE PROFESSION

The education profession is vested by the public with a trust and responsibility requiring the highest ideals of professional service.

In the belief that the quality of the services of the education profession directly influences the nation and its citizens, the educator shall exert every effort to raise professional standards, to promote a climate that encourages the exercise of professional judgment, to achieve conditions that attract persons worthy of the trust to careers in education, and to assist in preventing the practice of the profession by unqualified persons.

In fulfillment of the obligation to the profession, the educator—

9. Shall not in an application for a professional position deliberately make a false statement or fail to disclose a material fact related to competency and qualifications.
10. Shall not misrepresent his/her professional qualifications.
11. Shall not assist any entry into the profession of a person known to be unqualified in respect to character, education, or other relevant attribute.
12. Shall not knowingly make a false statement concerning the qualifications of a candidate for a professional position.
13. Shall not assist a noneducator in the unauthorized practice of teaching.
14. Shall not disclose information about colleagues obtained in the course of professional service unless disclosure serves a compelling professional purpose or is required by law.
15. Shall not knowingly make false or malicious statements about a colleague.
16. Shall not accept any gratuity, gift, or favor that might impair or appear to influence professional decisions or action.

Adopted by the NEA 1975 Representative Assembly

Teaching Job Websites

The Web has quickly become the major resource for finding education vacancies: through your college's career center website, school district websites, and state departments of education or related organizations. Many commercial sites also exist; be aware that some may have fees attached. These addresses are current as of July 2002, but may change.

AAEE sponsors two web-based services. First is Project Connect, a year-round vacancy listing service. Just go to www.aaee.org, click on Project Connect and follow the links. You will need a username (teacher) and password (aswan) to search for positions.

Alabama
www.alsde.edu/html/JobVacancies.asp?footer=general

Alaska
www.akeducationjobs.com

Arizona
www.arizonaeducationjobs.com

Arkansas
www.as-is.org/classifieds

California
www.calteach.com

Colorado
https://gateway.cde.state.co.us/portal/page?_pageid=33,34440&_dad=portal&_schema=PORTAL

Connecticut
www.state.ct.us/sde

Delaware
www.teachdelaware.com

Florida
www.teachinflorida.com

Georgia
www.teachgeorgia.org

Hawaii
http://doe.k12.hi.us/personnel/jobopportunities.htm

Idaho
www.jobservice.us/iw/jobsearch/js.asp

Illinois
www.isbe.state.il.us

Indiana
http://ideanet.doe.state.in.us/peer/welcome.html

Iowa
www.iowaeducationjobs.com

Kansas
www.kansasteachingjobs.com

Kentucky
www.kde.state.ky.us

Louisiana
www.louisianaschools.net/lde/index.html

Maine
www.state.me.us/education/jobs1.htm

Maryland
www.msde.state.md.us

Massachusetts
www.doe.masss.edu/jobs

Michigan
http://mtn.merit.edu/joblistings.html

Minnesota
www.mnasa.org/school_jobs

Mississippi
www.mde.k12.ms.us/mtc/vacancy.htm

Missouri
www.moteachingjobs.com

Montana
http://jobsforteachers.opi.state.mt.us

Nebraska
www.nebraskaeducationjobs.com

Nevada
www.nde.state.nv.us/hrt/hr/employment_department.html

New Hampshire
www.ed.state.nh.us/about/employ.htm

New Jersey
www.njhire.com

New Mexico
www.nmsba.org

New York
www.highered.nysed.gov/tcert/index.html

North Carolina
www.dpi.state.nc.us/employment.html

North Dakota
https://onestop.jobsnd.com

Ohio
www.ode.state.oh.us/jobs

Oklahoma
www.sde.state.ok.us/pro/job.html

Oregon
www.ospa.k12.or.us

Pennsylvania
www.teaching.state.pa.us/teaching/site/default.asp

Rhode Island
www.ridoe.net/teachers/ed_employment.htm

South Carolina
www.cerra.org/scctr_jobbank_submit.asp

South Dakota
www.state.sd.us/deca/jobs.htm

Tennessee
www.state.tn.us/education/mtjobs.htm

Texas
www.sbec.state.tx.us

Utah
www.utaheducationjobs.com

Vermont
www.state.vt.us/educ

Virginia
www.pen.k12.va.us/VDOE/JOVE/home.shtml

Washington
www.wateach.com

West Virginia
http://wvde.state.wv.us/jobs

Wisconsin
www.wisconsin.gov/state/app/employment

Wyoming
http://onestop.state.wy.us/appview/tt_home.asp

United States Department of Defense Dependents Schools
www.odedodea.edu/pers

Source: Job Websites. 2004 AAEE Job Search Handbook, American Association for Employment in Education, Inc.

Important Dates in the History of Western Education

ca. 4000 B.C.E.	Written language developed
ca. 2000	First known schools
1200	Trojan War
479–338	Period of Greek brilliance
469–399	Socrates
445–431	Greek Age of Pericles
427–346	Plato
404	Fall of Athens
384–322	Aristotle
336–323	Ascendancy of Alexander the Great
303	A few private Greek teachers set up schools in Rome
167	First Greek library in Rome
146	Fall of Corinth: Greece fell to Rome
C.E. 31–476	Empire of Rome
35–95	Quintilian
40–120	Plutarch
70	Destruction of Jerusalem
476	Fall of Rome in the West
734–804	Alcuin
800	Charlemagne crowned Emperor
980–1037	Avicenna
1100–1300	Crusades
1126–1198	Averroes
ca. 1150	Universities of Paris and Bologna
1209	Cambridge founded
1225–1274	St. Thomas Aquinas
1295	Voyage of Marco Polo
1384	Order of Brethren of the Common Life founded
ca. 1400	Thirty-eight universities; 108 by 1600
ca. 1423	Printing invented
ca. 1456	First book printed
1460–1536	Erasmus
1483–1546	Martin Luther
1487	Vasco da Gama discovered African route to India
1491–1556	Ignatius of Loyola
1492	Columbus landed in America
ca. 1492	Colonists began exploiting Native Americans
ca. 1500	250 Latin grammar schools in England
1517	Luther nailed theses to cathedral door; beginning of Reformation
1519–1521	Magellan first circumnavigated the globe
1534	Founding of Jesuits
1536	Sturm established his Gymnasium in Germany, the first classical secondary school

1568	Indian school established in Cuba by the Society of Jesus
1592–1670	Johann Comenius
1601	English Poor Law established principle of tax-supported schools
1618	Holland had compulsory school law
1620	Plymouth Colony, Massachusetts, settled
1635	Boston Latin Grammar School founded
1636	Harvard founded
1642	Massachusetts law of 1642 encouraged education
1632–1704	John Locke
1647	Massachusetts law of 1647 compelled establishment of schools
ca. 1600s	Hornbooks evolved
1661	First newspaper in England
1672	First teacher-training class in France, Father Demia, France
1684	Brothers of the Christian Schools founded
1685	First normal school, de la Salle, Rheims, France
1697	First teacher training in Germany, Francke's Seminary, Halle
1700–1790	Benjamin Franklin
1712–1778	Jean-Jacques Rousseau
1723	Indian student house opened by College of William and Mary
1746–1827	Johann Pestalozzi
1751	Benjamin Franklin established first academy in the United States
1758–1843	Noah Webster
1762	Rousseau's *Émile* published
1775–1783	Revolution, United States
1776–1841	Johann Herbart
1782–1852	Friedrich Froebel
1778–1870	Emma Willard
1789	Adoption of Constitution, United States
1796–1859	Horace Mann
1798	Joseph Lancaster developed monitorial plan of education
1799–1815	Ascendancy of Napoleon, Waterloo
1804	Pestalozzi's Institute at Yverdon established
1806	First Lancastrian School in New York
1811–1900	Henry Barnard
1819	Dartmouth College Decision
1821	First American high school
1821	Troy Seminary for Women, Emma Willard; first higher education for women in United States
1823	First private normal school in United States, founded by Rev. Hall in Concord, Vermont
1825	Labor unions came on the scene
1826	Froebel's *The Education of Man* published
1827	Massachusetts law compelled high schools
1837	Massachusetts had first state board, Horace Mann first secretary
1839	First public normal school in United States, Lexington, Massachusetts
1855	First kindergarten in United States, based on German model, founded by Margarethe Meyer Schurz at Oshkosh, Wisconsin
1856–1915	Booker T. Washington
1857–1952	John Dewey
1861–1865	Civil War
1861	Oswego (New York) Normal School, Edward Sheldon

1862	Morrill Land Grant Act: college of engineering, military science, agriculture in each state
1868	Herbartian Society founded
1870–1952	Maria Montessori
1872	Kalamazoo Decision made high schools legal
1875–1955	Mary Bethune
1888	Teachers College, Columbia University, founded
1892	Committee of Ten established
1896–1980	Jean Piaget
1904–1990	B. F. Skinner
1909–1910	First junior high schools established at Berkeley, California, and Columbus, Ohio
ca. 1910	First junior colleges established at Fresno, California, and Joliet, Illinois
1917	The Smith-Hughes Act encouraged agriculture, industry, and home economics education in the United States
1932–1940	The Eight-Year Study of thirty high schools completed by the Progressive Education Association
1941	Japanese bombed Pearl Harbor
1941	Lanham Act
1942	Progressive Education Association published the findings of the Eight-Year Study; reported favorably on the modern school
1944–1946	Legislation by 78th U.S. Congress provided subsistence allowance, tuition fees, and supplies for the education of veterans of World War II, the GI Bill
1945	The United Nations Educational, Scientific, and Cultural Organization (UNESCO) initiated efforts to improve educational standards throughout the world
ca. 1946–1947	Beginning of U.S. "baby boom"; eventually caused huge increase in school enrollments
1948	*McCollum v. Board of Education;* U.S. Supreme Court ruled it illegal to release children for religious classes in public school buildings
1948	Fulbright programs began; by 1966 involved 82,500 scholars in 136 nations
1950	National Science Foundation founded
1952	GI Bill's educational benefits extended to Korean War veterans
1954	U.S. Supreme Court decision required eventual racial integration of public schools
1954	Cooperative Research Program
1957	Soviet Union launched *Sputnik*
1958	Federal Congress passed the National Defense Education Act
1959	James B. Conant wrote *The American High School Today*
1961	Federal court ruled *de facto* racial segregation illegal
1961	Peace Corps established
1961	Approximately four million college students in the United States
1962	In *Engle v. Vitale,* U.S. Supreme Court ruled compulsory prayer in public school illegal
1963	Vocational Education Act
1963	Manpower Development and Training Act
1964	Economic Opportunity Act provided federal funds for such programs as Head Start
1964	Civil Rights Act
1965	Elementary and Secondary Education Act allowed more federal funds for public schools

1965   Higher Education Act

1966   GI Bill's educational benefits extended to Vietnam war veterans

1966   One million Americans travel abroad

1966   U.S. International Education Act

1966   Coleman Report suggested that racially balanced schools did not necessarily provide a better education

1967   Education Professions Development Act

1972   Indian Education Act, designed to help Native Americans help themselves

1972   Title IX Education Amendment outlawing discrimination on the basis of sex

1973   In *Rodriguez v. San Antonio Independent School*, U.S. Supreme Court ruled that a state's system for financing schools did not violate the Constitution although there were large disparities in per-pupil expenditure.

1975   Indochina Migration and Refugee Assistance Act (Public Law 94-23)

1975   Public Law 94-142, requiring local districts to provide education for children with special needs

1979   Department of Education Act

1980   U.S. Secretary of Education position became a cabinet post

1983   *High School: A Report on Secondary Education in America* by the Carnegie Foundation

1983   *A Nation at Risk: The Imperative for Educational Reform*, report by the National Commission on Excellence in Education

1983   Task Force on Education for Economic Growth, Action for Excellence, Education Commission of the States Report

1983   Task Force on Federal Elementary and Secondary Education Policy, Making the Grade, the Twentieth Century Fund Report

ca. 1980–1984   Fundamentalist religious movement advocating prayer in the schools and teaching of Biblical creation story

1984   Public Law 98-377 added new science and mathematics programs, magnet schools, and equal access to public schools

1984   Perkins Vocational Education Act to upgrade vocational programs in schools

1984   Public Law 98-558 created new teacher education scholarships and continued Head Start and Follow Through programs

1985   NCATE Redesign Standards published

1986   Holmes Group report published

1986   Carnegie Report of the Task Force on Teaching as a Profession

1989   Presidential Education Summit with governors

1990   U.S. Supreme Court decision to allow Bible clubs in schools

1992   U.S. Supreme Court decision finds officially sanctioned prayers or invocations unconstitutional

1994   National Educational Goals: 2000 adopted by federal government

ca. 1990s   Development of school voucher plans and charter schools

2001   President Bush promises to push school reform

2001   Federal No Child Left Behind Act

2003   U.S. Supreme Court reaffirms and clarifies affirmative action

Professional Education Associations: A Selected List

American Alliance for Health, Physical Education, Recreation, and Dance (AAHPERD)
www.aahperd.org

American Association of Physics Teachers (AAPT)
www.aapt.org

American Comparative Literature Association (ACLA)
www.acla.org

American Council on the Teaching of Foreign Languages (ACTFL)
www.actfl.org

American Federation of Teachers (AFT)
www.aft.org

American Library Association (ALA)
www.ala.org

American Speech-Language-Hearing Association (ASHA)
www.asha.org

American Association for Health Education (AAHE)
www.aahperd.org/aahe

Association for Childhood Education International (ACEI)
www.acei.org

Association for Education in Journalism and Mass Communications (AEJMC)
www.aejmc.org

Association for Educational Communications and Technology (AECT)
www.aect.org

Association for Supervision and Curriculum Development (ASCD)
www.ascd.org

Association of Christian Schools International (ACSI)
www.acsi.org

Council for Exceptional Children (CEC)
www.cec.sped.org

Education International (EI)
www.ei-ie.org/main/english/index.html

International Reading Association (IRA)
www.reading.org

International Society for Technology in Education (ISTE)
www.iste.org

International Technology Education Association (ITEA)
www.iteawww.org

Interstate New Teacher Assessment and Support Consortium (INTASC)
www.ccsso.org/Projects/interstate_new_teacher_assessment_and_support_consortium/780.cfm

Modern Language Association of America (MLA)
www.mla.org

Music Teachers National Association (MTNA)
www.mtna.org

National Art Education Association (NAEA)
www.naea-reston.org

National Association for Bilingual Education (NABE)
www.nabe.org

National Association for the Education of Young Children (NAEYC)
www.naeyc.org

National Association for Gifted Children (NAGC)
www.nagc.org

National Association for Multicultural Education (NAME)
www.nameorg.org

National Association for Sport & Physical Education (NASPE)
www.aahperd.org/naspe

National Association of Biology Teachers (NABT)
www.nabt.org

National Association of Episcopal Schools (NAES)
www.naes.org

National Board for Professional Teaching Standards (NBPTS)
www.nbpts.org

National Business Education Association (NBEA)
www.nbea.org

National Catholic Educational Association (NCEA)
www.ncea.org

National Council for Accreditation of Teacher Education (NCATE)
www.ncate.org

National Council for the Social Studies (NCSS)
www.ncss.org

National Council of Teachers of English (NCTE)
www.ncte.org

National Council of Teachers of Mathematics (NCTM)
www.nctm.org

National Education Association (NEA)
www.nea.org

National Middle School Association (NMSA)
www.nmsa.org

National Science Teachers Association (NSTA)
www.nsta.org

Phi Delta Kappa
www.pdkintl.org

Teachers of English to Speakers of Other Languages (TESOL)
www.tesol.org

Name Index

Subject Index

Photo Credits

Page xxxii, © Jim Cummins/CORBIS; p. 2, Comstock Royalty Free Division; p. 5, Lindfors Photography; p. 9, © Laura Dwight Photography; p. 10 (Top), © Jim Cummins/CORBIS; p. 10 (Bottom), © James Leynse/CORBIS SABA; p. 12, Photo by Dennis Nett/Syracuse Newspapers/The Image Works; p. 14, Stephen Marks; p. 16, © Jeffry Myers/Stock Boston; p. 18, Lindfors Photography; p. 23, © Will Faller; p. 40, © Lisette Le Bon/SuperStock; p. 42 © Paul Viant/Getty Images; p. 45, © Bluestone Productions/SuperStock; p. 48, © Jim Cummins/CORBIS; p. 49, © Dennis MacDonald/Photo Edit; p. 57, © Michael Newman/Photo Edit; p. 63, © Li-Hua Lan/The Image Works; p. 65, © Tony Freeman/Photo Edit; p. 68, © Lon C. Diehl/Photo Edit; p. 69, © Joe Bator/The Stock Market; p. 76, © Kevin Radford/SuperStock; p. 79, © Will and Deni McIntyre/CORBIS; p. 84, © Bob Daemmrich/The Image Works; p. 87, © Rob Crandall/The Image Works; p. 90, © David Young-Wolff/Photo Edit; p. 91, © Will Hart/PhotoEdit; p. 95, © David Young-Wolff/Photo Edit; p. 99, © Elyse Lewn/Getty Images; p. 100, © Robert Harbison; p. 110, © Laura Dwight Photography; p. 113, © Paul Chesley/Getty Images; p. 115, © Mike Maple/Woodfin Camp & Associates; p. 119, © Pete Saloutos/CORBIS; p. 121, © Jeffry Myers/Stock Boston; p. 123, © Laura Dwight Photography; p. 125, © Greg Pease/Getty Images; p. 131, © Laura Dwight Photography; p. 133, © Sylvia Johnson/Woodfin Camp & Associates; p. 138, © Bohdan Hrynewych/Stock Boston/PictureQuest; p. 140, © Michael Newman/Photo Edit; p. 144, © Laura Dwight Photography; p. 148, © Bob Daemmrich/The Image Works; p. 151, © Matthew McVay/Getty Images; p. 154, © Najlan Feanny/Stock Boston; p. 159, Sally & Derk Kuyper; p. 163, AP/Wide World Photos; p. 172, © Brian Parker/Tom Stack & Assoc.; p. 177, Lindfors Photography; p. 186, © Michael Newman/Photo Edit; p. 189, North Wind Picture Archives; p. 193, © Photo Disc/Getty Images; p. 194, © Annie Griffiths Belt/CORBIS; p. 198, © Will Hart; p. 207, © Jamea J. Bissell/SuperStock; p. 211, © Rashid/Monkmeyer; p. 216, © Will Hart; p. 220, © Michael Newman/PhotoEdit; p. 223, © Gabe Palmer/CORBIS; p. 226, © Bob Daemmrich/Stock Boston; p. 232, © Michael Krasowitz/Getty Images; p. 234, © Genevieve Naylor/CORBIS; p. 237, © R. W. Jones/CORBIS; p. 240, © Araldo de Luca/CORBIS; p. 244 (Both), 246, North Wind Picture Archives; p. 248, © Archivo Iconografico, S. A./CORBIS; p. 249 (Top), North Wind Picture Archives; p. 249 (Middle), Library of Congress; p. 249 (Bottom), © Bettmann/CORBIS; p. 253, Courtesy of the Blackwell Collection, Northern Illinois University; p. 257 (Both), 258, 259, North Wind Picture Archives; p. 260, © CORBIS; p. 262, Library of Congress; p. 263, North Wind Picture Archives; p. 270, © Kwame Zikomo/SuperStock; p. 273, Brown Brothers; p. 276, © Will Hart; p. 278, Culver Pictures; p. 281, © James Marshall/The Image Works; p. 282, © Robert Harbison; p. 288, © Minnesota Historical Society/CORBIS; p. 289, © CORBIS; p. 290, Courtesy of the Blackwell Collection, Northern Illinois University; p. 291, Library of Congress; p. 296 (Top), © CORBIS; p. 296 (Bottom), Lyrl Ahern; p. 302, © Pierre Tremblay/Masterfile; p. 304, © Charles Gupton/CORBIS; p. 312, © Gabe Palmer/CORBIS; p. 317 (Top), © Araldo de Luca/CORBIS; p. 317 (Bottom), 319 (Top), North Wind Picture Archives; p. 319 (Bottom), 320, 321, Courtesy of the Blackwell Collection, Northern Illinois University; p. 323, Courtesy of the Special Collections, Milbank Memorial Library, Teachers College, Columbia University; p. 327, North Wind Picture Archives; p. 329, © Lawrence Migdale/Stock Boston; p. 334, © Superstock/PictureQuest; p. 340, © Tom & Dee Ann McCarthy/CORBIS; p. 343, © Mark Richards/Photo Edit; p. 345 (Top), © Stockbyte/PictureQuest; p. 345 (Bottom), © ThinkStock/SuperStock; p. 347, Courtesy of the Blackwell Collection, Northern Illinois University; p. 349, © Myrleen Ferguson Cate/Photo Edit; p. 350, The Paulo Freire Archives; p. 351, © Archivo Iconografico, S. A./CORBIS; p. 352, © Laura Dwight Photography; p. 355, © David Young-Wolff/Photo Edit; p. 360, © Superstock/PictureQuest; p. 364, © Richard Hutchings/Photo Edit; p. 365, © Mary Kate Denny/Photo Edit; p. 368, © BananaStock/Superstock; p. 369, Lindfors Photography; p. 376, © Will Hart; p. 377 (Top), © Laura Dwight Photography; p. 377 (Bottom), Comstock Royalty Free Division; p. 379, © Mark Richards/Photo Edit; p. 384, © Stockbyte/Superstock; p. 386, © Steve Lyne, Rex Interstock/Stock Connection/PictureQuest; p. 389, © Spencer Grant/Photo Edit; p. 390, © Joe Sohm/The Image Works; p. 391, © Charles Gupton/CORBIS; p. 397, © Laura Dwight Photography; p. 399, © Charles Gupton/CORBIS; p. 401, © David Young-Wolff/Photo Edit; p. 402, © Mug Shots/CORBIS; p. 408, © Dennis MacDonald/Photo Edit; p. 420, © Tom Stewart/CORBIS; p. 423, © Jose Luis Pelaez Inc./CORBIS; p. 425, © Tom Stewart/CORBIS; p. 427, AP/Wide World Photos; p. 435, © Michelle D. Bridwell/Photo Edit; p. 437, © Tom Stewart/CORBIS; p. 444, © David Young-Wolff/Photo Edit; p. 455, © Robin Sachs/Photo Edit; p. 464, © Mary Kate Denny/Photo Edit; p. 470, © Steven Begleiter/IndexStock; p. 475, © Jeff Greenberg/IndexStock.

Interior Image Credits

Andrew Hall/Stone/Getty Images (magnifying glass) Digital Vision/Getty Images (globe)

Coverage of Interstate New Teacher Support Consortium (INTASC) Standards for Beginning Teacher Licensing and Development

INTASC Standards		Text Chapter/Page Number
Standard 1	Central concepts, tools of inquiry, and structures of the subject being taught	**Chapter 1:** 9, 10, 15–16 **Chapter 9:** 307–326 **Chapter 10:** 338–380 **Chapter 13:** 427–429
Standard 2	Children's learning and intellectual, social, and personal development	**Chapter 3:** 84–96, 98–101 **Chapter 8:** 294–296 **Chapter 9:** 315–326 **Chapter 10:** 339–355 **Chapter 11:** 376–377 **Chapter 12:** 397–398 **Chapter 13:** 445–449 **Chapter 14:** 469, 480–481
Standard 3	Student differences in their approaches to learning and adaptations for diverse learners	**Chapter 2:** 45, 47–48 **Chapter 4:** 120–124, 126–128 **Chapter 6:** 201–203 **Chapter 7:** 237–249, 260–263 **Chapter 8:** 275–278, 280, 284–285, 289 **Chapter 9:** 326–330 **Chapter 10:** 349–350 **Chapter 12:** 395–396, 413–416 **Chapter 13:** 442–444
Standard 4	Instructional strategies for students' development of critical thinking, problem solving, and performance skills	**Chapter 3:** 79–80, 98, 104–105 **Chapter 4:** 130–134 **Chapter 7:** 239–241, 242–249, 252–253, 261–263 **Chapter 8:** 289–291, 296 **Chapter 9:** 315–326 **Chapter 11:** 375–378 **Chapter 13:** 433–445 **Chapter 14:** 480–481
Standard 5	Individual and group motivation and behavior for positive social interaction, active engagement in learning, and self-motivation	**Chapter 3:** 85–86 **Chapter 9:** 315–326 **Chapter 10:** 339–355 **Chapter 11:** 366–374 **Chapter 14:** 471–472
Standard 6	Effective verbal, nonverbal, and media communication techniques for inquiry, collaboration, and supportive interaction in the classroom	**Chapter 4:** 121, 123–124, 128–130 **Chapter 7:** 257–260 **Chapter 11:** 375–376 **Chapter 13:** 449–460